THIRD EDITION

Theories of Personality

Richard M. Ryckman
University of Maine at Orono

Brooks/Cole Publishing Company 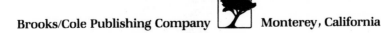 Monterey, California

To my mentor,
W. EDGAR VINACKE

Sponsoring Editor: Claire Verduin
Editorial Assistant: Pat Carnahan
Production Service: *Ex Libris* □ Julie Kranhold
Manuscript Editor: Lieselotte Hofmann
Interior Design: Wendy Calmenson
Cover Design: Koney Eng
Cover Illustration: Adolph Gottlieb, *HANDS OF OEDIPUS*, 1943, oil on linen,
□ 40"x35¹⁵⁄₁₆". ©Adolph and Esther Gottlieb Foundation, Inc., N.Y.
Typesetting: Graphic Typesetting Service, Los Angeles, California

Credits for Chapter Opening Photographs

2/Freud National Library of Medicine; **3/Jung** The Bettmann Archive; **4/Adler** The
Bettmann Archive; **5/Horney** Association for the Advancement of Psychoanalysis; **6/
Fromm** Erich Fromm; **7/Erikson** Harvard University Archives, William Tobey; **8/
Allport** Harvard University Archives; **9/Cattell** Raymond Cattell; **10/Kelly** Brandeis
University; **11/Skinner** Harvard University Archives; **12/Rotter** Julian Rotter; **13/Ban-
dura** Albert Bandura; **14/Maslow** William Carter; **15/Rogers** Nozizwe Siwundhla;
16/May Mark Kaufman; **17/Sheldon** Dorothy Paschal (Brown Bros.)

Brooks/Cole Publishing Company
A Division of Wadsworth, Inc.

Printed in the United States of America

10 9 8 7 6 5 4 3

Library of Congress Cataloging in Publication Data
Ryckman, Richard M.
   Theories of personality.

   Includes bibliographies and indexes.
   1. Personality.   I. Title.
BF698.R96   1985   155.2   84-23287

ISBN 0-534-04914-1

P R E F A C E

Theories of Personality has the primary purposes of reviewing basic concepts and principles of the major theories of personality and of assessing how well they meet criteria for judging the scientific worth of a theory. It also introduces students to the newest issues and developments in the discipline of personality psychology.

The material is presented in a clear and understandable manner for undergraduates who have had little or no exposure to the field of personality psychology. I have included many case studies to show how the theories are applied to the treatment of personality problems. There are also numerous examples from everyday life and unusual topics to stimulate student interest. Each major theoretical position is introduced by an objective overview of the theorist's basic concepts and propositions, so that comparisons of the theorists should follow rather easily.

The book is divided into eight parts. Part 1, "An Introduction to the Discipline," addresses the problem of establishing an acceptable definition of personality and the reasons for studying individual differences from a scientific stance. It provides basic information concerning the scientific process and the interrelatedness of theory and research. It also lists the criteria by which scientists judge the worth of a theory so that the student will be able to evaluate the theories reviewed in succeeding chapters.

Part 2, "Psychoanalytic and Neoanalytic Perspectives," reviews the seminal contributions of Freud and his psychoanalytic theory and the personality theories of neoanalytic theorists Jung, Adler, Horney, Fromm, and Erikson. The decision to discuss only these theorists was a difficult one. Jung and Adler are included because their views of personality represent, in many respects, significant and original departures from Freud's position. Horney's theory is reviewed because it focuses on values of central importance in many Western societies—that is, achievement, competition, and materialism—and because she discussed in an original manner (and in more detail than Adler) the ways in which excessive strivings for success often give rise to neurotic behavior. Fromm is included because his view of personality, with its strong elements of existentialism and humanistic psychology, also moves considerably beyond the Freudian viewpoint. Finally, Erikson is included because his theory is a prime example of ego psychology, a psychology that integrates biological, social, and cultural contributions to personality functioning.

The chapter on Freud focuses on the basic conflicts generated by the opposition between the needs of individuals and the needs and goals of society. To demonstrate the origins and operation of these conflicts, Freud's structural theory of personality is presented, along with a description of the major defense mechanisms people use to control the anxiety that issues from the conflicts. Freud's theory of psychosexual development is described, and the most recent research data consistent with that theory are reviewed. Finally, there is an examination of the theory of therapy, and how it is applied to the treatment of psychopathology.

In the Jung chapter, the structural components of the psyche are outlined, along with a description and explanation of the operation of the psyche's energy system. Primary attention is paid to the theory of types and to research supporting the position. Jung's theory of psychotherapy is described, and we examine the major techniques used in therapy to uncover unconscious conflicts and to facilitate movement toward self-realization.

The Adler chapter shows the important role played by members of society (especially parents) in influencing the development of the person and discusses Adler's view that psychological health can be attained only if individuals strive to realize their potentials in a manner that contributes to the community's welfare. Current research on birth order is highlighted.

The chapter on Horney describes the formation of the three major neurotic trends (that is, moving toward, against, and away from people) as a means of overcoming feelings of basic anxiety and how these contradictory trends operate in an interrelated way on an unconscious level to create a basic conflict. There is also a discussion of the irrational belief systems of neurotics and the applied value of Horney's seminal contributions in this area to modern cognitive-behavior therapy and research.

In the chapter on Fromm, the impetus for our striving to attain goals is traced to our attempts to explain our existence. The chapter also outlines the process of personality development, focusing on how the type of society largely determines whether predominantly healthy character orientations or unhealthy orientations will emerge. Fromm's view of the utopian society is described in detail.

The chapter on Erikson covers his theory of ego development and functioning, with special emphasis on the crises experienced by adolescents. Marcia's extensions of Erikson's thinking about identity status in adolescence are reviewed, along with the latest validational research evidence for the construct.

Part 3, "Trait Perspectives," covers the major trait theories of Allport and Cattell. The chapter on Allport includes a discussion of the contemporary humanistic psychology movement and shows his devotion to the construction of a psychology of personality that focuses on the uniqueness of the individual. The chapter on Cattell shows his commitment to establishing a personality theory based on sound measurement principles and procedures. It provides an introduction to factor analysis so that students can appreciate Cattel's use of the technique in his discovery of the major source traits of personality. It also presents Cattell's latest efforts to account for the role played by situational forces in the determination of personality functioning.

Part 4, "Cognitive Perspectives," is devoted to Kelly's theory of personal constructs. After a review of the fundamental philosophical assumptions underlying his theory, its basic concepts, postulates, and corollaries are discussed. We also examine Kelly's Role Construct Repertory test, an assessment procedure designed to measure the personal construct systems, and its use in therapy to appraise client experience.

Part 5, "Social-Behavioristic Perspectives," discusses the theories of Skinner, Rotter, and Bandura. The chapter on Skinner stresses recent changes in Skinner's thinking about the role of cognition and his willingness to incorporate cognitive constructs into his system, at least under certain circumstances. The Rotter chapter discusses the role of cognitive processes in the determination of personality functioning. We examine the basic concepts of Rotter's theory and consider their use in ascertaining the reasons for adjusted and maladjusted behavior. We also review some of the recent research evidence for Rotter's locus-of-control construct.

The chapter on Bandura discusses the basic assumptions underlying his social-learning theory and the reasons for his reliance on observational learning to account for individual differences. It also covers Bandura's recent postulation of the cognitive mechanism of self-efficacy to account for personality functioning and change.

Part 6, "Humanistic-Existential Perspectives," covers the positions of Rogers, Maslow, and May. The first point of emphasis in the chapter on Rogers is his insistence that healthy persons are those who rely on their own assessment of their experiences and feelings in making moral and behavioral decisions rather than yielding to the judgments of others. This discussion leads to an analysis of his organismic-wisdom hypothesis, a central conception in his theory as well as in Maslow's. A second focus in the chapter is on Rogers' recent extension of his views of the fully functioning person. Finally, we consider how Rogers' ideas apply to education and marriage.

For Maslow, I have presented his hierarchy of needs scheme and a discussion of the possible dangers of B-cognizing in order to make the important point that the self-actualizing process involves the integration of both D- and B-needs. This chapter also includes a discussion of the characteristics of self-actualizing people, along with comments about their imperfections. As Maslow pointed out, all too often people believe that self-actualizers are godlike individuals with no flaws, a misconception that this discussion will, I hope, remedy.

The chapter on May begins with a definition of existentialism and a survey of its roots in European philosophy. It describes the existentialists' disenchantment with our present views of science and discusses their belief that we should study issues more closely related to major concerns of human existence. To clarify the major concepts and principles in May's approach, some of the similarities and dissimilarities between existentialism and psychoanalysis are examined.

Part 7, "Constitutional Perspectives," is devoted to Sheldon's classic work on somatotyping. Highlighted here are Sheldon's concern with the liberal-environmentalist bias in contemporary psychology and his attempts to correct it by developing a biological theory of personality. Although contemporary personality psychologists pay homage to the role played by biology in determining behavior, in practice they have tended to ignore its contribution. As a result, we know very little about the ways in which genetic factors influence individual behavior. I hope the material here will make students aware of the importance of the biological determinants of personality.

Part 8, "The Future of Personality Psychology," reviews the most recent developments in the discipline of personality psychology. After years of debate, there is now a consensus among eminent scholars that the creation of an interactional model of personality would be a decided improvement over the person-oriented theories that currently dominate the field.

Each chapter concludes with a "Critical Comments" section (the first and last chapters are exceptions), which evaluates each theory; discussion questions; a list of suggested readings, which will aid instructors in substituting or adding other pertinent materials; and a glossary, whose terms are boldfaced in the text.

This new edition has profited immensely from the comments of my students as well as those at other colleges and unversities. The students' honest and provocative questioning has helped me tremendously. I also owe a debt to my colleagues Joel Gold, Max Hammer, Colin Martindale, William Stone, Alan Stubbs, and Geoffrey Thorpe for their helpful comments.

The constructive criticisms of reviewers have led to substantial changes in the chapters and the addition of new materials on Horney's social and cultural psychoanalysis. The discussions of the most recent developments in theory and the newest lines of research are also the fruitful result of their comments.

Reviewers who commented on various portions of the manuscript were Harold Beard, Central Missouri State University; John C. Brigham, Florida State University; Walter Heimer, C. W. Post Center, Long Island University; P. J. Hettema, Tilburg University (The Netherlands); Michael Hirt, Kent State University; Kathleen McCormick, Ocean County College; E. H. Olson, Lawrence University; Linda Silka, University of Lowell; Alexandra Symonds, Karen

Horney Institute in New York City; and Guus Van Heck, Tilburg University (The Netherlands).

It is also a pleasure to acknowledge the fine contributions of the staff at Brooks/Cole in the production of the text. My editor, Claire Verduin, has been most encouraging and helpful. I also wish to thank Marian Perry, Eva Benson, and Nancy England for the adept typing of several drafts of the manuscript.

Lastly, I once again express my appreciation and affection to my wife, Leona, who mercifully understands me (and understands me mercifully). To our sons, Bob and Mark, my thanks for their supportive comments about the text.

Richard M. Ryckman

CONTENTS

P A R T 1

An Introduction to the Discipline

Personality psychology has been blessed with an array of highly creative thinkers whose insights have been of immense value in helping us understand many aspects of personality functioning. However, no one theorist has ever been able to construct a completely adequate theory of personality. The task is clearly too complex and difficult. Instead, there are a variety of definitions of personality as well as a large number of different and often conflicting theoretical viewpoints. Yet investigators have recently been making substantive attempts to consolidate the contributions of the various theorists and to eliminate some of the weaknesses in their positions. There also has been a consensus among these investigators on a new theoretical framework for studying personality development and functioning. The result will very likely be the development of a more adequate theory and the creation of innovative methodologies to test the validity of the new theorizing, an outcome that will help increase our understanding of personality functioning even more.

To aid us in developing a more adequate theory, we can examine the strengths and weaknesses of the current positions to see how well these positions meet the standards ordinarily used by investigators to assess the worth of a scientific theory. Chapter 1 details these criteria of evaluation. It also describes the major concepts used in constructing scientific theories and the primary kinds of research procedures used to test them. Exposure to this basic information should enable you to evaluate the scientific usefulness of the theoretical positions presented in the succeeding chapters. It should also enhance your understanding of the debate described in the final chapter, a debate that has led prominent personality psychologists to recognize the need for the development of an interactional theory of personality.

CHAPTER 1

Personality and the Scientific Outlook

How Is Personality Defined?

Virtually all of us are fascinated by and interested in knowing more about ourselves and other people. In our attempts to make sense of our experiences, we tend to engage in naive analyses of our own behavior and that of others. We wonder, for example, why one of our friends refuses to date someone we find particularly attractive. We are puzzled by the student who is interested in learning everything possible about physics, when we find it difficult to listen to more than ten minutes of a lecture on the topic. We are curious about the actions of assassins and at a loss to explain why they went to such extremes, while countless others with similar or perhaps even greater frustrations and personal problems did not. We cannot imagine why a quiet, unassuming youth who is well liked by neighbors and relatives suddenly decides to buy a high-powered rifle and snipe at passengers on a passing commuter train; almost inevitably, neighbors, friends, and relatives are quoted in the media as saying that they would have expected such violence from any number of neighborhood kids the sniper's own age, but not from the sniper.

In each of these instances, we are concerned with generating explanations for the actions we observe. We want to know *why* these people behaved as they did. And so do psychologists who work in the discipline of personality. In seeking explanations for individual differences in behavior, they construct theoretical systems to account for a wide variety of behavior differences in many situations. Their efforts to understand human motivation and behavior throughout the entire developmental process range from attempts to gather information about individual differences in activity level at birth to the study of the attitudes of young and elderly people toward dying. Clearly, though, such a range of behavior is so great, and the kinds of phenomena examined are so complex, that no investigator, however knowledgeable or creative, can completely cover the ground.

Each investigator, therefore, brings to the discipline his or her own particular perspective on the subject matter. In other words, the investigators' unique theoretical orientations guide their efforts. These perspectives range from William Sheldon's almost total emphasis on the biological, or inherited, determinants of personality to J. B. Rotter's stress on the ways in which social learning experiences affect behavior. The upshot is that each investigator generates a particular definition of personality as well as working assumptions of the manner in which personality operates.

For the layperson, personality is often defined in terms of social attractiveness. The person with a "good" personality impresses others with his or her ability to get along well with people. Beauty pageant contestants are typically judged on their physical attractiveness, talent, and "personality." Here the judgment of a good personality is based on popularity with judges and other contestants and on social poise and sophistication. Some students also talk about each other in these terms: Laura is said to have a "great" personality, which usually means that she behaves in ways that the perceivers find acceptable; Henry is said to have "no" personality, which means that they find his behavior highly objectionable. Personality is sometimes also treated as a consolation prize by students: Bob encourages Joe to date an ugly female because she has a "great" personality; Jane encourages Linda to date an ugly male because his personality makes up for his looks.

A definition of personality in terms of social attractiveness is inadequate in two major respects. First, it limits the number and kinds of behavior considered worthy of incorporation into the investigation of personality. Second, it makes the absurd point that some individuals, who obviously have unique learning histories, are devoid of personality. There are several other deficiencies in such a definition: its inattention to the unique ways in which an individual's experiences are organized and its neglect of biological contributions to behavior. Of course, these criticisms also apply to many of the definitions of personality offered by investigators in the area.

Despite the plethora of definitions, there is basic agreement among investigators that personality is a **psychological construct**; that is, it is a complex abstraction that includes the person's unique learning history and genetic background (assuming that he or she is not an identical twin) and the ways in which these organized and integrated complexes of events influence his or her responses to certain stimuli in the environment. Thus many investigators see the study of personality as the scientific study of individual differences that help account for people's unique ways of responding to various situations. Providing explanations, buttressed eventually by **empirical evidence,** for each individual's ways of responding to his or her environment is the primary focus of interest in the discipline.

Why a Scientific Study of Personality?

In some segments of society today there seems to be a disenchantment with almost any endeavor associated with science and technology. It is held that these enterprises are to blame for many of our social problems, from the menace of industrial pollution to the terrifying possibility of world destruction by nuclear weapons. Although these problems are monumental and should provoke our utmost concern, it is not productive to place the blame on an abstraction—that is, on science—and to rail against it. There is nothing inherently evil about science and technology. They can produce instruments of life as well as death, depending on the interests and goals of society and government. Think of the incubators that prolong the lives of prematurely born infants, the sophisticated microscopes that allow surgeons to salvage the damaged brains of accident victims, the pacemakers that prolong the lives of patients with heart problems, the medications that prevent coma in diabetics and stroke in hypertensives, and so forth. An indiscriminate, antiscience viewpoint simplistically glosses over the fact that science and technology are primarily tools controlled and guided by people. These sophisticated and powerful instruments can be used either to further or to hinder human development.

Psychologists use the scientific approach to study individual differences because they believe it is the most effective way to gather accurate information. There is also the hope that such knowledge can be used to benefit people. In the final analysis, psychologists are convinced that a scientific orientation will lead us more directly and surely to beneficial, accurate information than will orientations that rely almost exclusively on rational speculation, mysticism, intuition, or common sense. This conviction, however, should not be interpreted as meaning that these alternative ways of knowing have no value and can never be used to help us understand human behavior. Insights stemming from the work of philosophers, novelists, poets, and theologians have always indicated otherwise.

Science and Common Sense

Some students believe that psychology, including personality psychology, is a discipline that only mirrors the observations of common sense. They argue that it really cannot contribute much to our understanding of people beyond what we all already know; thus there is not much point in devoting our energies to its study. The major flaw in this argument is that although many of the findings in psychology confirm our commonsense impressions, there are also countless instances when research results reveal our knowledge to be incomplete or inaccurate. We are, of course, never certain of the validity of these beliefs until we test them empirically.

A study by Darley and Latané (1968) illustrates this point by showing that reliance on common sense could even spell physical disaster for any one of us. They investigated the conditions under which it was more or less likely that a victim in an emergency situation would receive help from bystanders. Their interest in this problem had been aroused by a tragic incident in the spring of 1964 when a young woman named Kitty Genovese was repeatedly stabbed for over half an hour in the middle of a street in a residential area of New York City while 38 people, alerted by her screams, watched from their windows; no one called the police until she was dead. Although news commentators, clergy, and professors offered a variety of explanations for the nonintervention behavior, including calling it an indication of "moral decay," "existential despair," and "alienation," Darley and Latané focused on a more prosaic, but eventually more compelling, reason. Their explanation involved the number of witnesses to the event. In contrast to the commonsense belief that the more observers to an emergency, the more likely the victim will be to receive aid, they argued that the more bystanders there are in such a situation, the *less* likely it is that a victim will receive help. Their conjecture was based on the argument that the more bystanders there are in an emergency, the more the responsibility for intervention will be seen by an individual watcher to be shared among them. If there is only one observer, the burden for intervention rests squarely with him or her. As the number of bystanders increases, the less responsible any one of them will feel about failing to act. Consequently, the more observers, the less likely the victim will receive aid.

To test their hypothesis, Darley and Latané created an "emergency" situation in the laboratory by leading study participants to believe that another individual was undergoing an epileptic seizure during a discussion about personal problems of college students in a high-pressure academic environment. In one condition, the subject perceived that only one other person, the "victim," was present. In another condition, the subject believed the victim and one other person were present. In the final condition, six people were present: the subject, the victim, and four others. The results were in accord with the investigators' expectations and are shown in Table 1–1. The

Table 1–1
Effects of Variation in Group Size on Likelihood and
Speed of Intervention

Group Size	Sample Size	Percentage of Ss Responding to "Seizure"	Time in Seconds
2 (subject and victim)	13	85%	52
3 (subject, victim, and one other)	26	62%	93
6 (subject, victim, and four others)	13	31%	166

Adapted from Darley and Latané (1968, p. 380).

larger the group, the lower the percentage of subjects who came to the aid of the victim and the more slowly they reacted. This hypothesis has been retested in a variety of contexts with essentially the same result and does not, therefore, appear to be a finding that can easily be dismissed as a fluke occurrence.

An even more convincing example of the inaccuracy of some common-sense beliefs can be seen in Milgram's classic work on obedience to authority (Milgram, 1963). In his study, an experimenter ordered a naive subject to administer varying levels of electric shock to a "victim" as part of a learning experiment to study the effects of punishment on memory. The subject, as "teacher," was ordered to apply greater levels of shock to the "learner" every time the learner made an error on a paired-associates task. The shock levels varied in intensity from 15 to 450 volts. (In actuality, none of the learners experienced any shock, but subjects were convinced that the shocks were indeed being administered: many of them were observed to tremble, sweat, groan, and bite their lips as they meted out the punishment.)

Milgram was concerned with the extent to which subjects would comply with the commands of the experimenter and administer the highest degree of shock. He asked a group of psychiatrists and other mental-health professionals how many subjects in a group of a thousand would administer the highest level. Their estimate was that only one in a thousand would do so. A sample of senior psychology majors predicted that one out of a hundred persons, only 1%, would comply to the fullest degree. In actuality, 26 out of 40 subjects, or 65%, administered maximum shock, a finding in dramatic opposition to commonsense beliefs. More recent research by Shanab and Yahya (1977) shows even higher levels of obedience among young subjects (6 to 16 years of age). These researchers found that 73% of the subjects were willing to administer maximum shock in obedience to commands by an experimenter.

Thus it would appear that scientific effort can provide knowledge that may have important implications for each of us, knowledge that builds upon and often corrects the assumptions of common sense. At the very least, these findings suggest that we should be cautious in making indiscriminate statements about the obviousness of findings compiled by scientific psychology.

The Scientific Orientation: Theory and Research Methodology

Our next concern is with the nature of science, including the manner in which theories are constructed and tested through empirical research. Such information will prove useful in critically evaluating the positions presented in this book, with the aim of cogently relating them to our own lives and experiences.

What Is Science?

In general terms, science is concerned with the description, explanation, prediction, and control of events. The outcome of all the efforts by countless investigators is the accumulation of systematized knowledge based on the observation of **phenomena.** Science is grounded in human values and concerns from which investigators select certain problems for study. At its best, it is a process that excites their imagination and taxes their ingenuity. Often, it is frustrating—for example, when one's hypotheses are disconfirmed— but it is rarely dull. For each investigator, it is definitely not the passionless, automatic, and impersonal activity imagined by the uninitiated. In its essence, it involves an inevitable intertwining of two major processes—theory and method. There are, of course, a wide variety of research techniques available to investigators. We will focus on only three of them: the experimental method, correlational techniques, and case studies. But first let us briefly examine the nature of these processes.

Interrelatedness of Theory and Research

Scientific theories are conceptual systems constructed by researchers to help them make sense of existing information and, more important, to aid in the prediction of as yet unobserved relationships between events. Ideally, **theories** consist of a set of interrelated and internally consistent assumptions, or **propositions,** from which **hypotheses** are derived and made testable by the use of **operational definitions.** Thus the concepts in the hypotheses are defined in terms of the specific procedures, or operations, used to measure them. For example, a person's characteristic level of self-esteem may be measured by scoring his or her answers to a series of items on a questionnaire. Operational definitions are important because they allow other investigators to know precisely how the characteristics were measured, thus providing an objective basis for communication among investigators who use the concepts in their own theorizing or who want to replicate the results of another investigator's efforts. Although sometimes considered a trivial aspect of science, **replication** is critical and necessary because the outcomes of any research effort are considered not as facts in any absolute sense but as probability statements. On the basis of replication findings, investigators are better able to evaluate the worth of any one hypothesis. Successful replication tends to increase confidence in the findings; failure causes investigators to question the empirical validity of the relationship. One of the outcomes of persistent failures to replicate is that investigators may be forced to revise their theories and perhaps make new predictions.

In a theory of **cognitive dissonance** created by psychologist Leon Festinger, for example, the major propositions are that people tend to strive for consistency in their beliefs and behavior and that inconsistent or "nonfitting" cognitions about themselves or other people, inanimate objects, or events in the environment give rise to an aversive psychological state called dissonance (Festinger, 1957). Cognitions refer generally to opinions, beliefs, attitudes, behaviors, or feelings about one's environment or oneself. Once a dissonant state is generated, it is assumed there will be pressures to reduce it by various means and to avoid its increase. For example, a heavy smoker should experience dissonance when she learns, while reading the morning paper and smoking her fifth cigarette, that medical research has demonstrated that people who smoke heavily are ten times as likely to get cancer than are nonsmokers. The fact that she likes to smoke is dissonant with the report that her habit is very likely to be harmful to her health.

She can reduce the dissonance in various ways: (1) by telling herself that smoking is so enjoyable, it is clearly worth the risk; (2) by arguing that the results in the report are correlational in nature, thereby merely implying that some smokers (especially she) will never experience heart attack—after all, her father smoked three packages of cigarettes a day and lived to be 102; (3) by arguing that smoking helps calm her nerves and that without it she would turn to other potentially self-destructive activities, like overeating or drinking too much coffee; (4) by maintaining that the dangers of excessive smoking have been exaggerated; or (5) by reducing or stopping her smoking. Although several other alternatives are available, the general point is that the dissonance-reducing behaviors are ways of rationalizing or justifying one's actions to oneself *after* the behavior in question has occurred. We will now see how Festinger's theory has been tested by use of the experimental method.

Experimental Method

To test hypotheses based on theory in a precise and rigorous manner, investigators use the **experimental method**—specifically laboratory experiments. In these situations, the experimenter actively manipulates or systematically alters certain variables and checks their effects on other variables. The actively manipulated variables are called **independent variables;** the others are labeled **dependent variables.** In the traditional and strictest sense, such experiments demand the use of **control groups,** in which the independent variable is manipulated in one group but not in the other. In this way, a more accurate assessment of the effects of independent-variable manipulation on the dependent variable is possible. The basic function of control groups, however, is to allow investigators to make comparisons between the ways in which their manipulations affect dependent outcomes. Thus, in the broadest sense, experimental studies that allow such comparisons, even though they do not use a control group in the traditional sense, are considered to have utilized control (Kerlinger, 1979).

You might bear these points in mind as we discuss a classic example of laboratory research conducted by psychologists Aronson and Carlsmith and based on Festinger's dissonance formulations (Aronson and Carlsmith, 1962). These researchers were concerned with the relationship between individual differences in ability and task performance. They argued that once a person's ability level on a task was clearly established, future performances on that task at the same ability level would be pleasant and sought out, whereas performances that were inconsistent with the established level would be unpleasant and therefore avoided or minimized. Specifically, they maintained that people who expect to do well on a task and who instead do poorly will experience dissonance and will attempt to reduce it by minimizing the performance. We do not really need dissonance theory to help us make this rather uninteresting prediction, however, because people in our culture are usually rewarded for good performances and punished for poor ones. But dissonance theory did allow Aronson and Carlsmith to make an interesting and nonobvious prediction regarding the behavior of people who are incompetent at a task and who suddenly perform superbly. In such an obviously dissonant situation, they hypothesized, individuals would, if given the opportunity, change a superior performance to an inferior one to make it consistent with their poor task ability.

To test the prediction, a large sample of college students viewed 100 cards, each of which had three individual photographs of young men pasted on them. They were asked to judge which of the three on each card was schizophrenic. Some of them were led to believe that they were incompetent at the task over the first 80 cards; others, that they had considerable skill. Once their ability levels were clearly established, they viewed the remaining 20 cards and then scored their own performances, noting for each of the 20 cards the number of correct selections. A short time later, all the participants were told by the experimenter that she had forgotten to record the speed of the performance for the last 20 trials. Therefore, she explained, it would be necessary for the subjects to reexamine these cards and make their judgments as if they had never seen the cards before. The key question was, How many previously correct decisions would the low- and high-ability participants change to incorrect ones? As predicted, the low-ability participants made significantly more changes than did the high-ability ones. So there may be circumstances under which people with particular personality characteristics perform in unexpected and self-defeating ways.

Correlational Method

Much of the research in personality is correlational in nature; that is, it is concerned with establishing relationships between two variables. For example: Is the need for achievement related to students' performance? Is the need for achievement related to a person's chronic anxiety level? Is there a relationship between prejudice and self-esteem? In the **correlational method,** the direction and size of the relationship is expressed by a statistical device called the **correlation coefficient** (also known as Pearson's product-moment coefficient). The direction of the correlation coefficient tells us how scores on one variable are associated with scores on the other. Positive correlations indicate that low scores on one variable are associated with low scores on the other or that high scores tend to be associated with high scores. For example, research indicates that high scores on the dogmatism scale, a test designed to measure a person's general intolerance of the beliefs of others, are associated with high scores on **self-report** anxiety scales (Vacchiano, Strauss & Schiffman, 1968). So, intolerant people (high dogmatics) tend to be high in anxiety, whereas tolerant people (low dogmatics) tend to be low in anxiety. Negative correlations indicate that high scores on one variable are associated with low scores on another or that low scores tend to be associated with high scores. An example of a negative correlation is the research finding that high dogmatics are apt to have lower self-esteem. Conversely, low dogmatics tend to have higher self-esteem.

The size of a correlation indicates the degree of the relationship between two variables. A perfect positive correlation between variables would be written $+1.00$; a perfect negative relationship, -1.00; and a complete lack of association, .00. Perfect positive or negative correlations are, of course, rare.

Correlation coefficients do not provide us with any information about which variable *causes* the other. If we found a $+.60$ correlation between student ratings of the physical attractiveness of college men and their frequency of dating, we could not conclude that the large number of dates they had was a result of their physical attractiveness. Physical attractiveness may also be positively correlated with intellectual ability, "ego strength," or general self-confidence and dominance, so that any one or a combination of these variables may have produced the high dating frequency. One of the primary advantages of employing the experimental rather than the correlational method is that it allows us to make causal inferences about variables with a higher degree of confidence.

Singer (1964) has provided a good example of correlational research in personality in a study designed to determine whether or not there was a relationship between students' manipulative strategies and their academic grades. His study was based on the undergraduate belief that some students get high grades by manipulating their professors. Singer asked large numbers of students to fill out a paper-and-pencil test called the Machiavellianism Scale in order to measure individual differences in the use of manipulative strategies in a wide variety of situations. This scale was based primarily on information adapted from Machiavelli's *The Prince*, in which a 16th-century statesman offered advice to monarchs on the proper ways to rule. Items used in the scale included the following: (1) "It is wise to flatter important people." (2) "Never tell anyone the real reason you did something unless it is useful to do so." (3) "The best way to handle people is to tell them what they want to hear" (Christie & Geis, 1970, p. 17).

After obtaining the test scores, Singer proceeded to correlate them with grade-point averages. He found a correlation of $+.39$ for the men in his sample but not for women, which suggested that the men who used manipulative strategies to attain their goals had higher grade-point averages. The kinds of strategies they used were left unspecified. Among other possible explanations for the positive correlation was that bright people might tend to be manipulative, so that brightness (academic ability) contributed to their higher averages. This alternative was ruled out by using a partial correlation technique that allowed the investigator to hold ability test scores constant. The initial correlational relationship was still obtained.

But even though there was a positive association between Machiavellian skills and high grade averages for men, what about the lack of such a relationship for women? Does this mean that women do not use manipulative strategies to attain their goals? Singer argued that women also probably manipulate, but they use strategies involving physical attractiveness and appearance rather than verbal deceit. Singer tested his idea by using faculty ratings of the physical attractiveness of the women in his study and then correlating these ratings with grade-point averages, with academic ability held constant. The results showed a significant correlation of $+.37$ for first-born women, but a nonsignificant correlation of $-.04$ for later-borns. But why did he find the relationship for first-borns and not for later-borns? That question could not be answered precisely and directly, but further study did show that first-born women tended to sit at the front of the class, to see the instructor after class, and to visit him in his office more frequently than did later-borns. The general conclusion, then, was that college men and women probably do use manipulative strategies to secure their goals but that the *kinds* of strategies used differ by sex.

These results also imply that the professor is a poor soul at the mercy of students as he or she tries to fulfill academic responsibilities. As Singer note: "he [or she] is seemingly caught in a maelstrom of student intrigue and machination. The picture is bleak" (1964, p. 150). In the professor's defense, it should be noted that when faculty members were administered the Machiavellianism Scale, their scores were higher than those of the students, indicating that the faculty is even more manipulative than the students. Perhaps, as Singer pointed out, the "battle" is not all that one-sided.

Finally, we should note that psychologists use many other correlation techniques in their research, some of which are considerably more sophisticated than the Pearson product-moment coefficient. Examples include **partial** and **multiple correlation** techniques, as well as factor-analytic methods (see Chapter 9 for the rudiments of the factor-analytic procedure).

Case Study Method

Intensive study of an individual's behavior over a period of time and in various situations is called a case history or **case study.** Such studies are frequently used in clinical and medical research to provide descriptions of a person's actions. One of the primary advantages of the technique is that it allows for a "rich," or complex and integrated, treatment of the individual. Personality studies using the experimental method examine average or typical differences between individuals. The case method, then, provides a view of the uniqueness of the person, in the sense that it describes both the consistencies and the inconsistencies of individual behavior as well as the ways in which characteristic experiences are organized. Because it focuses on the unique characteristics of the individual, the data it yields are difficult, if not impossible, to apply to people in general. The procedure also lacks the systematic control of variables inherent in laboratory experiments. Although this lack is a major source of weakness because it makes causal inferences impossible, it is also a source of strength because it may lead to serendipitous findings that, in turn, may lead to new, testable hypotheses and further research.

A good example of the use of the case study method is Freud's analysis of Leonardo da Vinci's personality, with special focus on his alleged homosexuality. The famous genius of the Renaissance had been accused and subsequently acquitted by authorities of forbidden sexual relations with other boys while he was an apprentice in the house of his master, Verrocchio. From this information and a few other biographical fragments, Freud brilliantly reconstructed much of Leonardo's unconscious life in an attempt to determine the truth or falsity of the accusation. Since Freud assumed that early childhood experiences were critical determinants of later personality development, he focused on Leonardo's only written account of his earlier life. As Leonardo described the flight of the vulture, he interrupted himself to discuss an early memory:

It seems that it had been destined before that I should occupy myself so thoroughly with the vulture, for it comes to my mind as a very early memory, when I was still in the cradle, a vulture came down to me, opened my mouth with his tail and struck me many times with his tail against my lips. [Freud, 1947, pp. 33–34]

To Freud, this infantile fantasy meant that

[the] "tail," or "coda," is one of the most familiar symbols, as well as a sub-stitutive designation of the male member, in Italian no less than in other languages. The situation contained in the fantasy, that a vulture opened the mouth of the child and forcefully belabored it with its tail, corresponds to the idea of fellatio, a sexual act in which the member is placed into the mouth of the other person. Strangely enough, this fantasy is altogether of a passive character; it resembles certain dreams and fantasies of women and of passive homosexuals (who play the feminine part in sexual relations). [Freud, 1947, p. 38]

Freud then described this fantasy as an elaboration of another situation he assumed everyone had experienced—namely, the pleasurable sensations derived from sucking the mother's nipples during infancy. Thus, Da Vinci's fantasy suggested to Freud that Leonardo may have been a passive homosexual whose sexual life had been inhibited by an extraordinarily close relationship with his mother in the absence of his father. "Mother," according to Freud, was depicted in Egyptian hieroglyphics by the picture of a vulture, so that Leonardo's fantasy was a memory of a time when his own mother (the vulture) held him close and kissed him passionately on the lips many times. Since the erotic feelings of the young Leonardo for his mother could not continue to develop consciously, he repressed them by putting himself in her place and then mirroring her behavior in his selection of a sexual object. Furthermore, Leonardo sublimated much of his sexual feeling by taking "pretty" boys into his employment as apprentices. He selected strikingly handsome boys and "nursed" them as his mother had protected and cared for him during his childhood.

Some people concluded Freud had proved scientifically that Leonardo da Vinci was a homosexual. The conclusion is wrong. Freud presented an interesting and ingenious, but post hoc, interpretation of the dynamics of Leonardo's alleged homosexuality. It is an interpretation tacked on to certain information about the master's life. A retrospective analysis does not prove anything scientifically, although we cannot help but admire Freud's intriguing formulations. A scientific analysis, on the other hand, would demand that **a priori predictions** about the relationship between early childhood experiences and events be made and then the relevant data collected. These points are important because they tell us that we should be cautious in accepting conclusions made by the **post hoc method.** While we may marvel at the creativity involved in some of these speculations and acknowledge that they can be used to generate testable hypotheses, we should not assume that they provide absolute proof for a theory, despite claims to the contrary.

Criteria for the Evaluation of Scientific Theories

Comprehensiveness. There seems to be general agreement among theoreticians that a "good," or formally adequate, theory encompasses and accounts for a wide range and diversity of data—that is, it is **comprehensive.** Since no theory can cover all the phenomena related to human personality, decisions must be made concerning the importance of the events to be studied (Pervin, 1980, p. 21). For example, is it more important that the theory adequately describe and explain eyelid conditioning or human aggression? The answer seems obvious—investigators should focus on the study of aggression because an understanding of aggressive acts would allow us to account for behaviors that have important implications for human welfare. If we gain knowledge about the parameters, or characteristics, that control eye-blinking, what have we accomplished? The answer, for most people, is "Not much." Yet we should exercise some caution in making this judgment until we hear the other side of the argument. Many scientists have maintained that in science there is no unambiguous criterion that allows us safely to exclude phenomena from study on the basis of triviality. They argue that what may be a trivial undertaking for you may be an important research investigation for someone else, and vice versa. Further, and more important, no one knows for certain what will happen in the future. Work on a seemingly trivial problem may also bear fruit at some later time. In the eye-blink example, an understanding of the characteristics that control eye-blinking could give us information about the principles of classical conditioning, principles that can be used to explain the origins of many irrational fears and phobias.

As you can see, there is no clear-cut answer to this problem. But one prominent personality theorist, Salvatore Maddi, has suggested that investigators can minimize the risk of triviality by relying on naturalistic observation. Such observation would include gathering information about human behavior by studying people in their daily surroundings and, to a lesser extent, in therapeutic settings (Maddi, 1976, pp. 598–599). In this way, we can make tentative judgments about the worth of personality theories on the basis of comprehensiveness.

Precision and Testability. Besides being comprehensive, a good theory should contain concepts that are clearly and explicitly defined. It should also contain **relational statements** and propositions that are consistent and logically related to one another. It is generally recognized that in the early stages of theorizing, investigators may rely heavily on analogies and metaphors as an aid to thought, but in the final analysis they may create only inconsistencies and ambiguities that hamper understanding. Examples include Jung's *shadow*, which lurks around in the *darkness* of the collective unconscious, and Freud's treatment of the ego as a battlefield where mortal combat takes place between the forces of the id and superego.

Not only must the concepts in the theory be defined with **precision,** but the hypotheses containing them must be capable of being empirically studied—that is, they must be linked at some point with external reality (Hall & Lindzey, 1978, p. 20). The link between conceptualization and observation is made through the use of operational definitions. In brief, a good theory contains hypotheses that have **testability.**

Parsimony. A good theory should be **parsimonious,** or economical— that is, it should contain only those concepts and assumptions needed to explain the phenomena within its domain. The inclusion of unnecessary concepts or assumptions can lead an investigator to waste much effort studying meaningless relationships. A theory that contains more concepts and assumptions than are necessary is considered inadequate. A theory can also be regarded as inadequate if it contains *fewer* concepts and assumptions than are necessary to account completely for the phenomena in its domain. Thus the parsimony criterion is not met just because an investigator uses fewer concepts and assumptions in an absolute sense. He or she may have ignored the complexity of the data to be explained.

Empirical Validity. Good theory must be capable of generating predictions that have **empirical validity.** Ascertaining this validity is a key function of theory and involves the testing of hypotheses by making observations to find out if the investigator's conjectures are correct. Of course, the determination of validity is not always easy. First, research findings are always determined statistically. This means that we can place a certain amount of confidence in our findings, but we are never completely certain. If we confirm the hypothesis, it generally means that we have some confidence that the predicted relationship exists. As noted earlier, successful replications increase our confidence. On the other hand, failure to confirm may mean that we will not place much confidence in the existence of the relationship. Successive failures to replicate may make us even less certain.

Second, determining the validity of a theory is difficult because investigators can argue that the measures used to assess the concepts were unreliable and invalid, though they themselves may be measuring the concepts poorly or not at all. An investigator's claims involving faulty measurement may be legitimate or illegitimate. In fact, the measurement procedures may be unreliable and error-ridden. On the other hand, a few theorists and their advocates have such strongly vested interests in their own formulations that they dismiss out-of-hand any evidence disproving those theories on the ground that the concepts tested were not adequately measured. Such self-serving statements run counter to the ideals of science and in the long run are overruled by the body of evidence accumulated by independent researchers.

Heuristic Value. A good theory has **heuristic value** in that it stimulates investigators to do further research. Or, it may be the source of new ideas for some researchers and lead them into new paths that may prove enlightening and useful.

Applied Value. Finally, a good theory has **applied value;** that is, it leads to new approaches to the solution of people's problems (Kelly, 1955, p. 24). This criterion is not universally endorsed by scientists, especially not by those who work in the various areas of experimental psychology. Yet it seems particularly germane to theories in the area of personality. An adequate theory of personality will undoubtedly focus on abnormal as well as normal development, and an overriding concern of virtually all personality psychologists is to help people overcome their problems.

Now that we are equipped with information about the essential ingredients of the scientific process and the standards used to evaluate the worth of the various theories, we are ready to examine the major perspectives in the study of personality.

Discussion Questions

1. Why is the definition of personality in terms of social attractiveness inadequate for use by psychologists?
2. How would you define personality more adequately?
3. What is science? In what ways does the scientific enterprise involve the use of theory and research?
4. Why do most psychologists use the scientific approach to study problems of individual differences?
5. Discuss some of the inadequacies of the commonsense approach to the study of behavior.
6. Discuss the importance of operational definitions and replication in the study of personality.
7. What are the basic elements of the experimental method?
8. What is the correlational method, and when and how is it used in the investigation of scientific problems?
9. Explain the differences between the experimental and the case study methods.
10. List and describe six criteria commonly used by investigators for the evaluation of scientific theories.

References

Aronson, E., & Carlsmith, J. M. Performance expectancy as a determinant of actual performance. *Journal of Abnormal and Social Psychology*, 1962, *65*, 178–182.

Christie, R., & Geis, F. L. *Studies in Machiavellianism*. New York: Academic Press, 1970.

Darley, J. M., & Latané, B. Bystander intervention in emergencies: diffusion of responsibility. *Journal of Personality and Social Psychology*, 1968, *8*, 377–383.

Festinger, L. *A theory of cognition*. Evanston, Ill.: Row, Peterson, 1957.

Freud, S. *Leonardo da Vinci: A study in psychosexuality*. Translated by A. A. Brill. New York: Random House, 1947.

Hall, C. S., & Lindzey, G. *Theories of personality*. 3d ed. New York: Wiley, 1978.

Kelly, G. A. *The psychology of personal constructs*, vol. I. New York: Norton, 1955.

Kerlinger, F. N. *Behavioral research: A conceptual approach.* New York: Holt, Rinehart & Winston, 1979.

Maddi, S. R. *Personality theories: A comparative analysis.* 3d ed. Homewood, Ill.: Dorsey Press, 1976.

Milgram, S. Behavioral study of obedience. *Journal of Abnormal and Social Psychology*, 1963, 67, 371–378.

Pervin, L. A. *Personality: Theory, assessment and research.* 3d ed. New York: Wiley, 1980.

Shanab, M. E., & Yahya, K. A. A behavioral study of obedience in children. *Journal of Personality and Social Psychology*, 1977, 35, 530–536.

Singer, J. E. The use of manipulative strategies: Machiavellianism and attractiveness. *Sociometry*, 1964, 27, 128–150.

Vacchiano, R. B., Strauss, P. S., & Schiffman, D. D. Personality correlates of dogmatism. *Journal of Consulting and Clinical Psychology*, 1968, 32, 83–85.

Suggested Readings

Gold, J. A. *Principles of psychological research.* Homewood, Ill.: Dorsey Press, 1984.

Kerlinger, F. N. *Behavioral research: A conceptual approach.* New York: Holt, Rinehart & Winston, 1979.

Meyers, A. *Experimental Psychology.* New York: Van Nostrand, 1980.

Meyers, L. S., & Grossen, N. E. *Behavioral research: Theory, procedure, and design.* 2d ed. San Francisco: Freeman, 1978.

Neale, J. M., & Liebert, R. M. *Science and behavior: An introduction to methods of research.* 2d ed. Englewood Cliffs, N.J.: Prentice-Hall, 1980.

Glossary

Applied value   Criterion or standard for judging the scientific worth of a theory. An adequate theory is capable of providing creative solutions to problems that are of interest and concern to people.

A priori prediction   Hypothesis of the relationship between events that is made prior to the actual collection of data to test its validity.

Case study   Research technique involving the intensive study of a single person in order to understand his or her unique behavior.

Cognitive dissonance   Painful motivational state created within a person when two or more thoughts, attitudes, or behaviors are inconsistent with one another.

Comprehensiveness   Criterion or standard by which to judge the worth of a scientific theory. An adequate theory must encompass and account for a wide variety of phenomena.

Control group   In an experiment, the group that does not receive the experimental treatment. A control group is designed to provide baseline data against which the effects of the experimental manipulation can be judged.

Correlation coefficient   The statistic used to describe the direction and magnitude of the relation between two variables.

Correlational method   General procedure for establishing the noncausal nature of the association or relationship between events. Statistics involving correlations can vary in complexity from simple correlation coefficients to complicated factor-analytic techniques.

Dependent variable Change in behavior that occurs as a result of the manipulation of conditions by an experimenter. The changes depend on the manipulation of the independent variable(s).

Empirical evidence Observations of phenomena made by investigators.

Empirical validity Criterion used to judge the worth of a theory in which the various hypotheses are tested by experiments or observations to determine whether or not they are correct. Confirmation of the hypotheses lends support to the theory's validity.

Experimental method Scientific method for studying the nature of cause-and-effect relationships between variables. It involves the manipulation of independent variables and the observation of the effects on dependent variables.

Heuristic value Criterion or standard for judging the scientific worth of a theory. An adequate theory should stimulate new ideas and new research.

Hypothesis Tentative theoretical statement about how events are related to one another. Hypotheses are often stated as predictions about how the operation of one set of events will affect the operation of others.

Independent variable The variable actively manipulated by the experimenter so that its effects on individual behavior can be observed.

Multiple correlation Statistical technique in which it is possible to determine the relationship between one variable and a combination of two or more other variables.

Operational definition Procedures or operations used to define particular concepts. For example, a person's intelligence could be operationally defined by his or her scores on a verbal reasoning test.

Parsimony Criterion for judging the scientific worth of a theory. An adequate theory should be as parsimonious, or economical, as possible and still adequately account for the phenomena in its domain.

Partial correlation One of many correlational techniques designed to measure the nature of the association between events. The partial correlation technique allows the investigator to assess the nature of the relationship between two events by eliminating, or "partialing out," the influence of a third variable.

Phenomenon Observable fact or event capable of being studied scientifically.

Post hoc method Explanation of a phenomenon given *after* its occurrence. The explanation presumes that certain factors caused the occurrence of the phenomenon, but there is no evidence that they actually did. The proof that the explanation has validity would await the outcomes of further experimental testing.

Precision Criterion or standard for judging the scientific worth of a theory. An adequate theory should contain concepts and relational statements that are clearly and explicitly stated and measured.

Proposition General theoretical statement, which may be true or false, about the relationship between events.

Psychological construct A highly complex abstraction that encompasses a variety of components or dimensions. For example, intelligence is a construct that encompasses such components as reasoning ability, spatial ability, mechanical ability, and mathematical ability.

Relational statement Theoretical proposition or hypothesis that links or relates concepts. For example, the concepts of frustration and aggression might be linked as follows: Increases in frustration lead to increases in aggressive behavior.

Replication Duplication or repetition of an experiment to determine whether or not the original findings are reliable.

Self-report An individual's written or verbal description of his or her behavior.

Testability Criterion or standard for judging the scientific worth of a theory. An adequate theory must contain hypotheses that can be defined, measured, and checked by observable events.

Theory A number of interrelated conceptual statements that are created by investigators to account for a phenomenon or a set of phenomena.

Psychoanalytic and Neoanalytic Perspectives

Only a few people in the history of human endeavor have done work so creative and provocative that it shapes the course of human values and thought. Copernicus, the eminent 16th-century Polish astronomer, was such an individual because he discovered that the earth was not the center of the universe and forced us to reexamine our beliefs about our own omnipotence and omniscience. Darwin, the English naturalist of the 19th century, was another pioneer, for he made us realize that we are simply part of the natural world and governed to some extent by our biology.

Sigmund Freud belongs in this august company because he compelled us to acknowledge that we are often irrational and impulsive and characterized by conflicts of a sexual and aggressive nature. It was a shock to many scholars in the humanistic tradition of Western thought, which emphasized rationality and the virtues of ethical conduct, to learn that human beings are often irrational and that they continuously engage in internal struggles to keep their sexual and aggressive impulses in check. Freud bared the baseness of the human soul for everyone to see, and some people have never forgiven him his "treachery." He removed us from our pedestals and forced us to examine the dark and impulsive side of our natures. For his efforts, he was initially publicly reviled and scorned. Eventually, however, investigators in many disciplines began to explore the validity of his statements.

Today, Freud's influence is worldwide. Scholars in literature are fond of using psychoanalytic concepts to explain the motives of their characters. Anthropologists focus on child-rearing practices in various cultures and use a Freudian model to understand adult personality. Philosophers and sociologists have used the Freudian concepts of repression and anxiety in their analyses of problems confronting modern society. Freudian concepts have also been adopted by lay people. We are all aware of the importance of "Freudian slips" and the ways in which the unconscious influences behavior. Sometimes we talk glibly about ego trips, phallic symbols, penis envy, and Oedipal conflicts. Clearly, Freudian thinking has had a revolutionary impact on our lives. Freud deserves his place in history, whether we ultimately accept or reject his view of human behavior and functioning.

In Chapter 2, we review the basic concepts of Freud's theory. We examine his attempts to construct a theory of personality based on interpretations of self-reports by his patients. The chapter includes a description of the basic constructs (instincts, the unconscious, and the id, ego, and superego) in his model and some of the important ways in which they interact to produce internal conflict. We also consider the use of various defense mechanisms to protect the ego and reduce the anxiety generated by the conflicts. Freud's theory of psychosexual development is reviewed, with special emphasis on the origins and nature of the various character disorders. We then consider the research evidence for the theory of psychosexual development and show how this theory can be applied to cases involving psychopathology, including obsessive-compulsive neurosis. As do the chapters that follow, this chapter closes with an analysis of the strengths and weaknesses of the position discussed.

Chapter 3 on Carl Jung examines the nature of the individual's psyche, all the interacting systems within human personality that are needed to account for the mental life and behavior of the person, and the life-process energy that motivates the person to action. Although both Freud and Jung used the term *libido* to describe the energy that propels the person into action, Jung's conceptualization of it was much broader than Freud's. Jung thought of it not just in terms of sexual impulses that try to force their way into consciousness but as forces generated by continuous conflicts within the psyche. Once created, this energy can move in various directions. In short, Jung treated libido as a force that can split and move erratically and unpredictably through the psyche. The result is that the person may at times exhibit bizarre and impulsive behavior. This conceptualization also adds a certain mystery to the person, because autonomous forces, often operating capriciously, do not allow outside observers to clearly identify the causes of the person's behavior.

Following the discussion of libido, the chapter examines the major structures of the psyche and describes the evolution of the self as the conflicts between the various oppositional forces are resolved via transcendence. Jung believed that in the attempt to evolve toward selfhood, people adopt different orientations or attitudes toward life and utilize different psychological processes or functions to make sense out of their experiences. Eventually he combined the attitudes and functions in a theoretical scheme of psychological types and discussed the ways in which introverted and extraverted individuals try to deal with the world and their own conflicts. This theoretical scheme is examined in considerable detail and includes a review of the major research evidence based on it. The chapter then delves into Jung's views of disordered behavior and therapy.

In contrast to Freud and Jung, Alfred Adler, whose work is the subject of Chapter 4, presented a simplified scheme to account for the development of personality. He came to believe that all individuals feel inferior and strive to overcome these feelings and to become superior. Neurotic strivings are, in his view, associated with attempts to achieve personal superiority at the expense of others, whereas healthy strivings include attempts to reach for perfection via efforts to improve the lot of others. Although Adler emphasized human rationality and consciousness in making decisions and discussed in detail the ways in which our goals inspire us to improve ourselves, we should not conclude that his position was totally optimistic in tone. Specifically, Adler was never able to break completely with his Freudian origins, and so he concluded that our lifestyles are set by the end of our fifth year. Such a stance has pessimistic overtones, because it implies that there is not much one can do to change oneself drastically after early childhood. Thus a person with a destructive lifestyle is essentially doomed to a life of misery and conflict. Therapy can be beneficial but only to a certain extent. This point should be borne in mind when we consider the implications of Adler's position in relation to the treatment of human suffering.

Despite his adherence to this aspect of Freudian theory, the general tone of Adler's writings is optimistic. Chapter 4 reveals his essential humanism and points out his socialist political orientation as well as his constant attempts to help oppressed people. In particular, it focuses on his concept of social interest—that is, on his belief that we have an innate need to help others and on his wish for an ideal society in which cooperation, harmony, and equality would be the rule. The other major concepts in his theory are also presented. Then we review Adler's examination of the process of personality development, with special emphasis on his birth-order concept and the research that utilizes it. Discussion of abnormal development follows, along with a presentation of the ways in which Adler's theory can be applied to the treatment of psychopathology.

Chapter 5 presents the major concepts and principles in Karen Horney's revisionist view of Freudian theory. Her theory posits disturbed relationships between parents and their children as the primary cause of neurosis. Neurotics are pictured as insecure individuals with compulsive and rigid needs and strivings that are designed to reestablish the safety of their environments. Unfortunately, these strivings are almost invariably unsuccessful. They cause conflict and pain on an unconscious level and result in inefficient problem-solving. According to Horney, neurotics are alienated from their real selves and from other people. They identify with a false idealized self to avoid coping with the pain associated with an acknowledgment of their limitations. The chapter chronicles the development of this alienation process and the therapeutic procedures Horney used to reduce the alienation and to release the individual's potentials for growth.

In Chapter 6 we consider the basic concepts and principles in Erich Fromm's theory. Fromm was chosen in preference to other neo-Freudians such as Sullivan and Murray because he focused on the ways in which a society's political and economic structures influence development. Although in many respects he retained the Freudian focus on inner conflicts and attempted to cope with them, he attributed the origins of these conflicts not so much to underlying sexual and aggressive impulses as to the imposition of social and economic controls on the individual. This chapter also gives us an opportunity to examine the unique ways in which Fromm combined elements of existentialism and psychoanalysis in his theory of personality development.

The chapter begins with Fromm's view of the basic needs inherent in all human beings. If these needs are satisfied, the person becomes a productive citizen. If they are not, he or she develops nonproductive orientations. We review Fromm's analysis of the social and cultural conditions that influence development along productive or nonproductive lines and present research evidence in support of the theory of character types. Then we examine Fromm's view of the need for restructuring society to change nonproductive orientations into productive ones. Fromm argued for the development of a society based upon humanistic ethics in which working people would be active and responsible participants in the political and economic decision-making process. He maintained that such a society would help overcome much of the alienation workers currently experience in both totalitarian and capitalist countries. The chapter then considers the application of Fromm's theory to the treatment of disordered behavior. He saw the causes of pathology as primarily sociocultural in nature. To overcome their problems, people must raise their consciousness about the many familial and cultural conditions that stifle their development. They must then actively attempt to change those conditions responsible for their plight. More important, constructive change depends upon massive societal reform.

As the final chapter in this part, Chapter 7 considers the concepts and principles in Erik Erikson's psychoanalytic ego psychology. It begins by pointing out that Erikson's theory represents a systematic extension of Freud's view of the role played by the ego in personality development and functioning. In contrast to Freud, Erikson sees the ego as often operating autonomously from id motivations. He perceives it as an entity having nondefensive functions and as helping people to adapt constructively to the demands of their surroundings. Our primary focus is on Erikson's dynamic theory of ego development and functioning, with particular emphasis on the crises experienced by youths as they try to establish their identities. In Erikson's view, the major disturbance during this period of role confusion is youths' inability to decide on an occupational identity, and we present support for this theory. We also consider the primary techniques utilized by Erikson in the assessment of personality, review his pioneering efforts to use psychohistorical analysis to increase our understanding of the lives of important historical figures, and examine the application of the theory of ego development to the treatment of abnormal behavior.

CHAPTER 2

Freud's Psychoanalytic Theory

Biographical Sketch

Sigmund Freud was born in 1856 in Freiberg, Moravia (now Czechoslovakia), of Jewish parents. His father was a wool merchant who married twice, and Sigmund was the oldest son in the second marriage. The family consisted of five daughters and two other sons. Freud was a serious boy who excelled in his studies throughout his early schooling. Upon entering the University of Vienna, he reluctantly decided on a medical career and was graduated in 1883. He maintained that he never felt comfortable playing the "doctor game," but he was impressed with the scientific attitude of people in the medical profession. Freud yearned to answer the great problems of the world and to learn all he could about human nature (Jones, 1963, pp. 3–4, 22). He saw science as the means for satisfying such yearnings.

During his medical school days, Freud came under the influence of the eminent physiologist Ernst Brücke and worked as his assistant on neurological problems in lower animals. Although quite content in his work at Brücke's laboratory, Freud soon realized that his chances for advancement were poor and that the monetary rewards would always be minimal. As he was seriously interested in a lovely young woman at the time and believed he should be earning enough money to support her before committing himself to marriage, he was naturally quite distressed. After several attempts to secure money from his superiors failed, Freud, with Brücke's friendly encouragement, left the laboratory and entered private medical practice in the hope of raising his income. Shortly afterward, in 1885, he applied for a postgraduate traveling stipend to work with the renowned French neurologist Jean Charcot on the treatment of nervous disorders. The competition for the grant was fierce although it provided the winner with only $240 to cover traveling expenses from Vienna to Paris and all living expenses over a six-month period. Eventually, after much haggling and debate by the committee authorized to make the decision, Freud was declared the winner. Elated, he wrote the following note to his fiancée, who lived in Hamburg:

> Oh, how wonderful it is going to be. I am coming with money and am staying a long while with you and am bringing something lovely for you and shall then go to Paris and become a great savant and return to Vienna with a great, great nimbus. Then we will marry soon and I will cure all the incurable nervous patients and you will keep me well and I will kiss you till you are merry and happy—and they lived happily ever after. [Jones, 1963, p. 50]

It should be mentioned that Freud and Martha Bernays were married in 1886 and lived happily together for more than half a century.

Freud then tried hypnosis with his own patients at the suggestion of a mentor and physician named Joseph Breuer. Breuer had treated a young woman, Anna O., for a group of physical symptoms that had arisen in connection with the death of her father. The symptoms included paralysis of her limbs and disturbances of sight and speech. Breuer found, to his astonishment, that the woman's symptoms disappeared if she talked about them while in a hypnotic trance. In this state, she would relive the terrifying experiences that gave rise to her symptoms and express the accompanying emotions fully. This physical expression of emotion was labeled a **catharsis.** Eventually Freud and Breuer severed their relationship because of Freud's insistence that the basis of such disorders was sexual in nature (Jones, 1963, pp. 147, 165).

Between 1892 and 1895, the method of **free association** gradually evolved in Freud's thinking. He used the cathartic method in his treatment for several years, but he found there were many patients he could not hypnotize. As a consequence, he began to ask patients to concentrate on a particular symptom and to try to recall any early experiences that might explain its origins. Eventually he asked his patients to free-associate—that is, to express every thought that occurred to them, no matter how irrelevant, unimportant, or unpleasant (Jones, 1963, pp. 157–158). Although the patients' recollections seemed aimless and accidental, Freud felt intuitively that there must be some definite force controlling the thoughts. He had been thoroughly trained in medicine and neurology to accept the principles of **determinism** and causality, so that he could not now bring himself to believe that the thoughts of a patient were unrelated. In addition, Freud was impressed by the unwillingness of many patients to disclose memories that were painful to them. He labeled this opposition "resistance" and came to believe that his patients were "repressing" certain important memories. His job, then, was to probe their unconscious and uncover the reasons for their active resistance.

In the course of his analyses, Freud also discovered that patients insisted on tracing the origins of their traumatic experiences to early childhood. To his surprise, he found that many of these memories involved sexual experiences. Until this time, most people believed that childhood was a time of innocence, devoid of sexual urges. Freud disagreed strongly:

> We do wrong entirely to ignore the sexual life of children; in my experience children are capable of all the mental and many of the physical activities. Just as the whole sexual apparatus of man is not comprised in the external genital organs and the two reproductive glands, so his sexual life does not begin only with the onset of puberty, as to casual observation it may appear to do. [Jones, 1963, p. 172]

Freud at first believed that the early childhood seduction scenes his patients described were literally true. Eventually, however, he began to have doubts. He found it difficult to believe, for example, that all his women patients' fathers were sexually perverse. He also found that literal acceptance of these accounts and subsequent suggestions to the patients of how they must deal with them did not always have therapeutic benefits. He noted in a letter to a friend that he had to renounce his explanations of hysteria and his hopes of becoming a famous physician. But he eventually faced up to the situation and revised his **libido theory.** The major revision was his acceptance of the fact that the descriptions were not literally true; they were instead fantasies that were nevertheless psychically real and valid in their own right (Jones, 1963, pp. 172–173).

In asking his patients to free-associate, Freud also discovered that they often mentioned their dreams. He found that dreams provide the best means of unlocking the secrets of the **unconscious.** They yield invaluable information about the nature of the person's conflicts and the mechanisms by which they were concealed from awareness (Jones, 1963, p. 129). In 1900, Freud published *The Interpretation of Dreams*. In it he noted that dreaming is neither an idle activity nor as chaotic as it seems. Dreams serve as wish-fulfillment devices, and their latent content can be used to help a patient understand his or her problems.

In 1902, the Vienna Psychoanalytical Society was formed. Initially, a small group of scholars from various disciplines met in Freud's office to discuss their work. When the membership grew, this practice was abandoned for meetings in larger, more formal settings. The period 1905–1906 was a highly productive one for Freud; he published several books, including *Jokes and Their Connection with the Unconscious*, his well-known *The Psychopathology of Everyday Life*, and *Three Essays on the Theory of Sexuality* as well as some articles. *Three Essays* in particular made Freud almost universally unpopular. The book was labeled "shockingly wicked," and Freud was branded as a man with an obscene and evil mind. The primary focus of the criticism was Freud's assertion that children are born with sexual urges and that their parents are selected as their first sexual objects. Freud believed, however, that eventually his arguments would be accepted (Jones, 1963, pp. 240–243).

By 1910, Freud had gained an international reputation, but internal dissension was beginning to occur among members of the Psychoanalytical Society concerning his libido theory. The defections began with Adler and Wilhelm Stekel, who were followed by Jung and others. Adler's defection was precipitated by his disagreement with Freud over the importance of the sexual factor in determining behavior. Adler minimized its importance and elevated the concept of a struggle for power in its place. He also deemphasized or discarded the concepts of repression, the unconscious, and infantile sexuality. Such major differences led inevitably to a separation between the two men. The split with Jung was much more distressing for Freud. He had been closer personally to Jung than to Adler and believed that Jung was superior in intellect and knowledge, so he took the defection more seriously (Jones, 1963, pp. 313–314, 318).

Jung was disturbed by the uncompromising way Freud treated the question of sexuality in his public discussions of patients' neuroses. As Jung saw it:

> We should do well not to burst out with the theory of sexuality in the foreground. I have many thoughts about that, especially on the ethical aspects of the question. I believe that in publicly announcing certain things one would saw off the branch on which civilization rests; one undermines the impulse of sublimation.... Both with the students and with the patients, I get on further by not making the theme of sexuality prominent. [Jones, 1963, pp. 318–319]

Eventually, Jung deemphasized the sexual factor in the determination of neurosis. He considered libido, or sexual energy, as a designation of general tension and rejected Freud's belief that the Oedipal conflict involves incestuous yearnings on the part of the child. But despite the defection of some of his disciples, whose positions came to be known as the neoanalytic **perspective,** Freud's fame continued to grow and the Psychoanalytical Society flourished.

World War I had a profound impact on Freud's thinking and research. He was acutely distressed by the mass killing and suffering and eventually came to attribute these experiences to the operation of a universal death instinct among human beings. Despite his pessimism about the future of humankind, Freud continued to elaborate his ideas in a long series of books. Among the more important ones we find *Totem and Taboo* (1913), *Introductory Lectures on Psychoanalysis* (1917), *Beyond the Pleasure Principle* (1920), *The Ego and the Id* (1923), *Future of an Illusion* (1927), *Civilization and Its Discontents* (1930), *New Introductory Lectures on Psychoanalysis* (1933), and *An Outline of Psychoanalysis* (published posthumously in 1940). In the early 1930s, when Hitler came to power and anti-Semitism flourished, Freud's books were burned in Berlin and his supporters urged him to flee Vienna. With the Nazi invasion of Austria in 1938, Freud reluctantly left his home and took up residence in London. His last years were spent in considerable pain, as he had been suffering from cancer of the jaw and mouth since the mid-1920s. He persisted in his work, despite more than thirty operations, until the very end. He died in London on September 23, 1939.

Basic Concepts and Principles

Instincts: The Driving Forces in Personality

In Freud's view, human behavior is governed to a large extent by instincts. Instinctual drives are initiated by bodily needs that motivate people to seek gratification so that bodily processes can return to their prior state of equilibrium, or homeostasis. Painful feelings are associated with instinctual stimulation, while pleasurable feelings are associated with a decrease.

Instincts have four basic characteristics: (1) a *source* in some bodily deficit; (2) an *aim*—gratification of the need; (3) an *impetus* that propels the person to act; and (4) an *object* through which the instinct achieves its aim. As Freud perceived it, many objects in the external world can provide the outlet for the gratification of our biological needs. And because instincts are changeable, it is clearly possible for them to move from object to object in their attempt to gain maximum pleasure. If gratification is not forthcoming from a particular object, the object can be displaced by a substitute so that satisfaction can be obtained. For example, a college man may find a new girlfriend to love if his relationship with his current companion is not satisfying. A woman who has hostile feelings toward her boss may be prevented from expressing them because she fears the loss of her job. She may then come home and behave aggressively toward her family.

Instincts can even turn around on the individual, as when a person's aggressive feelings toward others are turned toward the self and result in acts of self-mutilation or even suicide. Sexual impulses can also be turned inward, as when an individual becomes self-absorbed and narcissistic and utilizes masturbation as the primary outlet.

Life and Death Instincts. Freud also theorized that each person has instinctive urges that seek to preserve life. Each of us is motivated to satisfy our hunger, thirst, and sexual needs. Without food and water, we obviously could not survive. And the effort to achieve sexual satisfaction helps perpetuate the species, for procreation is its typical consequence. **Libido** is the energy associated with these instincts. Originally, Freud maintained that libido was associated only with the sexual instincts, but he later revised his position and viewed libido as the psychic and pleasurable feelings associated with the gratification of the life instincts (Freud, 1952b).

In addition to the life instincts, Freud postulated the existence of opposing death instincts. He believed that "the goal of all life is death" (Freud, 1952b). Human beings strive to return to an inorganic state of balance that preceded life. In such a state, there would be no painful struggle to satisfy biological needs; the individual would be in a state of repose. The life instincts operate, however, to ensure that death is delayed as long as possible so that human beings can obtain many other satisfactions before attaining "nirvana."

Aggression is a major derivative of the death instincts: individuals try to destroy others or themselves. Freud believed that aggressive impulses are very strong in everyone. His appraisal of human beings was extremely negative. As he saw it,

> The ... truth ... is that men are not gentle, friendly creatures wishing for love, who simply defend themselves if they are attacked, but that a powerful measure of desire for aggression has to be reckoned as part of their instinctual endowment. The result is that their neighbor is to them not only a possible helper or sexual object, but also a temptation to them to gratify their aggressiveness on him, to exploit his capacity for work without recompense, to use him sexually without consent, to seize his possessions, to humiliate him, to cause him pain, to torture and kill him. Homo homini lupus [Man is to man a wolf]; who has the courage to dispute it in the face of all the evidence in his own life and in history? [Freud, 1952a, p. 787)]

It is not surprising that Freud remained quite pessimistic about the future of the species. Incidentally, although Freud maintained that libido is the psychic energy associated with the life instincts, he never postulated a corresponding energy source for the death instincts.

The Basic Conflict: The Individual's Instinctual Needs versus the Needs of Society

Freud recognized that society would not survive for long if its members were allowed to express all their impulses. Stronger individuals would take advantage of weaker ones, using their superior force to gain their ends. Social instability could also well be the outcome of allowing people to mate indiscriminately whenever the urge arose. Thus, even though people may wish to act out their sexual and aggressive impulses, society will not permit them to do so, and rightly so, in Freud's view. Problems for individuals occur, however, because society is often too harsh in its demand that people renounce their impulses. It maintains control over people by threatening punishment if they disobey. Eventually society (through the parents and others) instills its values in people so that they feel guilty if they do something inappropriate, thereby lessening the chances that they will repeat the behavior. They become anxious if they even contemplate behaving the wrong way. Yet despite these internal checks on people's behavior, their urges continually seek expression so that conflict between them and society is never-ending. In Freud's view, individuals must eventually learn to resolve their conflicts by seeking realistic ways of gratifying their impulses, by showing behavior that is in line with the proscriptions of society.

To understand the dynamics of an individual's conflicts, it was necessary for Freud to postulate constructs that allowed him to describe the ways in which these conflicts originated and influenced behavior.

Structural Theory of Personality

Conflicts originate as the three systems of the mind compete for the limited amount of psychic energy available, energy that has its starting point in the instinctual needs of the individual. These three systems are the id, ego, and superego, and we now turn to a description of them and how they function in relationship to one another.

Id. Freud conceptualized the **id** as the original aspect of personality and considered it to be rooted in the biology of the individual (Jones, 1963, p. 2). It was thought to consist primarily of unconscious sexual and aggressive instincts. These instincts might operate jointly in different situations to affect our behavior. For example, we might find ourselves hating and acting aggressively toward parents whom we dearly love, or we might feel sexually attracted to an arrogant, obnoxious person with whom we are continually arguing.

Freud likened the id to a "seething cauldron" that contains our powerful and primitive urges and desires. He believed that these urges insistently and indiscriminately seek expression in external reality. The id is thus amoral because it is unconcerned with the niceties and conventions of society. It operates according to the pleasure principle: The aim of these impulses is always immediate and complete discharge and satisfaction. The pleasure principle appears to be an outgrowth of philosophical hedonism, a doctrine that states that people always strive to maximize pleasure and minimize pain.

Ego. It is clear that we do not live in a social vacuum and cannot simply do whatever we wish whenever we wish. Adults who act impulsively are called immature or childish. Mature conduct, on the other hand, appears to demand that we control our impulses in a wide variety of situations. For Freud, this control became possible when the **ego** was differentiated from the id. The ego, in his view, is the organized aspect of id, formed to provide direction for the person's impulses. It comes into existence because the needs of the person require appropriate transactions with the environment if they are to be satisfied. The ego therefore develops partially to carry out the aims of the id. It also functions to keep the impulses of the id in check until a suitable object is found.

The conscious ego is characterized by realistic (logical and rational) thinking; and it copes not only with id impulses but also with the demands of the superego. As Freud saw it, the ego is similar to a battlefield where the "armies" of the id and superego continually clash. While much of the ego operates in consciousness, some of its processes are unconscious and serve to protect the person against anxiety caused by the demands of the id and superego (Freud, 1960, p. 7). To handle this anxiety, individuals employ many different defense mechanisms. Before discussing how these mechanisms operate as protective devices, let us consider the third system of the mind, the superego.

Superego. Freud used the construct of the **superego** to describe the individual's internalization of societal moral values. These values are instilled in the person primarily by parents, who teach which behaviors are appropriate or inappropriate in given situations. The superego represents learned ideals and was eventually conceptualized by Freud as having two primary components, conscience and the ego-ideal. **Conscience** is acquired through the use of punishment by the parents; the **ego-ideal** is learned through the use of rewards. For example, when a boy does something wrong, his conscience makes him feel guilty, but when he obeys his parents and wins their approval by performing in socially accepted ways, he feels proud. The main functions of the superego are to inhibit the urges of the id, to persuade the ego to substitute moralistic goals for realistic ones, and to strive for perfection.

Although the superego serves positive functions by preventing the individual from expressing primitive urges publicly and by encouraging the individual to set goals that would establish him or her in a career as a productive citizen, it also has negative implications. It may be too harsh and demanding. As a child, for example, a person could incorporate values from parents who view sex as dirty and sinful so that, as an adult, the person may be afraid to approach members of the other sex and be incapable of forming an intimate relationship with anyone. Or a person may learn from parents that one always must love one's neighbors, an impossible task, according to Freud, because many people are not worthy of one's respect and love. Adherence to such an exceedingly high standard, in Freud's opinion, would inevitably create problems for the individual.

Ego Defense Processes

One of Freud's key contributions to psychology involved his treatment of the many ways in which the individual uses protective maneuvers to reduce anxiety-arousing threats to the ego. **Anxiety** is a highly unpleasant state that signals a danger to the ego (self). The danger may be that the person's instinctual impulses are out of control and are threatening to overwhelm him or her. The danger may arise because the individual fears punishment from his or her conscience for thinking about doing something that the superego considers wrong. In the face of these dangers, the person's ego unconsciously attempts to regain control by activating defensive processes. These defensive processes involve a distortion of reality. We turn now to a discussion of the basic ego defenses Freud postulated.

Repression. Freud conceptualized **repression** as an attempt by the ego to keep undesirable id impulses from reaching consciousness. In the course of analyzing dreams, he discovered that certain thoughts were blocked from consciousness—repressed—because they were too painful to acknowledge and that attempts by him to make patients aware of these experiences met with "resistances." In Freudian terms, the battle for supremacy between the ego and the id involves an opposition between energy forces. The driving forces are called **cathexes;** the restraining forces, **anticathexes.** In other words, certain unconscious wishes or ideas are energized and strive for expression in consciousness but are met by other ideas energized by restraining forces seated in the ego. If the ego forces dominate, the wishes will be repressed—that is, forced back into the unconscious. If the id forces dominate, the person will "act out" his or her socially unacceptable impulses. For example, a person who hates her father might repress her hostility and anger and thus be totally unaware of her actual feelings. If these feelings were to break through to the surface, she might physically attack her father. The battle would be centered on her attempts to express her feelings and the ego's attempts to repress them because their expression could lead to serious problems. The ego would attempt to protect the individual by forcing her to repress her unpleasant thoughts. Freud considered repression the most fundamental of all defense mechanisms. As he put it, "The theory of repression is the pillar upon which the edifice of psychoanalysis rests" (Freud, 1938a, p. 939).

Freud also distinguished between repression and suppression. **Suppression** is the conscious blocking of unpleasant matters from awareness. Individuals have some control over their behaviors and actively try to avoid thinking about unpleasant matters. Repression, in contrast, occurs entirely on an unconscious level and involves unpleasant experiences that are repulsive to the ego. Memories that have been suppressed can be brought quite readily into awareness by cues from the environment, whereas repressed memories cannot be triggered into awareness in the same way.

Denial. A person's refusal to perceive an unpleasant event in external reality is called **denial.** For example, a loved one dies and the grieved partner refuses to accept it.

Often parents unwittingly teach children to use such a defense. They inform their little son that he is a "big boy" and that he is "just as strong as Father." They also reassure him after he is hurt that he is really "all right" or that he really "loves to play the piano" despite his protestations to the contrary. As a result, he may learn to apply such thinking to painful experiences (A. Freud, 1946, pp. 90–91).

The use of denial is not always harmful to the individual, as indicated by a study involving hospital patients by Levine and Zigler (1975). They found that stroke, lung cancer, and heart disease patients reported no greater amount of dissatisfaction with their present level of psychological and behavioral functioning than did healthy people who were used as control subjects. By denying, to some extent, the harmful impact of their disease on their functioning, these patients were evidently able to prevent further deterioration in their condition and postpone death. Although the occasional use of such a mechanism to protect the ego is healthy, it becomes unhealthy if it is used continually and indiscriminately.

Displacement. Freud used the term **displacement** to refer to the unconscious attempt by the individual to obtain gratification for id impulses by shifting to substitute objects if objects that would directly satisfy the impulses are not available. For example, a young boy insulted by a big and strong teenager may not be able to retaliate for fear of being physically hurt. As a result, he might then vent his anger on someone who is smaller and weaker than he. In this case, a substitute object is sought so that the impulse can be gratified, although it is clear that aggressing against the weaker child would not be as satisfying as aggressing against the teenage antagonist.

Sublimation. In Freudian terminology, **sublimation** is a form of displacement in which the unacceptable id impulses themselves, not the object at which they aim, are transformed. The unacceptable impulses are displaced by ones that are socially acceptable (A. Freud, 1946, p. 56). A woman with a strong need for aggression may channel her energies into activities that are socially acceptable. She may become, for example, an outstanding scientist or first-rate novelist. By so doing, she may demonstrate her superiority and domination of others, but in a way that contributes to society. In like manner, poets and painters may satisfy some of their sexual needs through their art.

Freud believed that creative sublimations of human instincts are necessary if civilized society is to exist and survive. He also believed, unfortunately, that such creativity is only available to the few people in society with special gifts and talents. Furthermore, in his rather pessimistic view, even the creative elite are subject to suffering because sublimated activities would not fully satisfy their primitive sexual and aggressive impulses (Freud, 1952a, pp. 773–774).

Projection. When a person protects the ego by attributing his or her own undesirable characteristics to others, we might infer that **projection** has taken place (Freud, 1938c, p. 625). For example, a student who is very stingy might claim that it is really other people who are stingy. A girl who hates her mother may be convinced that it is her mother who hates her. A student who cheats on examinations may continually assert that other students received high grades because they cheated.

Reaction Formation. Freud considered **reaction formation,** which involves the conversion of an undesirable impulse into its opposite, as a lower form of sublimation (Freud, 1938d, p. 625). There is the man who hates his wife and yet is exceedingly kind to her. He could be said to be "killing her with kindness." Another example is the mother who knows that her son hates violence of any kind and gives him a "gift" of karate lessons at the local YMCA for his birthday.

Rationalization. A widely used protective mechanism, **rationalization** is the justification of behavior through the use of plausible, but inaccurate, excuses. A young athlete fails to stay on the track team because of a lack of ability and concludes that he did not really want to stay on the team anyway because it is going to lose many games. Or a young woman flunks out of college and them claims that self-made women with practical experience are superior to college graduates with little "real-life" experience. Finally, a person who loses a tennis match and blames it on the inferior quality of the ball or racquet would be rationalizing if, in fact, the ball and racquet were superior in quality. All these examples illustrate the "sour grapes" form of rationalization. The other form has been called the "sweet lemon" rationalization. Here the person protects himself or herself against feelings of inadequacy by claiming that an unpleasant experience is exactly what he or she wanted. A man who wins a llama on a television program and proclaims that it is the answer to his dreams might be using this kind of defensive maneuver.

Intellectualization. The process of **intellectualization** allows individuals to protect themselves against unbearable pain. It involves a dissociation between one's thoughts and feelings. For example, a woman may conjure up an elaborate rational to "explain" the death of her young husband. By citing reasons and focusing on the logic of her argument, she may avoid, for a while at least, the tremendous pain associated with such a traumatic experience.

Undoing. In the defense mechanism called **undoing,** a person who thinks or acts on an undesirable impulse makes amends by performing some action trying to nullify the undesirable one. Such actions are typically irrational and can be seen in various superstitious rituals and in some religious ceremonies. By performing the undoing act, the person is convinced that the wrong he or she committed has been rectified. For example, a man who has continual thoughts about masturbation and believes that they are evil may wash his hands frequently as a means of "cleansing" himself.

Compromise Formation. When someone uses contradictory behaviors to gain some satisfaction for an undesirable impulse, he or she is indulging in **compromise formation.** Take the barbed compliment. Betty, who really hates Jane, comments, "My, what a pretty dress! How did *you* ever manage to select it?" Or a male student says to his professor, "That was an excellent test. How did *you* ever manage to construct it?" To apply the *coup de grace*, the student may add a few moments later, "Good lecture; I never expected it from you."

As we will see in the next section, Freud postulated other defense mechanisms, such as identification and fixation.

The Process of Personality Development

The Theory of Psychosexual Development

With this preliminary and rather sketchy review of the major structural components of personality completed, we turn to an examination of Freud's use of these constructs in his scheme of **psychosexual development.** Before discussing the theory, however, we should note that it is biological in nature and based on the inevitable unfolding of different stages at which particular behaviors occur. Normal development involves the coursing of libidinal or "sexual" energy through a variety of earlier stages to a final stage called, aptly enough, genital. Between the phallic and genital stages lies the latency period in which sexual energy is considered to lie dormant. Abnormal development, on the other hand, occurs if the person undergoes traumatic experiences, almost inevitably sexual in nature, in early childhood, that prevent the flow of significant amounts of libidinal energy through the various stages. The person's development is then said to be **fixated** at a particular stage so that he or she is more vulnerable to crisis later in life. When subjected to stress, for example, he or she might regress by showing infantile kinds of behavior. For each stage in which conflict occurs, Freud postulated a corresponding adult character pattern.

Oral Stage. The infant is practically all id, according to Freud, and cannot initially distinguish between the self and the environment. An infant is

controlled by biological impulses and is basically selfish. The focus of pleasurable sensations or "sexual" impulses during the first pregenital stage is
the mouth (Freud, 1969, p. 10). Of course, the mouth is also the source of
food and water intake and thus is critical for survival, but Freud did not
emphasize this fact. Obviously, the parents are typically the primary sources
of gratification for the infant, and their behavior is critical in determining
whether or not the infant will experience personal difficulties in later life.
These difficulties may occur as a result of parental overindulgence or under-
indulgence of the infant's needs during the first year or so. For example,
conflict could be generated if the mother resents nursing the baby and
proceeds to wean it abruptly. Portions of the libidinal energy available to
the individual then become fixated around this conflict while the remaining
energy flows through to the next stage.

Anal Stage. During the second and third years, pleasurable sensations
are focused on the anal cavity. In this **anal stage,** the chief pleasures for the
child involve retention or expulsion of feces (Freud, 1957, p. 324). It is during
this stage that ego processes are being differentiated from the id and the
child begins to assert independence. This independence does not, however,
involve rational decision-making in which the child weighs the conflicting
evidence and comes to reasonable conclusions. Rather, it is a negativistic
independence in which the child rejects out-of-hand whatever is being offered
by the parents. If the child is asked "Will you please tie your shoelaces?" the
answer is an immediate "No!" If the child is then asked "Do you want a
candy bar?" the answer, once again, is a resounding "No!" even though he
or she may be hungry and had been seen by the mother foraging in the
kitchen for candy only moments earlier. It is a period, in short, for a contest
of wills and the assertion of ego control.

According to Freud, the primary contest revolves around toilet training.
In this culture and others, cleanliness is a virtue, and parents typically place
heavy stress on regulating defecation and urination. The child can resist
these demands by retaining the waste matter or by expelling it inappropriately—for example, by wetting or soiling the pants. Conflicts during this
stage precipitate the occurrence of particular kinds of behavioral difficulties
in adolescence and adulthood, as we shall soon learn.

Phallic Stage. During the fourth and fifth years, sexual tension is focused
on the genital area. In this **phallic stage,** both boys and girls are considered
to derive pleasure from self-manipulation (Freud, 1957, p. 327). For boys,
there is a developing longing for sexual contact with the mother. In the
broadest sense, this longing involves seeking the mother's affection and love.
At the same time, the child becomes increasingly aware that there is a sexual
relationship between his parents and that his father is his rival. But the
father is bigger and stronger, and the child fears that he will be punished
for his desires and that his penis will be cut off. The child can alleviate his

castration anxiety by *identifying* with his father. His sexual desire is thereby shunted into more socially acceptable channels. These strong, conflicting feelings and the process by which they are more or less adequately resolved Freud called the **Oedipus complex,** a term borrowed from Sophocles' tragedy *Oedipus Rex*, in which the Greek king and hero, Oedipus, unwittingly kills his father and commits incest with his mother. The development of the superego is an outgrowth of the resolution of this complex, with the child taking on the values of his parents and their attitudes toward society.

Freud saw support for the Oedipus conflict in the kinship ties and practices within clans in various primitive societies (Freud, 1950, pp. 144–145). Using anthropological and historical evidence as a guide, he speculated that the brothers of a clan in a primal horde banded together in order to kill their father, their chief rival for the affection of the women. After committing the deed, they realized that a new social organization was necessary if they were ever going to live in harmony and avoid mutual destruction in a frantic effort to possess the women. As a consequence, a law against incest was implemented. Freud theorized that all cultures had instituted two taboos—namely, a law against incest and a law protecting the totem animal. The totem animal was seen by Freud as a symbol of the father, and worship of it allowed tribal members to allay their sense of guilt for their deed. In Freud's view, worship of the totem animal also symbolized a covenant between tribal members and their fathers. On the one hand, the father promised them protection and care; on the other hand, the members promised to respect the father's life. That is, they promised not to repeat the deed that had destroyed their real father. The covenant between tribal members and their fathers bears some resemblance to the male child's eventual **identification** with his father as a means of resolving his own basic conflict over the mother.

The process for girls is very different, according to Freud. The lack of a penis is the source of their problems. Girls are considered to envy boys their possession of a penis and to seek its attainment. At first they try to compensate for their "deficiency" by emulating boys and also by masturbation of what Freud calls their "stunted penis," their clitoris. Although the mother is their first love object, they come to resent her, in Freud's opinion, for bringing them into the world without a penis. They begin to love their father because he has the desired object. They then identify with their mothers as a means of vicariously obtaining the desired object (Freud, 1969, pp. 44–51). Although initially they seek the father's penis, Freud argued that this desire is transformed into another fantasy—the wish to have a baby by him as a gift. Finally, the girl wishes to have a male baby because he would bring the longed-for penis with him. As these desires can never be fulfilled, all girls were considered by Freud to have relatively inadequate superegos. These "mutilated little creatures," as he called them, had little sense of objectivity and justice. This special conflict process in girls was called the Electra complex by some of Freud's supporters. In Greek mythology, Electra induced her brother to murder their hated mother. Perhaps one reason Freud was reluctant to apply the term *Electra complex* to the conflict process in girls is that the analogy seems weak and at variance with his own description of the process.

In any event, for many people, the Freudian proposal concerning the mechanisms and outcomes of the Oedipus complex, especially for girls, is absolutely absurd. Freud has been severely criticized for maintaining that the Oedipal conflict is biologically based and occurs universally in all human beings. There is, for example, some cross-cultural evidence that the Oedipus complex is not universal in the species and that, in some cultures at least, the resentment of the boy toward his father is based on the father's powerful position in the family and not on sexual jealousy.

Next, advocates of the women's movement in this country have correctly pointed to Freud's chauvinistic outlook toward women, an attitude not unexpected of someone who lived in a strongly patriarchal society. Women in Vienna in Freud's time were second-class citizens and subject to all the degrading treatment that accrues to members of minority groups. His concept of "penis envy" is particularly galling to women because it implies that anatomy is destiny and that constructive personal growth is virtually impossible. If you are inherently inferior, it makes little sense to expend great amounts of effort to try and improve yourself.

Karen Horney, a prominent neoanalyst, took particular issue with Freud over this matter many years ago. Her arguments are, in general, echoed by leading feminists today. Horney maintained that the Freudian position is bogged down in faulty biology. She asked why a biologically healthy female would show such psychological qualities. Further, she maintained that the Freudian interpretation does not allow for the social and cultural factors that affect the psychology of women. Penis envy is presumed to manifest itself in the behavior of the "castrating female" by tendencies to dominate and humiliate men and to be ambitious and competitive. In the course of her observations, Horney noted that tendencies toward dictatorial power and egocentric ambition are characteristics of neurotic *men* as well as of neurotic women (Horney, 1937, p. 204). These problems stem, in her opinion, from an excessively competitive society in which status is conferred upon those who are achievement-oriented, dominant, and ambitious. What normal women actually envy is the status of men and the psychological and physical rewards associated with the positive aspects of its attainment. (See Chapter 5 for more details on Horney's position.)

Finally, some researchers question the validity of Freud's contention that women of all cultures desire a male child. Psychotherapist Max Hammer asked married and single college students and married noncollege adults, "If you knew for sure that you could have only one child, would you prefer that child to be a male or a female?" and recorded their answers (Hammer, 1970, pp. 54–56). Table 2.1 presents the results in detail. In general, Hammer found that the results for the noncollege adults disconfirmed the Freudian

Table 2.1
Preference for Sex of Child, by Social Factors and Sex of Adult Respondents

Preference	Unmarried College Students		Married College Students		Married Noncollege Adults	
	Men	Women	Men	Women	Men	Women
Boy	156 (90%)	184 (78%)	24 (83%)	15 (73%)	16 (90%)	8 (30%)
Girl	18 (10%)	52 (22%)	5 (17%)	6 (27%)	2 (10%)	18 (70%)
Number	174	236	29	21	18	26

Adapted from Hammer, 1970, p. 55.

hypothesis: 70% of these women said they would prefer a girl. Of course, a Freudian would probably disagree with this conclusion because it is based on individual self-reports. A Freudian would argue—and probably continue to do so even if one replicated this finding many times with large numbers of women—that the women who said they preferred a girl were actually repressing their true desires. Although there is no way actively and directly to disprove the Freudian contention, it does not seem reasonable to expect that *every* woman in the world has such desires, given the incredibly complex and varied motivational life of human beings.

Latency Stage. From the sixth year to puberty there is a period during which the sexual instincts were assumed by Freud to be dormant (Freud, 1969, p. 10). He believed that the person's characteristic ways of behaving are established during the first five years of life and that radical personality change is extremely difficult, if not impossible, thereafter. Sexual energy is not lessened during the **latency stage** but is sublimated or channeled into other pursuits, including the learning of various skills from school experiences.

Genital Stage. With the advent of puberty, sexual tension increases dramatically. The reproductive organs have matured and both sexes are now capable of procreation. The aims of the sexual instincts have been predominantly autoerotic, but now, in the **genital stage,** the goal is mating with an appropriate sex object. At this point, an adequate heterosexual adjustment depends on the amount of libidinal energy available to the person. If there have been no severe traumatic experiences in early childhood, with corresponding libido fixations, an adequate adjustment is possible. On reaching adulthood, the person typically marries and settles into family life. For Freud, the normal person is one who makes satisfactory adjustments in two major areas—love and work. On the other hand, an inadequate adjustment involves libidinal fixations and the development of particular character disorders (Freud, 1969, pp. 12–13). We turn now to a discussion of these character types.

Character Types

The Oral Character.   Persons who are fixated at the oral stage have problems in later life related primarily to receiving or taking of things from the external world. Concretely, individuals who have had their needs overindulged become habituated to receiving support and encouragement from other people. Having been overindulged, they are excessively dependent on others for gratification (Blum, 1953, p. 160). They tend to be trusting, accepting, and gullible. People with such characteristics tend to admire strength and leadership in others, but they make little attempt to fend for themselves. One could also conjecture that they tend to be rather incompetent because most of their gratification is derived from what others do for them and not from what they themselves accomplish. Such people are apt to be overoptimistic, with the corresponding feeling that "bad things can't happen to me." Obviously, a person with such a Pollyanna outlook will experience inevitable conflicts with others because not everyone is as nurturant and supportive as his or her mother. How long could you expect others to remain your friends if you kept demanding all of their time, effort, and affection without reciprocating in approximate measure?

Fixations also may occur because parents underindulge or severely frustrate their infants. In such instances, a person learns to exploit others. As neoanalyst Fenichel reported, people with such an orientation are apt to have sadistic attitudes (Fenichel, 1945, p. 489). They tend to envy others their success and to try, through the use of manipulative strategies, to dominate them. Further, such people tend to be stingy; they want "something for nothing." It is difficult to imagine liking and supporting a person who is continually manipulative and exploitative in interpersonal relations.

The Anal Character.   Difficulties during toilet training can lead to **anal eroticism.** According to Freud, anal characters have three primary characteristics. They are exceptionally stingy, orderly, and obstinate (Blum, 1953, p. 161). Further, each of these primary characteristics has a number of other traits associated with it. The anal character's sense of orderliness is associated with both bodily cleanliness and conscientiousness in the performance of the most trivial duties. The tendencies toward parsimony may be associated, in extreme cases, with avarice, and obstinacy may give rise to active defiance of others. All these characteristics may be an outgrowth of reaction-formation defenses in which these persons may be unconsciously renouncing socially unacceptable impulses such as messiness, dirtiness, and stinginess. These impulses, in turn, are considered to be based on the pleasurable sensations that accompanied early toilet training when the children kept their "prized possessions" from the parents and took delight in playing with their feces.

The Phallic Character. The difficulties experienced by phallic characters stem from inadequate resolution of the Oedipus complex. Phallic characters react to severe castration anxiety by behaving in a reckless, resolute, and self-assured manner (Blum, 1953, pp. 163–164). The penis is overvalued, as reflected in excessive vanity and exhibitionism. Such males have to prove they are "real men." One way of proving it is by continuous conquests of women—that is, by being Don Juans. For women, the primary motive is penis envy. Consequently, they are continuously striving for superiority over men. Such women are considered to be "castrating females."

The Genital Character. Freud viewed the genital character as the ideal type. Genital characters are sexually mature and capable of orgasm. Libidinal energies are no longer dammed up because such people have located appropriate love objects (Blum, 1953, p. 164). In Freud's view, the key to happiness is the ability to love and be loved. Sexual love is one aspect of intimacy that provides us with happiness and joy. Although the establishment of intimacy is central to happiness, Freud reminded us that it also makes us vulnerable. Specifically, we are vulnerable to rejection by, and the eventual loss of, the loved one. Yet Freud believed that love is necessary for healthy functioning and that love has to be pursued despite the suffering that it inevitably entails.

Genital characters are also capable of sublimating their id impulses by expressing them in the form of productive and creative work. The creative activities that bring happiness differ for each individual. Some pursue happiness by refining their intellectual skills and by seeking truth, as in the case of the scientist. Others seek it through direct action, as demonstrated by the artistic grace and agility of the prima ballerina. Thus each person has to find the course that is best for him or her (Freud, 1952a, pp. 772–776).

Research Evidence for the Theory of Psychosexual Development

We may agree that Freud created an interesting and provocative theory of human development, but the question of its empirical validity remains open and subject to examination. Even though the theory is rather vaguely stated, it is still possible to derive hypotheses from it for scientific testing. First, the theory suggests that certain clusters of personality traits exist in mature adults (Kline, 1972, p. 7). For example, hypothesized traits in the oral receptive character include optimism, dependency, impatience, talkativeness, love of soft foods, and an intense curiosity. For the anal character, key characteristics include an opposition to influence from others, a drive to clean things, minute attention to detail, and a love of self-control. For the phallic character, typical traits include recklessness, pride, vanity, self-assurance, and courage. Can we identify people who have any one set of these traits and not the others? After surveying a great deal of research on the subject, Kline concluded: "There is good evidence for the anal character . . . some evidence for the oral character . . . and almost no support for the other psychosexual syndromes (e.g., the phallic character)" (Kline 1972, p. 44). Since Kline's early review of the research literature, many more studies have been conducted that suggest his conclusions are in need of revision. The general impression of this literature currently is that there is good evidence for the oral character as well as for the anal character, with almost no support for the phallic character.

A good example of empirical support for the oral and anal character types is provided in a study by Tribich and Messer (1974). In accordance with psychoanalytic theory, they predicted that if oral people are submissive and dependent in general and even more so in the presence of authority figures, they should conform more to influence attempts by these individuals than do anal characters. Anal characters are, in fact, theorized to be hostile and resistant to influence attempts, so that not only should they not yield to the judgments of authority figures, but they should actively oppose their judgments by moving in a direction opposite to the one being advocated.

To test these hypotheses, Tribich and Messer first measured orality and anality in college men by administering a projective test called the Blacky Pictures. This test contains 12 cartoons depicting the adventures of a dog named Blacky. Subjects are asked to make up stories about Blacky, and their responses are then scored by trained assessors. An oral subject, for example, might look at one of the pictures and tell a story that involved Blacky "sucking vigorously at his mother's breast." Or he might look at another picture and say that he believed it meant that "Blacky will grow up to like eating more than anything else." (These are, in fact, two actual responses of a subject in the experiment.)

Once the personality type of the subject was determined, he was brought individually to a laboratory where he was introduced to a high-status authority figure (a psychiatrist). Each subject was then told that once the room was completely dark, a point of light would be shown and his task was to judge how far the point of light had moved in inches. He was told it would move between 1 and 23 inches. Before responding, however, the subject would hear the authority figure's judgment of how far it had moved. The results indicated that the orals' responses over a series of trials were an average of five inches closer to the authority figure's than were those of the anals, thereby confirming the prediction of the investigators. Studies by Kagan and Mussen (1956) and by Masling, Weiss, and Rothschild (1968) also found that oral types tend to conform highly to the judgment of others.

Psychoanalytic theory claims not only that oral characters are highly dependent on others, but that they have have strong needs for contact, affiliation, and nurturance. Recent research has provided evidence of their needs for company and emotional support by showing that oral types tend to experience aversive arousal when socially isolated (Masling et al., 1981). Specifically, these researchers found that people with oral dependency needs showed more anxiety when performing tasks alone in a soundproof chamber than when they performed them in the presence of others. Masling, O'Neill, and Katkin (1982) showed further that oral subjects forced to interact with a cold, impersonal individual experienced more stress than oral subjects who interacted with a warm, personal individual. Low oral subjects, in contrast, showed no differences in stress level between the cold and warm interaction conditions.

As for the orals' needs for contact and nurturance, Juni, Masling, and Brannon (1979) found that people high in orality used greater physical contact as a means of helping others solve a problem than people low in orality. Specifically, high and low oral individuals participated in an experiment on problem-solving. As part of the experiment, they were asked to coach (by any methods they wanted) a blindfolded subject through a maze as fast as they could. The investigators found that high oral individuals touched the blindfolded subjects more often as a means of coaching them than did low oral subjects and that the blindfolded subjects tended to complete the maze successfully more quickly under the guidance of the high oral individuals. Thus there is supportive evidence for Freud's theorizing about the existence of oral and anal character types but far less support for his theorizing about phallic and genital character types.

The second hypothesis that can be derived from Freud's theory of psychosexual development is that the character types are the outgrowth of specific child-rearing practices (Kline, 1972, p. 8). However, the results of a great many investigations show little or no support for this hypothesis. In fairness, though, we could maintain that the lack of support stems more from methodological inadequacies—for example, the use of unreliable and invalid measures—than from inadequacies of the theory (Kline, 1972, p. 94). In short, we could argue that the theory has never been put to a fair test. Another person could counterargue that many aspects of the theory itself are so vague that satisfactory measures of its constructs cannot be devised. Accordingly, it might be best to abandon the effort to test it. In any event, the evidence in support of this part of the theory is weak and unconvincing.

Techniques of Assessment

Freud relied primarily on the case study method to understand the personalities of his patients. As mentioned earlier, this technique involved exhaustive examination and analysis of the lives and past experiences of his patients and the subsequent utilization of this information to help them overcome their problems. Free association and dream analysis were the two major aspects of Freud's case study procedure. These techniques emerged only after considerable experimentation with lines of inquiry that focused on the physiological determinants of behavior and on hypnotic phenomena.

Free Association. Originally, Freud attempted to uncover the repressed memories of his patients by using hypnosis. He found that while in this altered state of consciousness, some patients were able to recall and relive their repressed experiences. As a result, their disturbing symptoms began to disappear. Many patients, however, were not susceptible to hypnosis, and Freud began to look elsewhere for a workable technique. Eventually he found it in the **free-association** procedure. This technique involved self-reports by the patients of whatever thoughts and memories occurred to them without any kind of self-censorship. The patients were told to report *all* thoughts, no matter how trivial, unimportant, mortifying, embarrassing, and illogical they seemed to be. Freud called this attempt at completely uncensored reporting the "fundamental rule" of **psychoanalysis.** During these sessions, Freud sat behind the patient, out of sight but in a position to watch facial expressions and gestures. Freud used this technique primarily because he wanted to be certain that he did not elicit particular forms of behavior from the patient through his own gestures and facial expressions. He wanted the patient's responses to be spontaneous and not to be controlled by him (Ford & Urban, 1963, p. 168). When resistances occurred, Freud believed that the analysis was definitely moving in the right direction—that is, uncovering the actual source of the patient's problems. Through the use of free association, Freud discovered that his patients' problems typically stemmed from traumatic experiences in early childhood.

Dream Analysis. Freud used **dream analysis** as another major technique to unravel the secrets of the patients' unconscious. Freud's task, as he saw it, was to analyze and interpret the symbols present in the manifest content of their dreams, in an attempt to discover the latent or hidden meanings. As a result of his extensive clinical experiences, he believed that these symbols have universal meanings. Sticks, tree trunks, umbrellas, and snakes, for example, symbolize the penis; boxes, doors, and furniture chests represent the vagina. Despite their universal nature, Freud also believed that all symbols have to be judged and interpreted in terms of the unique conflicts of the individual. Moreover, these symbols typically have multiple meanings, which makes analysis highly difficult.

In Freud's view, dreams are always disguised attempts at wish fulfillment. The wishes are unconscious motives that are unacceptable to the individual and are nearly always erotic in nature. During sleep, these impulses seek expression but are subject to censorship. As a result, they seek expression indirectly (via displacement) by taking on disguised symbolic forms, as seen in the manifest content of the person's dreams. Often the events in the manifest content appear totally unrelated to the actual wish.

Detailed analysis by Freud, however, eventually revealed the connection, as seen in the following case study.

Freud's patient, a young woman, told him that her sister had two sons, Otto and Charles, and that, unfortunately, Otto had died recently. Otto was the patient's favorite, but she claimed that she was fond of Charles as well. She then told Freud that the evening before her appointment, she had had a dream in which, she said,

> I saw Charles lying dead ... in his little coffin, his hands folded; there were candles all about; and, in short, it was just as it was at the time of little Otto's death, which gave me such a shock. [Freud, 1938b, pp. 229–230]

She then asked Freud what this strange dream meant. Did it mean, she asked, that she was so evil as to wish that her sister would lose the only child she had left? Or did it mean that she really wished that Charles had died instead of Otto, whom she loved so much more? Freud reassured her that neither interpretation was correct.

In the course of the analysis, Freud discovered that the young woman had been orphaned at an early age and gone to live with her sister. Several years later she was introduced to a very attractive man by her sister. The man made a lasting impression on her. She and the man even planned to marry but never did. Somehow her sister had intervened, and now the man no longer paid visits to the house. Subsequently, the young woman was unable to extend her affections to others although she had many other suitors. The man, it turned out, was a professor with literary talents who often gave public lectures on his specialty topic. The young woman always managed to get tickets to hear him speak. She sat unobserved in the audience. If she learned that her friends were going to attend a concert, she attended also so that she might observe him in case he was there. The last time she saw him was at little Otto's funeral, when he offered her and her sister his condolences. Even at the funeral, she could not suppress her feelings of affection for the professor. The motive of her dream about little Charles then became clear. It signified nothing more than her wish to see the man again. Thus, even though initially the dream seemed strange and inexplicable, Freud was able to ferret out the hidden wish, thus helping the woman by making her real motivation clear to her.

Transference. Besides free association and dream analysis, Freud relied heavily on **transference** to facilitate a cure for his patients. In the course of treatment, Freud discovered that patients inevitably began to relive their old conflicts and interactions with authority figures (most notably, the parents) in their relationship with him. In general, then, he maintained that patients begin to see their therapists as reincarnations of important figures in their past. As a result, they transfer to their therapists the kinds of feelings and behaviors they had shown to these early authority figures.

In Freud's view, this transference phenomenon could be of inestimable value in helping therapists cure their patients. Yet it could also be a possible source of danger if the patients decided to act out their old feelings of hostility and anger toward their parents with their therapists. In general, the transference process is characterized by the patients' **ambivalence.** That is, patients typically have attitudes of both affection and hostility toward their parents, and these positive and negative feelings are displaced onto the therapist. Freud found that positive feelings were displaced onto him first, negative feelings later. In **positive transference** the patients developed a special affectionate interest in him. He was trusted completely and praised lavishly. In his women patients, positive transference assumed various forms. For example, some of them fell passionately in love with him and made sexual demands. Others revealed a wish that he treat them as he would a favorite daughter. In all cases the women were highly jealous of anyone who was close to him. In his men patients, Freud also found evidence of sexual feelings toward him, although rarely in the direct form that it occurred in his women patients.

Under conditions of positive transference, the patients typically made fine progress toward a cure. They were receptive to his interpretations, understood them, and were fully engrossed in the analysis. Difficulties soon arose, however, because positive transference was followed by **negative transference.** That is, patients showed intense anger and hostility toward him, viewing his interpretations with much distrust. Under these conditions, Freud pointed out to his patients that their feelings did not arise from the present situation and that they were instead simply repeating negative experiences that had occurred earlier in their lives. To the extent that they accepted this explanation and explored its possibilities, they were likely to attain insight into their problems and to achieve psychological health. Thus Freud believed strongly that transference was a highly important phenomenon that could be used as a technique to facilitate psychological growth.

Application of the Theory to the Treatment of Psychopathology

Neurotics and psychotics are individuals who use various defense mechanisms to respond to anxiety created by the stifling of their instinctual impulses. As a result, normal growth has been arrested and their functioning is ineffective and stereotypic. To cure such individuals, it is necessary to reduce their conflicts and defenses by relieving their anxieties. Relief occurs when the energies are directed away from the maintenance of defenses and made available for constructive growth. These conditions are made possible by therapists who help these individuals understand the sources of their conflicts through the use of free association, dream analysis, and transference. The patients are made aware that these internal struggles have weakened the ego and prevented them from coping effectively with the demands of external reality. They are helped to see that they are repeating old behaviors and using ineffective strategies in current situations. After successful therapy, the patients have an increased self-understanding and a more accurate assessment of reality. In other terms, what is unconscious is made conscious and the ego is strengthened. The patients are then able to function more effectively in everyday life (Freud, 1969, pp. 31–35).

Let us examine an actual case of a man suffering from a **neurosis** to see more precisely how Freud diagnosed the problem and provided help for the patient.

Obsessive-Compulsive Neurosis in the Rat-Man

Freud reported a case in which a young man with a university education entered therapy because he suffered from various obsessions and compulsions (Freud, 1963, pp. 19–105). His primary fears were that his father might die and that a woman whom he loved would be hurt or killed. In addition, he had compulsions to cut his own throat with a razor and an impulse to kill an old woman. His attempts to cope with these problems caused him to expend considerable energy, and it was not surprising that his sexual life was less than adequate. He reported performing coitus irregularly and masturbating only rarely.

Freud secured a promise from the man to report everything that occurred to him, even if it was unpleasant or seemed senseless or irrelevant. According to Freud, the man was unfamiliar with the analytic emphasis on sexual matters but began a discussion of his problems by recalling sexual experiences in his childhood. These episodes involved his fondling the genitals of a willing young family governess and watching another family governess undress as she prepared for her bath. He reported further that he enjoyed these experiences immensely, especially the ones that involved looking at the nude woman. At the same time, however, he had an uncanny feeling that his parents knew his thoughts and that he could be punished by his father for them. In general terms, then, we have a case in which strong instinctual impulses are experienced but are warded off because the person anticipates superego-generated guilt feelings. In addition, Freud mentioned that the patient used other ego-defense mechanisms to protect himself.

In the course of the therapy, the patient also mentioned a recent experience he had had with a captain during military training maneuvers. The patient disliked and dreaded this man because the officer was obviously fond of cruelty and advocated corporal punishment. During a conversation, the officer had told the patient of a horrible method of torture used by the military in other countries. The patient resisted telling Freud about it but eventually relented and said that it involved putting a number of ravenous rats into a pot that was then turned upside down and attached to the person's buttocks. The rats then bored their way into his anus. Despite the patient's reluctance to repeat the story, Freud noticed that he showed horrified pleasure as he told it. Further, the patient mentioned that, as he related the captain's story to Freud, he had the idea that the punishment was happening to the woman he loved. Subsequently, the young man was forced to admit that the idea occurred to him that the punishment was being applied to his father as well. Why did the patient have these cruel and hostile feelings toward two people he loved?

Further probing by Freud eventually revealed the source of the patient's wish that the rat punishment happen to his father and loved one. First, the patient's father had been a noncommissioned officer who had been extremely cruel and violent at times. Freud suggested that the captain who related the rat punishment story was disliked because he resembled the patient's father. At base, then, the patient hated his father. Freud then turned to the unraveling of these feelings. He believed that the problem lay in the sphere of sexuality and that some traumatic experience was responsible for the patient's feelings toward his father.

An examination of the onanistic, or masturbatory, history of the patient provided Freud with an important clue concerning the nature of the patient's conflicts with his father. The patient did not masturbate to any great extent during puberty, but a compulsion to practice it started when he was 21, shortly *after* his father's death. In addition, the patient had fantasies that his father was alive and would reappear at any moment. Between 12 and 1 o'clock in the morning the patient would interrupt his work and take out his penis and look at it in the mirror. Freud conjectured that it was during this period that the patient expected his father's ghost to appear. Because the father would then witness his son's exposure and would disapprove of it, Freud inferred that the patient's actions were defiant ones. Further probing revealed that his father had caught the patient in a sexual act connected with masturbation during his early childhood and had beaten him severely for it. The patient had then repressed all memories of the event. Thus, the patient had perceived his father as trying to interfere with his sexual satisfaction and so wished secretly for his death.

Freud found that rats had many meanings for the patient, but three were especially important. First, the patient recalled that once when he visited his father's grave, he saw a rat gliding over the grave. He assumed that the rat had been inside his father's grave and had just finished eating part of the corpse. Second, rats were considered to be dirty and greedy animals and were mercilessly persecuted by people. He felt that he was much like the rat because as a child he had bitten people when he was in a rage, his rages sometimes being generated by his father's beatings. Third, rats were like children, in the patient's earliest recollections of them, and he was very fond of children. Unfortunately, though, his loved one could not have any children and this fact may have been the primary reason for his ambivalent feelings toward her.

Freud conjectured, finally, that the rat could be considered a symbol of the male sex organ. This organ could further be symbolized as a worm, because as a child the patient had had an illness in which large round worms had burrowed in his anus. Freud concluded that the rat obsession was also related to anal eroticism. Thus Freud eventually revealed to the patient the multiple sources of his anal conflicts and, with the patient's consent, concluded that he was cured.

Critical Comments

Freud's position can be evaluated on the basis of how well it meets the six criteria outlined in Chapter 1 for judging the worth of scientific theories.

Comprehensiveness. Freud was an astute and original thinker who created a highly comprehensive theory. The range and diversity of behavior and experience described and interpreted are remarkable. Freud sought to understand not only various kinds of emotional and behavioral disorders, but other phenomena such as humor, marriage, war, death, friendship, myths and fairy tales, incest, societal mores, dreams, slips of the tongue, "bungled actions," suicide, bed-wetting, creativity, competition, and absent-mindedness. In short, Freud developed a system that explicitly sought to explain virtually all human behavior. His theory remains, to the present day, the most comprehensive conceptual system ever created by a personality investigator.

Precision and Testability. Part of the major problem with Freudian theory centers on the relative vagueness of its concepts, the imprecision and ambiguities of its relational statements, and the difficulties it presents in allowing for the clear derivation and testing of hypotheses. Moreover, when results based on such loose theorizing are secured, it is impossible to know whether they support the theory. When the results are contrary to the theorizing, however, it is always possible for advocates to claim that such outcomes are meaningless because the hypotheses were not validly derived from the major theoretical propositions.

A related criticism is that much of the theory is presented in metaphors, or in terms that do not lend themselves to scientific testing—for example, the life and death instincts. Frequently, "explanations" for observations are offered after the fact. The theory postdicts well but has real difficulty in predicting how people will behave. Much of the evidence for it is post hoc and secured through uncontrolled case study methods. In addition, Freud did not record the patient's observations as he recited them, thereby opening the door to the criticism that the patient's memory of the events was distorted. Finally, the universal conclusions that Freud drew about human behavior on the basis of extensive observations of a few patients seem incredible and naive. They can, however, be better understood if we realize the implications of a theory that is strongly rooted in biology. It is clear, then, that Freud's theory has some difficulty in meeting the precision and testability criterion.

Parsimony. Freud's theory fails to meet the parsimony criterion. Although it utilizes a number of assumptions and concepts to account for the phenomena in its domain, its proposed explanatory scheme is highly restricted in nature. It is a theory that does not allow for different and more adequate explanations of behavior. It is a "nothing-but" theory. The nothing-but refers to the fact that sex and aggressive tendencies are the sole determinants of behavior. Thus the motivational base of the theory is limited. It ignores the fact that behavior is controlled by a variety of motives, not just sex and aggression.

In addition, the structure of human personality is divided into only three components, and the interactions among them are presumed to account for the nature of the underlying conflicts that hinder personality functioning.

Finally, Freud presented a generally pessimistic and one-sided view of human nature. People are seen as essentially irrational and controlled by amoral forces. Although he recognized fully that human beings can act rationally, he chose to focus almost entirely on the irrational side of human nature.

Empirical Validity. There have been literally thousands of investigations of various aspects of Freudian theorizing. These investigations can be divided generally into two categories: evidence for Freud's theory of psychotherapy and evidence for his theory of psychosexual development.

In regard to Freud's theory of psychotherapy, Eysenck (1952) did an early massive review of the clinical literature to assess the effectiveness of psychoanalysis in curing people. He examined over 7000 case histories of patients and concluded that psychoanalytic therapy did not significantly facilitate the recovery of neurotic patients. His data showed that 66% of the patients treated to completion by means of psychoanalysis were much improved or cured. This figure seems impressive, but Eysenck also found that 72% of the patients who were *not* treated by means of any formal therapy also were much improved or cured within two years of the onset of their illness. Thus approximately two-thirds of the patients improved or recovered to a marked extent whether they were treated psychoanalytically or not. Although numerous critics have attacked Eysenck's conclusions on theoretical and methodological grounds, recent reviews of all the evidence by Rachman (1971) and Erwin (1980) show that Eysenck's argument is still essentially valid today.

The evidence in support of Freud's theorizing on psychosexual development is more promising, as we have seen. In addition, there is evidence that the less adequate an individual's defenses against sexual and aggressive impulses, the greater the likelihood of the appearance of **psychopathology;** these data are consistent with Freud's theorizing (Silverman, 1976). There is also evidence that sexual conflicts are present in many neurotics and that some of these disturbances arise from experiences during early childhood. It is also apparent that these early experiences have a marked impact on later personality functioning in some cases. All in all, the research evidence in support of Freud's theory of neurosis is greater than many of his critics are willing to admit.

Heuristic Value. Freud's theory has had tremendous heuristic value. He has served as an inspiration to many scholars by showing them the kinds of contributions that can be made to our knowledge of behavior through painstaking and courageous investigation. His theory has proved fascinating and stimulating to people in many different disciplines. Scholars in literature, sociology, history, anthropology, religion, philosophy, and political science have all made use of Freudian concepts.

Much of this fascination lies in the complicated picture of human beings that Freud has painted. Men and women are not simply rational animals but curious mixtures of the irrational and rational. They often feel threatened by society and are continually searching for acceptable ways to express their innermost feelings. In an attempt to deal with their conflicts, they use various defense mechanisms that, while temporarily protective, prove damaging in the long run. Through painful confrontation with reality in a therapeutic setting, the limitations of their personalities are revealed and heroic attempts to overcome them are made with the help of the therapist. Such drama was destined to excite and interest observers of human behavior and experience. This is a major part of Freud's legacy.

Applied Value. In addition to his seminal contributions to therapy and the treatment of emotional disorders, Freud's insights have been applied by anthropologists to cross-cultural phenomena. For example, Freudian concepts have been used to explain the effects of different weaning and toilet-training schedules on later personality development as well as on incestuous behavior. They have also been employed by sociologists and social psychologists to help them understand the dynamics of family life and the functioning of small groups. Freudian concepts have also been used fruitfully by historians, theologians, novelists, and economists. Thus the psychoanalytic position has had considerable applied value.

Discussion Questions

1. In what ways do the interactions between and among the id, ego, and superego create difficulties for the individual?

2. What are the primary defense mechanisms as they were envisioned by Freud? Give possible examples of the operation of such mechanisms from your own experiences.
3. Cite some examples of the ways in which defense mechanisms can be used to help the person adjust to his or her environment.
4. What do you think might happen to a society in which id impulses were left unchecked by the superego?
5. Using the Freudian model of psychosexual development, how would you explain the behavior of a person who overeats continually?
6. Do you agree that cleanliness is a virtue in contemporary society? If so, what are the possible reasons that people value it? If not, cite your reasons.
7. Do you think that Freud's concept of penis envy has any merit?
8. What are the implications of the Freudian position for the ways in which society should treat homosexuals? Do you agree with Freud's position?
9. Do you agree with Freud that the normal individual is one who is satisfactorily adjusted in two major areas—love and work?
10. Do you agree with Freud that the two major human motives are sex and aggression? State your reasons.

References

Blum, G. S. *Psychoanalytic theories of personality*. New York: McGraw-Hill, 1953.

Erwin, E. Psychoanalytic therapy: The Eysenck argument. *American Psychologist*, 1980, *35*, 435–443.

Eysenck, H. J. The effects of psychotherapy: An evaluation. *Journal of Consulting Psychology*, 1952, *16*, 319–324.

Fenichel, O. *The psychoanalytic theory of neurosis*. New York: Norton, 1945.

Ford, D. H., & Urban, H. B. *Systems of psychotherapy: A comparative study*. New York: Wiley, 1963.

Freud, A. *The ego and the mechanisms of defense*. Translated by Cecil Baines. New York: International Universities Press, 1946.

Freud, S. The history of the psychoanalytic movement. In A. A. Brill (Ed.), *The basic writings of Sigmund Freud*. New York: Random House, 1938a.

Freud, S. The interpretation of dreams. In A. A. Brill (Ed.), *The basic writings of Sigmund Freud*. New York: Random House, 1938b.

Freud, S. Totem and taboo. In A. A. Brill (Ed.), *The basic writings of Sigmund Freud*. New York: Random House, 1938c.

Freud, S. Three contributions to the theory of sex. In A. A. Brill (Ed.), *The basic writings of Sigmund Freud*. New York: Random House, 1938d.

Freud, S. *Totem and taboo*. Translated by J. Strachey. New York: Norton, 1950.

Freud, S. Civilization and its discontents. In R. M. Hutchins (Ed.), *Great books of the Western world*. Chicago: Encyclopaedia Britannica, 1952a.

Freud, S. Instincts and their vicissitudes. In R. M. Hutchins (Ed.), *Great books of the Western world*. Chicago: Encyclopaedia Britannica, 1952b.

Freud, S. *A general introduction to psychoanalysis*. Translated by J. Riviere. New York: Permabooks, 1957.

Freud, S. *The ego and the id*. Translated by J. Riviere; revised and edited by J. Strachey. New York: Norton, 1960.

Freud, S. Three case histories. In P. Rieff (Ed.), *The collected papers of Sigmund Freud.* New York: Collier Books, 1963.

Freud, S. *An outline of psychoanalysis.* Translated and edited by J. Strachey. New York: Norton, 1969.

Hammer, M. Preference for a male child: Cultural factors. *Journal of Individual Psychology,* 1970, *26,* 54–56.

Horney, K. *The neurotic personality of our time.* New York: Norton, 1937.

Jones, E. *The life and work of Sigmund Freud.* Edited and abridged by L. Trilling & S. Marcus. Garden City, N.Y.: Anchor Books, 1963.

Juni, S., Masling, J., & Brannon, R. Interpersonal touching and orality. *Journal of Personality Assessment,* 1979, *43,* 235–237.

Kagan, J., & Mussen, P. Dependency themes on the TAT and group conformity. *Journal of Consulting Psychology.* 1956, *20,* 29–32.

Kline, P. *Fact and fantasy in Freudian theory.* London: Methuen, 1972.

Levine J., & Zigler, E. Denial and self-image in stroke, lung cancer, and heart disease patients. *Journal of Consulting and Clinical Psychology,* 1975, *43,* 751–757.

Masling, J., O'Neill, R., & Katkin, E. S. Autonomic arousal, interpersonal climate, and orality. *Journal of Personality and Social Psychology,* 1982, *42,* 529–534.

Masling, J., Price, J., Goldband, S., & Katkin, E. S. Oral imagery and autonomic arousal in social isolation. *Journal of Personality and Social Psychology,* 1981, *40,* 395–400.

Masling, J., Weiss, L., & Rothschild, B. Relationships of oral imagery to yielding behavior and birth order. *Journal of Consulting and Clinical Psychology,* 1968, *32,* 89–91.

Rachman, S. *The effects of psychotherapy.* Oxford: Pergamon, 1971.

Silverman, L. H. Psychoanalytic theory: The reports of my death are greatly exaggerated. *American Psychologist,* 1976, *31,* 621–637.

Tribich, D., & Messer, S. Psychoanalytic character type and status of authority as determiners of suggestibility. *Journal of Consulting and Clinical Psychology,* 1974, *42,* 842–848.

Suggested Readings

Erwin, E. Psychoanalytic therapy: The Eysenck argument. *American Psychologist,* 1980, *35,* 435–443.

Fenichel, O. *The psychoanalytic theory of neurosis.* New York: Norton, 1945.

Freud, S. *A general introduction to psychoanalysis* (English trans. of rev. ed. by J. Riviere). New York: Permabooks, 1957.

Freud, S. *The standard edition of the complete psychological works.* Edited by J. Strachey. London: Hogarth, 1953.

Kline, P. *Fact and fantasy in Freudian theory.* London: Methuen, 1972.

Silverman, L. H. Psychoanalytic theory: The reports of my death are greatly exaggerated. *American Psychologist,* 1976, *31,* 621–637.

Glossary

Ambivalence The mixed feelings of one person toward another that are characterized by alternation between love and hate.

Anal eroticism Feelings of sexual pleasure that have their source in the person's control over expulsion and retention of feces.

Anal stage Second pregenital stage of psychosexual development in which primary gratifications center around the anal cavity.

Anticathexis Restraining force within the personality designed to keep unwanted impulses from reaching consciousness or awareness.

Anxiety Painful feelings experienced by the person when the ego is threatened by unknown forces.

Catharsis A term based on the Greek word meaning purification. It refers to the process in which an emotional reliving of earlier traumatic experiences serves to reduce disturbing physical symptoms.

Cathexis Driving energy force that attaches itself to an idea or behavior.

Compromise formation Defense mechanism that involves the use of contradictory behavior to attain some satisfaction for an unacceptable impulse.

Conscience Punitive aspect of the superego, according to Freud.

Denial Primitive defense mechanism in which the person protects himself or herself against threats from the environment by blocking out their existence.

Determinism Philosophical doctrine that all behavior is caused by the operation of other events and does not occur freely.

Displacement Defense mechanism in which the person seeks gratification of impulses that are thwarted by shifting from the desired object to a substitute object.

Dream analysis Psychoanalytic technique used to probe the unconscious of the patient through the interpretation of his or her dreams.

Ego Agency postulated by Freud to help the individual satisfy his or her basic urges in ways deemed appropriate by the members of society.

Ego-ideal Positive aspect of the superego involving the standards of perfection taught to the child by the parents.

Fixation Defensive attachment to an earlier stage of psychosexual development that prevents the learning of new behaviors and the acquisition of new interpersonal relationships.

Free association Therapeutic technique pioneered by Freud in which the therapist encourages the patient to report without restriction any thoughts that occur to him or her.

Genital stage Final stage of psychosexual development in which an attempt is made to develop a mature love relationship with a member of the opposite sex.

Id Reservoir of unconscious forces or urges that blindly seek gratification.

Identification In Freudian theory, the defensive process whereby an individual takes on the characteristics of another to relieve his or her anxieties and reduce internal conflicts.

Intellectualization Defense mechanism in which persons protect themselves against pain by isolating their thoughts about painful events from their feelings about them.

Latency stage Psychosexual period during which libidinal energy lies dormant and the primary focus is on the development of interests and skills through contact with childhood peers.

Libido In Freudian theory, the basic energy source contained in the id that propels behavior. It was considered to consist of sexual impulses. For Jung, libido was conceptualized as a more general life-energy process consisting of sexual and self-preservative instincts.

Libido theory The view that the child has unconscious sexual urges that seek expression through intimacy with the parent of the opposite sex.

Negative transference Phenomenon that occurs during psychoanalytic therapy in which the patient redirects toward the therapist the unconscious feelings of anger and hostility retained from experiences with authority figures in childhood.

Neoanalytic perspective Theoretical positions that have their origins in Freudian psychoanalytic theory but that have evolved new concepts and ways of examining and understanding human personality that are significant departures from Freud's original theory.

Neurosis Behavioral disorder characterized by underlying conflicts and anxieties that prevent the individual from coping effectively with his or her everyday problems.

Obsessive-compulsive A kind of neurotic who experiences repetitive thoughts and actions he or she cannot control.

Oedipus complex The process during the phallic stage in which the male child desires sexual contact with the mother, feels threatened by the father, and eventually resolves the conflict by identifying with the father.

Oral stage First pregenital stage of psychosexual development in which primary gratifications center around the mouth.

Phallic stage Third pregenital stage of psychosexual development in which primary gratifications are derived from manipulation of the genitals.

Positive transference Phenomenon that occurs during therapy in which the patient redirects toward the therapist the unconscious feelings of love and affection retained from experiences with authority figures in childhood.

Projection Defense mechanism in which a person attributes his or her undesirable characteristics to others.

Psychoanalysis Theory of personality development, functioning, and change created by Freud. It places heavy emphasis on the roles of biological and unconscious factors in the determination of behavior.

Psychopathology Disordered behaviors, e.g., neuroses or psychoses.

Psychosexual development Theory devised by Freud to account for psychological and personality development in terms of changes in the biological function of the individual.

Psychosis Severe kind of behavior disorder characterized by an inability to relate effectively to other people.

Rationalization Defense mechanism in which the individual provides plausible, but inaccurate, justifications for his or her behavior.

Reaction formation Defense mechanism in which an impulse or behavior is converted into its opposite.

Repression Basic defense mechanism that keeps unpleasant experiences from entering consciousness.

Sublimation Form of displacement in which a socially acceptable goal replaces one that is unacceptable.

Superego Agency postulated by Freud to represent the incorporation by the individual of the moral standards of society and the ways in which the internalized standards control his or her behavior via reward and punishment.

Suppression Defense mechanism involving the conscious removal of unpleasant thoughts from awareness.

Transference Phenomenon postulated by Freud to account for the development of positive and negative feelings toward the therapist by the patient during the course of treatment—feelings originally presumed to be directed toward another person (usually one of the parents).

Unconscious In Freudian theory, the depository of hidden wishes and impulses that govern the behavior of the individual.

Undoing Defense mechanism in which a person makes amends for a socially unacceptable act by performing a related socially acceptable act that attempts to nullify the misdeed.

CHAPTER 3

Jung's Analytical Psychology

Biographical Sketch

Carl Jung was born in Kesswil, Switzerland, in 1875. His father, a pastor in the Swiss Reformed Church, was characterized by Jung as a weakling who was dominated by his wife. Jung described his mother as an insecure woman who frequently contradicted herself and treated members of the family inconsistently—that is, she alternated between being loving and kind and being harsh and aloof. When Jung was 3 years old, his mother entered a hospital for several months with an illness Jung attributed to the difficulty in her marriage (Storr, 1973, pp. 1–2). He reported in his autobiography that the separation from his mother had a profound impact on him.

> I was deeply troubled by my mother's being away. From then on, I always felt mistrustful when the word "love" was spoken. The feeling I associated with "woman" was for a long time that of innate unreliability. . . . "Father," on the other hand, meant reliability and powerlessness. That is the handicap I started off with. Later, these early impressions were revised: I have trusted men

friends and been disappointed by them, and I have mistrusted women and
was not disappointed. [Jung, 1963, p. 8]

He developed an ambivalent attitude of love and hate toward his mother,
and reflections of his conflict are found in his image of women in his later
works. In these works women are frequently portrayed as destroyers and
dominators as well as protectors; they are also depicted as unreliable and
mistrustful.

During his early school days, Jung lacked companionship, probably
because he was far more advanced intellectually than any of the other children. He reported that he was not athletically inclined and did not engage
in typical rough-and-tumble play with his peers. Instead, he spent much of
his time in solitary pursuits, in long walks during which he gloried in the
mysteries of nature. Jung reported that he became fully aware of his own
existence during one of his walks to school. As this awareness became clear
to him, he reveled in the knowledge that he was an autonomous being who
controlled his own life instead of being continually controlled by others:

> *I was taking the long road to school . . . when suddenly for a single moment*
> *I had the overwhelming impression of having just emerged from a dense*
> *cloud. I knew all at once: now I am myself! . . . Previously I had existed, too,*
> *but everything had merely happened to me. Now I happened to myself. Now*
> *I knew: I am myself now, now I exist. Previously I had been willed to do this*
> *and that: now I willed. This experience seemed to me tremendously impor-*
> *tant and new: there was "authority" in me. [Jung, 1963, pp. 32–33]*

In this recollection we can see the beginnings of Jung's later focus on
the importance of "inner experience." Another incident during his early
school days made a marked impression on Jung and may explain his later
reliance on the concept of the unconscious. Jung was assigned a composition topic in an English class. It interested him very much, so much so
that he spent a great deal of time and effort on it. He even hoped it would
receive one of the highest marks in the class. Instead, his teacher accused
him, in front of his classmates, of having copied it. Jung clung to his innocence, but the teacher persisted in his accusations and threatened to have
Jung dismissed from school. For days afterward, Jung thought about the
incident and tried to muster proof of his innocence. But there was no way
to prove he had written the composition himself. At this point, his grief and
rage were nearly out of control. Suddenly, he reported, he experienced an
"inner silence," and something deep down inside him (his unconscious)
began to speak. It said:

> *"What is really going on here? All right, you are excited. Of course the teacher*
> *is an idiot who doesn't understand your nature—that is, doesn't understand*
> *it any more than you do. Therefore he is as mistrustful as you are. You distrust*

yourself and others, and that is why you side with those who are naïve, simple,
and easily seen through. One gets excited when one doesn't understand things."
(Jung, 1963, pp. 65–66)

The picture that emerges of Jung as a boy is one of a person who was
sensitive and highly intelligent but who neither understood nor was understood by his parents, teachers, and peers. As a result, he withdrew as much
as he could from the world of people and began to rely on his own inner
experiences to help him understand the world.

During his teens Jung decided to become an archeologist, but his family
was too poor to send him to a university that included this specialty in its
curriculum. Instead, he entered the nearby University of Basel and majored
in medicine. He decided to specialize in psychiatry because it seemed to
provide an opportunity to reconcile two important opposing tendencies
within himself—an interest in natural science and a preoccupation with
religious and philosophical values. This concern with conflict between
opposites became a dominant theme in his later theorizing (Storr, 1973, p. 5).
In 1900, having obtained his medical degree, Jung took a position as an
assistant in a Zurich mental hospital. There he became interested in the
etiology of schizophrenia. An extensive study of the schizophrenic patients
led him to postulate the existence of a "collective unconscious" in people.
He found the fantasies and delusions of the patients were in many respects
similar to the myths and fantasies that guided people in contemporary and
ancient cultures. Jung believed that the materials his patients revealed to
him went beyond the recollection of their personal childhood and adult
experiences (Storr, 1973, pp. 8–9).

In 1906, he published *The Psychology of Dementia Praecox*, a psychoanalytic treatment of schizophrenia, and sent a copy of the book to Freud. A
year later, Jung went to Vienna to meet Freud. The visit marked the beginning
of a collaboration that lasted until 1913. The many reasons for the final split,
cataloged in Jung's *Psychology of the Unconscious*, include his basic disagreement with Freud over the importance of the sex instinct in people.
Jung could not accept Freud's belief that such an urge was virtually the only
determinant of behavior. He also grew tired of Freud's concern with the
pathological side of human nature. Jung wanted to develop a psychology
that dealt with human aspirations and spiritual needs. In this respect he
was an important forerunner of the humanist movement. He also argued
that the way to self-realization was through the rediscovery of the spiritual
self (Storr, 1973, pp. 12–13).

Between 1913 and 1917, Jung went through a mental crisis in his own
life that culminated in his resigning from a lectureship at the University of
Zurich. The crisis was precipitated by the break with Freud. Jung felt he
could no longer rely on Freud's approach to therapy, that he needed to
develop a new attitude or orientation toward treatment. He decided to let
his patients tell him everything about their fantasies and dreams and tried

not to interpret their self-reports in Freudian terms. Then Jung himself began to have dreams of a frightening nature. For example, he dreamed of dead bodies placed in crematory ovens, bodies that were then discovered to be alive. He also dreamed of monstrous catastrophes befalling Europe and felt vindicated when World War I broke out (Jung, 1963, pp. 170–176).

This flight into grotesque fantasies and dreams soon caused Jung to resign his lectureship. He did so consciously and deliberately because he "felt that something great was happening" to him (Jung, 1963, p. 194). In short, Jung began an attempt to probe the secrets of his unconscious and to unlock the mystery of his own personality. He was obsessed with understanding both sides of his personality—that is, the inner world of subjective experience and the unconscious and the outer world of contact with other people and material objects. Since he was already successful in his academic and writing career (in his outer world), an exploration of his unconscious and inner world beckoned. In other words, Jung felt that his development was too one-sided; he was overdeveloped in regard to the outer world but underdeveloped in regard to his knowledge of the inner world. He began a quest for "wholeness," for an integrated personality in which both sides of his nature would be brought into harmony or balance with each other. Part of this journey of self-exploration also involved an acceptance of the inevitability of death and the fact that its occurrence was beyond the control of his ego. As a result, Jung eventually adopted a "religious" attitude toward life in the sense that he had a greater appreciation of it and its mysteries. This inward turning and self-analysis at the middle stage of life is clearly reflected in his description of the individuation, or self-realization, process. This process is difficult and painful. In Jung's view, the person is "forged between hammer and anvil." Self-realization involves acknowledging everything you wish not to acknowledge about yourself.

It was only toward the end of World War I that Jung emerged from his inward journey. In his opinion, the principal factor in the resolution of his crisis was that he began to understand his mandala drawings, which symbolized the self. The rest of his life was relatively uneventful, except for one period during World War II when some critics accused him of being a Nazi sympathizer. Jung vigorously denied the charges and was eventually exonerated. He spent much of his time traveling and lecturing throughout the world and died in 1961 at the age of eighty-five (Fordham, 1966, p. 145).

The Complexity of Jung's Position

Jung's **analytical psychology** may be the most unusual in the entire body of work on personality. Although it provides numerous insights into personality functioning, it is also very difficult to understand. In many respects, it is complex, esoteric, and obscure. Part of the problem stems from the fact that Jung read widely in a number of different disciplines. As a result, he drew upon materials from psychology, psychiatry, literature, physics, chemistry, biology, archeology, philosophy, theology, mythology, history, anthropology, alchemy, and astrology in his attempts to understand human functioning. Since few investigators or readers have the background necessary to evaluate the materials he utilized, it has been easier for many people to ignore or dismiss his theorizing than to grapple with the incredible array of complex ideas that are an integral part of it. Still another difficulty lies in Jung's own failure to write clearly. He often used conventional terms in idiosyncratic ways without fully explaining the arbitrary shifts he had made in their meanings. With these difficulties clearly in mind, we present a review of the basic ideas of the theory.

Basic Concepts and Principles

The Psyche and Life-Process Energy

For Jung, the total personality is called the **psyche.** In his conceptualization, it is a nonphysical space that has its own special reality. Through the psyche, energy flows continuously in various directions from consciousness to unconsciousness and back and from inner to outer reality and back. This psychic energy was also thought by Jung to be real. He considered the terms *psychic energy* and *libido* to be interchangeable. He also considered libido to signify a general **life-process energy,** of which sexual urges are only one aspect (Jung, 1969, p. 17). Psychic energy, like physical energy, is an abstraction representing something real that cannot be touched or felt but that we know exists through its effects. Just as physical energy manifests itself in the heating and lighting of the rooms in our homes, so psychic energy manifests itself in our various feelings, thoughts, and behaviors.

Most important, psychic energy is considered an outcome of the conflict between forces within the personality. Without conflict there is no energy and no life. Love and hatred of a person can exist within a psyche, creating tension and new energy that seek expression in behavior. Other values may also conflict, such as a desire to have premarital intercourse when one knows that significant others may strongly disapprove. The number of potential conflicts is virtually unlimited. Jung also maintained that the various structures of the psyche are continually opposed to one another. For example, consciousness and unconsciousness are interdependent. Further, the shadow—that is, the unconscious and often evil side of our nature—may conflict with the ego, while ego processes may operate to keep unpleasant memories from awareness. The psyche is therefore conceived of as a general entity that operates according to the **principle of opposites.**

Once energy is created, it moves in a variety of directions (Progoff, 1953,

p. 63). It can be dissipated in outward behavior or it can continue to move within the psyche, first in one direction, then in another. It may split and move unsystematically through the psyche, go into the unconscious, or attach itself to other energy sources that could then manifest themselves in bizarre psychological forms—for example, in hallucinations and delusions of "unaccountable" moods. The point is, some of the libidinal energy that courses through the psyche operates autonomously, and hence unpredictably, with various results.

Libido also operates according to the principles of equivalence and entropy. These psychological formulations are based on the first and second laws of thermodynamics in physics. The **principle of equivalence** states that "for a given quantity of energy expended or consumed in bringing about a certain condition, an equal quantity of the same or another form of energy will appear elsewhere" (Jung, 1969, p. 18). In other words, an increase in some aspect of psychic functioning is met by a compensatory decrease in functioning in another part of the psyche, and a decrease in some aspect of psychic functioning is met by a compensatory increase in functioning in another area of the psyche. An increase in concern with achievement of occupational success might mean an equivalent loss of concern with one's spiritual life, and vice versa. In the area of sexuality, an erotic feeling for a person that cannot be freely expressed would be repressed but would continue to be active at the same level of intensity in the unconscious. In another person, the expression of the same feeling might be sublimated or transformed into creative work. Jung's notion is similar in this respect to Freud's notion of displacement.

The **principle of entropy** refers to the process within the psyche by which elements of unequal strength seek psychological equilibrium. If energy, for example, is concentrated in the ego, tension will be generated in the psyche to move the energy from the conscious to the unconscious in order to create a balance. The critical point is that any one-sided development of the personality creates conflict, tension, and strain. An even distribution, on the other hand, produces harmony and contentment. The aim of individual development is self-realization, which involves the integration of all aspects of the psyche. In such a harmonious state, the person would presumably be maximally happy and productive. This balanced state would also involve the evolution of a new center (the self) to replace the old one (the ego). The ego should not be considered useless or obsolete in the final system; it would exist, but in harmony with the other aspects of the psyche.

At this point, a review of the major structural components of the theory and their functions is in order.

Ego

Jung believed that the ego is a "complex of representations which constitutes the centrum of [the] field of consciousness and appears to possess a very high degree of continuity and identity" (Jung, 1923, p. 540). The term

complex refers to a collection of thoughts that are united, often by a common feeling. Ego is a complex that is not synonymous with the psyche but is only as aspect of it (Jung, 1969, p. 324). Nor is it identical with consciousness. Instead, the ego is a unifying force in the psyche, which is at the center of consciousness. It is responsible for our feelings of identity and continuity as human beings. Thus the ego contains the conscious thoughts of our own behavior and feelings as well as memories of our experiences.

The Personal Unconscious

The region next to the ego is the **personal unconscious** (see Figure 3.1). It consists of all the forgotten experiences that have lost their intensity for some reason, possibly because of their unpleasantness. It also includes sense impressions that are too weak to be perceived consciously (Jung, 1969, p. 376). These unconscious materials are accessible to the person's consciousness under certain circumstances. For example, they could be elicited by a skillful therapist with the help of the patient.

The Collective Unconscious

Still deeper within the psyche lies the **collective unconscious.** It was characterized by Jung as "a deposit of world-processes embedded in the structure of the brain and the sympathetic nervous system . . . [which] constitutes, in its totality, a sort of timeless and eternal world-image which counterbalances our conscious momentary picture of the world" (Jung, 1969, p. 370). In other words, it is the storehouse of latent memories of our human and prehuman ancestry. It consists of instincts and archetypes that we inherit as possibilities and that often affect our behavior. The archetypes are themes that have existed in all cultures throughout history. According to Jung, such collective memories are universal in nature because of our common evolution and brain structure.

This concept has often been misunderstood. Writers usually refer to it as one of Jung's original contributions to psychology, although Freud had already utilized a similar concept he called the racial unconscious. Second and more important, Jung did not accept the idea, espoused by the French naturalist J. B. Lamarck, that a person's characteristics are inherited directly. Instead, he argued that we inherit pathways that carry with them a tendency or predisposition to respond to certain experiences in specific ways (Progoff, 1953, p. 70). These tendencies come forth, sometimes spontaneously and sometimes when the person is under stress, in the form of archetypal motifs or themes. For example, Jung stated that men and women in every culture have inherited the tendency to respond in ambiguous and threatening situations with some form of an all-powerful being that we call God. In Jung's words:

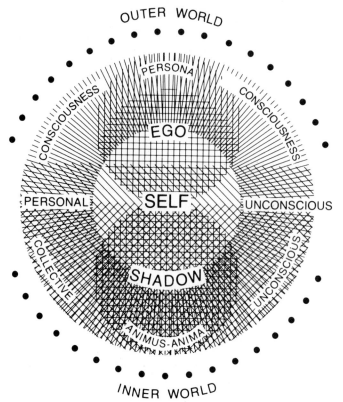

Figure 3.1 Structural components of the psyche. Adapted from J. Jacobi, *The Psychology of C. G. Jung* (New Haven: Yale University Press, 1962), p. 126, Diagram 6.

> *God is an absolute, necessary function of an irrational nature, which has nothing whatever to do with the question of God's existence. The human intellect can never answer this question, still less give any any proof of God. Moreover, such proof is superfluous, for the idea of an all-powerful divine Being is present everywhere, unconsciously if not consciously, because it is an archetype. [Jung, 1964, p. 81]*

Jung then proceeded to argue that a person who renounces the idea of God will experience personal difficulties. Human beings must come to grips with such an idea if they are ever to achieve inner harmony. Thus Jung would probably characterize atheists as people who have developed in a one-sided fashion and who are bound to experience difficulties eventually because they have failed to acknowledge this nonrational aspect of their nature. Searching for a rational answer in an irrational realm is a doomed quest. Jung seems to suggest that we accept the idea of an all-powerful being on faith; yet he also seems to contradict himself by suggesting that since the idea of God has a reality within the psyche as an archetype, it is potentially knowable. This difficulty disappears if we keep the distinction between internal and external reality clearly in view. Jung maintained that we can never offer objective proof of God's existence—that is, tangible, material proof shared by others in the external world—but the idea of God has validity in a subjective or inner reality sense because it has its roots in human experience on a universal basis.

The idea of God is not, however, like the idea of a chair with its clearly discernible properties. God is a universal symbol; and such symbols, though real, can never be fully understood (Jung, 1958c, p. 118). We may gain valuable information about their reality through persistent self-analysis, but we will never know them completely. They are really processes that take different forms. They have a kind of shadowy existence, a mysterious quality about them that, perhaps, we must at some point come to accept. In brief, their reality is so complex and bewildering that rational inquiry is helpful only to a point. Beyond that, only faith and acceptance of their unknown and unknowable aspects are demanded if movement toward a balanced psyche is to be achieved.

The Archetype

Although we discussed the concept of the archetype earlier, more elaboration is needed because of its central position in Jung's theory. As we now know, **archetypes** are universal themes that affect our behavior. At various points in his writings, Jung referred to such themes as "imagoes" (images), "primordial images," "root-images," "dominants," and "behavior patterns." Archetypes are, essentially, thought forms or ideas that give rise to visions projected onto current experiences. For example, one of the primary archetypes is the mother–child relationship, which is characterized by the mother's protection of the child. Dissolution of this bond must ultimately occur if the child is to attain adulthood. Jung maintained that the bond is broken in many primitive cultures when young men undergo rituals of rebirth and visits to men's houses (Jung, 1964, p. 208). We do not have comparable rituals in our culture. As a result, many men have never solved their basic dependency on their mothers. In married life, a man may project the mother image onto his wife by acting in childish, dependent, and submissive ways. Or he may react in an opposite manner by acting in hypermasculine ways, rejecting any offers of help from his spouse.

It should also be noted that not all archetypes are equally developed within the psyche. Some are well formed and exert a strong influence on personality functioning; others are not well developed and exert only minimal influence. Other major archetypes in the Jungian system include the persona, shadow, the anima and animus, the self, and the major attitudes of introversion and extraversion. Although introversion and extraversion are not considered by many theorists to be archetypes, Jung believed that they are: they are innate dispositions, but ones often molded by experience (Jung, 1923, p. 286).

The Persona. For Jung, the **persona** is "a compromise ... between the demands of the environment and the necessities of the individual's inner constitution" (Jacobi, 1962, p. 19). It is the mask we wear to function adequately in our relationships with other people. This mask may take as many forms as the roles we play in our daily routines. It also aids in controlling evil forces in the collective unconscious. Presumably, the persona is an archetype because it is a universal manifestation of our attempt to deal appropriately with other people.

But the persona also has negative features. We can, for instance, learn to hide our real selves behind these masks. Our persona can become split off from potentially enlightening forces in the personal and collective unconscious. From another perspective, we may become so committed to a particular role that we lose sight of our individuality. Jacobi provides an example of the stultifying aspects of such automatic and rigid role-playing: "We all know the professor ... whose individuality is exhausted in playing the professor's role; behind this mask one finds nothing but a bundle of peevishness and infantilism" (Jacobi, 1962, pp. 19–20).

In the Jungian view, so inflexible a man would have to become more accepting of his own and other people's feelings. He would further have to recognize and accept the limits of his rationality and intellect. He would also have to become more receptive to archetypes like the wise old man who might teach him something about human fallibility, because this archetype is the embodiment of wisdom and understanding. Of course, the professor might argue that such a view is sheer nonsense and that he is feeling fine and functioning well. Jungians would probably retort that the professor is simply rationalizing. In any event, the point is that in Jung's system excessive identification with the persona may have harmful effects on personal development.

The Shadow. Introduction of the shadow to students usually is met with chuckles and amused expressions; but for Jung the concept had important and serious meanings. The term was chosen by him to indicate the dark, sinister, Mr. Hyde side of our natures. In contrast to the persona's affiliation with the ego and consciousness and its role in personal adaptation to the external world, the **shadow** represents the evil, unadapted, unconscious, and inferior part of our psyches. It has two primary aspects—one associated with the personal unconscious, the other with the collective unconscious (Dry, 1961, p. 95). In relation to the personal unconscious, the shadow consists of all those experiences that the person rejects on moral and/or aesthetic grounds. For example, our egos may reject our sadistic impulses, or we may repress socially unacceptable sexual or aggressive impulses. Jung believed, incidentally, that the shadow incorporates both Freud's sexual instinct and Adler's will to power.

In relation to the collective unconscious, the shadow consists of universal personifications of evil within our psyches. The Devil, in its various forms, would be a prime example. Jung maintained that we may never fully understand this unadapted side of our personality because we can never bring ourselves to confront absolute evil. Nevertheless, the shadow exists in all of us, and it manifests itself in a variety of ways—unaccountable moods, pains of unexplained origin, feelings of self-destruction, and desires to harm others. It should be clearly understood that we do not, at base, have control over these impulses. Jung believed that these repressed feelings operate independently in the unconscious, where they join forces with other impulses. The result may be a complex with sufficient force to erupt into consciousness and momentarily to subdue the ego. For example, a dignified and sophisticated executive may suddenly become highly abusive toward his colleagues during an important meeting. His arguments may become totally irrational, irresponsible, and not at all related to the issues under consideration.

Finally, as with all of Jung's concepts, there are positive features to the shadow as well as the negative ones we have discussed. Some examples of the positive side are the murderer who decides impulsively to spare his victim because the victim reminds him of a loved one; the selfish woman who spends virtually all her time making money and who then donates a large percentage of her earnings to a local charity, even though she does not realize a tax break from her action; and the "sinner" who suddenly becomes "good" and is concerned with helping others. More generally, the positive side of the shadow is sometimes evident when a person feels unaccountably vital, spontaneous, and creative.

The Anima and Animus. Like Freud, Jung believed that all men and women have elements of the opposite sex within them. Each man has a feminine side, while each woman has unconscious masculine qualities. This concept was based, at least partially, on the fact that both men and women have varying amounts of male and female hormones. The feminine archetype in man Jung called the **anima;** the masculine archetype in woman he labeled the **animus.** Like all archetypes, the anima and animus can function in either constructive or destructive ways. Jung stated that the anima operates positively in man when it serves as "his inspiration . . . [when] her [anima's] intuitive capacity, often superior to man's, can give him timely warning [presumably about harmful events], and her feelings, always directed towards the personal, can show him ways which his own less personally accepted feeling would never have discovered" (Jung, 1964, p. 199). The negative aspects of the anima concept are seen when men act in moody, "bitchy," and "catty" ways. The animus in women has positive manifestations when it produces arguments based on reason and logic. The negative side of the animus can be seen in these behaviors:

> *In intellectual women . . . [when it] . . . encourages a critical disputatiousness and would-be high-browism, which . . . consists essentially in harping on some*

irrelevant weak point and nonsensically making it the main point. Or a per-
fectly lucid discussion gets tangled up in the most maddening way through
the introduction of a quite different and if possible perverse point of view.
Without knowing it, such women are solely intent upon exasperating the man
and are, in consequence, . . . completely at the mercy of the animus. [Jung,
1964, p. 220]

Despite Jung's claims that the anima and animus are universal phenomena, the descriptions sound suspiciously like our cultural stereotypes of the
sexes. The masculine archetype includes those characteristics we associate
traditionally with the male role—reason, logic, forceful argument, and social
insensitivity, among others. The feminine archetype and traditional feminine
behavior are closely associated with attributes such as emotionality, social
sensitivity, intuition, vanity, moodiness, and irrationality. Although Jung did
catalog the presumed negative characteristics of the animus, his major detailed
arguments about the "weaknesses" of the anima suggest a patriarchal bias
that we have already seen in the writings of Freud.

These a priori images may operate in dreams and fantasies, according
to Jung, but often they are projected onto real-life objects. For example, the
anima in a man could be projected onto his lover, producing a discrepancy
between them that could be harmful to both parties. Perhaps he sees his
lover as the universal mother, a compassionate and sensitive being who will
always protect him and look out for his interests. In actuality, however, his
lover may be a boor who is concerned only with exploiting him sexually.
From another perspective, the animus may take the form of the evil con-
queror who, when projected on a kindly and sensitive suitor, will inevitably
produce conflicts and problems. The ability to differentiate these universal
images from their real-life counterparts is an extremely difficult task, but
one that is important if each of us is to progress toward selfhood.

The Self. An archetypal potentiality in all of us is the **self.** It is conceptualized as an innate blueprint that, theoretically at least, is capable of being
realized. This "destiny within us" involves a process that Jung called the
"way of individuation" (Jacobi, 1962, p. 100). Individuation is a "process by
which a [person] . . . becomes the definite, unique being that he in fact is. In
doing so he does not become 'selfish' in the ordinary sense of the word, but
is merely fulfilling the peculiarity of his nature, and this . . . is vastly different
from egotism or individualism" (Jung, 1964, p. 183).

Thus the self is the final goal of our striving and, in this sense at least,
is similar to the goal of perfection in Adler's system, as we shall soon learn.
The movement toward **self-realization** is a difficult process, one Jung believed
could not be attained by young people. It takes time and considerable effort
to resolve the many conflicts between opposites within the psyche, so that
the few people who come closest to the attainment of selfhood would be
middle-aged at a minimum. With the attainment of harmony, a new center
or midpoint evolves within the personality—namely the self, which replaces

the old one, the ego. The ego now becomes a satellite of the self, much like the earth in rotation around the sun. Consciousness does not replace unconsciousness within the psyche. Instead, the principle of opposites remains viable with consciousness and unconsciousness balancing each other.

In such a state, the self is conceptualized as the unifying force that has a **transcendent function** that provides stability and balance to the various systems of the personality. In other words, as individuals explore the unconscious aspects of their individual psyche, each learns more about it and its functions and thus begins to feel more comfortable with this side of their nature. For example, a woman begins to understand how her shadow operates to make her moody or impulsive; a man begins to understand how his anima forces him to idealize his girlfriend and to ignore her faults. This understanding involves a resolution, not a solution, of their conflicts. Through their new understanding, they transcend these conflicts and begin to live more harmoniously within themselves and with others.

Much of Jung's interest in **symbols** like the shadow and the anima stemmed from his attempt to find the ways in which the self has been described and expressed in various religious and occult systems, psychologies, arts, and philosophies throughout history (Progoff, 1953, p. 153). The most important representations of the self are the **mandalas,** or magic circles, symbols found in the writing and art of all cultures (see Figure 3.2). These mandalas represent a synthesis or union between opposites within the psyche when individuals attain self-realization. According to Jung, the oldest mandala is a paleolithic sun wheel drawing based on the principle of four (Jung, 1958a, p. 326). Mandalas are also found in Buddhism and Taoism and in other religions of the Orient.

In these religions, the golden flower is often placed in the center of the mandala, signifying the "heavenly mansion, the realm of the highest bliss, the boundless land, and the altar on which consciousness and life are brought forth." In the Middle Ages, mandalas often included Christ with four evangelists around him (Jacobi, 1962, pp. 128–131).

Medieval alchemy was also involved in Jung's search for unique expressions of the self. He saw the alchemists' transmutation of base metals into gold, for example, as similar to the "transformation of personality through the blending and fusion of the noble with the base components, of the differentiated with the inferior functions, of the conscious with the unconscious" (Jung, 1964, p. 232). Finally, Jung stated that many of his patients spontaneously reported mandalas in their dreams and also painted them during therapy sessions. Thus, by drawing upon materials from an incredible variety of sources, Jung believed he had discovered a universal synthesizing phenomenon that transcended personal experience.

Jung believed that, in an attempt to evolve toward selfhood, people adopt different ways of relating to experience; that is, they adopted different attitudes toward life and utilized different psychological processes or functions

Figure 3.2 Mandala of awakening consciousness. Adapted from J. Jacobi, *The Psychology of C. G. Jung* (New Haven: Yale University Press, 1962), p. 114, Plate 14.

to make sense out of their experiences. Jung spelled out the details of the basic attitudes and functions used by people in his theory of psychological types.

The Theory of Psychological Types

Basic Attitudes

The two fundamental attitudes in Jung's typology are extraversion and introversion. **Extraversion** refers to "an outgoing, candid, and accommodating nature that adapts easily to a given situation, quickly forms attachments, and, setting aside any possible misgivings, often ventures forth with careless confidence into an unknown situation." **Introversion,** in contrast, signifies "a hesitant, reflective, retiring nature that keeps itself to itself, shrinks from objects, is always slightly on the defensive, and prefers to hide behind mistrustful scrutiny" (Jung, p. 52). Jung pointed out that people are not purely introverted or extraverted. Instead, each person has both introverted and extraverted aspects to his or her nature, and both factors involve complex variations. One set of characteristics, however, is **dominant** (that is, conscious), while the other set is **inferior** (that is, unconscious). The dominant side is compensated for by the inferior side, and vice versa. If too much libido is invested in the dominant side, for example, energy forces are set up and activated in the unconscious, typically with harmful results for the individual.

Jung's typology is based on his conceptualization of the flow of libido within the psyche. One way in which energy can flow is outward toward life; another is inward toward subjective experience. For Jung, however, extraversion and introversion are not to be equated with outward libidinal flow or progression and inward flow or regression, respectively. Instead,

> movement can occur in two different forms; either extraverted, when the progression is predominately influenced by objects and environmental conditions, or introverted, when it has to adapt itself to the conditions of the ego (or, more accurately, of the "subjective factor"). Similarly, regression can proceed along two lines, either as a retreat from the outside world (introversion), or as a flight into extravagant experience of the outside world (extraversion). [Jung, 1969, pp. 40–41]

Thus extraversion and introversion have their own "special dynamics," and both attitudes have progressive and regressive properties. What precisely is Jung talking about here? He is arguing that introversion and extraversion can have both "good" (healthy) and "bad" (unhealthy) consequences for our development. Like all of Jung's concepts, this one has positive and negative features, as the following examples demonstrate. Introversion may have progressive effects when a person creates a unique and useful product, like a first-rate novel. Introversion may have regressive effects when it leads to excessive brooding and indecisiveness in an individual who needs to make a firm judgment. Witness the student who is doing poorly in a course and hesitates to ask a more competent classmate or the instructor for help; failure in the course may well be the outcome. Extraversion may have progressive effects when it leads us to make sensible decisions, like the decision to ask for assistance. Extraversion may have regressive effects when it causes people to act injudiciously, like accepting virtually every pronouncement of authority in order to secure approval. Such people are so committed to the "object"—the authority figure—that they accept his or her comments uncritically. Witness the student who changes her or his career on the advice of neurotic relatives.

The Four Functions

In addition to his ideas about introversion and extraversion, Jung postulated the existence of four functions or ways in which people make sense of their experiences. As modes of relating to the world, these functions include sensing, thinking, feeling, and intuiting. Sensation is our initial experiencing of phenomena, without evaluation. Thinking proceeds from this point and is the interpretation of events through the use of reason and logic. Such interpretations also involve evaluation along an affective, or feeling, dimension. Finally, in the mode of intuition we relate to the world directly, with a minimum of interpretation and reasoning (Progoff, 1953, p. 100).

Jung called thinking and feeling the **rational functions** because they involve a process of making judgments about experiences. Sensation and intuition are the **irrational functions** because they involve passively recording, but not evaluating or interpreting, experience. Although many of us tend stereotypically to associate thinking with rationality and feeling with irrationality, Jung pointed out that both thinking and feeling involve the assessment of the worth of any experience. Thinking is primarily concerned with the truth or falsity of our experience; feeling implies the degree to which we like or dislike something. There is a further semantic difficulty in that Jung did not want the term *irrational* to convey the idea of excessive or "mindless" emotionality. Instead, he used the term to mean modes of relating to experience that are unrelated to reason. Perhaps "nonrational" would have been a more suitable designation for Jung to have used.

The rational and irrational functions are articulated or differentiated to varying degrees within the psyche. As Jung envisioned it, one function of the rational or irrational pair is dominant, or superior, with its counterpart being inferior. The members of the remaining pair exist in a kind of twilight zone, partly conscious and partly unconscious. The superior function is the most highly differentiated, followed by the auxiliary pair, with the inferior function being least differentiated. It should be noted that any one of the functions can be dominant; that is, there are thinking, feeling, sensing, and intuiting kinds of individuals. Of course, each of these types lacks full development. The "whole," or integrated, person would be one capable of utilizing all the functions in dealing with his or her experiences.

Typology Derived from the Basic Attitudes and Functions

Out of the two major attitudes and four functions, Jung fashioned an eightfold classification scheme of **psychological types.** In reality, there are 16 possible personality types, if we consider that either member of the auxiliary pair can exist in a somewhat differentiated and conscious form. In his classic work on the subject, however, Jung focused his attention on eight of the possibilities—both the introverted and the extraverted thinking, feeling, sensing, and intuitive types.

The Extraverted Thinking Type. As Jung saw it, the **extraverted think-ing type** is characterized by a need

> *to make all his life-activities dependent on intellectual conclusions, which in the last resort are always oriented by objective data.... This kind of man ... [lives by an] ... intellectual formula. By this formula are good and evil mea-sured and beauty and ugliness determined.... If the formula is wide enough, this type may play a very useful role in social life, either as a reformer or [as] a ventilator of public wrongs ... or as the propagator of important innova-tions. But the more rigid the formula, the more does he develop into a grumbler, a crafty reasoner, and a self-righteous critic. [Jung, 1923, pp. 346–347]*

Such a person also has repressed feelings in his or her pursuit of ideas and ideals and tends to deny "aesthetic activities, taste, artistic sense, cul-tivation of friends, etc." (Jung, 1923, p. 348). Jung argued further that a person who is developing in such a negative fashion may appear concerned about the welfare of other people but in reality is concerned only with the attain-ment of his or her goals. The self-serving activist who exploits the friendship of other people to further his or her aims is an example.

The Introverted Thinking Type. According to Jung, the **introverted thinking type,**

> *like his extraverted counterpart, is strongly influenced by ideas, though his ideas have their origin not in objective data but in his subjective foundation. He will follow his ideas like the extravert, but in the reverse direction: inwards and not outwards. [Jung, 1923, p. 383]*

The subjective foundation of the introverted thinker is the collective unconscious. Creative ideas spring from this source and not from outside sources like traditional moral authority. As a result of this concern with internal forces, the introverted thinker appears cold, aloof, and inconsider-ate of others. In addition, he or she tends to be socially inept and inarticulate in attempts to communicate ideas.

The Extraverted Feeling Type. Jung described the **extraverted feeling type** as one who lives according to "objective situations and general values" (Jung, 1923, p. 356). In other words, their feelings and behavior are controlled by social norms—that is, by the expectations of others. As a consequence, their feelings change from situation to situation and from person to person. Jung believed women to be the best examples of this type. A prime example would be a college woman who breaks her engagement because her parents object to the man. Her feelings toward him are based on her parents' judg-ments. If they like him, fine; if they do not, she feels compelled to reject him. In such people, thinking is largely repressed.

On the plus side of the ledger, Jung maintained that extraverted feeling women can make adequate marriages. "These women are good companions and excellent mothers, so long as [their] husbands and children are blessed with the conventional psychic constitution" (Jung, 1923, p. 357). By "conventional psychic constitution," Jung seems to mean husbands and children who conform to the rules and regulations society prescribes for the "well-adjusted" family.

The Introverted Feeling Type. Jung cited women as being the prime examples of the **introverted feeling type** also:

> They are mostly silent, inaccessible, and hard to understand: often they hide behind a childish or banal mask, and their temperament is inclined to melancholy. They neither shine nor reveal themselves. [Jung, 1923, p. 389]

Although they may appear unfeeling to others, in reality they are capable of intense emotion, but their feelings have origins in the collective unconscious. They have the depth of emotion that could erupt in religious or poetic form.

The Extraverted Sensing Type. Jung visualized men as the prime examples of the **extraverted sensing type.** They are primarily reality-oriented and typically shun thinking and contemplation. Experiencing sensations becomes almost an end in itself. Each experience serves as a guide to new experience. Such people are usually outgoing and jolly and have a considerable capacity for enjoyment, some of which revolves around good food. In addition, they are often refined aesthetes, concerned with matters of good taste in painting, sculpture, and literature as well as with food and physical appearance. When they become overenamored with the object—for example, in the area of food or physical appearance—they develop into "crude pleasure-seeker[s] or . . . unscrupulous, effete aesthete[s]" (Jung, 1923, p. 365). The novelist Rabelais' young fictional character, Gargantua, presents a perfect example of the negative aspects of extraverted sensing types:

> He spent his time like other small children: namely, in drinking, eating and sleeping; in eating, sleeping and drinking; in sleeping, drinking and eating. He was forever wallowing in dirt, covering his nose with filth and begriming his face. . . . He used to piddle on his shoes, brown up his shirt-tails, wipe his nose on his sleeve and clear his nostrils into his soup. . . . Often he coughed up, figuratively and literally. Fat? Another ounce of wind and he would have exploded. Appreciative? He would piss, full-bladdered, at the sun. . . . Cautious? He used to hide under water for fear of the rain. [Rabelais, 1936, p. 36]

The Introverted Sensing Type. In Jung's view, **introverted sensing types** are irrational types guided by the "intensity of the subjective sensation—excited by the objective stimulus" (Jung, 1923, p. 395). These appear to be people who overreact to outside stimuli. They may take innocuous comments from others and interpret them in imaginative or bizarre ways. They may also appear rational and in complete control of their actions because of their unrelatedness to objects—for example, people in the environment. Such people may also treat the objective world (external reality) as mere appearance and even as a joke. Libido from primordial images affects their perception of events. Positive manifestations of libido are found in creative persons, whereas negative manifestations are seen in psychotics.

The Extraverted Intuitive Type. Exploiting external opportunities is the chief concern of **extraverted intuitive types.** In Jung's words, they have "keen nose[s] for anything new and in the making" (Jung, 1923, p. 368). Politicians, merchants, contractors, and speculators are examples. Women are more likely than men to have such orientations (Jung, 1923, p. 369).

Among the positive features of this type are that they are the initiators and promoters of promising enterprises, and that they often inspire others to great accomplishments. But there are also serious dangers for people with this orientation. Although they may enliven and encourage others, they do little for themselves. In addition, they are impatient and always seeking new possibilities. Consequently, they often do not see their actions through to completion.

The Introverted Intuitive Type. In the **introverted intuitive type** of person, there is an intensification of intuition that often results in estrangement from external reality. Such people may be considered enigmatic even by close friends. On a positive level, they may become great visionairies and mystics; on the negative level, they may develop into artistic cranks who espouse their own idiosyncratic language and visions. Such people cannot be understood by others and, since their judgment functions (their thinking and feelings) are relatively repressed, they are incapable of communicating effectively with others.

Research Evidence for the Theory of Psychological Types

To assess the validity of Jung's proposed typology, it was necessary for investigators to construct a scale that measured the various concepts. A personality inventory called the Gray-Wheelwright was developed first by Jungian analysts, but it has been largely replaced by the more popular **Myers-Briggs Type Indicator (MBTI).** Considerable work has been done with the MBTI to establish its reliability and validity. It is an inventory that consists of 166 items with a forced-choice format. Sample items for use in identifying introverts and extraverts and the sensing, thinking, feeling, and intuitive types are presented in Table 3.1.

Table 3.1
Sample Items from the Myers-Briggs Type Indicator
(MBTI)

Introversion (I)—Extraversion (E) Items

1. When you have to meet strangers, do you find it
   a. pleasant, or at least easy (E), or
   b. something that takes a good deal of effort? (I)

2. Are you naturally
   a. a "good mixer" (E) or
   b. rather quiet and reserved in company? (I)

3. In a large group, do you more often
   a. introduce others (E) or
   b. get introduced? (I)

Sensing (S)—Intuition (N) Items

1. Do you usually get along better with
   a. imaginative people (N) or
   b. realistic people? (S)

2. Do you get more annoyed at
   a. fancy theories (S) or
   b. people who don't like theories? (N)

3. Would you rather be considered
   a. a practical person (S) or
   b. an ingenious person? (N)

Thinking (T)—Feeling (F) Items

1. Which of these two is the higher compliment
   a. he is a person of real feeling (F) or
   b. he is consistently reasonable? (T)

2. Do you think it is a worse fault
   a. to show too much warmth (T) or
   b. not to have enough warmth? (F)

3. Do you more often let
   a. your heart rule your head (F) or
   b. your head rule your heart? (T)

Reproduced by special permission from the Myers-Briggs Type Indicator by Katherine C. Briggs and
Isabel Briggs Myers, copyright 1943, 1944, 1957, and 1976; published by Consulting Psychologists Press,
Inc., Palo Alto, Calif.

In their research with the typology, Fling, Thomas, and Gallaher (1981) have
shown that undergraduate volunteers for a meditation research study were
more likely to be introverted than extraverted, feeling than thinking, and
intuitive than sensing, in comparison with a matched sample of nonvolun-
teer undergraduates.

Research also has shown that occupational interests among college students are related in many instances to the Jungian typology. For example, one study showed that introverts had strong interests in mathematics and technical-scientific occupations, whereas extraverts gravitated toward sales and public relations jobs. Students who were intuitive preferred jobs as musicians and psychologists, whereas feeling, thinking, and sensing types leaned toward the occupations of minister, certified public accountant, and banker, respectively (Stricker & Ross, 1962).

Other research has provided additional evidence in support of Jung's typology. Carlson and Levy (1973) found that introverted thinkers were more effective in memorizing emotionally neutral stimulus material (a number or series of digits) than were introverted and extraverted feeling types and extraverted thinkers. Extraverted feeling types were more accurate than the others in remembering new, emotionally toned material (a series of pictures of a female model's portrayals of different emotions). A number of other predictions derived from Jung's theory were also confirmed, including one that showed that extraverted intuitive types were overrepresented among social volunteers as compared with a matched sample of nonvolunteers.

Interesting research by Carlson (1980) has shown further that the kinds of memories that introverted thinkers and extraverted feelers report as significant moments in their lives differ considerably. Introverted thinking and extraverted feeling adults were asked to describe the most vivid experiences they had in the past that made them feel joyful, excited, or ashamed. In line with Jung's theory, extraverted feelers most often mentioned memories that involved experiences with other people (social experiences), while introverted thinkers most often mentioned experiences that they had had while alone (individual experiences). For example, some of the experiences of joy recollected by introverted thinkers were reported as (1) graduating from junior college, (2) awakening in the hospital and seeing my new baby, and (3) shooting my first rabbit (age 10). In contrast, extraverted feelers reported (1) meeting my girlfriend in a group attending the Rose Parade, (2) having my boyfriend propose marriage, and (3) being chosen the most popular counselor at the church camp.

Experiences of excitement for introverted thinkers included (1) anticipating a trip to San Francisco, and (2) beginning a new job in a program for the mentally retarded. Extraverted feelers reported (1) cheering for a friend at a cross-country track meet, and (2) embarking on a small business venture with my spouse. Shameful experiences for introverted thinkers included (1) drinking too much and then becoming "too candid" at a party, and (2) getting plastered and throwing up at a party. Extraverted feelers reported (1) being arrested for shoplifting with a friend (age 12), and (2) calling my mother an "old hag" and being reprimanded by my father.

Thus there is strong support for the Jungian scheme of psychological types. From the research just described, it is clear that some complex Jungian concepts can be translated into terms that allow for empirical testing and verification.

The Process of Personality Development

In earlier sections of the chapter we discussed in a rather sporadic fashion some of Jung's thinking about the process of personality development. Here we will present a more focused summary of his views.

First, Jung conceived of personal development as a dynamic and evolving process that occurs throughout one's life. The person is continually developing and learning new skills and moving toward self-realization. Although Jung had little to say about the developmental process in childhood, he obviously did not accept Freud's view that the individual's personality is relatively fixed by the end of early childhood. Neither did he accept Freud's view that only past events determine the person's behavior. For Jung, the individual's behavior is determined not only by past experiences but also by future goals. He saw the person as one who continually plans for the future. But although the person can progress toward selfhood by developing differentiated psychological functions, he or she can also move backward. Such backward movement need not, however, necessarily have detrimental effects on the individual. As we have learned, some retreats into the psyche can provide the impetus for creative growth.

The movement toward actualization is often a difficult and painful process. It involves continual attempts by the individual to understand his or her experiences and to develop healthy attitudes. The person is often beset by crises, and Jung believed that many individuals experience their most severe crises during the middle years. Adequate resolution of these crises helps move the person toward an accurate perception and full understanding of himself or herself. Under these conditions, the person becomes individuated; that is, the person becomes all he or she is capable of becoming as a human being. The person is then able to reconcile the opposing forces within the psyche through transcendence.

Progress toward self-actualization is not automatic. If the person grows up in an unhealthy and threatening environment, where the parents use harsh and unreasonable punishment, growth will likely be stifled. It is also possible that repressed evil forces within the psyche can erupt without warning to produce personality dysfunction. Under these conditions, the outcomes may be neurosis or psychosis. We turn now to a discussion of these disorders.

Neurosis and Psychosis

Jung considered neurosis and psychosis to be disorders that differ primarily in the severity of their consequences for people. Both result from one-sided development in which repressed forces create problems in functioning. In all the eight types discussed earlier, for example, intense repression of one of the four functions would probably result in a form of neurosis. More specifically, when thinking is repressed in the introverted feeling type,

Jung argued, the thinking function may eventually project itself onto objects, thus creating problems for the person. Why? Because the thinking function is archaic and undifferentiated, so the person's judgment about the object or objects is bound to be gross and inaccurate. Such a person is unable to reason accurately about the intentions of others. As a consequence,

> other people are [assumed to be] thinking all sorts of mean things, scheming evil, contriving plots, secret intrigues, etc. In order to forestall them, she herself is obliged to start counter-intrigues, to suspect others ... and [to] weave counterplots. Beset by rumours, she must make frantic efforts to be top dog. Endless clandestine rivalries spring up, and in these embittered struggles she will shrink from no baseness or meanness, and will even prostitute her virtues in order to play the trump card. Such a state of affairs must end in exhaustion. [Jung, 1923, p. 391]

The resulting form of neurosis is neurasthenia, a disorder characterized by listlessness and fatigue. Jung saw psychosis as an extension of neurosis that occurs when repressed and unconscious forces overpower consciousness. In his view, consciousness is a secondary phenomenon derived from unconsciousness. Therefore consciousness is a rather fragile entity that can be "swallowed up" by unleashed forces in the unconscious. In such instances, the person collapses and the ego loses control when attacked by elements of the collective unconscious. Jung provided an illustration of the onset of psychosis with the case of a quiet young man who imagined that a woman was in love with him. When he discovered his love was unrequited, he

> was so desperate that he went straight to the river to drown himself. It was late at night, and the stars gleamed up at him from the dark water. It seemed to him that the stars were swimming two by two down the river, and a wonderful feeling came over him. He forgot his suicidal intentions and gazed fascinated at the strange, sweet drama, and gradually he became aware that every star was a face and that all these pairs were lovers who were carried along locked in a dreaming embrace. An entirely new understanding came to him: all had changed—his fate, his disappointment, even his love receded and fell away. The memory of the girl grew distant, blurred; but instead, he felt with complete certainty that untold riches were promised him. He knew that an immense treasure lay hidden for him in the neighboring observatory. The result was that he was arrested by the police at four o'clock in the morning, attempting to break into the observatory.
>
> What had happened? His poor head had glimpsed a Dantesque picture whose loveliness he could never have grasped had he read it in a poem.... For his poor turnip-head it was too much. He did not drown in the river but in an eternal image, and its beauty perished with him. [Jung, 1959, p. 126]

This illustration also shows that in Jung's scheme the collective unconscious has its attractive elements and can sometimes lure a person into its essentially fathomless inner reality.

Techniques of Assessment

Like Freud, Jung relied primarily on the case study as a personality assessment technique. He also showed his Freudian roots by utilizing dream analysis and by making use of patients' self-reports about significant early experiences. Yet, in a number of important respects, Jung's use of these techniques differed from his mentor's. In addition, Jung developed a few highly original procedures.

Dream Analysis. In Jung's view, dreams are involuntary and sponta-neous eruptions of repressed materials that are rooted in both the personal and the collective unconscious. However, their manifest content is not always a disguised attempt at wish-fulfillment of sexual and/or aggressive needs. Instead, dreams are more often attempts at resolving current problems and conflicts being experienced by people and providing them with a means of furthering their own development in a healthy direction. For example, Jung reported that a young man dreamt that his father was behaving in a drunken and disorderly manner. The son stated that his father was actually a highly virtuous man and that he and his father had an ideal relationship. Jung interpreted the dream to mean that the son's admiration for his father pre-vented him from having the confidence to develop his own personality. He was, in fact, too close to his father and therefore was unable to develop his own identity. It was almost as if the dream were informing the son that his father was not so virtuous after all and that there was no need for the son to feel inferior (Fordham, 1966, p. 103).

According to Jung, dreams are also compensatory in nature. They are efforts at adjustment, attempts at rectifying deficiencies in personality. People who are very shy, for example, may have dreams in which they are the "life of the party." Failures in business may dream of great financial ventures and successes. Mediocre actors may dream about receiving a standing ovation for their performance in a Broadway play. Although the idea of compensa-tion in dreams is intriguing, initial research findings have not been very supportive of its validity (Domino, 1976).

Method of Amplification. Dreams are replete with various kinds of sym-bols that typically have multiple meanings and are very difficult to interpret. To reveal their meanings as far as was possible, Jung utilized the **method of amplification.** Unlike free association, which involves starting with a particular symbol and moving further and further away from it, the method of amplification involves adhering to a given symbol and giving numerous associations to it. In the process, the symbol's multiple meanings become clearer and provide patients with insights into their problems. These asso-ciations are given by both the patient and the analyst. Often the associations provided by the analyst determine the direction of the patient's own associations (Jacobi, 1962, p. 82). Moreover, patients usually provide the subjective or personal meanings of the symbols, while the therapist provides the universal meanings of the symbols as revealed in mythology, religion, alchemy, art, history, and so forth (Jacobi, 1962, p. 87).

Analysis involves examination of not just one dream but of a series of dreams. Jung believed that analysis of a series of dreams is important because it provides a means of achieving more accurate interpretations of the problems confronting the patient. He thought that the analysis of a single dream could prove misleading. The in-depth analysis of a series of dreams also allows the patient and therapist to move from the personal meanings embedded in the symbols to their deeper meanings as archetypal images.

Word-Association Test. Jung pioneered an experimental technique called the **word-association test,** which he used in conjunction with dream analysis. This procedure involved having the patient respond to stimulus words with whatever words occurred to him or her. Jung recorded the time that elapsed between the initial presentation of the stimulus and the eventual response and used the time latency as an indicator of possible areas of resistance and conflict within the person. The assumption was that the longer the time interval, the greater the likelihood that important complexes or areas of conflict within the psyche were being tapped. In addition, areas of conflict were assumed to be present under the following conditions: (1) the patients repeated the stimulus word several times as though they had not heard it; (2) they misheard the word as some other word; (3) they gave a response of more than one word; (4) they gave a meaningless reaction (that is, a made-up word); or (5) they failed to respond at all. Jung also required his patients to recall all their responses to the word stimuli after a rest interval. Failing to reproduce the words or reporting distorted reproductions were also considered reflective of underlying conflict (Jacobi, 1962, p. 38).

Painting Therapy. Another technique Jung used in conjunction with dream analysis was painting therapy. He relied heavily on paintings by his patients as a means of further encouraging them to express their unconscious feelings or thoughts. He maintained that these paintings had little artistic merit and was careful to point out that fact to the patients. As the paintings were artistically worthless, the patients made sense out of them by concluding that they must be expressions of their innermost selves. The painting exercises were conducted to help the patients clarify the symbols they had seen in their dreams and to force patients to cope actively with their problems. In Jung's view, painting had real therapeutic effects. It moved patients off dead center and started them on the road to self-realization.

Application of the Theory to the Treatment of Psychopathology. Jung believed that neurosis is a severe disorder in which the person's growth toward self-realization is halted. Yet, in his view, neurosis has a positive aspect to it as well. It is a "warning sign" that the person's personality is desperately in need of broadening and that this could happen only if the therapist and patient utilized the correct therapeutic procedures.

These procedures would differ depending on, for example, the age of the patient. Jung thought that the forms of neurosis in young and middle-aged people are radically different:

> The life of a young person is characterized by a general expansion and striving towards concrete ends; and his neurosis seems mainly to rest on his hesitation or shrinking back from this necessity. But the life of an older person is characterized by a contraction of forces, by the affirmation of what has been achieved, and by the curtailment of further growth. His neurosis comes mainly from his clinging to a youthful attitude which is now out of season. Just as the young neurotic is afraid of life, so the older one shrinks back from death. [Jung, 1954, p. 39]

Thus it is clear that therapy has to be tailored to the age of the person. For the most part, Jung confined his efforts to treatment of the problems of the middle-aged. His analytical therapy is really a "psychology of the afternoon."

The middle-aged people who visited Jung had special problems. Unlike many neurotics who suffer because they lack a strong ego, the men and women treated by Jung were usually highly successful people, often of outstanding ability. Yet they were restless and discontented. At this stage in their development, they typically began to ask themselves whether there might not be more to life than material success. They began to search for the meaning of their existence (Storr, 1973, p. 80). This search involved an exploration of their unconscious as a means of correcting an overdeveloped consciousness. In other words, they made an effort to rediscover those aspects of themselves that had been neglected. They began to realize that they must stop their relentless pursuit of success in order to rediscover the spiritual meaning of their existence. They must cultivate their inner life, come to grips with its secrets, and assimilate them into consciousness. They must also come to accept the inevitability of death.

Jung viewed therapy as the process by which patients are able, through exploration of their inner life, to broaden their personalities and to develop a spiritual or religious attitude toward their existence. It was not only patients, however, who gained insights into themselves as a result of analysis. Therapists were equally involved in the process and could obtain positive benefits. Jung maintained that both analysts and patients have many limitations and that both are struggling toward self-realization. Consequently, he maintained that therapists must give up all claims to superior knowledge as well as desires to influence their patients if substantial progress toward the Tao, or fulfillment and harmony, are ever to be obtained. Progress toward the Tao refers to a process described by Chinese philosophers whereby individual conflicts and anxieties are transcended so that people can live in a state of perfect harmony and bliss.

Jung seemed to contradict himself slightly when he spoke later of therapists as guides for patients. A guide is defined as a person who has some special skills and knowledge that someone else can utilize for personal benefit. A guide should also, of course, be thoroughly familiar with the task he or she is undertaking. Hunters do not, for example hire a guide who is ignorant of the woods where they will be camping. In the best sense, though, Jung seemed to adopt a genuine attitude of humility toward an arduous and uncertain spiritual journey, the outcome of which is essentially unknown to the participants.

In Jung's view, the therapeutic process has four key stages: confession, elucidation, education, and transformation (Jung, 1954, p. 55). Confession is a necessary first step in the healing process because it forces the individual to acknowledge his or her limitations to another. The person also becomes aware of his or her universal ties to humankind in the sense that all men and women possess certain weaknesses. The cathartic process also leads to the patient's reliance on the therapist; that is, transference occurs. In the process of understanding this transference, the patient brings to the surface certain contents of the unconscious that the therapist clarifies; this is elucidation. During this stage, the person learns the origins of his or her problems. In the third stage, education, the person incorporates the insights into his or her personality in order to adapt to the social environment. Transformation occurs when the therapist and the patient have been through the first three stages. At this point, the dynamic interplay between the two can lead to exciting changes that move beyond adaptation to the environment and toward self-realization.

Self-realization is an ideal state and not something to be actually attained. It is the process that is important, not the achievement of the goal. By undergoing this painful struggle to reconcile the conflicting sides of their nature, patients become more integrated, whole personalities. They do not become perfect human beings; they become, instead, what they are destined to become—individuals with unique sets of strengths and limitations. Self-realization involves the acceptance of these limitations. It is a religious experience in the sense that reconciliation of the opposites within individuals may occur when they subordinate themselves to a higher authority whom they believe will make all things well in the end (Storr, 1973, p. 91). However, this religious attitude does not necessarily entail allegiance to a particular orthodox creed. It may involve subordination to a set of rules or moral principles that help resolve their conflicts and bring them to a state of peace and harmony.

Finally, self-realization is not a state of total passivity. Rather, the person accepts the reality of each situation and adapts accordingly. The person may work to control and change those situations in life that can be realistically shaped, but he or she knows that not every situation is controllable or should be controlled. There are some situations in which an accepting attitude is healthiest.

Critical Comments

Let us now utilize our six criteria to evaluate the scientific worth of Jung's theory.

Comprehensiveness. Jung's position comes close to matching the one created by Freud in the sheer number and diversity of phenomena it examines. In many instances, however, it is not as detailed in its treatment of the phenomena in its domain as is Freud's. Nevertheless, Jung's theory is quite comprehensive. At various points in his career, he addressed himself to such diverse phenomena as marriage, creativity, religion, education, and the occult.

Precision and Testability. Jung's theory fails generally to meet the criterion of precision and testability. Many of its relational statements are vague and riddled with inconsistencies. Many of its concepts are highly ambiguous. For example, the archetypes are metaphysical concepts that have multiple meanings and few clear referents in external reality. As Jung himself put it:

> *They can only be roughly circumscribed at best.... Every attempt to focus them more sharply is immediately punished by the intangible core of meaning losing its luminosity. No archetype can be reduced to a simple formula. It is a vessel which we can never empty and never fill. It has a potential existence only, and when it takes shape in matter, it is no longer what it was. It persists throughout the ages and requires interpreting ever anew. The archetypes are the imperishable elements of the unconscious, but they change their shape continuously. [Jung, 1958b, p. 145]*

In addition to this inherent vagueness, Jung argued that some of our behavior is controlled by "autonomous forces" in the collective unconscious—forces that operate unpredictably. For instance, a man and a woman may be having an enjoyable discussion about the virtues of the sexes when they suddenly find themselves embroiled in a bitter controversy about the inherent superiority of one sex over the other. Jung might account for this unexpected shift in behavior by maintaining that the negative aspects of the anima in the man and the animus in the woman had projected themselves onto their behavior. The man might begin to argue in a "womanish" way and become completely irrational and emotional about the innate superiority of men, whereas the woman might become "mannish" and begin to argue dogmatically and in a domineering fashion about the natural superiority of women. The bitter argument might continue unabated for an hour or so and then suddenly subside. Jung would maintain that the man was anima-possessed and the woman animus-possessed. The point at which such "possessions" occur is completely unpredictable.

To scientists, such an assumption is totally unacceptable because it violates their belief that all behavior is caused by previous events. Although Jung believed that determinism was a useful concept in the explanation of behavior, he also maintained that it had its limitations. In his view, people live by aims as well as by causes. Furthermore, Jung maintained that some behavior is produced according to a **principle of synchronicity.** This principle refers to Jung's belief that sometimes two events occur together in time, but one event does not cause the other. For example, a man may dream of the death of his uncle and then learn the next day via telephone that his uncle has just died. Clearly, dreaming about the death did not cause it. But neither was the nearly simultaneous occurrence of the events a chance happening. Instead, Jung believed that the co-occurrence is a meaningful coincidence. In his view, it is possible that an archetypal death image in some form had knowledge of the uncle's death and that it had penetrated the man's dream to make him aware of its impending occurrence. How could the archetype have known with certainty that the death would occur? Jung believed that space and time are relative to archetypes and that they can readily move through and embrace the past, present, and future as one in space and time. The underlying mechanism and process that explain how archetypes are capable of transcending space and time boundaries is left unexplained by Jung. It is a mysterious process, but one that Jung felt had validity.

Despite the ambiguity in Jung's work and his advocacy of acausal explanations for some phenomena, explanations that are scientifically unacceptable, scientists are increasingly becoming interested in testing some of Jung's complex and original ideas.

Parsimony. Jung's theory also fails to meet the parsimony criterion. There seem to be more concepts than are necessary to explain its phenomena. Given kinds of behavior are readily "explained" by invoking a variety of archetypes. If a person behaves aggressively, for example, it could be the result of the activation of his or her shadow, animus or anima, a mother archetype, a father archetype, and so forth. The behavior could be the result of the operation of one of these archetypes, several of them, all of them, or none of them. It could be due simply to the operation of unknown and uncontrollable forces within the psyche. When it is caused by the operation of an archetype, there is no systematic explanation of why or how one archetype takes precedence over another.

Empirical Validity. Many aspects of Jung's theory are difficult to test, and, as a result, empirical support is currently lacking. However, as mentioned earlier, his position has been generating some interest among scientists recently. Most of the investigations have focused on the verification of his theory of psychological types, and the evidence for its validity has been consistently supportive.

Heuristic Value. Jung's theory has considerable heuristic value. Although it has not been accorded high status by most scientists, it has been accepted by professionals from a variety of disciplines, including history, literature, art, anthropology, religion, and certain segments of the clinical psychology community. The ties between his position and religion have been especially close since, for Jung, spiritual concerns were the highest human value. He felt that Western people were too overdeveloped in the rational realm and grossly underdeveloped in the spiritual arena. Accordingly, he believed that many of us need to turn inward and to meditate in a search for the meaning of our existence. It is not too surprising, then, that Jung has enjoyed popular success among many idealistic, middle-class students surfeited with material possessions and shaken by a crisis of faith in dealing with authority figures.

Applied Value. Jung's theorizing about the nature of psychopathology and its treatment has had a highly positive impact on the work of many therapists. The theory has also proved useful to the members of many other disciplines, including theologians, artists, photographers, and historians. The Myers-Briggs Type Indicator, which is an outgrowth of Jung's theorizing about psychological types, has also been used to good advantage by vocational counselors. Thus Jung's theory has had considerable practical impact.

Discussion Questions

1. What is the psyche? How does psychic energy originate and how does it affect the person's behavior?
2. Some examples were given in the chapter to show how the principle of equivalence operates in the personality. Can you think of any additional examples?
3. Do you believe that the collective unconscious exists?
4. One example of an archetype is the mother-child relationship. Can you think of any other experiences that are universal in nature?
5. How would you define the shadow? Is it possible to measure it objectively?
6. What kinds of individuals believe in the existence of evil forces within a person that control his or her behavior?
7. What is the nature of the relationship between the anima/animus and our cultural sex-role stereotypes?
8. Have you ever had a transcendent experience that helped you resolve a personal problem? Describe it as best you can and tell how it helped you overcome the difficulty.
9. Can you think of other examples of mandalas that are part of our culture?
10. Are you primarily an introvert or an extravert? In what ways?
11. Cite examples that show the negative qualities of introversion and extraversion.
12. What are superior and inferior functions? What are some of the problems an individual could experience if his or her thinking function was undifferentiated?
13. List the characteristics of the eight different personality types postulated by Jung. What kind of personality type are you?

14. Do you agree with Jung that neurosis in young people is due to their avoidance of setting and trying to attain concrete external goals?
15. In what ways is Jung's position compatible with contemporary religion? Would you agree that there is a need for spiritual awakening among young people and adults?

References

Carlson, R. Studies of Jungian typology: II. Representations of the personal world. *Journal of Personality and Social Psychology*, 1980, *38*, 801–810.

Carlson, R., & Levy, N. Studies of Jungian typology: I. Memory, social perception, and social action. *Journal of Personality*, 1973, *41*, 559–576.

Domino, G. Compensatory aspects of dreams: An empirical test of Jung's theory. *Journal of Personality and Social Psychology*, 1976, *34*, 658–662.

Dry, A. M. *The psychology of Jung*. New York: Wiley, 1961.

Fling, S., Thomas, A., & Gallaher, M. Participant characteristics and the effects of two types of meditation vs. quiet sitting. *Journal of Clinical Psychology*, 1981, *37*, 784–790.

Fordham, F. *An introduction to Jung's psychology*. Middlesex, England: Penguin Books, 1966.

Jacobi, J. *The psychology of Jung*. New Haven: Yale University Press, 1962.

Jung, C. G. *Psychological types*. New York: Harcourt, 1923.

Jung, C. G. The practice of psychotherapy. In *The Collected Works of C. G. Jung*, Vol. 16. London: Routledge & Kegan Paul, 1954.

Jung, C. G. Commentary on "Secret of the golden flower." In V. S. de Laszlo (Ed.), *Psyche and Symbol*. Garden City, N.Y.: Doubleday Anchor, 1958a.

Jung, C. G. The special phenomenology of the child archetype. In V. S. de Laszlo (Ed.), *Psyche and Symbol*. Garden City, N.Y.: Doubleday Anchor, 1958b.

Jung, C. G. The psychology of the child archetype. In V. S. de Laszlo (Ed.), *Psyche and Symbol*. Garden City, N.Y.: Doubleday Anchor, 1958c.

Jung, C. G. The relations between the ego and the unconscious. In V. S. de Laszlo (Ed.), *The Basic Writings of C. G. Jung* New York: Modern Library, 1959.

Jung, C. G. *Memories, dreams, reflections*. New York: Pantheon, 1963.

Jung, C. G. *Two essays on analytical psychology*. New York: Meridian, 1964.

Jung, C. G. *The structure and dynamics of the psyche* (2nd ed.). Princeton: Princeton University Press, 1969.

Progoff, I. *Jung's psychology and its social meaning*. London: Routledge & Kegan Paul, 1953.

Rabelais, F. The five books of Gargantua and Pantagruel. In *The Complete Works of Rabelais*. Translated by J. LeClerog. New York: Random House, 1936.

Storr, A. *C. G. Jung*. New York: Viking, 1973.

Stricker, L. J., & Ross, J. A description and evaluation of the Myers-Briggs Type Indicator. *Research Bulletin* (Princeton: Educational Testing Service), 1962.

Suggested Readings

Brome, V. *Jung*, New York: Atheneum, 1978.

Dry, A. M. *The psychology of Jung*. New York: Wiley, 1961.

Jacobi, J. *The psychology of Jung*. New Haven: Yale University Press, 1962.
Jung, C. G. *Collected Works*. H. Read, M. Fordham, & G. Adler (Eds.). Princeton: Princeton University Press, 1953.
Jung, C. G. *Memories, dreams, reflections*. New York: Pantheon, 1963.
Storr, A. *C. G. Jung*. New York: Viking, 1973.

Glossary

Analytical Psychology Jung's unique brand of psychology that emphasizes the complex interplay between oppositional forces within the psyche and the ways in which these internal conflicts affect personality development.

Anima The feminine archetype in men. It includes both positive and negative characteristics of the transpersonal female. In a positive sense, the anima involves a sense of warmth and intuitive understanding. In a negative sense, it involves moodiness and irritability.

Animus The masculine archetype in women. It includes both positive and negative characteristics of the transpersonal male. In a positive sense, the animus involves an ability to reason and use logic to solve problems. In a negative sense, it involves an uncritical and dogmatic adherence to certain ideas and an irrationality in solving problems.

Archetype Universal theme or symbol that can be activated by forces operating in the psyche, thereby generating visions that are projected onto current experiences.

Collective unconscious The depository of instincts and archetypes that go beyond personal experience. These transpersonal experiences are the residue of human evolutionary development and can be activated under the proper conditions.

Complex Collection of thoughts united by a common feeling.

Dominant characteristic In Jung's theory, a developed, differentiated, and conscious part of the psyche.

Extraversion Basic attitude postulated by Jung to account for people's attempts to relate to the world. Extraversion implies an outgoing and relatively confident approach to life.

Extraverted feeling type Individual characterized positively by an acceptance of the standards of society and negatively by a change in emotions from situation to situation, along with an indiscriminate yielding to the expectations of others.

Extraverted intuitive type Individual characterized positively by a quick grasp of the creative possibilities in various ventures and negatively by impatience and flightiness.

Extraverted sensing type Individual characterized positively by an appreciation for the arts and negatively by crude pleasure seeking.

Extraverted thinking type Individual characterized in a positive way by a concern for social reform and in a negative way by a selfish and exploitative attitude toward others.

Inferior characteristic In Jung's theory, an underdeveloped, undifferentiated and unconscious part of the psyche.

Introversion Basic attitude that implies a retiring and reflective approach to life.

Introverted feeling type Individual characterized positively by intense feelings of sympathy for others who have experienced misfortune and negatively by shyness and inaccessibility.

Introverted intuitive type Individual characterized positively by the ability to envision the future and negatively by an inability to communicate effectively with others.

Introverted sensing type Individual characterized positively by the intensity of subjective sensations and negatively by oversensitivity and obtuseness.

Introverted thinking type Individual characterized positively by imagination and a willingness to think originally and boldly and characterized negatively by social ineptness.

Irrational functions Modes of apprehending events in the world without evaluating them. For Jung, sensation and intuition were the irrational (nonrational) functions.

Life-process energy All the urges that are derived from conflict between forces in the psyche.

Mandala Symbolic representation of the self or of the world.

Method of amplification Therapeutic technique in which the patient and analyst continue to reassess and reinterpret the same symbols in an attempt to broaden their understanding of them.

Myers-Briggs Type Indicator (MBTI) Paper-and-pencil test designed to measure the various types of individuals postulated to exist by Jung in his theory of psychological types.

Persona Archetype consisting of the role human beings play in order to meet the demands of others. The persona also allows them to express their innermost feelings in ways acceptable to other people.

Personal unconscious In Jung's theory, the region that contains all the personal experiences that have been blocked from awareness.

Principle of entropy In Jungian theory, the idea that energy is redistributed in the psyche in order to achieve equilibrium or balance.

Principle of equivalence The idea that energy expended in one part of the psyche will be compensated for by an equal amount of energy in the same or different form in another part of the psyche. Thus energy is neither created nor lost but simply shifted from one region of the psyche to another.

Principle of opposites The idea that energy that propels personality and behavior is derived from the interplay between opposite forces within the psyche.

Principle of synchronicity The idea that there is an acausal order in the world that has meaning and that goes beyond causality. *Deja Vu*

Psyche For Jung, a construct that was postulated to represent all of the interacting systems within human personality that were needed to account for the mental life and behavior of the person.

Psychological types Theory proposed by Jung in which people could be classified in terms of eight types based on a combination of attitudes and functions.

Rational functions Modes of making judgments or evaluations of events in the world. For Jung, thinking and feeling were rational functions.

Self For Jung, an archetype that leads people to search for ways in which to maximize the development of their potential.

Self-realization. Process that involves the healthy development of the capabilities of people so that they can fulfill their own unique natures.

Shadow The inferior, evil, and repulsive side of human nature.

Symbol In Jung's psychology, a representation of a psychic fact. Each symbol is thought to have multiple meanings and to be incapable of being understood completely.

Transcendent function The process by which a conflict is resolved by bringing opposing forces into harmony or balance with each other through understanding.

Word-association test. Therapeutic technique in which patients are presented with stimulus words and asked to give responses to them. Greater time latencies in responding are assumed to be reflective of the existence of underlying problems.

CHAPTER 4

Adler's Individual Psychology

Biographical Sketch

Alfred Adler was born in Vienna in 1870, of Jewish parents. His father was a grain merchant whose work allowed the family to live an affluent, middle-class life. Alfred was the third of seven children, five boys and two girls, of whom the oldest was a boy and the second a girl. His early schooling proceeded without difficulty and without special academic distinction.

Later, at the Vienna Medical School, he came under the influence of a famous internist who stressed that the physician must always treat the patient as a whole, not just the ailment. He also was fond of saying, "If you want to be a good doctor, you have to be a kind person." They were two lessons Adler never forgot. During his university days, he also acquired a socialist political orientation and endorsed many of Karl Marx's contentions about the nature of men and women but not Marxist economic policies. Adler was attracted to the humanistic side of socialism, the side that stresses equality and cooperation between human beings and the maintenance of the democratic tradition in society. He became an unflagging champion of the common person and fought against oppression of the masses all his adult life.

Once he had received his medical degree, Adler established a private practice in a lower-middle-class Vienna neighborhood near a famous amusement park. His patients included artists and acrobats from the park shows. Some of these extraordinary physical specimens told Adler that they had achieved their powers as a reaction to weakness and illness in childhood. It was these experiences that, at least partly, led Adler to focus on the concept of overcompensation in his theorizing.

Adler's association with Freud apparently grew out of his defense of Freud's view on dreams, which had been attacked by critics in the local press. In 1902, Adler was elected the first president of the Vienna Psychoanalytic Society. He never established a warm personal relationship with Freud nor with most of the other members of the group. Adler was not a person to worship at the feet of the master, and his forthright questioning and criticism of some of Freud's concepts led to his resignation from the society in 1911.

Soon after, Adler formed a group called the Society for Free Psycho-Analytic Research, a title chosen to show his obvious displeasure with what he considered Freud's dictatorial ways. In 1913, Adler changed the name of the association to Individual Psychology to reflect his concern with understanding the whole personality, not just isolated aspects of behavior. One of the meanings of the word *individual* is total entity or indivisible entity, and it is this meaning that best reflects Adler's concern. Unfortunately, the term also suggests a study of the individual as contrasted with the study of group behavior. But Adler's theory is, in many respects, sociopsychological in nature, so that for him the individual can be understood only in terms of his or her participation with other members of the society.

During World War I, Adler worked as an army doctor in a Vienna hospital. Largely as a result of this experience, he discovered the importance of the concept of social interest. He saw the savage effects of the war on people, effects generated by lack of trust and cooperation. He returned to his writing and research activities with renewed purpose, focusing much of his energy on disseminating information to the "common man" about the need for cooperation, love, and respect between people. He was also instrumental in helping to establish in the Vienna school system some 30 child-guidance clinics in which counseling with the entire family was conducted. By the early 1920s, Adler had gained international recognition and acceptance. He began to accept invitations to lecture in European cities and later discussed his views with audiences in the United States. He succumbed to a heart attack while on a European lecture tour in Aberdeen, Scotland, in May 1937 (Furtmuller, 1973, pp. 330–394).

Basic Concepts and Principles

The Aims of the Theory

According to Adler, **individual psychology** is a science that attempts to understand the experiences and behavior of each person as an organized entity. He believed further that all actions are guided by a person's fundamental attitudes toward life. True to his interest in improving the lot of humankind, he said that he also aimed at the correction of faulty or mistaken attitudes through use of the basic knowledge accumulated by tests of the theory. Thus, in addition to collecting basic information about human behavior, Adler was greatly interested in applying such knowledge in a practical way.

Basic Theoretical Scheme

Out of Adler's efforts to understand "that mysterious creative power of life—that power which expresses itself in the desire to develop, to strive and to achieve—and even to compensate for defeats in one direction by striving for success in another" came a simple, yet interesting, set of theoretical propositions (Adler, 1969, p. 1). These propositions emphasized that an understanding of human personality is possible only if we are aware of the person's goals. In contrast to Freud, who was a strict determinist, Adler adopted the **teleological** position that it is the individual's goals that direct his or her current behavior. People have a purpose in life—namely, to attain perfection or completion. That is, they are motivated to strive toward fulfillment of their own unique potentials. Further, this movement toward perfection is generated by feelings of inferiority. We are continually struggling, according to Adler, from "minus to plus." We are all engaged in the "great upward drive."

In his earliest writings, the final goal of our struggle was to be aggressive and all-powerful, to dominate others. Humans were seen as selfish and concerned only with self-aggrandizement. Later, Adler revised his thinking and claimed that the final goal is to be superior.

This goal of **superiority** can be formulated by individuals so that it guides them along either a constructive or destructive path. If the goal is formulated in a destructive way, it will cause individuals to attempt to dominate and exploit others. According to Adler, only neurotics strive for such a mistaken goal. If, on the other hand, the goal is formulated in a constructive way, it will cause people to relate to others with cooperation and goodwill. The striving for superiority by healthy people involves movement toward perfection in a way that contributes to the welfare of others. Healthy people act in accordance with social interest. Furthermore, the development of healthy or unhealthy goals is shaped to a considerable extent by the kinds of experiences people had during the first five years of life.

Creative Evolution and Social Interest

The essence of Adler's position is that people's mental health depends directly on their efforts to contribute to the betterment of the community. As he saw it, the species could not exist for long without sustained cooperation among its members. The life of each infant depends, for example, on the willingness of adults to extend themselves and to minister to the needs of these helpless creatures. The survival of the species also depends on the willingness of individuals to relate to one another on an intimate basis and to engage in procreative acts. In a complex society, the needs of the members can be gratified only through a division of labor and the coordination of effort among workers. Thus, without cooperative effort and goodwill, humanity would perish.

Adler discussed the necessity for such cooperation in the context of the evolution of the species. He claimed that there is a creative evolution in all living things that aims at the goal of perfection. Active, continous movement and adaptation to the external world has therefore always existed. It is a compulsion to create a better adaptation to the environment, to master it. All of us are in the midst of this creative evolution, according to Adler. We benefit tremendously from the massive efforts and contributions of our ancestors as we continue to strive in our own unique ways to improve the living conditions of us all. The ultimate goal, in Adler's view, is the creation of an ideal community.

We are all born with the potential for social feeling or interest, but it can come to fruition only with the proper guidance and training. **Social interest,** as Adler defined it, "means a striving for a form of community which must be thought of as everlasting, as it could be thought of if mankind had reached the goal of perfection" (Adler, 1973c, pp. 34–35). By striving for the completion of the goals of others, we help ourselves toward the same goal. This striving would also imply that we have respect and consideration for all human beings. As Brennan maintained, "We remain open to the other and welcome him as a host would a guest, according to his own meaning, whose life is respected as equally valid as one's own" (Brennan, 1969, p. 10). It is this humanistic view that Adler strongly defended throughout his later writings, the implications of which we will examine in greater detail throughout the remainder of this chapter.

Feelings of Inferiority and the Striving for Superiority

While he was still involved in the practice of medicine, Adler noted that individuals with defective organs typically tried to compensate for their weaknesses by intensive training. A girl with a speech impediment might try to overcome her problem by intensive and persistent practice until, one day, she is able to excel, perhaps by becoming a national news broadcaster. Or a boy with puny legs might strive to become an outstanding distance runner. The qualifiers in these examples are necessary because Adler firmly believed that it is not the defect itself that produces the striving but the person's **attitude** toward it. The person is free to interpret the deficiency in many ways or even to ignore it. If he or she ignores it, it will not result in overwhelming striving behavior.

Adler later expanded the concept of **organ inferiority** to include exaggerated strivings caused by feelings of unmanliness. **Masculine protest** was the term he used to describe these compensation behaviors. In Adler's thinking, superiority tended to be equated with masculinity and behaviors such as assertiveness, independence, and dominance, while inferiority tended to be equated with femininity. Feminine behavior included passivity, submissiveness, and dependence. Adler's thinking was probably based on the roles enacted by males and females in Viennese society at the time. Adler was not a male chauvinist. He used the concept of masculine protest to show that women were placed in an inferior position by society and that, as a consequence, they often tried to overcome feelings of inadequacy by aping masculine behavior, as in the case of women who spouted obscenities continuously and who often swaggered and acted tough. Lesbianism was considered an extreme manifestation of the masculine protest. On the other hand, similar compensatory behavior could be found in women who acted in an exaggeratedly feminine manner. These "superfeminine" women may have adopted their lifestyle as a means of luring and then dominating and humiliating men.

Adler's concept described the behavior of men as well as women. Men who felt insecure could also acquire exaggerated ways of behaving to prove that they were "real men." The Don Juan type would try to "prove" his manhood by countless seductions. For either sex, then, such manifestations were neurotic in character. In line with his egalitarian orientation, Adler abhorred the thought of treating anyone, male or female, as inferior and argued vigorously that such bias had to be eliminated (see Adler, 1927, pp. 120–148).

Eventually he broadened the concept of organ inferiority even more and argued that all of us experience feelings of psychological and social inferiority, beginning with our earliest participation in family life. Our parents and most others are not only bigger physically than we are, but also more sophisticated and adept at solving problems. Out of these feelings of inferiority, whatever the basis, comes a striving for superiority. Feelings of inferiority can be largely constructive or largely destructive. Acknowledging that we all feel inferior at some point in our lives could serve as a basis for mutual help and cooperation to overcome problems in living. But if we dwell excessively on our inferiorities, real or imagined, we are less likely to trust others or ourselves. As a consequence, we are apt to operate on the "useless side" of life; we are more likely to **overcompensate** for our deficiencies and develop an exaggerated sense of superiority that others find loathsome.

Fictional Finalisms

Adler's **fictional finalism** concept is based on the writings of the philosopher Hans Vaihinger. Vaihinger published a book entitled *The Philosophy of "As-If."* In it, he argued that people create ideas that guide their behavior. Adler adopted this view and came to the conclusion that no one's various strivings could occur without the perception of goals. Goals give direction to all our behavior and are necessary for individual advancement and development. These goals, Adler believed, are ideals and not something tangible. They can be healthy fictions or mistaken ones. For example, you could believe that your goal was to help people and to engage in activities that would prove beneficial to others. Or you could believe that you are Casanova and that your goal is to "prove" your superiority over women through an endless and indiscriminate procession of seductions.

Style of Life and the Creative Self

Two concepts—the style of life and the creative self—are closely interrelated in Adlerian theorizing. The **style of life,** originally called the "life plan" or "guiding image," refers to the unique ways in which people pursue their goals. An actress attempts to attain perfection through study and through stage and film appearances. A scholar tries to become superior by intensive reading, studying, and thinking and by discussing ideas with her colleagues. Our unique styles of life are formed during our first five years. All our later experiences are then assimilated and interpreted in accordance with these established patterns of behaving. These styles emerge as reactions to our inferiorities, real or imagined. Once established, they are virtually impossible to modify.

The concept of the **creative self** appears to be an outgrowth of Adler's concern with the mechanistic nature of his style-of-life construct. That is, Adler was probably dissatisfied with the idea that the individual acquires unique behavior patterns strictly through stimulus-response learning, because this idea implies that the person is a passive recipient who does not interpret or act on his or her experiences. The concept of the creative self, on the other hand, implies that we each create our own personality, that we actively construct it out of our experiences and heredities. People are, in the final analysis, responsible for their destinies. They are often quite aware of the alternatives available to them in solving problems and act in a rational and responsible manner. It is primarily the neurotic whose goals are unconscious and who is often unaware of the available alternatives in given situations.

The Process of Personality Development

The Importance of Early Childhood Experiences

Adler believed that both parents played crucial roles in discouraging or encouraging the development of the distinctive lifestyles of their children (Ansbacher & Ansbacher, 1956, pp. 372–381). The parents are charged with nourishing the child's increasing awareness with accurate conceptions of work, friendship, and love. In Adler's view, these are the three basic problems of life, and the healthy or courageous person is the one who confronts and attempts to cope with them.

The mother's role is particularly important because she is usually the first person to have extended, intimate contact with the child. She introduces the child to social life. If she loves the child, she is likely to be interested in teaching the skills necessary to secure his or her welfare. If she is dissatisfied with her role, on the other hand, she may be preoccupied with trying to prove her own superiority through the achievements of her child. She may then try to prove to everyone that her child is more intelligent and good-looking than all others and that he or she crawled, stood, and walked sooner than anyone else. Unfortunately, most children react adversely to such pressure, and the typical result is hostility and resentment.

For the father, the primary task is to prove that he is a worthwhile human being by contributing to the welfare of his wife, his children, and his society. Furthermore, he must treat his wife as an equal and cooperate with her in meeting the problems of life. Of course, she must also value him as an equal. If she is afraid of losing the affection of her children and forces him to be the sole administrator of punishment for their misdeeds, she is not fulfilling her obligations as a wife and mother and is acting, instead, on the "useless side" of life. She is guilty of pampering her children because of her own weaknesses and of exploiting her husband. The same argument would apply to a husband who pampers his children.

Adler believed further that each child is treated uniquely by his or her parents, depending on his order of birth within the family. The first-born tends to be the center of attention in the family before the birth of the second child. The oldest child is then placed in the position of the "dethroned monarch" who has to share the affection and attention of the parents with the new baby and eventually, perhaps, more babies. As a consequence, the oldest child may feel resentment and hostility toward the younger ones. Such negative feelings are likely to occur if the parents have not properly prepared the child for the arrival of one or more siblings. If they have made adequate preparations, the oldest child may adopt a protective and supportive attitude instead. He or she will often play the part of father or mother with the younger ones and feel responsible for their welfare.

According to Adler, the oldest child understands best the importance of power and authority because he or she has to undergo their loss within the family. Consequently, the oldest child will be highly supportive of and dependent on authorities in later life and will be a person who tends to desire the maintenance of the status quo. Such a person is likely to be politically conservative. The second child is likely to view the oldest brother or sister as a competitor to be overcome. If the oldest child is protective and supportive of the younger sibling's attempts to excel, healthy development is more probable. If the eldest resents the second child and acts maliciously, the younger one is more likely to move toward neurosis. Adler also felt that the second child may set unrealistically high goals, thereby virtually ensuring ultimate failure.

The youngest child has many models and tends to develop a competitive orientation, according to Adler. He or she tends to commandeer most of the family's attention. Adler believed that parents tend to pamper and spoil the youngest members of their families. The result is a person who is excessively dependent on others for support and protection, yet who wants to excel in everything he or she does. Such a child tends to suffer from extreme feelings of inferiority because others are bigger and more experienced.

The only child has no models or rivals and is likely to be the center of attention in the family, assuming that his or her birth was a welcome event. If the child was unwanted, neglect or active rejection by the parents will probably occur. In most instances, however, the only child is likely to pampered by the parents, especially the mother. Later, the child may experience considerable difficulty if he or she is not universally liked and admired.

Birth-Order Research

It is encouraging to report that recent tests of Adler's birth order thesis have yielded strong support for some of his major arguments. Although Schooler's (1972) review of the research literature on **birth-order effects** revealed a general lack of consistent findings, more recent research results have been more supportive.

As mentioned earlier, Adler believed that first-borns understand best the importance of power and authority, because they have had to undergo their loss with the birth of the second child. Adler maintained that, as a result, first-borns spend their lives trying to regain power and authority through outstanding achievement. They want to rule over others (Ansbacher & Ansbacher, 1956, p. 379). Thus we would expect first-borns to excel in intellectual activities, to attain higher levels of achievement and eminence, and to be outstanding in general. There is considerable support for these predictions. Belmont and Marolla (1973) found a strong, positive correlation between birth order and intellectual performance for nearly 400,000 subjects, the entire male population of the Netherlands who attained 19 years of age during the period 1963–1966. First-borns outstripped later-borns in intellectual achievement in families where the number of children ranged between two and nine. Breland (1974) demonstrated further that this positive relationship between birth order and intellectual achievement held true, irrespective of the level of schooling achieved by their parents, the family's income, or the age of the mother.

Zajonc and Markus (1975) explained the greater intellectual development of first-borns by maintaining that they are thrust into positions of "teachers" in the family. They are expected to tutor their lesser-skilled brothers and sisters in a variety of activities. As a result, they have to learn more themselves, and their intellectual development is accelerated. Younger children do not have these demands placed on them to the same degree. It is the oldest child instead who is looked to for advice and help. Younger children do not have the wherewithal to educate their older siblings. As a result, their intellectual development does not tend to be as great. The youngest child in particular suffers from a lack of opportunity to tutor others.

Only children are in a strange position. Although they have no opportunity to tutor brothers and sisters, thereby suggesting lower intellectual development, they nevertheless have the undivided attention of their parents, who might spend large amounts of time instructing them, thereby ensuring high intellectual development. In a review of the research literature examining the intellectual development of only-borns, Falbo (1977) found that they were more intellectually advanced than later-borns from large families, but not as advanced as first-borns from small families.

Other investigations have revealed that first-borns are overrepresented among college students, graduate students, university faculty, and eminent people in science and government. Wagner and Schubert (1977), for example, found that oldest sons were overrepresented among United States Presidents. Also-rans for President did not show such an overrepresentation of first-borns. Zweigenhaft (1975) also found first-borns overrepresented among U.S. Congressmen. Recently, Melillo (1983) showed that first-borns were overrepresented among women with doctorates (Ph.D., Ed.D., D.S.W., and M.D.).

Adler maintained that first-borns are often the center of attention and are then made anxious by the loss of their central position to younger rivals. As a consequence, they make attempts to regain their original status by performing in accordance with parental expectations. Under stress, they may reach out to others for support. Thus theoretical argument leads to the prediction that first-borns tend to become more anxious than later-borns in threatening situations and, as a result, tend to affiliate more with others.

The earliest support for this hypothesis was found in an investigation by Schachter (1959). In his study, female subjects were introduced to a medical doctor who informed them that they were about to participate in an experiment concerned with the effects of electric shock on pulse rates and blood pressures. In one condition, the experimenter informed half the subjects that the shocks would be very mild and would only tickle. All subjects were then informed that they would have to wait ten minutes before the part of the experiment that involved shocking would begin and were given the option of waiting alone or together with other women. In addition, a third category on their checklist was available for those subjects who did not care whether they waited alone or together. (Incidentally, none of the subjects ever received any shock.) As expected, first-borns not only reported being more anxious than later-borns, but a larger percentage of them chose to affiliate with other women. Figure 4.1 depicts the data in graphic form. Other research has also shown that first-borns perform less effectively under stress and that they are less likely than later-borns to participate in dangerous sports.

Adler also maintained that the youngest child was likely to be the most pampered member of the family (Ansbacher & Ansbacher, 1956, p. 380). This pampering, he thought, would lead to excessive dependence on others and a search for easy, immediate solutions to problems. Excessive dependence, furthermore, would be seen most clearly in families in which the youngest child was a male and his older siblings were sisters rather than brothers. Therefore the youngest members of families were likely to have a conflict

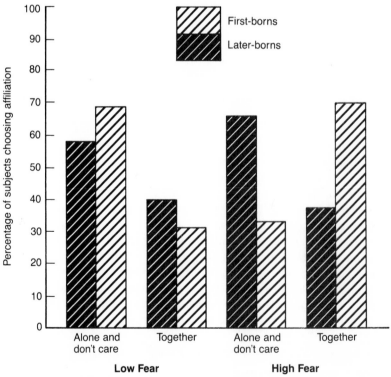

Figure 4.1 Percentage of first-borns and later-borns choosing to affiliate under nonstress and stress conditions. Adapted from Schachter, *The Psychology of Affiliation*, 1959, pp. 44, 45.

between needing independence and seeing dependence on others as providing a convenient, hassle-free source of gratification.

In a related way, alcoholics are frequently people who use the bottle as a means of quick and easy "solutions" to their immediate problems. Thus we would expect the youngest members of families to be overrepresented among alcoholics. In a review of 27 studies examining the birth-order position of alcoholics, Barry and Blane (1977) found support for this prediction. There was a higher incidence of alcoholics among last-borns in 20 out of the 27 studies.

It is necessary to note that not all of the research findings testing Adler's birth-order thesis have been supportive. Several studies in the research literature do not support the idea of a greater need for affiliation among first-borns (Schooler, 1972). In addition, Falbo (1978) has found no support for Adler's contention that only children are highly selfish and concerned primarily with being the center of attention. In a study using college students as subjects, she found that only children were likely to be more cooperative than first- or last-born children when engaging in a mixed-motive game against an opponent where either party had the option of acting competitively or cooperatively. Nevertheless, the research findings have been generally supportive of much of Adler's theorizing, and research on birth-order effects continues at an unprecedented rate.

Personality Development of the Neurotic

Out of this incredible welter of family experience and the person's interpretation of it emerges a guiding goal and a distinctive style of life that can be changed only rarely. As hinted earlier, the three major sets of environmental factors that may give rise to severely mistaken or neurotic life goals are (1) organ inferiority, (2) neglect or rejection, and (3) pampering. Adler believed that pampering is especially damaging. In any event, neurotic persons are those who feel acutely their inferiority and who compensate for this feeling by establishing unrealistically high goals that they believe will enable them to demonstrate personal superiority over others. Neurotics are characterized further as persons who are grossly inaccurate in their self-evaluations. They may continually either underestimate or overestimate their own worth. They are continually tense and fearful. They fear decisions, tests, and defeats. In the final analysis, they are terrified of being unmasked and recognized by others as inferior. Such persons do not act in accordance with social interest; they are not courageous. Instead, they continually adopt safeguarding or defensive strategies to protect themselves.

To make this developmental process clear, let us briefly examine some of the experiences of a hypothetical male student. He is a first-born who received a great deal of attention from his parents, who always told him he was more intelligent than any of the other boys or girls his age, that he was superior to other children at solving problems, and that he was destined to become a great leader. They almost invariably praised him for his successes. Relatedly, they ignored, minimized, or distorted his failures by blaming someone else or some aspect of the environment. If he struck out in a Little League baseball game, for instance, it was because the umpire made a poor call or because he neglected to use his favorite bat. If he did not receive the highest marks on his school tests, it was because the teacher was incompetent. Although he felt keenly inadequate and inferior at times in a variety of situations, he told himself that his parents were correct in their exaggerated appraisal of his skills. He did this as a means of safeguarding himself from the painful knowledge of his limitations. Beginning at an early age, then, his faulty style of life was set and he began to focus most of his energies on his goal to become a godlike person. His fictional goal would not permit him to admit mistakes. He came to believe that he was personally superior to others and to expect success in all his activities.

In college, he dated a few girls, invariably with poor results. He expected them to acknowledge his personal superiority and his vast knowledge of events and to pay attention to his pronouncements. When they became resistive and resentful, he dimissed them as too simple-minded to understand the profundity of his thinking. Sex was considered a weapon one used to demonstrate complete superiority over women. Women were supposed to acknowledge his mastery of them, and he was surprised when they refused to comply with his demands. Eventually, he stopped dating altogether and concentrated instead on "proving" his superiority by excelling in his studies. He began to narrow his activities to those in which he was certain to excel. His competitiveness for grades was incredibly intense, and he continually downgraded his fellow students for their academic shortcomings. He began to turn his social activities with them into competitive battles. For example, he would turn a casual stroll to a morning class with a classmate into a competitive race in order to prove his superiority. He would not lend books to other students for fear they would attain higher grades. His professors were hardly worthy of him, and unless they praised his brilliance, he considered them incompetents who should be expelled from the university. Eventually, he was graduated and got a job as a journalist. Persistent conflicts with his boss and co-workers, however, finally led him to seek therapy. Examination of the origins of his faulty lifestyle eventually produced a willingness to attempt to correct his mistakes. He came to understand the sources of some of his conflicts and to modify, to a certain extent, his lifestyle.

Personal Development of a Constructive Lifestyle

The person who develops a healthy lifestyle, according to Adler, is one who experienced a family life in which the parents treated him or her with respect and consideration. Under such conditions, Adler believed, the person is likely to learn the importance of equality and cooperation between people. Such a person would, therefore, be apt to acquire a lifestyle that had as its aim the attainment of goals in accordance with social interest. Adler often left the nature of these goals unspecified; they could vary from adoption of the principles of "honesty is the best policy" and "do unto others as you would have them do unto you" to movement toward specific occupational goals such as professor, doctor, silversmith, auto mechanic, used car salesperson, and television repairperson. Although research by this author and psychologist Martin Sherman has shown that members of the general public have little respect for the last three occupations (Ryckman & Sherman, 1974), Adler would suggest that individuals could fill these roles in line with social interest—that is, by expending maximum effort and utilizing their abilities for the welfare of society.

Adler also maintained that the healthy person could change his or her fictional goals if circumstances demanded it. Would you act dishonestly and steal a loaf of bread to feed a starving child? Adler would probably answer yes but only if you had exhausted every other avenue in trying to solve the problem. The healthy person is one who lives by principles, yet is realistic enough to modify them under exceptional circumstances.

We turn now to a presentation of a simple classification scheme that Adler employed to help people better understand the nature of healthy and unhealthy personality. He provided this typology reluctantly because he did not consider human beings as types, because each person has a unique style of life (Ansbacher & Ansbacher, 1956, p. 166). Nevertheless, he felt that such a typology had some educational value, and he presented it, having made his disclaimer.

Adler's Four Major Types

The Ruling Type. Individuals of the **ruling type,** according to Adler, lack social interest and courage. When threatened, they try to reduce feelings of anxiety by acting in an antisocial way. Their striving for personal superiority and power is so intense that they typically exploit and harm others to accomplish their goals. Adler believed juvenile delinquents, suicidal individuals, and drug addicts to be prime examples of this type.

The Getting Type. Individuals of the **getting type** are relatively passive and make little effort to solve their own problems. Instead they use their charm to persuade others to help them. Adler felt that such parasitism is clearly unhealthy.

The Avoiding Type. People of the **avoiding type** do not have the confidence necessary for solving their own problems. Thus, instead of struggling with their problems, they typically try to sidestep them, thereby avoiding defeat.

The Socially Useful Type. People of the **socially useful type** face life confidently. They are prepared to cooperate with others and to contribute to the welfare of others. Their activities are in agreement with the needs of others. They help to build a better community and are psychologically healthy.

Techniques of Assessment

Like Freud, Adler sought to understand the individual's personality by focusing on an examination and analysis of early childhood experiences. He used three major techniques to gain access to these crucial experiences: early recollections, dream analysis, and knowledge of birth order.

Early Recollections. Adler believed that reports by patients of their earliest memories provided valuable insights into their unique styles of life. He maintained that patients were very willing to discuss these memories. Often the memories were based on actual experiences, but sometimes they were fanciful. Whether they were real or imaginary, Adler thought they still revealed important meanings, giving clues into the person's strivings for superiority (Ansbacher & Ansbacher, 1956, pp. 351–352).

To illustrate the importance of these memories, Adler recounted one of his cases in which a woman patient recalled receiving a pony as a gift from her father when she was 3 years old. Her sister also received a pony from him on this particular occasion. She recalled further that the sister took the straps from her father and led the pony triumphantly down the street. Her own pony, however, hurrying after the other, went too fast for her and she fell down in the dirt. She then told Adler that later in life she surpassed her sister as a horsewoman but never forgot her humiliating experience in the least (Ansbacher & Ansbacher, 1956, pp. 354–355).

Adler first noted that the woman mentioned her father and not her mother in recalling this incident. This meant that as a child the woman was not particularly satisfied with her home life and that perhaps her mother favored her older sister. This information could prove useful in her treatment.

Next Adler mentioned that the incident seems to be one in which the older sister has triumphed. This implied an unhealthy competition between the two sisters and that the younger sister (the patient) believed she was continually being humiliated in the relationship. The fact that she mentioned she later surpassed her sister as a horsewoman meant she felt the need to triumph over her, but that, unfortunately, her "victory" did not diminish her feelings about the original experience in the least. Adler maintained that the patient's memory simply reinforced her attitude: "If anyone is ahead of me I am endangered. I must always be the first." Thus, striving is typical, in Adler's view, of second children who are always trying to over-take the pacemaker, the oldest child. It was this unhealthy attitude toward life and others that was causing the patient needless pain. By revealing to her her basic attitude, Adler enabled her to begin making changes that would lead to a more satisfying outlook on life.

Dream Analysis. Adler also utilized dream analysis as a major technique for understanding each patient's personality. Unlike Freud, however, he did not focus on sexual interpretations of manifest dream content. Instead, he thought that the person's dreams are determined by his or her goal of supe-riority. More specifically, dreams reflect the individual's unconscious attempts to achieve personal goals in accordance with his or her unique style of life. The goal of a given individual may be constructive or destructive, of course. The student who is courageous and unafraid of examinations, for example, may have dreams about successfully climbing a mountain and enjoying the view from the top, whereas the student who is a quitter and who wants to postpone examinations may have dreams of falling off the mountain (Adler, 1969, p. 70). Each student's dreams are those controlled by his or her unique style of life.

For Adler, dreams also provide glimpses of the future. They suggest potential solutions to the person's problems. For example, Adler cited the case of a man who was very disappointed in his wife. His primary complaint was that she did not take adequate care of their children. Adler saw the complaint as a symptom of a deeper, underlying hostility toward the wife because the man believed she had not married him out of love.

During the course of analysis, the man reported a dream in which the youngest of his three children got lost (he actually had only two children) and could not be found. The man interpreted his dream as meaning that the lost third child was a warning to him not to have more children because his wife would neglect it and it would become lost. Though Adler acknowl-edged the plausibility of this interpretation, he also pointed out that the dream about a third child might suggest a desire for a reconciliation with his wife and the development of a more satisfying relationship with her (Mairet, 1964, pp. 164–166).

Birth Order. Adler's third technique was birth-order analysis as a means of understanding the patient's personality. Adler believed that a correct analysis of the effects the patient's birth position in the family had on his behavior would help win his confidence. Such an analysis also enables the therapist to convince the patient that he is simply reacting to the circum-stances of his childhood position so that he should not blame himself entirely for developing a faulty lifestyle (Forer, 1977, p. 110). By reducing self-blame and resistance, this analysis helps the patient adopt a more constructive way of life.

All three of these major techniques were used in conjunction with one another by Adler to gather important information and insights into his patients' personalities and to help them correct their mistaken styles of life.

Application of the Theory to the Treatment of Psychopathology

Neurotics and psychotics, according to Adler, are people who have faulty lifestyles, usually acquired via contact with parents who either pampered, neglected, or rejected them during early childhood. In many instances, these parents showed erratic behavior, sometimes mixing pampering and rejection. Adler believed that, as a consequence of this treatment, these children became highly anxious, felt insecure, and began to develop protective devices to cope with feelings of inferiority. Most often, they developed a striving for personal superiority to compensate for these feelings. Thus neurotic individuals begin to believe in an arrogant way that they are actually superior to others and to act in ways consistent with that belief. For example, they may strive to be perfect and belittle others. They avoid failure and being wrong at all costs. Other people are thus perceived as competitors who must be defeated in order for neurotics to feel satisfied, no matter how short-lived the feeling. Psychotics, too, view others with suspicion but do not validate their worth so much through comparison with others as through the use of private logic and reasoning and delusions of grandeur.

According to Adler, the goal of therapy is the reorganization of the patients' mistaken beliefs about themselves and others, the elimination of faulty goals, and the implementation of new goals that will help them realize their potential as human beings. To accomplish these objectives, Adler believed that the patient "must be guided away from himself, toward productivity for others; he must be educated toward social interest; he must be brought to the only correct insight, that he is as important to the community as anyone else; he must get to feel at home on this earth" (Adler, 1973d, p. 200).

The therapist acts as the client's guide to facilitate movement toward these ends. First, they jointly learn to understand the childhood origins of the person's difficulties and the reasons for the development of a faulty lifestyle. They begin to see why the patient feels he or she *must* be superior to others and that this orientation is destructive. Encouraged by the therapist, the patient moves away from competitive self-centeredness and comes to realize that psychological health is contingent on the development of a cooperative attitude toward others and on attempts to contribute to the welfare of society. The patient begins to see that he or she is worthwhile and part of the community and that there is great joy in accepting responsibility for one's own actions. Under these conditions, the person is no longer a "taker," but a "giver." Slowly, the patient moves toward reorganization of his or her perceptions and begins to behave differently toward others.

Implications of the Adlerian Position for Our Society

Much of Adler's theorizing has an authentic ring to it, especially when it is considered in the context of our highly competitive and power-oriented culture. Many of us can see ourselves and others engaged in a race to outdo one another and to secure more prestige and status than our neighbors. In the words of one prominent Adlerian, Rudolph Dreikurs,

> *Everyone tries to be more . . . to reach higher and, as a consequence, we are all neurotic, in a neurotic society which pays a premium to the overambitious search for prestige and striving for superiority. This search inspires a desire for self-evaluation and personal glory, thereby restricting our ability for cooperation and our sense of human fellowship. Yet underneath we are all frightened people, not sure of ourselves. . . . It is this doubt of oneself, expressed in a feeling of inadequacy and inferiority, which restricts our Social Interest and which is at the root of all maladjustment and psychopathology. [Dreikurs, 1963, p. 245]*

From a very early age, children are taught the importance of winning and of avoiding failure. Comparisons between individuals are continuously made, and although warnings are sometimes given not to feel bad or think less of oneself after losing and not to downgrade a defeated opponent, such distinctions are tremendously difficult to maintain. As a consequence, many individuals who acquire notable skills tend to feel smug and personally superior to others, while the inept tend to feel unworthy and inadequate. Even persons with superior skills are not spared these feelings of inadequacy, for they have been taught by their parents and others never to be satisfied with their accomplishments.

The harmful effects of excessive competition are manifested in a variety of ways. Cheating and lying may become ways of ensuring the maintenance or the enhancement of personal success. Consider as just two examples the large numbers of students who routinely cheat on examinations to achieve higher grades and do not feel guilty about it and the perhaps equally large number of academics who have lied and cheated in similar situations and who now pontificate about the deceptions practiced by their students.

The overwhelming moral suggestion in most of Adler's writings and those of his followers is that cooperation is "good" and competition is "bad." It would be easy to conclude, as a consequence, that adequate social interest involves only cooperation and equality. But can cooperation have negative consequences for people and competition positive ones? Is competition in any form compatible with adequate social interest and cooperation incompatible with it? A closer look at Adler's definition of social interest indicates that the answers to these questions may be yes, for his definition includes striving not only for personal superiority but also for superiority in the sense of realizing one's potential. In this latter sense of the term, an argument could be made that the healthy person acts in accordance with social interest to attain standards that move him or her toward completion. This private competition would involve setting new standards as old ones are attained. Thus a painter or a craftsworker could compete in this restricted sense of the term and have the products of his or her labor contribute to the welfare and happiness of others. These attempts would be in harmony with Adler's idea that the attainment of perfection involves overcoming the environmental resistances confronting the organism (Adler, 1973c, p. 75).

Although such arguments may make some sense, they do not address the problem directly because most competitive events involve interpersonal comparisons and evaluations. But even here an argument can be made for the idea that competition may be compatible with social interest. Such an outcome could theoretically be obtained if a person competed *with* others rather than *against* them. Such competition would involve feelings of accomplishment or defeat but without the accompanying feelings of personal superiority or inferiority in relationship to others. Perhaps such an outcome is possible where there is mutual respect and esteem between opponents before the onset of the competition. There would still be a winner and a loser, but neither party would feel any compulsion to gloat after winning or to feel inferior after losing. Instead, each might even rejoice in the other's success or be dejected when the other lost. Both parties would also benefit from the testing of their skills. The winner would be likely to improve as a result of the contest, while the "loser" would learn something from the failure that could be used to enhance performance in the future.

Interpersonal competition can also serve to energize and motivate individuals, to push them beyond previous levels of performance, and to force them to find creative solutions to seemingly insoluble problems. Inventions, for example, are often the products of healthy competition between individuals and research teams in the marketplace of ideas and have served to better the lives of the members of society. Such competitive outcomes would be totally compatible with an emerging social interest.

In contrast, cooperation may be incompatible with social interest to the extent that it prevents personal movement toward perfection. When groups force individuals to sacrifice their opportunities to excel, such coercion would be seen as incongruent with social interest. An example is the bright student who settles for "C" grades because his friends would ridicule him if he obtained mostly "A" grades. He may cooperate with them, but to the detriment of his personal development. The "team player" in business organizations may also at times stifle her own creative urges in the interest of cooperation. In such instances, participants appear interchangeable, and equality between people becomes a synonym for sameness. Adler considered equality an essential quality of adequate social interest, but he did not equate it with sameness. He recognized individual differences in abilities and advocated equality in the sense of our recognizing the essential validity of everyone's existence and the fact that there should be equality of opportunity for every person. People should, in Adler's view, have full opportunity to realize their potential, an ideal that is also fundamental in our democratically oriented society.

Critical Comments

We turn now to an assessment of the scientific worth of Adler's theory in terms of our six criteria.

Comprehensiveness. Adler addressed himself to a wide range of phenomena involving disordered behavior; and in this respect, his position rivals Freud's. He discussed at length the etiology and cure of many different kinds of neuroses and psychoses. But Adler also applied his thinking to an understanding of the ways in which political, educational, and religious institutions affect personality development. In his discussions, he tried not only to assess the impact of the destructive elements of these institutions on the individual but also to outline the ways in which they could be restructured to promote psychological health and well-being. In general, then, Adler's theory is comprehensive in nature, although, like Freud's theory, its motivational base is very limited.

Precision and Testability. The concepts in Adler's theory are generally global in nature and poorly defined. For example, some individuals are thought to have "proof complexes." A proof complex, according to Adler, is "found in many people who want to prove that they also have a right to exist or that they have no faults" (Adler, 1973b, p. 75). How would you measure the proof complex in people? Even if you could develop an adequate measure, it obviously would be an extremely difficult task. Then think of the difficulties in operationalizing Adlerian concepts like the style of life and—to mention some we have not touched upon—the redeemer complex, the exclusion complex, the predestination complex, and creative power.

The relational statements of the theory are also vaguely stated. Consider a hypothesis such as "The law of movement and its direction originate from the creative power of the individual and use, in free choice, one's experiences of one's body and of external effects, within the limits of human capacity" (Adler, 1973a, p. 51). How much creative power is needed to affect the person's unique movements? How much movement occurs if the creative power of the person is utilized? It is interesting to note that Adler believed this hypothesis had already been empirically validated.

Parsimony. Adler made a diligent effort to construct a scientific theory that was understandable to the ordinary person. The result was a "commonsense" psychology that utilizes only a few constructs. But although parsimony of explanation is considered a virtue in scientific psychology, the set of constructs must be adequate to the task of accounting for human behavior in all its complexity. Because Adler postulated a master motive— that is, the striving for superiority—his position has a reductionist quality that fails to do justice to the great diversity of reinforcers that motivate us. Relatedly, the paucity of constructs in the theory means that they are going to be applied in highly general and imprecise ways. For example, we have already reviewed a number of problems with various constructs in the theory, including the fact that they are defined so loosely that it is often unclear what dimensions they encompass and how those that can be identified are related to everyday situations.

Empirical Validity. There has been a healthy upsurge of interest recently in testing various aspects of Adler's theory. To accomplish this goal, however, investigators must first attempt to construct adequate measures of key concepts before trying to test some of the hypotheses that can be derived from the theory. Noteworthy efforts to construct a reliable and valid measure of social interest, for example, have been made (Crandall, 1980; Greever, Tseng, & Friedland, 1973). In addition, preliminary efforts have been made to construct and validate a measure of Adler's typology concerning the lifestyles of healthy and unhealthy people (Kannarkat & Bayton, 1979). Thus, research on much of Adler's theory is still exploratory. Aside from the recent strong support for many of his ideas about birth order effects, much of his theory lies fallow and untested. However, the current interest in operationalizing key concepts augurs well for eventual hypothesis testing. At present, though, empirical support generally is not very strong.

Heuristic Value. Clearly, the chief contribution of Adler's theory is the number of subsequent investigators of human personality who have been influenced by it. Adler's position has made contributions to work done by theorists in the areas of existential psychology and psychiatry, neo-Freudian psychoanalysis, personality diagnosis including dream interpretation, the practice of psychotherapy, and the theory of positive mental health (Ansbacher & Ansbacher, 1973, p. 3). Adler has directly or indirectly influenced such prominent psychologists and psychiatrists as Carl Rogers, Abraham Maslow, Rollo May, and Victor Frankl. He has also had considerable impact on the experimental work of Julian Rotter, as will become evident in the discussion of Rotter's position, which is discussed in Chapter 12.

Applied Value. In addition to its considerable heuristic value, Adler's theory focuses on phenomena that could reasonably be considered to be crucially involved in the development of people in a highly competitive and achievement-oriented society. In short, it is a theory that addresses itself to problems and issues that matter in a culture such as ours. His theory has had considerable applied usefulness in the areas of psychopathology, psychotherapy, education, and family life.

Discussion Questions

1. Do you agree with Adler that all of us have an innate need for achievement? Does any cross-cultural evidence cast doubt upon Adler's contention?
2. Adler maintained that we all have had feelings of inferiority. Do you agree? If so, what were the primary sources of these feelings for you and your friends?
3. What is the relationship between a person's attitude and his or her behavior, as Adler saw it?
4. What is the masculine protest? Explain why the concept is relevant in explaining the behavior of both men and women.
5. Do you agree with Adler that our behavior is guided by our goals? What are some of the major goals of college-educated people in America today?
6. Adler's view of the healthy society is based on his concept of social interest. What is social interest? Does the concept differ in any way from the concept of "enlightened self-interest"?
7. One of Adler's most interesting concepts is that of birth order. Do you agree with him that a person's order of birth can have a dramatic impact on personality development because parents tend to treat older and younger children differently? How many children are there in your family? Have your parents treated you and your brothers and/or sisters differently? If you are an only child, do you think that fact has made any difference in the way your parents reacted to you?
8. Do you think that we are all neurotic and that we strive too much for success?
9. Is competition necessarily destructive? How is social interest compatible with competition?
10. Is it possible for people to treat one another as equals in a capitalistic society such as ours?

References

Adler, A. *Understanding human nature.* New York: Greenberg, 1927.

Adler, A. *The science of living.* Garden City, N.Y.: Doubleday Anchor, 1969.

Adler, A. Advantages and disadvantages of the inferiority feeling. In H. L. Ansbacher & R. R. Ansbacher, (Eds.), *Superiority and social interest.* New York: Viking, 1973a.

Adler, A. Complex compulsion as part of personality and neurosis. In H. L. Ansbacher & R. R. Ansbacher (Eds.), *Superiority and social interest.* New York: Viking, 1973b.

Adler, A. On the origins of the striving for superiority and of social interest. In H. L. Ansbacher & R. R. Ansbacher (Eds.), *Superiority and social interest*. New York: Viking, 1973c.

Adler, A. Technique of treatment. In H. L. Ansbacher & R. R. Ansbacher, (Eds.), *Superiority and Social Interest*. New York: Viking, 1973d.

Ansbacher, H. L., & Ansbacher, R. R. (Eds.). *The individual psychology of Alfred Adler*. New York: Basic Books, 1956.

Ansbacher, H. L., & Ansbacher, R. R. (Eds.). *Superiority and social interest: A collection of later writings*. New York: Viking, 1973.

Barry, H., III, & Blane, H. T. Birth order of alcoholics. *Journal of Individual Psychology*, 1977, *62*, 62–79.

Belmont, L., & Marolla, F. A. Birth order, family size, and intelligence. *Science*, 1973, *182*, 1096–1101.

Breland, H. M. Birth order, family configuration, and verbal achievement. *Child Development*, 1974, *45*, 1011–1019.

Brennan, J. F. Autoeroticism or social feeling as basis of human development. *Journal of Individual Psychology*, 1969, *25*, 3–18.

Crandall, J. E. Adler's concept of social interest: Theory, measurement, and implications for adjustment. *Journal of Personality and Social Psychology*, 1980, *39*, 481–495.

Dreikurs, R. Individual psychology: The Adlerian point of view. In J. M. Wepman & R. W. Heine (Eds.), *Concepts of personality*. Chicago: Aldine, 1963.

Falbo, T. The only child: A review. *Journal of Individual Psychology*, 1977, *33*, 47–61.

Falbo, T. Only children and interpersonal behavior: An experimental and survey study. *Journal of Applied Social Psychology*, 1978, *8*, 244–253.

Forer, L. K. The use of birth order information in psychotherapy. *Journal of Individual Psychology*, 1977, *62*, 105–113.

Furtmuller, C. Alfred Adler: A biographical essay. In H. L. Ansbacher & R. R. Ansbacher (Eds.), *Superiority and social interest*. New York: Viking, 1973.

Greever, K. B., Tseng, M. S., & Friedland, B. U. Development of the Social Interest Index. *Journal of Consulting and Clinical Psychology*, 1973, *41*, 454–458.

Kannarkat, J. P., & Bayton, J. A. Validity of Adler's active-constructive, active-destructive, passive-constructive, and passive-destructive typology. *Journal of Research in Personality*, 1979, *13*, 351–360.

Mairet, P. (Ed.). *Alfred Adler: Problems of neurosis; A book of case studies*. New York: Harper & Row, 1964.

Mellilo, D. Birth order, perceived birth order, and family position of academic women. *Individual Psychology*, 1983, *39*, 57–62.

Ryckman, R. M., & Sherman, M. F. Locus of control and attitudes of workers and college students toward members of selected occupations. *Journal of Applied Social Psychology*, 1974, *4*, 351–364.

Schachter, S. *The psychology of affiliation*. Stanford: Stanford University Press, 1959.

Schooler, C. Birth order effects: Not here, not now! *Psychological Bulletin*, 1972, *78*, 161–175.

Wagner, M. E., & Schubert, H. J. P. Sibship variables and United States Presidents. *Journal of Individual Psychology*, 1977, *62*, 78–85.

Zajonc, R. B., & Markus, G. B. Birth order and intellectual development. *Psychological Review*, 1975, *82*, 74–88.

Zweigenhaft, R. L. Birth order, approval seeking, and membership in Congress. *Journal of Individual Psychology*, 1975, *31*, 205–210.

Suggested Readings

Adler, A. *The practice and theory of individual psychology.* New York: Harcourt, Brace & World, 1927.

Adler, A. *The science of living.* Garden Gity, N.Y.: Doubleday Anchor, 1969.

Ansbacher, H. L., & Ansbacher, R. R. (Eds.). *The individual psychology of Alfred Adler.* New York: Basic Books, 1956.

Ansbacher, H. L., & Ansbacher, R. R. (Eds.). *Superiority and social interest: A collection of later writings.* New York: Viking, 1973.

Glossary

Attitude Learned tendency to respond to an object in a consistently favorable or unfavorable way.

Avoiding type An unhealthy person who avoids confronting problems, thereby assuring defeat.

Birth-order effects Adler's belief that each child is treated uniquely by the parents depending on the order of his or her birth within the family. As a result, order of birth is considered to be an important personality determinant of behavior.

Creative self Term used by Adler to reflect his belief that people have the ability to create actively their own destinies and personalities.

Fictional finalism Imagined goal that guides the person's behavior.

Getting type An unhealthy person who attains personal goals by relying indiscriminately on others for help.

Individual psychology The name for a psychology advocated by Adler that seeks to understand human behavior by recognizing its complexity and organization.

Masculine protest Attempt by a male or female to compensate for feelings of inferiority by acting superior.

Organ inferiority Biologically based defect of an organ of the body that causes the individual to feel inadequate.

Overcompensation Exaggerated attempts by individuals to overcome their feelings of inferiority by acting as though they were superior to others.

Ruling type An unhealthy person who strives for personal superiority by exploiting others.

Social interest Innate tendency in human beings to help and cooperate with one another as a means of establishing a harmonious and productive society.

Socially useful type A healthy person who actively confronts and solves his or her problems in accordance with social interest.

Style of life The distinctive personality pattern of the individual that is basically established by the end of early childhood.

Superiority The striving to attain perfection. For Adler, superiority is categorized into two types: personal superiority and superiority in a perfection sense. Personal superiority is considered harmful because it implies attempts to achieve satisfaction at the expense of others, whereas superiority strivings in the perfection sense are considered healthy because they imply the fulfillment of the individual's potential as a result of helping others.

Teleology Belief that goals determine behavior. More generally, the doctrine that behavior is directed and shaped by a designing force.

CHAPTER 5

Horney's Social and Cultural Psychoanalysis

Biographical Sketch

Karen Horney was born in 1885 in Blankenese, a village located on the north bank of the Elbe River, approximately 12 miles west of Hamburg, Germany. Her father, Berndt Wackels, was a Norwegian sea captain who was employed by one of the large shipping lines located in Hamburg. Horney's mother, Clotilde van Ronzelen, was a member of a prominent Dutch-German family. She married Captain Wackels, a man who was 18 years her senior and who had four children from a previous marriage. Their first child was a son, Berndt, born in 1881, followed four years later by Karen.

As a child, Karen had very ambivalent feelings toward her father. He took her on several boat trips throughout the world and instilled in her a love of the sea and travel and a cosmopolitan outlook on life. She loved him deeply but felt intimidated by his stern, self-righteous manner. Wackels was a God-fearing, religious fundamentalist who strongly believed that women were inferior to men. He restricted Karen's activities, while granting Berndt various freedoms and privileges. While her father vehemently opposed her ambitions, especially her educational goals, her mother was more encouraging and protected her from her father's authoritarianism. Although Karen's mother was clearly the more supportive of the two parents, neither parent apparently gave Karen much affection. Thus, wracked by doubts about her self-worth, she uncritically accepted the protection of her mother and became a clinging, highly compliant daughter, presumably as a means of feeling safe and wanted. Horney's feelings of inadequacy were heightened by her perception that she was physically unattractive, although others did not see her that way. She reacted strongly to this negative self-image by investing all her energies in her studies. As she said many years later in retrospect, "If I couldn't be beautiful, I decided I would be smart." She was always an excellent student.

She entered medical school in Freiburg in 1906 and was the only woman in her class. The male-dominated atmosphere at the medical school presented some difficulties for her, in the sense that she felt sometimes that she had to prove she was just as competent, if not more so, as her male friends and associates. Yet her social life during this period was full, exciting, and rewarding. She was introduced to Oskar Horney, a student majoring in economics, and married him while still undergoing her medical training. After finishing his studies, Oskar went to work in an investment firm and was promoted rapidly to manager of company operations. In the meantime, Karen was finishing her medical studies while trying simultaneously to fulfill roles as homemaker and mother to a baby daughter (she eventually bore two other daughters).

The conflict inherent in these activities, coupled with the death of her mother and emerging difficulties in her marriage (she eventually divorced her husband in 1939), plunged Horney into depression, and she entered therapy with a psychoanalyst, Dr. Karl Abraham. Somewhat disappointed with the results of the analysis, Horney began to question the basic tenets of psychoanalysis. Her questioning also led her to participate in weekly evening sessions with other analysts for several years at Dr. Abraham's home to discuss psychoanalytic concepts, principles, and therapeutic practices. These informal sessions eventuated in the formation of the Berlin Psychoanalytic Institute, of which Horney remained an active member from 1918 to 1932.

During this period Horney also became more outspoken about the limitations of orthodox psychoanalysis. She believed strongly that Freud had placed too much stress on the role played by the sexual instincts in the formation of neurosis and not enough on the cultural and social conditions that fostered pathology. For Freud, neurosis was essentially an outgrowth of the person's inability to cope with his or her sexual impulses and strivings, while for Horney it was primarily the result of disturbed human relationships. In her view, neurosis and sexual disturbance were often, but not inevitably, intertwined. When they were, it was the neurosis, based upon faulty character structure, that produced impaired sexual functioning, while for Freud (in direct contradiction) it was impaired sexual functioning that was the primary cause of the neurosis. Horney believed further that each culture generates its own unique set of fears in its people. In one culture, fears might be created by nature (for instance, living at the base of an unpredictable volcano or in the scorching desert), in another by warlike neighbors. In our culture, the heavy emphasis on competition and the achievement of individual success sometimes leads to a fear of failure or of being inferior to others. The normal person, according to Horney, is capable of adjusting to these threatening conditions and in making the best use of what the culture has to offer. The neurotic, in contrast, is unable to adjust and uses defenses rigidly and indiscriminately to lessen his or her fears and to feel safe. Interwoven with the problems generated by living in a given culture are the problems and fears created by the unique social or interpersonal conditions of a person's life. Mistreatment by one's parents, siblings, peers, authority figures, and others may all contribute in complicated fashion to maladjusted functioning. Thus, in Horney's judgment, sociocultural conditions have a tremendous impact on the individual's development and functioning. This emphasis on the role of the socialization process in producing neuroses and the deemphasis (but not elimination) of the role of biology caused Horney to reinterpret much of Freud's thinking and observations, including his libido theory, his theory of psychosexual development, and his theory of therapy. Her new theory germinated under the stimulation of debates with her colleagues and students at the Berlin Psychoanalytic Institute and can be seen in its evolutionary form by reading her books in chronological order: *The Neurotic Personality of Our Time* (1937), *New Ways in Psychoanalysis* (1939), *Self-Analysis* (1942), *Our Inner Conflicts* (1945), *Neurosis and Human Growth* (1950), and the posthumous *Feminine Psychology* (1967).

In 1932, Horney left the Berlin Psychoanalytic Institute and came to the United States, where she became associate director of the Chicago Psychoanalytic Institute. Two years later she moved to New York to establish a private practice and to work and teach courses at the New York Psychoanalytic Institute. While in New York, she had many opportunities to meet and exchange ideas with prominent social scientists, including Erich Fromm, Clara Thompson, Margaret Mead, H. S. Sullivan, Ruth Benedict, and John Dollard. She continued to refine her theories and to write books and journal articles. She also gave many lectures on her ideas to various professional societies. Her ideas, unfortunately, rankled some of her more orthodox Freudian colleagues at the New York Psychoanalytic Institute and eventually she felt obligated to resign. Several other members resigned in sympathy with her. Shortly afterwards she helped found the American Institute of Psychoanalysis as a vehicle for promoting her own theories. She succumbed to cancer in 1952 after a lengthy illness (Rubins, 1978).

Basic Concepts and Principles

The Etiology of Neuroses and the Creation of Basic Anxiety

According to Horney, neuroses typically originate in disturbed relationships between parents and children. Among the attitudes and behaviors of parents that cause disturbed relationships are the following:

> *direct or indirect domination, indifference, erratic behavior, lack of respect for the child's individual needs, lack of real guidance, disparaging attitudes, too much admiration or the absence of it, lack of reliable warmth, having to take sides in parental disagreements, too much or too little responsibility, overprotection, isolation from other children, injustice, discrimination, unkept promises, hostile atmosphere, and so on and so on. [Horney, 1945, p. 41]*

Horney believed further that it rarely, if ever, is only one of these factors that operates to produce pathology in a particular person. Rather, behavior is invariably multidetermined so that several of the factors operate jointly to produce disturbance. The operation of these negative factors creates **basic anxiety** in children, which means that they have a feeling of being isolated and helpless in a potentially hostile world. Their social environment is dreaded because it is felt to be unfair, unpredictable, begrudging, and merciless. These children also feel that their freedom is being taken away by parents and other adult authority figures and that their happiness is being prevented. Thus their self-esteem and self-reliance are continually being undermined. Fear is instilled in them by intimidation and isolation, and their natural exuberance and curiosity are stifled through brutality or overprotective "love" (Horney, 1939, p. 75).

The Use of Neurotic Strategies to Cope with Feelings of Basic Anxiety

To cope with the feelings of insecurity, isolation, and hostility that accompany basic anxiety, children often resort to the use of certain defensive attitudes. These protective devices ensure the temporary alleviation of pain and make them feel safe. They must be utilized so that the children can survive their distressful feelings (Horney, 1942, p. 45). Horney discussed these defenses as neurotic needs or strivings designed to reestablish the safety of their environments. They are distinguished from normal needs by their compulsiveness, rigidity, and indiscriminate usage and by the fact that they are unconscious (Horney, 1945, pp. 30–31). She outlined and discussed ten neurotic needs as follows (Horney, 1942, pp. 54–60):

1. *The Neurotic Need for Affection and Approval.* Although we all wish to be liked and appreciated by people of whom we are fond, neurotics show an indiscriminate hunger for affection, regardless of whether they care for the person concerned or whether the person has any positive feelings toward them. Thus they are overly sensitive to any criticism or indication that the attention they want and need from others is not forthcoming. They will sever a budding relationship with someone, for example, if the person does not accept their invitation for supper, even though he mentioned that he wanted to attend but could not owing to circumstances beyond his control. They may also terminate a relationship if someone disagrees with them about some trivial issue. Such individuals also have strong inhibitions about expressing their wishes or asking for favors. Moreover, they are incapable of saying no to demands from people. For example, they can readily be persuaded by salespeople to buy things they really do not need, or they can be coaxed into having premarital sex, even though it is a violation of their moral principles and causes them considerable anguish afterward (Horney, 1937, pp. 35–38).

2. *The Neurotic Need for a "Partner" Who Will Take Over One's Life.* In Horney's judgment, many neurotics are excessively dependent on others. They feel very lonely and inadequate without the presence, benevolence, love, and friendship of a "partner." Driven by the strong need for a "partner," they select an individual without much prior reflection and consequently discover that he or she does not meet their expectations. Whereas a genuine and mature partnership involves mutual caring, sharing, and love, neurotics are incapable of such behavior and typically become associated with others who are bound by the same limitations. Their relationships are therefore disturbed and unsatisfying (Horney, 1939, p. 251).

3. *The Neurotic Need to Restrict One's Life within Narrow Borders.* Neurotics are generally not risk-takers. They are afraid of expressing their wishes for fear of receiving disapproval and ridicule. Even in situations where spontaneity and expansiveness are valued and accepted (for example, parties and athletic contests), neurotics may be unable to assert themselves. Thus they may avoid such situations by claiming that they are boring and not worthwhile. They may avoid accepting jobs as teachers or as business executives because they are afraid that they will fail and face public humiliation. As a result, many neurotics feel safe only by living a highly circumscribed life where routine and orderliness are paramount. Safety is also achieved through compulsive modesty and submission to the will of others.

4. *The Neurotic Need for Power.* In normal individuals, the need for power manifests itself in the realistic realization of their physical strength, reasoning capacities, maturity, and wisdom. Their striving for power is typically associated with a worthy cause—for example, the betterment of their

family, professional group, or country. In power-oriented neurotics, in contrast, striving does not spring from strength, but from anxiety, weakness, and feelings of inferiority. Neurotic striving for power serves as a protection against helplessness, one of the key elements of basic anxiety. Neurotics, according to Horney, hate any appearance of weakness, so they avoid situations where they would have to ask for help or where they would be expected to yield to the wishes of others. Their feelings of insignificance cause them also to conjure up a rigid ideal image of themselves that makes them believe they should be able to master any situation, no matter how objectively difficult, and master it immediately or with little effort. They believe that they are clearly superior to others, and this belief implies that they should control the direction and outcomes of their relationships. These tendencies to control, however, may be masked or repressed to such a degree that they (and others) are unaware of them. Instead they may appear to be highly generous and supportive of others' freedom, while in fact they may unconsciously be striving to control others' lives in very subtle ways. If this is not possible, such neurotics may become depressed or have severe headaches or stomach upsets caused by the extreme frustration in not being able to control the situation.

The strong belief of personal superiority also causes power-oriented neurotics to want to be right all the time. They become irritated at being proven wrong, even in trivial matters. Moreover, they need to be able to predict what will happen in the future. There is a strong aversion to any situation involving uncontrollable factors. Power-oriented neurotics see self-control as a virtue and feel contempt for anyone who cannot control his or her emotions. Thus their own relationships are impaired severely because they must control their emotions at all times and because they view signs of affection from their partners as indications of weakness. Further, their relationships are permeated by conflict because they must always be right and must never give in (Horney, 1937, pp. 160–171).

5. *The Neurotic Need to Exploit Others.* Horney believed that exploitative neurotics are hostile, distrustful individuals who need to exploit others in order to feel safe. For instance, they may steal other people's ideas, jobs, or partners to obtain relief from their feelings of insecurity. They lead a parasitic kind of existence, expecting others to do favors for them and to lend them money. They live as though they had a right to expect good things to happen to them and to blame others for bad things.

Unfortunately, a frequent correlate of the need to exploit others is the fear that they will cheat or exploit you. As a consequence, such neurotics live in constant fear that others will take advantage of them. They may, for example, react with anger that borders on rage if there is the slightest delay in getting back work tools they lent their neighbors or if a cashier in a grocery store makes an honest mistake and overcharges them 50 cents for some item (Horney, 1937, pp. 183–186).

6. *The Neurotic Need for Social Recognition and Prestige.* According to Horney, normal individuals take pride in being popular and in being recognized by others for their accomplishments. Yet their lives do not revolve totally around these events nor do they devote virtually all of their energies to the attainment of recognition and prestige. Pathological individuals, in contrast, are often driven by the need to be admired and respected by others. They evaluate all things—ideas, people, possessions, groups, and so on—in terms of their prestige value. For these people it is imperative that they know prominent people, belong to prestigious groups, read the latest books and see the latest plays, and have friends and spouses who enhance their prestige (Horney, 1937, p. 172). The loss of status is their primary fear.

7. *The Neurotic Need for Personal Admiration.* Horney observed that neurotic individuals are filled with self-contempt and loathing. As a means of avoiding these painful feelings, they are driven to create an idealized image of themselves. These essentially unrealistic images operate largely on an unconscious level and vary depending upon the neurotics' unique prior experiences and their character structure. Some neurotics unconsciously strive to be exquisite human beings, devoid of flaws and limitations. They act as though they were paragons of virtue or intelligence and are forced thereby to deny the fact that they are not always generous, loving, caring, or brilliant. Such neurotics are not concerned primarily with the recognition by others of their status and material possessions, but with having others admire their idealized selves—for example, recognize that they are saintly or geniuses (Horney, 1945, pp. 96–99).

8. *The Neurotic Ambition for Personal Achievement.* Related to the needs for prestige, social recognition, and personal admiration is the neurotics' need for personal achievement. While it is perfectly normal for people to want to be best in their chosen occupation, neurotics are characterized by indiscriminate ambition and striving to be the best in too many areas. For instance, a neurotic may want simultaneously to be a great painter, an out-standing physician, a prominent musician, and a world-renowned architect. Since neurotics expect too much and are obligated to divide their energies as a means of moving toward the attainment of these goals, they are doomed to failure and are inevitably disappointed. Moreover, their indiscriminate strivings force them not only to seek to be superior in several occupations, but to seek the defeat of others. That is, such neurotics have the hostile attitude that "no one but I shall be beautiful, capable, [and] successful" (Horney, 1937, p. 192). According to Horney, ambitious neurotics even act *as if* it is more important for them to defeat others than to succeed themselves. Because they are not very likely to be highly successful, they must at least feel superior to others by tearing others down—that is, by bringing their "opponents" down to their level or beneath it (Horney, 1937, pp. 188–194).

9. *The Neurotic Need for Self-Sufficiency and Independence.* We all have a need for privacy and solitude at times. When the stresses associated with our daily interpersonal interactions become too overwhelming, we sometimes retire to the privacy of our rooms, or take a vacation, or distract ourselves by engaging in constructive solitary activities—perhaps jogging, reading, or woodworking. When we are refreshed, we rejoin the fray and are usually better able to cope with the situation. In contrast, many neurotics are permanently estranged from others. They are afraid to express emotional feelings toward others lest they be placed in a vulnerable position to learn negative things about themselves that would be shattering. Consequently, long-term obligations are avoided. Marriage, for example, is a precarious proposition because it demands intimacy. Thus it is avoided.

By remaining distant from others, neurotics also maintain their illusion of personal superiority. In their fantasies, they are clearly superior to others, and they jealously guard this illusion by trying to avoid interpersonal comparisons, especially competition. They are convinced that others should simply recognize their greatness. So the basis for their imagined superiority over others is unlikely to be tested against reality or by actual performance (Horney, 1945, pp. 73–80).

10. *The Neurotic Need for Perfection and Unassailability.* Horney thinks that the need for perfection typically has its origins in early childhood. Perfectionistic neurotics often have self-righteous, authoritarian parents who exercised unquestioned control over their lives and who instilled in them the need to attain lofty goals and to apply excessively high standards to their actions. Such individuals were often criticized and ridiculed for failure to measure up to these unrealistic goals. Unfortunately, these neurotics adopt their parents' values and spend much of their lives trying to act in ways that leave them beyond reproach and criticism. Obviously, no human being can be completely moral and virtuous in every respect, so there is a tendency for such neurotics to maintain an appearance of perfection and virtue (Horney, 1939, pp. 215–219). In their minds, they equate *knowing* about moral ideals with *being* a good person (Horney, 1950, p. 196). Because they see themselves as fair, just, and responsible (although they often are not), they demand respect from others. They are therefore hypersensitive to any opinion from others that suggests they have flaws and limitations.

Moving Toward, Against, or Away from People: The Three Basic Neurotic Trends

While Horney felt that her descriptions of the ten needs were valid, she also perceived certain similarities and commonalities among them. As a result, she classified them into three basic types: compliant, aggressive, and detached.

Compliant Types. All the traits and needs associated with **"moving toward people"** are manifested by *compliant types.* They have neurotic needs for affection and approval, for a partner to control their lives, and for a life they can live within restricted borders. These types, as Horney saw it, need to be liked, wanted, loved, appreciated, protected, and guided by others (Horney, 1945, p. 51). As a result, they tend to be self-effacing and submissive and are likely to devalue their own talents and abilities. Compliant types try desperately to live up to the expectations of others as a means of receiving approval. Any criticism, rejection, or desertion by others is terrifying, and they will make the most pitiable efforts to win back the positive regard of the person threatening them (Horney, 1945, p. 54).

Aggressive Types. Persons who have neurotic needs for power and exploitation, for social recognition and prestige, personal admiration, and personal achievement are *aggressive types.* Their needs are all associated with a tendency to **"move against people."** While compliant types assume everyone is nice, aggressive types believe that others are essentially hostile and untrustworthy. Aggressive types believe, in the Darwinian sense, that only the fittest survive and that the strong annihilate the weak. So their primary aim is to be tough or at least to appear tough. They regard all feelings, their own as well as others', as "sloppy sentimentality" (Horney, 1945, pp. 64–65). They make especially poor marriage partners because their prime concern is not the expression of positive and joyous feelings toward the partner but on having a mate who can enhance their own prestige, wealth, or position.

Aggressive neurotics also are always driven to demonstrate they are the strongest, the smartest, or the shrewdest. They are highly competitive and extremely hardworking, putting all of their intelligence and zest into their work in order to be successful. Yet their interest in their work may be misleading because for them work is only a means to an end—that is, an effort to enhance their prestige and wealth.

Detached Types. Indiscriminate needs for self-sufficiency, perfection, and unassailability characterize *detached types.* These needs are associated with **"moving away from people."** Detached types tend to shroud themselves in secrecy. They are reluctant to divulge even the most trivial details of their lives (for instance, their birthplace or the number of children in their family), and most of their activities are solitary ones. They prefer to work, eat, and sleep alone to avoid being disturbed by others. In their favor, detached types are not conforming automatons. They will fight for their beliefs and to maintain their integrity. Unfortunately, their independence has a negative aspect to it: it is aimed at *never* being influenced or obligated (Horney, 1945, p. 77).

The Basic Conflict in Neurosis. Our descriptions of the three personality types may have suggested that each one is independent of the others. That is, some people are compliant types who move only toward people, some are aggressive types who move only against people, and still others are detached types who move only away from people. Horney rejected this idea. For her, neurotics have within them all three attitudes or trends or strivings, although one may predominate. Thus in compliant types we can observe aggressive tendencies and a need for detachment at times. In aggressive types we discern underlying strong needs for affection (obtained through compliance) and a need to be self-sufficient, while in detached types we see elements of hostility and a desire for affection. In Horney's view, these fundamental attitudes are present in every neurotic individual to some degree. The attitudes are contradictory and constitute the **basic conflict** in neurosis. For neurotics, these contradictory attitudes cause turmoil and conflict on an unconscious level, sap their energies, and result in fatigue and inefficiencies in solving problems. In normal persons, the three trends are also present, but they complement one another and make for inner harmony. There is much more flexibility in normal people: they can alternatively give in to others, fight others, or keep to themselves when and where it is appropriate to do so. Neurotic individuals, on the other hand, are driven to fight, to comply, to be aloof, regardless of whether or not their behavior is appropriate in particular circumstances (Horney, 1945, pp. 34–47).

A Basic Conflict in a Neurotic: The Case Study of Claire

To understand more completely how the three contradictory attitudes operate in interrelated fashion on an unconscious level to create a basic conflict in the neurotic, we will describe the underlying personality dynamics of one of Horney's patients, a woman named Claire.

Claire was a 30-year-old magazine editor who entered therapy because she was easily overcome by a paralyzing fatigue that interfered with her work and social life. She could do only routine work, being unable to finish any difficult tasks. Claire had been married when she was 23, but her husband had died three years later. She had, however, now established another relationship with a man that continued throughout the period of psychoanalysis. According to Claire, both relationships were satisfying sexually as well as otherwise.

During the course of the analysis, Horney discovered that Claire had a compulsive modesty, a need to force others to recognize her superiority, and a compulsive dependence upon her partner. Claire was unaware of any of these trends in herself at the outset of therapy.

Horney made the diagnosis of a compulsive modesty by listening carefully to Claire's reports about herself. She continually described herself as being not very intelligent, attractive, or gifted and tended to dismiss any evidence to the contrary. She claimed that others were clearly superior to her. If others disagreed with her, she automatically assumed that they were right. She recalled that when her husband had started an affair with another woman, she said nothing in opposition, although the experience was highly painful. She even managed to consider his behavior justified on the grounds that the other woman was more attractive and affectionate. She also found it impossible to spend money on herself. She could not bring herself to buy dresses or books or to take trips. And even though she was an executive, it was impossible for her to give orders. If she was forced to do so, she did so in a very apologetic way.

The consequences of this self-effacing trend were a general lowering of her self-confidence and a discontentment with her life. She was basically unaware of her discontentment and was truly surprised when she had spells of crying. Eventually she began to realize that intense anxiety lurked behind her facade of modesty. The realization came when she was about to offer a suggestion for improving her magazine to other company executives. As she was about to make her recommendation, she experienced intense panic. Nevertheless, she made the suggestion and as discussion of it ensued she had to leave the room because of a sudden diarrhea. When she returned, she found that the discussion was moving in her favor and her panic subsided. Her plan was finally accepted and she felt elated.

The next day she came to Horney's office for a session and told the therapist of her experience. When Horney remarked that the adoption of her suggestion was a triumph for her, she became annoyed and rejected it. She said that it was presumptuous of her to offer such a plan. Who was she to know better than the others?! But gradually she began to realize that by suggesting a plan, she had ventured forth from her narrow lifestyle by taking a risk. She realized also that she was ambitious and did strongly want social recognition and success, but that these needs had been repressed. They were, however, continually operating on an unconscious level and striving for expression. The facade of modesty was a means of making her feel safe. It prevented her from having to test her ideas and abilities in direct competition with others in an open forum and, most important, from having to cope with anticipated failure or rejection by others. The result of these insights was that Claire began to have more confidence in herself.

Claire also was highly dependent on men, although she did not realize it initially and claimed that there was nothing wrong in her relationships with them. Yet analysis revealed evidence to the contrary. For example, she was totally devoted to her current lover. Her thoughts centered on a call or letter or visit from him. Hours that she spent without him were considered boring and empty, and she felt totally miserable about incidents that she interpreted as utter neglect by him. She fantasized about him, seeing him as a great and masterful man and herself as his slave. In her dreams, he gave her anything she wanted and made her into a famous writer.

The main feature of her compulsive dependence was an entirely repressed parasitic attitude, an unconscious wish to have the "partner" supply the content of her life, to take responsibility for her, to solve all her problems, and to make her into a great person without any effort on her part. This neurotic striving alienated her from him because the inevitable disappointments she felt when he could not fulfill her unrealistic expectations caused her to become intensely angry with him. For fear of losing him, much of this anger was repressed, but some of it emerged in occasional explosions. Eventually, through analysis, Claire began to understand her deep dependency on her friend and the reasons for her hostility and anger. Her fatigue appeared only occasionally, not continually as it had before. She also became more capable of productive writing, although she still suffered occasionally from "writer's block." Her relationship with her partner also became more spontaneous and honest. Much of her behavior became less compulsive and defensive, and both she and Horney were pleased with the substantial progress she had made at the time the analysis was terminated (Horney, 1942, pp. 75–88).

The Process of Personality Development

Horney's Critique of Freud's View of Development

Horney agreed with Freud that adult personality structure and functioning are influenced tremendously by early childhood experiences. Like him, she also believed that unconscious processes play an important role in the formation of character and that the use of defenses is an inevitable outgrowth of people's attempts to cope with inner conflicts and anxiety. She also agreed that the removal of these defenses is essential for adequate and effective functioning. Despite this common ground, Horney disagreed with Freud that an inherited set of sexual and aggressive strivings is more important than the environment in the development of adult character, that the important experiences in the formation of character are primarily sexual in nature, and that people are doomed to compulsively repeat in adulthood ways of behaving learned in childhood (Horney, 1939, p. 33). Finally, Horney believed Freud's theory of psychosexual development to be essentially invalid. In particular, she strongly criticized Freud's explanations of the role played by the Oedipus conflict and **penis envy** in the formation of female character and his theory of **female masochism.** Let us examine her criticisms of Freud's explanations of these phenomena.

Penis Envy: Do Women Really Want to Be Men?

According to Freud, as we noted in Chapter 2, many abnormalities seen in women grow out of their frustrated wishes to be men. He maintained that the most upsetting event in the development of girls is their discovery that, while boys have penises, they do not. They react to this discovery with the wish to have a penis too and with envy toward the more fortunate male sex. Since their "deficiency" is an unalterable fact, they transfer the wish for a penis to a wish for a child, particularly a male child who will bring the penis with him. They then identify with their mothers, hoping to become mothers themselves someday, as a means of indirectly obtaining the desired object.

In Freud's view, women's most significant attitudes and wishes derive their energy from a wish for a penis. For example, happiness during pregnancy is thought to be caused by the symbolic possession of the penis (the penis being the child in the womb). Cramps during menstruation are interpreted as being the result of fantasies in which the father's penis has been swallowed. Disturbances in relationships with men are interpreted also in terms of penis envy. Women who try to surpass men or to disparage them are said to be "castrating females." Defloration during sex may arouse hostility toward the partner because it is experienced as a castration. Women's physical modesty is seen ultimately as a wish to hide the "deficiency" of her genitals (Horney, 1939, pp. 101–104).

In sum, the Freudian view of the development of women leads to the unequivocal conclusion that they are inferior creatures. Feminine inferiority feelings are regarded as an expression of contempt for their own sex because of their lack of a penis. Furthermore, not much can be done to eliminate this self-loathing because the "defect" is biologically based and cannot be altered. Anatomy is destiny, according to Freud.

Horney's criticism of Freud's view of penis envy was a complicated one. She thought Freud was a genius who had identified an important phenomenon in women. Yet she questioned his explanation of the phenomenon as deriving completely from instinctual sources. She thought that penis envy does derive to some extent from anatomical differences between the sexes, but that its more important source resides in cultural and social forces in a patriarchal society that indoctrinates both sexes with the view of male superiority and female inferiority.

On anatomical grounds, she maintained that penis envy has its origins in women's desire to urinate as men do. She believed that fantasies of omnipotence are more easily associated with the jet of urine passed by the male. As "evidence," she cited a game played by European boys in which they would stand at right angles to one another and urinate to make a cross, while concentrating their thoughts simultaneously on a particular person and wishing he or she would die. This experience was laden with feelings of magic and power. The significance of the cross was heightened by its religious connotation and by the importance of the idea that X marks the spot. In addition, males are able to look at themselves in the act of urinating, thereby satisfying their sexual curiosity, while females are unable to see or perform in the same way because their genitals are hidden. Thus women, according to Horney, may actively envy males because of the ready visibility of their genitals. Finally, males derive pleasure from holding their penis while urinating, and the fact that they hold their penis during the act may be construed as permission to masturbate. Females, in contrast, are often forbidden to touch or manipulate their vaginas and clitorises (Horney, 1967, pp. 39–41).

On sociocultural grounds, Horney maintained that our whole civilization is essentially masculine. The laws, religion, morality, science, and art are the creation of men. Men are clearly in the dominant, or superior, position, while women occupy an inferior place. Unfortunately, in Horney's judgment, women have adapted themselves to the inferior status assigned to them by men and judged themselves as inferior (Horney, 1967, pp. 55–57). This perverse adaptation results not only in self-hatred and contempt, but in hatred of other women and resentment and hostility toward men. It results in a lack of faith in women's capacity for any real achievement and in a minimizing of success whenever it occurs. Even motherhood appears as an unfair burden to women who have adopted the masculine disregard and disrespect for the accomplishments of women. The feelings of having been discriminated against by fate result also in women's unconscious claims for compensation. In their fantasies, there is a rejection of the feminine role and a wish for all the qualities and privileges that in our culture are regarded as masculine—that is, strength, courage, success, sexual freedom, and independence (Horney, 1939, p. 108). Therefore penis envy should not be seen as being based on a castration complex in which the penis has been cut off, thus creating wishes and fantasies for its symbolic replacement, but rather on a justifiable envy of qualities associated with certain aspects of masculinity in our culture. Women, according to Horney, must realize that their inferiority feelings are based on their unconscious acceptance of a male superiority ideology and that their feelings about themselves can be changed only if efforts are made to make society itself more democratic and egalitarian. Anatomy is not necessarily destiny, in Horney's opinion, although it does play a part.

Female Masochism: Do Women Really Enjoy Suffering?

Before discussing Horney's criticisms of Freud's explanation of masochism, we must first carefully examine the definition of the phenomenon because much confusion surrounds it (Caplan, 1984). Some authorities define it as a wish to suffer pain and to be subjected to it by force; pain is pursued because it is, in itself, pleasurable. Others see it as a condition in which sexual gratification depends on suffering physical pain and humiliation; pain is endured because it is associated with pleasure, and pleasure can be experienced only if pain is experienced as well. This second definition seems closest to Freud's conception because he discussed the topic in terms of a *fusion* of life instincts (the drive toward pleasure) and death instincts (the drive toward death—that is, pain).

Freud identified masochism with femininity. He maintained that women were sexually passive by nature and that their passivity caused them to repress their aggressiveness (which is a manifestation of their drive toward death), thereby "binding erotically the destructive tendencies which have been turned inwards" (Freud, 1952, p. 855). Thus sexual intercourse for women involves masochistic gratification because it fuses pleasurable sensations with pain (the penetration of the vagina). Childbirth also mixes pleasure with pain and is thus considered to give women unconscious masochistic satisfaction. In addition, the orthodox psychoanalytic view holds that girls' early sexual wishes and fantasies concerning the father involve the desire to be mutilated and castrated by him. Women may also fantasize about being raped, beaten, and humiliated. In short, the standard Freudian view of women, as we have seen, is one of an inferior and incompetent creature who takes secret pleasure in being abused physically and psychologically.

Horney's view of female masochism was very different from Freud's, although she thought that his position had merit in some respects. Compatible with Freud's view, for example, she thought that certain biological differences between the sexes could provide a basis for female masochism. Specifically, she thought that men's greater size and strength could give women a sense of inferiority. Moreover, a sense of inferiority could easily be fueled by women's knowledge that they can be raped and by the pain that accompanies menstruation, intercourse, and childbirth.

Horney nevertheless believed that these anatomical and physiological differences were not sufficient in themselves to create female masochism. These conditions simply *prepare* women to adopt a masochistic role. It is primarily society itself that serves to shape women's behaviors and experiences and that leads them to define themselves in masochistic terms. As Horney put it: "The problem of feminine masochism cannot be related to factors inherent in the anatomical-physiological-psychic characteristics of woman alone, but must be considered as importantly conditioned by the culture-complex or social organization in which the particular masochistic woman has developed" (Horney, 1967, pp. 232–233).

Thus society influences women's conception of themselves as inferior. It does so in several ways: (1) by blocking their strivings for achievement in male-dominated occupations; (2) by fostering their economic dependence on men; (3) by restricting their activities to life spheres that are built upon emotional bonds, such as family life, religion, or charity; and (4) by fostering an estimation of themselves as beings who are, in general, inferior to men (Horney, 1967, p. 230).

Although feminists today endorse Horney's view of female masochism as being grounded primarily in social and cultural experiences, they challenge her arguments about the contributions of anatomical and physiological differences to the development of the phenomenon. As Caplan (1984) cogently maintained:

> *The fact that men often have greater physical strength than women might well lead some women to feel physically inferior, but that is worlds away from leading women to want to suffer, which is masochism. Next, the possibility that women can be raped need not lead women to enjoy pain, any more than the possibility that men can be stabbed, murdered, or raped needs to lead men to enjoy pain. To suggest that biological differences in intercourse lead women to be masochistic reflects, first of all, a mistaken assumption that intercourse has to take place—for biological reasons—with the woman beneath the man, and it reflects furthermore a narrow focus on penile penetration as the essence and totality of sexuality, to the exclusion of other aspects of sexuality and sensuality. For many women the moment of penetration is not the crux of their experience of sexuality, and since there are various opportunities for pleasure, and specifically for sexual pleasure, in women's lives, the focus on penetration as the foundation of a woman's personality, thus supposedly leading her to become generally masochistic, seems curious. [Caplan, 1984, p. 136]*

Thus modern feminists believe that, although Horney made a significant departure from the focus on biological factors as "proof" of women's innate masochism (and a significant contribution to our understanding of the phenomenon), they also believe that she unfortunately did not go far enough. Similarly, they believe that her view of penis envy as having a base in anatomical differences between the sexes is incorrect. In brief, feminists agree with Horney's assessment of the cultural and social origins of female masochism and penis envy but disagree with her view that these phenomena are partially rooted in biology.

Let us examine other aspects of Horney's revisionist views of personality development.

Horney's Revised, Humanistic View of Development

As mentioned earlier, Horney thought that the unique social and cultural experiences of children are crucial in the determination of their adult personalities. She felt that harsh and arbitrary treatment of children by parents lays the foundation for neurosis. Healthy development, in contrast, was seen as being predicated on warm, fair, considerate, supportive, and respectful treatment by the parents. In her **humanistic view of development,** Horney strongly believed that everyone is special and has a unique set of potentials that would flourish under wise parental guidance. These intrinsic potentialities she called the *real self.* With proper support, she believed everyone could develop toward self-realization. That is, they could develop the depth and clarity of their own feelings, thoughts, wishes, and interests, the ability to tap their own resources and gifts, the faculty to express themselves, and the ability to relate to others spontaneously (Horney, 1950, p. 17). Unfortunately, however, many people do not receive proper guidance. Instead, they are treated arbitrarily and with a lack of respect, and the result is alienation from the real self.

Alienation and the Formation of the Idealized Self

Horney maintained that unfavorable environmental conditions impair the realistic inner confidence of people and force them to evolve defenses to cope with others. Because their major energies are directed toward the development of defenses as a means of feeling safe, attempts to develop their real selves are overridden. To the extent that safety is paramount, people's innermost feelings and thoughts recede in importance and become blurred. They are in a sense no longer the masters of their destiny but are driven by their neurotic needs. Alienation from their real selves causes people to seek a sense of stability and identity, a sense that they are significant and worthwhile.

The answer for neurotics revolves around the use of their imaginations to create **idealized images** for themselves. These images endow them with unlimited abilities and powers. In their imaginations they become heroes, geniuses, supreme lovers, saints, and gods. The images provide an avenue for "solving" their basic conflicts. According to Horney, eventually neurotics try to actualize their **idealized selves** in regard to the outside world through achievement and the attainment of success, glory, and triumph. They are relentlessly and painfully driven to be perfect, feeling that they *should* be able to do and to know everything and to like everyone. Horney calls this compulsive need "the **tyranny of the shoulds.**" The neurotic, according to Horney, unconsciously believes the following:

> *He should be the [epitome] of honesty, generosity, considerateness, justice, dignity, courage, unselfishness. He should be the perfect lover, husband, teacher. He should be able to endure everything, should like everybody, should love his parents, his wife, his country; or, he should not be attached to anything or anybody, nothing should matter to him, he should never feel hurt, and he should always be serene and unruffled. He should always enjoy life; or, he should be above pleasure and enjoyment. He should be spontaneous; he should always control his feelings. He should know, understand, and foresee everything. He should be able to solve every problem of his own, or of others, in no time. He should be able to overcome every difficulty of his as soon as he sees it. He should never be tired or fall ill. He should always be able to find a job. He should be able to do things in one hour which can only be done in two to three hours. [Horney, 1950, p. 65]*

Neurotics cling to these impossible standards because their attainment promises to satisfy all their inner conflicts and to eliminate all pain and anxiety. Unfortunately, self-idealization does not work. When neurotics compare their **actual selves** (selves as they are at the moment) against the measuring rod of their idealized selves, they inevitably fall short. For example, their frequent impotence during lovemaking belies their belief that they are great lovers. Their hesitation and stammering while asking their boss for a promotion and a raise is clearly at variance with their view of themselves as articulate speakers. The fact that they are working at menial jobs is a constant reminder that they have not achieved high occupational status and success. As a result of these experienced discrepancies between their actual and idealized selves, neurotics are filled with self-contempt and hatred. Although they are aware of the *results* of self-hate—that is, feeling inferior, tormented, guilty—they are completely unaware that they themselves have brought about these painful feelings and self-evaluations (Horney, 1950, p. 116). Thus self-hate is essentially an unconscious process. Rather than examine themselves critically, neurotics are prone to externalize their hatred and to see it as emanating from other people, institutions, or fate.

Externalization: The Attempt to Keep the Idealized Self Intact. As we have seen, neurotics seek refuge from their inner conflicts by creating and identifying with an idealized self. Yet when the discrepancies between their idealized selves and their actual selves reach a point where the tensions are unbearable, neurotics run away from themselves and see everything as if it lay outside (Horney, 1945, p. 116). **Externalization** is the tendency of neurotics to experience internal processes as if they occurred outside the self and to hold external factors responsible for their difficulties. Part of externalization involves projection—that is, the tendency to attribute to others one's own failings and shortcomings. It also involves "experiencing" many feelings in others rather than in one's self. For example, neurotics tend to perceive that others are angry with them when actually they are angry with themselves. They will also attribute good feelings in themselves to the weather or to fate. Successes are attributed to good luck, and so forth. Most important, the neurotic's own self-contempt is externalized. In the aggressive type, the tendency is to despise others. Aggressive neurotics feel superior to others and reinforce their feelings of superiority by seeing others as inferior and worthy of contempt. In the compliant type, the tendency is to see others as filled with contempt for them. Horney believed that this projection is particularly damaging to compliant types. It makes them shy, inhibited, and withdrawn (Horney, 1945, p. 118).

In conclusion, externalization is a process of self-obliteration (obliteration of the actual and real selves) designed to ensure that the idealized self remains intact. It does not work very well, however, and neurotics are forced to rely on other defenses for support.

Auxiliary Approaches to Artificial Harmony. Horney described seven defenses used by neurotics to help themselves cope with their inner conflicts and with disturbances in their interpersonal relationships (Horney, 1945, pp. 131–140). We will discuss each one briefly.

1. *Blind Spots.* Horney stated that many lay people wonder how neurotics can keep from seeing the discrepancies between their actual and idealized selves since the discrepancies are so blatant. Neurotics seem to have **blind spots,** or areas in which obvious contradictions are blotted out or ignored. The reason, according to Horney, is that neurotics are often inordinately numb to their own experiences (Horney, 1945, p. 133).

2. *Compartmentalization.* The defense called **compartmentalization** refers to the separation of beliefs and/or actions into categories or compartments so that they do not appear inconsistent with one another. Take the Ku Klux Klan member who is convinced that he is a Christian. By maintaining that his Christian beliefs of love and tolerance extend only to humans and that Blacks are clearly animals, and therefore inhuman, he can continue to hate and persecute them without feeling great stress.

3. *Rationalization.* As we noted in Chapter 2, **rationalization** is defined as self-deception by the use of plausible, but inaccurate, excuses to justify one's perceived weaknesses or failures. For example, aggressive neurotics view feelings of remorse and sympathy for others as weakness. Therefore an aggressive neurotic who has sent flowers to his long-time colleague's widow as an expression of his sympathy might justify his action by claiming that he sent them only because it was his duty as a fellow employee to do so.

4. *Excessive Self-Control.* The protective device called **excessive self-control** refers to the neurotics' compulsive need to restrict expression of their emotions. As Horney put it:

   Persons who exert such control will not allow themselves to be carried away, whether by enthusiasm, sexual excitement, self-pity, or rage. In analysis they have the greatest difficulty in associating freely; they will not permit alcohol to lift their spirits and frequently prefer to endure pain rather than undergo anesthesia. In short, they seek to check all spontaneity. [Horney, 1945, p. 136]

   Since the most destructive actions are violent ones prompted by rage, most of the neurotics' energy is directed toward control of this emotion. But a **vicious circle** is set up. Suppression of rage leads to the unconscious buildup of even more rage, which, in turn, entails even more self-control to choke it.

5. *Arbitrary Rightness.* Doubt and indecision characterize the neurotic. The feelings they engender are intolerable and, as a result, neurotics employ **arbitrary rightness** as a protective device. It is an attempt by the neurotic to settle all disputes by declaring dogmatically that he or she is invariably right.

6. *Elusiveness.* Neurotics who use **elusiveness** as a means of protection can never be pinned down to any statement; they deny ever having made the statement or claim that the other person misinterpreted the meaning of what they said (thus they can never be wrong). They are continually equivocating and are unable to give a concrete report of any incident. As a result, the listener is confused over just what really did happen.

Horney maintained that the same confusion reigns in the lives of neurotics. At times, they are overly considerate, yet at other times ruthlessly inconsiderate. They can be highly domineering in some respects, self-effacing in others. Because of these inconsistencies, it is sometimes difficult for an analyst to guide them to the accurate identification of their underlying conflicts.

7. *Cynicism.* As the final protective device, **cynicism** involves the denying and deriding of moral values. In Horney's opinion, neurotics tend to be Machiavellian in their outlook. They believe people are not to be trusted. Small wonder, since they think that they can do whatever they please as long as they do not get caught. They are people of expedience, not principle.

In conclusion, all these irrational defenses help (at least temporarily) to maintain the neurotics' idealized conception of themselves. It is not surprising that healthy growth is virtually impossible.

Research Evidence for the Association between Irrational Beliefs and Psychopathology

A common theme in Horney's theorizing about neurosis is that abnormal people have numerous irrational beliefs about themselves and others that create and increase their suffering and ineffective ways of behaving in relationships with others. In regard to their idealized selves, for example, they irrationally believe they are paragons of virtue, brilliant people, and great lovers. They also defend further against feelings of insecurity by blaming other people, fate, or institutions for their failures, by claiming that they are invariably right, and by convincing themselves that no one can be trusted. Moreover, neurotics are driven by moral absolutes ("the tyranny of the shoulds") that require them to act as though they were completely honest, courageous, and unselfish.

There is considerable correlational evidence in modern cognitive therapy psychology that supports Horney's assertions concerning the link between irrational beliefs and psychopathology. For example, the greater the number of irrational beliefs held by individuals, the more likely they are to be depressed (Dobson & Breiter, 1983; LaPointe & Crandell, 1980; Lewinsohn et al., 1981; Nelson, 1977; Thorpe & Barnes, 1981), socially inept (Hayden & Nasby, 1977), poor at problem solving (Schill et al., 1978), and unhappy in their marriages

(Eidelson & Epstein, 1982). Eidelson and Epstein compared couples in marital therapy with couples not in therapy in terms of the beliefs they endorsed concerning their relationships. They found that the couples experiencing marital difficulties held a variety of dysfunctional beliefs. They believed, for instance, that disagreement with their spouses was destructive and that such conflict was a sign of a lack of love or even imminent divorce, even though conflicts based upon interpersonal differences are an inevitable part of any relationship. Furthermore, unhappy couples believed irrationally that partners who truly care about and know each other should be able to sense each other's needs and preferences without explicit, direct communication. Their reliance on "mindreading" led them to put less effort into clear communication and resulted in disappointment and escalation of conflict. Unhappy couples also believed that they could not change themselves nor could their partners change. Such an extreme belief led to feelings of helplessness and diminished satisfaction with the relationship. Finally, Eidelson and Epstein found that unhappy couples thought that they must be perfect sex partners. (Recall Horney's point that many neurotics believe that they are great lovers.) Such a belief led to anxiety and inhibition in the sexual sphere.

Finally, Horney maintained that, to change these irrational thoughts so that the patients' mental health would be improved, it was necessary for therapists to actively challenge the beliefs and to replace them with more realistic thoughts and feelings. Cognitive therapists generally agree with Horney's contention, and there is some evidence that such therapy is effective (Ellis & Greiger, 1977; Smith, 1983; Smith, in press). D'Alelio and Murray (1981), for example, used this form of cognitive therapy to reduce test anxiety in college students. Specifically, therapists taught groups of test-anxious college students to identify and challenge the distracting and irrational thoughts that were interfering with their exam performances and to replace them with more constructive thoughts. For example, a student might report the self-defeating statement "Since I don't know the answer to the first question, I won't know the others and will fail." This statement is challenged and replaced with coping statements such as "Just because I don't know the answer to the first question doesn't mean I don't know the others. I will skip this question and come back to it later. I won't spend time worrying."

This kind of cognitive therapy was administered in group sessions by different therapists. Each group met for 1½ hours once a week. Some groups met over a four-week period, while others met for eight weeks. The groups that trained for eight weeks showed the greatest reductions in test anxiety and worrying; the four-week groups followed, with the least reductions being associated with control groups of subjects who received no training. (Control subjects, however, were offered similar therapeutic treatment at the end of the semester.) Unfortunately, although the students who went through the therapy sessions showed reductions in test anxiety and worrying, their grade-point averages did not improve during the school year. But a similar study by Holroyd (1976), using more highly motivated subjects, did find an increase in grade-point average from the end of the fall semester to the end of the spring semester after cognitive therapy (1.25 points on the average for the treatment groups), while the control groups showed no statistically significant gains (there was actually a slight decrease of .30 in grade-point average).

Techniques of Assessment

Horney believed that free association and dream analysis were techniques that could help therapists identify the sources of neurotics' problems. Although she agreed with Freud that these procedures were indispensable for the uncovering of conflicts, she disagreed with him in many of her interpretations of the problems uncovered by the use of these devices. Whereas Freud continually interpreted the patients' free associations and dream reports in terms of thwarted sexual and/or aggressive strivings, Horney's interpretations focused on the disturbances experienced by patients in their interpersonal relationships and on the neurotic trends utilized by them to cope with their basic anxieties and fears.

She also saw the personal relationship between the analyst and the patient differently than Freud. Freud believed strongly that psychoanalysis was a science. Accordingly, he adopted the stance of an objective scientist while treating patients. That is, he tried not to impose his personal moral values on them. Rather, he perceived himself as an objective observer who was collecting data and presenting them to the patients for their consideration and use. This dispassionate orientation meant that the analyst would be highly tolerant in the sense that he or she would refrain from making value judgments about the patients' personal qualities and experiences. The expectation was that the analyst's forbearance would allay the patients' fears of condemnation and thereby encourage freer expression of their thoughts and feelings. Horney thought it was impossible for an analyst to refrain from making such value judgments during the course of therapy. Moreover, she believed that patients could sense that the analyst was indeed making such judgments and that trying to hide the fact only served to make the relationship worse. She thought that the analyst should be more active and directive in offering suggestions to patients and more honest and open with them. In Horney's view, such an outlook would facilitate the growth of the relationship and lead more readily to a cure.

Application of the Theory to the Treatment of Psychopathology

Neurotics are alienated from their real selves and from others. They have identified with their idealized selves and become pretenders who are afraid of having their limitations exposed by others. Horney believed that only when they are able to relinquish their illusions about themselves and their illusory goals will they have a chance to find their real potentialities and to develop them. The process of removing the obstructive factors hindering growth, however, is a long and difficult one, for neurotics are strongly committed to defending their illusions. Aggressive types, for example, hope the analysis will remove all impediments to their having unqualified triumphs and an unquestioned sainthood. Thus they think only of perfecting their idealized selves, while the analyst seeks, in contrast, to help remove their idealized selves and to promote the growth of their real selves.

For Horney, therapy is a human relationship, and all the difficulties that neurotics have in their relationships with other people operate during the therapeutic process. Patients may become argumentative, sarcastic, and/or assaultive. They may be evasive, refuse to discuss a subject, or talk with emotionless intelligence about their problems as if they were unimportant. They may react with rage and become abusive toward the analyst. Yet many of these actions act as signposts directing the therapist's inquiries. That is, the actions provide clues that point to the presence of underlying conflicts. Patients tend also to be highly threatened by the therapist's inquiries and to experience considerable anxiety. For the patients, this anxiety is terribly painful, but for the therapist it may also have a positive meaning. It may indicate that the patients are now strong enough to take the risk of confronting their problems more directly. According to Horney, the therapist's inquiries also help patients become more aware of all the obstructive forces operating within them. She believed, however, that this self-knowledge must not remain an intellectual knowledge only but must become an emotional experience as well if it is to promote growth. In her opinion, intellectual realization is important, but it does not have sufficient impact on patients to promote change. Only when patients feel the intensity of the unconscious forces operating within them will they be motivated to change and to relinquish their illusions.

Once their illusions have been given up, the therapist focuses on helping the patients find their real selves. Through the use of free association and dream analysis their real selves may begin to emerge. Patients are reinforced also for any sign they give of greater independence in their thinking, of assuming responsibility for themselves, and of being interested in the truth about themselves. They are encouraged to make attempts at finding their identities through self-analysis outside of the therapeutic setting. The analyst also points out any signs of progress made by patients in their human relationships. These glimpses of growth have a highly positive impact on patients. They have a sense of fulfillment that is different from anything they have known before. It acts as the best incentive for them to work harder at their own growth, toward greater self-realization. As they grow, they begin to realize that there are other problems in the world beside their own. They begin to extend themselves to others—to members of their family, to members of their community, nation, and other countries. They become more willing to accept responsibility not only for themselves but for others as well. They become contributors to others and find the inner certainty that comes from the feeling of belonging through active and unselfish participation (Horney, 1950, pp. 333–365).

Critical Comments

We turn now to an evaluation of Horney's theory on the basis of our six criteria.

Comprehensiveness. Horney created a comprehensive theory that encompasses a variety of normal and abnormal phenomena. She discussed in great detail the etiology and cure for different forms of neurosis. Her discussions centered on the impact that complicated social and cultural forces have on the development and maintenance of neurosis. Accordingly, the explanatory base for her theory was much richer than the one utilized by Freud. Possibly the most original aspect of her theorizing about neurosis centered on the concept of the idealized self and the discrepancy between it and the real self. In this theorizing we see her humanistic concerns with trying to understand, not only how to eliminate the forces that produce and maintain neurosis, but how to develop a theory about positive growth and optimal personality functioning.

Precision and Testability. Many of the concepts utilized by Horney are abstract and difficult to define precisely. To her credit, Horney made a strenuous effort to define her terms. Unfortunately, some of them remained relatively imprecise and unclear (for example, potentialities, inner dictates, inner forces, and shallow living). Given these definitional ambiguities, it would be very difficult to design adequate tests of the theory.

Parsimony. Horney's theory is clearly not overly simple. Her explanations of the origins and development of neurosis are rich and complicated and seem generally adequate to the task. Thus her theory seems parsimonious.

Empirical Validity. Although there have been only a few direct tests of Horney's theory, some of the research by prominent cognitive therapists, especially Ellis and his colleagues, relies heavily on several of Horney's concepts and formulations. The research evidence in this work generally supports, albeit indirectly, Horney's views.

Heuristic Value. Horney's ideas about the "tyranny of the shoulds" are highly original and have been utilized by many cognitive therapists in their descriptions of the etiology and maintenance of various forms of neurosis.

Although cognitive therapists and researchers employ many kinds of therapeutic procedures to reduce emotional suffering and impaired ways of behaving that cannot be directly traced to Horney's theory of psychotherapy, Ellis' *rational-emotive therapy* procedures are in many respects an outgrowth of the consideration of Horney's formulations and recommendations concerning the treatment of patients. Moreover, Horney's theorizing about human growth and self-realization marks her as an important early contributor to the development of the humanistic psychology movement.

Applied Value. In addition to its heuristic value, Horney's theory has had an important impact on the work of cognitive therapists who help alleviate the suffering of many clinical patients.

Discussion Questions

1. Horney believed that competitiveness and neuroticism are positively associated. Is competition necessarily destructive? What distinguishes healthy from unhealthy competition?
2. Why is this country so obsessed with competition and achievement?
3. Horney thought that each person has a real self consisting of worthwhile, intrinsic potentialities that await further development. Have you been able to identify such potential strengths in yourself? What are they?
4. Do you know many people who think they are invariably right? How do you cope with them?
5. Why can Horney's views on the development of women be seen as generally consistent with the teachings of feminists today?
6. Why are the spontaneity and expansiveness that characterize the healthy person missing in the neurotic?
7. Is it always unhealthy or inappropriate to blame others for your failures, as much of Horney's writings suggest?
8. Under what conditions or situational circumstances is it healthy to distort reality?
9. Do you agree with Horney that it is impossible for a therapist to avoid making value judgments during therapy sessions with patients?
10. Assuming that Horney's sociocultural explanations of penis envy and female masochism are valid, in what ways could penis envy and masochistic attitudes lead to mistrust and hostility between the sexes?

References

Caplan, P. J. The myth of women's masochism. *American Psychologist*, 1984, *39*, 130–139.

D'Alelio, W. A., & Murray, E. J. Cognitive therapy for test anxiety. *Cognitive Therapy and Research*, 1981, *5*, 299–307.

Dobson, K. S., & Breiter, H. J. Cognitive assessment of depression: Reliability and validity of three measures. *Journal of Abnormal Psychology*, 1983, *92*, 107–109.

Eidelson, R. J., & Epstein, N. Cognition and relationship maladjustment: Development of a measure of dysfunctional relationship beliefs. *Journal of Consulting and Clinical Psychology*, 1982, *50*, 715–720.

Ellis, A., & Greiger, R. *Handbook of rational emotive therapy*. New York: Julian Press, 1977.

Freud, S. New introductory lectures on psychoanalysis. In R. M. Hutchins (Ed.), *Great books of the Western world*. Chicago: Encyclopaedia Britannica, 1952.

Hayden, B., & Nasby, W. Interpersonal conceptual structures, predictive accuracy, and social adjustment of emotionally disturbed boys. *Journal of Abnormal Psychology*, 1977, *86*, 315–320.

Holroyd, K. A. Cognition and desensitization in the group treatment of test anxiety. *Journal of Consulting and Clinical Psychology.* 1976, *44*, 991–1001.

Horney, K. *The neurotic personality of our time*. New York: Norton, 1937.

Horney, K. *New ways in psychoanalysis*. New York: Norton, 1939.

Horney, K. *Self-analysis*. New York: Norton, 1942.

Horney, K. *Our inner conflicts*. New York: Norton, 1945.

Horney, K. *Neurosis and human growth*. New York: Norton, 1950.

Horney, K. *Feminine psychology*. New York: Norton, 1967.

LaPointe, K. A., & Crandell, C. J. Relationship of irrational beliefs to self-reported depression. *Cognitive Therapy and Research*, 1980, *4*, 247–250.

Lewinsohn, P. M., Steinmetz, J. L., Larson, D.W., & Franklin, J. Depression-related cognitions: Antecedent or consequence? *Journal of Abnormal Psychology*, 1981, *90*, 213–219.

Nelson, R. E. Irrational beliefs in depression. *Journal of Consulting and Clinical Psychology*, 1977, *45*, 1190–1191.

Rubins, J. L. *Karen Horney: Gentle rebel of psychoanalysis*. New York: Dial, 1978.

Schill, T., Monroe, S., Evans, R., & Ramanaiah, N. The effects of self-verbalizations on performance: A test of the rational-emotive position. *Psychotherapy: Theory Research and Practice*, 1978, *15*, 2–7.

Smith, T. W. Changes in irrational beliefs and the outcome of rational-emotive psychotherapy. *Journal of Consulting and Clinical Psychology*, 1983, *51*, 156–157.

Smith, T. W. Irrational beliefs in the cause and treatment of emotional distress: A critical review of the rational-emotive model. *Clinical Psychology Review*, in press.

Thorpe, G. L., & Barnes, G. S. Relationships between self-reported emotionality and rationality in two clinical and two non-clinical samples. Unpublished manuscript, University of Maine, 1981.

Suggested Readings

Horney, K. *The neurotic personality of our time*. New York: Norton, 1937.
Horney, K. *Our inner conflicts*. New York: Norton, 1945.
Horney, K. *Neurosis and human growth*. New York: Norton, 1950.
Horney, K. *Feminine psychology*. New York: Norton, 1967.

Glossary

Actual self The self as it is at the moment, including all of the person's actual strengths and weaknesses.

Aggressive types Neurotic individuals who protect themselves against feelings of insecurity by exploiting others in order to feel superior.

Arbitrary rightness Protective device by which people are convinced they are invariably correct in all their judgments.

Basic anxiety The painful psychological state in which a person feels isolated and helpless toward a potentially hostile world.

Basic conflict The clash within neurotics caused by the incompatibility and inconsistency between their unconscious tendencies to move toward, against, and away from others.

Blind spots Defense mechanism by which painful experiences are denied or ignored because they are at variance with the idealized self.

Compartmentalization Defense mechanism by which neurotics alleviate tensions by disconnecting incompatible neurotic trends within themselves.

Compliant types Neurotic individuals who cope with feelings of basic anxiety by indiscriminately seeking the approval and affection of others through excessive conformity.

Cynicism Defense mechanism by which the person believes in nothing and therefore cannot be hurt or disappointed by others.

Detached types Neurotic individuals who protect themselves by avoiding others.

Elusiveness Defense mechanism whereby a person refuses to take a position on anything so that he/she can never be proven wrong and criticized or ridiculed by others.

Excessive self-control Defense mechanism whereby a person exercises willpower, consciously or unconsciously, to keep conflicting emotional impulses under control.

Externalization Defense mechanism whereby a person experiences inner emotions externally and blames others for his or her own weaknesses and failings.

Female masochism For Freud, a perversion in which women experience a blending of pleasure and pain during certain activities and fantasies. He believed that male masochism occurred only in males with feminine (passive) natures.

Humanistic view of development An optimistic view of development that sees each person as having intrinsic and unique potentials for constructive growth.

Idealized images Fantasies of neurotic individuals in which they visualize themselves as perfect beings.

Idealized self The defensive identification of neurotics with their idealized images.

Moving against people A major neurotic trend that aims at the control of basic anxiety through the domination and exploitation of others.

Moving away from people A major neurotic trend that protects the person against basic anxiety by utter detachment and extreme self-sufficiency.

Moving toward people A major neurotic trend that protects the person against feelings of basic anxiety by self-effacement and obliteration.

Penis envy In Horney's view, penis envy is primarily a sociocultural phenomenon in which women are indoctrinated to see themselves as inferior and men as superior. They therefore unconsciously strive to emulate masculine goals and values and to obtain the advantages and privileges that accrue to males.

Rationalization Defense by which people ward off the anxiety created by a threatening situation by offering plausible, but inaccurate, excuses for their conduct.

Rational-Emotive Therapy A cognitive restructuring therapy in which the faulty beliefs of neurotics that lead to emotional disturbance are identified, challenged, and then replaced with more constructive, rational ways of thinking.

Real self The potentials within a person for constructive growth. It encompasses also the person's current strengths and limitations (actual self).

Tyranny of the shoulds Concept used by Horney to describe the moral imperatives that relentlessly drive neurotics to accept nothing less than perfection for themselves.

Vicious circle Circular process by which inner emotional conflicts create defenses to control them, which, in turn, serve to repress and to exacerbate them, thereby creating the need for even stronger defenses to control them, and so on ad infinitum.

C H A P T E R   6

Fromm's Humanistic Psychoanalysis

Biographical Sketch

Erich Fromm was born in Frankfurt, Germany, in 1900, the only child of Jewish parents. His father was an independent businessman, his mother a homemaker. As a boy, Fromm was an ardent student of the Old Testament. He was aroused by the compassion and the possibility of human redemption in the stories of Abraham and Jonah and of Adam and Eve and in the words of the prophets. In particular, he was impressed by the promise that one day nations "shall beat their swords into ploughshares and their spears into pruning hooks: nation shall not lift sword against nation, neither shall they learn war any more" (Hausdorff, 1972, p. 11). This prophecy had special meaning for Fromm because of the anti-Semitism and isolation he experienced. He sought consolation in the Old Testament and began to long for a universal peace and brotherhood he hoped would help him transcend the present. This longing can be seen clearly in his later writings about the nature of mature love and the establishment of a utopian social order.

Fromm's family life was not one of harmony. A strong concern with spiritual values was matched by an equally strong concern with the attainment of material success. He described his household as "tense," his father as "over-anxious and moody," and his mother as "depression-prone" (Hausdorff, 1972, p. 12). Fromm believed, retrospectively, that this conflict between spiritual and secular values in his boyhood provided the impetus for his later search for a harmonious social order. His concern with understanding the fundamental questions of life and society was increased dramatically at age 12 when a friend of the family, a beautiful and talented woman, committed suicide. Her death seemed incredible and senseless to him (Hausdorff, 1972, p. 13).

At 13, Fromm began 14 years of study of the Talmud under two humanistic and socialistic rabbis. He then left organized Judaism but retained a lifelong interest in religious writings (Hausdorff, 1972, p. 13. He entered the University of Heidelberg at a time when the social sciences were enlivened by a burst of new ideas. Karl Marx's theories on the ways in which the political and social order affected the individual's development were by then widely known, and it is clear that Fromm was influenced by them, as will become apparent later in the chapter. Darwin's theory of biological evolution was also sweeping the academic world, as were Freud's new and startling formulations of human personality (Hausdorff, 1972, pp. 14–15). Freud's ideas were particularly intriguing to Fromm because they seemed to offer insights into problems he could not resolve. For example, Freud's concepts helped Fromm understand the suicide of the family friend. As he put it, "When I became acquainted with Freud's theories, they seemed to be the answer to a puzzling and frightening experience" (Hausdorff, 1972, p. 16). Although he then continued his studies in sociology and received his Ph.D. from Heidelberg in 1922, his interest in psychoanalysis soon became paramount.

In 1925, Fromm went through instruction in psychoanalysis and later was analyzed by Hans Sachs. He never had any formal medical training, a fact that has led some of his critics to speculate that this "lack" in his education accounted for his "de-biologizing" the Freudian position (Hausdorff, 1972, p. 16). Fromm underwent still further psychoanalytic training in Berlin at the Psychoanalytic Institute in 1932. His teachers included some prominent Freudians—for example, Karl Abraham, Sandor Rado, Theodor Reik, and Franz Alexander—although he never met Freud himself (Hausdorff, 1972, pp. 20–21).

While increasing his knowledge of psychoanalysis, Fromm lectured at several institutes in Frankfurt and wrote papers utilizing both Marxist and Freudian ideas. It was at this point that he began to develop his theory of character formation. In 1931, Fromm wrote *The Development of the Dogma of Christ*, in which he adhered to the Freudian idea that religion is illusory, an infantile attempt to seek psychic gratification (Hausdorff, 1972, p. 22). He continued to publish papers compatible with orthodox psychoanalytic ideas throughout the 1930s.

In 1934, Fromm immigrated to the United States and became an American citizen. Several years later, he published the beginnings of his new theory in a popular book called *Escape from Freedom.* In it, Fromm discussed the ways in which modern society and ideologies mold the social character of the individual. In his view, men and women are primarily social beings who have been historically conditioned but who also have human needs that occur prior to the socialization process. We are born with certain potentialities whose development is fostered or hindered by the prevailing social order. Fromm believed Freud was correct in his contention that the family is the primary agent of society but wrong in his assumption that instincts govern the behavior of the individual. Likewise, Fromm thought that Marx's emphasis on the power of ideas in bringing about social change was incorrect. For Fromm, ideas "are answers to specific human needs prominent in a given social character" (Hausdorff, 1972, p. 36). In general terms, Fromm's analysis is truly sociopsychological in nature. It is an attempt to construct a theory in which the physiological and psychological needs of the individual and the needs and goals of society are mutually satisfied. His ideas about the development of social character are more precisely formulated in *Man for Himself* (1947). Most of the types he postulates bear a close resemblance to the Freudian character types, as we shall see. Numerous other books followed: *Psychoanalysis and Religion* (1950), *The Forgotten Language: An Introduction to the Understanding of Dreams, Fairy Tales, and Myths* (1951), *The Dogma of Christ* (1955), *The Sane Society* (1955), *The Art of Loving* (1956), *May Man Prevail?* (1961), *Sigmund Freud's Mission: An Analysis of His Personality and Influence* (1962), *The Heart of Man* (1964), *The Revolution of Hope* (1968), *The Crisis of Psychoanalysis* (1970), *Social Character in a Mexican Village* (with M. Maccoby) (1970), *The Anatomy of Human Destructiveness* (1973), and *To Have or to Be?* (1976).

Throughout his highly productive life, Fromm held important academic and clinical psychology positions. He lectured at Columbia University, Bennington College, Yale University, Michigan State University, New York University, and the National University in Mexico. He also held positions at the International Institute of Social Research in New York City, the American Institute of Psychoanalysis, the William Alanson White Institute of Psychiatry, and the Mexican Institute of Psychoanalysis.

After his retirement in 1965 as professor of psychiatry at the National University in Mexico, Fromm continued commuting between the United States and Mexico for many years to continue his teaching and consulting activities. Then, in 1976, Professor Fromm and his wife moved to Switzerland. He died in 1980 at his home in Muralto, Switzerland.

Basic Concepts and Principles

Human Beings, "Freaks" of Nature

For Fromm, the most powerful motivating force for men's and women's behavior stems from their attempts to find a reason for their existence. In his view, we are all animals with certain biological needs that must be satisfied—and yet, we are more than animals. We can be aware of ourselves and we can also use reason to solve our problems. In addition, we have the capacity to imagine and to create new and useful products. These abilities, according to Fromm, are both a blessing and a curse. Although our self-awareness and reason can be used to solve our problems, they also make us conscious of our limitations, including the fact that we must inevitably die (Fromm, 1947, p. 49). Each of us must deal with this problem, and we all resolve it in relatively constructive or destructive ways. Our reason makes us aware of other problems, including the fact that we cannot possibly realize all our potentialities in the time available to us. It also informs us that we can no longer be unified with nature like the other animals. It impels us to deal with our frailties and to engage in a painful struggle with life.

In Fromm's view, these capacities provide us with a fundamental choice. We can choose to lead healthy and productive lives by developing our potentialities, or we can choose to escape from our freedom by submitting ourselves to others or by trying to destroy them. Using our freedom to develop into productive citizens can be painful, but it is also genuinely satisfying. On the other hand, escaping from freedom by blind obedience to others produces temporary security, but in the long run it is counterproductive and stifles our basic nature. We need to relate productively to one another if we are to maintain our sanity.

Human Needs

Fromm argued that, because we are no longer one with nature, we all feel isolated and alone at times (Fromm, 1955b, p. 35). We are aware of our ignorance, our limitations, and the role of chance in our births and deaths. To remain in such a state would lead to insanity; we must unite ourselves with others if we are to survive. Thus, the **need for relatedness** is a direct outgrowth of our existential condition. This relatedness can be comparatively constructive or destructive in nature. We can achieve union by submission or by domination over others. In Fromm's view, both forms of relatedness are symbiotic and involve harmful dependencies. The passive form of symbiotic fusion is masochism (Fromm, 1956, p. 16). The person with masochistic tendencies feels alive only when he or she submits to the commands of others. It is almost as if the person says "You are everything: I am nothing." Perhaps you have known someone like this. Such a person tends to worship or adore others; the other is absolute perfection and can do no wrong. The masochistic individual feels alive primarily when he or she is being hurt by the other. Fromm also maintained that one can masochistically submit to fate, sickness, and to the orgiastic state produced by drugs. The active aspect of symbiotic relatedness is sadism. The sadistic person overcomes his aloneness, according to Fromm, by dominating and humiliating others. "I am everything and you are nothing" seems to be the battle cry (Fromm, 1956, p. 16).

Both these character types provide evidence of union without love. In contrast, Fromm believed that **mature love** is the embodiment of productive relatedness. He defined such love as "union under the condition of preserving one's integrity, one's individuality" (Fromm, 1956, p. 17). Its basic elements are "care, responsibility, respect and knowledge" (Fromm, 1956, p. 22). Mature love involves care and concern for the welfare of others. Although we often think of responsibility as a duty imposed by others, Fromm viewed it as the ability to respond voluntarily to the needs of others. Respect is also a term that sometimes has negative connotations, but Fromm used it in the root sense of an ability to see others as they are and to be concerned with their growth and unfolding. Finally, Fromm maintained that we cannot respect and love people if we do not know them (Fromm, 1956, p. 24). Such a criterion means that mature love requires considerable time and effort as well as a gradual, mutual self-disclosure.

In contrast, Fromm treated romantic love as pseudolove because of its immediacy and the fact that it requires no effort. Such "love" is based primarily on physical attractiveness and not on intimate knowledge of the "loved" one. Although there is intense commitment, the commitment is usually temporary. Fromm's definition of mature love suggests that we be leery of "instantaneous friendships" or situations in which we arrive at the simplistic conclusion that we truly love someone we have known only for six months. Mature love should be treated as an ideal goal to be sought instead of one presumptuously claimed. In a positive sense, Fromm's conception tells us that there is always something to be known about ourselves and the other person and that we can delight in the exploration of the mysteries of another.

Another aspect of the human condition is the **need for transcendence.** For Fromm, we overcome our passive natures by acting creatively. To act creatively, however, we must love ourselves as well as others. The negative side of transcendence is destruction. Fromm maintained that the impotent person—that is, the one who feels powerless and incapable of creation—can transcend the environment only by destroying it. People have within them the potential for happiness and the capacity for self-destruction (Fromm, 1955b, pp. 41–42).

The **need for rootedness** is also one of our basic needs. In discussing this aspect of our natures, Fromm built on Freud's treatment of the potentially incestuous ties between mothers and their children and on historical evidence of the relationships between individuals in patriarchal and matriarchal societies. Fromm maintained that our most fundamental relationship is with our mothers. As infants, we are physically helpless and completely dependent on them for the gratification of our needs. As he put it: "Mother is food; she is love; she is warmth; she is earth. To be loved by her means to be alive, to be rooted, to be home" (Fromm, 1955b, p. 43). It is therefore extremely difficult to separate ourselves from her so that, even as adults, we sometimes long for this former security. Fromm credited Freud with recognizing the importance of the relationship between mother and child in his formulation of the Oedipal conflict, but he said that Freud placed too much emphasis on its sexual roots and not enough on its irrational, affective origins. In brief, Fromm maintained that an intense and irrational dependency on the mother, which may or may not have sexual overtones, is a universal problem for people (Fromm, 1955b, pp. 45–46).

In continuing his discussion of rootedness, he examined the positive and negative features of the individual's historical behavior in matriarchal and patriarchal cultures. In cultures ruled by women, Fromm claimed there is a positive sense of equality and freedom. In his words, "the mother (in the generic sense) loves her children not because one is better than the other, not because one fulfills her expectations more than the other, but because they are her children, and in that quality they are all alike and have the same right to love and care" (Fromm, 1955b, p. 48). In the negative sense, a matriarchal structure implies an unanswering loyalty to blood and soil (mother earth), so that creative development is stifled. In patriarchal cultures, people look on male authority figures with fear and awe. Such relationships were and are negative because they encourage inequality and oppression. Positively, such cultures promote reason, individualism, and discipline. Fromm believed that loyalty to authority, when it places country above humanity, is destructive. In his judgment, a world of peace and understanding is possible only when we can experience rootedness in our brothers and sisters. In short, we must transcend boundaries that cripple us and keep us from experiencing solidarity with others (Fromm, 1955b, pp. 60–61).

People also have a **need for identity.** They have to be able to say to others "I am I" and not "I am as you desire me." Each of us has a degree of self-awareness and a knowledge about our capabilities. Fromm would maintain that we should value our abilities and use them productively. We should also avoid, at all costs, basing our identities on what others expect of us. Such identities are shaky and create problems. In Fromm's view, identity based on "herd conformity" is unfortunately widely present in our culture. We learn to accept uncritically the pronouncements of authority and to "buy" truth as others see it without engaging in our own thinking.

Finally, we all need a perspective on reality or, in Fromm's terms, a **frame of orientation and devotion,** if we are to live productively. Such orientations are necessary because we need to make sense of our many experiences. The frame of orientation develops gradually in early childhood to the point where we learn to use reason and imagination effectively in coping with our problems or to rely instead on rationalization to help us justify our behavior. Productive individuals utilize reason as well as feelings in their attempt at adaptation. In addition, Fromm maintained that we need an object of devotion and that the form and content of that object differ widely among peoples. Some use systems of animism and totemism; others worship monotheistically (Fromm, 1955b, p. 66). Devotion to a humanistic ethic, an ethic in which "there is nothing higher and nothing more dignified than human existence," is apparent in Fromm's orientation (Fromm, 1955b,

p. 23). For him, God is seen not in traditional terms but in the form of ideals such as love, truth, and justice that we all struggle to attain. Consequently, Fromm believed that "God is I, inasmuch as I am human" (Fromm, 1956, p. 59).

The Process of Personality Development

The Development of Character Orientations

In his formulations of the developmental process, Fromm discarded Freudian libido theory. Instead, he focused on the unique social and cultural conditions that affect the character development process and the satisfaction of our basic, existential needs. This process parallels Freud's position in some respects, as will become clear, but the etiological factors underlying it differ. It would be tempting to conclude that whereas Freud emphasized the biological determinants of personality, Fromm was concerned only with the cultural aspects. Such a conclusion would be incorrect for two reasons. First, Fromm did recognize individual differences in temperament; he argued that character, which is based on one's experiences, and temperament, which is constitutional, combine to affect behavior. Despite the lack of scientific evidence for the typology of temperaments developed in ancient Greece by Hippocrates, Fromm utilized it in his theorizing. For example, choleric individuals who are capable of mature love would tend to react very strongly and quickly when they love (Fromm, 1947, p. 60).

Second, and more important, Fromm argued that people have innate needs and potentialities that unfold in the course of development, provided social conditions are right. In particular, Fromm maintained that the norms of society are initially communicated to the child through the parents. The development of nonproductive orientations in children is the result of living with parents who are largely incapable of love. The acquisition of a productive orientation stems from experiences with loving parents. Although the following descriptions are presented as though they were ideal types, Fromm made it clear that people are typically blends of these orientations, although one type tends to predominate (Fromm, 1947, p. 69).

Nonproductive Orientations

Receptive Character Type. In Fromm's view, receptive character types are people who believe that the source of all good or satisfying events lies outside of themselves. A similar formulation is seen in Freud's description of the behavior of infants during the oral-receptive stage of development. Recall that neo-Freudian Karen Horney also described a similar character type in her discussion of individuals who attempt to adjust to feelings of basic anxiety by indiscriminately "moving toward people."

Receptive characters are always looking for a "magic helper." They need desperately to be loved, yet are incapable of truly loving anyone themselves. They are also highly dependent people. They are dependent not only on authorities for knowledge and help but on people in general for any kind of support. Most often, receptive characters are friendly, cheerful, and optimistic under many conditions. When subjected to threat, however, they become distraught and rely on others and not on their own intellectual resources for the solution to their problems (Fromm, 1947, pp. 70–71).

Exploitative Character Type. Exploitative characters are people who believe that the source of all satisfaction lies beyond themselves. They do not, however, wait passively to be gratified but instead they actively take whatever they want from others by force or cunning. A similar description is found in Freud's treatment of the oral-aggressive person and in Horney's description of the aggressive type. Such people, according to Horney, experience momentary satisfaction by "moving against people" (see Chapter 5).

moving against people

Fromm believed that individuals with an exploitative character relate to others symbiotically and that they themselves are not productive (Evans, 1966, p. 4). As a result, they rob and exploit others to attain their ends. Examples are the plagiarizer and the man who "steals" the affections of another's wife (Fromm, 1947, pp. 71–73).

Hoarding Character Type. Hoarding characters have little faith in the goodness of the outside world. Instead they "relate" to the world in a negative fashion, usually by withdrawing from others. People with hoarding orientations have characteristics similar to the ones attributed by Freud to the anal character. Horney's detached type, who tries to adjust by "moving away from people," also bears a close resemblance to Fromm's hoarding type (see Chapter 5).

moving away from people

Hoarding types are obstinate, orderly, and obsessed with cleanliness. Obstinacy is a logical reaction to any attempt by others to intrude into their private space. Orderliness signifies the attempt to keep the world in its proper place as a means of avoiding threats from the outside world. The outside world is also seen as dangerous and unclean so that hoarding types tend to try to annul the menacing contacts with it by compulsive washing (Fromm, 1947, pp. 73–75).

Necrophilous Character Type. In 1973, Fromm discussed the existence of another character type more closely related to Freud's anal character. In Fromm's view, necrophilia is the malignant form of the anal character (Fromm, 1973, p. 387). Whereas hoarding types show their destructiveness by withdrawal and passivity, necrophiles exhibit destructiveness by actively exploiting and destroying people and things.
Necrophilous characters are people who are attracted to and fascinated by all that is dead: corpses, decay, feces, dirt. They enjoy talking about

e.g., Ozzie Osborne, Alice Cooper — rock star

sickness, burials, and death. Moreover, they are truly enamored with force and power (Fromm, 1964, p. 38). They believe that the only way to solve a problem is through violence (Fromm, 1973, pp. 375–376). Severely necrophilous individuals are racial bigots, terrorists, warmongers, executioners, and torturers of innocent people. e.g. k k k ?

In Fromm's view, necrophiles also worship technology. They have used technology to create nuclear weapons and other instruments of death. In the name of progress, they have also continually created new things for us to use and consume and, in the process, have polluted the planet. Their approach to the world is intellectual and unfeeling. They have pushed us to the edge of destruction. What is needed, in his opinion, is reason, not mere intelligence. Reason combines intelligence and feeling and would help us to act constructively. It would turn us from the path of death and destruction (Fromm, 1973, pp. 380–398).

Marketing Character Type. Fromm's description of the marketing character represents a clean break with Freudian theorizing. He stated that this orientation has developed only recently in industrial societies. In such societies, people learn to treat themselves and others as commodities with a certain exchange value in a way that parallels the interchanges in the economic marketplace. In short, we all become buyers and sellers in an ever-fluctuating and uncertain "personality market." Appearance becomes the reality for us; substance becomes illusion. Commercials bombard us with messages about products that, if used, would make us more acceptable to others. Many of us go to considerable lengths to heed the current pronouncements. Films and popular magazines tell us how to dress and act if we are to be "successful." Business executives and other professionals have a definite image of how they should appear if they are to win promotions. Like professionals, college students also bow to such social pressures; they indiscriminately wear the "uniform of the day."

Finally, people with marketing orientations have little genuine interest in the welfare of other people. Others are treated as "objects" to be used for their own selfish purposes. As a consequence, marketing relationships are typically characterized by indifference.

The Productive Orientation

Biophilous Character Type. In Fromm's view, **biophilous characters** are people who love life and who want to mold and influence others by love, by reason, and by example, not by force and not by treating people in bureaucratic terms as though they were things (Fromm, 1964, p. 49). Biophiles have a productive attitude. Such an attitude encompasses their "mental, emotional and sensory responses to another, to [themselves], and to things"

(Fromm, 1947, p. 49). It involves the use of their powers and the maximum realization of inherent potentialities. Fromm believed that biophiles can use their powers only if they are free and independent of control by others. Under these conditions, they are able to use their reason and imagination to penetrate to the essence of their experiences. They are capable of mature love, of understanding another on an intelligent and emotional level.

A love of life is shaped by association with people who themselves love life, according to Fromm. Parents and others communicate to the child through gestures and tone of voice their feelings about life; they do not need to preach to the child that he or she ought to love life. Instead, they need only provide a warm, supportive, nonthreatening environment in which they act as ethical role models (Fromm, 1964, p. 55).

Research Evidence for the Theory of Character Types

Fromm and Maccoby (1970) found evidence confirming the theory of character types in an extensive field study using Mexican villagers as subjects. Through the use of questionnaires, projective testing, and interviews, they were able to show that the main types of social character postulated in Fromm's theory were present in the populace—the receptive, hoarding, and exploitative types. There were also some individuals who possessed a highly productive orientation. Furthermore, the investigators found, as Fromm's theory would predict, that receptive types were more likely than the other types to have intense mother-fixations and to depend on heavy drinking to deal with their stress. Over 80% of the 28 alcoholics in the village of nearly 500 people had a receptive orientation.

Fromm and Maccoby also found that exploitative characters were the village's first modern entrepreneurs, creating new capitalistic businesses that had the effect of destroying village traditions. Such character types also took advantage of the workers, most of whom were economically dependent on these entrepreneurs for survival.

The data also indicated that hoarding types were rebellious and destructive. This tendency toward destructiveness was consistent with Fromm's theory about the traits associated with necrophilia. Destructiveness was seen in sadistic treatment by necrophiles of members of their family. They often used either physical attacks, severe criticism, or isolation to punish their children for wrongdoing. The result was that initiative was deadened in the children.

Productive villagers possessed both democratic and traditional attitudes. For example, they expressed a traditional respect for authorities who had worked hard to help the villagers. They did not feel they were superior in any way to other community members. Instead, they were the people who most respected the rights and wishes of others. Productive people were also loving, caring parents who respected their children and did not use heavy physical punishment to discipline them.

Society and Human Productiveness

Although the character types postulated by Fromm are acquired initially through contact with parents, he also discussed the ways in which the nature and organization of society dramatically affect the development of individual potentialities. At the risk of oversimplification, Fromm argued that we live in a "sick" society in which indiscriminate competition and exploitation prevail and in which individuals feel powerless to correct the situation. In Fromm's view, a sick society tends to produce sick people, while a healthy one produces healthy people. Like Marx, he believed that work and mental health are intimately linked. In a sick or insane society such as ours, men and women tend to be alienated from their work. They are exploited by members of the ruling class—for example, entrepreneurs and powerful politicians—and treated like commodities. These "rulers" live by the sweat of the workers and treat them as inferiors. Such exploitation leads workers to feel intense resentment and hostility toward their "oppressors," with revolution as the outcome. For Marx, the goal of the workers should be personal liberation from such tyranny through violent revolution. Fromm appears to be much more of a moderate in this regard, calling instead for reform via the humanization of the means of production. Such reform will not be easy, in Fromm's opinion, because people are generally unaware of the forces that determine their behavior. Yet the task must be undertaken if we are ever to live in harmony with one another.

To understand the process by which society hinders our self-development, Fromm conducted a historical and Marxist analysis of capitalism. He noted that 19th-century capitalism was characterized by ruthless exploitation of the workers. It was considered virtuous to maximize profits at the workers' expense. The workers presumably had a choice—to work or not to work. In reality, of course, they had to work in order to survive, and so they accepted the wages offered by the boss. Not only were the wages low, but there was also little correlation between personal effort and pay, so there was little incentive to improve oneself. Exploitation also took other forms, including the abuses of child labor and the callous unwillingness of many owners to rectify unsafe working conditions. Capitalists then used their profits to seize new opportunities for expansion and to acquire property for production and consumption (Fromm, 1955b, pp. 86–87).

The result of such social and economic tyranny was the formation of exploitative and hoarding types among the elite—people who were "unimaginative, stingy, suspicious, pedantic, obsessional and possessive" (Fromm, 1955b, p. 87). The exploitative types were characterized by arrogance, conceit, exploitativeness, and egocentricity (Fromm, 1947, p. 120). Each type also had a positive side. For example, the positive aspects of the hoarding orientation included the need to be "practical, economical, careful, reserved, cautious, tenacious, imperturbable, orderly, methodical, and loyal" (Fromm, 1955b, p. 87). The positive features of the exploitative character included initiative, pride, and self-confidence (Fromm, 1947, p. 120).

Vestiges of the hoarding and exploitative types are found today, according to Fromm, but they are not the primary types. Instead, the 20th century is characterized by the emergence of the receptive, marketing, and necrophilous orientations. Capital and the means of production have come under the control of fewer and fewer companies. These companies have grown so large that management has been separated from ownership. We are also living in an era of big government. Bureaucracy reigns supreme under these conditions, and the result is increased **alienation** among the workers. The current emphasis, Fromm believed, is on efficiency and smooth operation. As a consequence, capitalism in our time seeks men and women with marketing orientations, people who mesh well with the organization. The bureaucratic mentality does not tolerate the risk-taker. Such people are perceived as troublemakers who need to be replaced by others who are more "adjusted." In brief, bureaucracy demands conformity from its personnel.

In addition, Fromm saw the necrophilous character as the product of the second half of this century. Such individuals have turned their interests away from life, people, nature, and ideas and have instead transformed life into things. Sexuality becomes a technical skill in which men and women often feel obligated to perform on cue and then judge their adequacy in terms of frequency of "performance" each week. Love and tenderness are directed toward machines and gadgets. We aspire to make the creation of robots one of our great achievements, robots who will be virtually indistinguishable from human beings. We are, in Fromm's judgment, beginning to sacrifice all life in the worship of "progress" (Fromm, 1973, p. 389).

Fromm also thought that the emphasis on bigness in institutions and in the media has led to a relative standardization of tastes and interests among the citizenry. We read the same papers, watch the same television programs and films, and listen to the same radio broadcasts. We are more concerned with consuming goods passively and with having entertainment spoon-fed to us than we are with actively participating in the process. More specifically, we rely in rather uncritical fashion on instant analyses of political events by news commentators instead of trying to do our own thinking about these issues. We also pay people large sums of money to entertain us so that we do not have to make the effort to create our own diversions. Many of us buy art for investment purposes and have not the slightest knowledge of aesthetics. In all these areas, and many more, the indiscriminate and passive incorporation of events has led to the formation of a receptive orientation. In the final analysis, then, these social conditions have produced people who are alienated from themselves and others. They are security-conscious to the point of dullness. Most of all, they feel powerless.

Humanistic Communitarian Socialism as the Solution to Alienation

How, then, do we satisfy our psychic needs and learn to substitute a productive orientation for a nonproductive one? According to Fromm, the answer lies in a drastic reordering of society and in an awakening on our part. It involves creating "an industrial organization in which *every working person would be an active and responsible participant, where work would be attractive and meaningful, where capital would not employ labor, but labor would employ capital*" (Fromm, 1955b, p. 248). Under such conditions, men and women would be productively related to one another. Fromm contended that, to ensure relatedness, workers should be organized into groups sufficiently small so that they can learn to know one another, even though there may be thousands of workers in the factory. In addition, the worker should be informed not only about the various aspects of his or her job but also about the various facets of the entire production process. The worker should know how the organization is related to the economic needs of the entire society. Most important, the worker must be given an active role in the decision-making process of the organization. Fromm pointed out that he was not advocating that workers own the means of production but that they participate in the formulation and review of company policy. His solution involves a blend of centralization and decentralization in which all individuals participate actively in the process—a **humanistic communitarian socialism.** Finally, the primary purpose of any organization, according to Fromm, is to "serve people and not make a profit" (Fromm, 1955b, p. 35).

In addition to massive changes in the area of work, Fromm urged the transformation of the political system. He noted that the voter today is alienated from politics; the whole situation is beyond comprehension. As Fromm put it: "[N]othing makes real sense or carries real meaning [to the citizen]. He reads of billions of dollars being spent, of millions of people being killed; figures, abstractions which are in no way a concrete, meaningful picture of the world" (Fromm, 1955b, p. 295).

To overcome this impersonal and unreal situation, we must recognize that the best decisions cannot be made via mass voting. Instead, we can make good decisions only in relatively small groups, much like the old town meetings (Fromm, 1955b, p. 296). The voters must also have the necessary information to make meaningful decisions. Above all, their decisions must be capable of influencing our leaders.

Finally, Fromm stated that society will also have to be changed on a cultural level. There must be an "opportunity for people to sing together, walk together, dance together, [and] admire together" (Fromm, 1955b, p. 303). There must also be a spiritual renewal. This renewal would involve an increased commitment to the aims of Judaism and Christianity that includes "the dignity of man as an aim and end in itself, of brotherly love, of reason and of the supremacy of spiritual over material values" (Fromm, 1955b, p. 304). A commitment to these ideals, whether one believes in a monotheistic God or not, would eventually lead to a sane society in which all people would be productively related.

Techniques of Assessment

In some respects, Fromm remained close to his Freudian roots in his attempts to assess personality functioning. Like Freud, he focused on the ways in which traumatic experiences in early childhood hinder personality development. He also agreed with Freud that the unconscious conflicts responsible for the patient's problems must be made known if he or she is ever to recover and that free association and dream analysis are useful tools for achieving that objective.

Yet Fromm went well beyond Freud in his assessment attempts. In addition to his use of psychological methods of inquiry, he also employed a historical method that emphasizes the role that political, religious, economic, sociological, and anthropological factors play in molding personality. It is this continued and systematic effort at utilizing a multilevel approach to the understanding of personality that makes Fromm and his **humanistic** ←focus **psychoanalysis** unique. The goal he sought is a theoretical construction of human nature through the observation and interpretation of actual behavior in a cross-cultural and historic context (Fromm, 1947, p. 33). In more concrete terms, he hoped to infer our basic natures by watching our behaviors in a variety of contexts.

Application of the Theory to the Treatment of Psychopathology

According to Fromm, the causes of pathology are primarily sociocultural in nature. On a microscopic level, they involve symbiotic relationships between parents and children. On a macroscopic level, they involve those economic and political forces within society that stifle personal growth. These diverse forces are largely responsible for the individual's inability to achieve a productive orientation. They create repressions of his or her needs for love and relatedness and generate, instead, brutal and exploitative strivings. The person comes to see others as threats to personal existence—that is, as obstacles to be overcome or removed. Under these conditions, the person is alienated from self and from others. Such persons do not understand the sources of the problems or that their behavior is at variance with their basic nature.

To achieve positive growth, these persons must be made aware of the many family and societal conditions that have stifled their development. In addition to self-awareness, they must actively change those life conditions responsible for the illness. They must change their values and the norms and ideals that block their growth (Fromm, 1955b, p. 240). Further, in Fromm's view, chances for positive growth depend not only on changes within the person and in his or her particular life circumstances but on more general changes within society. As mentioned earlier, a sane society, according to Fromm, produces sane people, and a society based on humanistic ethics is desperately needed. In such a society, qualities like greed, narcissism, and exploitativeness would be nonexistent, and people would live in harmony and cooperation (Fromm, 1955b, p. 242).

Critical Comments

We now evaluate Fromm's theory on the basis of our six criteria.

Comprehensiveness. Fromm created a comprehensive theory that attempts to show how biological and sociocultural forces mold our personalities. He focused on the conditions responsible for positive mental health as well as those that produce pathology, and in the process he discussed many different phenomena—for example, work performance, ethics, justice, cooperation and competition, self-love, power, and prestige.

Precision and Testability. Fromm's theory is dotted with imprecise terms—for example, "potentiality," "inner voice," and "love." Love is defined as "primarily giving, not receiving" (Fromm, 1956, p. 18). Fromm himself pointed out that this definition is ambiguous. He then attempted to clarify the meaning of the term and ended his arguments by declaring that "giving is more joyous than receiving, not because it is a deprivation but because in the act of giving lies the expression of my aliveness" (Fromm, 1956, p. 9). Even here the meaning is not very clear. Other definitions are equally confusing. Note, for example, his definition of conscience:

> *Conscience is thus a reaction of ourselves to ourselves. It is the voice of our true selves which summons us back to ourselves, to live productively, to develop fully and harmoniously—that is, to become what we potentially are.* [Fromm, 1947, p. 163]

Parsimony. Fromm's theory is not very parsimonious. It seems as though he was reluctant to abandon concepts of dubious value in helping us understand personality functioning. For example, he still utilized the typology of temperament proposed by Hippocrates many centuries ago (see Chapter 17). In addition, he continued to employ Freudian concepts in his discussions of the causes of nonproductive orientations when it is clear that he favored the use of sociocultural explanations. Are both sets of concepts necessary for the adequate explanation of individual behavior? Even if they are, the criticism may still be valid since Fromm also employed a set of existential concepts to explain the same behaviors.

Empirical Validity. There have been very few attempts to test Fromm's theory of character development. The interdisciplinary field study conducted by Fromm and his colleague, Michael Maccoby, however, was strongly supportive. There are also studies in the sociopsychological research literature that support Fromm's claims that workers are most satisfied with their work situations when they have actively and fully participated in decision-making related to their jobs. In addition, there is a considerable body of evidence showing that self-alienation is associated with other socially undesirable characteristics; for example, low self-esteem and high anxiety are directly associated with poor performance in a variety of situations.

Despite this empirical support, many of Fromm's major arguments about the dehumanizing influences of modern society on human experience and the ways in which society must be restructured to produce healthy, creative citizens are stated as metaphysical questions, so they cannot be empirically investigated (for example, may man prevail? to have or to be? where are we now and where are we headed?). Other arguments are stated so globally that they cannot be investigated empirically in their present form. They remain interesting, insightful speculations by a person who was clearly more of a social philosopher than a scientist. In general, then, empirical support for most of Fromm's theory is minimal.

Heuristic Value. The primary value of Fromm's theory is its ability to stimulate the thinking of others. It is a complex set of formulations that rests firmly on moral issues that are important to each of us and that Fromm correctly concluded must be grasped and understood if we are to live in a more harmonious relationship with one another.

Applied Value. Fromm's writings have been read by countless academicians and their students and by millions of lay people as well. It is difficult to assess whether they have had a positive impact on the lives of those readers, but editorial comment in the media has been generally favorable, and his readership has continued to increase. In personal terms, I and many of my students have found Fromm's writings highly provocative. They strike a responsive chord in us because they encourage us to aspire to the creation of a more humane society. Thus, Fromm's theorizing seems to have considerable applied value for many people.

Discussion Questions

1. In what ways are human beings "freaks" of nature? What are our fundamental existential concerns?
2. Do you believe that most people have a need to relate to others? If so, why do they?
3. What is meant by the "need for transcendence"? In what ways have you acted creatively?
4. Do you agree with Fromm that we must place love of humanity before love of country if we are to behave productively?
5. Have you ever engaged in "herd conformity"? What were the determinants and consequences of your actions?
6. List the nonproductive character orientations, as envisioned by Fromm, and describe the ways in which they are similar to the Freudian character types.
7. Is the marketing personality type obsolete in contemporary society?
8. Would you agree that the owners of big business are oppressing poor people? Can you muster arguments that show both the harmful and the beneficial results of the consolidation of power in the hands of a relatively few large corporations?
9. Do you feel that many people today can be characterized as receptive in their orientations? Do you and your friends take primarily an active or passive part in recreational activities?
10. Is Fromm's utopian dream of a humanistic communitarian socialist society possible or desirable?

REFERENCES

Evans, R. I. *Dialogue with Erich Fromm.* New York: Harper & Row, 1966.

Fromm, E. *Man for himself.* New York: Holt, Rinehart & Winston, 1947.

Fromm, E. *Psychoanalysis and religion.* New Haven: Yale University Press, 1950.

Fromm, E. *The forgotten language: An introduction to the understanding of dreams, fairy tales, and myths.* New York: Grove Press, 1951.

Fromm, E. *The dogma of Christ.* Garden City, N.Y.: Doubleday, 1955a.

Fromm, E. *The sane society.* New York: Holt, Rinehart & Winston, 1955b.

Fromm, E. *The art of loving.* New York: Harper & Row, 1956.

Fromm, E. *May man prevail?* Garden City, N.Y.: Doubleday, 1961.

Fromm, E. *Sigmund Freud's mission: An analysis of his personality and influence.* New York: Simon & Schuster, 1962.

Fromm, E. *The heart of man.* New York: Perennial Library, 1964.

Fromm, E. *The revolution of hope.* New York: Bantom Books, 1968.

Fromm, E. *The crisis of psychoanalysis.* Greenwich, Conn.: Faucett Books, 1970.

Fromm, E. *The anatomy of human destructiveness.* New York: Faucett Crest, 1973.

Fromm, E. *To have or to be?* New York: Harper & Row, 1976.

Fromm, E., & Maccoby, M. *Social character in a Mexican village.* Engelwood Cliffs, N.J.: Prentice-Hall, 1970.

Hausdorff, D. *Erich Fromm.* New York: Twayne, 1972.

Suggested Readings

Fromm, E. *Escape from freedom.* New York: Rinehart, 1941.

Fromm, E. *Man for himself.* New York: Holt, Rinehart & Winston, 1947.

Fromm, E. *The sane society.* New York: Holt, Rinehart & Winston, 1955.

Fromm, E. *The art of loving.* New York: Harper & Row, 1956.

Fromm, E. *The heart of man.* New York: Perennial Library, 1964.

Fromm, E. *The anatomy of human destructiveness.* New York: Faucett Crest, 1973.

Fromm, E. *To have or to be?* New York: Harper & Row, 1976.

Glossary

Alienation Feelings of powerlessness and aloneness experienced by individuals who have rejected traditional values of society and are incapable of instituting a social and political system compatible with their own values and principles.

Biophilous character Person oriented toward promoting life.

Frame of orientation and devotion Development of a consistent and meaningful set of values and principles that help individuals make sense of their worlds.

Humanistic communitarian socialism An ideal democratic society in which all individuals would have input into the decisions that affect their lives and be able to develop their potential to the fullest, without fear of exploitation.

Humanistic psychoanalysis Theoretical position advocated by Fromm that draws on Freudian principles to explain the conditions within early family life and within society that restrict or facilitate the healthy development of the individual.

Mature love An active concern for the well-being of the other person and the ability to give generously of oneself for the benefit of the other without expectation of return. It also involves a knowledge of the other and an acceptance of the other's weaknesses as well as strengths.

Necrophilous character Person attracted to death and destruction.

Need for identity Need on the part of a person to become aware of his or her own characteristics and capabilities.

Need for relatedness Basic human need to be in contact and share experiences with other people.

Need for rootedness Basic human need to feel that we have a place within society.

Need for transcendence Need on the part of the person to resolve conflicts by acting in a creative or destructive manner.

C H A P T E R   7

Erikson's Psychoanalytic Ego Psychology

Biographical Sketch

Erik Homburger Erikson was born in 1902 near Frankfurt, Germany. His parents were Danish. Erikson never knew his natural father because the man abandoned Erik and his mother before Erik was born. Although Erikson (1975, p. 27) maintained that his parents were legally married at the time of their separation, one prominent biographer thinks they were not and that Erik was probably an illegitimate child (Roazen, 1976, p. 96). In any event, soon after the abandonment, his mother left Denmark for Germany to be near friends and to await the birth of her child.

A few years after Erik's birth, she took him to a local Jewish pediatrician, Dr. Theodor Homburger, for treatment of a minor illness. The mother and doctor soon became friends, eventually fell in love, and were married. Erik was given his stepfather's name and taken to live in the doctor's home. To ensure that Erik would be comfortable in his new life, his mother and step-father decided not to tell him of his natural father's abandonment. Still, Erikson reported that he quickly developed an acute sense that something

was wrong: Although his mother and stepfather were Jewish, his own physical appearance was clearly Scandinavian; that is, he was tall and had blue
eyes and blond hair. Adding to his confusion about his identity was the fact
that he was called "goy" by members of his stepfather's temple, while he
was identified as a Jew by his classmates. Later, when he found out the truth
about his heritage, his identity crisis worsened. Although he kept his stepfather's surname until well into adulthood, he eventually took the surname
Erikson. The reason for his decision to change his surname remains obscure.
Perhaps it was because such a name—Erikson—is consistent with a Scandinavian heritage, and it thus served as a way to finally establish his identification with the Danish father who had abandoned him (Roazen, 1976, pp.
98–99).

His early life was apparently serene in most other respects. Erik went
to primary school from ages six to ten, then, until eighteen, he attended a
humanistic Gymnasium, an institution roughly equivalent to our high school.
Erikson did not, however, take well to the strict and formal academic atmosphere, and he was not a good student (Coles, 1970, p. 14). His aversion to
formal education continued throughout his life; he never attained a university degree.

Rejecting his stepfather's pleas for him to become a physician, Erikson
left home after graduation from the Gymnasium and wandered through
Europe, free of attempts by his family and friends to convince him to make
something of himself. During this moratorium, Erikson was besieged by
doubts concerning the choice of an occupation. After a year of wandering,
he returned home and enrolled in an art school. He stayed for approximately
a year, became restless again, and traveled to Munich, where he enrolled in
another art school. After two years in Munich he went to live in Florence,
Italy, a city he loved. While there, he gave up sketching completely and
simply wandered about the city, learning about its culture and history. It
should be noted that during this period he was not considered odd or "sick"
by his family or friends but rather simply as a wandering artist who was
engaged in a natural struggle to find himself (Coles, 1970, pp. 14–15).

After his stay in Florence, he returned home and at twenty-five prepared
to settle down to study and teach art for a living. At this point, however, fate
intervened. Erikson was asked by a former high school friend, Peter Blos, to
join him as a teacher at a small, experimental American nursery school in
Vienna. While at the school, Erikson met Anna Freud and her famous father,
Sigmund, and was introduced into their circle of friends. Miss Freud was
trying to convert a psychoanalytic interest in the childhood of adults into
a concern with understanding the dynamics of childhood itself (Coles, 1970).
Erikson shared her pioneering endeavor and was eventually trained by her
as a child analyst. Erikson was also fully accepted by the psychoanalytic
group surrounding Freud, but he was not sure that he wanted to earn his
living as a psychoanalyst. He still wanted to paint and draw. But as his
clinical experiences with children became more numerous, he began to

change his opinion. He saw the connection between psychoanalysis and art. For example, he reports that children's dreams and play involve important visual images that only later are translated into words in therapy (Coles, 1970, pp. 22–23). Moreover, Freud himself was becoming increasingly interested in the application of psychoanalysis to art, and this made a deep impression on Erikson (Coles, 1970, p. 24). Finally, Erikson began to think seriously about a career as an analyst because he had acquired a new set of responsibilities. At a party he had met a young woman of mixed Canadian and American background, Joan Serson, and promptly fell in love with her. A few months later they were married. Approximately four years after that he finished his training at the Vienna Psychoanalytic Society and was elected a member in 1933.

Later that year Erikson, his wife, and their two young sons immigrated to the United States and settled in Boston. He became the first child analyst in Massachusetts. He was given a position at both Harvard Medical School and Massachusetts General Hospital and became associated with the Harvard Psychological Clinic. The Harvard intellectual community had a tremendous influence on his thinking and his professional development. Especially noteworthy were anthropologists Margaret Mead, Gregory Bateson, Ruth Benedict, and Scudder Mekeel and psychologists Kurt Lewin, Henry Murray, and Lawrence Frank. In 1936, Erikson left Cambridge for New Haven. He accepted a position in the Yale University Institute of Human Relations. In 1938, his third child, Sue, was born. That same year, stimulated by his conversations with his anthropologist colleagues, Erikson left New Haven to observe the behavior of children of Sioux Indians living on the Pine Ridge Reservation in South Dakota.

In 1939, Erikson moved to California, where he continued his analytic work with children. He became affiliated with the Institute of Child Welfare at the University of California. In his work with children, Erikson devised "experimental play situations" designed to demonstrate the hopes and fears, struggles and defeats, and victories of growing children. He was seeking to understand the crucial events in the life process. During this period he also went north to observe the children of another Indian tribe, the Yurok. His anthropological work began to convince him that the members of these cultures were not "savages" or "sick" simply because they utilized rituals and ceremonies to express their underlying needs. It was just that their rituals and ceremonies differed from the ones used in our own culture. He also refused to label their behavior with such orthodox psychoanalytic terms as "neurotic" or to engage in fatalistic diagnoses such as calling the Yuroks an "anal" people as some analysts were prone to do. He rejected the idea that their unusual ritualistic behavior could be explained *only* by reference to unresolved conflicts surrounding toilet training during early childhood. Instead, he began to see that the Yurok and Sioux went through a series of developmental crises similar to the ones that people in our own society experienced and that successful resolution of these crises strengthened the members and moved them toward psychological health (Evans, 1967, p. 62). Thus Erikson's anthropological experiences caused him to recognize the limitations of Freud's theory of infantile sexuality and to replace it with a more general life-span theory of ego development that posited that the development of the person is marked by the unfolding of a series of stages that are universal to humankind.

In 1950, Erikson published *Childhood and Society*, a text that soon brought him international recognition as a leading spokesman of ego psychology. (A second edition of the book was published in 1963.) In it he presented the details of his theory of human development based on his many years of cross-cultural research and clinical experience. He convincingly showed how various developmental stages unfold and how the ego changes, grows, and synthesizes a myriad of experiences. He also expanded on Freud's theory of infantile sexuality by placing and analyzing its basic propositions within a broader historical and sociocultural context. In brief, in his classic text, Erikson for the first time integrates psychoanalysis with history and anthropology.

While the *Childhood and Society* manuscript was in press, Erikson, then on the faculty of the University of California, became involved in a political struggle with the California Board of Regents. The regents required that all faculty sign a loyalty oath swearing that they were not members of the Communist Party nor did they support any party or organization that advocated the violent overthrow of the government. This requirement was the outgrowth of public hysteria during the McCarthy years when fears about Communist conspiracies and rumored Communist attempts to overthrow the government gripped Americans. Erikson courageously refused to sign the oath. Instead, he resigned his university position and wrote an explanatory statement that was read to the members of the American Psychoanalytic Association. The letter read in part:

Dear Sirs:

I deeply appreciate the privilege of a free hearing before a committee of colleagues. With you I shall not play hide-and-seek regarding a question which must be implicit in what you wish to ask me and which must be explicit in what I shall have to say: I am not and have never been a Communist, inside "the party" or outside, in this country or abroad.

One may say, then, why not acquiesce in an empty gesture if it saves the faces of very important personages, helps to allay public hysteria, and hurts nobody? My answer is that of a psychologist. I do believe that this gesture, which now saves face for some important people, will, in the long run, hurt people who are much more important: the students. Too much has been said of academic freedom for the faculty; I am concerned about certain dangers to the spirit of the student body, dangers which may emanate from such "compromises" as we have been asked to accept.

For many students, their years of study represent their contact with thought and theory, their only contact with men who teach them how to see two sides of a question and yet to be decisive in their conclusions, how to understand and yet to act with conviction. Young people are rightfully suspicious and embarrassingly discerning. I do not believe they can remain unimpressed by the fact that the men who are to teach them to think and to act judiciously and spontaneously must undergo a political test; must sign a statement which implicitly questions the validity of their own oath of office; must abrogate "commitments" so undefined that they must forever suspect themselves and one another; and must confess to an "objective truth" which they know only too well is elusive. Older people like ourselves can laugh this off; in younger people, however—and especially in those more important students who are motivated to go into teaching—a dangerous rift may well occur between the "official truth" and those deep and often radical doubts which are the necessary condition for the development of thought.

I realize that the University of California is a big place with many purposes. In many departments the danger which I have outlined will not interfere with the finding and teaching of facts. Mine is a highly specialized place in an area of knowledge still considered rather marginal to true science. My field includes the study of "hysteria," private and public, in "personality" and "culture." It includes the study of the tremendous waste in human energy which proceeds from irrational fear and from irrational gestures which are part of what we call "history." I would find it difficult to ask my subject of investigation (people) and my students to work with me if I were to participate without protest in a vague, fearful, and somewhat vindictive gesture devised to ban an evil in some magic way—an evil which must be met with much more searching and concerted effort.

In this sense, I may say that my conscience did not not permit me to sign the contract after having sworn that I would do my job to the best of my ability. [Quoted in Coles, 1970, pp. 157–158]

In 1951, Erikson moved east once more and worked at the Austen-Riggs Center in Stockbridge, Massachusetts, an institute for psychoanalytic training and research. In 1958, he published a psychohistorical account of the life of theologian Martin Luther: *Young Man Luther: A Study in Psychoanalysis and History*. His work became increasingly popular among psychologists, historians, psychiatrists, anthropologists, philosophers, theologians, and biologists as well as among students, and he was invited to lecture in colleges and universities all over the world (Coles, 1970, p. 255).

In 1960, Erikson returned to Harvard, where he taught an extremely popular undergraduate course entitled "The Human Life Cycle." (Undergraduates irreverently dubbed it "From Womb to Tomb," according to Erikson.) Erikson remained at Harvard until his retirement in 1970. During his tenure at Harvard and in the years following his retirement, he continued to be highly productive. Among the noteworthy texts he wrote during this time we find *Insight and Responsibility* (1964), *Identity: Youth and Crisis* (1968b), and *Gandhi's Truth* (1969), a brilliant account of the life of India's nonviolent political leader, Mahatma Gandhi. This psychohistorical analysis earned Erikson the National Book Award and a Pulitzer Prize. He also published *In Search of Common Ground* (1973), *Dimensions of a New Identity: The 1973 Jefferson Lectures in the Humanities* (1974), *Life History and the Historical Moment* (1975), *Toys and Reasons: Stages in the Ritualization of Experience* (1977), and, most recently, *Identity and the Life Cycle: A Reissue* (1979). At present, Erikson is a visiting professor at the University of Pennsylvania, where he is working on a research project on applying his stage theory of development to rehabilitation in a geriatric population.

Basic Concepts and Principles

Ego Psychology: Liberalizing the Traditional Psychoanalytic Position

Erikson's position represents a systematic extension and liberalization of Freud's view of the role played by the ego in personality functioning. Freud saw the ego as a relatively weak agency that operated in the service of the powerful id. In his judgment, ego functioning was primarily concerned with satisfying the person's biological needs by seeking realistic outlets or by inhibiting the id's urges when suitable objects for impulse gratification were not available. In addition, the beleaguered ego was expected to seek suitable objects for impulse satisfaction without offending the moral prescriptions of a largely punitive superego.

In contrast to this traditional view of the ego as a set of defenses against strong inner drives, Erikson conceptualized the ego as often operating independently of id emotions and motivations. In his view, there are portions of ego functioning that are neither defensive in nature nor concerned with the control of biological urges. Instead, the ego often functions to help individuals adapt constructively to the challenges presented by their surroundings. This new perspective examines ego function in relation to society. It provides a more positive view of personality, seeing the ego as having organizing and synthesizing functions that help people resolve inner conflicts as well as the environmental difficulties. Within this elaborated framework, the ego is a powerful agency that typically operates to promote health. **Ego psychology** therefore involves examining, analyzing, and explaining personality functioning and change in a way that is radically different from the one offered by orthodox psychoanalysis. It emphasizes the integration of biological and psychosocial forces in the determination of personality functioning. Special attention is given to the unique interpersonal, cultural, and historical experiences present as people face a variety of developmental crises in the course of socialization. These experiences do not necessarily operate to restrict growth. Rather, each culture, in Erikson's view, has evolved unique ways of helping individuals resolve their crises so that their egos can be strengthened. Thus the focus in Erikson's psychology is on the emergence of a strong ego identity as individuals resolve crises inherent in the developmental process. This process operates according to the epigenetic principle.

The Epigenetic Principle

Like Freud, Erikson postulated that human development is characterized by a series of stages that are universal to humankind and unfold in a predetermined way. Unlike Freud, however, he placed much greater emphasis on the growth and positive functioning of the ego. He posited that ego development occurs throughout one's lifetime and not just in the early part of life. This process of development, according to Erikson, is governed by the **epigenetic principle**, which states that human growth has a ground plan and operates in stages that unfold in an invariant sequence. Erikson believed that at critical points in the maturational process, people everywhere have

> a readiness to be driven toward, to be aware of, and to interact with a widening
> social radius and . . . that society, in principle, tends to be so constituted as
> to meet and invite this succession of potentialities for interaction and attempts
> to safeguard and to encourage the proper rate and the proper sequence of
> their unfolding. [Erikson, 1963, p. 270]

Each stage, then, is marked by a particular psychosocial "crisis" that must be confronted. The word **crisis** is used by Erikson in a developmental sense to connote not a threat of catastrophe but a turning point, a crucial period in which a decisive turn one way or another is unavoidable (Erikson, 1964, pp. 138–139). Crises are moments of decision between progress or regression in development. Erikson optimistically thinks that the general tendency is toward resolving the crisis in order to move toward the establishment of a strong self-identity. He maintains that all "such developmental and normative crises differ from imposed, traumatic, and neurotic crises in that the very process of growth provides new energy even as society offers new and specific opportunities according to its dominant conception of the phases of life" (Erikson, 1968b, pp. 162–163). Although Erikson is optimistic that there is an inherent tendency toward successful resolution of the developmental crises, whether this is the actual result for individuals depends to a considerable degree on the quality of their psychosocial experiences. It also depends on their active attempts to analyze and integrate their experiences and to utilize their emerging abilities and skills. This last comment is particularly important because it implies that Erikson does not see people as passively buffeted around by outside forces. Rather, he sees people as actively attempting to deal with their experiences in a constructive, growth-promoting way—and often succeeding.

Positive resolutions of each crisis contribute to a progressive strengthening of the ego, whereas negative resolution results in its weakening. A positive resolution at one stage also increases the chances of resolving crises at other stages. Conversely, an inability to resolve a crisis at a given stage reduces the chances of successful adaptation during succeeding stages. The stages are therefore interrelated and dependent on one another (Erikson, 1963, p. 272). Each one builds on the ones that precede it.

In describing ego strength, Erikson uses the term **virtue.** In its original meaning, virtue meant "inherent strength or active quality," and Erikson uses the term in this sense. Virtues are human qualities or strengths that are the outgrowth of successful resolution of conflicts associated with the various developmental stages (Erikson, 1964, p. 113). In his view, each stage provides the opportunity for the establishment of a unique strength or virtue. The establishment of each of these virtues, however, is not to be seen as a final achievement accomplished once and for all at a given stage. It also does not mean that the establishment of a virtue makes the individual impervious to new conflicts later in the developmental process (Erikson, 1963, pp. 273–274). The resolutions to conflicts are not completely positive or negative either, in Erikson's view (Evans, 1967, p. 15). Rather, each conflict resolution carries with it both positive and negative learning about events and people. Positive crisis resolution occurs when the ratio of positive to negative learning is weighted in favor of the positive.

Let us now examine in more detail Erikson's theory of ego development and how individuals attempt to cope with and resolve their conflicts at each stage.

The Process of Personality Development

Ego Development Theory

Erikson postulates the existence of eight stages of ego development. The first four are closely wedded to Freud's oral, anal, phallic, and latency stages, although Erikson places less emphasis on the sexual causes of conflicts in these stages than does Freud. Instead, he chooses to discuss them primarily in terms of the individual's social experiences. The remaining four stages show little reliance on Freud's theorizing. Table 7.1 presents a schema of the various stages.

1. Oral-Sensory Stage: Basic Trust versus Mistrust. The first stage corresponds closely to Freud's oral stage and occurs during the first year of life. Pleasurable sensations center on the mouth, and the focal activity is feeding. The infant lives and "loves" through its mouth. The mother is the one who typically ministers to the infant's needs, and healthy development

Table 7.1
The Eight Stages of Ego Development

Stage	Age (Estimated)	Ego Crisis	Ego Strength
1. Oral-Sensory	birth–1	Basic Trust versus Mistrust	Hope
2. Muscular-Anal	2–3	Autonomy versus Shame and Doubt	Will
3. Locomotor-Genital	4–5	Initiative versus Guilt	Purpose
4. Latency	6–12	Industry versus Inferiority	Competence
5. Adolescence	13–19	Identity versus Role Confusion	Fidelity
6. Young Adulthood	20–24	Intimacy versus Isolation	Love
7. Middle Adulthood	25–64	Generativity versus Stagnation	Care
8. Late Adulthood	65–death	Ego Integrity versus Despair	Wisdom

Adapted from *Childhood and Society* by Erik H. Erikson, with the permission of W. W. Norton & Company, Inc. Copyright 1950, © 1963 by W. W. Norton & Company, Inc.

in the infant depends on the quality of her care. The mother's attitude toward her child-care function is shaped by the society in which she lives. If the society downgrades the status of motherhood, the result will likely be a caretaker who resents her role. If society, in contrast, praises and extols the virtues of motherhood, her attitude is apt to be healthy and constructive.

In Erikson's view, if the mother acts in a loving and consistent way, the infant is likely to develop a sense of **basic trust**. The infant's first social achievement, according to Erikson, is its eventual willingness to let the mother out of its sight without becoming unduly anxious, because it has an inner certainty that she will return to feed and care for it. Such certainty provides the rudiments of an ego identity because it depends on the infant's recognition that people are dependable (Erikson, 1963, p. 247). The basic trust that develops between mother and child is not totally one-sided, though. It is truly an interpersonal experience, for the infant also begins to act in a trustworthy way. As it develops teeth, it is driven to bite. It must, however, learn not to engage in this behavior, lest the mother withdraw in anger and pain. If it learns properly, the mother will come to trust her infant and both parties can engage in a relaxed and mutually gratifying set of experiences.

In contrast, a sense of **basic mistrust** is created if the mother has a poor attitude and therefore acts in an unreliable, aloof, and rejecting way. The mother's lack of dependability and care is likely to frustrate, anger, and enrage the infant, leading it to be more demanding and unpredictable. The feeling of being deprived also leaves a residue of mistrust that continues to have effects later on in the developmental process.

If the interpersonal experiences with the mother are generally more positive than negative, the child develops an attitude toward others that is more trusting than mistrusting. The healthy person is not one who is completely trusting, however. In principle, such a person would be too naive, gullible, and easily hurt by others. A certain amount of mistrust is healthy. There are people who are dangerous, so precautions must be taken to ensure survival.

Finally, if the resolution in this stage is a positive one—that is, more trust than mistrust emerges—the outcome is a sense of confidence and **hope**. It is clear that this sense of hope can be dashed later if new pressures or conflicts arise. Conversely, the beginnings of hope established during the first stage of life can also be strengthened substantially by subsequent, positive experience. Society, in Erikson's judgment, provides an opportunity for the perpetuation and strengthening of trust through its religious institutions. Trust, in his view, becomes the capacity for faith. Unlike Freud, who viewed the religious beliefs of people as unhealthy delusions that prevent them from dealing constructively with reality, Erikson has a much more positive outlook. For him religious institutions succeed in "giving concerted expression to adult man's need to provide the young and the weak with a world-image sustaining hope" (Erikson, 1964, p. 153). Erikson's view of organized religion, however, is not entirely positive. He does recognize that all too often the church has exploited, for its own self-aggrandizement, the most infantile strivings in human beings (Erikson, 1964, p. 153).

2. Muscular-Anal Stage: Autonomy versus Shame and Doubt. The second stage is closely related to Freud's anal stage and occurs during the second and third years of life. During this period, the child's muscles begin to mature and he or she starts to learn how to exercise control over them. This is the period during which toilet training occurs in our society. Youngsters must learn to control their anal sphincter muscles so that elimination of waste materials can be accomplished in a manner deemed appropriate by society. Erikson points out that intense conflicts do not arise in all societies over whether to "hold on" or "let go." In many agrarian cultures, for example, parents ignore anal behavior and leave it to older children to take toddlers out to the bushes to perform the elimination function. The toddlers learn by imitating the behavior of the older children. In our society, however, the scene is set for intense conflict, according to Erikson, because we have as our ideal the always clean, punctual, and deodorized body (Erikson, 1968b, pp. 107–108). Thus children must be trained to obey, and this leads to a power struggle between parents and children and to a conflict of wills. Ironically, just as children have learned to trust their parents and the world, they must now learn how to assert their independence. They must become self-willed and take chances with their trust in order to establish what they can do by themselves (Evans, 1967, p. 19).

A sense of **autonomy** and self-control is engendered if parents guide their children's behavior gradually and firmly. When this is predominantly the treatment, children experience an increased sense of pride in their accomplishments and good feelings toward others. The virtue of **will** emerges, defined as "the unbroken determination to exercise free choice as well as self-restraint." (Erikson, 1964, p. 119). It is the gradual increase in the power to exercise judgment and decision.

On the other hand, if parents are either too permissive or too harsh and demanding, children experience a sense of defeat that can lead to **shame and doubt**—deep shame and a compulsive doubt concerning their ability to make effective judgments and to exercise control over their lives. One result may be the neurotic attempt to regain control by compulsive action (Erikson, 1963, p. 252).

Individuals who develop a sense of control over their lives tend later to support our legal institutions to the extent that they are equitable in the administration of the law. They see that only through adherence to the law can they and others preserve their own freedom, independence, and sense of rightful dignity (Erikson, 1963, p. 254).

3. Locomotor-Genital Stage: Initiative versus Guilt. The third stage occurs from ages 4 through 5 and bears some resemblance to Freud's phallic stage. If the resolution of conflict in the previous stage has been successful, children feel that they are now individuals in their own right. During the third stage, then, their **initiative** is sparked, and they must find out what kind of people they may become (Erikson, 1968b, p. 115). Children thus become curious about their parents, their friends, and their surroundings. Their developing bodies allow them to move about more freely. They independently seek out more contact with others beyond the family circle. They engage in play and other experimental activities with their peers. Their language becomes refined, and they ask incessant questions about innumerable things. Their imaginations are very active, and they fantasize about being adults. There is also a great deal of playacting as children start trying out a variety of adult roles (Erikson, 1968b, p. 115).

Children during this stage are intrusive. Besides exploring their environments and trying out new roles, Erikson believes, like Freud, that they show an overconcern with sexual matters. Children attempt (largely in fantasy form) to possess the parent of the opposite sex, with an accompanying feeling of rivalry toward the parent of the same sex. If children are severely punished by the parents for these "advances," they develop a sense of **guilt.** If, on the other hand, the parents are understanding and guide the children's motives and desires into socially acceptable activities, the result is the development of a sense of **purpose.** This virtue involves setting major life goals. It involves "thinking big" and identifying with parents.

Play activities greatly affect the development of these goals. Children playact being mothers or fathers and achieving success as doctors, nurses, lawyers, judges, dentists, and so forth. The kind of play activities and fantasies engaged in differ for the sexes, according to Erikson, and are, in part, the result of biology. He found, for example, that boys and girls differed in the kinds of constructions they made when playing at building. Boys tended, in using toys, to build high towers and large buildings and to use animals, human figures, and cars in their construction. Girls, in contrast, rarely built towers. When they did, they made the towers lean against the background. Girls usually made simple enclosures with low walls and tended to build houses. According to Erikson, children's toy constructions closely paralleled the morphology of their sex organs. In males, the penis, being erectable and intrusive in character, is represented by high buildings and towers that "stand out" in comparison to other objects in a setting. In females, the vagina is represented by static house interiors and low enclosures. Erikson believes further that the boys' tendency to picture upward movement (high towers) and mobility (fast cars) could be the expression of their need to prove themselves strong and aggressive and to achieve "high standing." The girls' representations of house interiors, in contrast, could reflect their need to concentrate on the anticipated task of taking care of a home and rearing children (Erikson, 1963, pp. 97–107).

As you might suspect, these statements did not endear Erikson to feminists (see, for instance, Weisstein, 1975). They thought he was claiming that "anatomy is destiny." In their opinion, this view, if accepted, would then result in the restriction of opportunities for women and keep them in a subservient position. They also maintained that the differences between the sexes could be better explained as being the result of cultural conditioning rather than as an expression of genetic endowment.

Erikson responded to this criticism by saying he had been misunderstood and quoted selectively by feminists. He reports that in his original article he did not say that *only* anatomy is destiny. What he did say, in fact, was that anatomy was *only one* determinant of our behavior. His words were as follows:

> *Am I saying, then, that "anatomy is destiny"? Yes, it is destiny, insofar as it determines not only the range and configuration of physiological functioning and its limitation but also, to an extent, personality configurations. The basic modalities of woman's commitment and involvement naturally also reflect the ground plan of her body . . . [but] . . . a human being, in addition to having a body, is somebody, which means an indivisible personality and a defined member of a group. . . . In other words: anatomy, history, and personality are our combined destiny. [Erikson, 1968b, p. 285]*

Assumption

In Erikson's view, society, culture, and biology jointly determine our behavior. He thinks the feminists have oversimplified his position. In his opinion, our bodies predispose us to certain activities, but this does not necessarily mean we must perform only these activities and no others. For example, women's bodies are built for childbearing and nursing. Yet, the historical period and society in which we live may not actively encourage women to develop along these lines. Instead society may encourage women to develop their other capacities by entering careers and performing jobs that are traditionally considered masculine. Erikson would welcome this breaking down of cultural stereotypes. (The same argument would apply for men entering "women's occupations.") At the same time, however, he would maintain that, owing to their biology, women still have maternal feelings, desires, and unique capabilities that, if repressed because of societal pressures, could restrict their personal growth. In his opinion, feminists have placed too much emphasis on the cultural and social determinants of behavior and, in their zeal to lift the oppression of women, have denied the positive aspects of their bodies and the fact that they alone can contribute to society by being mothers and teachers of the very young (Erikson, 1975, pp. 225–247).

4. *Latency Stage: Industry versus Inferiority.* The fourth stage loosely parallels Freud's latency period and occurs from ages 6 to 12. There is a lull in sexual desires and feelings. In the meantime, children turn from the home to school life, whether school is classroom or jungle or field (Erikson, 1963, p. 258). It is a period of learning new skills and of making things. Children develop a sense of **industry,** which means they are industrious and busy learning how to complete jobs (Evans, 1967, p. 28). Teachers become important in their lives during this time. They prepare children for the future and for careers by teaching them things that make them literate. They introduce children to the technology of the culture. The danger in this period is that children may fail to develop the virtue of **competence**. They may fail to learn to do new things and thus may feel **inferior**. Failure to learn may be caused by an insufficient resolution of the conflicts in the preceding stage. Children may, for instance, still want their mothers more than knowledge. They may still compare themselves to their bigger and more skilled fathers and thereby suffer acute feelings of inadequacy. In Erikson's view, parents can help to minimize these feelings by gradually preparing children for the rigors of the school environment and by encouraging them to trust their prospective mentors. Erikson believes that a positive identification with their teachers is necessary if children are to develop a strong ego. Teachers who know how to emphasize what children can do and who are trustworthy and encouraging are needed (Erikson, 1968b, p. 125). The positive outcome of such sensitive treatment is the emergence of a sense of competence, which provides children with a healthy preparation for their roles as workers in later life.

5. *Adolescence: Identity versus Role Confusion.* The fifth state of development occurs from the ages 13 through 19. Individuals who have ade-

quately resolved the conflicts inherent in the prior stages bring into adolescence a growing sense of self-identity. Their mothers and fathers see them as trustworthy and are trusted in return. The parents make their child feel he or she is *somebody*. The parents have given the child a name and have reacted with consistency and love. Young people know that they are an integral part of the family, and yet, they also have a budding sense of independence and personal efficacy. They recognize their own competence, can take initiative, and are able to see tasks through to completion. Therefore adolescence is entered into with a variety of loosely related segments of identity based on experiences in the earlier stages. Mixed in with the individual's sense of positive identity is a negative identity, according to Erikson. It consists of all the things the individual has done for which he or she has been punished and therefore feels guilty or ashamed. It also consists of feelings of incompetence and inadequacy based on past failures (Evans, 1967, pp. 35–36).

During adolescence these prior identifications are questioned and then restructured by an ego that is concerned with integrating these identifications with strong, emerging sexual feelings and the social roles that are available to the individual. As Erikson puts it,

> The integration now taking place in the form of ego identity is . . . more than the sum of the childhood identifications. It is the accrued experience of the ego's ability to integrate all identifications with the vicissitudes of the libido and with the opportunities offered in social roles. The sense of ego identity, then, is the accrued confidence that the inner sameness and continuity prepared in the past are matched by the sameness and continuity of one's meaning for others, as evidenced in the tangible promise of a "career." [Erikson, 1963, pp. 261–262]

We can see from the preceding discussion that **identity** is a multifaceted concept. At base, however, it refers to a conscious sense of direction and uniqueness derived from a mélange of psychosocial experiences that are integrated by the ego. That is, identity involves an integration by the ego of all our previous identifications learned as a participant in a variety of groups (for instance, family, church, school, peers) and all our self-images (Evans, 1967, p. 36). It involves the sense that we have made an adequate heterosexual choice and have found a suitable partner to love. It also encompasses our connection with the future when we opt for specific careers and become recognized as responsible members of society by others. A large part of our identity rests on what we do for a living, on the support we receive from society, and on our internalization of the ideals of our class, our nation, and our culture (Erikson, 1964, p. 93). Identity consists, therefore, of the things we are and the things we want to become and are supposed to become. It also consists of the "things which we do not want to be or which we know we are not supposed to be" (Evans, 1967, p. 32).

Identity is not, however, achieved once and for all during adolescence. Instead, adolescence is the period during which an **identity crisis** is normative. It is a **moratorium** between childhood and adulthood in which individuals attempt to solve special problems. If these problems are not resolved satisfactorily, a frantic search for identity could be started anew, even in old age.

In Erikson's judgment, the identity crises experienced by youths stem from **role confusion** concerning who they are and what they will become. For many youths, adolescence is a period of torturous self-consciousness characterized by awakening sexual drives and rapid growth of the body, by doubts and shame over what they are already sure they are and what they might become.

The most disturbing part of life during this period, according to Erikson, is youths' inability to decide on an occupational identity. Although they have a strong need to commit themselves to a set of goals and principles that would give direction and meaning to their lives, many of them find it extremely difficult to make satisfactory choices.

Erikson maintains that in such an unsettled period, confused youths try to establish their identities by overidentifying with an assortment of heroes. They also become very defensive in a variety of ways:

> To keep themselves together, they temporarily overidentify . . . with the heroes of cliques and crowds. On the other hand, they become remarkably clannish, intolerant, and cruel in their exclusion of others who are "different," in skin color, cultural background . . . and often in entirely petty aspects of dress and gesture arbitrarily selected as the sign of an in-grouper or out-grouper. It is important to understand . . . such intolerance as the necessary defense against a sense of identity diffusion, which is unavoidable at a time of life when the body changes its proportions radically . . . and when life lies before one with a variety of conflicting possibilities and choices. Adolescents temporarily help one another through such discomfort by forming cliques and by stereotyping themselves, their ideals, and their enemies. . . . It is difficult to be tolerant if deep down you are not quite sure that you are a man (or a woman), that you will ever grow together again and be attractive, that you will be able to master your drives, that you really know who you are, that you know what you want to be . . . and that you will know how to make the right decision without, once [and] for all, committing yourself to the wrong friend, sexual partner, leaders, or career. [Erikson, 1968a, p. 200]

The behavior of many young people, according to Erikson, is therefore characterized by **totalism**—setting absolute boundaries to one's values and beliefs and interpersonal relationships (Erikson, 1964, p. 92). Simplistic ideologies are embraced and followed with little questioning. For example, many youths accept the values mouthed by "heroes" in the drug culture, by delinquent gangs and fanatic religious cults, and by political groups because these seem to provide answers to difficult and threatening problems. Erikson cautions us, however, from simply labeling such behavior as pathological. Instead, he maintains that we should try to understand it as an alternative way of dealing with experience. Although such behavior has destructive outcomes that cannot be condoned, it also has survival value for many young people (Erikson, 1964, p. 93). Erikson's view of young people and their development is generally optimistic. He thinks that some of their confusion and failure to act constructively is not their fault but rather the result of rapid political, cultural, and technological changes that have led to the questioning of established values that no longer seem to work. It can also be traced to a generation of adults, some of whom are unclear about their own values and cannot, therefore, provide proper guidance. Lastly, some adults precipitate protest in young people because these adults behave in corrupt and evil ways and are not worthy of emulation. Erikson also stresses that adults need young people as much as young people need adults. Young people are the caretakers of the future. Through their protests, they also force the older generation to restructure its own value system.

The successful resolution of the crisis of adolescence leads to the emergence of a sense of fidelity. **Fidelity,** in Erikson's opinion, is "the ability to sustain loyalties freely pledged in spite of the inevitable contradictions of value systems" (Erikson, 1964, p. 125). Young people select friends, mates, and co-workers and commit themselves to these people. Young people develop a loyalty to a vision of the future and move to meet it (Erikson, 1975, p. 209). They are ready to take their place in a technological society not just as guardians of traditions and customs but as rejuvenators and innovators of the culture. Youths who have not adequately resolved their conflicts unfortunately develop **negative identities** in which they act in scornful and hostile ways toward roles offered as proper and desirable by the community (Erikson, 1968b, pp. 172–173). Their loyalties are to groups, people, and ideologies that are destructive to themselves and to society.

6. *Young Adulthood: Intimacy versus Isolation.* The sixth stage spans the ages of 20 to 24. Healthy young adults have established a stable self-identity during adolescence that makes it possible for them now to enter into intimate relationships with others. They are eager and ready to fuse their identity with others. An effort is made to commit themselves to partnerships, and there is the strength to abide by such commitments even though they call for significant compromises and sacrifices (Erikson, 1963, p. 263).

Erikson points out that the establishment of intimate relationships is not to be confused with the "intimacies" involved in sexual intercourse (Roazen, 1976, p. 103). Intimate relationships involve something more than sexual closeness. Erikson thinks that a truly intimate relationship is possible only between partners who have clearly established identities and loyalties. Because adolescents are still struggling to establish their identities, it follows that they cannot love (be intimate) in the truest sense. Erikson sees adolescents as engaged in passionate infatuations with each other that can result in "intimacies" (sexual closeness), but it is only young adults who are capable of loving—in other words, establishing intimate relationships with other persons. Mature love, for the young adult, involves "mutuality of mates and partners in a shared identity, for the mutual verification through an experience of finding oneself, as one loses oneself, in another" (Erikson, 1964, p. 128).

Healthy intimate relationships are beneficial to both the person and society. According to Erikson, such relationships meet the following standards. There is a

1. *mutuality or orgasm*
2. *with a loved partner*
3. *of the opposite sex*
4. *with whom one is able and willing to share a mutual trust*
5. *and with whom one is able and willing to regulate the cycles of*
   a. *work*
   b. *procreation*
   c. *recreation*
6. *so as to secure to the offspring, too, all the stages of a satisfactory development. [Erikson, 1963, p. 266]*

Young adults who cannot develop a capacity for **intimacy** and productive work, in Erikson's opinion, experience a sense of **isolation**—the inability to take chances with one's identity by sharing true intimacy (Erikson, 1968b, p. 137). Such individuals unfortunately are self-absorbed and engage in interpersonal relationships on a very superficial level.

If young adults develop their capacity for intimacy more than for isolation, however, the result is the emergence of the virtue of **love.**

7. Middle Adulthood: Generativity versus Stagnation. The seventh stage spans the middle years from ages 25 to 64. Healthy adults have a strong ego identity, have established mature relationships with others, and have followed a career. Their primary responsibility, in Erikson's judgment, is to establish and guide the next generation. **Generativity** encompasses not only the production of children and the guidance of the younger generation but also the creation of ideas, art, products, and so forth (Evans, 1967, p. 51). The crisis centers on the question of whether adults are going to be productive or whether they are going to stagnate. **Stagnation** involves a lack of productivity, boredom, and interpersonal impoverishment (Erikson, 1968b, p. 138). If the capacity of adults for generativity exceeds their sense of stagnation, the virtue of **care** emerges. The older generation is thus concerned with helping the younger generation develop in constructive ways. Although it is clear that generativity includes having children as a means of ensuring the survival of society, Erikson stresses that people can be generative even if they are childless. Such individuals can help ensure the higher development of society by contributing to its members through productive work and through active demonstration of concern with the betterment of young people.

8. Late Adulthood: Ego Integrity versus Despair. The final stage lasts from age 65 to death. Healthy people are those who have adapted to the triumphs and disappointments of their lives, who have been the originators of others, and/or the generators of products and ideas. They are able to look back at their lives and conclude that they were special and had meaning. They are also able to accept the inevitability of death as a necessary part of the life cycle and not fear it. In brief, elderly people who are functioning well see a unity and meaning in their lives. They have **ego integrity.**

In contrast, individuals who have not been able to accept some of the inevitable failures in their lives and who have led selfish, uncaring lives experience **despair** because they realize life is now short and there is no time to start a new life or try out new paths to integrity (Erikson, 1963, p. 269).

Finally, the virtue of **wisdom** is associated with a meaningful old age. According to Erikson, "wisdom is detached concern with life itself in the face of death itself" (Erikson, 1964, p. 133). It conveys the integrity of experience despite a decline in bodily and mental functioning. It allows the person to envisage human problems in their entirety and to communicate to the younger generation a constructive living example of the ending period of the life of a unique human being (Erikson, 1964, pp. 133–134).

Research Support for the Theory of Ego Development

Erikson's complicated theorizing about ego development has not lent itself readily to empirical verification because his hypotheses are often not stated clearly. Validation of much of his theorizing also requires extensive longitudinal studies to gauge changes in development as people proceed through the life cycle. Such research is costly and difficult. Consequently, there has been relatively little research to date that aims at verifying Erikson's elaborate explanations of the ways in which the eight stages of development operate, interlock, and influence one another. In addition, empirical verification of the theory is difficult because many of the constructs Erikson uses are highly abstract and difficult to measure adequately. One notable exception is in the area of the identity crisis in adolescence, where acceptable measures of various aspects of ego identity have been constructed and where important research based on extensions and crystallizations of Erikson's theorizing have occurred.

Refinements in Erikson's Theorizing about Ego Identity. Marcia (1966) has maintained that four distinct positions, or statuses, are implicit in Erikson's writings about identity development in adolescence. They are (1) identity diffusion, (2) foreclosure, (3) moratorium, and (4) identity achievement. These statuses are defined in terms of two dimensions: crisis and commitment. As mentioned earlier, crisis refers to an active period of struggle that individuals experience as they try to resolve questions of career choice and a set of values or principles to follow. Commitment involves making firm decisions in these areas and then pursuing goals consistent with the decisions. **Identity diffusion** individuals are people who lack firm commitments and are not actively in crisis. They may never have experienced crisis, or they may have experienced a period of struggle in the past and been unable to resolve it by making a decision. **Foreclosure** individuals have never experienced a crisis but have nevertheless made firm commitments to certain goals, beliefs, and values. A good example is the college freshman who is uncritically following her parents' wishes and pursuing a degree in medicine without examining whether this goal is actually the best one for her in terms of her needs and abilities. **Moratorium** individuals are those who are currently in a state of crisis and are actively considering alternatives in an attempt to arrive at a decision. Finally, **identity achievement** people are those who have undergone a period of crisis and, as a consequence, have developed firm commitments.

In addition to clarifying and making explicit Erikson's theorizing about the four phases of ego identity development in adolescence, Marcia (1966) has created an elaborate interview procedure to measure them. The availability of this instrument has allowed investigators to identify the interpersonal relationships of individuals occupying particular identity statuses and also to assess some of the major implications that location in a particular status has for personality functioning and performance. It has also spurred the construction of several other less complicated, yet useful, measures of the ego identity construct (Bourne, 1978; Rosenthal, Gurney, & Moore, 1981).

Research on the Four Identity Statuses. Several investigations have examined the nature of differences in family relationships and parenting styles of individuals occupying each of the identity statuses. In general, this research shows that foreclosures have the closest relationships with their parents: they rate their parents most favorably and strongly endorse parental authority and values. These individuals do not actively explore alternatives, and they have low ego identity. In contrast, identity diffusers report the most distance between themselves and their parents, whom they perceive as indifferent and rejecting. These adolescents feel ambivalent about their parents, owing to differences in opinion concerning the goals and values thought worthy and appropriate for pursuit by teenagers. In times of crisis, these young people are unlikely to turn to their parents for support and advice. Once the crises have been resolved and identity achieved, however, the establishment of warmer relationships may be possible (Waterman, 1982, pp. 351–352).

In much of the research on identity status, there is an assumption that a progressive strengthening in the sense of identity occurs during adolescence and into adulthood. Marcia (1966) maintained that this progressive strengthening proceeds from low to high ego maturity, as follows: diffusion, foreclosure, moratorium, and identity achievement. Within this global perspective, however, different people follow different sequential patterns. For example, sometimes one person in the moratorium phase moves progressively toward attainment of identity achievement, while another person may move regressively from moratorium status to ego diffusion. Or, alternately, an adolescent in a foreclosure state may simply remain there into adulthood. Some of these possible developmental pathways are presented in Figure 7.1.

Both sexes undergo similar patterns of identity development, according to the majority of studies in the research literature on this aspect. The sexes may differ, however, in some of the goals that are an integral part of their emerging identities. For instance, male identity has been found to center primarily on the attainment of a career, while female identity has a multiple and varying base, revolving around career and/or marriage and/or childbearing.

In some interesting research on female identity, O'Connell (1976) has shown that the traditional woman defines herself in terms of the man she marries and the children she raises. Thus her sense of identity is to a considerable degree a reflection of her roles as wife and mother. Her worth and sense of esteem are derived from her participation in the lives of significant others. Her sense of reflected identity is therefore strong, while her personal identity, which is based on her unique endowments, capabilities, and needs, is weak. O'Connell has shown, however, that the sense of personal identity does strengthen once the traditional women's childbearing duties diminish and her children reach elementary school age.

For the nontraditional married woman, whose identity centers on career goals, the sense of personal identity is strong and remains so, according to O'Connell, throughout the childbearing, preschool, and elementary school

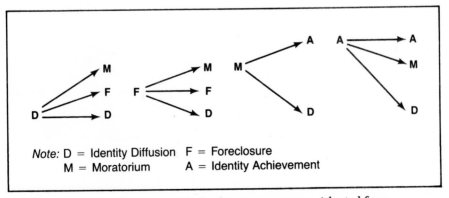

Note: D = Identity Diffusion   F = Foreclosure
      M = Moratorium   A = Identity Achievement

Figure 7.1 Possible sequential development patterns. Adapted from Waterman, 1982, p. 343.

stages. Finally, unlike the traditional woman, who experiences a moratorium during adolescence (before marriage and childbearing), the nontraditional woman does not experience such a moratorium at any point during the period from adolescence to adulthood.

Although the sexes show variability in the sources of their respective identities, recent research by Tesch and Whitbourne (1982) on young single adults (average age of 25) shows that the ability to achieve intimacy with members of the other sex is found for *both* sexes with advanced identity statuses. That is, both men and women who had attained enduring relationships characterized by a high degree of involvement, open communication, and high commitment were more likely to be identity achievers than those with moratorium or diffuse identities. These findings contradict the stereotypic view of some people that the ability to achieve enduring, intimate relationships is more characteristic of women than of men.

Finally, researchers have devoted considerable attention to the academic motivation, goals, and achievements of college students who occupy various identity statuses. For example, Adams and Fitch (1983) have shown that identity achievers are more attracted to scholastic or academically oriented departments than to departments that emphasize social activities and the material benefits (for example, getting high-paying jobs upon graduation) of pursuing degrees. Consistent with these data is a study by Marcia and Friedman (1970) which shows that identity achievers choose more difficult academic majors than do identity diffuse students. That is, students with strong identities more often chose to major in engineering, chemistry, pharmacy, biology, and mathematics, while identity diffusers preferred to major in sociology, anthropology, education, and physical education. Waterman and Waterman (1970) have found also that students with clear commitments to occupational goals had more favorable evaluations of their educational experiences than did students who were unclear about those goals. Identity achievers also have higher grades than members of the other statuses (Cross & Allen, 1970). Moreover, in line with Erikson's theorizing, Marcia (1966) found that college men who had successfully resolved their identity crises (and therefore had a clear sense of ego identity) performed better on an intellectually challenging task than did students with diffuse identities. Students with strong ego identities also lost less self-esteem when they failed on tasks they thought to be associated with academic success (Marcia, 1967). Identity achievers also show greater cultural sophistication and tolerance for outgroups, as well as higher levels of logical and moral reasoning than members of the other statuses (Cote & Levine, 1983; Rowe & Marcia, 1980; Waterman 1982).

Waterman, Geary, and Waterman (1974) and Adams and Fitch (1982) have also provided support for Erikson's idea that adolescence is characterized by psychosocial growth. They found significant increases in the number of students who achieved identity for both occupation and ideology (a set of values and principles to guide one's life) from their freshman to senior years.

Most students had achieved strong identities by the second half of their senior year.

In conclusion, there is considerable evidence validating Erikson's theorizing about identity development and functioning in adolescence, but research investigations testing hypotheses associated with several of the other developmental stages, particularly middle adulthood and old age, are relatively few.

Techniques of Assessment

Erikson has always identified himself as a psychoanalyst and paid homage to Freud's insights into the human condition and to his creation of various techniques to illuminate the sources of people's difficulties. At the same time, he has extended and modified many of Freud's concepts and techniques and forged new ones.

One basic difference in technique involves Erikson's view of the nature of the relationship between therapist and patient. He adopts a more egalitarian and personal stance toward his patients than did Freud. Unlike Freud, who tried to foster an impersonal, objective atmosphere by requiring his patients to recline on a couch while he remained seated in a chair out of sight, Erikson asks many of his patients to sit across from him in an easy chair. Freud was guided by his view of the consulting room as a psychologist's scientific laboratory; it was only secondarily a healing sanctuary. Erikson, however, believes that such neutrality on the part of the therapist can prove harmful to patients because it may induce in them fears of losing their identities. He thinks that the patient can be helped only to the extent that the therapist becomes actual (or real) to him or her (Roazen, 1976, pp. 67–69). Thus Erikson advocates a stance of "disciplined subjectivity" for the therapist. It is from this unique subjective perspective that the therapist should try to analyze and understand the patient's problems through empathy and by examining historical events that occurred during and affected the patient's life.

Erikson makes use of the Freudian concepts and procedures of transference, free association, and dream analysis in his work, but his usage differs in several respects from his mentor's. Especially different is his view of dreams and their meanings. Whereas Freud interpreted dreams as wish fulfillments of sexual needs, Erikson typically interprets them in psychosocial terms as attempts to preserve and enhance identity. He agrees with Freud that dreams can be viewed as indicators of people's struggles to understand prior developmental crises. For Freud, though, the crises revolve around sexuality; for Erikson, they often center on questions of identity. Erikson also differs from Freud in that he attaches considerable importance to the therapist's efforts to understand the manifest content of dreams. He thinks that Freud often treated the manifest content of patients' dreams as superficial, preferring instead to delve into the "depths" of dreamers' psyches to get at latent contents and their meanings. In Erikson's view, analyses of manifest content sometimes reveal important information about the dreamer's current life problems and about the dreamer's view of his or her relationship with the therapist. Although Erikson acknowledges that analyses of dreams can lead to the discovery of important information about the sources of prior conflicts, he also thinks that they have a healing function. He believes that any successful dream provides suggestions about solutions to problems. Dreams point to the future and provide clues about how to cope with it as well as the past (Roazen, 1976, p. 56).

Freud worked primarily with neurotic adults; Erikson is essentially a child analyst and as such has had to use techniques appropriate to that age group. Thus Erikson utilizes a variety of play therapy techniques to increase his understanding of the unique problems of his young patients (Erikson, 1977). For example, he encourages his patients to use toys to construct exciting scenes from their own imaginations. He finds that these play constructions offer important clues to the sources of the child's problems. They also provide an opportunity for the child to create ideal situations and to master reality by experiment and planning (Erikson, 1963, p. 222). Play, therefore, allows youngsters to relive their past, to redeem their failures, and to strengthen their hopes for the future. It is not a recreational activity but rather a work activity designed to enhance mastery.

Finally, Erikson is a pioneer in the use of **psychohistorical analysis**. He uses this technique as a means of increasing his understanding of the lives of important historical figures. Erikson created the procedure because he was interested in building a bridge between psychoanalysis and history. He maintains that all too often historians have ignored the role of individual development in their attempts to explain historical events, while analysts have focused too narrowly on early personal development and have deemphasized the role of broader historical processes in their efforts to explain the behavior of individuals. Psychohistorical analysis therefore is Erikson's attempt to overcome such myopia by applying his theory of ego development and its various crises throughout the life cycle to the biographies of prominent people like Thomas Jefferson, Maxim Gorky, George Bernard Shaw, Martin Luther, Mahatma Gandhi, and Adolf Hitler. Through it, he also seeks to better understand their lives by judging them in the context of the unique historical periods in which they lived. Psychohistorical analysis emphasizes the need for analysts to judge the meaning of these lives from a broadened perspective that includes an awareness and appreciation of the tremendous impact of political, economic, social, and cultural forces on the development and personalities of historical figures. Analysts should also recognize and take into account the subtle ways in which their own values and experiences as well as the influences of their own historical period guide their interpretations of these people's lives (Erikson, 1974, pp. 14–15).

Application of the Theory to the Treatment of Psychopathology

For Erikson, neurotics and psychotics are people with confused identities who lack a sense of mastery over their experiences. Their egos are fragmented and weak, and they are unable to relate well to others or to take their place in society. This pathetic situation is an outgrowth of their failure to successfully resolve one or more of the crises inherent in their life cycles. For example, failure to develop a sense of basic trust in the first stage of life has negative consequences because it is the source of several different kinds of pathology in later life. Specifically, Erikson maintains that schizophrenia is at least partially based on a failure to establish trust in others. Eventually such a failure leads the person to break with external reality. To help such a person, Erikson believes that the therapist must teach that patient to trust the world again (Evans, 1967, p. 55).

A lack of trust can also be seen in the paranoid individual, according to Erikson. But in this illness, Erikson sees a fixation in development "somewhere between the hope and will state" (Evans, 1967, p. 56). That is, the paranoid is unable to overcome the suspicion that the adults who tried to train his will during the anal stage were really trying to break it. If confronted later in life with restricted opportunities (for example, the person is unable to find a job), such an individual is likely to believe that others are out to "get him"—that is, to stop him or her from demonstrating the ability to succeed independently (Evans, 1967, pp. 56–57).

Obsessive-compulsive neuroses also result from fixations at the anal stage. Erikson thinks that this illness may occur because parents have been too harsh in their training procedures. As a result, the person is given to stubbornness, procrastination, and ritualistic repetitions as a means of regaining control of his or her life (Erikson, 1968b, p. 111). In treating this person, the therapist would rely not only on identifying the sources of the conflict with parents but also on encouraging the patient to use his or her capabilities and freedom to exercise will without feelings of shame and doubt (Evans, 1967, p. 58).

Major adjustment problems in adolescence typically center on the lack of clarity about occupational goals. Part of the difficulty in making this crucial decision may be traced to a failure to develop a sense of self-control over one's choices and/or a lack of imagination and direction concerning one's ideals and goals during the muscular-anal and locomotor-genital stages, respectively. Finally, there may also be a strong sense of inferiority about one's competence in performing tasks well as a result of failure to grow during the latency period. Thus the confused young person faced with the tremendous pressures of making a decision may react badly. He or she may drop out of school, leave jobs, stay out all night, turn to destructive acts like vandalism and robbery, or withdraw into bizarre and horrible moods. Erik-

not this personality level

son thinks the adolescent's only salvation in this situation is for friends, family, therapist, and judiciary personnel to refuse to type him or her with diagnostic labels like "borderline psychotic" or "schizoid" and for them to accept the fact that there are special social and cultural conditions that trigger such behavior (Erikson, 1968b, p. 132). The use of labels may in fact force the young person to embrace a negative identity more strongly, thereby exacerbating his or her problems. Instead, the adolescent must be treated sympathetically and given encouragement by the therapist. At the core of therapeutic treatment is the patient's need to rebuild his or her identity. This is an extremely difficult task, and because it is so painful Erikson reports that patients typically engage in resistive behavior. The patient usually tries to convince the therapist that his or her negative identity is real and necessary. Although Erikson thinks the therapist should acknowledge the validity of this contention, he or she should not let the patient conclude that this negative identity is "all there is to me." Instead, the therapist should treat the patient with understanding and affection (but not permissively), firmly point out the patient's strengths, and indicate direction for positive growth (Erikson, 1968b, pp. 212–216). The therapist should encourage the patient to develop his or her talents through social experimentation. Such activities typically result in an increase in ego strength.

A major contributing factor to the development of neurosis in young adults is their failure to relate intimately to others. Neurotics are often lonely, isolated people who have been unable to accept the risks and responsibilities associated with the establishment of truly intimate relationships. They lack the ability to love and to have deep, enduring friendships. Because sexual relations are part of the expression of mature love, we might expect such individuals to experience difficulties in the form of impotence, premature ejaculation, or frigidity. These problems can be overcome only when these disturbed and distressed individuals have undergone therapeutic experiences that strengthen their sense of identity. Erikson believes only people with strong egos are capable of coping with the disappointments, hurts, and possibilities of rejection associated with opening oneself up to another.

Neurosis during middle adulthood is associated with the frustration of the universal need to contribute to society and to the next generation. Neurotic adults are unable to experience satisfaction in guiding and helping the next generation. Such self-absorbed individuals feel strongly that life should have greater meaning and joy, yet there is instead a feeling of boredom and stagnation. Treatment of these individuals focuses on the origins of their excessive self-love and lack of trust in others: it is believed that during early childhood they experienced an arrest in growth that prevented them from extending themselves to others.

Finally, pathology in late adulthood is correlated with fragmentation of the ego. Elderly neurotics are still unable to adapt themselves to earlier defeats. Thus they are incapable of integrating these experiences into their self-concepts. They are also likely to feel that they have not accomplished all their goals and that there is not enough time to rectify the situation. Death is also feared. Treatment is aimed at getting the patient to see that a life cycle is unique and that it is something that has to be. The patient must also come to accept the fact that the life cycle permits no substitutions and that death is an inevitable part of it (Erikson, 1968b, p. 139).

Critical Comments

We now turn to an examination of the scientific worth of Erikson's theory.

Comprehensiveness. Erikson is an imaginative and original thinker who has created a highly comprehensive theory. It seeks to account for the biological, social, cultural, and historical factors that jointly determine personality development and functioning. His position addresses itself to a wide variety of phenomena, both normal and abnormal. It covers phenomena such as race relations, mythology, national identity, play activities, marriage, divorce, incest, sexual relations, occupational choice, academic success and failure, love, womanhood, and cross-cultural rituals, in addition to its focus on different types of psychopathology. It also makes an effort to describe and explain healthy personality functioning.

Precision and Testability. Erikson's theory definitely fails to meet the criterion of precision and testability. It is populated by highly abstract concepts that have few clear referents. The identity concept, for example, is particularly nebulous. It refers to

> *wholeheartedness, wholemindedness, wholesomeness, and the like. As a Gestalt, then, wholeness emphasizes a sound, organic, progressive mutuality between diversified functions and parts within an entirety, the boundaries of which are open and fluent. [Erikson, 1964, p. 92]*

In other contexts, Erikson defines the same term differently as "the capacity of the ego to sustain sameness and continuity in the face of changing fate" (Erikson, 1964, p. 96). It also refers to the "things which we want to become, and we know we are supposed to be, and which ... we can fulfill" (Evans, 1967, p. 32). As you can see from these quotes, the concept is extremely complex and does not lend itself readily to precise measurement. As a result, the theory is difficult to test. Difficulties in testing it also arise because the propositions in it are usually vaguely stated and the hypotheses associated with them are often not stated explicitly enough. For example, Erikson maintains that fixations that occur during specific stages influence later character development in special ways. Thus we would assume there should be a number of distinct character types, each of which should have a unique set of personality characteristics, or traits, but nowhere does Erikson have much to say about these implications of his theorizing. In fairness to Erikson, those ambiguities should be seen in the context of the enormously difficult task that he has tackled—the description and explanation of the operation of the eight stages of ego development as they are influenced by complicated biological, social, cultural, and historical forces.

Parsimony. Though we can admire the scope of Erikson's theory, it is clear that its explanatory base is rather limited. Most phenomena are explained in terms of identity formation, disintegration, or integration. The identity concept therefore seems to carry too heavy a burden. It is also often used in post hoc fashion by Erikson to explain his clinical and/or cross-cultural observations.

Empirical Validity. In general, there has not been much research conducted to test the richness of Erikson's theorizing. We have already mentioned several major reasons for this state of affairs. First, Erikson's formulations are highly abstract, so that it is hard to convert them into testable terms. Second, it is difficult and costly to conduct the longitudinal studies needed to adequately determine whether his theorizing about the developmental process has validity. Third, psychologists tend to use readily available populations for their research. This fact could explain why most of the tests of Erikson's theory have focused on adolescents and not on middle-aged adults and the elderly. Empirical research on the identity crisis in adolescence has provided findings that are generally consistent with Erikson's theorizing, although much more work remains to be done.

Heuristic Value. Erikson's theory has had strong heuristic value. It has generated interest in scholars in many disciplines. Erikson's ethical concerns, as evident in his discussions of the virtues associated with development, have stimulated thinking among theologians and moral philosophers. His extensive analysis of the meaning of rituals in various societies has influenced the thinking of cultural anthropologists. It is also apparent that his use of psychohistorical analysis to study political, religious, and literary figures has had a considerable impact on the work of historians. Perhaps most significantly, Erikson's ego-psychology formulations have broadened the theoretical base of psychoanalysis and have influenced the thinking of colleagues in the psychoanalytic community.

Applied Value. Erikson's work has had tremendous practical impact in the areas of child psychology and psychiatry, vocational counseling, marriage counseling, education, social work, and business. For example, his ideas about the stages of ego development and the conflicts inherent in them have been used to help clinically treat children, adolescents, and older adults. Vocational counselors also make use of Erikson's work in advising young people about occupational goals. Mental health consultants also conduct workshops with business employees to discuss ways to overcome the sense of stagnation that many of them experience midway through their careers. Erikson's work provides many suggestions for increasing feelings of generativity among such individuals.

Erikson's work has also been popular with students and other members of the general public, helping to increase their understanding of the kinds of stresses they are likely to experience at a given stage in their lives and providing them with recommendations for alleviating the stresses so that positive growth can be achieved.

Discussion Questions

1. What is an identity crisis? Is it a typical experience for adolescents as Erikson claims?
2. Do you think, as Erikson maintains, that women have innate maternal feelings that, if repressed, produce feelings of anxiety and dissatisfaction?
3. Erikson emphasizes the role of the mother in creating a sense of basic trust or mistrust in children. What is the role of the father in child care? Is it as important as the mother's? Is it different? If so, in what ways?
4. Erikson thinks that the ability to love someone presupposes a strong identity and that because adolescents have confused identities, they can not truly love anyone. Do you agree or disagree with him? Why?
5. If healthy, intimate relationships involve a mutuality of orgasm with a loved partner of the opposite sex, what is Erikson's view of homosexual relationships?
6. In your opinion, does organized religion exploit the masses in order to achieve its own selfish ends? Cite reasons for your answer.
7. Do you agree with Erikson's belief that the most disturbing part of adolescence centers on youth's inability to decide on an occupational identity? Is this a major problem for you or any of your friends?
8. In what ways are youths with weak egos remarkably clannish, intolerant, and cruel in their exclusion of people who are different?
9. Which one of Marcia's identity statuses, if any, characterizes you and/or your friends? Do you agree that foreclosures are closest to their parents?
10. Why is Erikson's theory of ego development and functioning more optimistic in its view of human beings than Freud's position? Do you think that Erikson's optimism is warranted?

References

Adams, G. R., & Fitch, S. A. Ego stage and identity status development: A cross-sequential analysis. *Journal of Personality and Social Psychology*, 1982, 43, 574–583.

Adams, G. R., & Fitch, S. A. Psychological environments of university departments: Effects on college students' identity status and ego stage development. *Journal of Personality and Social Psychology*, 1983, 44, 1266–1275.

Bourne, E. The state of research on ego identity: A review and appraisal, Part I. *Journal of Youth and Adolescence*, 1978, 7, 223–251.

Coles, R. *Erik H. Erikson: The growth of his work.* Boston: Little, Brown, 1970.

Cote, J. E. & Levine, C. Marcia and Erikson: The relationships among ego identity status, neuroticism, dogmatism, and purpose in life. *Journal of Youth and Adolescence*, 1983, *12*, 43–53.

Cross, H. J., & Allen, J. G. Ego identity status, adjustment, and academic achievement. *Journal of Consulting and Clinical Psychology*, 1970, *34*, 288.

Erikson, E. *Young man Luther: A study in psychoanalysis and history.* New York: Norton, 1958.

Erikson, E. *Childhood and society* (2nd ed.). New York: Norton, 1963.

Erikson, E. *Insight and responsibility.* New York: Norton, 1964.

Erikson, E. Identity and identity diffusion. In C. Gordon & K. J. Gergen (Eds.), *The self in social interaction.* New York: Wiley, 1968a.

Erikson, E. *Identity: Youth and crisis.* New York: Norton, 1968b.

Erikson, E. *Gandhi's truth.* New York: Norton, 1969.

Erikson, E. *In search of common ground.* New York: Norton, 1973.

Erikson, E. *Dimensions of a new identity: The 1973 Jefferson Lectures in the Humanities.* New York: Norton, 1974.

Erikson, E. *Life history and the historical moment.* New York: Norton, 1975.

Erikson, E. *Toys and reasons: Stages in the ritualization of experience.* New York: Norton, 1977.

Erikson, E. *Identity and the life cycle: A reissue.* New York: Norton, 1979.

Evans, R. *Dialogue with Erik Erikson.* New York: Harper & Row, 1967.

Marcia, J. Development and validation of ego identity status. *Journal of Personality and Social Psychology*, 1966, *3*, 551–558.

Marcia, J. Ego identity status: Relationship to change in self-esteem, "general maladjustment" and authoritarianism. *Journal of Personality*, 1967, *35*, 188–193.

Marcia, J., & Friedman, M. L. Ego identity status in college women. *Journal of Personality*, 1970, *38*, 249–263.

O'Connell, A. N. The relationship between life style and identity synthesis and resynthesis in traditional, neo-traditional, and non-traditional women. *Journal of Personality*, 1976, *44*, 675–688.

Roazen, P. *Erik H. Erikson: The power and limits of a vision.* New York: Free Press, 1976.

Rosenthal, D. A., Gurney, R. M., & Moore, S. M. From trust to intimacy: A new inventory for examining Erikson's stages of psychosocial development. *Journal of Youth and Adolescence*, 1981, *10*, 525–537.

Rowe, I., & Marcia, J. E. Ego identity status, formal operations, and moral development. *Journal of Youth and Adolescence*, 1980, *9*, 87–99.

Tesch, S. A., & Whitbourne, S. K. Intimacy and identity status in young adults. *Journal of Personality and Social Psychology*, 1982, *43*, 1041–1051.

Waterman, A. Identity development from adolescence to adulthood: An extension of theory and a review of research. *Developmental Psychology*, 1982, *18*, 341–358.

Waterman, A. S., Geary, P. S., & Waterman, C. K. Longitudinal study of changes in ego identity status from the freshman to the senior year at college. *Developmental Psychology*, 1974, *10*, 387–392.

Waterman, A. S., & Waterman, C. The relationship between ego identity status and satisfaction with college. *The Journal of Education Research*, 1970, *64*, 165–168.

Weisstein, N. Psychology constructs the female, or the fantasy life of the male psychologist (with some attention to the fantasies of his friends, the male biologist and the male anthropologist). In I. Cohen (Ed.), *Perspectives on psychology.* New York: Praeger, 1975.

Suggested Readings

Erikson, E. *Childhood and society* (2nd ed.). New York: Norton, 1963.

Erikson, E. *Insight and responsibility*. New York: Norton, 1964.

Erikson, E. *Identity: Youth and crisis*. New York, Norton, 1968.

Evans, R. *Dialogue with Erik Erikson*. New York: Harper & Row, 1967.

Roazen, P. *Erik H. Erikson: The power and limits of a vision*. New York: Free Press, 1976.

Glossary

Autonomy The sense of independence that individuals experience if they successfully resolve conflicts during the second stage of life.

Basic mistrust The belief that others cannot be trusted. It is the result of the failure of mothers to act in a consistent and affectionate manner toward their infants.

Basic trust The belief that others are reliable. It stems from the receipt of consistent and affectionate treatment by mothers during the first stage of development.

Care A strength in healthy, middle-aged people whereby they feel a concern for the welfare of the younger generation.

Competence A strength in healthy children involving the ability to make things and complete tasks.

Crisis A turning point in individual development in which conflicts can be resolved positively, thereby strengthening the ego, or negatively, thereby weakening it.

Despair The negative outcome in the last stage of life for individuals who have been unable to resolve their conflicts constructively. These conflicts involve the fear of death and the belief that their lives have been failures and that they are unable to rectify the situation.

Ego integrity The feeling by the elderly that their lives have had meaning and have been worth living.

Ego psychology The theory that the ego is not always controlled by id impulses, but that it often functions independently of these urges, thereby providing the individual with an opportunity for positive growth.

Epigenetic principle The principle that human development is genetically determined and operates in stages that unfold in an invariant sequence.

Fidelity A sense of loyalty and commitment to friends, mates, and co-workers, and a value system that is the outgrowth of the positive resolution of conflicts during adolescence.

Foreclosure An identity status within adolescence in which individuals who have never experienced a crisis concerning their goals have nevertheless made firm commitments concerning them.

Generativity The term used to indicate the productivity of middle-aged adults in a variety of areas. It includes the production of children and the guidance of the younger generation as well as the production of ideas, art, books, and so forth.

Guilt The feeling of wrong-doing that youngsters have when they show inappropriate behavior and are punished for it.

Hope The belief that persistent wishes and goals can be attained.

Identity The multifaceted concept that essentially involves knowing who you are and where you are going as well as what you are not and do not want to be. It is the unified sense of self as uniquely different from others.

Identity achievement The most advanced identity status within adolescence in which individuals have undergone a period of crisis and, as a result, have developed firm commitments concerning their life goals.

Identity crisis The experience of confusion in adolescence, characterized by the agonizing inability to make definite choices concerning a career or a mate or an ideology to live by.

Identity diffusion An identity status within adolescence in which individuals are not actively in crisis about their life goals and have not made any commitments concerning them.

Industry The sense of satisfaction that accrues to children as a result of being actively engaged in learning new skills and completing jobs.

Inferiority The negative outcome of the fourth stage of development when children feel they are incompetent failures and, thus, feel inferior.

Initiative The feeling that one has control over one's outcomes and can therefore be the source of ideas and action.

Intimacy The ability of people with mature egos to merge their identities with their partners without feeling threatened or overwhelmed.

Isolation The result of being unable to take chances with one's identity by sharing true intimacy.

Love The ability to trust and share one's experiences and identity with a partner so that both parties are enhanced.

Moratorium A time of exploration during adolescence in which individuals are experiencing a crisis concerning their life goals and are actively considering alternatives in an attempt to arrive at a decision.

Negative identity A commitment to values and roles that are unacceptable to society.

Psychohistorical analysis The technique used by Erikson to increase understanding of historical figures. In general, it involves the use of his theory of ego development in the analysis of their lives.

Purpose The virtue that emerges when parents guide their children into socially desirable activities. The result is the setting of life goals by the children.

Role confusion The state in adolescence in which young people cannot decide on the proper life roles for themselves.

Shame and doubt The negative result of faulty parental training in the anal stage, causing youngsters to feel they do not have the ability to make their own judgments or to exercise control over their lives.

Stagnation The feeling of being unproductive and useless that stems from the inability of the person to care for something or someone.

Totalism The premature, unquestioning commitment by adolescents to simplistic ideologies and ideas as a means of reducing their own painful feelings of confusion.

Virtue A strengthening of the ego that emerges following the successful resolution of a conflict associated with one of the developmental stages.

Will The virtue that involves the determination by youngsters to exercise free choice in making decisions and not be controlled by others.

Wisdom The virtue that emerges following successful resolution of the crisis of old age. It involves the ability to put one's life and experiences into a life-cycle perspective, to see that this life had unity and meaning and that it was worth living.

PART 3

Trait Perspectives

The earliest attempts to explain human behavior involved the use of typologies and traits. Typologies are the classification of behavior into discrete or all-or-nothing categories—for example, Hippocrates' classic distinctions among choleric, melancholic, sanguine, and phlegmatic types. Trait classifications involve the use of graduated dimensions along which individual differences can be quantitatively arranged. These quantitative arrangements reflect the degree to which people are assumed to possess a given amount of some particular characteristic. For example, people may vary considerably in laziness, intelligence, and dominance. Some people are not very intelligent, most are moderately intelligent, and only a few possess great intellectual abilities.

In their attempts to understand personality functioning in terms of traits, theorists have sometimes found themselves in disagreement about the definition of the word *traits* and about whether traits cause or are correlated with behavior. Specifically, some investigators view traits as having real existence within the person and as being capable of causing behavior once they are activated. Allport falls into this category. Other investigators, in contrast, treat traits as convenient constructs that are used to describe patterns of behavior. For example, if we observe a man intentionally harming others in various situations, we might conveniently summarize his behavior as aggressive. We could then utilize this information to predict his behavior in a new situation. That is, we could predict that, because he showed aggressive behavior in the past in many situations, he should also be aggressive in the new situation. But we are very aware that the trait label that we applied to his past behavior did not cause him to be aggressive in the new situation, assuming that it is how he behaved. Rather, his past behavior (labeled generally as aggressive) is simply correlated with behavior in the new situation. Investigators who adopt this stance do not consider traits to have real existence nor do they see traits as causes of behavior. Cattell does not adopt this position in its entirety. Instead, he thinks that traits have a neurological basis (are real), but he says that we do not currently have sufficient scientific information about their physiological basis, so that it is best to consider them as constructs whose physical basis will be discovered someday.

Part 3 reviews and evaluates the positions of two of the most prominent trait theorists, Allport and Cattell. Like the Freudian and neo-Freudian theorists we considered in Part 2, Allport and Cattell focus most of their attention and effort on internal, underlying personality states. Both psychodynamic and trait theorists assume that those underlying characteristics and motives exert considerable influence on behavior. In the content of their positions, Allport and Cattell endorse some of the Freudian concepts. Both accept the notion that people sometimes act defensively and that some behavior is determined by unconscious motives. But Allport, more than Cattell, shows a clear and basic break with the Freudian model in the extent to which he focuses on unconscious and defensive behavior. He believed Freud and others placed far too much emphasis on the irrational in personality functioning and not enough on the rational. For him, the Freudian model best describes the behavior of people with behavioral disorders but has little of substance to say about the behavior of healthy, mature individuals.

Allport set out to correct this imbalance by establishing the broad outlines of a humanistic psychology that focused on the uniqueness of the individual and on the creative and rational aspirations of most people to realize their potentials. In this regard, Allport must be seen as an important forerunner of the humanistic movement, popular in psychology today. A discussion of his work could have been placed quite readily and appropriately in Part 6, where we will discuss the humanistic-existential positions. Because Allport believed the trait concept to be the most important one in the construction of an adequate theory of personality, his position belongs within the trait perspective framework. Chapter 8 does, however, pay considerable attention to Allport's humanistic roots. It also details Allport's attempts to create an adequate definition of personality, and it outlines his theory of traits. The major gap in his theorizing about the developmental process of becoming and about the role that traits play in this emergent process is presented. The review of the process of development focuses on this conception of the mature personality. In his view, the development of maturity takes considerable time, so that only adults are capable of coming close to self-actualization. The developmental process involves abrupt shifts so that the mature individual is qualitatively different from the abnormal or immature one. Mature people have been able to free themselves from excessive reliance on the immediate gratification of basic impulses and drives. They are emotionally secure and are characterized by self-acceptance and tolerance toward others. In our coverage of the many techniques Allport used to assess personality, the major differences between idiographic and nomothetic approaches to data collection are reviewed.

In Chapter 9, the key focus is on Cattell's belief that an adequate theory of personality must rest on solid measurement and statistical procedures. The chapter provides an introduction to the complex factor analytic methods he utilizes to "discover" the basic traits of personality. Originally, Cattell maintained that there were 16 source traits that could be used to explain personality functioning. Recently, however, he has found, through extensive research, that there are seven new factors. In addition, his new Clinical Analysis Questionnaire (CAQ) can be used to measure 12 new psychopathology factors. He now believes that he has uncovered the major source traits found in normal and abnormal people.

We also focus on Cattell's new econetic model that describes the ways in which the physical, social, and cultural environments affect individuals and their subsequent behavior. Then there is a discussion of the specification equation, which is an attempt to combine traits and situations as a means of predicting behavior more accurately. This multidimensional model includes a complex representation of the ways in which traits are dynamically interrelated within the person and how they operate across a variety of situations. Next, we outline Cattell's emphasis on the role of heredity in personality development and functioning. As for the role of learning in personality development, Cattell not only presents the usual ways in which classical and instrumental conditioning affect personality formation, but he also stresses in original fashion the role of a complex form of learning called integration learning in changing personality. Our discussion continues with the ways in which personality diagnosis through the use of precise measurement procedures can be used to identify disordered behavior so that the clinician is in a better position to help clients. We will show why Cattell thinks that the P-technique (which involves testing the client repeatedly on a large number of personality dimensions over a long period) is the procedure best able to provide an accurate assessment of changes occurring in the client during the course of therapy.

C H A P T E R 8

Allport's Trait Theory

Biographical Sketch

Gordon Allport was born in 1897 in Montezuma, Indiana, the son of a country doctor. There were four boys in the Allport family, and Gordon was the youngest. He characterized his family life as marked by trust and affection along with a strong emphasis on the virtue of hard work. Allport was scholarly from an early age; he was good with words but poor at sports. He did not get along very well with his peers. In a show of utter contempt, one of his classmates even said of the young scholar, "Aw, that guy swallowed a dictionary" (Allport, 1968, p. 378).

Although he finished second highest academically in his high school class of 100 students, Allport insisted that he was "a good routine student, but definitely uninspired ... about anything beyond the usual adolescent concerns" (Allport, 1968, p. 379). Following his older brother Floyd, who had graduated from Harvard, Allport squeezed through the entrance tests and matriculated there in 1915. The years at Harvard were stimulating and enlightening, according to Allport. He was overwhelmed by the intellectual

197

atmosphere and the strict adherence to the highest academic standards. It was a real intellectual awakening for the small-town boy from the Midwest. Allport followed the example of his older brother and majored in psychology. Besides enrolling in courses taught by prominent psychology professors and being influenced by them, he also participated in a number of volunteer service projects (Allport, 1968, p. 381).

After receiving his baccalaureate in 1919, Allport took an opportunity to teach English and sociology at Robert College in Constantinople, Turkey. The following year he won a fellowship for graduate study at Harvard. Before returning to Cambridge, however, he decided to visit a brother who was working in Vienna at the time. He also decided to see if he could arrange a private meeting with Sigmund Freud. With the audacity of youth, he wrote a letter to Freud announcing that he was in Vienna and implying that Freud would no doubt be glad to meet him. To his great surprise, Freud replied in his own handwriting and invited Allport to visit him at his office.

When Allport arrived, Freud ushered him into his famous inner office and sat staring at him expectantly. Not anticipating the silence and not knowing what to say, Allport thought fast and told him of an episode on a streetcar on his way to the office. He reported that he had seen a 4-year-old boy who displayed a conspicuous dirt phobia. The boy kept saying to his mother, "I don't want to sit there . . . don't let that dirty man sit beside me" (Allport, 1968, p. 383). Since the mother was so clean and dominant-looking, Allport assumed Freud would quickly see the point of the story—that the boy's abhorrence of dirt was a result of his mother's obsession with cleanliness. Instead, when he had finished the story, Freud hesitated and said kindly, "And was that little boy you?" (Allport, 1968, p. 383). Allport, flabbergasted, realized that Freud was accustomed to thinking in terms of neurotic defenses, so that Allport's manifest motivation had completely escaped him. Allport reported that the experience taught him that depth psychology often plunged too deeply into the psyche and that psychologists might understand people better if they paid more attention to their patients' manifest, conscious motives before probing into their unconscious natures.

Allport entered graduate school in psychology and finished the work for his doctorate in two years. He received his Ph.D. in 1922, at the age of 24 (Allport, 1968, p. 384). He was interested in developing a psychology of personality, but practically no one else in academic life had similar interests; he reported that his thesis was perhaps the first one devoted to an examination of the traits of personality. Immediately after receiving the degree, Allport had a shattering experience that he claimed was a turning point in his life and career. He was invited to attend a meeting of a group of experimental psychologists at Clark University to discuss current problems and issues in sensory psychology. After two days of discussions, the eminent psychologist Edward Titchener allotted three minutes to each graduate student to describe his own investigations. Allport reported his work on traits of personality and was punished by total silence and stares. Titchener strongly disapproved of his presentation and demanded of Allport's major professor, "Why did you let him work on that problem?" Allport was mortified at this remark, but later, when they had returned to Harvard, his professor consoled him by saying, "You don't care what Titchener thinks." And Allport found that in fact he did not (Allport, 1968, p. 385). The experience taught him another lesson—namely, not to be unnecessarily bothered by rebukes or professional slights and to pursue his own interests. From that point on, Allport remained a maverick in psychology, a person who thought deeply and originally about issues and who stated his views candidly, no matter how controversial they were in the eyes of others.

Except for a brief stint at Dartmouth, most of Allport's professional life was spent at Harvard. During this period, from 1930 to his death in 1967, he wrote many scholarly theoretical and research articles on such topics as prejudice, expressive movements, rumor, and attitudes and values. He also published a number of books, including *Personality: A Psychological Interpretation* (1937), *The Nature of Prejudice* (1954), *Becoming: Basic Considerations for a Psychology of Personality* (1955), and *Pattern and Growth in Personality* (1961). Fittingly, his work was recognized by his colleagues, and he was awarded many honors. He was elected president of the American Psychological Association in 1939 and given the Distinguished Scientific Contribution Award in 1964. He said, though, that he valued one honor above all others: at the 17th International Congress of Psychology, in Washington, D.C., in 1963, 55 of his former Ph.D. students presented him with two handsomely bound volumes of their own writings with the dedicatory inscription: "From his students—in appreciation of his respect for their individuality" (Allport, 1968, p. 407).

Basic Concepts and Principles

Personality as Seen by a Humanist

Allport, like many investigators in the discipline, commented on the virtual impossibility of defining the term *personality* precisely. After reviewing definitions offered by theologians, philosophers, lawyers, poets, sociologists, and psychologists, Allport proposed his own version in his first book: personality is "what a man really is." But this, too, was still too brief and vague. Accordingly, he presented a more precise definition: "Personality is the dynamic organization within the individual of those psychophysical systems that determine his unique adjustments to his environment" (Allport, 1937, p. 48). In a later book, he again revised his definition: "Personality is the dynamic organization within the individual of those psychophysical systems that determine his characteristic behavior and thought" (Allport, 1961, p. 28).

For Allport, the "dynamic organization" of personality refers to his belief that it is fruitless to consider personality as consisting of fragmented components independent of one another. Instead, personality is unified and constantly evolving and changing. Personality is also seen as caused by forces within the person. Although he did not deny that situational influences have an effect, he still felt it is the individual's own perception of these forces that determine his or her behavior. Furthermore, some behavior that seems to be controlled by external forces is really controlled by internal forces. For example, Allport maintained that "if a child is a hellion at home, and an angel outside, he obviously has two contradictory tendencies in his nature or perhaps a deeper genotype that would explain the opposing phenotypes" (Allport, 1968, p. 46). A situationist would simply predict that the child would behave differently depending on which situation was salient. Allport argued that the differences in behavior may be caused by opposing tendencies or traits in the person's nature—for example, by the learned predispositions to act as a hellion or an angel in such situations.

Allport became more Freudian by suggesting that a unifying **genotype** may actually be responsible for the two **phenotypes** (behaving as a hellion at home and an angel outside). For example, the actual underlying tendency, or genotype, might be one of expedience; that is, the child may have the trait of expedience or the tendency to perform behaviors advantageous to him or her. Behaving like an angel at home might be pleasing to the child's parents; behaving like a hellion outside may win the approval of peers. As you can readily see, such trait "explanations" can be invoked easily on a post hoc basis and can be made to fit virtually any data under consideration. Another important point to remember in connection with this example is that although Allport recognized the role the situation plays in behavior, his primary allegiance remained with the ways in which the person's unique traits and other characteristics determine his or her behavior.

The reference to **psychophysical systems** in Allport's definition shows that he considered personality to consist of neither mental nor physical events exclusively but of both "mind" and "body" elements in an inextricable unity. These events are also organized into a complex he called a system.

Personality involves the characteristic or unique behavior or thought of the person. Allport argued that all the traits we apparently share with others are, at base, idiosyncratic and unique. He acknowledged that this aspect of the definition is very broad, but he wanted to take into account the fact that we not only adjust to our environment by behaving in certain ways, but we also reflect on it. By so doing, we ensure not only survival but growth.

Other Characteristics of Allport's Humanistic Psychology

Allport's emphasis on the uniqueness of the person is only one of the features of his position. In addition, there is a strong focus on the ways in which the internal cognitive and motivational processes of the person influence and cause behavior. These internal processes and structures include reflexes, drives, habits and skills, beliefs, intentions, attitudes, values, and traits. The person is conceived of as being active, creative, and characteristically rational. As the person matures, he or she becomes increasingly capable of making conscious and deliberate choices among the various alternatives for behavior. The person is seen as a self-reliant being who is relatively independent of the influence of others and who pursues goals in a thoughtful way. Allport chose this positive and optimistic approach to the person in reaction to the more pessimistic conceptualizations current when he was postulating his position. He believed these views of the person were too static, reductionistic, and mechanistic and placed too much emphasis on the unconscious and irrational side of human personality. Allport's theory was an attempt to provide a much needed corrective for this one-sided view.

The Theory of Traits

The major concepts in Allport's theory revolve around the different kinds of traits possessed by each of us and the different properties of the **proprium,** or self. We consider first his theory of traits and follow it with his treatment of the proprium and the developmental process, although it should be noted that Allport never systematically related his trait concepts to his concepts of human development. Later we will try to make some sense out of this irregularity in his theorizing, but first we should consider the basic concepts in his **trait theory**.

What Precisely Is a Trait? For Allport, a trait is "a generalized and focalized neuropsychic system (peculiar to the individual) with the capacity to render many stimuli functionally equivalent and to initiate and guide consistent (equivalent) forms of adaptive and expressive behavior" (Allport, 1937, p. 295). Thus a trait is something that actually exists but is invisible. It is located in certain parts of the nervous system. Although we do not see it, we infer its existence by observing the consistencies in a person's behavior. Dissimilar stimuli are all capable of arousing a trait readiness within the person. The trait then manifests itself through different responses. All these different responses are equivalent, however, in the sense that they serve the same function—that is, expression of the trait. Figure 8.1 illustrates the manner in which a trait generally operates. For example, a college man's shyness is inferred from his inability to establish friendships with other students, his avoidance of social gatherings, his enjoyment of solitary recreational activities like reading and stamp collecting, and his hesitancy in participating in seminar discussions.

Cardinal, Central, and Secondary Traits. Allport also made a number of distinctions among various kinds of traits. Characteristics that are pervasive and dominant in a person's life he called **cardinal traits**. These are master motives, ruling passions, eminent traits (Allport, 1961, p. 365). For

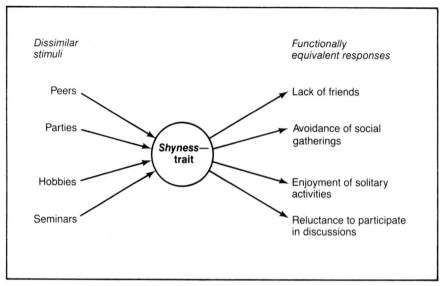

Figure 8.1 The trait in action. Dissimilar stimuli arouse the trait. The trait then provides a variety of functionally equivalent responses.

example, a person may have an overwhelming need to be powerful, and this need could be inferred from virtually all his behavior. Such a person would not only strive to attain a position of power within society but would also interact with his golf partner, his mail carrier, his children, and his wife in a similar fashion. He would try to dominate his wife and would even try desperately to win a game of Ping-Pong with his 5-year-old daughter. A casual conversation with an acquaintance might lead him to a bitter struggle to win on some trivial issue.

Characteristics that control less of a person's behavior but are nevertheless important are called **central traits**. Such traits include possessiveness, ambitiousness, competitiveness, and kindness. Although they do control the person's behavior in various situations, they do not possess the generality of a cardinal trait. Characteristics that are peripheral to the person are called **secondary traits**. Preferences, for example, are secondary traits. A person might "love" banana cream pie; this preference is aroused by a limited variety of situational stimuli around suppertime. He or she may prefer to vacation in Maine or Nova Scotia and therefore may respond with favorable comments to advertising and conversation with friends about vacations in these areas.

Common Traits versus Personal Dispositions. Allport made yet another distinction among traits: they could be considered categories for classifying groups of people on a particular dimension (Allport, 1961, p. 349). We might say, for example, that some people are more dominant than others or that some people are more polite than others. Such comparative designations are really abstractions based on an identification of given dimensions. In short, they are **common traits,** or traits we share with others. They are generalized dispositions and, in Allport's view, of limited usefulness in a science of personality.

Much more to his liking was the concept of the **personal disposition**. In contrast to the common or generalized trait, the personal disposition, or individual trait, concerns a unique characteristic of the person, a trait not shared with others (Allport, 1961, p. 358). Allport hoped that psychologists would stop paying so much attention to the role of common traits in a science of personality and focus instead on those characteristics unique to the individual. His hope was based on his belief that common traits are categories into which the individual is forced, whereas personal dispositions more accurately reflect the individual's own personality structure. As he stated it,

> by common trait methods, we find that Peter stands high in esthetic interest and anxiety, but low in leadership and need-achievement. The truth is that all these common traits have a special coloring in his life, and—still more important—they interact with one another. Thus, it might be more accurate to say that his personal disposition is a kind of artistic and self-sufficient solitude. His separate scores on common traits do not fully reflect this pattern. [Allport, 1961, p. 359]

For Allport, only by adopting an approach to the study of personality focused on the uniqueness of the person can we hope to make substantial advances in our understanding. By and large, though, investigators have argued that unique or individual constructs are impossible to imagine. If we used constructs that were unique to the individual, there would be no words in the language for them. We would continually have to invent new terms to describe each individual's motives and behavior—a hopeless undertaking. Of course, we can and do talk about the unique configurations or patterns of traits within an individual's personality, but even here critics have argued that a science focused on general differences between people can handle this problem; there is no need for Allport's highly personalized approach (Holt, 1962). Perhaps, though, in their zeal to prove him wrong, these critics miss Allport's fundamental point about trying to focus more clearly on the uniqueness of the individual. (We will discuss this issue further in the section "Techniques of Assessment.")

The Process of Personality Development

At this point, you know that there are various ways of conceptualizing the development process. Freud, for example, focused on the development of strong sexual and aggressive needs as they related to various areas of the

body—the oral, anal, phallic, and genital areas. Jung considered development in terms of the conflict between opposites within the individual that
facilitated movement toward self-realization. For Allport, the discussion of
the developmental process centers on the concept of the self. He acknowledged that the concept is a slippery one and that it has been used by different investigators in different ways. It has also encountered vigorous opposition from many psychologists. Wilhelm Wundt, the eminent 19th-century
structuralist, thought the concept of self or ego or soul was hindering progress in psychology and declared that he favored a "psychology without a
soul" (Allport, 1955, p. 36). Wundt's objection, and the objection of many
behaviorists who came after him, was that there was a tendency on the part
of some investigators to assign a primary role to the term *self* in their theories
and to discuss it as a mysterious central agency that unified our actions. In
short, the term was reified by many investigators and treated as though it
actually existed and could direct behavior. For example, a reified use of the
term might be found in the following "explanation" of a person's behavior:
"Her strong sense of self caused her to give up smoking." In other words,
she gave up smoking because of her strong ego.

Allport agreed that such reification is damaging to psychology, but he
thought we could avoid this pitfall and still make good use of the term. In
fact, he even maintained that we *must* use the term for two reasons. First,
the one certain criterion we have of our identity and existence is our sense
of self. It is a fundamental experience; if we discard it, we discard the essence
of personality. Second, contemporary theories of learning motivation and
development need some form of the concept of self to account for differences in behavior produced by differences in individual experiences, relevant or irrelevant to the self. Another way of stating this belief is that differences in learning and performance will occur as a function of the degree of
"ego involvement" of individuals. If they are very ego-involved or if the task
has greater self-relevance, they may learn to master it more quickly. Of course,
theorists with a behavioral perspective would probably argue that Allport
comes very close to reifying the concept of self in this kind of example.

A simpler and more precise way of discussing the differences in performance in this case might be to translate self-relevance into reinforcement
terms and say that we might expect differences in performance if the person
places different values or degrees of importance on the outcomes of the
performance. He or she works quickly to master a task that yields valuable
reinforcers but does not learn as efficiently a task in which the outcomes
are relatively unimportant (see Chapter 12, for a more detailed discussion
of this point).

The Proprium, or Self

Allport substituted the term *proprium* for self in his theorizing and used
it to mean a sense of what is "peculiarly ours." It includes "all aspects of
personality that make for inward unity" (Allport, 1955, p. 40). The proprium,

or self, is continuously developing from infancy to death and moves through the stages described next. (Note how the term has been endowed with magical powers in the previous sentences. It should be clear that we use it in this way because it is convenient to do so, not because we believe an actual entity called the proprium guides our development.)

The Bodily Self. In infancy, the bodily sense, the first aspect of selfhood, becomes salient, according to Allport. As infants, we are continually receiving sensory information from our internal organs and our muscles, joints, and tendons. These sensations become particularly acute when we are hungry, when we are frustrated, and when we bump into things. In such situations, we learn the limits of our own bodies. As we mature, these recurrent bodily sensations provide information that confirms our own existence. In Allport's opinion, these sensations of the **bodily self** provide an "anchor" for our self-awareness. When we are healthy, we hardly notice the sensations; when we are ill, we are keenly aware of our bodies (Allport, 1961, p. 114). How intimate these sensations are is shown by Allport in an interesting example:

> Think first of swallowing the saliva in your mouth, or do so. Then imagine expectorating it into a tumbler and drinking it! What seemed natural and "mine" suddenly becomes disgusting and alien. Or picture yourself sucking blood from a prick in your finger; then imagine sucking blood from a bandage around your finger! What I perceive as belonging intimately to my body is warm and welcome; what I perceive as separate from my body becomes in the twinkling of an eye, cold and foreign. [Allport, 1955, p. 43]

Later in the developmental process, we experience sensations from our bodily growth. In adolescence, when these changes are abrupt, some of us feel we are puny, ugly, and awkward; the rest of us feel we are strong, beautiful, and graceful. Some girls may try to test their ability to attract boys by accentuating female physical attributes. Some boys may test their prowess in physical games and exaggerate their sexual exploits. Allport believed strongly that this bodily sense forms the core of the self and is an important aspect of selfhood throughout life.

Self-Identity. The second aspect of the proprium also occurs during the first 18 months of life and is called **self-identity.** Despite the vast changes that occur in our lives as we grow older, there is a certain continuity and sameness in the way we perceive ourselves. As Allport saw it: "Today I remember some of my thoughts of yesterday; and tomorrow I shall remember some of my thoughts of both yesterday and today; and I am certain that they are the thoughts of the same person—of myself" (Allport, 1961, p. 114). This information about self-identity seems obvious and even trite, but there have been useful and interesting discussions by neoanalyst Erik Erikson of the crises faced by people, especially adolescents, who doubt or are confused by their identities (recall materials on ego identity in Chapter 7).

Self-Esteem. The third aspect of the proprium to emerge from the second through the third year of life, according to Allport, is feelings of **self-esteem.** At this point, we have become more familiar with our environments; we experience pride when we master available tasks and humiliation when we fail. Allport also thought that one symptom of our growing self-awareness is the outpouring of opposition to virtually any suggestion our parents may make. It is a time for testing the limits of our environment and for refusing to take orders from others. In Allport's view, we are typically very negativistic at this stage. Moreover, many of us do not outgrow our oppositional tendencies and they reappear, usually in adolescence. Then our "enemies" typically are our parents and other members of the "establishment."

Self-Extension. From approximately 4 to 6 years of age, we are in a phase in which our primary concern is possessions. We are typically very egocentric. "I know the moon is following us, Daddy!" "No, I want *all* of the candy!" "He can't come into *my* house!" "Get out of *my* room, Billy!" These are just some of the manifestations of our unreasoning selfishness. We also become immersed in material possessions. It is not that unusual to see adolescents and adults kissing their cars, patting them, and encouraging them to perform in superior fashion. Imagine the symbolism a Freudian would see in such behavior! All these possessions become warm, acceptable parts of ourselves. To praise them is to praise the owner; ridicule them and you ridicule the owner. Later, as we mature, we extend our loyalties and concerns to other groups, people, churches, and nations. We no longer see these objects from a selfish perspective (What can they do for me?), but rather we become more concerned about benefiting them. We develop concerns about these groups and people based on moral principles and ideals (Allport, 1955, p. 45). Thus **self-extension** in the earliest phases of development is selfish; in the later phases it is unselfish.

Self-Image. The next aspect of the proprium is the **self-image.** This part of ourselves evolves during the same period as our sense of self-extension. The self-image has two components, according to Allport: learned expectations of the roles we are required to enact and the kinds of aspirations for the future we seek to attain (Allport, 1955, p. 47). The self-image evolves slowly in conjunction with the development of conscience. We learn to do things that others expect of us and to avoid behaviors that will bring disapproval. We begin to formulate plans for the future and to make tentative decisions about careers and the values we will embrace.

The Self as Rational Coper. During the period between 6 and 12, we begin to engage in reflective thought. We devise strategies to cope with problems, and we delight in testing our skills, particularly our intellectual ones. We are also capable of distortion and defense. Nevertheless, the thrust of Allport's argument is that we are, at this stage, beginning to be aware of the **self as rational coper,** to sense our rational powers and to exercise them (Allport, 1955, p. 46).

Propriate Striving. Finally, Allport discussed the aspect of the self called **propriate striving**. This facet of the self occurs from 12 on and can be understood if we concentrate on Allport's treatment of human motivation. He distinguished between propriate and peripheral motives. Peripheral motives are our impulses and drives and our striving toward the immediate gratification of our needs. They include our attempts at tension reduction. We are hungry; we eat. We are thirsty; we drink. We are cold; we put on clothing. We are fatigued; we go to sleep. These are simple and automatic acts aimed at reducing our tensions. Propriate motives, in contrast, consist of our "ego-involved" behavior. They include our attempts to increase or maintain rather than decrease tensions and our striving for important goals. We strive to attain a college degree, sometimes at tremendous personal cost. We may try to become the best athlete in a given sport. We may yearn to be a great artist or novelist. Propriate striving is characterized by the unification of personality as we pursue our major goals. In Allport's view, "The possession of long-range goals, regarded as central to one's personal existence, distinguishes the human being from the animal, the adult from the child, and in many cases the healthy from the sick" (Allport, 1955, p. 51).

The emergence of propriate striving is closely related to the development of conscience. In the child, the evolving conscience is a "must" conscience, or what Fromm called an "authoritarian conscience" (Fromm, 1947, p. 148). It is also similar to Freud's conception. It is a conscience based on fear of punishment. The child begins to incorporate or internalize the parents' values and standards and feels guilty if he or she violates their rules. As the person matures, however, there is a marked change in his or her perception of the world and other people. There is an emergence of the "ought" conscience, or what Fromm called the "humanistic conscience." In this stage, obedience to the external standards of authority gives way to internal, or self-generated, rules. The person's conduct is guided by his or her own values and self-image.

The shift from a "must" to an "ought" conscience is not automatic. Many people who are adults in age are still children in conduct. They are still reacting to parental prohibitions. They still suffer from unresolved guilt feelings and a rehashing of old conflicts with authority figures (Allport, 1955, p. 74). They have not learned to rely on their own judgment and to orient themselves toward the attainment of challenging goals.

Although the seven aspects of the proprium seem to emerge at different stages of life, Allport felt that they do not function separately. Several, even all of them, can operate simultaneously, as the following example shows.

Suppose that you are facing a difficult and critical examination. No doubt you are aware of the butterflies in your stomach (bodily self); also of the significance of the exam in terms of your past and future (self-identity); of your prideful involvement (self-esteem); of what success or failure may mean to your family (self-extension); of your hopes and aspirations (self-image); of your role as the solver of problems on the examination (rational agent); and of the relevance of the whole situation to your long-range goals (propriate striving). In actual life, then, a fusion of propriate states is the rule. [Allport, 1961, p. 137]1

The Development of the Mature Personality

Allport talked about the developmental process as one of **becoming.** The development of the mature personality takes time, according to him, so that only the adult is capable of coming close to self-realization. These shifts in development are not always smooth and even; they are, instead, often abrupt and discontinuous. The normal or mature person is qualitatively different from the abnormal or immature one.

Initially, the infant is an unsocialized being:

Even at the age of two the child is, when measured by standards applied to adults, an unsocialized horror. Picture, if you can, an adult who is extremely destructive of property, insistent and demanding that every desire be instantly gratified, helpless and dependent on others, unable to share his possessions, violent and uninhibited in the display of all his feelings. Such behavior, normal to a two year old, would be monstrous in a man. Unless these qualities are markedly altered in the process of becoming, we have on our hands an infantile and potentially evil personality. [Allport, 1955, pp. 28–29]

During this early stage of development not only are the persons dependent on others, but most of their behavior is designed to aid their adjustment or, in more understandable terms, to help them survive. They perform those behaviors that will reduce hunger and thirst, for instance. They also learn what Allport called our "tribal conformities"—for example, wearing clothes or brushing of teeth (Allport, 1955, p. 63).

As their propriums develop, they also learn to protect themselves against threats through the use of various defensive strategies. In this regard, Allport accepted the validity of the Freudian ego-defense mechanisms, but he felt that excessive and indiscriminate use of these strategies is indicative of an abnormal or immature personality. The mature personality, in contrast, is characterized as being relatively free of these debilitating tactics. Allport granted that sometimes adults behavior is motivated by sexual and aggressive needs, but once again he felt that such motivation plays a relatively small part in the functioning of the mature person. In his view, the mature individual's functioning is directed more by events that affect him or her currently. Thus, if you want to understand behavior, focus on current rather than past motives. For example, students may eat too little not because they are fixated at the oral stage but because they have a contract with the college to eat in the dining halls and the food there is relatively unappetizing.

Functional Autonomy. The early development of the person, then, is characterized by the presence of peripheral motives. Later, as the proprium develops, there is a shift from reliance on such learnings and motives to reliance on ones that are more central to ourselves. These propriate strivings include the use of our creative and spontaneous energies to move us toward full maturity. The key question now becomes "How do we free ourselves from these infantile motives so that we can function as mature adults?" The answer, according to Allport, is found in his general law of motivation called **functional autonomy**. As he put it, "Functional autonomy regards adult motives as varied and as self-sustaining, contemporary systems growing out of antecedent systems but functionally independent of them" (Allport, 1961, p. 227). Through the use of this concept, Allport hoped to show that, as persons mature, their bonds with the past are broken. Mature persons no longer depend on parents. They have become functionally autonomous— that is, their behavior is independent of the parents' wishes. They also no longer need to use defensive tactics to protect their self-esteem from attacks by others. They are independent of them because they are now capable of judging their conduct by self-generated rules. A few examples may clarify the concept:

> An ex-sailor has a craving for the sea, a musician longs to return to his instrument after an enforced absence, a miser continues to build up his useless pile. Now the sailor may have first acquired his love for the sea as an incident in his struggle to earn a living. The sea was "secondary reinforce-ment" for his hunger drive. But now the ex-sailor is perhaps a wealthy banker; the original motive is destroyed and yet the hunger for the sea persists and even increases in intensity. The musician may first have been stung by a slur on his inferior performance into mastering his instrument; but now he is safely beyond these taunts, and finds that he loves his instrument more than anything else in the world. The miser perhaps learned his habit of thrift in dire necessity, but the miserliness persists and becomes stronger with the years even after the necessity has been relieved. [Allport, 1961, p. 227]

Thus Allport's concept of functional autonomy serves as a bridge between the phase of development controlled by immature strivings and that char-acterized by mature motives. It should be noted that Allport's concept pro-vides a description of shifts in the developmental process and not an expla-nation of *why* the shift occurs. Allport struggled mightily to provide an adequate explanation of the phenomenon. He saw its basic roots as biological, but concluded that we lack knowledge of the specific neurological mechanisms that may be involved (Allport, 1961, pp. 244–245). Speculating further, he thought that each person has a creative energy level that must be satisfied.

If it is not, then new interests and motives must develop. These new developments are qualitatively different from motives that operate simply to satisfy our basic hunger, thirst, and sex needs. People are, in Allport's view, innately curious and seek to understand themselves, others, and their environments. They are continually trying to discover their place in the world, to establish their unique identities. This creative quest for growth, meaning, and selfhood is part of our nature (Evans, 1970, p. 32). It is a movement toward becoming and, in the final analysis, it underlies the phenomenon of functional autonomy and helps explain the radical shifts in our motives as we move toward maturity. To be sure, this creative urge for meaning is influenced and modified by our experiences with others and the environment. For example, a person has no fully formed, innate need to be a physician, but instead acquires an interest in medicine through reading, friends, teachers, and parents. The creative urge simply provides the impetus for doing something that is challenging and capable of fulfilling his or her potentials.

Finally, for Allport, the mature person is one who is able to free himself or herself from excessive reliance on earlier motives. Allport developed six criteria for judging whether or not a person is mature (Allport, 1961, p. 283). A discussion of each follows.

Extension of the Sense of Self. Truly mature persons, according to Allport, are able to participate in activities that go beyond themselves. They are concerned not only about their own welfare but also about the welfare of others. As Allport saw it:

> True participation gives direction to life. Maturity advances in proportion as lives are decentered from the clamorous immediacy of the body and of ego-centeredness. Self-love is a prominent and inescapable factor in every life, but it need not dominate. Everyone has self-love, but only self-extension is the earmark of maturity. [Allport, 1961, p. 285]

Warm Relatedness to Others. The mature individual is also capable of relating warmly to others. Allport distinguished between two kinds of warmth. The first is intimacy. The mature person is characterized by the capacity for love whether it be love of family or friends. The second kind is compassion. Allport believed that mature persons have a certain detachment in their dealings with others that allow them to be respectful and appreciative of individual differences in behavior and thought.

Both kinds of warmth suggest that the mature person would not be possessive, gossipy, or intrusive on the privacy or rights of others. He or she would avoid constant complaining, criticizing, and sarcasm. Putting it another way, the mature person, according to Allport, would follow the rule "Do not poison the air that other people have to breathe." Such respect for other people is in evidence because the mature person *comes to know that all mortals are in the same human situation: They did not ask to come into the world; they are saddled with an urge to survive and are buffeted by drives and passions; they encounter failure, suffer, but somehow carry on. No one knows for sure the meaning of life; everyone is growing older as he sails to an unknown destination. [Allport, 1961, p. 285]*

Self-Acceptance. Mature persons are also emotionally secure. They avoid overreacting on matters that are beyond their control. They have a high frustration tolerance level, for they have reached the point of **self-acceptance.** Immature persons, in contrast, tend to act impulsively and to blame others for their own mistakes. Unlike mature persons, they do not bide their time or make plans to circumvent obstacles in their path. In brief, they lack the kind of self-control that characterizes the mature person.

Realistic Perception of Reality. Mature persons are also accurate in their perception of events. They do not continually distort reality. They have the knowledge and skills that are necessary for effective performance and living. Along with these skills, they also have the capacity to lose themselves in their work. In short, they are problem-centered, not ego-centered.

Self-Objectification. Mature persons know themselves. They are blessed with **self-objectification**—insight into their own abilities and limitations. Correlated with their insight is a sense of humor. Mature individuals have the ability to see the absurdity in life and not be overwhelmed by it. They can be amused by their own mistakes and not deceived by their own pretentiousness.

Unifying Philosophy of Life. The mature individual also has developed "a clear comprehension of life's purpose in terms of an intelligible theory" (Allport, 1961, p. 294). Allport noted that the sense of "directedness" is present in mature people and that such a set of life goals is typically vaguely defined in adolescents. Young people do have ideals, but these are sometimes not clearly delineated. Moreover, once they seek to implement these ideals and fall short, they begin to experience disappointment. In their late 20s they begin to learn that they must compromise with reality. They find that their jobs are not as challenging or rewarding as they had hoped, that their marriages or living arrangements fall far short of their desires, and that they have not been able to overcome some of their personal limitations (Allport, 1961, p. 295). They find their goals and values changing and a revised and clearer set of principles beginning to emerge. The mature person has a fairly clear self-image and a set of standards that guide his or her conduct.

In regard to the relationship between traits and the proprium, we can only speculate. As the beginning of the proprium occurs in infancy and most of our complex traits are learned later in the developmental cycle, it seems reasonable to assume that the proprium is the guiding force in our lives, whereas traits are more an outgrowth of its functioning. Because some of our traits are cardinal or central ones, some of our characteristics are clearly bound in important ways to proprium functioning. In short, some traits are integral parts of ourselves. It is also clear that, although the proprium guides our conduct, new experiences can also have an impact. For example, a person may be guided by a self-image that requires him or her to be kind to others, but changes in both the self-image and the central trait of kindness may be modified by experiences with a series of exploitive individuals.

Techniques of Assessment

Because Allport considered personality to be a dynamic and interrelated entity, he thought it pointless to focus only on one or two of its facets. Since it is so complex, he believed that investigators must employ every "legitimate method" to study it (Allport, 1961, p. 395). Legitimate methods include reliable and valid assessment procedures based on objective and systematic observations of given phenomena. Illegitimate methods, according to him, include "gossip, prejudiced inference, the exaggerated single instance, unverified anecdote . . . [and] 'character reading'" (Allport, 1961, pp. 395–396).

Some of the legitimate methods are (1) constitutional and physiological diagnosis; (2) studies of sociocultural membership, status, and roles; (3) personal documents and case studies; (4) self-appraisal techniques such as self-ratings and Q-sorts (see Chapter 15); (5) conduct samplings such as behavior assessments in everyday situations; (6) observer ratings; (7) personality tests and scales; (8) projective tests; (9) depth analysis, such as free association and dream analysis; (10) expressive behavior measures; and (11) synaptic procedures (Allport, 1961, p. 458). Synaptic procedures involve combining the outcomes of a variety of assessment techniques to produce a general profile of the individual's personality (Allport, 1961, p. 445).

Although some of these techniques focus on the typical case or the average person, Allport's own orientation centered on the uniqueness of the individual. As he said, "Each person is an idiom unto himself, an apparent violation of the syntax of the species" (Allport, 1955, p. 19). As a result, he fought an uphill battle against the prevailing view in American psychology that a science of personality should seek to establish universal laws of human functioning. It should seek, according to Allport's opponents, to understand the behavior and experience of people in general, to focus on the typical case or the average person. Such an approach Allport labeled **nomothetic.** He distinguished this approach from one in which the primary goal is to understand the functioning of a specific individual. Such a science he labeled **idiographic.**

The two views also generate different kinds of information about people. The nomothetic approach, for example, relies heavily on the use of statistics in the analysis of human behavior. It can tell us that in comparison to Bill or Jane, John has a lower need for achievement because he scored only at the 10th percentile on a paper-and-pencil test designed to measure this characteristic, whereas the other two people scored well above the 95th percentile. Further testing could tell us that John is above average in intelligence as compared to other adolescents of the same age. But Allport argued that although such testing may give us information about John that is useful, its usefulness is quite limited; it does not tell us anything about John's uniqueness. The information we obtained is abstracted from a unique personality. The idiographic approach, in contrast, would provide us with information about the ways in which these and many other characteristics interact with John's personality. It would give us a view of the dynamic and organized personality that is peculiar to John. Thus Allport would seek to establish the lawfulness in John's behavior and experiences through the use of such techniques as personal records, pattern analysis of expressive movements, graphology, and case studies (Allport, 1937, pp. 369–399).

We turn now to a consideration of an attempt by Allport to understand the unique functioning of an individual through an analysis of personal documents.

Jennie Gove Masterson: An Idiographic Analysis. A prime example of the use of personal documents to facilitate understanding of an individual's personality and life is seen in Allport's pioneering analysis of the correspondence of Jennie Gove Masterson. Between the ages of 58 and 70, Mrs. Masterson wrote a series of 301 letters to two friends of her son, Ross. The letters provide insight into her personality and her tempestuous and strange relationship with Ross.

As a young woman, Jenny married an American railway inspector, a Henry Masterson. Before her marriage, she earned her own living and now she found it very irritating to remain at home idle all day. She complained often to her husband about her situation, but to no avail. Like most men who lived in the early part of the 1900s, he was vehemently opposed to his wife seeking employment. Before the issue was resolved, her husband died. A month later, her son was born.

Shortly afterward, she went to work as a telegrapher to support herself and her infant son. She did not complain about widowhood but was very happy to have a child to whom she could give her undivided attention. Jenny was so content with this arrangement that she rejected several desirable offers of marriage. She lavished affection on Ross and was his constant companion. Several of her relatives claimed she spoiled him, but she replied that she would gladly scrub floors to buy him the things he said he wanted. After several quarrels with her relatives about her pampering of Ross, she severed her relationship with them for 25 years.

When Ross reached puberty, Jenny sent him to an expensive boarding school. She took a position as a librarian so that she could cover his educational expenses. She lived chiefly on cereal and milk in a small, windowless room for several years to cut costs. She remained Ross' closest companion. This overprotectiveness continued for several more years until Ross rebelled. He began to see other women, and quarrels with Jenny about them were frequent and very bitter. Eventually Ross married but kept it a secret from his mother. She soon discovered his deception, however, and was furious. She drove him out of her home with violent denunciations and threatened to have him arrested if he tried to see her again. A few years later she relented and began to see and correspond with him until his untimely death.

Following is a sample of four letters she wrote to Ross' two friends, Glenn and Isabel, about him and other people in her life over this stormy period of more than a decade.

At the time of the first letter written in 1928, Ross had abandoned his wife and begun a relationship with another woman. Jenny is despondent and turns to Glenn and Isabel for support, explaining why she is so unhappy with Ross and why there is antagonism between them.

> "But it isn't money that stands between Ross and me—not by any means— it's women—more women. (My writing is awful—I'm all nerves.) Sometimes I wonder if Ross is a trifle off balance—sex mad. At first he talked lovely about saving money, building up a character in business and that sort of thing, and I was in the 7th Heaven. He has saved money, it's in our joint names in a bank, several hundred dollars. That's why I skimped so. But all the time he was carrying on an affair with a woman, ... a very bad affair, and before he got out of it, he wasn't so far from the Pen. I helped him out of that—

> "Now, it's Marie, the Butcher's daughter from Toledo. ... When Ross ditched his wife he wrote to Marie. [Now] Marie [speaks] of coming to N.Y. this winter and renting a room. Ross and I had a scrap—I refuse to do it. Marie will never enter any house that I am in. ...

> "I did not intend to say so much, but I'm heartsore, and sick, and truly discouraged. Ross cares absolutely nothing at all for me—I am a great drawback and burden to him." [Allport, 1965, pp. 51–53]

In the second letter written in 1929, Jenny mentions Ross' poor health. He suffered from an infected ear, had an operation, and the doctors found a large mastoid on the inner ear and an abscess on the outer covering of the brain. She also mentions her resentment of Ross' girlfriend, who she calls a chip (whore).

> "Ross called to see me last week—he is still in the Dr.'s hands. He looks very poorly. I invited him to ... have luncheon with me, and he did. ... It was a swell luncheon, and he seemed to enjoy it. You know ... the way to bring Ross to his senses is to give him what he wants and then leave him alone.

> "I wish now that I had left him last May when he moved the Chip to the Bronx. But even if he marries her now (she may force him into it) he will not remain with her long. And that is where I come in, and why I invited him to

luncheon—so that he may not be quite alone until he finds a new chip. Right well I know that he hasn't a bit of use for me—is ashamed of me, and despises me, but still the tie of blood is there, and I cannot believe that he is altogether insensible to it." [Allport, 1965, p. 70]

Unfortunately, Ross did not recover from his illness and died shortly afterward. In the third letter written at the end of 1929, Jenny's hostility toward Ross' girlfriend erupts, and she blames her for Ross' death.

"My affairs. Oh, they are all in a turmoil. The chip lady [although] all dissolved in tears, and of course heartbroken, is not too liquid to forget that material things count in this mundane sphere, and lo! she claimed Ross's clothes, and Ross's car . . . [She claims to be Ross's closest relative.] If she is Ross's nearest relative it is she who will receive the [Veteran Administration's] compensation, and that would be tragic enough to make one die of laughter. She has only known him 6 months. February was the beginning of their "Great Romance"—dirty and low as they are made—the low contemptible street dog. She killed Ross—morally and physically." [Allport, 1965, pp. 73–74]

Following Ross' death, Jenny entered into a series of legal entanglements with his girlfriend over his estate, from which Jenny emerged victorious. In her fourth letter written in 1930 on Ross' birthday, Jenny recalls the happy time she and Ross experienced on his birthday the year before his death.

"This month has been pretty hard on me—I had to move—it cost a lot— then came Ross's birthday, October 16. Last October 16 Ross spent with me— I watched for him all morning, my heart in my mouth. Then early in the afternoon he came, carrying a lovely bunch of red roses—my favorites—he always got red roses for me. I was in Heaven. He had not forgotten me—he chose to have dinner with me—not with the Chip. He took me to a nice place . . . on Broadway, and then to a show—a splendid show—he came to my room on the roof, and kissed [me] goodnight under the stars—how little we dreamed of what the next year would bring! I am always thinking of him— always wishing that I had done something I did not do—or left something undone, or unsaid, that I did do, and said." [Allport, 1965, p. 88]

In 1931 Jenny entered a home for women. She described it as similar to a good hotel. She lived there until her death in 1937. The superintendent of the home said that she had become unbearably difficult during the year before her death. She had taken to sweeping her dinner onto the floor from the dining-room table if it displeased her and had even attacked one of the boarders, hitting her over the head with a pail. The boarders were afraid of her, and the superintendent had been considering her removal to an institution for the insane just before her death.

An Analysis of the Correspondence: Jenny's Traits. Allport asked 36 judges to read Jenny's letters and then to characterize her in trait terms.

The judges assigned a total of 198 trait names, which were subsequently reduced to eight major, central traits considered important for understanding her personality: quarrelsome-suspicious, self-centered, independent, dramatic, aesthetic-artistic, aggressive, cynical-morbid, and sentimental.

Allport believed that the judges' evaluations of Jenny's letters provided some insights into her personality that went beyond a commonsense interpretation of her character gained by a casual reading of the letters. But he maintained that the judges' assessments were nevertheless still primarily intuitive. He then reported a follow-up study in which content analysis was used to assess the structure of Jenny's personality. Content analysis is a research technique for the objective, systematic, and quantitative description of communications (Allport, 1965, p. 197). The content of her letters was coded; that is, what she said was classified into many distinct categories, such as hostility, art appreciation, and affection. Then, for each category, a frequency count was recorded—for example, the number of times a hostile remark was made, that Jenny mentioned her love of art, and that she made comments about her affection for people. These data were then subjected to a complex statistical analysis called factor analysis (see Chapter 9) to discover the major traits of Jenny's personality.

The results obtained with this relatively objective analysis were quite similar to the findings produced by the more intuitive approach (the judges' ratings). Allport cautioned us to remember that, although these two approaches provide us with insight into the uniqueness of Jenny's personality, they by no means provide all the answers about her.

Application of the Theory to the Treatment of Psychopathology

For Allport, the healthy or mature person is one who is continually in a state of becoming; the unhealthy or immature person is one whose growth has been stifled. He believed, like Freud, that the person's development could be arrested as a result of faulty relationships with his or her parents, especially the mother, in early childhood. Allport believed that each of us needs to be secure and protected and that deprivations of love and affection can have a lasting and harmful impact on our growth:

All in all a generous minimum of security seems required in early years for a start toward a productive life-style. Without it the individual develops a pathological craving for security, and is less able than others to tolerate setbacks in maturity. Through his insistent demanding, jealousy, depredation, and egoism he betrays the craving that still haunts him. By contrast, the child who receives adequate gratification of his infant needs is more likely to be prepared to give up his habits of demanding, and to learn tolerance for his later frustrations. Having completed successfully one stage of development

*he is free to abandon the habits appropriate to this stage and to enter the
mature reaches of becoming. [Allport, 1955, p. 32]*

To overcome these deprivations, Allport believed that the person must
come to feel "accepted and wanted by therapist, family, and associates."
The person must feel loved and must learn to love. As Allport put it, "Love
received and love given comprise the best form of therapy" (Allport, 1955,
p. 33).

But this is only one side of the picture. There are many people who have
had secure and loving backgrounds who later become neurotic. Although
their secure backgrounds make them free to grow, other problems crop up.
Pressures are exerted on individuals to adjust to the norms of society, and
often these adjustments preclude positive growth. Why? The reason, according to Allport:

*Society itself is sick. Why . . . make a patient content with its injustices, hypoc-
risies, and wars? And to what society shall we adjust the patient? To his
social class, thus making him provincial and depriving him of aspiration? To
his nation, thus giving him no vision of mankind as a whole? It is doubtful
that we can accept society (any society) as a standard for a healthy personality.
A head-hunter society demands well-adjusted head-hunters as citizens, but
is the deviant in this group who questions the value of decapitation necessarily an immature human being? [Allport, 1961, p. 305]*

Indiscriminate acceptance of these demands produces persons with
restricted self-extension, a distorted self-image, a defensive self, and stunted
propriate striving. That is, their loyalties become circumscribed, producing
an intolerance of other people and groups outside the favored few. They
also see themselves and their goals in terms of the values established by
others. For example, a person may see himself as a lawyer and pursue that
goal because his parents demand that he do so. In the process, important
goals that he actually desires to pursue are shunted aside. He experiences
considerable conflict and uses defensive maneuvers to alleviate the suffering.
Movement toward self-realization is hindered. The task of the therapist, in
Allport's view, is to help such persons become aware of the sources of their
distorted goals and to assist them in the attainment of maturity and well-
being.

Critical Comments

We turn now to a consideration of the scientific worth of Allport's theory.

Comprehensiveness. Allport's theory is comprehensive in the sense that
it is incredibly eclectic, borrowing and using concepts from learning theory,
psychoanalysis, and existentialism; but, technically speaking, most of its

focus is on healthy development. In addition, the various developmental stages of the proprium are described in general terms, and there is little attempt to specify precisely the variables that control the occurrence, maintenance, or modification of self-phenomena. The theory is also restricted in the sense that it recognizes the influence of the environment in the development of personality but does not specify the ways in which the environment operates to affect functioning.

Precision and Testability. Allport's theory is populated with vague and ill-defined concepts and relational statements. Terms like *propriate striving* and the *self as rational coper* do not lend themselves readily to operational definitions. We have already seen that Allport was not explicit in stating the ways in which his trait concepts were related to his formulations about the development of the proprium. Given these problems, it is apparent that it would be difficult to design adequate tests of his theory.

Parsimony. Allport's theory fails to meet the parsimony criterion not because it is surfeited with excess concepts but because it has too few concepts to account for the phenomena within its domain. It is doubtful that the complexities of the developmental process can be described adequately in terms of the seven major concepts he utilized in portraying the properties of the self.

Empirical Validity. There have been few attempts to determine the validity of Allport's theory of traits and self-development. Perhaps the chief reason for this neglect has been that the theory of traits is primarily descriptive and does not contain general propositions that could lead to the derivation of testable hypotheses. His theory of self-development is also primarily descriptive, and much of it is stated in such global terms that it does not lend itself readily to empirical testing. Thus empirical support for his theory is weak.

Heuristic Value. Although Allport's theory has not generated much research, his arguments concerning the necessity of accounting for the role of individual traits (personal dispositions) in the development of an adequate theory of personality remain relevant and provocative to investigators to the present day (see Maddi, 1980, pp. 342–344). He remains the champion of the idiographic approach to the study of personality. As he put it:

> Psychology is truly itself only when it can deal with individuality. It is vain to plead that other sciences do not do so, that they are allowed to brush off the bothersome issue of uniqueness. The truth is that psychology is assigned the task of being curious about human persons, and persons exist only in concrete and unique patterns. . . .
>
> We study the human person most fully when we take him as an individual. He is more than a bundle of habits, more than a point of intersection of

abstract dimensions. He is more than a representative of his species, more than a citizen of the state, more than an incident in the movements of mankind. He transcends them all. The individual, striving ever for integrity and fulfillment, has existed under all forms of social life-forms as varied as the nomadic and feudal, capitalist and communist. No society holds together for long without the respect man shows to man. The individual today struggles on even under oppression, always hoping and planning for a more perfect democracy where the dignity and growth of each personality will be prized above all else. [Allport, 1961, p. 573]

Many investigators have been forced by Allport's clear voice to reconsider their acceptance of the tenets of a nomothetic science and to agree with him that any worthwhile theory of personality has to focus on the uniqueness of the individual.

Applied Value. Allport's theory has not had much impact on disciplines outside psychology. Within psychology, however, his theory of self-development has proved highly useful to clinical psychologists in their treatment of patients.

Discussion Questions

1. Compare and contrast the nomothetic and idiographic approaches to the study of personality. What are the advantages and disadvantages of each view?
2. In what ways is Allport an important forerunner of the humanistic movement in psychology?
3. Describe the various phases of the developmental process as postulated by Allport. How much research support is there for his theory of development?
4. Is it always healthy to live by your own standards or values and not by the standards of others?
5. List the inadequacies of utilizing the notion of functional autonomy as an explanatory concept of behavior.
6. Describe the criteria used by Allport to characterize the mature person. Can you think of any others?
7. What is a trait? What kinds of traits are there, according to Allport? Give concrete examples of the operation of each kind in people you know.
8. Is it truly possible to have traits that are unique to the individual?
9. Do you agree with Allport that young children are "unsocialized horrors"? What are the implications of Allport's belief for the disciplining of children?
10. What are some of the major problems in utilizing trait concepts to explain behavior?

References

Allport, G. W. *Personality: A psychological interpretation.* New York: Holt, 1937.
Allport, G. W. *The nature of prejudice.* Reading, Mass.: Addison-Wesley, 1954.

Allport, G. W. *Becoming: Basic considerations for a psychology of personality.* New Haven: Yale University Press, 1955.

Allport, G. W. *Pattern and growth in personality.* New York: Holt, Rinehart & Winston, 1961.

Allport, G. W. *Letters from Jenny.* New York: Harcourt, Brace & World, 1965.

Allport, G. W. An autobiography. In G. W. Allport (Ed.), *The person in psychology: Selected essays.* Boston: Beacon Press, 1968.

Evans, R. I. *Gordon Allport: The Man and His Ideas.* N.Y.: Dutton, 1970.

Fromm, E. *Man for himself.* New York: Holt, Rinehart & Winston, 1947.

Holt, R. R. Individuality and generalization in the psychology of personality. *Journal of Personality,* 1962, *30,* 377–402.

Maddi, S. R. The uses of theorizing in personality. In E. Staub (Ed.), *Personality: Basic aspects and current research.* Englewood Cliffs, N. J.: Prentice-Hall, 1980.

Suggested Readings

Allport, G. W. *Personality: A psychological interpretation.* New York: Holt, 1937.

Allport, G. W. *Becoming: Basic considerations for a psychology of personality.* New Haven: Yale University Press, 1955.

Allport, G. W. *Personality and social encounter.* Boston: Beacon Press, 1960.

Allport, G. W. *Pattern and growth in personality.* New York: Holt, Rinehart and Winston, 1961.

Allport, G. W. *Letters from Jenny.* New York: Harcourt, Brace & World, 1965.

Allport, G. W. *The person in psychology: Selected essays.* Boston: Beacon Press, 1968.

Glossary

Becoming   Developmental process involving movement toward self-realization.

Bodily self   Feelings that people have about themselves as a result of feedback from their physical senses.

Cardinal trait   Characteristic of the individual that serves as the motivating force for virtually all of his or her behavior.

Central trait   Important characteristic that controls the behavior of an individual in a variety of situations.

Common trait   Disposition we share with others.

Functional autonomy   Process whereby a behavior that was once controlled by a motive no longer is dependent on the operation of that motive for its occurrence. It is now said to function or operate independently of the motive.

Genotype   Inherited characteristics that may or may not be reflected in the phenotype, or outward appearance of the individual.

Idiographic view   Approach to science that seeks to understand the uniqueness of a given individual's behavior through intensive investigation.

Nomothetic view   Scientific approach to the study of behavior that seeks to establish laws by specifying the general relationships between variables.

Personal disposition   Trait unique to the individual.

Phenotype   Outward appearance of a particular characteristic that may or may not reflect the underlying inherited genotype.

Propriate striving   Motive that propels the individual toward attainment of important, long-range goals. These drives involve an increase, rather than a decrease, in tension.

Proprium Term used by Allport to signify all the various aspects of the person that make him or her unique. A synonym for the self.

Psychophysical system Way of conceptualizing the organization of inner experience through the use of psychological concepts to represent actual underlying states in the nervous system.

Secondary trait Peripheral characteristic such as a preference.

Self-acceptance The person's tolerance and understanding of his or her limitations, as well as a recognition of his or her strengths.

Self as rational coper Describes the period during which individuals see themselves as capable of rationally formulating and utilizing strategies to attain personal goals.

Self-esteem Feelings a person has about his or her worth.

Self-extension A sense of identity that people have with their possessions, family, home, and country. In the immature person, self-extension involves egocentricity. The person sees other objects (e.g., family, people) in terms of their contribution to his welfare and security. In the mature person, self-extension involves the need to contribute to the welfare of other people and groups that are central to his existence.

Self-identity Feelings people have about themselves, that they are established human beings who have a past that is unique and that guides their judgments.

Self-image Role people play to win the approval of others; also the formulation of plans and behavioral strategies for the future that help people attain their goals.

Self-objectification Ability of an individual to divorce himself or herself from emotional entanglements in problems and to see them realistically. It also involves a recognition of one's own abilities and limitations.

Trait theory Conception of personality that postulates the existence of underlying dispositions or characteristics that direct behavior.

CHAPTER 9

Cattell's Factor Analytic Theory

Biographical Sketch

Raymond Bernard Cattell was born in Staffordshire, England, in 1905. He received a bachelor of science degree in chemistry from the University of London when he was 19 and his Ph.D. in psychology from the same institution in 1929. While at the university, he served as a research assistant to the famous psychologist-mathematician Charles Spearman, who was keenly interested in determining whether there was one general ability or intelligence or whether people were made up of many different and specific abilities. To answer that question, he gave a large series of tests pertinent to the issue, intercorrelated the test scores, and came to the conclusion that there was, indeed, a single general intelligence factor. Today in psychology the tendency is to focus more on the specific abilities people possess and to utilize their scores for particular skill measures to predict specific types of performance; but the point is, in attempting to answer the question of general versus specific abilities, Spearman devised the method of factor analysis. Cattell has relied heavily on this technique in developing his own theory of personality.

Through Spearman and his intellectual predecessors, British scientist Sir Francis Galton and statistician Karl Pearson, Cattell was introduced to the statistical study of personality and ability functioning. Galton conducted pioneer work on the origins of genius and used statistical analyses of biological data to show associations between phenomena. Pearson later developed a formal, mathematical technique called the Pearson product-moment correlation coefficient to measure the size and direction of the association between two events. This procedure was later used in the creation of the factor analytic method.

Following his graduation, Cattell served as director of a psychology clinic in England before going to New York to become a research associate of the learning theorist E. L. Thorndike at Columbia University. Following his brief stay at Columbia, he held positions at Clark University, Harvard, and Duke before accepting a post at the University of Illinois in 1944. He remained at Illinois until 1973, when he left to establish the Institute for Research on Morality and Self-Realization in Boulder, Colorado. Currently Professor Cattell is a visiting professor at the University of Hawaii at Manoa.

Two other influences on Cattell's thinking should be mentioned. First, his clinical experience has led him to accept many of the psychoanalytic formulations, so that his theory is an interesting blend of rigorous experimental work and clinical observation. Second, it is clear that Cattell has been greatly influenced by the British social psychologist William McDougall, who espoused an instinct doctrine of social behavior. McDougall made an attempt to "explain" social behavior by postulating seven basic instincts: repulsion, curiosity, flight, pugnacity, self-abasement, self-assertion, and parenting. Through extensive factor-analytic research, Cattell has shown that there are ten clearly identifiable ergs (innate motives that influence behavior). They include food-seeking, mating, gregariousness, parental protectiveness, exploration, escape to security, self-assertion, narcissistic sex, pugnacity, and acquisitiveness. He has also tentatively identified several others but wants to wait for more confirmatory research before assigning them independent status. Cattell also relies heavily on McDougall's concept of sentiment in his theoretical formulations, as will become apparent.

Over a period of 50 years, Cattell has published approximately 35 books and well over 400 research articles. He has also been the author or coauthor of numerous personality tests, including the Culture Fair Intelligence Tests, the Eight State Questionnaire, the Motivation Analysis Test, the Object-Analytic (O-A) Personality Test Battery, the Institute for Personality and Ability Testing (IPAT) Anxiety Scale Questionnaire, the Clinical Analysis Questionnaire (CAQ), and the popular Sixteen Personality Factor Test (16 PF test).

Among his more notable books, *Description and Measurement of Personality* (1946) is an early attempt to encourage good, solid, empirical research in the area of personality by presenting the basic concepts of his theory and attendant research findings. In *Personality: A Systematic Theoretical and Factual Study* (1950), Cattell attempted to build on the foundation laid in the earlier work and, in addition, to evaluate data and theories other than his own. These other positions included psychoanalysis, observations from cultural and physical anthropology, and formulations from sociology. Next, Cattell published *Personality and Motivation: Structure and Measurement* (1957), which presented the most comprehensive treatment of his position to that date. In 1965, he published a popular version of his theory in *The Scientific Analysis of Personality.* (He further developed this book with P. Kline and published an updated version, *The Scientific Analysis of Personality and Motivation*, in 1977.) Some of his opinions on the usefulness of the multivariate approach to the study of personality are found in a text he edited called the *Handbook of Multivariate Experimental Psychology* (1966a). He also edited the *Handbook of Modern Personality Theory* with R. M. Dreger in 1977. Shortly thereafter, Cattell published *Personality and Learning Theory* in two volumes: Volume 1, *The Structure of Personality in Its Environment* (1979), and Volume 2, *A Systems Theory of Maturation and Structured Learning* (1980). These two impressive volumes represent Cattell's monumental attempt to integrate his earlier theoretical and research efforts. He also presented an expanded theory of personality development that takes into account both biological and environmental influences. Finally, Cattell published *The Inheritance of Personality and Ability* in 1982. The text aims at demonstrating the highly important role played by genetic factors in the determination of personality functioning and features the newest methodologies for assessing that role.

Basic Concepts and Principles

The Importance of Multivariate Experiments

To fully appreciate Cattell's perspective on personality, we must recognize his intense commitment to measurement and statistical analysis in the development of theory. For him, the methodological tail wags the theoretical dog. In other words, Cattell strongly believes that all scientific advances depend on exact measurement (Cattell, 1950, p. 4). Thus he is disdainful of "armchair speculation" that has no ties to measurement. Measurement provides the foundation from which theories spring and not the reverse. Before we try to determine why a person behaves as he or she does, we need to be able to accurately describe and measure the behavior itself (Cattell, 1950, p. 3).

To build a theory, then, we start with empirical observation and description and then generate tentative hypotheses based on this procedure. This procedure, in turn, leads to certain deductions that we then test empirically. Following our observations, the process begins again. Cattell calls the entire process the **inductive-hypothetico-deductive spiral** (see Figure 9.1). This

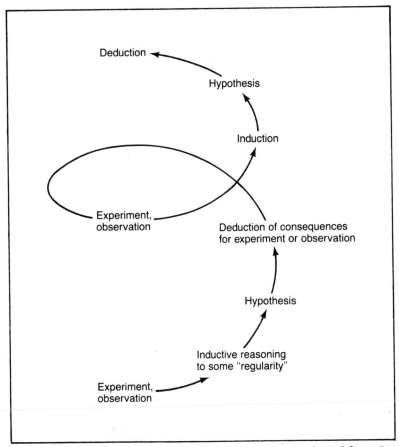

Figure 9.1 The inductive-hypothetico-deductive spiral. Adapted from Cattell, 1966b, p. 16.

theory-building technique is in contrast to the hypothetico-deductive model presented in Chapter 1, because it begins with a set of general propositions from which hypotheses are then deduced and tested. Although this model is the one generally employed in the social sciences, Cattell's point is that all too often such theories demand that the researcher have a fully developed hypothesis before starting the research. First, such a requirement fails to teach neophyte investigators about research as an exploratory process. Second, it leads them to believe that confirmation of their hypothesis rests on some single measurement difference. According to Cattell, this latter belief is particularly misleading because it encourages the researcher to think that the behavior under consideration was caused by a single event when in fact it had multiple origins. Of course, Cattell may be knocking down a straw man—few investigators in contemporary psychology are naive enough to believe that behavior is usually caused by a single event. Nevertheless, two important and cogent points Cattell raises are (1) that excessive reliance on **bivariate experiments** to test hypotheses leads to oversimplified interpretations of the way events operate in reality, and (2) that only **multivariate experiments** allow investigators to analyze and interpret complex behavior adequately.

In making his case for the use of multivariate experiments in psychology, Cattell argues that the bivariate method—that is, the method that relies on the manipulation of an independent variable and the assessment of its impact on a dependent measure—artificially considers "bits" of human behavior and ignores studying the "total organism" (Cattell, 1965, p. 20). In contrast, the multivariate experimenter considers the "whole person" and the complexity of his or her behavior. The investigator "actually measures all the variables and . . . then set[s] an electronic computer to abstract the regularities which exist" (Cattell, 1965, p. 22).

Cattell's arguments should not lead you to conclude that he considers bivariate experimentation worthless. He simply believes that it is a far more rewarding strategy to utilize multivariate techniques first in initial, exploratory research on some problem in order to identify the key variables and to generate hypotheses that can then be tested with bivariate and manipulative experimental designs (Cattell, 1979, p. 7). To study multiple-variable problems, Cattell relies heavily on various forms of factor analysis.

What Is Factor Analysis?

A highly complicated statistical procedure, **factor analysis** is concerned with the isolation and identification of a limited number of variables, or factors, that underlie a larger group of observed, interrelated variables. Factor analysis has a number of forms, but Cattell utilizes two of them primarily— the R technique and the P technique—in the bulk of his work.

R Technique. The most common form of factor analysis is the **R technique.** It usually involves giving large groups of subjects a variety of personality tests, then intercorrelating their scores. If, for example, we administered to a large introductory psychology class several tests measuring indecisiveness, tendency to brood, depression, aggressiveness, competitiveness, and conceit, then scored each of them, and then intercorrelated all of the subjects' scores, we might find a series of correlations like those in Table 9.1. We can see, for example, that subjects who had high scores on the test designed to measure indecisiveness also had high scores on the brooding test and on the depression test. In brief, these three tests are highly intercorrelated. They are, however, essentially unrelated (have very low correlations) to subjects' scores on the remaining three tests (that is, the aggressiveness, competitiveness, and conceit tests). These latter three tests are, however, highly intercorrelated. High intercorrelations, or clustering, among variables suggest the presence of some underlying factor(s) that caused sub-

Table 9.1
Intercorrelations between Six Test Variables

Test	A	B	C	D	E	F
A Indecisiveness	—					
B Brooding	.72	—				
C Depression	.85	.67	—			
D Aggressiveness	.02	.04	.07	—		
E Competitiveness	.08	.18	.00	.83	—	
F Conceit	.16	.04	.10	.92	.68	—

jects to respond the way they did on the tests that cluster together. Thus the investigator starts with a large number of surface variables (surface traits) and seeks to reduce them to a few common source factors (source traits) that can be used to predict the variation in the original surface variable measures. Variables that are strongly intercorrelated are considered to be measuring, to a great extent, the same entity, or factor. The problem facing investigators is that they must then eventually label these underlying factors. As the judgments are subjectively based interpretations that have important implications for future theorizing and research, considerable skill and care must be exercised in the labeling process. Inaccurate interpretations can be costly.

Once the intercorrelations have been determined, further factor-analytic computations are employed to derive a factor matrix such as the one shown in Table 9.2. The degree of association between each surface variable and the factors are called **factor loadings.** Loadings of .30 and above are usually considered substantial and significant. In Table 9.2 we can see that indecisiveness, brooding, and depression all load significantly on Factor I, which

Table 9.2
Loading of Six Tests on Two Factors Labeled Guilt-Proneness (Factor I) and Dominance (Factor II)

Test	Factor I	Factor II
A Indecisiveness	.68	.14
B Brooding	.76	.08
C Depression	.86	.04
D Aggressiveness	.11	.88
E Competitiveness	.03	.69
F Conceit	.15	.52

we can tentatively label "guilt-proneness." Likewise, aggressiveness, competitiveness, and conceit load significantly on Factor II, which we can label "dominance."

Once the factors have been tentatively identified, further research on other samples of subjects is usually conducted in an attempt to refine the factors even more. There will also be attempts to cross-validate the factors by using subjects of different ages, ethnic and cultural backgrounds, and so forth. In addition, other tests may be thrown into the factor analytic "basket" in an effort to discover new variables that load significantly on the factor. Interestingly, too, the primary factors themselves may be further analyzed to yield what Cattell calls **second-order factors.** These higher-order factors or strata control even more of the variation in test-score behavior than the **primary factors.** Anxiety and introversion/extraversion are two key exam ples of second-order factors. Thus primary factors such as ego weakness, guilt-proneness, innate tension, and suspiciousness all load on the general second-order anxiety factor.

P Technique. While the *R* technique allows investigators to assess the existence of common traits in large populations, the **P technique** is designed to discover the unique trait structure of the person (Cattell, 1961, p. 415; 1965, p. 372). It involves repeatedly testing a given individual by using a large number of personality dimensions on a number of different occasions. Thus an attempt is made to correlate the surface traits within one person and to discover via factor analysis his or her unique underlying traits. Using the technique, Cattell can also assess the process of change in an individual's motivation. For example, it tracks changes in the person's feelings of fatigue, guilt, arousal, and anxiety.

With this preliminary information about the mechanics of factor analysis in hand, let us examine Cattell's definition of personality and some of the other major concepts in his theory.

The Formula for Defining Personality

Personality is defined as "that which tells what [a person] will do when placed in a given situation" (Cattell, 1965, pp. 117–118). In line with his concern with the mathematical analysis of personality, Cattell then presents the definition in terms of the formula

$$R = f(S, P)$$

The formula signifies that the behavioral response (R) is a function (f) of the situation (S) that confronts the person and the nature of his or her personality (P). Although most trait theorists deemphasize the role played by situational parameters in influencing our behavior, Cattell has recently expanded his theorizing to include the ways in which situations, in conjunction with personality traits, influence behavior (Cattell, 1979; 1980). To account for situational influences, he has constructed an econetic model consisting of a system for classifying situations and for assessing their impact on the individual. Before examining this model in more detail, however, we turn to Cattell's treatment of the major personality factors, including ergs, sentiments, attitudes, interests, emotional states, and, especially, traits.

What Are Traits and How Do They Come into Being? According to Cattell, **traits** are relatively permanent and broad reaction tendencies and serve as the building blocks of personality. He makes distinctions between constitutional and environmental-mold traits, between ability, temperament, and dynamic traits, and between surface and source traits. Let us consider each of these major distinctions in turn.

Constitutional Traits and Environmental-Mold Traits. As Cattell sees it, **constitutional traits** are determined by biology, whereas **environmental-mold traits** are determined by experience—that is, by interactions with the environment. In other words, some traits are determined by nature, others by nurture.

Cattell has created a complicated statistical procedure called **Multiple Abstract Variance Analysis (MAVA)** to assess the degree to which various traits are determined genetically and environmentally. The method is based on comparisons between people of the same family either raised together or raised apart or between members of different families (that is, unrelated people) raised either together or apart. Each person is given a test to assess a particular trait. Specifically, the test for a given trait is administered to identical twins raised together, identical twins raised apart, fraternal twins raised together, fraternal twins raised apart, siblings raised together, siblings raised apart, unrelated children raised together, and unrelated children raised apart (Cattell, 1982, p. 90). The percentage of genes in common for members of these groupings, ranging from most to least, is identical twins, fraternal twins and siblings, and unrelated children. The test scores of the individuals in each of these groupings are then correlated with each other, through a technique known as intraclass correlations. Whereas ordinary correlations (see Chapter 1) are obtained by examining the associations between scores on different tests for the same individuals, intraclass correlations involve an examination of the associations between the scores of different individuals on the same test. Then, by using a number of complex mathematical equations, researchers can determine the precise amounts of contributions that genetic and environmental factors make in the development of a trait.

This complicated procedure can be understood better on logical grounds through the following example. If a researcher is interested in determining the contributions of genetic and environmental factors to the development of the trait of intelligence, he or she would give an intelligence test to members of the various groupings (or classes) just outlined. As identical twins have the same genes, any differences in intelligence between them are presumably due (primarily) to differences in their environments. Thus the correlation between identical twins, even those raised in radically different environments, for a trait entirely based on heredity should theoretically be +1.00. In reality, the correlation will be slightly lower owing to errors in measurement; the test will not be perfectly reliable. (In contrast, fraternal twins have only 50% of their genes in common, and therefore the correlation for a trait that is totally genetically determined would be lower than the one for identical twins.)

If, for example, the correlation between the scores on the intelligence test for identical twins raised together is actually + .86 and the correlation for identical twins raised apart is + .72, then, because these correlations are so high and similar in magnitude, they suggest that intelligence is largely hereditary. If, on the other hand, the correlation for identical twins raised together is + .86 and for identical twins raised apart is only + .22, then, because these correlations differ so radically in magnitude, they suggest that the environment has a much greater impact than heredity.

Pursuing the same problem from another perspective, if the correlation is + .86 for identical twins raised together, + .60 for fraternal twins raised together, + .47 for siblings raised together, and + .32 for unrelated individuals raised together, then the data suggest that intelligence is largely hereditary. This conclusion is based on the idea that, in general, the further away we get from close hereditary connections (high percentage of common genes), the smaller the correlations will become.

It turns out that the correlations used in the preceding example are based on actual data and have led the investigators who compiled them to conclude that approximately 70% of the variation in intelligence among individuals is due to genetic factors and the remaining 30% to environmental factors and errors of measurement (McGee & Wilson, 1984, p. 320).

One important feature of MAVA is that it allows researchers to make more precise determinations of the contributions of genetic and environmental factors to the development of traits than do other methods. This information can then be used to help clinicians make decisions about the kinds of treatment that should be used to maximize the chances of recovery of patients. Cattell points out that clinicians only ask for trouble if they try to change a largely genetic trait; instead, they should shrewdly use the trait as a fulcrum for levering some other trait that *is* susceptible to change—that is, an environmentally based trait. For example, if clinicians know that a client has an IQ of 140, they can utilize that fact to facilitate insights into his or her emotional problems. A different strategy would be pursued if the client's IQ was only 80 (Cattell, 1982, p. 396).

Ability Traits, Temperament Traits, and Dynamic Traits. Traits can be further subdivided into ability, temperament, and dynamic traits. **Ability**

traits refer to the person's skill in dealing with the complexity of a given situation. Intelligence is a good example. **Temperament traits** refer to the stylistic tendencies of the individual. For instance, people may be either chronically irritable, moody, easygoing, or bold. **Dynamic traits** refer to the motivation and interests of the person. A person may be characterized, for example, as ambitious, power-oriented, or interested in athletics (Cattell, 1965, p. 28).

In addition to these distinctions, Cattell, like Allport, thinks that categorizing traits as either common or unique is useful. Common traits refer to characteristics shared by many people—for example, intelligence, confidence, powerlessness. Unique traits are those specific to one person—for example, Bill is the only person with an interest in collecting 1898 census records for the cities of Baltimore and Los Angeles. Virtually all of Cattell's work focuses on common traits, but the incorporation of the unique-trait concept into his theory provides a means for him to emphasize that our personalities are unique. He also points out that the organization of common traits within our personalities is always unique.

Surface versus Source Traits. The distinction between surface and source traits is perhaps the most important one Cattell makes. In his view, **surface traits** are "simply a collection of trait elements, of greater or lesser width of representation which obviously 'go together' in many different individuals and circumstances" (Cattell, 1950, p. 21). These are variables that, when intercorrelated, cluster together. The **source trait,** in contrast, is the underlying factor that controls the variation in the surface cluster of traits. Surface and source traits are measured by the methods of factor analysis. Once we have accurately identified the major source traits controlling behavior, we should be in a better position to predict the person's behavior accurately, assuming, of course, that we have sufficient information about his or her ways of reacting in a given situation.

Major Source Traits

Cattell maintains that any attempt to discover the major source traits of personality must begin with an adequate sampling of all the personality traits that can be used to describe individuals. He calls this total domain of personality traits the **personality sphere** and maintains that the only practical source for such a listing is found in language. Cattell argues that over the centuries every aspect of one human being's behavior that is likely to affect another has been handled by some verbal symbol—that is, a trait name (Cattell, 1957, p. 71). Thus Cattell began by examining the 4500 trait names found in the English language by Allport and Odbert (1936) and then reduced them to 171 by eliminating synonyms. Observers then rated individuals on these traits. Using this procedure, 36 clusters of correlations—surface traits— were identified. Subsequently, ten other surface traits were added, a few from the psychiatric literature and some that appeared in experiments over the years. Thus Cattell maintains that 46 surface traits embrace the whole personality sphere (Cattell & Kline, 1977, pp. 30–31).

Later, personality questionnaires consisting of items incorporating the surface traits were constructed, administered to subjects, scored, and factor-analyzed to yield the underlying source traits of personality. (These traits were also assessed by using other data-collection techniques outlined in the "Techniques of Assessment" section.)

Initially, Cattell and his co-workers were able to identify 16 major source traits (Cattell, 1965, p. 64). These source traits were initially labeled factors A, B, C, D, E, and so on, but later, as more and more supportive evidence accumulated, the factors were more clearly identified and given labels. These 16 basic traits were then used in the construction of the **Sixteen Personality Factor Test (16 PF test).** The trait names of these factors are shown in Table 9.3. The traits are listed in order of their importance in controlling variation in behavior, starting with factor A and ending with factor Q. Thus the possession of information about a person's intelligence (factor B) would allow an investigator to predict that person's performance on given tasks more effectively than would knowledge about his or her dominance (factor E). To measure the traits, study participants are given hundreds, even thousands, of items. Then their scores are factor analyzed. Some sample items for factor A are given in Table 9.4. Once the factors begin to emerge, other items are added and given to additional large groups of normal study participants to refine the factors. That is, the items that load most heavily on each factor are retained; the ones that do not are eliminated.

Factor A. The largest factor, factor A, turned out to be a dimension long recognized by psychiatrists as important in the differentiation of individuals who had been committed to mental hospitals. As Cattell notes, the German psychiatrist Emil Kraepelin first defined schizophrenia in terms of withdrawal, and later the Swiss psychiatrist Eugen Bleuler devised a classification scheme in which "insane" people were categorized as either cyclic or schizophrenic types. In the 1920s, Ernst Kretschmer, a German psychiatrist who did pioneering research on the relationship between physique and psychopathology, insisted that the types recognized by Bleuler were also found in a less extreme form in normal individuals. Kretschmer showed that these types were associated with certain body builds; schizothymes (schizophrenics) tended to be tall and thin, while cyclothymes (manic-depressives) tended to be plump (Cattell, 1965, pp. 65–66). Thus a long history of clinical observation and research findings supports the differentiation of individuals as either reserved or outgoing.

Factor C. Another main personality factor that emerged via statistical analysis was ego strength (factor C). This source trait is very similar to the psychoanalytic concept of ego strength. Research in many different laboratories in this country and in Great Britain shows that people who are

Table 9.3
Major Source Traits on the Sixteen Personality
Factor Test

Low-Score Description	Factor		Factor	High-Score Description
Reserved* (schizothymia)	$A-$	vs	$A+$	Outgoing (affectothymia)
Less Intelligent (low "8")	$B-$	vs	$B+$	More Intelligent (high "8")
Emotional (low ego strength)	$C-$	vs	$C+$	Stable (high ego strength)
Humble (submissiveness)	$E-$	vs	$E+$	Assertive (dominance)
Sober (desurgency)	$F-$	vs	$F+$	Happy-go-lucky (surgency)
Expedient (low superego)	$G-$	vs	$G+$	Conscientious (high superego)
Shy (threctia)	$H-$	vs	$H+$	Venturesome (parmia)
Tough-minded (harria)	$I-$	vs	$I+$	Tender-minded (premsia)
Trusting (alaxia)	$L-$	vs	$L+$	Suspicious (protension)
Practical (praxernia)	$M-$	vs	$M+$	Imaginative (autia)
Forthright (artlessness)	$N-$	vs	$N+$	Shrewd (shrewdness)
Placid (assurance)	$O-$	vs	$O+$	Apprehensive (guilt-proneness)
Conservative (conservatism)	Q_1-	vs	Q_1+	Experimenting (radicalism)
Group-tied (group adherence)	Q_2-	vs	Q_2+	Self-Sufficiency (self-sufficiency)
Casual (low integration)	Q_3-	vs	Q_3+	Controlled (high self-concept)
Relaxed (low ergic tension)	Q_4-	vs	Q_4+	Tense (ergic tension)

*Popular terms are not enclosed in parentheses; technical terms are. Adapted from Cattell, 1965, p. 365.

Table 9.4
Sample Items on the 16 PF for Factor A (Reserved versus Outgoing)

1. I would rather work as:
   a. an engineer   b. **a social science teacher***

2. I could stand being a hermit.
   a. True   b. **False**

3. I am careful to turn up when
   someone expects me.
   a. **True**   b. False

4. I would prefer to marry someone
   who is:
   a. a thoughtful companion   b. **effective in a social group**

5. I would prefer to read a book on:
   a. **national social service**   b. new scientific weapons

6. I trust strangers.
   a. sometimes   b. **practically always**

*A person who answers the items by choosing the boldfaced alternatives has an outgoing temperament. Adapted from Cattell, 1965, p. 70.

neurotic or highly anxious also tend to have low ego strength. Cattell points out that alcoholics, narcotics addicts, juvenile delinquents, and school drop-outs are abnormally low in ego strength. The essence of the factor involves an inability to control one's impulses and to deal realistically with problems (Cattell, 1965, p. 73–74).

Factor E. People who have scores high on factor E, submissiveness-dominance, show these characteristics: Those who are dominant (E +) are self-assertive, boastful, conceited, aggressive, vigorous, forceful, willful, and egotistical; those who are submissive (E −) tend to be unsure, modest, retiring, meek, quiet, and obedient. Note that almost all source traits have good and bad aspects at either pole. This means that a person whose scores load on the E + pole may have both positive and negative characteristics, as may a person whose scores load on E − (Cattell, 1965, pp. 90–91). For example, a person whose scores indicate dominance (E +) has the positive characteristics of vigor and forcefulness and the negative characteristics of conceit and egotism. Similarly, a submissive individual (E −) has the positive traits of modesty and quietness and the negative traits of uncertainty and excessive meekness.

Cattell mentions that men and boys score higher on dominance than women and girls; so do firefighters, Olympic champions, and pilots. Neurotics who are improving also show increases in dominance. But dominance is also prevalent in psychopaths—for example, in con artists and incorrigible criminals (Cattell, 1965, p. 92).

Factor F. The largest single factor in children is factor F, surgency-desurgency, and it is quite important in the personalities of adults. Cattell estimates that heredity determines 55% of the variation in this trait (Cattell, 1980, p. 58). High-surgency people are characterized as cheerful, joyous, sociable, responsive, energetic, witty, humorous, and talkative. Those high in desurgency are characterized as depressed, pessimistic, seclusive, retiring, subdued, introspective, and worrying. In connection with his discussion of the surgency factor, Cattell poses the rhetorical question of why psychology creates so many neologisms like surgency; his answer is that the popular counterparts of these terms are often misleading. Although "sociable" might seem adequate to describe surgency, for example, Cattell argues that surgency includes not only sociability but other traits as well. In addition, the *quality* of the person's sociability will vary depending on whether we are talking about the test scores on factor A or on factor F. The sociability incorporated in factor A refers to a warm, gentle, "liking to be around people" orientation, whereas the sociability covered in factor F refers to a person who is slightly exhibitionistic, the "life of the party," with a practical-joking side bordering on crudeness (Cattell, 1965, pp. 92–93). These are the reasons, then, for Cattell's frequent invention of terms.

Factors G and H. In many respects factor G, superego strength, is similar to Freud's concept of the superego. People who are high in superego strength tend to be persistent in their pursuit of ideals and concerned with exercising self-control over their actions (Cattell, 1965, p. 94).

Factor H, parmia versus threctia, refers to a source trait that has a moderate degree of inheritance—approximately 40%. This contention is based on the cumulative findings of several different investigations, using a variety of statistical techniques to assess genetic and environmental contributions to the development of the trait (Cattell, 1982, p. 341). The label "parmia" is derived from the contention that "the H + person is one in whom the normal parasympathetic performance predominance is not easily shaken by sympathetic system (threat) or other interrupting responses" (Cattell, 1957, p. 130). "Parmia" is based on a shortening of the term *parasympathetic immunity,* and "threctia" comes from the term *threat reactivity.* The parmic individual is characterized as bold, adventurous, gregarious, genial, and responsive; the threctic person tends to be shy, timid, aloof, and self-contained (Cattell, 1965, p. 95).

Factor I. Source trait I is labeled premsia (tender-mindedness) versus harria (tough-mindedness). "Premsia" is short for *protected emotional sensitivity;* "harria" comes from *hard realism.* According to Cattell, people learn to be either tender-minded or tough-minded. Tender-mindedness is associated with parental overprotection and indulgence, whereas tough-mindedness is related to strict parental disciplining. I + individuals are impatient, demanding, immature, gentle, sentimental, imaginative, and anxious. I – people are mature, independent-minded, realistic, and self-sufficient. Cattell has also found that I+ people are more creative and more neurotic. In addition, he notes that older cultures tend to be more premsic, whereas pioneer cultures such as those of the United States and Australia are more harric (Cattell, 1965, pp. 96–98).

Factor L. In Cattell's scheme, factor L is labeled alaxia versus protension. "Alaxia" is apparently a shortening of the term *relaxation,* while "protension" is derived from *pro*jection and *tension.* Protensives tend to be suspicious, jealous, and withdrawn; alaxics are trusting, understanding, and composed (Cattell, 1957, p. 143).

Factor M. Cattell labels factor M as praxernia versus autia. "Autia" (M +) is derived from *aut*istic and refers to people who are unconventional, fastidious, absorbed, highly imaginative, and intellectual. "Praxernia" is derived from *pra*ctical and conc*ern*ed and refers to individuals who are conventional, practical, conscientious, logical, and worrying. In the neurotic, M + persons have a tendency to become completely absorbed in their own thoughts and to have a disregard for practical planning. In other words, they are persons who tend to be removed, at times, from the demands of external reality. The M − person, in contrast, is very much concerned with the demands of the environment and tends to pay excessive attention to detail. Cattell contends that M − may be the basis for obsessive-compulsiveness (Cattell, 1957, pp. 147–149).

Factor N. Natural forthrightness (N −) characterizes people who are naive, unpretentious, and spontaneous, while shrewdness (N +) characterizes those who are worldly, astute, insightful, and smart (Cattell & Kline, 1977, p. 116).

Factor O. According to Cattell, guilt-proneness (O +) is a trait found in pathological individuals—for example, alcoholics, criminals, and manic-depressives. They have few friends and are often critical of group life and standards. O − individuals are self-confident, resilient, and placid (Cattell & Kline, 1977, p. 116).

Factors Q_1–Q_4. The remaining factors account for a small proportion of the variation in behavior and have labels that are largely self-explanatory. One factor of considerable interest to the general public and scientific investigators alike, however, is radicalism-conservatism (Q_1). Cattell found that radicals tend to believe in evolution rather than in judgments given by authority figures in the Old Testament. They also rely less on conventional rules than conservatives—that is, they conform less to society's expectations of them. Cattell also reports that other research has shown that radicals like to engage in self-analysis, prefer dealing with complicated problems, and enjoy discussing the serious questions of life with friends more than do conservatives (Cattell, 1957, p. 209).

In an early study, investigators first hypothesized that conservatives have a generalized fear of uncertainty and, as a consequence, would be more likely than liberals to express an aversion to complex and abstract art works. They had college students express their feelings toward 20 paintings judged by an art expert to differ in uncertainty. The paintings were categorized as simple representational, simple abstract, complex representational, and complex abstract. As expected, conservatives preferred paintings that were simple and representational (literal) in nature and strongly disliked paintings that were complex and abstract. Liberals, in contrast, tended to prefer the more complex and abstract paintings (Wilson, Ausman, & Mathews, 1973).

Research with the 16 PF

Once the preceding major factors had been identified and utilized in the construction of a reliable measure of personality, attempts were made to use it in generating hypotheses about the behavior of people. In one study, for example, researchers were concerned with examining the relationship between the quality of the marriage relationship and the personality of husbands and wives. Marriages were first defined as stable or unstable, and then the personality traits of husbands and wives in both groups were compared. Instability was operationally defined as "any known step being taken toward dissolution." It was found that stable marriages were characterized by similarities in the personality traits of the couples, whereas unstable marriages were composed of individuals with dissimilar characteristics (Cattell & Nesselroade, 1967).

Another study (Burton & Cattell, 1972) tried to refine the work of the earlier researchers by looking at specific marital dimensions and personality traits instead of at the global concept of stability-instability. The marital dimensions included ratings by married couples of the degree of sexual gratification in the marriage, the amount of togetherness and role sharing, wife adequacy (measured by the degree of interest shown by the wife in keeping her home neat and clean and in doing most of the housework), the degree of participation in community affairs, the degree of social and intellectual equality between the spouses, the stability of the marriage, the amount of social integration, work performance, social influence, masculine dominance, wife adequacy II, and division of influence. Amount of social integration referred to the number of activities that all family members, including the children, could do together. Work performance was measured by items that revealed whether or not each member of the family had his or her own set of jobs to do. Social influence referred to the party who had more influence over the other in social matters. Wife adequacy II referred to the degree of participation by the wife in decision-making, and division of influence assessed which spouse was the main source of influence in such matters as sex, child rearing, spending, and so forth. Married students filled out the

Marriage Role Questionnaire (MRQ), which contained these dimensions, and the 16 PF test. The data were then analyzed to determine how the personality traits were related to the specific marital dimensions.

In general, the results were as follows: Spouses who were guilt-prone, highly anxious, and low in ego strength were dissatisfied sexually, a finding that is not too surprising. In regard to the "togetherness and role sharing" factor, couples who were highly anxious, guilt-ridden, and shy were more likely to have difficulty in agreeing with their mates on a variety of issues and in sharing problems. Couples who were high on exvia (extraversion) and low on anxiety reported high participation in community activities. Spouses who were highly anxious also reported that they had marriages in which job responsibilities were clearly established but that they did not have much say in choice of friends and in other matters relating to the household. Spouses who controlled such matters as number of children planned and the way money should be spent tended to be dominant, enthusiastic, and venturesome. Such subjects were also high on contertia—that is, they tended to use cognition rather than feelings in problem solving. Not unexpectedly, their marriages were most unstable.

Finally, in regard to the "home devotion" factor, spouses high on superego strength (conscientious and responsible spouses) and on extraversion and compulsivity were the ones who scored high on home devotion. The authors speculated that perhaps an easygoing nature is important because such a trait could help the person combat the repetition and drudgery involved in keeping a home neat and tidy (Burton & Cattell, 1972). Attention to detail would also be an asset, assuming that it did not permeate the person's life and keep her or him from functioning effectively in other areas.

It should be mentioned in connection with this study and with many others involving factor-analytic technique that it is impossible to establish causal directions in these relationships. For example, it is possible that the lack of sharing of problems between the partners caused them to be anxious and not that their anxiety caused them to disagree and to withdraw from each other. Of course, other extraneous variables could have produced the relationship between high anxiety and high disagreement. In addition, we have to exercise caution in accepting the labels the authors attach to their factors. This is largely an impressionistic undertaking and could mislead you. Is a wife's adequacy really measured by the degree of interest she shows in keeping her house neat and tidy and by her doing most of the work? Not only women's liberationists would take strong issue with that assessment! Perhaps a more appropriate label for the factor would be "traditional homemaker's responsibilities."

Newly Discovered Source Traits

Additions to the 16 PF. Recently Cattell has found, through extensive research, seven new factors in addition to the 16 factors measured by his personality test. They include excitability, zeppia versus coasthenia, boorishness versus mature socialization, sanguine casualness, group dedication with sensed inadequacy, and social panache versus explicit self-expression.

Excitability, a factor found in children, increases until early adolescence and then decreases through adulthood. Cattell stresses that this factor is not to be confused with emotionality and instability. Rather, it refers to a cognitive excitability, a restlessness in which people become hyperactive (Cattell & Kline, 1977, p. 113).

People with high scores on zeppia are zestful, like attention, and like group action, while coasthenics are individuals who lack energy and are reflective and restrained in their behavior.

People high in boorishness are ignorant of social requirements, awkward, and unconcerned about others, while people characterized by mature socialization are self-disciplined, polished, and alert to their social responsibilities (Cattell, 1979, p. 66–67).

Sanguine casual individuals are unambitious, self-assured, modest, and casual.

High scorers on group dedication with sensed inadequacy are devoted to groups but think that others do not see them as successful.

People high in social panache feel persecuted by society, while explicit self-expression people like drama and the heady discourse of avant-garde ideas (Cattell & Kline, 1977, p. 119).

Abnormal Traits. Although the source traits utilized in the 16 PF test can distinguish between normals and neurotics, they do not measure all aspects of deviant behavior and do not assess the characteristics of psychotics. Cattell, however, has once again applied factor analysis to surface traits in the normal and abnormal personality spheres and has found 12 new factors that measure psychopathology. These primary source factors are listed in Table 9.5.

These 12 factors have been utilized in the construction of a new test, the **Clinical Analysis Questionnaire (CAQ).** It consists of 28 scales. Sixteen of these are dimensions previously included in the 16 PF, and 12 assess pathological behavior. This test should be of considerable interest and use to clinical psychologists.

In conclusion, Cattell has identified the major source traits of normal and abnormal personality. These traits are organized within the person and propel him or her into action. He applies the concept of the dynamic lattice in discussing the dynamic relationships between these traits.

Dynamic Traits and the Dynamic Lattice

In Cattell's theory, dynamic traits are further subdivided into attitudes, sentiments, and ergs. Attitudes are defined as specific interests in particular courses of action toward certain objects in a given situation (Cattell, 1965, p. 175). Cattell views them as hypothetical constructs that intervene between

Table 9.5
Major Abnormal Source Traits Assessed by the
Clinical Analysis Questionnaire

Factor		
D_1	Is happy, mind works well, does not find ill health frightening LOW HYPOCHONDRIASIS	Shows overconcern with bodily functions, health, or disabilities HIGH HYPOCHONDRIASIS
D_2	Is contented about life and surroundings, has no death wishes ZESTFULNESS	Is disgusted with life, harbors thoughts or acts of self-destruction SUICIDAL DISGUST
D_3	Avoids dangerous and adventurous undertakings, has little need for excitement LOW BROODING DISCONTENT	Seeks excitement, is restless, takes risks, tries new things HIGH BROODING DISCONTENT
D_4	Is calm in emergency, confident about surroundings, poised LOW ANXIOUS DEPRESSION	Has disturbing dreams, is clumsy in handling things, tense, easily upset HIGH ANXIOUS DEPRESSION
D_5	Shows enthusiasm for work, is energetic, sleeps soundly HIGH ENERGY EUPHORIA	Has feelings of weariness, worries, lacks energy to cope LOW ENERGY DEPRESSION
D_6	Is not troubled by guilt feelings, can sleep no matter what is left undone LOW GUILT AND RESENTMENT	Has feelings of guilt, blames self for everything that goes wrong, is critical of himself HIGH GUILT AND RESENTMENT
D_7	Is relaxed, considerate, cheerful with people LOW BORED DEPRESSION	Avoids contact and involvement with people, seeks isolation, shows discomfort with people HIGH BORED DEPRESSION

environmental stimuli and eventual external responses. The attitude of a woman student, for example, might be "I want very much to kiss this handsome guy the next time we go out together." The attitude shows an intense interest (I want very much) in a particular course of action (to kiss) toward a specific object (this handsome guy) in a given situation (the next time we go out together). Ergs and sentiments are inferred from the factor-analytic study of attitudes. For example, a man may have a timid disposition that is based on an underlying fear erg (Cattell, 1950, p. 84).

Sentiments are large and complex attitudes, according to Cattell. Sentiments incorporate a host of interests, opinions, and minor attitudes. For instance, a man's sentiment about his home may be seen in his attitudes

Table 9.5 (continued)
Major Abnormal Source Traits Assessed by the
Clinical Analysis Questionnaire

Factor		
P_a	Is trusting, not bothered by jealousy or envy LOW PARANOIA	Believes he or she is being persecuted, poisoned, controlled, spied on, mistreated HIGH PARANOIA
P_p	Avoids engagement in illegal acts or breaking rules, sensitive LOW PSYCHOPATHIC DEVIATION	Has complacent attitude towards own or others' antisocial behavior, is not hurt by criticism, likes crowds HIGH PSYCHOPATHIC DEVIATION
S_c	Makes realistic appraisals of self and others, shows emotional harmony and absence of regressive behavior LOW SCHIZOPHRENIA	Hears voices or sounds without apparent source outside self, retreats from reality, has uncontrolled and sudden impulses HIGH SCHIZOPHRENIA
A_s	Is not bothered by unwelcome thoughts or ideas or compulsive habits LOW PSYCHASTHENIA	Suffers insistent, repetitive ideas and impulses to perform certain acts HIGH PSYCHASTHENIA
P_s	Considers self as good, dependable, and smart as most others LOW GENERAL PSYCHOSIS	Has feelings of inferiority and unworthiness, timid, loses control easily HIGH GENERAL PSYCHOSIS

Reproduced by special permission of the Institute for Personality and Ability Testing.

about his wife, his children, and about marriage in general as well as in his interests in home repairs and landscaping and so forth (Cattell, 1950, pp. 161–162). Such a sentiment would be learned over a long period. Cattell characterizes sentiments as environmental-mold traits—that is, traits learned via experience with people.

An **erg,** according to Cattell, is "an innate psychophysical disposition which permits its possessor to acquire reactivity (attention, recognition) to certain classes of objects more readily than others, to experience a specific emotion in regard to them, and to start on a course of action which ceases more completely at a certain specific goal activity than at any other" (Cattell, 1950, p. 199). In short, an erg is an innate drive triggered by environmental stimuli that ceases when its goal is reached. For example, the parental erg is released by cries of distress from children and satisfied when they are out of danger. (See the biographical sketch for a list of the other drives Cattell maintains are innate.)

Why does Cattell think these drives are innate? He bases his judgment on findings in both naturalistic and clinical observation studies. Naturalistic studies involve observation of behavior in lower mammals analogous to behavior in human beings and general observations of human behavior in a wide variety of situations and cultures (Cattell, 1979, p. 155). It is inconceivable to Cattell that human beings, who are clearly related structurally and functionally to the mammals and primates, could lack the instinctual equipment they possess.

The dynamic traits he uses in his personality theory are further postulated to be organized in complex ways within the cognitive and motivational structure of the organism. The traits are interrelated in a **dynamic lattice.** Cattell also relies heavily on Murray's concept of **subsidiation** to explain how the traits are intertwined. Subsidiation refers to a process whereby certain traits control and lead to the occurrence of other traits. For example, to achieve the goal of becoming a great concert pianist, the person must first learn to serve deferentially as an apprentice to a master pianist. We say that this deference to the master is subsidiated to the achievement drive. We are, in brief, describing a step sequence of traits in which the occurrence of a particular trait is necessary before another trait can occur. Thus Cattell believes that we must not only be able to describe and measure the various kinds of traits possessed by the person but also be able to show how they are interconnected (Cattell, 1950, p. 156). To accomplish this latter goal, Cattell thinks, we must ask the person why a particular habit or trait is being shown. He also thinks that, although people may not know the answer to the question or may even distort their answers to protect themselves, often they will be able accurately to describe the process by which their traits are linked.

When they have described the process, we are left with a complicated and often bewildering intertwining of interests, attitudes, sentiments, goals, and drives. Figure 9.2 presents only a fragment of a dynamic lattice for a hypothetical person involving attitude subsidiation, sentiment, structure, and innate goals. At the right of the diagram, we see the ergs; in the middle are the various sentiments; and at the left are a variety of attitudes. We can also note that numerous ergs give expression to various sentiments, that the sentiments are related to one another, that several attitudes converge on the same sentiment, and that a few attitudes are common to different sentiments. For the hypothetical person under consideration, we might speculate that love of his wife is based on the fact that she satisfies his needs for sex, protection, and companionship. In addition, he knows that he must maintain a healthy bank account to ensure his security and to secure the material goods his wife needs to be happy. When all these facts are registered on a conscious level, the person may perceive a need to voluntarily change

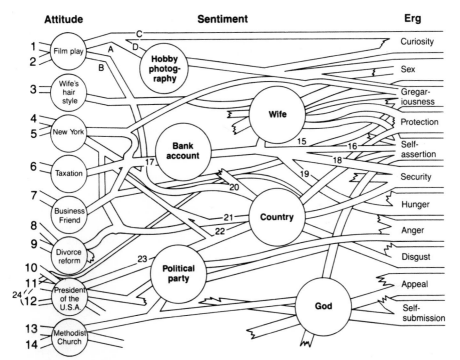

Figure 9.2 Fragment of a dynamic lattice, showing attitude subsidiation, sentiment, structure, and ergic goal. Adapted from Cattell, 1950, p. 158.

his dynamic lattice. Perhaps, then, he will discontinue his frequent recreational trips to New York City for fear they will deplete his account and create unhappiness for him. Alternatively, he may wish to talk to his business friend as a means of securing a higher rate of monetary return. Such a tactic, if possible, would ensure maximum satisfaction for both his wife and him.

Changes in the dynamic lattice can also be brought about by various moods and emotional states. That is, the person's traits, attitudes, sentiments, interests, and even goals can be modified by such states as fatigue, guilt, anxiety, depression, arousal, extraversion, stress, and regression. (For example, the person feels confused and therefore acts impulsively.) These states can be measured by the **Eight State Questionnaire** (Cattell & Kline, 1977, p. 22). Changes in the dynamic lattice can be brought about, too, by changes in the person's environment. (For example, a serious setback in business forces the person to drastically change his or her lifestyle.)

Sentiments are less susceptible to change than attitudes, according to Cattell, because sentiments are the deeper, underlying structures in personality. Occasionally, though, changes in personality can occur. A man may lose his family in a catastrophe, for instance, and this traumatic event will trigger major changes in his functioning (Cattell, 1950, p. 160).

It should be mentioned that a master motive, which Cattell calls the **self-sentiment,** integrates the various attitudes, sentiments, and interests of the person and also regulates the expression of the ergs.

Econetic Model

As mentioned earlier, a major criticism of trait theories has been that they neglect the contributions made by the environment to the prediction of behavior. The **econetic model** represents Cattell's efforts to remedy this deficiency. It postulates that human behavior is the result of a complex and subtle interplay between traits and situations. As a first step in trying to understand this complicated interaction, it is necessary to construct a taxonomy of situations or environments. Cattell has made exploratory moves to map this vast **environmental sphere** by taking note of situations mentioned on every tenth page of the encyclopedia of a given culture. (This procedure is similar to his efforts to map the traits in the personality sphere.) This approach has yielded some encouraging consistencies in the kinds of situations commonly found in a culture when different encyclopedic sources are used; but thus far, investigators have not followed up on Cattell's pioneering efforts (Cattell, 1979, p. 218). Nevertheless, Cattell believes that econetics (or the study of the ecology) is likely to develop rapidly in the future as investigators in various disciplines in the social sciences cooperate. The result should eventually be the construction of a reliable and objective taxonomic scheme.

Cattell maintains that once this task is completed, the impact of these situations on the individual must be assessed. Some situations have relevance for the individual; others do not. Of the situations that do play a role in the person's life, some have tremendous impact, others only minimal impact. Some objects in situations are accessible to the individual; others are not. What these situations mean to the individual also depends on his or her moods. In brief, once the classification task is complete, the unique psychological meaning of various situations for the individual must be established (Cattell, 1979, p. 220). It should be recognized that the assessments of environmental effects are complex. They involve measurements of the effects of other people and of the physical, social, and cultural environments on the individual. Each of these components is typically weighted differently and contributes differentially to the modulation of the person's traits and subsequent behavior. In addition, the relative contributions of these factors change over time and must be assessed.

Specification Equation

The prediction of behavior can be achieved by means of use of a **specification equation** that takes into account the multiple traits that influence behavior as well as the impact of the environment. It is called a specification equation because it specifies the ways in which traits and situations are to be combined to predict any performance. In actuality, the specification equation is highly complicated, taking into account a number of factors not discussed in our treatment of Cattell's theory. (See Cattell, 1979 and 1980, for a detailed discussion of the basic equations and their derivations.) In the most general terms, however, the equation is as follows:

$$R = b_1A_1 + b_2B_2 + b_3C_3 + \ldots + b_nK_n$$

In the formula, R is the performance, or "response," of individuals in a given situation. It is determined by the weighted combination of (1) persons' source traits (b_1A_1); (2) their states and moods (b_2B_2); and (3) the social and cultural meaning of this situation for them (b_3C_3). It could also include the weighted combination of any other factors that have not been specified yet (b_nK_n).

The small b's are weights, or behavioral situation indices. These beta weights are unique to each factor and show the degree to which each is involved in the person's performance in the situation under consideration (Cattell, 1965, pp. 78–80). Weights for traits are generated by experiments in which the performances of large groups of comparable individuals are assessed and the relative importance of the traits is determined by factor analysis. Then these weights are used in the general equation, along with the person's own scores, as a means of predicting performance. Other statistical procedures—for example, the P technique—are used to establish the weights for states and the unique meaning of the situation for the individual.

Now suppose that we are interested in predicting Brent's performance on a math test. On the basis of testing, let us assume that we know that intelligence is the most important source trait in predicting success on the test, followed by conscientiousness and self-sufficiency. Let us also assume that it has been possible for us to establish the weights for states (for example, Brent's anxiety and fatigue levels) and the unique meaning of the situation—that is, its relevance and importance—to him.

If the weights on these factors can vary from .00 to 1.00 (with a weight of 1.00 signifying maximum loading or highest importance) and if scores could vary between zero and 100, then we might find a distribution of weights and scores for Brent as follows:

$$R = [.8(90) + .6(80) + .3(30)]$$
$$+ [.6(90) + .8(100)] + [.9(70) + .8(100)]$$

In this equation, high scores of 100 indicate maximum intelligence, conscientiousness, and self-sufficiency, while low scores indicate minimum anxiety and fatigue. High scores also indicate that success on math tests is highly relevant and important to Brent. Working through the equation gives us Brent's expected performance:

$$R = [.8(90) + .6(80) + .3(30)]$$
$$+ [.6(90) + .8(100)] + [.9(70) + .8(100)]$$
$$R = (72 + 48 + 9) + (54 + 80) + (63 + 80)$$
$$R = 129 + 134 + 143$$
$$R = 406$$

Maximum performance on the test would be predicted as follows:

$$R = [.8(100) + .6(100) + .3(100)]$$
$$+ [.6(100) + .8(100)] + [.9(100) + .8(100)]$$
$$R = (80 + 60 + 30) + (60 + 80) + (90 + 80)$$
$$R = 170 + 140 + 170$$
$$R = 480$$

Since a maximum performance score is 480 and Brent's score was 406, we conclude that Brent will perform well.

The combination model just presented is linear in nature. Cattell says that we should use it if it helps us predict behavior accurately, and we should modify or even abandon it if it does not. At this point, however, Cattell thinks that a linear model and not a curvilinear one is adequate for the prediction of much of our behavior (Cattell, 1965, p. 252). We could use it to predict academic performance and job success, for example. It is a multidimensional model that includes a complex representation of the ways in which traits and situations are dynamically interrelated.

The Process of Personality Development

The Role of Heredity and the Environment

Unlike any of the other theorists reviewed in this text, Cattell discusses in detail the physiological influences of the mother on the behavior of the embryo. He believes that such influences can have a tremendous effect on personality. For example, he notes that children born with **Down's syndrome** have limited intelligence and personalities with severely restricted behavioral patterns. In addition, abnormalities in the person's metabolism can lead to mental retardation. Cattell also points out that the birth process can have a definite effect on personality. For example, injuries to the head at birth may produce deficiencies in intelligence and motor coordination or even paralysis. In regard to temperament, Cattell believes that it is related to the endocrine condition of the mother during the gestation period, although he is not sure about the nature of the relationship. Thus personality seems to be shaped by the operation of the physiological condition of the mother on the normal nervous system maturation of the individual *in utero* (Cattell, 1950, pp. 557–559).

In addition to biological influences on personality, Cattell discusses the tremendous impact of the environment after the first year of life. At first, biological and maturational influences are paramount. Cattell points out research that shows that in both motor and verbal learning, untaught twins quickly achieve the same levels of performance as those who have been thoroughly trained (Cattell, 1950, p. 561). His point is that untrained children may learn particular skills very rapidly once they are mature enough to do so and that they can quickly achieve levels of proficiency that equal those of their well-trained counterparts. As the person grows older, however, the environment does have an increasing impact on the formation of personality.

The Role of Learning

Cattell distinguishes between three kinds of learning that are involved in personality formation: classical conditioning, **instrumental conditioning** (reward learning), and integration learning. As you probably know from your introductory psychology course, **classical conditioning** involves pairing a neutral stimulus with a stimulus that provokes a particular response until the presentation of the neutral stimulus itself is capable of evoking the response. A classical-conditioning interpretation has been used to account for the acquisition of many fears and phobias. Cattell believes that classical conditioning can account for some of our individual learning but not for most of it. He thinks it plays a role in unconscious learning, in the formation of phobias, and in the acquisition of deep and powerful emotional attachments (Cattell, 1965, p. 268).

Much more of our personality learning, according to Cattell, occurs via reward learning. We perform a certain action to reach a goal. The rat in the Skinner box presses a bar and receives food pellets. It quickly learns to press the bar. Bar pressing is instrumental to the attainment of the goal. Under other conditions, the animal presses the bar and is shocked. It quickly learns to avoid pressing the bar. Similarly, a man learns to diet because his friends and his doctor will approve the weight loss. Or a little girl takes a cookie without her parents' permission and is spanked. She rapidly learns to leave the cookie jar alone, at least when her parents are in the vicinity.

Cattell argues that reward learning is paramount in the formation of dynamic lattices (Cattell, 1965, p. 269). A student may have a sentiment about her athletic prowess, for instance, and train hard and long. Such training may prove highly rewarding if she subsequently wins a race at a track meet. As a consequence, her sentiment toward athletic prowess is satisfied and so is her erg for self-assertion—that is, her innate need to feel proud. The formation and maintenance of the dynamic lattice will depend on **confluence learning**—that is, the acquisition of behaviors and attitudes that simultaneously contribute to the satisfaction of two or more different goals (Cattell, 1965, p. 270). For example, the student athlete may develop a positive attitude toward dieting and physical exercise because they satisfy her need for pride (self-assertion erg) and her need to do something different (curiosity erg). Thus learning may involve the satisfaction of a number of goals within the person's dynamic lattice. The sentiments themselves are learned via reward learning. For example, the student's interest in proving her athletic prowess is perhaps acquired through successful performance.

Cattell also postulates a complex form of learning called **integration learning.** It appears to be a form of cognitive and instrumental learning in which the developing person uses ego and superego processes to maximize long-term satisfactions. The person learns to seek realistic satisfactions (Cattell, 1965, p. 276). The similarity to Freud's position should be readily apparent. Cattell agrees that the development of the ego and superego occurs during the second through the fifth years of life. Cattell accepts as well Freud's observations that this period is marked by conflicts and is critical in the development of personality (Cattell, 1950, pp. 573–575).

With the shift in loyalty from parents to peers, Cattell sees the period of 6 through 13 years as a carefree one in which children continue to strengthen their egos and extend love beyond their parents and themselves to others. It is a period of consolidation. During adolescence, there are rapid physical changes in boys and girls and increases in emotional instability, social awkwardness, and sex interests, along with augmented concerns about being altruistic and contributing to society. The primary sources of conflict during this period are "(a) the task of gaining independence from the parents; (b) the task of gaining status in an occupation, preparing for that occupation, and achieving economic self-support; (c) achieving satisfactory sex expression by winning a mate; and (d) achieving a stable, integrated personality and satisfactory self-concept" (Cattell, 1950, p. 594). These conflicts are due, in Cattell's opinion, to both biological and environmental influences.

Maturity is the period from 25 to 55 and is a time of little basic personality change. Although there is a slight decline in biological efficiency (for example, increased problems with hearing and vision and a slowing of the metabolic rate), Cattell believes that, thanks to learning and experience, increases in creativity are possible. Both sexes have greater emotional stability (Cattell, 1950, pp. 610–613). Maturity also is a period in which adjustments need to be made. There is the discovery that adolescent dreams and aspirations are, in many respects, unrealistic. Near the end of maturity, when there is more leisure time, there is a tendency to revive romantic interests. Cattell cites the Kinsey Report as showing that men tend to have a renewed interest in extramarital affairs. In women, with the approach of the menopause, a wistful longing for romance occurs (Cattell, 1950, p. 616).

In old age, there is more rapid decline in physical power. Performance on tasks demanding ingenuity suffers, whereas performance on tasks requiring experience remains steady. Cattell supports the views of some modern psychiatrists who argue that the following characteristics are typical of people in old age:

Worry over finances
Worry over health
Feeling[(s) of being] unwanted, isolated, lonely
Feeling [of] suspicion
Narrowing of interest
Loss of memory
Mental rigidity
Overtalkativeness, especially of the past
Hoarding, often of trivial things
Feeling(s) of inadequacy, leading to feelings of insecurity and anxiety
Feeling(s) of guilt, irritability
Reduction of sexual activity but increased sexual interest, especially in the male
Untidiness, uncleanliness
Conservatism
Inability to adjust to changed conditions
Decreased social contacts and participation (Cattell, 1950, pp. 618–619)

Although it is impossible to deny that there is physical deterioration in old age and that this deterioration may manifest itself in lessened performance in various situations, it is not at all clear that the negative characteristics frequently attributed to the elderly are accurate. Old people do not necessarily lack confidence or feel powerless, and they are not necessarily wracked by guilt and anxiety. Indeed, there are many old people who are competent, satisfied with their situations, and actively engaged in meaningful activities. In the final analysis, a more realistic appraisal of both the strengths and deficiencies associated with old age is needed. We need to move away from the concept of the elderly as "doddering old codgers" who cannot tie their shoelaces and also from the glorification of the period as the "golden years" when "senior citizens" flower and prosper without a care in the world.

The Theory of Abnormal Development

Cattell accepts the clinical notion that neurosis and psychosis are based on unresolved conflicts within the person, and he seeks to develop quantitative techniques to aid the therapist in diagnosis and treatment. He envisions the conflicts of the person in Freudian terms—as involving struggles between the id, ego, and superego—and calls for the development of a "quantitative psychoanalysis" (Cattell, 1965, p. 230). For example, a man's interest in marrying one of two women is based on the operation of a number of ergs and other personality factors. Cattell gives a simplified version of the formulas that could be utilized by a clinician to predict the way in which the man would resolve his conflict. The formulas, with slight modifications, are as follows:

$$I_{\text{Jane}} = 0.6E_{\text{sex}} + 0.5E_{\text{greg}} + 0.3M_{\text{superego}}$$
$$I_{\text{Sally}} = 0.6E_{\text{sex}} + 0.3E_{\text{greg}} + 0.3M_{\text{superego}}$$

In this example, the man is in real conflict because the various ergs and the superego sentiment are approximately equal in strength. Yet, because the gregariousness erg is slightly stronger for Jane, the decision would be in her favor. In ordinary language, both women satisfy the man's needs for sex equally and are respectable in the eyes of others, but Jane is a more pleasing companion socially than Sally, so he decides to marry Jane (Cattell, 1965, p. 232).

The situation that faces the clinician is much more complicated than this simplified example would suggest, of course. Cattell also proposes that the clinician, in trying to understand the client's conflicts, rely on diagnostic tools that have been empirically validated. These tools—for example, the 16 PF test and the CAQ—provide a means of assessing the major factors in personality that include not only the Freudian structures of id, ego, and superego but also the various attitudes, interests, and sentiments of the client (Cattell, 1961, chap. 14).

Definition of Neurosis. For Cattell, a neurosis is the "pattern of behavior shown by those individuals who come to a clinic for aid because they feel themselves to be in emotional difficulties (and who do not have that kind of disorder that a psychiatrist recognizes as psychosis)" (Cattell, 1965, p. 209). He uses such an operational definition because he is convinced that our understanding of neurosis must begin by identifying those measurements that differentiate this group from normal members of the general population. Using this initial criterion, both he and Hans Jurgen Eysenck, another prominent factor-analytic theorist, have found that neurotics do indeed differ from both psychotics and normals on a number of personality dimensions. Thus neuroticism and psychoticism are not just illnesses that differ in degree. They are different kinds of illness (Cattell, 1965, p. 210). Let us consider the primary factors that have been identified as contributing to neurosis before considering the factors involved in psychosis.

Factors Contributing to Neurosis. Cattell presents evidence that neurotics grow up in families characterized by conflict, inconsistent discipline, and insufficient affection. They are also subjected to parental demands to adhere to excessively high moral standards. This family background coupled with their genetically based lower-than-average emotional stability, leads eventually to neurosis (Cattell, 1950, p. 497).

On the basis of countless factor-analytic studies by Cattell and scores of other investigators, the following factors have been tentatively identified as contributing to neurosis. Neurotics have been found to be low in ego strength or emotional stability, high on autia and premsia, and low on surgency and dominance (Cattell, 1965, p. 211). In regard to autia, Cattell has found that neurotics tend to disregard externals and social necessities and refuse to change their ideas to bring them into line with acknowledged facts. They are also high in premsia on the I factor, showing extreme and indiscriminate emotional sensitivity to others and a considerable amount of capricious behavior. Furthermore, Cattell claims that neurotics are shy and inhibited generally. He also points out that their low ego strength means that they are easily overcome by their emotions, are subject to moods, and cannot adjust their behavior to the realities of given situations (Cattell, 1965, p. 212).

Above all, neurotics tend to be highly anxious. Cattell traces their anxiety to various sources. It may arise because the ergic tension of the person is unsatisfied. Cattell is true to his Freudian roots when he notes that ergic drives for sex and pugnacity (aggression) are more frequently punished in our society and, as a consequence, can give rise to high levels of anxiety. Also consistent with the orthodox Freudian position, Cattell maintains that anxiety can arise as a result of low ego strength and a highly punitive superego. In very original fashion, Cattell also makes the major point that the high levels of anxiety most neurotics show may be partially a result of a constitutional proneness to threat reactivity. In other words, neurotics may be biologically more sensitive to threats than normals. Furthermore, Cattell argues that these high levels of anxiety may be partially caused by a self-sentiment with breadth. In short, a person who is committed to a great variety of activities is more vulnerable to threats than one who does not have such a broad range of pursuits. Finally, high levels of anxiety can arise if the individual is forced to deal with many trivial details in life to achieve ergic and self-sentiment satisfactions (Cattell, 1961, pp. 18–22).

Although generally in agreement with Cattell on the kinds of variables that contribute to neuroticism, Eysenck maintains Cattell has exaggerated the number of factors needed to account for neurosis. He claims that there are fewer factors and that Cattell found more because he failed to use a factor-analytic method to extract second-order factors (Eysenck, 1953, p. 66). The important point, however, is that two major theorists, working independently, are in substantial agreement about the kinds of traits that characterize the neurotic.

Definition of Psychosis. According to Cattell, psychosis is "a form of mental disorder different from neurosis, in which the individual loses contact with reality and needs hospitalization for his own protection and that of others" (Cattell, 1965, p. 373). In comparison to the neurotic, the psychotic lacks insight into his problems, is unable to take care of himself, and may be a threat to others.

Factors Contributing to Psychosis. Cattell points out that manic-depressive psychosis and schizophrenia are highly inheritable (Cattell, 1982, p. 28). Yet he also notes that differences in family environments contribute to the onset of the two types of psychosis. He reviews evidence that shows that the parents of manic-depressives are warmer and much more overprotective of their children than are the parents of schizophrenics. In contrast, the parents of schizophrenics have been found to be much more ambivalent in their attitudes toward their children (Cattell, 1950, p. 542). In regard to scores on the 16 PF test, Cattell reports on the findings of other investigators that show that schizophrenics are low in ego strength, low in drive tension, and highly introverted and conceited. Manic-depressives, in contrast, are low in intelligence, conservative in temperament, and high on superego (Cattell, 1965, p. 225).

Finally, a factor labeled, appropriately enough, "psychoticism" has been found by Eysenck to distinguish powerfully between psychotics and normals. Regarding personality traits, Eysenck found that, in comparison to normals, psychotics were less articulate, were poorer at solving mathematical problems, were slower in tracing lines with a stylus, had poorer memories, and had less ability to concentrate on the task at hand. They also read more slowly, tended to overestimate distances and test scores, and showed unrealistic levels of aspiration (Eysenck, 1952, p. 217). Cattell is in substantial agreement with Eysenck on these points.

Techniques of Assessment

Cattell can rightfully be called a "psychometrist of personality," because he places such heavy emphasis on the use of various testing and statistical techniques. We have already seen how he uses factor analysis to derive the major traits of personality, for example. To apply the factor-analytic procedures, however, masses of data must first be collected from large numbers of people. Cattell relies on three major procedures to obtain such data. He calls them the L-data, Q-data, and T-data methods. **L-data,** or life-record data, refer to the measurement of behavior in actual, everyday situations. Ideally, such data would be collected without using rater judgments. Instead, the investigator would collect unobtrusive data, such as the number of automobile accidents a woman had over the past 20 years, her marks in school, the number of civic organizations of which she is or has been a member, and so forth. However, Cattell believes such data would be difficult to obtain, so the investigator is forced to take secondhand data—that is, data in the form of a rating by someone who knows the woman well. Different aspects of the woman's behavior, such as her dependability on the job and her friendliness, would be obtained via trait ratings from co-workers and friends on, for example, 10-point, Likert-type scales.

The second source of information is called **Q-data,** or questionnaire data.

Such information is often gathered in an interview situation in which respondents fill out paper-and-pencil tests from which trait scores can be derived. The 16 PF test is an excellent example of a source of Q-data.

The third type of data is based on objective tests and is called **T-data.** T-data are gathered by an observer in a standard test situation from a subject who performs without being aware of the dimensions on which he or she is being scored. Whereas Q-data refer to information that can potentially be faked by subjects, T-data refer to information that cannot essentially be faked. For example, if a man is asked on a questionnaire whether or not he ever cheats on examinations and he is either too frightened or embarrassed to admit to such behavior, he may fake his answer and report that he never does so, even though he may on rare occasions. In regard to T-data, however, the man may be asked to respond to a Rorschach test in which the inkblots do not provide him with unambiguous information he can fake. That is, he does not know the dimensions on which he will eventually be scored by clinical psychologists (Cattell, 1965, pp. 60–62).

Application of the Theory to the Treatment of Psychopathology

Cattell insists that skillful treatment of mental disorders relies on personality-factor assessments that will provide not only a profile for diagnosis but also a statement about the kinds of constitutional factors that influence behavior (Cattell, 1965, p. 288). In addition, it should not surprise you to learn that he believes the availability of reliable and valid measuring instruments can help the clinician make better judgments about the efficacy of treatment procedures. These judgments can be made by assessing the client's personality before and after therapeutic intervention and noting the amount of change in behavior (Cattell, 1961, p. 413). The *P* technique is further suggested as the procedure best able to provide an accurate assessment of the complex changes occurring in the client as he or she moves through therapy. As mentioned earlier, through this technique the client is repeatedly tested by use of many personality dimensions on a number of different occasions, so that his or her unique trait structure emerges (Cattell, 1965, p. 372; 1961, p. 415).

Although all therapy should rest on precise measurement, Cattell believes that astute clinical observation has merit and should be used, but always in conjunction with testing procedures. In this respect and in others he is an eclectic. He appreciates and accepts many of Freud's clinical insights, but he maintains that a therapy built on pronouncements and not on measurement can, in the long run, do serious harm to society. In general, he is contemptuous of the "fanciful and presumptuous theorizing of pre-metric, pre-experimental" theorists (Cattell, 1965, p. 333).

He thinks further that a search by the therapist for the causes of a disorder in early traumatic experiences, à la Freud, may be beneficial to the client. By reliving the experiences, the client is in a better position to re-evaluate his or her own emotional reactions and eventually to change de-structive behavior. Some of these changes can be effected, in Cattell's view, via behavior therapy in which the person is taught new responses to threat-ening stimuli. Thus, to a limited degree, he accepts as valid therapeutic approaches that utilize historical analysis (for example, psychoanalysis) or a direct reconditioning approach (for example, behavior therapy).

Yet, in the final analysis, Cattell opts for a view of therapy that recognizes that people with severe disorders are defective throughout their personality functioning (Cattell, 1965, p. 335). Measurement procedures must focus on the entirety of the person's trait structure; we cannot focus simply on trau-matic experiences involving sex and aggression, nor can we focus only on certain limited and specific areas of behavior change. We must address ourselves to the full range of constitutional personality factors that set limits on the person's performance and to the complex interweaving of traits and sentiments that influence behavior patterns. Obviously, then, we need com-plex measurement procedures to assess complex underlying structures. Accordingly, some kinds of therapy will prove more effective than others, depending on the kinds of factors that are causing the specific types of neuroses and psychoses. For example, in psychoses based largely on the operation of constitutional factors, therapy might involve the use of drugs, electric shock, and lobotomy (Cattell, 1950, p. 543). In certain neuroses, on the other hand, therapy might start with analyses of dreams and the reliving of traumatic experiences (Cattell, 1961, p. 415). Where the problem is of a minor and relatively restricted nature, in the sense that it does not involve deep-rooted trauma, behavior therapy might be effective. Thus Cattell is clearly eclectic in his attitude toward the kinds of treatment to be used in therapy. But he is single-minded in his determination that all therapy should be based on solid measurement procedures.

Critical Comments

We turn now to an examination of the scientific worth of Cattell's theory.

Comprehensiveness. There is little doubt that Cattell has devised a comprehensive theory of personality. His theory addresses itself to a wide range of diverse phenomena, both normal and abnormal. Beyond that, it attempts to account for both the biological and the sociocultural factors that jointly influence behavior. We cannot help but be impressed by the range of his interests and efforts in pursuing this formidable task.

Cattell also fully recognizes the complexity of the motives that determine behavior and the fact that an adequate science of psychology must utilize measurement procedures that are equal to the task. As he notes, we can no longer afford to rely so heavily on the bivariate experiment in our research efforts, for three reasons. First, one of its primary shortcomings is that it sometimes precludes the study of vital human matters. Try to imagine doing controlled experiments on bereavement, for example. Second, many important psychological concepts, such as love, justice, and neurosis, cannot be adequately measured operationally by single variables. Third, investigators are occasionally presumptuous in assuming that controlled experiments can lead to results in which the causal connection between events can be determined absolutely. Such outcomes are, of course, extremely unlikely; in reality, investigators never know whether this kind of control has been achieved (Cattell, 1957, p. 25).

Fortunately, Cattell has not taken an either-or position on the merits of the multivariate approach and the deficiencies of the controlled experiment. He does not suggest that investigators abandon the bivariate approach. Instead, he recognizes that both approaches have unique assets. The bivariate approach does, for example, allow investigators to make cause-and-effect inferences with greater certainty than do other approaches.

It is thus reasonable to conclude that Cattell recognizes the complexity of personality, has developed a theory that seeks to approximate that reality, and attempts to utilize measurement procedures commensurate with the task.

Precision and Testability. Of all the theorists in this text, Cattell has demonstrated the most concern with the construction of a theory based on precise measurement. He has steadfastly and painstakingly worked to define and refine his concepts through the use of sophisticated and elaborate factor-analytic procedures. Nevertheless, critics have argued that his data are fraught with ambiguities and subjectivity. They maintain that he is the one who made the decision to include only certain traits in his factor analyses. Therefore it should not surprise anyone that he got out of the analyses the traits that he put in. Cattell says this is a platitudinous argument because he made painstaking efforts initially to include virtually all the traits known to human beings in his factor analyses. Recall that his construction of the personality sphere was an attempt to examine all the traits that could be used to describe behavior. It is a good bet that he has covered most of them.

Another criticism of the factor-analytic approach concerns the subjectivity involved in labeling factors. Despite all the concern with objectivity in his measurement procedures, Cattell must still, in the final analysis, use subjective judgment in interpreting the meaning of the factors by labeling them. Cattell, however, recognizes this limitation and advocates caution in applying labels until many different analyses are completed. Thus he has proceeded to apply labels to the factors he has found only after several replications have provided supportive evidence. He has also sought evidence for the clear existence of the factors through cross-validational work with different populations. Therefore, through continual attempts at refinement via research, the labeling of the factors becomes more readily apparent, and subjectivity becomes less of a factor.

Despite these criticisms (and several others that have been leveled at his work), Cattell's theory appears to be a model of elegance and precision when compared to the various psychodynamic and humanistic-existential theories.

Parsimony. Cattell has attempted to construct a theory that is parsimonious by using factor-analytic techniques to "uncover" the major source traits of normal and abnormal behavior. In addition, his econetic model provides a number of concepts that help him explain the impact of the environment on behavior. Thus Cattell's theory seems economical without being overly simplistic.

Empirical Validity. Cattell has spent most of his research career establishing the reliability and validity of the trait concepts to be utilized in the construction of an adequate theory of personality. Thus there is considerable empirical support for these basic concepts, as well as some support for various hypotheses based on them. Yet there is still only minimal support for the new econetic model.

Heuristic Value. Many psychologists agree that there is a great deal to admire about Cattell and his efforts as a scientific investigator. He is seen as a first-rate scholar with wide-ranging interests and expertise in a variety of areas. There is little question that he has been incredibly productive as a researcher and prolific as a writer. He is perceived as a person with the kind of curiosity, intelligence, and boldness necessary in the pioneering investigator. Despite this approbation, Cattell's theory has not had much impact on the thinking and work of investigators within psychology. There are several possible reasons for this situation. First, like Jung's, Cattell's work is difficult to understand. The language of the theory is often technical and forbidding, and his penchant for using neologisms is not designed to endear him to readers. Second, although factor analysis is a relatively objective and precise statistical technique, some investigators believe that the investigator's own biases can influence the outcomes, so they look askance at the research results compiled by Cattell and his colleagues. Third, and perhaps most important, until recently Cattell had made little effort to expand his theory to include contributions made by the environment to the accurate prediction of behavior. To experimentalists wedded to a strong environmentalism, his emphasis on the primacy of inner traits has been unappealing. Perhaps, however, Cattell's new work on the econetic model will arouse investigators' interest in the theory and stimulate research.

Applied Value. Cattell's work has had considerable impact on the clinical diagnosis of psychopathology and in the assessment of therapeutic growth; it has had an even greater impact on occupational psychology. For example, it has provided vocational counselors with reliable personality-testing procedures that have been used to provide information to youth and adults concerning the kinds of occupations that might be suitable for them and compatible with their own interests and abilities. Management supervisors in business and industry have also utilized Cattell's tests in making decisions about the placement of workers in jobs suited to their talents and personalities.

Discussion Questions

1. What is the inductive-hypothetico-deductive spiral? How does this approach to the construction of personality theory differ from the hypothetico-deductive model used by most investigators?
2. What is factor analysis? What are some of its strengths and weaknesses as a personality assessment procedure?
3. What is a trait? What are the primary sources of traits in personality?
4. How do source traits differ from surface traits? What are the major source traits?
5. Why does Cattell think it is necessary to invent new terms like *parmia* and *threctia* to describe personal dispositions?
6. What is Cattell's specification equation? Describe its use in the prediction of behavior.
7. What are the major aspects of the dynamic lattice?
8. List the three kinds of learning involved in the information of personality. Give examples of each type.
9. Is there necessarily a decrease in physical and mental powers with the onset of old age? Do the elderly always feel powerless?
10. What kinds of family backgrounds are likely to give rise to neuroticism?
11. How do neurotics differ from psychotics? What are the major factors contributing to psychoticism, as espoused by Cattell?
12. What is the *P* technique? How is it utilized in the treatment of people with behavioral disorders?
13. What are some of the advantages of using multivariate rather than bivariate experimental techniques to study human behavior?
14. What primary source traits would you attribute to the partners in stable and successful marriages? What primary source traits characterize people you like or dislike?
15. How does Cattell define personality? What are some of the limitations of his definition?

References

Allport, G. W., & Odbert, H. S. Trait names: A psycholexical study. *Psychological Monograph*, 1936, 47, 171–220.

Burton, K., & Cattell, R. B. Marriage dimensions and personality. *Journal of Personality and Social Psychology*, 1972, 21, 369–375.

Cattell, R. B. *Description and measurement of personality*. London: Harrap, 1946.

Cattell, R. B. *Personality: A systematic theoretical and factual study.* New York: McGraw-Hill, 1950.

Cattell, R. B. *Personality and motivation: Structure and measurement.* New York: Harcourt, Brace & World, 1957.

Cattell, R. B. *The Meaning and measurement of neuroticism and anxiety.* New York: Ronald, 1961.

Cattell, R. B. *The scientific analysis of personality.* Baltimore: Penguin Books, 1965.

Cattell, R. B. (Ed.). *Handbook of multivariate experimental psychology.* Chicago: Rand McNally, 1966a.

Cattell, R. B. *Personality and learning theory,* Vols. 1 and 2. New York: Springer, 1979; 1980.

Cattell, R. B. *The inheritance of personality and ability.* New York: Academic Press, 1982.

Cattell, R. B., & Dreger, R. M. (Eds.). *Handbook of modern personality theory.* Washington, D.C.: Hemisphere Publishing, 1977.

Cattell, R. B., & Kline, P. *The scientific analysis of personality and motivation.* New York: Academic Press, 1977.

Cattell, R. B., & Nesselroade, J. R. Likeness and completeness theories examined by sixteen personality factors measured by stably and unstably married couples. *Journal of Personality and Social Psychology,* 1967, 7, 351–361.

Eysenck, H. J. *The scientific study of personality.* London: Routledge & Kegan Paul, 1952.

Eysenck, H. J. *The structure of human personality.* London: Methuen, 1953.

McGee, M. G., & Wilson, D. W. *Psychology: Science and application.* New York: West Publishing Co., 1984.

Wilson, G. D., Ausman, J., & Mathews, T. R. Conservatism and art preferences. *Journal of Personality and Social Psychology,* 1973, 25, 286–288.

Suggested Readings

Cattell, R. B. *The scientific analysis of personality.* Baltimore: Penguin Books, 1965.

Cattell, R. B. Psychological theory and scientific method. In R. B. Cattell (Ed.), *Handbook of multivariate experimental psychology.* Chicago: Rand McNally, 1966b.

Cattell, R. B. *The inheritance of personality and ability.* New York: Academic Press, 1982.

Cattell, R. B., & Kline, P. *The scientific analysis of personality and motivation.* New York: Academic Press, 1977.

Glossary

Ability trait Skill possessed by individuals that enables them to cope effectively with problems posed by the environment.

Bivariate experiment Investigation in which the experimenter tries to assess the impact of one variable on another.

Classical conditioning Type of learning pioneered by Pavlov in which an initially neutral stimulus becomes capable of evoking a response after continued pairing with a stimulus that naturally produces the response. This type of learning is also called respondent conditioning.

Clinical Analysis Questionnaire (CAQ) New personality test designed to measure deviant forms of behavior.

Confluence learning Acquisition of attitudes and behaviors that simultaneously contribute to the satisfaction of two or more goals.

Constitutional trait Characteristic that is rooted in biology and is very resistant to change.

Down's syndrome A chromosomal abnormality in which children are born with 47 chromosomes instead of 46. They have three instead of two chromosomes in group 21. (Approximately 95% of all Down's syndrome children have a trisomy-21 condition.)

Dynamic lattice Complicated and organized system of traits that exist within human personality.

Dynamic trait Characteristic that embraces the motives and interests of people.

Econetic model Model that postulates the manner in which the physical, social, and cultural environments modulate traits and contribute to the accurate prediction of behavior.

Eight State Questionnaire Personality test that measures basic moods and emotional states of individuals.

Environmental-mold trait Characteristic learned through experiences with the environment.

Environmental sphere A listing of all the terms used in a culture to designate situations or environments.

Erg Innate drive that controls behavior.

Factor analysis Statistical techniques designed to yield the intercorrelations between a number of variables. Factor analysis attempts to account for these intercorrelations in terms of underlying factors, usually fewer in number than the original number of variables.

Factor loading Term used in factor analysis to indicate the degree of association between a specific variable and a general factor.

Inductive-hypothetico-deductive spiral Approach to theory construction and validation in which facts are collected first and then generalized into hypotheses that can lead to deduction that can be tested empirically.

Instrumental conditioning Type of learning in which the presentation of a reinforcing stimulus is made contingent on the occurrence of a response (operant conditioning, reward learning). Responses are strengthened or weakened by the application of various kinds of reinforcers.

Integration learning Form of learning proposed by Cattell in which the person utilizes his or her reasoning abilities and value system in making judgments as a means of maximizing the attainment of long-range goals.

L-data Life-record information obtained through observation of behavior in everyday situations.

Multiple Abstract Variance Analysis (MAVA) Statistical procedure used to determine the precise contributions of genetic and environmental factors to the development of traits.

Multivariate experiment Investigation in which the experimenter tries to assess the impact of a variety of variables on a given behavior.

Personality sphere A listing of all the traits used to describe behavior in a culture.

Primary factor General factor that emerges following an analysis of the correlations between a number of surface variables.

P technique Form of factor analysis that allows assessment of the unique trait structure of the person.

Q-data Questionnaire information obtained through a subject's self-reports of behavior.

R technique Form of factor analysis that allows assessment of the underlying source traits in large populations.

Second-order factor Higher-order factor that emerges after an analysis of the associations between a number of primary factors.

Self-sentiment Concept used by Cattell to account for the organization of the various attitudes, sentiments, and motives of the person.

Sixteen Personality Factor Test (16 PF test) Questionnaire derived from factor analysis and created by Cattell to measure basic underlying traits of personality.

Source trait Underlying characteristic found as a result of conducting a factor analysis on a number of variables and finding that they are all interrelated. The commonality, or unity, among the variables is then interpreted as indicating the existence of a source trait.

Specification equation Formula that specifies the ways in which traits are weighted in relation to given situations and then combined to predict behavior.

Subsidiation Process involving the interrelatedness of traits whereby the gratification of one motive is necessary before a related motive can be satisfied.

Surface trait Trait that is observable and controlled by an underlying source trait.

T-data Objective-test information based on an observer's judgments of a person's tendency to react to the environment in a particular way.

Temperament trait Innate tendency of the individual to react to the environment in a particular way.

Trait Relatively permanent and broad reaction tendency that serves as a building block of personality.

PART 4

Cognitive Perspectives

To understand the role of cognition in current theories of personality, it is first necessary to examine the meaning of the term. In ordinary language, cognition refers to the thoughts or ideas we have about the world around us. Thus, in the broadest sense, we are talking about events that occur inside us that help us make sense of the world. Technically, theories of cognition are concerned with the problem of how we gain information about events and how we act on our environments on the basis of our processing of this information.

Since cognition involves internal events, it could be argued that the various psychodynamic and trait theories we have considered thus far should be studied here. After all, Freud's concept of the ego deals in large measure with our attempts to understand external reality and to perform those behaviors that will result in maximum pleasure for us. The conflicts between the id and superego also involve the use of internalized rules to restrict the expression of inappropriate id impulses. These rules are frequently utilized in our decision-making and can be construed as cognitive in nature.

The concept of trait employed by Allport and Cattell to account for personality functioning is also a cognitive construct. Traits are motives assumed to guide behaviors and influence judgments about the environment. Allport goes beyond Cattell in postulating a developmental process of "becoming" that is largely cognitive. As we know, for him the mature person is one who is capable of making use of information in a rational way. The self-actualization theories created by Maslow and Rogers can also be construed as cognitive, as we shall see later in the text. So can the work of some of the social learning theorists reviewed in Part 5. These positions incorporate cognitive constructs like expectancy, imitation, verbal and pictorial imagery, and memory.

Why, then, not include these theorists and their positions in this section of the text? Why do we include only Kelly's theory? The answer is, although many of these theories have elements of cognition, Kelly stands alone as the creator of a comprehensive and "pure" cognitive theory of personality. His attention is focused solely on the ways in which we process information as a means of increasing our understanding of the world. His is an intellectualized view of personality that sees all of us acting as scientists in order to predict and control events. In Kelly's view, we are all continually trying to make sense of our world by forming hypotheses about how it works, by testing them in the real world, and then revising them if they do not fit or work. Our aim, according to him, is to maximize our predictive accuracy about the ways in which the world operates.

To present this view, he built a theory with a brand-new terminology and claimed that he had done away with many traditional concepts in psychology. For example, Kelly did not talk about learning, ego, motivation, reinforcement, drive, the unconscious, or need. Yet if one looks closely at his position, concepts like motivation, reinforcement, and drive are subtly present but not emphasized or discussed in a traditional way. For example, although Kelly did not focus on a drive-reduction concept of human thirst and hunger motivation, as some of the traditional learning theorists do, he did maintain that we seek to improve our constructs by increasing the number of concepts in our cognitive systems and by altering concepts at variance with our experiences. We have, in brief, a need to know, a desire to make accurate predictions about phenomena. These aims show clearly that Kelly believed human beings are motivated, but he focused on cognitive motivation and not on biological drives.

Kelly also rejected the empirical law of effect, which states that behavior is more likely to occur if it has been followed by the application of a positive reinforcer and less likely to occur if it has been followed by a punishing stimulus. He rejected this view of reinforcement because it suggests that our behavior is under the control of external reinforcers, whereas he believed our actions are controlled by cognitive processes. Yet Kelly did talk about reinforcement; but he discussed it indirectly in terms of the accuracy of the match between our conceptualization of the world and its actual state. In other words, it is positively reinforcing when we predict events accurately and punishing when we do not. For example, we tend to feel satisfied if we can predict accurately that someone we dislike will behave despicably toward either us or others, whereas we will be unhappy if our enemy behaves kindly and generously toward us or others because we do not expect such behavior. But this concept of reinforcement seems to have its limitations. Would we continue to be unhappy if our enemy presented us with a check for a million dollars or if he or she saved our lives during a catastrophe? Moreover, recent studies in social psychology have suggested that some people enjoy inconsistency and abhor consistency. Too much predictability is boring for many people.

Chapter 10 provides a close look at Kelly's unique and clearly stated theory. It begins by examining the fundamental assumption underlying the theory: the philosophical stance called constructive alternativism. After outlining the basic terms of the theory, we present the fundamental postulate and the many corollaries of Kelly's personal construct position. Next, there is a detailed examination of his Role Construct Repertory Test (RCRT), which is designed to measure personal construct systems. We then discuss Kelly's view of psychotherapy and the role of the therapist and client. An actual case history illustrates how Kelly's theory is applied to psychopathology. Our research review then shows how investigators have utilized variants of Kelly's RCRT to study the cognitive functioning and behavior of schizophrenic patients.

CHAPTER 10

Kelly's Theory of Personal Constructs

Biographical Sketch

George Alexander Kelly was born in a small town in Kansas in 1905, the only child of a Presbyterian minister and his wife. He attended high school in Wichita, Kansas, and then Friends University, where he enrolled in courses in music and public debating. He was graduated from Park College in 1926 with a degree in mathematics and physics. He flirted with the idea of becoming an aeronautical engineer but eventually committed himself to education. He then held a variety of jobs, including teaching speechmaking to students in a labor college and teaching Americanization to a class of recent immigrants.

In 1929 he was awarded an exchange scholarship and spent a year at the University of Edinburgh. He earned a bachelor's degree in education and returned to the United States with a developing interest in psychology. As a consequence, he entered the graduate program in that field at the University of Iowa. In 1931, he was awarded his Ph.D. for a dissertation in the area of speech and reading disabilities.

His professional career in psychology began with his acceptance of a position at Fort Hays State College in Kansas. Soon afterward, he began an attempt to develop psychological services for the state of Kansas by establishing a network of traveling clinics throughout the state. It was during this period that Kelly largely abandoned the psychoanalytic approach to the understanding of human personality. He reported that his clinical experiences had taught him that people in the Midwest were paralyzed by prolonged drought, dust storms, and economic consideration, not by overflowing libidinal forces. He began to develop this theory and based it partly on the observation of a friend who took a part in a dramatic production in college, "lived it" for the two or three weeks the play was in rehearsal, and was profoundly influenced by it. Kelly noted that although many people would dismiss his friend's efforts as "sheer affectation," his behavior was, in fact, not false or without substance. It eventually expressed his "real self." This experience led Kelly to formulate a fixed-role-therapy technique designed to help the person overcome his or her own limitations.

The crux of his theory of personal **constructs** was created when he observed that "people tended to have the symptoms they had read about or had seen in other people." When the terms, or constructs of, *inferiority complex* and *anxiety* were popular in the 1920s and 1930s, people began to describe themselves as having inferiority complexes or anxieties. These self-descriptions were subsequently used in their interpretations of reality. Kelly's preoccupation with the structure of language and the impact of language and roles on behavior led him to read the works of the eminent linguist Alfred Korzybski and those of Jacob Moreno, a theorist of role playing, and resulted in the refinement of his theory (Kelly, 1955, Vol. 1, pp. 360–366).

After a stint in the navy as an aviation psychologist during World War II, Kelly was appointed associate professor at the University of Maryland. He left Maryland in 1946 to become professor of psychology and director of clinical psychology at Ohio State University. During the next two decades, he completed his major theoretical work, *The Psychology of Personal Constructs* (1955). He also traveled widely and lectured at many universities throughout the world. In 1965 he accepted the Riklis chair of Behavioral Science at Brandeis University. He died in 1967.

Basic Concepts and Principles

Constructive Alternativism

The concept of **constructive alternativism** underlies Kelly's theory of cognition. Although it is an imposing term, the concept is really not too difficult to understand. It refers to the assumption that all of us are capable of changing or replacing our present interpretation of events (Kelly, 1955, Vol. 1, p. 15). In colloquial terms, we can always change our minds. But the assumption also implies that our behavior is never completely determined. We are always free to some extent to reinterpret our experiences. Thus it is clear that Kelly believed in the primacy of the individual. Yet Kelly also believed that some of our thoughts and behavior are determined by other phenomena. In other words, his theory is constructed on a joint freedom-determinism base. As he put it, "Determinism and freedom are inseparable, for that which determines another is, by the same token, free of the other" (Kelly, 1955, Vol. 1, p. 21). A concrete example might make his point clearer. A student decides that the attainment of a college degree summa cum laude is important to her. As a result, this subjective fact will determine certain other behaviors; for example, she will curtail her social activities and spend many hours studying in the library or her dormitory room. In brief, she was free to choose her goal, but once chosen, the goal determines certain related behaviors.

In the terminology used by Kelly, we can say that the **superordinate construct**—the attainment of the college degree—was freely chosen, and it then acted to subordinate or control certain other constructs—the number of social activities and the number of hours spent studying. As this is such an important point, because it sets the stage for the description of his personal-construct theory, we quote Kelly to make certain it is fully understood.

> The relation established by a construct or a construction system over its subordinate elements is deterministic. In this sense the tendency to subordinate constitutes determinism. The natural events themselves do not subordinate our constructions of them, we can look at them in any way we like . . . The structure we erect is what rules us. [Kelly, 1955, Vol. 1, p. 20)

Theorists who adopt a behavioral stance claim that Kelly's argument is inadequate. They maintain instead that all behavior is determined and would ask Kelly simply, "How did the young woman come to 'choose' her goal of graduating with highest honors?" They would then suggest that this goal too was determined by certain experiences she had had or was currently undergoing.

Every Person as "Scientist"

Kelly believed that each of us, like the scientist, attempts to predict and control events. We are continually in the process of evaluating and reevaluating our experiences and trying to use our interpretations to understand and control the world around us. We have our own "theories" about human behavior. We "test" hypotheses based on the theories, and we subsequently weigh the experimental evidence (Kelly, 1955, Vol. 1, p. 5). On the basis of this evidence, the world becomes more predictable or it becomes clear that we must change our concepts or constructs about it if we are to function effectively.

Of course, Kelly considered us scientists in a very special and limited way. As individuals and "scientists," we use our own highly personalized view of reality in making our judgments. These judgments and their revisions are rarely open to the scrutiny of others. Our constructs are also not as objectively defined as those used by research scientists, and our "theories," rarely meet the criteria set by conventional science. In short, we have rather commonsense views of ourselves and reality, and the possibilities for distortion and error are great (see Chapter 1 for a review of some of these points). Nevertheless, Kelly maintained that there are certain similarities between us and scientists, so that an understanding of these commonalities may help us appreciate his system better. We should be cautious in accepting the scientist analogy because, as you undoubtedly know, every analogy has its own limitations.

In Kelly's view, then, we operate *like* scientists as we make efforts to understand the world. He also noted that many of us continually shift our view of reality to fit the "data." No matter how distorted our views of reality are, they are still real to us and we operate accordingly. As Kelly explained:

> *A person may misrepresent a real phenomenon, such as his income or his ills, and yet his misrepresentation will itself be entirely real. This applies even to the badly deluded patient: what he perceives may not exist, but his perception does. [Kelly, 1955, Vol. 1, p. 8]*

Thus Kelly embraced the phenomenologist position that characterizes the works of the humanist theorists reviewed in Part 6. Like the humanists, Kelly believed we are not passive organisms but, instead, that we actively relate to the environment, often in a creative way.

The Nature of Constructs and Construing

In building our systems of personal constructs, we place interpretations on events. Through an abstraction process, we construct the meaning of events for ourselves (Kelly, 1955, Vol. 1, p. 50). We then utilize our constructions for dealing with new information from the environment. These interpretations are reality for us and determine how we act. They are also highly personalized; we may have the same experiences as others do, but we often interpret them differently.

The constructs that we form to make sense out of our experiences and that we use to deal with new experiences are based on our previous experiences. For Kelly, constructs are ways in which we organize experiences according to similarities and contrasts. He noted that "in its minimum context, a construct is a way in which at least two elements are similar and contrast with a third" (Kelly, 1955, Vol. 1, p. 61). In addition, he argued that constructs must contain at least three elements and may contain many more. As we have noted, constructs are also bipolar: they are construed in terms of contrasts as well as similarities. To say that an object is a chair implies, of necessity, that it is not also a table. To say that bearded men tend to be virile is to imply that clean-shaven men are impotent. To say that Beth and Marie are intelligent is to imply that someone else, perhaps Jane, is stupid.

Since constructs are primarily personal, people may apply different labels to the same experiences. For example, events that certain people call "dependent," others may label "pleasant." An individual may believe that he or she is being pleasant in interpersonal relationships when in fact his or her willingness to yield indiscriminately to the wishes of others to avoid their anger would be labeled "excessive dependence" by others. Kelly argued that there is also the possibility that although two people may label an experience similarly, the contrast end of the dimension may differ. For example, Bill and Jim may label certain of their behaviors and the behavior of others as "sincere," but Bill may see behavior on the opposite end of the spectrum as "insincere," whereas Jim may label it "morally degenerate." Thus Bill might react to certain contrast behaviors of his construct with mild disapproval, whereas Jim would probably become angry and upset under the same circumstances. Their subsequent behavior toward the person exhibiting the contrast behavior may also vary. Bill might try to reason with the "insincere" person; Jim might attack or avoid the "moral degenerate."

Finally, Kelly believed that constructs are not identical to verbal labels (that is, the words of our language), although these labels are used very frequently to convey the meanings of particular experiences to others. Specifically, constructs are actual discriminations people make on an experiential level between varieties of experiences (Bannister, 1977, p. 33). Thus sometimes people formulate constructs before they can verbalize them. This is particularly true of children. For example, some children are capable of showing affection toward loved ones but incapable of verbalizing their feelings. Kelly also maintained that people who are disturbed often "repress" or distort certain experiences and are unable or unwilling to deal with them on a verbal level. As a consequence, they undergo therapy with an expert who may be able to help them deal with the limitations inherent in their construct systems. A detailed example of how Kelly applied his theory of personal constructs in a therapeutic setting will appear later in the chapter.

Additional Characteristics of Constructs

Constructs are arranged in a hierarchical manner within a particular person's cognitive world. There are ordinal relationships between them; that is, one construct may subsume one or more other constructs (Kelly, 1955, Vol. 1, p. 57). For example, a person seen by others as a "moralizer" may actually use a superordinate construct of "good versus bad" to control his or her other concepts: a "good" person might be intelligent, cooperative, kind, ambitious, and sincere; a "bad" person might be stupid, competitive, cruel, unambitious, and insincere.

Constructs may also vary in their range of convenience. By **range of convenience**, Kelly meant that a particular construct might be related to some constructs but not to others (Kelly, 1955, Vol. 1, p. 68). A person might use the good-bad dichotomy to control many constructs but would not be likely to apply it to every construct. The good-bad dichotomy probably has a wide range of convenience for many people, but other constructs are much more limited. Consider, for instance, the construct of fat-thin. We might think of fat people versus thin people or fat lions versus thin lions. But we do not ordinarily think of fat light versus thin light, fat weather versus thin weather, or fat crying versus thin crying.

Related to the notion of range of convenience is Kelly's idea about the **permeability** of constructs. A construct is considered permeable if it will allow additional new elements—that is, constructs currently excluded from its range of convenience—to be construed within that framework (Kelly, 1955, Vol. 1, p. 79). For example, a man's construct of right versus wrong may allow him to include new ideas and behavior by other people as right or wrong. He may be prepared to make a judgment concerning, say, the moral validity of euthanasia, a topic about which he has previously been ignorant. On the other hand, if the construct were impermeable, he would be incapable of making such a moral evaluation. Of course, a construct is rarely completely impermeable; usually there are various degrees of permeability. By introducing the notion of permeability, Kelly made allowances for change in the system. Other ways of talking about change include making allowance for "growth," "personal development," and "the realization of the self."

In short, Kelly has posited a complicated, hierarchical system of cognition populated by personal constructs derived from experience that now control or determine the ways in which the person will react to incoming stimuli or information. Although much of the person's behavior is determined by such constructs, there is also room within his or her system for change, because the superordinate concepts are free and often permeable. Change in these permeable constructs would then produce changes in the superordinate-construct system.

Kelly also proposed that constructs could be characterized as preemptive, constellatory, and propositional. A concept that includes only its own elements and maintains that these elements cannot be part of other constructs is called a **preemptive construct.** For instance, Kelly noted that a person may argue, "Anything that's a ball can be nothing but a ball." So balls cannot be "pellets," "spheres," or "shots" (Kelly, 1955, Vol. 1, p. 153). Unfortunately, such black-or-white thinking sometimes characterizes our interpersonal relationships as well. Occasionally we hear someone claim that "capitalism is nothing but exploitation of the masses by big business," or that "the women's movement is nothing but an attempt by a few frustrated and ugly hags to castrate men."

Kelly described a **constellatory construct** as one that permits it elements to belong to other realms concurrently, but fixes their realm memberships" (Kelly, 1955, Vol. 1, p. 155). Stereotypes belong to this category.

Once we identify persons or objects as members of a given category, we then attribute a cluster, or constellation, of other characteristics to them. Although we are fully aware that we tend to stereotype people according to ethnic and cultural backgrounds, we also do so on the basis of other, seemingly less weighty characteristics, like hair color. For example, Lawson (1971) asked college men and women to rate fictitious people with different hair colors on a variety of personality characteristics. He found that men tended to see blondes as more beautiful, delicate, and feminine than either brunettes or redheads. Overall men and women rated brunettes most favorably and artificial or "bleached" blondes most unfavorably (for instance, as stupid or lazy). Brunettes were seen almost in Girl Scout terms—that is, intelligent, ambitious, sincere, strong, "safe," valuable, and effective. In attributing personality characteristics to men, both men and women also rated dark-haired men most favorably. They saw them as more handsome, intelligent, ambitious, sincere, strong, rugged, valuable, effective, and masculine than men with blonde or red hair. Men with blonde hair were generally rated more favorably than redheads. The tragic implication is that a stereotype may, under certain circumstances, produce unnecessary pain for the possessor of a particular genetically endowed trait when he or she comes into contact with someone who has a constellatory construct of that trait.

Finally, Kelly stated that a construct that left its elements open to construction in every respect be called a **propositional construct**. "Any round object can be considered, among other things, to be a ball." But a ball can, for such a person, also be elliptical, worn, or small. Propositional thinking is flexible thinking. The person is continuously open to new experience and is capable of modifying existing constructs. For Kelly, the person best equipped to deal with the environment is the one who knows the circumstances under which propositional, or preemptive, thinking is appropriate. He pointed out that if we relied exclusively on propositional thinking, we would be immobilized. We would continually be reevaluating and reconstruing our experiences and, as a result, would be indecisive. A star receiver on a professional football team, for instance, might best consider the object being hurled at him as a football and nothing else. In such a case, preemptive thinking would be a necessity. On the other hand, sole reliance on preemptive thinking would lead a person to make dogmatic and unyielding judgments. Such a way of thinking would be fraught with danger for the person: Imagine what would happen to the low-ability student who maintained that he or she was brilliant and never needed to study for examinations.

The Fundamental Postulate of the Theory

The basic assumption underlying Kelly's theory is that "a person's processes are psychologically channelized by the ways in which he anticipates events" (Kelly, 1955, Vol. 1, p. 46). This statement suggests that Kelly believed we are behaving, changing organisms who operate according to our expectations about events. In short, our expectations channel or direct our actions. They provide the motivation for our behavior. In Kelly's man-as-scientist analogy, we seek prediction and verification for our views of events. We generate a construct system by construing events; then we act on the basis of that framework.

The following corollaries or propositions were derived, in part, from the fundamental postulate as a means of elaborating the system.

Individuality Corollary. We not only anticipate events, but we may also differ from one another in our anticipations. According to Kelly, this prop-osition, the **individuality corollary**, lays the groundwork for the study of individual differences. People differ because they have had different expe-riences and also because there are different approaches to the anticipation of the same event (Kelly, 1955, Vol. 1, p. 55). The construct systems people generate are idiosyncratic in many respects, but there are also commonal-ities between people in the way they construe events. People can and do share experiences.

Organization Corollary. Next, Kelly proposed the **organization corol-lary**, maintaining that "each person characteristically evolves, for his con-venience in anticipating events, a construction system embracing ordinal relationships between constructs" (Kelly, 1955, Vol. 1, p. 56). People differ not only in their constructs but also in the way in which they organize them. Organization of constructs also serves to reduce conflict for the person. If a man knows that his wife and family come first, even before his mother, potential conflicts can be minimized. Doubt as to which construct is super-ordinate can be painful, as many husbands have learned.

Choice Corollary. Kelly assumed that all of us are continually making choices between the poles of our constructs. In proposing the **choice cor-ollary**, he assumed further that we tend to make a choice among those alternatives that will allow us to deal most effectively with ensuing events. Should we be cautious or risk-taking in given situations? Should we marry or not marry? Should we pursue a college degree or drop out? Kelly main-tained that people tend, in general, to make choices that define and "elab-orate" the system. In short, given an option, we choose alternatives designed to increase our confidence in our interpretations of the world, alternatives that also increase our understanding of it through "personal growth."

Fragmentation Corollary. According to Kelly, our construct systems are in a continual state of flux. Yet, within these systems, we may successively use a variety of subsystems that are inferentially incompatible with one another (Kelly, 1955, Vol. 1, p. 104). What precisely is Kelly talking about here? He is saying, in effect, that our construct systems are not always completely consistent with one another and that we may sometimes show behaviors that are inconsistent with our most recent experiences—the **fragmentation corollary**. For example, a young woman may decide that she loves a man and declare to friends that she has agreed to marry him. The following day, although we might expect her to show affection toward him, she might begin to revile him in front of friends, pointing out his limitations, and declare that the marriage is off. Here we have construct subsystems that are incompatible. Kelly might explain the inconsistency in her behavior by pointing out that although she loves him, she also knows that he is selfish and inconsiderate and that he will eventually hurt her badly. Thinking about these limitations forced her to terminate the marriage plans. In brief, the construct "fiancé" subsumed the construct of "love" and also the construct of "despising his personal characteristics." Such fragmented and inconsistent construct systems can exist side by side within a person's cognitive world and show up in successive behaviors because other constructs in the larger system trigger them. In this case, the incompatible systems may have been triggered by the superordinate construct "mother" if it was her mother who brought the man's failings to her attention.

The important point to note here is that in trying to predict behavior, we have to discover such ruling constructs and show how, in the final analysis, they control the person's behavior. Kelly is taking issue here with some of the traditional learning views of the determinants of behavior. For some of the early learning theorists, behavior was determined by its immediate antecedents. What Kelly is saying is that the prediction of behavior is much more complicated and involves an assessment of the meanderings of the individual's "cognitive world" and that this world is not always composed of logical and consistent subsystems.

Commonality Corollary. Kelly also maintained that "to the extent that one person employs a construction of experience which is similar to that employed by another, his psychological processes are similar to those of the other person" (Kelly, 1955, Vol. 1, p. 90). Kelly proposed this **commonality corollary** to show that although people who differ in their construction of events will behave differently (the individuality corollary), those who interpret events similarly will behave alike. Thus it is possible for people to act alike even if they have been exposed to different stimuli, if their constructs are similar.

Sociality Corollary. Finally, Kelly maintained, in his **sociality corollary**, that "to the extent that one person construes the construction processes of another, he may play a role in a social process involving the other person (Kelly, 1955, Vol. 1, p. 95). In other words, insofar as you could understand another person's construct system, you would be able to predict accurately what he or she would do and to adjust your own behavior accordingly. Much of our behavior, Kelly maintained, consists of such mutual adjustment. These mutual understandings allow us to function effectively in society. Imagine what would happen if we disagreed about the meaning of traffic signals, for example. If the construct "red" implied "go" for some people while the construct "green" implied "go" for others, we would soon learn the shattering consequences of our lack of mutual understanding and adjustment.

The Process of Personality Development

Kelly assumed that the development of each person revolved around attempts to maximize understanding of the world through the continuing definition and elaboration of his or her construct system. The rationale on which this assumption is based is unclear. It may be that Kelly, like other major humanistic psychologists, simply considered this tendency to be innate. Certainly he did not believe that it was learned, although the person's interaction with the environment was assumed to play the major role in helping him or her move toward personal growth. Yet this point must be clarified if we are truly to understand Kelly's views on the relationship between the environment and personal development. He rejected outright the mechanistic learning view that behavior was determined solely by the operation of environmental events. Individuals do not simply react to the environment. Instead, they actively, uniquely, and systematically construe it and then utilize these constructions to anticipate events. They use previous experiences to create hypotheses about the possible occurrences of new outcomes. In Kelly's opinion, they do not respond to the environment to maximize pleasure and avoid pain, as reinforcement theorists assume. Instead, they actively seek to maximize the accuracy of their views.

Kelly developed several models to illustrate the ways in which the individual utilizes information from the environment in deciding on a course of action. One of the more important ones he termed the circumspection-preemption-control (C-P-C) cycle. The cycle begins, according to Kelly, when the person considers all the possible ways to construe a given situation. That is, you consider a series of propositional constructs that might help you deal with the situation at hand. The preemption phase comes into play next when you reduce the number of constructs available to you and consider seriously only those that will help you solve the problem. Finally, you decide on a course of action by making a choice of that alternative in a single construct you believe will lead to action that will solve the problem (Kelly, 1955, Vol. 1, pp. 516–517). As an illustration, consider the case of a young woman who wants to become a world-renowned violinist. There are various ways she could construe herself in the situation. She could see herself as a "future tennis great," a "lazy person," or a "popular local actress." Until she rejects these self-constructs and settles on one that paints her as a "dedicated student of music," she is unlikely ever to become successful and to realize her ambition. By making that choice, she exercises control over her behavior and anticipates the extension of her construct system.

In Kelly's view, people are continually acting in this way. That is, they are continually considering the alternatives in given situations, reducing the possibilities to those that will work, and acting in accordance with their choices. He sees the developmental process, then, as a creative and dynamic interchange between individual and environment. It involves constructions and reconstructions in the light of new experiences. Its aim is to maximize the person's understanding and therefore his or her control over the environment. The healthy person is one who has an accurate and valid construct system and a flexible view of the world. We will discuss Kelly's beliefs about the unhealthy individual in a later section.

Techniques of Assessment

Kelly used many different techniques to assess personality and promote positive growth in his clients. He devised some of these procedures; others he borrowed and adapted from the works of other major personality theorists.

One of the primary methods Kelly employed was the interview or conference. During a series of therapeutic conferences, therapists attempt not only to assess the realities of their clients' lives but also to point out the directions in which they can proceed toward the solution of their problems (Kelly, 1955, Vol. 2, pp. 774–775). They also encourage clients to discuss their problems by acting in a supportive, reassuring, and accepting manner. Acceptance of clients does not mean, however, approval of their construct systems nor their views of themselves (Kelly, 1955, Vol. 2, p. 587). Instead, it means that therapists are capable of understanding their clients and of anticipating events the way clients anticipate them. In any event, in such nonthreatening environments, clients are expected to feel free to experiment with new ideas or beliefs and/or to revise or discard existing ones that work poorly or not at all without fear of suffering devastating consequences if their experiments go awry (Kelly, 1955, Vol. 2, p. 581).

A large part of this experimentation involves role playing. In Kelly's view, clients' invalid construct systems can be changed through participation in this procedure. Role enactment provides clients with insights into their maladaptive behavior and with new and more satisfying ways of behaving. Clients are typically assigned these roles by their therapists, who often engage in complementary role playing to clarify their clients' feelings about themselves and to provide them with an opportunity for self-insight. Clients are not passive, however. They may also cast their therapists into a variety of roles. For example, therapists may be asked to play the role of parent, teacher, or child. This situation, along with the process it entails, is similar to Freudian transference in the sense that clients may act toward their therapists as though they were actually significant authority figures from their past. During this intellectual and emotional process, they may achieve needed insight into their own problems. The emphasis in Kelly's therapy, however, is not on reliving the past. Rather, the therapy aims to provide clients with new roles to play and perfect that will promote growth and allow them to participate more fully and effectively in current life situations. This emphasis on providing opportunities for change and growth is an integral part of Kelly's fixed-role therapy, as we shall soon see.

Kelly viewed therapy as a creative process, and role playing is the major technique that enables clients to act creatively. Although playing new roles seems artificial and stultifying at first, this feeling soon dissipates and clients become more spontaneous. Role playing makes them more susceptible to change. Loosening of constructs can also be achieved, in Kelly's judgment, by use of relaxation techniques, free association, and dream analysis.

Although Kelly did make considerable use of personality testing as an aid in diagnosing problems and in assessing therapy effectiveness, he made it very clear that it should not be used to classify or "pigeonhole" the individual in any fixed way. It should not interfere with the ongoing therapeutic process. Thus, in his view, testing should occur early in the process. If, for example, it occurs after a client has participated in several months of therapy, it might leave him or her with the mistaken impression that all the therapeutic gains did not mean much. Why else would the therapist be testing at this stage in the process unless he or she was uncertain about the client's progress and needed more diagnostic information?

Even if testing were done early in the process, Kelly felt, it still could do irreparable harm to the clients if not administered properly. Thus clients should be made to see that testing can provide helpful information to therapists, information that is needed to guide the therapy in a positive direction. Clients should also be reassured that there are no right or wrong answers to the questions and that their therapists will continue to see them as worthwhile individuals no matter what the test results show.

The Role Construct Repertory Test. One test that proved extremely useful to Kelly in his therapeutic work was the **Role Construct Repertory Test (RCRT).** He devised this test as his major diagnostic tool for assessing the personal construct systems of people in clinical settings. A matrix, or grid, is created in which clients first list the names of the important people in their social environments. They are then asked to sort these people by successively considering three of them at a time, to make circles under their names, and to mark down in a space to the right of each row in the grid the way in which two of them are alike and yet different from the third. They are asked to put an X in the two circles corresponding to the ones who are alike. This procedure identifies the "similarity" part of the construct. Next, clients are asked to write in a space to the right the way in which the third person is different from the other two. This procedure identifies the "contrast" part of the construct.

Clients are then asked to consider the other prominent persons in their environments and to place a checkmark (√), *not* an X, under the name of each. If they do not place a checkmark under some of these important people, it means that the contrast part of the construct applies to them. Clients then proceed to sort all these people again on new dimensions. The number of constructs to be utilized depends on the clients. Some clients will use only a few; others, many.

For an illustration of how this assessment procedure works, turn to Table 10.1. This table represents the cognitive matrix of one of Kelly's clients. The columns list the important individuals in this person's life. The rows represent the constructs used by the client to construe them. Construct 2 can be termed an "education" construct. The client sees both a teacher he accepts (⊗) and one he rejects (⊗) as similar in educational level. He sees his boss, in contrast, as having a different educational background (○). His brother (√), sister (√), friend (√), and a successful person he knows (√) are all similar to his teachers in educational background. The remaining figures (voids), including himself, mother, father, spouse, ex-girlfriend, ex-friend, a rejecting person, a pitied person, a threatening person, an attractive person, a happy person, and an ethical person, all have an educational background that is different from his teachers'.

Once the task has been completed by a subject, it is possible to devise a score in a variety of ways. One simple method used by psychologist James Bieri was to examine the check patterns across the various rows and to assume that similar patterns signified a lack of differentiation in the client's perception of others (cognitive simplicity). On the other hand, if the patterns were highly dissimilar, it was assumed that the person had a highly differentiated view of others (cognitive complexity) (Bieri, 1955). In a clinical setting, the person's cognitive complexity score can be interpreted by the therapist, along with other testing information, to illuminate his or her problems. An example of such an interpretation is given in the next section. Here we will consider the use of the test in an experimental setting.

In his study, Bieri sought to test the validity of Kelly's RCRT by first classifying the college students who participated as either "cognitively complex" or "cognitively simple" on the basis of their scores on the RCRT. Using Kelly's assumptions that a basic characteristic of human beings is to move toward greater predictability of their environments and that each person has a set of constructs to use in making those predictions, Bieri argued that those who are cognitively complex would be better able to predict the behavior of others than those who are cognitively simple. He reasoned that those who can differentiate among many different events in the environment would be more capable of making discerning and accurate judgments than those who see many events in their environments as similar and who apply the same labels to them.

To test this hypothesis, Bieri had cognitively complex and cognitively simple subjects respond to a questionnaire depicting 12 social situations in which four alternatives were given. A typical item follows:

You are working intently to finish a paper in the library when two people sit down across from you and distract you with their continual loud talking. Would you most likely:

a. Move to another seat?
b. Let them know how you feel by your facial expression?
c. Try to finish up in spite of their talking?
d. Ask them to stop talking?

After the subjects completed the questionnaire, they were asked to guess how two of their classmates would respond in the same situations. The subjects' predictive accuracy was assessed by noting the number of times their predictions matched the responses of their classmates. As expected, the cognitively complex students were much more accurate in their predictions than the cognitively simple ones. It was also found that the cognitively simple or undifferentiated subjects were more likely than the complex subjects to perceive inaccurate similarities between themselves and others; that is, they tended to assume that the predictions they made for themselves would also apply to others, even though this was not the case. In brief, cognitively simple subjects tended to be quite egocentric. This is but one example of research based on Kelly's theorizing. There have been many other studies, and the findings tend to support Kelly's formulations (Bonarius, 1965).

In addition to the RCRT, Kelly used other techniques to assess personality. Two of the major ones, self-characterization sketches and fixed-role therapy, will be explored shortly.

Application of the Theory to the Treatment of Psychopathology

The Aim of Psychotherapy and the Roles of Therapist and Client

In Kelly's opinion, the sick person is best construed as one who continues to use constructs that are invalid. Thus the basic aim of psychotherapy is to help clients form new constructs or revise old ones so that they may deal more effectively with their environment. The therapist is concerned primarily with opening up the possibility of continual change in the clients' construct system so that they can regain their health. The therapist's job is to diagnose the illness and to throw light on the "paths" by which the client can become well (Kelly, 1955, Vol. 2, p. 582).

To achieve these objectives, Kelly believed, the clinician should conceptualize his or her role quite broadly. The therapeutic process, in Kelly's view, begins as both parties try to define their roles. If a man begins to concep-

Table 10.1
Client's Repertory Grid

#	Similarity Pole	Contrast Pole	Self	Mother	Father	Brother	Sister	Spouse	Ex-girlfriend	Friend	Ex-friend	Rejected person	Pitied person	Threatening person	Attractive person	Accepted teacher	Rejected teacher	Boss	Successful person	Happy person	Ethical person
1	Don't believe in God	Very religious	✓						✓			✓		✓					⊗	⊗	○
2	Same sort of education	Completely different education	✓	✓	✓	✓	✓			✓		⊗	○			⊗	⊗	○	✓		
3	Not athletic	Athletic				✓	✓	✓	⊗		✓			✓	⊗	✓			✓		
4	Both girls	A boy		⊗	⊗	○		⊗		○											
5	Parents	Ideas different	✓			○	✓	✓		✓						✓	✓	✓	✓	✓	✓
6	Understand me better	Don't understand me at all			○	✓	○			✓						⊗	✓			⊗	
7	Teach the right way	Teach the wrong way		⊗		✓	✓				○					⊗	✓	✓		✓	✓
8	Achieved a lot	Hasn't achieved a lot		✓		✓	✓									✓	⊗	⊗	⊗		✓
9	Higher education	No education	✓			⊗			✓	✓		○				✓		✓	✓		
10	Don't like other people	Like other people				⊗						⊗					○		✓		
11	More religious	Not religious	✓	✓	✓	⊗		✓		✓			○	✓		✓	✓		✓	✓	⊗

278

Table 10.1
(continued)

Constructs

No.	Similarity Pole	Contrast Pole
12	Believe in higher education	Don't believe in much education
13	More sociable	Not sociable
14	Both girls	Not girls
15	More understanding	Less understanding
16	Both have high morals	Low morals
17	Think alike	Think differently
18	Same age	Different ages
19	Both friends	Not friends
20	Both appreciate music	Don't understand music

Important People in Client's Life	12	13	14	15	16	17	18	19	20
Self	√			√	√	⊗			⊗
Mother	√	√	○	√					
Father	√	√		√	√	√			
Brother	⊗	√		√	⊗	√		√	√
Sister			√	○	√				○
Spouse		○	⊗			√	⊗	√	
Ex-girlfriend	√	⊗	○				⊗	⊗	
Friend	√			√	⊗	√		√	
Ex-friend	○			○				√	
Rejected person	√	√						√	
Pitied person	√	√					○		
Threatening person	⊗	⊗				√		√	
Attractive person	√				⊗	√			
Accepted teacher	√	√		⊗	√	√			
Rejected teacher	√			⊗	√	√		√	
Boss	√	√		√			⊗		
Successful person	√			√	√		⊗		√
Happy person	√	⊗		√	√	√	√		
Ethical person	√			√	√	√	○		√

Note: Circles containing Xs and checkmarks—similarity: empty circles and blanks—contrast. From Kelly, Vol. 1, 1955, p. 270.

tualize therapy as involving minor adjustments on his part, it will be virtually impossible for the therapist to get him to see the need for drastic change. The therapist, therefore, must begin with the client's limited view of psychotherapy and try to show him the need for revising it. The therapist does this by listening closely to the client's complaints and by using a variety of techniques to produce change. Techniques that produce minor changes include (1) threat, (2) invalidation, and (3) exhortation (Kelly, 1955, Vol. 2, pp. 583–587). By threat, Kelly meant that the client becomes aware of the possibility of imminent change in his construct structures. Under such conditions, Kelly thought the therapist could take advantage of the situation by pointing out new ways for the client to construe his experiences to facilitate constructive growth. Change could also be produced if the therapist invalidated the client's constructs—that is, showed why and how his or her constructs wouldn't work. Last, the therapist could produce minor change by admonishing the client's actions and suggesting ways to behave differently and more effectively.

To produce major change, it must be clear to clients that the therapist accepts them and is willing to help them "think through" their problems. Kelly's view of acceptance differs from that of other nondirective therapists, however. In the traditional view, the therapist assumes that everyone has the right to choose to become anything that he or she desires. Kelly would like to accept this view in principle but is uncertain where such a commitment by the therapist would lead. In his view, acceptance involves not so much approval of the clients' characteristics *en toto* as a readiness to understand the clients' construct system and to use it to help them get well. One of the implications of this stance is that therapists must have a clear and firm understanding of their own construct system. Further, they must empathize with the clients but not surrender their own viewpoint. Therapists should instead try to subsume much of the clients' system into their own viewpoint (Kelly, 1955, Vol. 2, pp. 585–587).

Kelly believed that major change could be effected if the therapist asked the client to "think through" his or her problems and to see how they would turn out in the end. He called such a procedure **controlled elaboration**. Its aim was to make the clients construct system internally consistent and communicable so that it could eventually be validated or invalidated by new experiences.

During the "thinking through" process, the therapist is not simply passive and accepting. He or she actively tries to help the client revise or discard old constructs and formulate new ones. The therapist does this by skillfully suggesting that new elements be added to the old constructs (for example, "Your view of your brother should also include the fact that he is highly considerate of your friends") or by helping the person formulate new constructs (for example, "Your minister is a person who might help you better understand why you doubt the existence of God"). The therapist also tries to challenge the client's system without precipitating a catastrophe (Kelly, 1955, Vol. 2, pp. 589–590).

The role of the therapist also requires that the client use current constructs to deal with problems experienced in childhood. Kelly maintained that all too often therapists allowed their clients to dwell on the past and to recount their experiences in childish terms. He proposed that revision of these constructs could happen only if client and therapist were willing to use new, adult thinking about the old experiences. The therapist also helps the client to design new "experiments," to "test" hypotheses with courage, and to weigh the "evidence" critically. The role of the therapist, therefore, is like the role of the experienced scientific investigator who is helping initiate a beginner into the realm of science. The therapist also acts as a validator of the evidence the client accumulates. As Kelly put it:

> It is ... important that the therapist play his role, not only with an acceptance and a generosity possibly rare in the client's interpersonal world but always with a kind of naturalness and faithfulness to reality which will not mislead the client who uses him as a validator. In a sense, the therapist must play a part as a reasonably faithful example of natural human reactions, rather than one which is superhuman or divested of all human spontaneity. In a sense, the therapist takes the best to be found in human nature and portrays it in such a way as to enable the client to validate his constructs against it. Having identified the therapist's generalization of the acceptable values in human nature, the client may seek them out among his companions. [Kelly, 1955, Vol. 2, p. 593]

In conclusion, therapists must have a clear idea of their own system and its constructs. They must also be alert and sensitive to a variety of cues emanating from their clients. As scientists, they must engage in propositional thinking and be willing to change their views on the basis of the evidence. They must, in brief, be flexible. They must also be courageous, according to Kelly, because psychotherapy is often a distressing experience for them as well as for their clients. Finally, therapists must possess verbal skills and an ability to utilize them, and they must be creative and energetic in the pursuit of their hypothesis, if their clients are ever to get well (Kelly, 1955, Vol. 2, pp. 595–605).

Use of the RCRT to Appraise Client Experience

Kelly noted that there were two general approaches to the appraisal of the client's experiences. One focused on the client's past; the other tended to deemphasize the past and to concentrate instead on the present. Kelly agreed that the therapist should not dwell exclusively on the past, but he did think the clinician should make some use of it via the case history method. As he saw it, the past was important because

> [its] events are the validational evidence against which [the client] won and lost his wagers, against which he tested his personal constructs. They are the

checkpoints he had to use in charting the course of his life. To understand what they actually were is to get some notion of the ranges of convenience of the client's constructs, what the system was designed to deal with, one way or another. Moreover, many of these events will have to be given some stabilizing interpretation in the new construct system produced under therapeutic intervention. [Kelly, 1955, Vol. 2, p. 688]

Moreover, for Kelly, this procedure would give the clinician evidence of how the person's culture affected his or her life. He believed that the culture provided the person with much evidence of what is "true" or "false" in life. To assess the effects of culture on the person, Kelly turned to the RCRT.

At this point, let us examine possible interpretations of the RCRT as they apply to the actual client's matrix shown in Table 10.1. If we proceed down column 1 ("Self") and simply note the incidents ($\checkmark$, $\otimes$) and the voids (blanks) and empty circles, we can get some idea of how this person sees himself. Remember that the incidents refer to the similarity poles, and the blanks and empty circles to the contrast poles, of the constructs. The client describes himself as a male who is similar in a few respects to his parents, who, like him, are very religious. Unfortunately, he claims that he doesn't understand himself, nor do his parents nor his wife nor his ex-girlfriend understand him. He is not friends with his parents or his sister. He sees his brother as one of the few people who understand him. Although his brother has accomplished a great deal, the client does not think that he himself has been very successful. Unfortunately, although the client seems to admire his brother very much, he does not consider him a friend or, alternately, his brother does not see him as a friend. He sees his friend and his wife as friends (see construct 19), but he does not see the person he calls "friend" as a real friend.

We might want tentatively to interpret his construct system to mean that the client sees himself negatively, as being alone and isolated, even among people who are supposed to be close to him. He is convinced that his parents do not understand him, and even though he believes his brother and his "friend" do understand him, he does not really see them as friends. Part of his problem might stem from his view of himself as not sociable. We have, then, a clinical picture of a young man who may be lonely either because his family and friends have failed to communicate with him or because they cannot communicate with someone so unsociable and withdrawn. Of course, it is also possible that his feelings of isolation are being produced by still other factors. In any event, his responses on the RCRT provide the clinician with only a clue to his problems. Other diagnostic techniques such as the self-characterization, which will be discussed next, as well as detailed interviews help the clinician make more definite judgments. You may be able to see other ways of interpreting this RCRT protocol. The interpretation here was designed simply to give you some idea of Kelly's approach.

Self-Characterization Sketches and Fixed-Role Therapy as Aids to Effect Change

Once Kelly had made his diagnosis of the client's difficulties, techniques had to be devised to bring about needed change. We have already reviewed briefly some of the procedures that could be used to produce both major and minor adjustment changes.

The therapist not only accepts what the client says, but asks the man to elaborate on his constructs through the use of a **self-characterization sketch**. It is a simple approach based on Kelly's belief that "if you do not know what is wrong with a person, ask him; he may tell you" (Kelly, 1955, Vol. 1, pp. 322–323). Thus the clinician directly asks the client to write a character sketch of another person, say John Bolling, as if he were the principal character in a play. The client is asked to write it as a friend who knew the character intimately and sympathetically. This third-person format is followed to make the task as nonthreatening as possible.

After the client has written the sketch and the therapist has interpreted it, the therapist uses the interpretation to write a fixed-role sketch for the client, which he is asked to enact. The sketch is designed to produce major changes in the client by making it a script that contrasts sharply with his current perception of himself, as revealed in the self-characterization sketch (Kelly, 1955, Vol. 1, p. 370). To accomplish this goal, the therapist focuses on those constructs in the self-characterization sketch that imply immobility. The fixed-role sketch is designed to protect the client by leading him to believe it is only a fictitious character he is enacting. Kelly found that with this disclaimer clients were willing to try out the new role and that later they began to see its implication for them and to act accordingly.

Kelly also provided a clear example of how the self-characterization and **fixed-role therapy** techniques worked in the case of an actual client he called Ronald Barrett. An analysis of the self-characterization sketch revealed that Ronald was a compulsive individual who believed dogmatically that there was a reason behind all existence and that the only way to understand the causes of one's existence was to rely on rational thought and logic. Thus the only way for Ronald to solve problems was to maintain control over his feelings and to rely solely on reason. Despite his attempt at maintaining strict control, however, Ronald saw himself "ready to explode" on any occasion and was disturbed by his feelings because they would bring disapproval from others. Although he had no warm and friendly relationships with people, he thought that he must have their approval. Such approval could be gained, he reasoned, only by keeping his emotions in check and appearing calm and restrained. His concern with restraining his feelings even extended to his relationships with girls. To quote directly from his self-characterization sketch:

> He [Ronald] has some ideas concerning girls that seem odd or just plain crazy to most people. He completely refrains from calling a girl "beautiful."

She may be cute, pretty, attractive, or some other adjective in his mind, but he uses the word "beautiful" only [to] describe material things that have no "feeling" as humans have. Although he listens attentively to stories or general discussions about sex, he rarely enters into the conversation. One may say that he puts too much meaning and thought into kissing a girl. If he has gone out with a girl a couple of times, or even once, and doesn't continue to go out with her or to call her, he is very hesitant about asking her for a date again, say two or three months later. He is usually lost for conversation when meeting someone new, or seeing a girl he knows, but if he once "breaks the ice," he can usually talk freely. However, when he calls a girl on the telephone, no matter how well he knows her, he hates to have anyone around him or even within hearing distance. Furthermore, he doesn't like to practice anything, such as a musical instrument, any place where he can be seen or heard. [Kelly, 1955, Vol. 1, p. 328]

Kelly noted that Ronald was himself disturbed by some of his ideas about girls. He also mentioned that Ronald did attribute "feeling" to girls, but not to beautiful ones. This suggested that he saw girls, and all feeling things, as imperfect. As a consequence, he continually was hesitant and awkward in his relationships with women. To help Ronald overcome his problems, Kelly wrote a fixed-role sketch for him to enact in his daily life. The sketch was about a man called Kenneth Norton. The sketch was as follows:

Kenneth Norton

Kenneth Norton is the kind of man who, after a few minutes of conversation, somehow makes you feel that he must have known you intimately for a long time. This comes about not by any particular questions that he asks but by the understanding way in which he listens. It is as if he had a knack of seeing the world through your eyes. The things which you have come to see as being important he, too, soon seems to sense as similarly important. Thus, he catches not only your words but the punctuations of feeling with which they are formed and the little accents of meaning with which they are chosen. . . .

Girls he finds attractive for many reasons, not the least of which is the exciting opportunity they provide for his understanding the feminine point of view. Unlike some men, he does not "throw the ladies a line," but, so skillful a listener is he, soon has them throwing him one—and he is thoroughly enjoying it.

With his own parents and in his own home he is somewhat more expressive of his own ideas and feelings. Thus, his parents are given an opportunity to share and supplement his new enthusiasms and accomplishments. [Kelly, 1955, Vol. 1, pp. 374–375]

According to Kelly, the sketch centered on a simple theme—the seeking of answers in the feelings of other people rather than in argument with them

(Kelly, 1955, Vol. 1, p. 375). He asked Ronald to become Kenneth Norton for two weeks. First, however, Kelly let Ronald rehearse in his office a number of times until he was thoroughly familiar with the sketch (Kelly, 1955, Vol. 1, p. 387). Of course, Kelly insisted on addressing the client as Kenneth throughout the rehearsal and enactment period. Kelly also held therapy sessions during the enactment period to assess Ronald's progress or lack of it. Progress was uncertain at first, but by the 12th interview, Ronald reported feeling much less insecure in social situations and more willing to express his feelings. Shortly afterward, the therapist "broke" the client's Kenneth Norton role and told him how Kenneth Norton was, in a sense, supposed to be Ronald Barrett. Ronald accepted this opinion after some discussion and then thanked the therapist for all his help. Ronald returned to his everyday situation with a changed set of constructs and a more realistic assessment of his own behavior and the behavior of others (Kelly, 1955, Vol. 1, pp. 394–395).

Assessment and Modification of the Construct Systems of Schizophrenics. Although the preceding discussion focused on the problem of a single client, much of the research utilizing Kelly's theory has employed variants of his RCRT to study psychiatric patients who have been diagnosed as schizophrenic. Kelly (1955) originally proposed that the thinking of schizophrenics involves the use of loosened constructions. **Loose constructions** are those that lead to varying predictions. They are weak and unstable ideas and networks of ideas. Bannister and colleagues (1975) have attempted to explain the origins of these loose constructions in schizophrenics. They maintain that schizophrenics, like normals, utilize constructs to make predictions about how the world operates; but, unfortunately, the predictions of schizophrenics, unlike those of normals, do not work very well. That is, many of their predictions are invalid. The consequence of being wrong is to receive punishment from others. Bannister and colleagues maintain that, to avoid more punishment, schizophrenics weaken the constructs themselves and the associations between them and begin, as a consequence, to live subjectively in a highly fluid and largely meaningless (for them) universe. Specifically, as children, schizophrenics may have lived in a family situation riddled with inconsistencies, with their parents sometimes behaving with kindness toward them and at other times with cruelty. Tremendous doubt could have been created, for example, if their parents rewarded them for a particular behavior at times and punished them for the same behavior at other times. Perhaps their parents also ridiculed them unexpectedly in front of their peers and arbitrarily reneged on their promises. The consequence of this severe and erratic treatment could be the development of highly fluid constructs about their parents and an unwillingness and inability to make definite predictions about how their parents would behave toward them. After all, why try to make predictions about them if the predictions are continually incorrect? Incorrect predictions are punishing.

To assess the validity of the assertion that schizophrenia is associated with disordered thinking, Bannister and Fransella (1966) measured the thinking of schizophrenics and compared it with that of depressives, neurotics, patients with mild forms of brain damage (organics), and normal individuals. A variant of the RCRT was used to measure disordered thinking. All subjects were tested individually. Each person studied eight photos of strangers, one at a time. Then he or she rank-ordered each photo according to how kind the person in the photo appeared to be, with the most kind person being ranked 1 and the least kind one ranked 8. Then the eight photos were reshuffled and each subject was asked to rank-order them again along a dimension of stupidity. The photos were again reshuffled and then rank-ordered along a dimension of selfishness. This same rating procedure was used several more times to elicit judgments of the degree of sincerity, meanness, and honesty of the people in the photos.

After this task was complete (administration 1), the subjects were given the same set of photos and were asked to repeat the entire procedure (administration 2). That is, subjects were asked to rank-order the same eight people on the same six personality dimensions.

Correlational analyses were then made between the ratings of the photos on the six dimensions for each group of subjects for administrations 1 and 2. More specifically, separate correlations were computed for each group— the schizophrenics, the depressives, the neurotics, the brain-damaged patients, and the normal subjects—to determine the extent to which the various groups were consistent in their ratings from administration 1 to administration 2. A consistent rating would involve rating a given person as most kind the first time and as most kind the second time. An inconsistent rating would involve rating a particular person as highly honest the first time and highly dishonest the second time. In brief, the assessment was one of the degree of consistency in the ratings from administration 1 to 2. The results: normals ($r = +.80$), depressives ($r = +.75$), neurotics ($r = +.74$), organics ($r = +.73$), and schizophrenics ($r = +.18$). The high correlations for the first four groups indicate highly consistent ratings, whereas the low correlation for the schizophrenics indicates a lack of consistency in their ratings, even though the second set of ratings was made *immediately* after completion of the first set. These results suggest that schizophrenics have a problem in thinking. Bannister, Fransella, and Agnew (1971) showed further that not only is the structure (organization and consistency) of the thinking in schizophrenics poor, but the content (the kind of beliefs they hold) of their thinking is bizarre. That is, much of their thinking is characterized by paranoid delusions and by illogical connections between constructs.

Schizophrenics also have difficulties in categorizing people in terms of their personal qualities (for instance, their abilities, motives, traits) when making judgments. Specifically, schizophrenics who were asked to look at photos of people and react to them made their judgments in impersonal terms. For example, they would report that the person in the photo was standing. In judging a second photo, they would not comment on the person in the photo at all, but would simply report that there was a book in the photo. Normals, in contrast, looked at the photos and made many more judgments in personal terms—for example, the person looked kind, sincere, or competitive (McPherson, Barden, & Buckley, 1970; McPherson, Buckley, & Draffan, 1971).

Finally, Bannister and co-workers (1975) have maintained that it is possible to reverse the process of thought-disorder in schizophrenics by providing them with new experiences that are consistently accurate. They reasoned that, if thought-disorder is the long-term consequence of the schizophrenics' repeated failures to predict accurately the behavior of others and themselves, then implementing therapeutic procedures in which patients are provided with evidence that they can accurately predict their own behavior and that of others should result in an improvement in their health and functioning. Accordingly, they recruited therapists to help these patients over a two-year period to identify beliefs that were weak and then proceeded to strengthen them. For instance, if a woman very tentatively believed that loud-mouthed people were mean, the therapist would enlist the support of the staff (psychologists and nurses) to present themselves in a loud-mouthed way to the patient whenever she requested cigarettes or candy and to refuse to give either to her. If a male patient believed that it was manly to be aggressive, the therapist would work to convince him that this belief was faulty and that it was manly to act like a gentleman. Situations were then arranged in which members of the staff would praise the patient and call him a fine gentleman for acting in a cooperative and nonaggressive way. Although the results of this long-term project were not completely positive, they were generally supportive of the investigators' theorizing, and there was evidence of some improvement in the thinking and psychological health of the patients.

Critical Comments

We turn now to an examination of the scientific worth of Kelly's theory.

Comprehensiveness. Kelly's theory is not very comprehensive, although it has the potential to handle far more phenomena than it currently does. Its perspective is primarily cognitive in nature, and it tends to deemphasize the role the situation plays in determining behavior. It is, in short, a personalistic (person-oriented) rather than a situationist or interactionist approach to the study of behavior. The emphasis on rationality is one-sided. It tends to downplay the irrational thoughts and desires that sometimes control our behavior. It is an intellectualized way of conceptualizing human functioning. People do not often act as scientists. They are not always objective; they do not always weigh evidence critically. Most important, even if they do weigh it, they sometimes remain unaffected by it.

It is important to note, however, that Kelly could not bring himself to dismiss out of hand some of the Freudian constructs that allow investigators to account for irrational behavior. Instead, he tried to retranslate some of the Freudian terms into terms compatible with his psychology of personal constructs. The concept of the unconscious is discussed, in part, as "pre-verbal constructs," for instance. These are concepts, because of their poor symbolization, the person cannot articulate. Another way of talking about the unconscious is to apply the concept of submergence. Kelly assumed that some of our biopolar constructs have poles that are not readily available to us (Kelly, 1955, Vol. 1, pp. 466–467). For example, a client may believe that "everyone is kind." This construct implies that nobody is ever cruel to her, an unlikely possibility. The therapist might argue that the contrast end of the construct (cruel people) is submerged and that his or her job is to make this aspect of the construct conscious before the client can begin to regain her health. Of course, although Kelly believed his concepts of preverbal constructs and submergence were more specific and clearly defined than Freud's concept of the unconscious, it is not readily apparent that this is indeed the case. Much of Kelly's discussion of the ways in which the therapist comes to understand the mechanisms by which clients submerge their constructs to avoid dealing with them is just as muddied as the interpretations offered by some psychoanalysts.

Precision and Testability. In comparison to most of the theories reviewed in the text, Kelly's position is unusually clear and testable. The theory is housed within an explicitly stated framework so that hypotheses can be derived and tested. In addition, the RCRT provides a precise and reliable way of measuring many of the basic ideas in the theory.

Parsimony. Kelly's position seems too economical. It has too few concepts to account for personality functioning. There are relatively few concepts used to describe the developmental process, for example. Kelly said little of an explicit nature about the kinds of learning experiences that move individuals toward maximum understanding of their world. It seems highly unlikely that the concepts of motivation and reinforcement are totally superfluous and do not help us understand personality functioning.

Empirical Validity. The experimental evidence in support of certain aspects of Kelly's theory is strong. Much of this research has been concerned with establishing the reliability and validity of the RCRT and with testing some of the basic propositions of the theory (Bonarius, 1965). In the clinical area, much of the research has centered on Kelly's seminal ideas about thought-disorder in schizophrenia, and it has provided general support for Kelly's theorizing.

Despite these facts, two points should be made. First, this evidence is largely correlational and paper-and-pencil in nature. Thus there is a definite need for more sophisticated experimental work in which measures of behavioral criteria are used and interaction effects between cognitive functionings of the individual in specific situations are assessed. There is also a need to move beyond the laboratory to test the theory in natural settings. Despite the provocative nature of Kelly's formulations, research efforts have remained at a fairly unsophisticated level. Perhaps investigators will remedy this problem in the near future so that the worth of Kelly's theory can be assessed more adequately.

Second, the RCRT is primarily a descriptive device; that is, it describes the constructs the client claims to use in articulating and ordering experiences. Interpretations of the meanings of the constructs, however, rest on the clinician's skills and sensitivity. Kelly claimed that the measure can be used to help clients improve their behavior, but the "evidence" he offered is traditional in nature; that is, it is based on the therapist's subjective judgment that the client has improved. In this respect, Kelly's use of case history materials to "prove" the validity of his views on psychotherapy is limited.

Heuristic Value. Kelly's theory has proved very interesting and challenging to British psychologists, who have been most active in testing various aspects of its. Research by American psychologists has been remarkably sparse, given the originality and provocative nature of much of Kelly's thinking. Perhaps part of the difficulty is that the theory is abruptly different from other existing positions in American psychology. Nor is it clear to many American psychologists that the elimination of important traditional concepts, like motivation and reinforcement, is a move in the right direction. Moreover, some of these psychologists believe that the theory is too cognitive and presents a view of personality that is too one-sided and simplistic, although efforts have been made recently by a British advocate of the theory to convince psychologists that such a view is erroneous (Bannister, 1977).

Applied Value. Kelly's theory has had little impact on disciplines outside psychology and has not contributed much to the solution of social problems. The theory is currently in its initial stages of verification, so it may have more impact in the future, especially in the clinical area.

Discussion Questions

1. Why do many people want to believe their behavior is free and not determined?
2. In what ways do we act as scientists in the prediction of our behavior? Cite limitations in applying this analogy as an aid in understanding our behavior.
3. What is a personal construct? Why must constructs contain at least three elements? Can you think of constructs that contain only two elements?
4. How do propositional and constellatory constructs differ? Give examples of each type of construct.

5. Make up a repertory grid that describes your own constructs in relation to the important people in your life. Did the exercise provide you with any insights about your personality?

6. What are some of the strengths and weaknesses of using Kelly's Role Construct Repertory Test (RCRT) to assess personality?

7. What are some of the potentially harmful consequences to other people of using stereotypes about hair color?

8. Are the traits associated with stereotypes always negative ones? Can you think of sex-role traits that are positive, for example? Why do people rely on stereotypes to guide their behavior?

9. What are some of your superordinate constructs? In your view, is your social success superordinate to academic success or vice versa? Why?

10. Do you agree with Kelly that people are generally rational in their behavior?

References

Bannister, D. (Ed.). *New perspectives in personal construct theory.* New York: Academic Press, 1977.

Bannister, D., Adams-Webber, J. R., Penn, W. I., & Radley, A. R. Reversing the process of thought-disorder: A serial validation experiment. *British Journal of Social and Clinical Psychology,* 1975, *14,* 169–180.

Bannister, D., & Fransella, F. A grid test of schizophrenic thought disorder. *British Journal of Social and Clinical Psychology,* 1966, *5,* 95–102.

Bannister, D., Fransella, F., & Agnew, J. Characteristics and validity of the grid test on thought disorder. *British Journal of Social and Clinical Psychology,* 1971, *10,* 144–151.

Bieri, J. Cognitive complexity-simplicity and predictive behavior. *Journal of Abnormal and Social Psychology,* 1955, *51,* 263–268.

Bonarius, J. Research in the personal construct theory of George A. Kelly: Role Construct Repertory Test and basic theory. In B. Maher (Ed.), *Progress in experimental personality research.* New York: Academic Press, 1965.

Kelly, G. A. *The psychology of personal constructs,* Vols. 1 and 2. New York: Norton, 1955.

Lawson, E. D. Hair color, personality and the observer. *Psychological Reports,* 1971, *28,* 311–322.

McPherson, F. M., Barden, V., & Buckley, F. The use of "psychological" constructs by affectively flattened schizophrenics. *British Journal of Medical Psychology,* 1970, *43,* 291–293.

McPherson, F. M., Buckley, F., & Draffan, J. "Psychological" constructs and delusions of persecution and "non-integration" in schizophrenia. *British Journal of Medical Psychology,* 1971, *44,* 277–280.

Suggested Readings

Bannister, D. (Ed.). *New perspectives in personal construct theory.* New York: Academic Press, 1977.

Bonarius, J. Research in the personal construct theory of George A. Kelly: Role Construct Repertory Test and basic theory. In B. Maher (Ed.), *Progress in experimental personality research.* New York: Academic Press, 1965.

Kelly, G. A. *The psychology of personal constructs,* Vols. 1 and 2. New York: Norton, 1955.

Mancuso, J. C. (Ed.). *Readings for a cognitive theory of personality.* New York: Holt, Rinehart & Winston, 1970.

Glossary

Choice corollary Proposition that people select between alternatives in making their judgments about the ways in which reality operates.

Commonality corollary Proposition that similar construct systems between individuals may lead to similarities or commonalities in behavior.

Constellatory construct Type of construct that allows its elements to belong to other constructs concurrently; but once identified in a particular way, these elements are fixed.

Construct Abstraction defined in terms of the similarity and contrast of its elements.

Constructive alternativism Fundamental assumption that human beings are capable of changing their interpretations of events.

Controlled elaboration Therapeutic technique in which clients are encouraged to clarify and "think through" their problems in consultation with the therapist. One of the outcomes of this consultation is the revision or discarding of old construct elements and the formulation of new and more effective ones.

Fixed-role therapy Therapeutic procedure used by Kelly to produce personality changes in clients by constructing roles for them that help them overcome their weaknesses. It helps the clients reconstrue themselves and their life situations.

Fragmentation corollary Proposition that the personal construct subsystems of individuals may be disjointed and incompatible with one another.

Individuality corollary Proposition that people differ in their constructions of reality.

Loose construction Belief that is unstable and weak, with little definition, and that leads to erratic and often invalid predictions about the way in which the world operates.

Organization corollary Proposition that the individual's constructs are arranged in particular ways within his or her personal system.

Permeability Dimension concerned with the issue of whether new elements will or will not be admitted within the boundaries of a construct. A permeable construct can admit new elements; an impermeable one cannot.

Preemptive construct Type of construct that includes only its elements and maintains that these elements cannot apply to other constructs.

Propositional construct Type of construct that leaves all of its elements open to modification.

Range of convenience All the events encompassed by a given construct.

Role Construct Repertory Test (RCRT) Test devised by Kelly to assess the personal construct system of an individual.

Self-characterization sketch Initial step in fixed-role therapy in which the client is asked to write a brief character outline of himself or herself but to phrase it in the third person so as to minimize threat to the client.

Sociality corollary Proposition that constructive interpersonal relationships depend on the participants' mutual understanding of each other's construct system.

Superordinate construct Construct that generally controls or subordinates many different constructs.

P A R T   5

Social-Behavioristic Perspectives

Historically, two major lines of thought and investigation have shaped the course of personality psychology. One grew out of clinical practice, beginning with the work of the French physicians Jean Martin Charcot and Pierre Janet, and culminated in the efforts of Freud and his disciples. These investigators were medical men concerned primarily with understanding the etiology of their patients' abnormal behavior in order to help them overcome their problems. Thus they emphasized behavior change. They also focused on some of the most interesting, important, and complicated phenomena in human functioning: love, hate, death, sexual behavior, aggressiveness, and so forth.

In contrast to this medical orientation, the other major line of investigation had its roots in the experimental laboratory. Theorists in this tradition were concerned primarily with the scientific understanding of the learning process. They assumed that most of our behavior was acquired and that the task of the psychologist was to specify the environmental conditions responsible for producing behavior. They were proponents of a simple stimulus-response (S-R) psychology in which an attempt was made to understand how given stimuli became linked to given responses.

The most important proponent of the S-R model in psychology was John B. Watson. Watson originally had been educated at the University of Chicago as a functionalist. The functionalists explained behavior in terms of "mental functions." Borrowing from Darwin's evolutionary theory, they maintained that human beings, like the lower animals, were engaged in a constant struggle to survive. To survive, they had to learn to "adjust" their behavior. Such adjustment was possible because human beings possessed "minds" that encompassed the "ability to reason" and helped them solve problems presented by the environment.

Later Watson said that such a position did little to advance psychology as a science. He believed that terms like "mind," "spirit," "soul," and "consciousness" were useless because the private events to which they referred could not be measured objectively and reliably. Psychology would advance only if it got rid of such "mentalism" and focused on public events that could be objectively validated. As a result, Watson proclaimed that psychology was the study of observable behavior and that references to private events were unscientific and unworthy of scientific investigation.

Watson's pronouncements had a significant effect on psychology during his lifetime, and vestiges of his viewpoint can be seen in the work of the various contemporary social-behavioristic theorists discussed in this part of the text. This statement is especially true of Skinner's work (Chapter 11), but it also applies in certain respects to the positions taken by Rotter and Bandura (Chapters 12 and 13).

Like Watson, Skinner has a basic aversion to the study of private events, even though he has recently concluded that such phenomena are important and would have to be included in any comprehensive theory of behavior. He would prefer to focus on observable behavior that can be reliably recorded. Like Watson, he is concerned primarily with trying to understand how environmental stimuli influence behavior, his hope being to generate fundamental laws. To accomplish this goal, Skinner believes that systematic observation and experimentation are necessary and that the experimentation must occur under controlled conditions. Such control can best be exercised by studying the behavior of lower animals in the laboratory. Because the behaviors most amenable to control are simple ones, Skinner believes that the investigator should proceed from the simple to the complex.

Such a position means that his followers will concern themselves primarily with a restricted set of phenomena and will not be actively engaged in attempts to explain phenomena like love and hate. Skinner thinks that his approach has paid off handsomely, as principles of behavior painstakingly discovered in laboratory work with lower animals have been successfully applied to people in therapeutic and educational settings. It is only in recent years that Skinner's operant analysis has been applied to human problems, but we can now say with some conviction that he is gradually moving from a simple behaviorism focused only on lower animals to a more complex social behaviorism that addresses itself to important human issues. In line with this new development, we even see the tough-minded Skinner beginning to recognize, however reluctantly, the role that cognitive variables play in behavior.

Chapter 11 reviews Skinner's arguments about the need for a scientific technology of behavior and the dangers of mentalism. He does not, however, equate mentalism with cognition. Mentalism has a pejorative meaning for Skinner, but cognition is a far less negative term for him. What Skinner objects to specifically are "mentalistic" explanations that seem to help us understand behavior but, in fact, impede our understanding. Statements like "He was kind to you because he has a *pure soul*," or "She scored an 'A' on her chemistry exam because she has a good *mind*" are two examples of mentalistic explanations that lack scientific explanatory power. They are invoked on a post hoc basis and are meaningless from a scientific standpoint, as we pointed out in Chapter 1. Cognition and mentalism are similar in that both refer to private events; but whereas mentalism describes events that cannot be studied scientifically, cognition refers to events that can be objectively and reliably recorded and communicated clearly among scientists. The primary method of studying cognitive events is verbal reports, and Skinner accepts their use, as do Rotter and Bandura.

Chapter 11 also focuses on the major terms and principles in Skinner's operant analysis of personality. Of particular importance is his treatment of the effects of various kinds of reinforcers and reinforcement schedules on the acquisition and modification of behavior. Skinner is frequently lambasted by critics as advocating the use of punishment to control behavior, but this accusation is simply not true. As we shall see, Skinner does not consider punishment an effective means of altering behavior. The chapter includes a discussion of the development of normal and abnormal personalities within Skinner's unique framework. There is also an extensive discussion of the ways in which operant principles can be applied in therapeutic and educational settings.

The work of Rotter and Bandura also has a number of features in common with the psychology advocated by Watson. Both Rotter and Bandura believe that most of our behavior is learned. They also believe that the advancement of psychology as a science will depend on the establishment of precise measurement procedures and the systematic observation of behavior under controlled conditions. Yet the theories advocated by both men rely heavily on the use of cognitive constructs, a position clearly in opposition to Watson's dictum that the study of such events has no place in psychology. Thus their positions go far beyond Watson's simple, mechanistic model of human functioning.

Whereas Watson leaned heavily on Pavlov's classical conditioning paradigm to explain the acquisition of behavior, Rotter and Bandura expand this position by incorporating the role of organismic variables into their formulas. Their position is a neobehavioristic one that includes such cognitive constructs as expectancy, imitation, covert rehearsal of events, self-efficacy, value, memory, and habits. These stimulus-organism-response (S-O-R) models attempt to deal with more complex phenomena than the ones studied by Watson and, to a certain extent, by Skinner. At the same time, however, Rotter and Bandura insist on accurate and objective measurement of these complex phenomena.

The positions of Rotter and Bandura are a more direct outgrowth of learning theories propounded after Watson. Rotter himself traces the origins of his position to the work of the learning theorists E. L. Thorndike, Edward C. Tolman, and Clark L. Hull. From Thorndike, Rotter adopted the view that behavior is subject to modification by its consequences. In other words, Rotter accepts the concept of instrumental, or operant, conditioning, which is, as we have noted, the cornerstone of Skinner's theory. (For a fuller review of Thorndike's position, see the biographical material on Skinner in Chapter 11.)

From Tolman and Hull, Rotter borrowed the notion that behavior is purposive—that is, we are guided by our motives to attain certain goals. Rotter's thinking is particularly close to Hull's in this regard. For Hull, the formula to predict the probability of the occurrence of behavior was as follows:

$$E = H \times D$$

E refers to the "excitatory potential" of behavior (the probability of behavior), H to habit strength, and D to drive strength. Thus, for Hull, the probability of a given response or movement toward a goal was seen to be a function of the animal's drive state (motive) multiplied by its habit strength. In Rotter's scheme, excitatory potential becomes "behavioral potential," habit strength is roughly translated as "expectancy of the occurence of reinforcement," and drive strength is reinterpreted as the "value of the reinforcement." Therefore the probability that a given behavior will occur is a function of the expectancies or habits that we acquire, primarily as a result of the number of experiences we undergo in a given situation and the importance of the reinforcer that will affect our drive level as we move toward our goal.

Chapter 12 includes a review of these and other concepts in Rotter's theory. The chapter focuses on one construct of particular importance in his social learning position—internal-external control of reinforcement—and provides a sampling of recent research findings based on the measurement of individual differences in locus of control.

Bandura's work, like Rotter's, places heavy emphasis on the role played by cognition in the acquisition, retention, regulation, maintenance, and modification of behavior. This does not mean, however, that he rejects the concept of reinforcement. He simply utilizes it differently in his theorizing and research. Thus, unlike Skinner, who sees reinforcers and punishers as automatically strengthening and weakening responses, respectively, Bandura sees response consequences as providing people with information concerning the kinds of behaviors they must show as a means of gaining beneficial outcomes and avoiding punishing ones. Learning from response consequences is therefore largely a cognitive process. Within this framework, observational learning plays a primary role in the acquisition, maintenance, and modification of behavior. As Bandura rightly notes, the study of imitation learning has been relatively ignored by traditional learning theorists. Historically, the concept can be traced to the work of L. Morgan in 1896, Gabriel Tarde in 1903, and William McDougall in 1908. All these theorists believed that imitation was an innate tendency in human beings. As the instinct doctrine fell into disrepute because of the popularity of Watsonian behaviorism, however, a few learning theorists, such as G. Humphrey, F. H. Allport, and E. B. Holt, tried to account for imitation as being due to Pavlovian conditioning. According to this learning paradigm, imitative responses were the simple result of a person's matching his or her behavior to the behavior of another. In other words, imitation involved contiguous association between social stimuli.

Soon, however, the behaviorist focus shifted from classical conditioning to instrumental, or operant, learning. This new view was advocated primarily by Miller and Dollard in their classic text *Social Learning and Imitation* (1941). In essence, their position was that imitation learning occurred when a motivated person was positively reinforced for matching the behavior of a model during a sequence of random trial-and-error responses.

Bandura's main objection to both the classical and instrumental conditioning explanations of imitation is that they fail to account for the acquisition of new responses through observation. In regard to the operant position, for example, Bandura contends the assumption is that the person makes a long series of random responses that are eventually shaped through reinforcement until they match the behavior of the model. Bandura believes this process is too cumbersome to account for the many responses we learn in the course of our lives. He suggests instead that imitative learning can often occur in the absence of external reinforcement. We acquire behavior without performing it overtly and without being reinforced for it. We simply watch the behavior of others, represent it cognitively (that is, symbolically), then perform it under the appropriate conditions.

Chapter 13 begins by elaborating on these points in a discussion of the major assumptions underlying Bandura's social-learning position. Then the basic concepts and principles of his theory are outlined. The focus is on the ways in which behavior is learned when the person is exposed to single and multiple models with varying personality characteristics. It is noted that the impact of multiple models on children's behavior is often complicated and difficult to assess, because the models often show contradictory behaviors. There is also a detailed discussion of the role of self-control processes in the acquisition of behavior. This is followed by an examination of some applications of modeling principles and research to two major social problems—violence in the media and problem behaviors, especially phobias in children. We then review Bandura's recommendations for bringing violence under control and the use of modeling as a therapeutic technique. In examining Bandura's treatment of the developmental process, we cover the concepts of imitation, successive approximation, and schedule of reinforcement used by Bandura to help us understand this process. Bandura's new theorizing about self-efficacy and its role in the development and change of pathological behavior is also presented, along with supporting empirical evidence.

Reference

Miller, N. E., & Dollard, J. *Social learning and imitation.* New Haven: Yale University Press, 1941.

CHAPTER 11

Skinner's Operant Analysis

Biographical Sketch

Burrhus Frederick Skinner was born in Susquehanna, Pennsylvania, in 1904. In his autobiography, he reports that his home life was warm and stable. He was never physically punished by his lawyer father and only once by his mother, and that was when she washed his mouth with soap and water after he said a "bad" word. Skinner also mentions that he liked school and acquired a strong background in English and literature, mathematics, and the sciences from a few fine teachers. As a boy, he was always building and creating things. He built roller-skate scooters, wagons, sleds, seesaws, merry-go-rounds, slingshots, blow guns, kites, and model airplanes. This fascination with mechanical objects can be seen in his invention and use of various devices in his experimental work. These devices include the Skinner box, an apparatus designed to help investigators study the effects of different reinforcement schedules on animal behavior; the cumulative recorder, a device to assess the rate of organisms' responses; and the teaching machine, an instrument designed to facilitate learning in students.

Because he had a thorough grounding in literature, Skinner decided to major in English when he enrolled at Hamilton College in New York State.

He notes, however, that he never really adjusted to student life. He joined a fraternity but knew little about fraternity life. He was also inept at sports. Like many students then and now, he complained bitterly about unnecessary curriculum requirements. By his senior year he was in open revolt. He participated in a number of activities designed to humiliate some faculty members the students thought pompous and arrogant. One of these incidents is particularly noteworthy. To deflate a name-dropping English professor, Skinner and another student printed posters that read, in part: "Charles Chaplin, the famous cinema comedian, will deliver his lecture 'Moving Pictures as a Career' in the Hamilton College Chapel on Friday, October 9." The lecture was reported to be under the professor's auspices. They plastered posters all over town, then returned to the campus and went to bed. The next morning the other student called the local newspaper and told reporters that the college president wanted the lecture publicly announced. By noon the situation was completely out of hand. Swarms of children were taken by their parents to the railway station to greet the famous actor. In spite of police roadblocks, approximately 400 cars got through to the campus. There were other escapades, along with threats of expulsion by the college president, but Skinner was finally permitted to graduate.

After college, Skinner pursued a career as a writer. As a senior, he had met the famous poet Robert Frost, who requested that Skinner send him samples of his work. Skinner sent him three short stories and received encouraging comments in reply. He then spent approximately two years in Greenwich Village in New York City and in Europe. Eventually he realized he would not be successful as a writer, presumably because he had nothing important to say. His interest in human behavior then led him to enter Harvard to study psychology.

Skinner found the intellectual atmosphere at Harvard stimulating and challenging and states that, to improve his skills in a new field, he set up a rigorous study schedule and adhered to it for almost two years. He read nothing that did not pertain to psychology and physiology. Some of his academic mentors included the historian E. G. Boring, the clinician Henry Murray, and the physiologist W. J. Crozier. The writings of J. B. Watson, Ivan Pavlov, and E. L. Thorndike also had a considerable impact on the young psychologist. For example, he was impressed by Watson's concern with devising a technology of behavior. In one fell swoop, Watson had thrown out all "mentalistic" concepts, including mind, spirit, and consciousness, and proclaimed instead that psychology was the scientific study of observable behavior. Skinner, too, has maintained that psychologists should focus on behavior that is observable and verifiable, but, unlike Watson, he believes that psychologists must also account for internal, or private, events, as long as they can be measured objectively and reliably.

The work of the Russian physiologist Ivan Pavlov on the conditioned reflex was also important to Skinner. Pavlov was originally interested in the process of digestion in lower animals and the conditions under which digestive juices were secreted. In the course of his work, he discovered that the animals salivated not only when food was actually in their mouths but also when it was shown to them by the experimenter. He called this phenomenon a "psychic secretion." His next step was to control the conditions under which such secretions occurred. As virtually every psychology student knows, by designing a room that minimized the intrusion of extraneous stimuli, Pavlov was eventually able to demonstrate, through a precise series of maneuvers, that salivation could be brought under the control of specific stimuli such as a light or a bell. Previously neutral stimuli acquired the power to evoke responses originally evoked by other stimuli. The animals were "classically conditioned." Besides the fact that such respondent conditioning can account for a variety of behaviors, Skinner was impressed by the procedure Pavlov used to bring the behavior under control. He reports accepting fully then and now Pavlov's dictum "Control your conditions and you will see order."

Although some of our behavior is learned via classical conditioning, most of it is learned after we behave voluntarily and find that our actions are followed by positive or negative experiences. Skinner's interest in operant behavior—that is, behavior that operates on the environment—was piqued by animal experiments conducted by the learning theorist E. L. Thorndike. Typically, cats were deprived of food, then placed in problem boxes, and left there until they accidentally moved a mechanism that opened a door and allowed them to escape. The animals usually made a variety of responses before making the correct one. Thorndike explained this trial-and-error learning by maintaining that an association was established between the animals' responses and the reinforcing consequences. Thorndike considered responses that resulted in pleasurable sensations to be "stamped in," whereas he considered responses followed by an annoying state of affairs to be "stamped out." Skinner has adopted a modification of this **law of effect** to explain the acquisition of behavior. A primary aspect of his modification is the focus on changes in the probability of responding produced by the application of reinforcers.

After years of intensive study, Skinner received his Ph.D. from Harvard in 1931, then spent five postdoctoral years working in Crozier's laboratory. In 1936, he accepted his first academic position, at the University of Minnesota; two years later, he wrote his first book, *The Behavior of Organisms*, a work that presents his initial formulations for an **operant analysis** of behavior. While at Minnesota, Skinner also found the time to begin a novel entitled *Walden Two*, a story about a miniature utopian society based on reinforcement principles. *Walden Two* was eventually published in 1948.

After a brief stint as chairman of the psychology department at Indiana University, he returned to Harvard in 1948 and has remained affiliated with that institution ever since. Besides being accorded many honors by his fellow psychologists, Skinner was also one of the few behavioral scientists to win the President's Medal of Science. He has also been a prolific writer; his books include *Science and Human Behavior* (1953), *Verbal Behavior* (1957), a book written in collaboration with C. B. Ferster titled *Schedules of Reinforcement* (1957), *Cumulative Record* (1961), *The Technology of Teaching* (1968), *Contingencies of Reinforcement* (1969), a book written with J. G. Holland titled *The Analysis of Behavior* (1961), *Beyond Freedom and Dignity* (1971), *About Behaviorism* (1974), *Particulars of My Life* (1976), *Reflections on Behaviorism and Society* (1978), *The Shaping of a Behaviorist* (1979), *A Matter of Consequences* (1983), and *Enjoy Old Age* (1983), written with colleague M. E. Vaughan. In this last book, Skinner offers advice to the elderly on how to manage their environments as a means of maximizing their enjoyment of old age, despite declines in their physical prowess and health. Apparently, Professor Skinner has taken his own advice: he continues to write (and to be positively reinforced by the consequences) and to be actively interested and involved in the promotion and advancement of psychology to benefit human beings (Skinner, 1970, pp. 1–21).

The Need for a Scientific Technology of Behavior

Like virtually all of us, Skinner believes we are faced today with problems that threaten our very existence. But although we often misuse the products of a scientific technology, he argues that we can in fact utilize the same technological prowess to solve our problems. We have even taken a few small steps in that direction. To contain the population explosion, we are turning to a variety of birth-control methods. We are beginning to utilize pollution control devices to clean up the environment. We are attempting to lessen the threat of world famine by devising better methods of crop production. We are continuously making attempts, sometimes with success, to control various kinds of diseases (Skinner, 1971, p. 1). Yet, in each of these areas we have only scratched the surface. Why is this so? In Skinner's opinion, it is because the solutions to these problems lie not in the application of our physical and biological knowledge but in an understanding of human behavior. He points out, for example, that birth-control devices are useless if people do not use them. Pollution control procedures also are not helpful if people continue to ignore or resist them. What we need are drastic changes in our behavior (Skinner, 1971, p. 4).

The Dangers of Mentalism

If we grant the legitimacy of Skinner's argument, why have we not made more progress in understanding human behavior and using this knowledge to alleviate suffering? The answer, Skinner believes, lies in our refusal to give up "mentalistic" explanations of behavior that give the *appearance* of helping us understand our actions, but in fact hinder us in our quest. In Skinner's words,

> *We are told that to control the number of people in the world we need to change* attitudes *toward children, overcome* pride *in size of family or in sexual potency, build some* sense *of responsibility* toward offspring, *and reduce the role played by a large family in allaying* concern *for old age. To work for peace we must deal with the* will to power *or the* paranoid delusions *of leaders; we must remember that wars begin in the* minds *of men, that there is something suicidal in man—a* death instinct *perhaps—which leads to war, and that man is aggressive by* nature. *To solve the problems of the poor we must inspire self-respect, encourage* initiative, *and reduce* frustration.... *This is staple fare. Almost no one questions it. Yet there is nothing like it in modern physics or most of biology, and that fact may well explain why a science and a technology of behavior have been so long delayed. [Skinner, 1971, pp. 9–10]*

Such explanations are post hoc in nature, according to Skinner. They seem to provide answers to questions, but they do not. Further, such **mentalism** also brings curiosity to an end (Skinner, 1971, p. 12). The problem seems to be solved. For example, if someone asks us, "Why didn't you study last night?" and we reply, "Because I didn't feel like it," she is likely to take our reply as a satisfactory explanation of our behavior. In fact, however, it would be much more revealing to know what in our past might have made studying aversive for us. Perhaps we did not do well on previous exams in the course, or perhaps we were looking forward to a party in the dormitory and studying for the exam would have prevented us from enjoying this experience. The possibilities are virtually endless. But the person accepts our comment "I didn't feel like it" and does not inquire further into the details of our behavior. Of course, in ordinary conversation we may not want more information. What we should realize, however, is that the person could have learned much more about the causes of our behavior if she had asked additional questions. She may have been lulled into accepting minimal information as an adequate explanation. Skinner maintains that a scientific approach to the study of human behavior must reject such false security. We must give up nebulous inner "explanations" and search instead for the precise antecedant events that, in reality, produce our behavior.

Skinner does not, as we have pointed out, categorically reject the study of all private events. In *About Behaviorism*, he takes pains to point out that Watson, in his zeal to establish psychology as a science, made an exaggerated and incorrect commitment eliminating the study of introspective life (Skinner, 1974, p. 5). Skinner believes, albeit half-heartedly, that psychologists must provide adequate explanations of private events, but the events studied must be capable of being reliably and objectively recorded. Thus verbal reports might provide acceptable data for Skinner and his followers if the scientific criteria were met (Skinner, 1974, p. 31). But because other people have difficulty teaching us the appropriate labels for our private experiences, we must be cautious in accepting such reports at face value. Thus, contrary to popular belief, Skinner does not just accept Watson's simplistic stimulus-response formulation. Skinner maintains that such an approach is obsolete and that he has been unfairly attacked. His critics, he says, are ignorant of the major changes in psychology in the past 60 years and continue mistakenly to criticize him for treating human beings as robots. Skinner says he recognizes the complexity of behavior and suggests that people, especially those in the humanities, "stop beating a dead horse."

It seems clear, then, that Skinner does not reject or accept the study of inner events in an all-or-nothing fashion. An example may help clarify what he would find objectionable or acceptable. Imagine a person sitting down at a table in a restaurant and eating a meal consisting of Fettuccini Alfredo, Beaujolais, spumoni, and coffee. For illustrative purposes, a basic question might be: Why did he eat? The typical answer is that he ate *because* he was hungry. Skinner would reject this interpretation as mentalistic if we considered this explanation adequate. He would say that the term *hunger* would have to be explained by linking it to antecedent events in the environment— for example, to the number of hours since the time of the previous meal. His hunger did *not* cause the person to eat; rather, food deprivation, along with a host of other environmental variables (the decor of the restaurant, the price and attractiveness of the food), contributed to the probability that he would eat that meal at that particular time.

A behavioristic analysis would force us to focus on those events in the environment that help produce the behavior. The events can be either current ones or past ones. This information, coupled with data about our genetic endowments, where it is pertinent to the explanation of a given behavior, helps us in prediction. For example, if the diner had been allergic to the starch in the fettuccini, he might have decided not to eat at all or to eat different food. Thus, inner events—that is, our prior histories, which are based on transactions with the environment, and our unique genetic heritages—contribute to the prediction of behavior. You should be aware that, although Skinner recognizes the legitimacy of such inner events for a behavioral psychology, he nevertheless deemphasizes them in his own analysis. He accords the same legitimacy to physiological events but again pays little actual attention to them in experimental analysis. Besides the difficulty of reliable measurement, the scientist cannot systematically manipulate physiological events and watch their effects on behavior. Skinner believes that major advances will occur only when psychologists focus on the ways in which behavior and external environmental variables are causally related. What is needed, in brief, is a functional analysis of behavior.

Free Will versus Determinism

According to Skinner, this search for order among events is offensive to many people. It is offensive because, once these relationships are specified, scientists can begin to anticipate and determine our actions (Skinner, 1953, p. 6). They can start to exercise control over our behavior. Such an idea runs counter to the long tradition we have of viewing ourselves as free agents.

We do not like to believe our actions are the product of specifiable anteced-ent conditions; we prefer to believe we are free and capable of spontaneous inner change (Skinner, 1953, p. 7). As members of a democratically oriented society, we also resist anyone who says he or she wants to control our behavior. Skinner states that this belief in our own autonomy has a number of unfortunate implications.

First, acceptance of the belief may mean that behavior is not caused by events in the environment. We alone are responsible for our own actions, and thus we should be rewarded for behaving well and punished when we behave badly. This view, however, often obscures our perception of the envi-ronmental variables that in fact control our behavior (Skinner, 1971, pp. 19–20). For example, some of us "know" that members of minority groups are responsible for their own situation. We say that they should show some initiative and work as we do. We sometimes hear people say of juvenile delinquents, "Well, they got themselves into it; let them get themselves out of it!" The part played by oppressive environments is lost in such accounts. The focus on the inner man and woman prevents us from seeing clearly the possible contributing causes of their behaviors. It is interesting that although many of Skinner's critics consider him a fascist, a reactionary, a Machiavel-lian, and the like because of his stand on determinism, he emerges instead, at least in this instance, more like a superliberal.

A science of behavior that questions our autonomy also threatens beliefs about personal worth and dignity. A scientific analysis shifts the credit as well as the blame for our actions to the environment (Skinner, 1971, p. 21). We may not object to an analysis that absolves us of blame, but we would probably object to one that deprives us of a chance to be admired and loved (Skinner, 1971, p. 75). In addition, Skinner points out that the amount of credit we give someone for a performance is typically inversely proportional to the conspicuousness of the causes of the behavior: "We stand in awe of the inexplicable, and it is therefore not surprising that we are likely to admire behavior more as we understand it less" (Skinner, 1971, p. 53). For example, we may be more impressed by the performance of a young figure skater if we do not know that she practiced six hours a day every day of the week for the past 11 years to attain her current status. We also are probably much more impressed with the "bright" and "creative" novelist if we do not know that he began writing at age 10 and had received 28 rejection slips from publishers before one of his manuscripts was accepted.

The rejection of ourselves as autonomous beings may also be threat-ening because it implies that we come under the control of others. Why should we fear such a consequence? First, the loss of freedom means for many of us that we will not be able to do what we want (Carpenter, 1974, p. 87). Skinner maintains that such an argument is false because it implies that we have free will. In reality, our wants are conditioned by external events. A homemaker, for example, does not buy a dishwasher because she simply and freely wants one. Instead, she may buy one because her old one is broken down or because she learns of a new model through advertise-ments in the media. Perhaps her mother-in-law has been pressuring her to sell "the old eyesore." Whatever the reason or reasons, her behavior is deter-mined by events in the past or current environment.

Second, many of us have been taught to believe that all control of behav-ior is bad (Carpenter, 1974, p. 89). Skinner maintains that such a belief is stereotypic. There are many instances in which control is exerted over our behavior, and we do not complain or think it bad. Parents restrain small children from diving into the 12-foot end of the pool. Society controls driving behavior with elaborate rules and regulations. State governments require auto-safety inspections. Compulsory vaccinations protect us against disease. Doctors exercise control when they operate on people. The list is endless.

Yet Skinner's critics continue to insist that a particular form of control—coercion—is bad because it involves the exploitation of one party by another. Skinner agrees wholeheartedly with this statement; he too would oppose control of this sort. What, then, are the objections to his position? There seem to be two primary points: one, that Skinner wants to manipulate people without their being aware of it; and two, that Skinner wants to set himself up as the arbiter of good and evil (Carpenter, 1974, p. 90). Skinner answers by pointing out that all our behavior is determined whether we are aware of it or not. In addition, he says we already have a general consensus on what is good and bad. Virtually everyone is against disease, poverty, war, and indiscriminate destruction of the environment. Conversely, nearly all of us prefer politeness to rudeness, generosity to greed, love to selfishness, and so on. Why quarrel over the obvious?

Despite the cogency of Skinner's arguments for a thoroughgoing deter-minism, the fact remains that the deterministic viewpoint is an assumption on his part, even though there is considerable evidence to support it. Most of the evidence is based on studies with lower animals in which it is possible to control conditions and observe systematic changes in behavior. For human beings, however, the problem is much more complicated: the scientist usu-ally does not have control over our previous environments and thus cannot observe the same changes in behavior that might occur in lower animals as a function of the manipulation of events in the current environment. In short, there is too much "noise" in the human system for us to argue con-clusively that determinism is scientifically proved. Nevertheless, it appears to be a reasonable working assumption in light of the fact that it continues to lead to the accumulation of data that advances our understanding of human behavior.

Personality from the Perspective of a Radical Behaviorist

We have considered some of the major reasons why Skinner opts for a scientific approach to the study of behavior, along with some of the provoc-ative philosophical implications of his position. But what about the study of personality? Is it lost in Skinner's strict emphasis on a cause-and-effect analysis of behavior? The answer to the latter question is no, but Skinner considers the study of personality legitimate only if established scientific criteria are met. He will not, for example, accept the idea of a personality or self that guides or directs behavior. He considers such an approach a vestige of animism, a doctrine that presupposes the existence of spirits within the body that move it (Skinner, 1974, p. 167). Nor would he be satisfied with dead-end "explanations" of behavior such as the answer here: "Why did the robbers kill those helpless people?" "Because they are crazy."

Skinner considers the study of personality to involve a systematic examination of the idiosyncratic learning history and unique genetic background of the individual:

> In a behavioral analysis, a person is an organism ... which has acquired a repertoire of behavior.... [He] is not an originating agent; he is a locus, a point at which many genetic and environmental conditions come together in a joint effect. As such, he remains unquestionably unique. No one else (unless he has an identical twin) has his genetic endowment, and without exception no one else has his personal history. Hence no one else will behave in precisely the same way. [Skinner, 1974, pp. 167–168]

The study of personality, then, would involve the discovery of the unique set of relationships between the behavior of an organism and its reinforcing consequences. Of course, such an analysis would have to be consistent with the organism's genetic capacity to respond to events in the environment.

Basic Concepts and Principles

Operant Behavior and Conditioning

All our behavior takes place in situations and produces outcomes. According to Skinner's system, we operate on the environment to generate consequences (Skinner, 1953, p. 65). The occurrence of reinforcers is said to be contingent or dependent on our behavior. Operant behavior includes talking to people, reading, walking, writing, eating, kissing, dressing, hitting a baseball, singing a song, and countless other activities. If we are deprived of water and then some behavior on our part causes water to be made available to us for drinking, that behavior is reinforced. We kiss another person and are reinforced for our behavior by the joyful acceptance of the kiss. Turning the house thermostat from 55 to 70 degrees on a winter morning is also reinforcing. The establishment of the linkage between the behavior and its consequences is called **conditioning**. Through operant conditioning, the occurrence of behavior is made more or less probable.

Operant Reinforcement and the Probability of Response

Behavior is made more probable if it is followed by the presentation of **positive reinforcers**—for example, food, water, or affection. It is also strengthened by the removal of aversive stimuli from the situation—for example, the cessation of electric shock, of criticism, of extremes in temperature. These latter stimuli are called **negative reinforcers**. Both positive and negative reinforcers strengthen behavior. Behavior is made less probable through the application of punishing stimuli (say, spanking a child) or through the removal of positive reinforcers (say, taking a toy away from a child) (Skinner, 1953, p. 73).

The Effects of Punishment

Skinner says that **punishment** is the most common technique of control in modern life. Its use is familiar to all of us:

> If a man does not behave as you wish, knock him down; if a child misbehaves, spank him; if the people of a country misbehave, bomb them. Legal and police systems are based upon such punishments as fines . . . incarceration and hard labor. Religious control is exerted through penances, threats of excommunication, and consignment to hell-fire. Education has not wholly abandoned the birch rod. In everyday personal contact we control through censure, snubbing, disapproval, or banishment. . . . All of this is done with the intention of reducing tendencies to behave in certain ways. [Skinner, 1953, p. 182]

But why is the use of punishment so pervasive? Probably because it is easy to apply and because it has immediate, observable, and satisfying effects for the punisher. In addition, the technique is easily learned, whereas alternative positive measures are more difficult to acquire. The need for punishment also has the ostensible support of history, according to Skinner (1971, p. 80). For all these reasons, many of us resort to it.

But does punishment work? Certainly in the short run it seems to be effective. It stops the undesired behavior. Skinner maintains that this effect may be misleading because the reduction in the strength of the behavior may not be permanent (Skinner, 1953, p. 183). The evidence for his contention is a study he conducted in which he trained rats of the same sex, age, and genetic strain to press a lever in a Skinner box as a means of obtaining food pellets (Skinner, 1938, pp. 151–160). After establishing the bar-pressing response, Skinner withheld the reinforcers from these animals to bring about **extinction** of the behavior. Skinner let some of the animals in a control group continue to press the bar without punishment until they stopped responding completely. In the experimental group, each time the animals pressed the lever, they were punished by a "slap" on the paws administered mechanically. This punishment continued for the first ten minutes of the extinction period and then was terminated. Skinner found an initial decrease in the rate of response for the animals while they were being punished. When the punishment was ended, however, the experimental group began to respond again. Eventually, this group produced as many responses as the controls. For Skinner, the general point of the study was that punishment temporarily suppresses behavior, but the behavior will reappear when the punishing contingencies are withdrawn. It should be noted, however, that, despite Skinner's belief, there is impressive evidence that punishment can effectively stop undesired behavior when it is properly applied (Walters & Grusec, 1977).

In any event, punishment also has two other undesirable effects, according to Skinner. First, it may give rise to emotional responses that are incompatible with appropriate behavior (Skinner, 1953, pp. 186–187). For example, a man who, as an adolescent, is punished severely for masturbating while looking at pictures of nude women may later experience strong feelings of guilt in a situation with a woman in which sexual behavior is appropriate. Or a child who has been beaten by her parents for reading poorly may later experience considerable resentment toward teachers who are trying to help her improve her reading skills. The feelings of resentment may then be correlated with behavior such as refusing to read, which leads to a continuation of the reading difficulties.

Second, punishment may also create strong conflict in people (Skinner, 1953, p. 190). It should be clear that such conflict would not, in a Skinnerian analysis, involve an "inner struggle" but rather an incompatibility between responses, one being positively reinforcing and the other being potentially punishing. The male student who has been rejected by several women students but who continues to seek a relationship with women on campus is a pertinent example. Such a person might be labeled in traditional personality terms as awkward, indecisive, and timid.

For all these reasons, Skinner believes we should shun the use of punishment to control behavior. Instead, we should focus on the use of positive reinforcers. (A detailed examination of Skinner's position in regard to the use of positive reinforcers in education will appear later in the chapter.)

Operant Extinction

The failure to reinforce a response affects the probability of responding by making its occurrence less and less frequent. Skinner points out that, under such extinction conditions,

> [a] person is . . . said to suffer a loss of confidence, certainty, or sense of power. . . . [He] is said to be unable to go to work because he is discouraged or depressed, although his not going, together with what he feels [discouragement and depression], is due to a lack of reinforcement—either in his work or in some other part of his life. [Skinner, 1974, p. 58]

We control the behavior of others through the use of such a procedure. For example, to eliminate behavior we consider undesirable, we ignore it. If our roommate acts in obnoxious ways, we may simply not pay attention to him. If a child has a temper tantrum, the parents may ignore her by reading a newspaper or turning on the television set. Such a procedure seems to make sense, but unfortunately it is often unworkable in practice. The reason is simply that the undesirable behavior is often very strong because it has been reinforced many times in the past. As a consequence, it is highly resistant to extinction. Thus the mother who tries to eliminate temper tantrums by ignoring her child's behavior is likely to give in eventually by listening to her, comforting her, and giving her what she wants. The mother's action not only positively reinforces her daughter's behavior but also ensures that it will continue. An alternate strategy in this situation might be to send the child to her room for a brief period, a procedure known technically as a "time out," until she stops whining and complaining and then to show her a more constructive way to solve her problem and reinforce her behavior when she uses that way.

Schedules of Reinforcement and the Acquisition of Unique Repertoires

All of us are exposed to different environments and to different schedules or arrangements of **reinforcement** in our daily lives. Some parents, for example, consistently reinforce their children's behavior; others supply only intermittent reinforcers. These schedules have a tremendous impact on our responses. Numerous studies with lower animals, for example, have shown that behavior learned on a schedule of **continuous reinforcement**—that is, a schedule in which each performance is followed by a reinforcer—produces higher rates of response than behavior reinforced only intermittently. Behavior learned on a schedule of **intermittent** (or partial) **reinforcement**, however, is much more resistant to extinction than behavior acquired on a continuous schedule (Skinner, 1953, p. 99). Animals trained on a continuous-reinforcement schedule also show greater signs of "emotional reaction" or "low frustration tolerance" when their behaviors are subjected to extinction than do animals trained on intermittent schedules.

The implications for human functioning are quite straightforward. Affluent parents who raise their children on continuous-reinforcement schedules should not be surprised when their offspring are called spoiled, soft, weak-willed, and lazy, among other things. These children do not show behaviors we can label persistent, hardworking, ambitious, and competitive, descriptions that are more likely to be applicable to children who have been subjected to partial or intermittent schedules of reinforcement (Carpenter, 1974, pp. 27–28).

There are various forms of intermittent reinforcement. Two of the major ones are the fixed-ratio schedule and the fixed-interval schedule. In a **fixed-ratio schedule**, an absolute number of behaviors is required before reinforcement is applied (Ferster & Perrott, 1968, p. 525). For example, a student may have to complete two class projects before receiving a grade in the course. Or a worker may be placed on a fixed-ratio schedule by an employer. Such a schedule is commonly known as piecework pay. Unfortunately, a high rate of responding may be required by the employer before she pays her employees. Such an unfavorable schedule may in some instances be detrimental to the health of the workers. In addition, we might find that morale and interest in the job is very low. In traditional personality terms, we might say that the workers are discouraged or apathetic.

In a **fixed-interval schedule**, the first performance that occurs after an absolute amount of time has elapsed is reinforced (Ferster & Perrott, 1968, p. 526). There are many examples of the operation of such schedules in our daily lives. We eat at certain times of the day; we go to bed and get up at a regular time. Sometimes we get paid by the hour. One of the interesting features of behavior regulated on fixed-interval schedules is that the rate of responding tends to be low just after reinforcement but increases rapidly as the time for reinforcement approaches. A person whose behavior is reinforced on such a schedule could be characterized as inconsistent, erratic, opportunistic, or even "moody."

Self-Control Processes

Skinner has been interested not only in the ways in which schedules of reinforcement determine behavior but also in the role of **self-control processes.** For him self-control involves an analysis of "how the individual acts to alter the variables of which other parts of his behavior are functions" (Skinner, 1953, p. 229). Individuals are said to exercise self-control when they actively change those variables or "things" that determine their behavior. For example, we may find that we cannot study when there is a stereo blaring music. We get up and shut it off. We have actively changed the nature of the variable (loud music) that affected our behavior. Another example is the obese man who exercises control over his behavior by buying and eating only low-calorie foods. He can also politely refuse to heat high-calorie foods when they are offered to him by others.

Skinner has outlined a number of the techniques we use to control our behavior (Skinner, 1953, pp. 231–241), many of which have subsequently been studied by social-learning theorists interested in modeling and behavior modification (see Chapter 13). Let us examine each of them in detail.

Physical Restraints. Sometimes, according to Skinner, we control our behavior through the use of physical restraints. For instance, some of us clap our hands over our mouths to avoid laughing at someone else's mistakes. Others put their hands in their pockets to keep from biting their fingernails. In unusual cases, people who feel strongly tempted to commit criminal or psychotic acts may present themselves at the door of an institution for incarceration.

According to Skinner, people sometimes engage in another form of physical restraint by simply moving out of situations in which the behavior to be controlled takes place. We walk away from someone who has insulted us lest we lose control and physically attack him or her. Parents often prevent the occurrence of undesirable behavior (for instance, fights, ridicule, criticism, or taunts) between their children by separating them. They may order one child to go outside to play and the other to stay inside and watch television.

Physical Aids. In Skinner's view, physical aids can also be used to control behavior. Sometimes people use drugs to control undesirable behavior. Truckers take stimulants to avoid falling asleep at the wheel on long interstate-road trips. Students often drink large amounts of coffee after all-night study sessions in an effort to remain alert during their early-morning exams.

Physical aids can also be used to facilitate certain behavior, as evidenced by situations in which people with sight problems put on eyeglasses or the partially deaf make use of hearing aids.

Changing the Stimulus Conditions. Another technique we use to control our behavior is to change the **stimuli** responsible for it. Overweight people put a box of candy out of sight so that they can restrain themselves. Some alcoholics avoid temptation by giving their liquor supply away. Some athlete-students put their athletic equipment out of sight when they sit down to study. Other students in a similar situation may draw the curtains in their rooms to avoid being lured outdoors on a bright spring day. Smokers sometimes try to reduce their smoking behavior by destroying their cigarettes. Other smokers adopt more moderate strategies (Williams & Long, 1979, p. 117). If they ordinarily carry their cigarettes in their right-hand shirt pocket, they shift them to their left-hand pocket or to their coat to make them more difficult to obtain. Sometimes they deliberately neglect to carry matches or a lighter so that they must ask someone for a light each time they want a smoke. The object of these strategies, of course, is to disrupt the smokers' habits, making it more difficult for them to engage in the unhealthy behavior.

Another way to reduce smoking frequency is to reduce the range of stimuli associated with it. Smokers typically have favorite times and situations when they smoke. For example, they use cigarettes while they are studying, working, eating, partying, and watching television. Various studies have shown that if they can break these associations, they can reduce their smoking drastically. (Williams & Long, 1979, p. 118).

In each of our examples, people are removing **discriminative stimuli** that induce unwanted behavior. But, according to Skinner, we not only remove certain stimuli in given situations, we also present stimuli in order to make certain behaviors more probable. We may, for example, use a mirror to master a difficult dance step. We may also listen to tapes of our voices in an attempt to improve our diction. Sometimes we enter dates and times in an appointment book to remind ourselves of our responsibilities.

Manipulating Emotional Conditions. Skinner maintains that we sometimes induce emotional changes in ourselves for purposes of control. Some people employ meditation techniques to alleviate stress. Similarly, we may work ourselves into a "good mood" before a stressful meeting to increase the probability of emitting the "right" behaviors. Athletes frequently use this method of control when they "psych themselves up" before an important game.

Performing Alternative Responses. Skinner also thinks that we often keep ourselves from engaging in behavior that leads to punishment by energetically engaging in something else. The overweight person may turn to an intensive jogging regimen to burn off excess calories and to keep from overeating. Widows or widowers may be advised by friends to keep very busy after the death of a spouse as a means of avoiding depressing thoughts. To keep from verbally or physically attacking people we dislike intensely, we may find ourselves thinking and performing actions unrelated to our opinions about them. In addition, we may avoid talking about such taboo topics as telling nuns about the right of women to have abortion on demand by talking about the less threatening subject of how to play a good game of bridge.

Positive Self-Reinforcement. Another technique we use to control behavior, according to Skinner, is positive self-reinforcement. We reward ourselves for commendable behavior. For example, a student may reward himself for studying hard and doing well on an exam by going to see a film acclaimed by the critics. Or an athlete may promise herself an expensive meal at a favorite local restaurant if she surpasses her old record in the 100-meter dash.

Self-Punishment. Finally, individuals may mete out punishment to themselves for failure to reach self-generated goals. For instance, a student may punish herself for failing to do as well as she thought she would do on an exam by giving away valuable tickets to a concert. College football players often jog extra laps around the track Monday morning as punishment for failure to perform adequately during a game on Saturday afternoon.

The Process of Personality Development

A Schedule of Reinforcement Approach

It should be clear at this point that Skinner would prefer to discuss changes in the individual's personality over time that involve his or her exposure to unique environmental schedules of reinforcement rather than discuss the emergence of maturational stages, à la Freud and Piaget. Although he thinks maturation theories have some predictive value, Skinner generally opposes them because they do not allow for the control or manipulation of events, a procedure he considers crucial for a science of behavior (Skinner, 1974, p. 12). Such theories tend to be descriptive, not explanatory, and, as Skinner sees it, the primary goal of science is the prediction and control of events (Skinner, 1953, p. 6). An example may clarify his position.

In stage 1 of Piaget's stage theory, children from birth to about 3 years of age are observed to play games without any attempt to adapt to social rules. In stage 2, children between the ages of 3 and 5 simply imitate the play of the rule-regulated behavior of adults and regard the rules as sacred and immutable. In stage 3, children who range in age from 7 to adolescence play the game with a mutually agreed-on set of rules but understand that the rules can always be changed with the approval of the other players (Flavell, 1963, pp. 291–292). Now, with these descriptions of behavior at the various age levels, we can predict the kind of behavior children will exhibit if we know their age. But we do not have an adequate explanation for their behavior. We have descriptive information of limited usefulness, not causal information. To ascertain why children behave as they do, we must be able to control and manipulate events that have an effect on their game-playing behavior.

For these reasons, Skinner prefers to study personality by focusing on the learning of a multitude of behaviors that allow the individual to survive and prosper in his or her transactions with the environment. In rough terms, the person is learning throughout life which contingencies provide satisfaction and which produce pain in given situations. The child learns to discriminate between stimuli or situations that are occasions for the reinforcement of specific behaviors and those that do not lead to reinforcement for the same behaviors. Learned behaviors are then said to be under **stimulus control**. A child, for example, may learn to cry in public and not at home, since crying in public usually brings immediate attention and comfort from his or her mother, whereas crying at home is generally ignored. Or a student may quickly learn that studying in a library and not in a noisy dormitory leads to passing grades. Simple skills are learned at first; later on, more and more complex behaviors are acquired and utilized. But people are not seen as passive organisms who simply respond automatically to reinforcement cues. Instead, they exercise self-control over their environments by actively selecting and changing environmental variables to satisfy their own needs.

The "Development" of Normal and Abnormal Personalities

Some people have had a unique set of transactions with the environment that results in the acquisition of **repertoires** we might label "normal." Others have had a set of experiences that result in the acquisition of unique response patterns we might label "abnormal." In Skinner's view, there is no qualitative difference between so-called normal and abnormal individuals. We do not need to devise a different set of reinforcement principles to account for their behaviors. He maintains that the same set of principles can account for the behavior of all individuals, irrespective of the labels we might use in describing their actions. According to him, we should focus more on the environmental determinants of behavior than on the inner determinants. We need to eliminate references to a "mental apparatus" such as the one employed by Freud. Such theorizing is imprecise, ambiguous, and leads to pseudoexplanations of behavior.

Skinner believes, however, that Freud contributed much to our understanding of behavior and that many of his ideas can profitably be translated into terms amenable to scientific inquiry. For example, the various ego-defense mechanisms Freud postulated can be examined in the case of a person's attempts to avoid or escape punishment. In Skinner's view, punishment makes the stimuli created by punished behavior aversive. As a consequence, any behavior that reduces or eliminates that stimulation is subsequently positively reinforcing. Thus repression simply involves the fact that "behavior which is punished becomes aversive, and by not engaging in it or by not 'seeing' it, a person avoids conditioned aversive stimulation" (Skinner, 1974, p. 155). There is no need to talk about an inner process in which id impulses incapable of fulfillment are kept lurking in the unconscious. Another example is sublimation. In Freudian terms, sublimation is the "discharge of instinctual energy and especially that associated with pregenital impulses through socially approved activities" (Skinner, 1974, p. 156). In Skinnerian terms, sublimation is translated in the following way: If two forms of behavior are positively reinforcing, but one of them is punished, the other is more likely to occur. For Freud, conversion involves "the transformation of an unconscious conflict into a symbolically equivalent somatic symptom" (Skinner, 1974, p. 156). Such mental events are presumed to have the power to produce physical illness. Inner-directed rage, for example, is said to produce ulcers. Skinner maintains that "the condition felt as rage is medically related to the ulcer, and that a complex social situation causes both" (Skinner, 1974, pp. 156–157). Of course, "complex social situation" would have to be precisely and adequately defined. It might hypothetically, however, include a punishing boss, a nagging wife or husband, whiny kids, loss of a loved one, and so on. Once again, the general point is that many of the traditional clinical concepts can be translated into terms that make them amenable to scientific investigation.

Techniques of Assessment

Skinner is primarily interested in the experimental analysis of behavior. This means he is concerned with identifying those environmental variables that control the emission of behavior. These variables include situational factors that signal the organism that the emission of particular behaviors will lead to the occurrence of reinforcers and the reinforcement schedules themselves. As the **functional analysis** of behavior is a complicated matter that involves the interplay of a multitude of variables, Skinner proceeds by focusing on specific behaviors and those environmental events considered to be controlling influences. In short, Skinner attempts to discover the nature of the cause-and-effect relationships between events. To accomplish this goal, Skinner first focuses on simple, observable behaviors that can be readily and reliably quantified and on those environmental stimuli thought to control the emission of these behaviors. Other variables thought to be irrelevant are eliminated or held constant.

Skinner believes that his approach can be implemented best by focusing on the behavior of nonhuman species because their environments are relatively easy to control and many of their behaviors are simple and can be quantified. The environment usually used for study purposes is the so-called Skinner box, and behavior is quantified through the use of a cumulative recorder. The Skinner box is a small, soundproofed chamber usually containing a lever or bar that an animal such as a rat can depress to obtain food reinforcers. For work with pigeons, translucent disks that can be lighted with different colors are mounted on the wall. When the pigeon pecks at the "right" disk—that is, a disk of a particular color chosen by the experimenter as correct—food is delivered via a feeding disk. The frequency and rate of response are recorded precisely and automatically by the cumulative recorder wired to the apparatus. A stylus or pen moves along a paper attached to a revolving drum.

Skinner maintains that the use of lower animals like the pigeon and rat to establish the principles of behavior is a good strategy because these principles are generalizable to the behavior of human beings. In his view, a single set of principles can account for much, but not all, of the behavior of both nonhuman and human organisms.

Application of the Theory to the Treatment of Psychopathology

Psychopathology and Behavior Modification

Reinforcement procedures are the cornerstone of **behavior modification**, which is an attempt to change undesirable behavior by applying learning principles derived from laboratory experiments (Krasner, 1970, p. 89). These principles are based on research in classical conditioning and observational learning as well as in operant conditioning. For our purposes, however, the focus will be on the use of operant techniques that have been utilized successfully in a number of problem areas. For example, investigators have demonstrated that it is possible to increase the social skills of retardates, to lessen the aggressive behavior of delinquents, to improve the study habits of students, to enable obese individuals to lose weight, to curtail smoking in cigarette smokers, to reduce stuttering in children and adults who stutter, and—as we discuss next—to control the undesirable behavior of psychotics.

The Token Economy. To alter the behavior of psychotics, investigators have designed special environments within institutions in which patients can earn tokens for performing socially appropriate tasks and then exchange these tokens for goods and activities that are positively reinforcing. Such incentive systems are commonly known as **token economies**.

Let us examine the classical attempt by Ayllon and Azrin to design such an environment as a means of strengthening key behaviors in psychotics in a mental hospital (Ayllon & Azrin, 1965). They pointed out that the most important limitation in trying to develop a technology of behavior is the lack of standardization, because untrained personnel are used to observe and record the behavior as well as administer reinforcers. For example, attendants may define "grooming behavior" in different ways. One attendant might define satisfactory grooming as combing hair, brushing teeth, and wearing clean clothes. Another may not check a patient's teeth or clothing and yet conclude that she has earned a number of tokens for appropriate grooming. It would not be unreasonable to find the second attendant swamped with requests from patients to check their grooming.

In addition, it is difficult to record and reinforce desired activities on a ward of approximately 45 patients when they are all engaging in a variety of activities at the same time. Research has shown that reinforcers have the greatest impact on behavior and are most effective if they are applied immediately following the desired response. If different attendants reinforced the patients at varying time intervals following responses, the impact on behavior would be lessened or even nonexistent. If the attendants do not know which behaviors to reinforce, how much to reinforce, or when to reinforce, it seems unlikely that there will be much improvement. Accordingly, the investigators spent 18 months developing their program in order to eliminate these and other problems. The final program included a standard list of behaviors to be changed as well as a list of the reinforcers. The behaviors to be strengthened differed among patients and included helping serve meals to the other patients; washing dishes; cleaning tables; typing letters; answering the telephone and calling hospital personnel to the phone; and washing sheets, pillow cases, and towels in the laundry. A list of the reinforcers to be given in exchange for tokens is shown in Table 11.1.

The results of the program showed, in general, significant improvement in patient behaviors over a 42-day period. In another experiment within the same program, the investigators demonstrated that once the tokens were withdrawn, the behavior of the patients deteriorated. When the system was

Table 11.1
List of Reinforcers Available to Patients for Tokens

Reinforcer	Number of Tokens Daily
I. *Privacy*	
Selection of room 1	0
Selection of room 2	4
Selection of room 3	8
Selection of room 4	15
Selection of room 5	30
Personal chair	1
Screen (room divider)	1
Choice of bedspreads	1
Coat rack	1
II. *Leave from the ward*	
Twenty-minute walk on hospital grounds (with escort)	2
Thirty-minute grounds pass	10
Trip to town (with escort)	100
III. *Social interaction with staff*	
Private audience with ward psychologist	20
Private audience with social worker	100
IV. *Devotional opportunities*	
Extra religious services on ward	1
Extra religious services off ward	10
V. *Recreational opportunities*	
Movie on ward	1
Exclusive use of a radio	1
Television (choice of program)	3
VI. *Commissary items*	
Candy, milk, cigarettes, coffee, and sandwich	1–5
Toilet articles such as toothpaste, comb, lipstick, and talcum powder	1–10
Clothing such as gloves, scarf, and skirt	12–400
Reading and writing materials such as pen, greeting card, newspaper, and magazine	2–5
Miscellaneous items such as ashtray, potted plant, picture holder, and stuffed animal	1–50

Adapted from Ayllon and Azrin, 1965, p. 360.

reinstated, performance levels rose again. This shift in performance shows the powerful impact of the tokens in changing behavior.

But this study and other experiments with token economies, although generally successful (see Kazdin, 1977), have spawned a number of serious questions. For example, the behaviors that are changed sometimes seem trivial and unrelated to the major problems confronting psychotics. What is so wonderful about getting a patient to comb her hair or wash some dishes? The answer is that although major problem behaviors remain untouched, the behaviors that were strengthened represent a significant shift in functioning for the patients. In the beginning of these experiments, some of the patients refused to wash or groom themselves. A few of them lay in their own excrement. Some refused to utter a word. The application of operant techniques changed this state of affairs and was the first step toward recovery. It also increased the freedom of the patients, in the sense of providing them with an opportunity to perform a variety of activities for positive payoffs rather than simply sitting all day doing nothing. The changes in appearance are also beneficial because the staff may begin to treat patients better. As psychologist Krasner put it, "If you can't tell the patient from the staff without a score card, you will most likely react to him (or her) as if he (or she) were normal just like you" (Krasner, 1970, p. 97). The effort to establish and implement a method of treatment is monumentally preferable to providing no treatment at all, as is all too often true of most mental institutions. Behavior modification is not the only therapeutic method that can be employed to overcome this impasse, but it is at least one and it does work.

On the debit side of the ledger, there is the problem of changing patients' more serious behavior problems and teaching them behaviors that will allow them to function adequately in the larger society. There is also the problem of determining whether behaviors that have changed actually generalize to extratreatment settings such as the community, home, and place of employment. As Kazdin (1977, p. 177) points out, although a few studies have demonstrated such transfer of training, most investigations have been unable to show such generalization once the training program has been withdrawn.

Aversive Techniques. Behavior modification confronts us with some serious ethical questions, one of which concerns the use of aversive techniques. Is it morally correct to use punishment, for example, to change behavior? This is a complicated question, but it does not seem to be enough to argue, as some authorities do, that it is ethically legitimate to do so because society itself tends to rely more heavily on aversive control than on the use of positive-reinforcement procedures (Kazdin, 1975, p. 237). That would be like the student who argues that cheating on exams is all right because "everybody does it and thinks it's OK."

The second argument often used is that behavior modification "*deemphasizes* the use of aversive techniques in applied settings" (Kazdin, 1975, p. 237). The reasons include the undesirable side effects of punishment and its interference with other, socially appropriate behavior. But this argument sidesteps the issue of whether punishment can be effective in changing behavior. In fact, there is considerable research evidence that aversive techniques can be used effectively to change undesirable behavior (Kushner, 1970, pp. 26–51).

At this point, let us examine an actual case history in which aversive-control techniques were used so that you can decide for yourself whether or not the use of punishment can be justified under certain circumstances. The case involved self-destructive behavior in a severely retarded 7-year-old boy who was nonverbal and who functioned like a 2-year-old (Kushner, 1970, pp. 42–44). The self-destructive behavior consisted of hand-biting severe enough to cause bleeding and infection. Hospital personnel tried to prevent the behavior by placing boxing gloves on the boy's hands, but when they were removed, he simply went back to biting his hands. The child also tried to prevent the behavior by sitting on his hands or by holding onto his nurse's hand. This strategy worked only temporarily, and he continued to bite his hands when they were free. Observation by the investigator indicated that the nurses' reaction to his crying following the hand-biting was to become very solicitous, to pick him up, and to give him a great deal of attention and affection, very much in the tradition of the Rogerian's giving of "unconditional positive regard" (see Chapter 15). Discussion with the nurses about the reinforcing properties of their behavior met with great resistance. Because it was obvious that the nurses could not be convinced of the necessity to ignore the behavior and because the extinction process would be so slow that much more damage would be inflicted, the investigator decided to use electric shock to prevent the behavior. Electrodes were placed on the child's thigh, and shock was administered following any hand-biting behavior. After the initial application of shock, the mother was brought into the room and was asked to use the word *no* at the same time that the shock was being administered. The decline in hand-biting was rapid and dramatic. Later the nurses were instructed to use the word *no* whenever the child moved his hand to his mouth and to call him a "good boy" when he moved his hand away. Other behavioral methods were then applied to maintain the low rate of hand-biting.

Would you condone the use of punishment in this case? This is a difficult judgment to make. Was there an alternative, positively reinforcing method that would have worked as well? If there was, it should have been employed (Kazdin, 1975, p. 241). In this example, however, the nurses had tried a number of less punishing strategies, and none of them had worked satisfactorily. Of course, this does not mean that they or the investigator exhausted all the possibilities before proceeding. If all possibilities were tried and found wanting, however, aversive control might be considered as a serious alternative. Even then, however, it would be unethical to use cruel and unusual punishment as a means of controlling the behavior. Thus, if aversive stimuli are used, they should obviously not be immobilizing or have serious and permanent side effects (Kazdin, 1975, p. 239). If all these conditions are met and the rights of the patients are protected, perhaps the use of punishment can be justified in certain instances. Obviously, any investigator employing aversive-control techniques must continually be aware of his or her ethical obligations and act accordingly. There are no easy answers in this situation, but progress in helping people is not made by denying the efficacy of punishment in producing behavioral change no matter how noble or worthwhile it makes us feel.

There have been abuses of the rights of patients in the past in programs using behavior-modification techniques. Occasionally, cruel and unusual punishment has been administered by investigators. In one study, for example, patients were shocked without their consent and deprived of meals for a number of days. Even in the Ayllon and Azrin study reviewed in this chapter, there is a question of the abuse of patients' rights. A reexamination of Table 11.1, which shows the kinds of reinforcers that could be bought with earned tokens, indicates that attendance at "extra" religious services could, theoretically at least, be prohibited by the investigators if the patient had not earned any tokens. This kind of prohibition comes very close to an abridgment of the patient's constitutional rights concerning freedom of religion. We should not conclude simplistically from these examples, however, that denial of patients' rights or the administration of cruel and unusual punishment is pervasive and, therefore, that behavior-modification procedures should be abandoned. Abuses are relatively few, and the benefits to thousands and thousands of people have been tremendous. Instead, investigators must work to eliminate abusive practices and uphold to the best of their abilities the ethical ideals of the profession.

Education and Behavioral Technology

For Skinner, the history of education in this country and in many others shows clearly that teachers and administrators have tended to rely on aversive practices to control the behavior of students. According to him, 50 years ago, children learned the prescribed materials to escape the cane or birch rod. Today the rod is seldom used, but Skinner (1969, p. 149) maintains that we have not actually shifted from aversive to positive control, but rather from one kind of aversive control to another. In the lower grades, for example, the child fills in a workbook to avoid the teacher's displeasure or criticism as well as the ridicule of his classmates. Not infrequently, low marks result in staying after school, a trip to the principal's office, or admonishments or spankings by parents. Homework is imposed by the teacher and is sometimes used as punishment for troublemaking. Many of the same practices occur at the college and university level, but in place of the principal, students face the college dean. In addition, the competition for marks in higher education is especially keen, and high marks for one student often mean low marks for another because many teachers unfortunately continue to grade according to the traditional bell curve.

These and many other practices are painful for large numbers of students and generate many unwanted by-products (Skinner, 1968, p. 97). Students may try to escape from the punishing situation by being tardy. Or they may eventually drop out of school altogether. Students who commit suicide have often experienced difficulties in school. Subtler forms of escape include chronic daydreaming and "restlessness." A student may not be able to sit still for a few minutes in class but will spend hours playing in the neighborhood park or watching television. Another serious result of aversive control, in Skinner's view, is that students may attempt to verbally attack their controllers: they may become defiant, rude, or impudent to their teachers and use obscene language. In the more serious cases, they may even physically attack their teachers. For Skinner, vandalism is another indirect manifestation of attempts by students to weaken the control of powerful others.

As a consequence of the detrimental nature of aversive practices, many well-intentioned and concerned teachers have sought alternatives. According to Skinner, one major alternative to punishment accepted by educators in practice, if not in theory, is permissiveness. He maintains that permissiveness has a number of seeming advantages, including the fact that it saves the practitioners the labor of supervision and the enforcement of standards. But he suggests that

> permissiveness is not ... a policy; it is the abandonment of policy; and its apparent advantages are illusory. To refuse to control is to leave control not to the person himself but to other parts of the social and nonsocial environments. [Skinner, 1968, p. 84]

Another major alternative, which is related in many respects to permissiveness, is guidance, and its effects on the educational process are usually described with a horticultural metaphor. A person is said "to grow" like a flower or tree if his experiences occur in the right "soil." Behavior can be "cultivated" but only under the right conditions. It is also "developed" until "maturity" (Skinner, 1968, p. 87). You might want to review Chapters 14 and 15 on Maslow and Rogers at this point for good examples of the guidance position. Skinner says that this position has some convenient advantages for its practitioners:

> One who merely guides a natural development cannot easily be accused of trying to control it. Growth remains an achievement of the individual, testifying to his freedom and worth, his "hidden propensities," and as the gardener is not responsible for the ultimate form of what he grows, so one who merely guides is exonerated when things go wrong. [Skinner, 1968, pp. 87-88]

In Skinner's view, the primary disadvantage of this position is that it obscures the reinforcements actually responsible for the changes in behavior by attributing them to "the unfolding of some predetermined pattern" (Skinner, 1968, p. 88).

Skinner himself opts for a detailed examination of the environmental determinants of behavior. In his opinion, education involves "the arrangement of (the) contingencies of reinforcement under which students learn" (Skinner, 1968, p. 64). These contingencies can be effectively arranged through the use of teaching machines and other programmed instruction techniques, such as computer-assisted instruction. Complex subject matter is presented to the student in a series of small, easy-to-learn steps. In one form of programmed learning, a question is presented and the student writes her answer in a space provided by the program. Then she lifts a lever that moves her answer under a transparent cover and simultaneously exposes the correct answer. If the two answers match, the student punches a hole in the paper near her response to indicate that she has answered correctly. This procedure instructs the machine to allow the next question to appear. The student answers all the questions by the same procedure. She then starts the series again and attempts to answer correctly those questions she answered incorrectly at first. The process is repeated until she has mastered the program materials (Skinner, 1969, p. 162).

Skinner maintains that such a format has many advantages over the traditional system. It is more efficient than the traditional instructional procedures. It is a labor-saving device because it can bring many students into contact with one programmer (Skinner, 1968, p. 37). Although programming may suggest mass production to some people, in reality it acts almost like a private tutor for the student. Unlike lectures and films, there is a continual interplay between the student and the materials. Programming does not eliminate the need for the teacher either. The teacher is the key person who arranges the contingencies of reinforcement for the students, but now he or she will make these arrangements pay off in effective learning. In addition, the teacher will still have the tremendous responsibility of weaning the students from the machine and showing them how the facts and principles they have learned can be related to other areas of life.

The teaching machine is programmed in such a way that it ensures the student thoroughly understands a point before he or she can proceed. One of the tragedies of traditional educational practices is that all too often the teacher is faced with the task of educating large numbers of students simultaneously. Under such "massed madness" conditions, it is impossible for even the best teacher to give each student the amount of attention he or she needs to learn the materials well. Still another advantage is that the machine reinforces the student sufficiently for each response and does it immediately (Skinner, 1968, p. 39). Very often the teacher in the traditional setting knows the value of immediate and adequate reinforcement but cannot provide it. Finally, the programmed-learning approach recognizes the importance of individual differences. Skinner (1968, p. 242) maintains that failure to account for these differences is the greatest single inefficiency in education today.

For all these reasons, Skinner strongly advocates the adoption of his programmed-learning approach. But although he is hopeful of eventual change in our educational system, his innovations may be resisted by educators:

Many of those charged with the improvement of education are unaware that . . .
technical help is available, and many are afraid of it when it is pointed out.

*They resist any new practice which does not have the familiar and reassuring
character of day-to-day communication. They continue to discuss learning
and teaching in the language of the layman. [Skinner, 1968, p. 259]*

Skinner is recommending the application of a scientific analysis of behavior
to educational practices. Now, almost two decades after his recommendation appeared, and thanks largely to the computer boom, it seems that his
approach is gaining some support among educators, as evidenced by the
large numbers of academic institutions now using the programmed-learning
format to help educate students.

Skinner's View of Utopia: The Behaviorally Engineered Society

In his book *Walden Two* Skinner tries to apply operant principles not
only to education and psychopathology but to the extremely complicated
problem of creating an ideal society. Skinner envisages Walden Two as this
utopia. It is portrayed as a rural community with cooperative housing and
dining systems for its nearly 1000 members. Such a communal arrangement
avoids the unnecessary duplication of facilities and the great expense associated with building separate houses. Because of the relatively small size of
the living arrangements, it is possible to interconnect all the bedroom quarters with common lounge areas, dining rooms, a theater, and a library. Thus
members can avoid, for the most part, going out in bad weather. These
protected arrangements are consistent with Skinner's emphasis on changing
the environment to meet individual needs. They permit more control of
undesirable weather conditions, thus making community members masters
of their own situation rather than the victims of it.

An additional benefit of living in such a small, largely self-contained
community is that there is no long-distance commuting to work along con-
gested and polluted highways, a nerve-wracking practice that continues to
plague many contemporary workers (Freedman, 1972, p. 3 in Chap. 2). A few
trucks simply ferry some of the workers back and forth over the short distance from the living quarters to the workshops (where, for example, furniture is made or repaired), the gardens, and the poultry, cattle, sheep, and
pig houses where the food resources are located.

Skinner insists that his utopia is not founded on the simplistic and
romanticized "return to the farm" philosophy of the 1800s. He maintains
further that his utopia does not spring from a rejection of modern life. For
example, the farming done for food and clothing relies on the best equipment available. This is bought from the larger, outside community, which
also supplies the power to run these machines (including the trucks). The
emphasis in Walden Two is on minimizing uncreative and uninteresting

work for its members. This orientation demands the best that technology can offer.

Although money may be necessary at times for transactions with the larger community, it is not needed or used within Walden Two. Money earned by members as a result of work done for outsiders is placed in a community fund to be used for future purchases from outsiders. Within Walden Two, food, clothing, shelter, recreation, and medical services are provided, so there is no need for money. To keep the system operating, however, members are required to contribute 1200 labor credits a year (or 4 credits for each of 300 workdays) in return for the goods and services provided to them. In general, one credit is given for each hour of work resulting in a four-hour workday for each member, thus leaving ample time for recreational activities and the satisfaction of curiosities (for instance, games, theatrical plays, reading, writing, art, science, hobbies). To ensure that unpleasant jobs get done and that some members do not feel resentful that they are doing jobs that are much more aversive than ones done by others for the same number of credits, the values of the labor credits are adjusted to make all kinds of work equally desirable. For example, cleaning sewers receives 1.5 credits per hour, while working in the community flower garden receives only 0.7 or 0.8 credits per hour (Skinner, 1948, p. 52). For several reasons, such an economy is viable even though each member works an average of only 20 hours per week. There is little unnecessary duplication of goods (for instance, there are community automobiles but not everyone owns one); and unnecessary services are eliminated (for instance, there are no bars or taverns because Skinner believes that the satisfied people of his utopia have no need to drink) (Freedman, 1972, p. 3 in Chap. 2). Waste is reduced in other ways. For instance, community members are not bombarded daily by advertisers interested primarily in making money by imposing frequent changes in clothing styles on consumers. Thus clothing styles change more slowly in Walden Two, so that members do not throw away clothes in good condition (Skinner, 1948, p. 35). There is no unemployment, thereby eliminating the bureaucratic burden and cost of administering benefits to the unemployed.

Walden Two also makes efficient use of all of its citizens, including women. Skinner is unequivocally egalitarian in his views on the relationships and roles of men and women, a view that predates the current women's liberation movement by approximately 20 years. There is no division of labor in terms of sex in Walden Two. The equal sharing by community members of tasks involving the preparation and serving of food, the cleaning of living quarters, and the education of the young, irrespective of sex, frees women to participate equally with men in all areas of communal life. Child care is also shared by members of the community and is performed by experts of both sexes.

Child care is of particular concern to Skinner, and he devotes considerable attention to it. Children in Walden Two do not live with their natural parents, nor are they raised by them. Instead group members share the responsibility of raising children. In the nursery, infants are raised by community experts, male and female. They live in a controlled environment so that they never know fear, frustration, or anxiety. After the first year of life, they are placed in dormitory quarters and annoyances are introduced on a gradual basis to develop tolerance for a certain degree of frustration. For example, Skinner cites a situation in which a group of children come home tired and hungry after a long walk. But rather than eating immediately, they must stand for five minutes in front of steaming bowls of soup before they are allowed to eat (Skinner, 1948, p. 109). Children are encouraged also to have a sense of humor and not to take annoyances too seriously. These lessons in self-control are taught so that children can handle any unhappiness that they might experience later in life. Whereas in our culture children may meet with uncontrolled frustration and subsequent defeat, in Walden Two the degree of frustration is carefully controlled so that success can be assumed (Freedman, 1972, p. 3 in Chap. 3).

Group care of children does weaken the relationship between parent and child, and this state of affairs is encouraged in Walden Two. Skinner believes that in the typical home parents do not know how to raise their children properly. Such care is best left in the hands of experts. By having children regard all adult members of Walden Two as their parents, several benefits accrue. For instance, children are discouraged from being too dependent on their biological parents. Foster children and stepchildren are loved as dearly as one's own. If the biological parents divorce, children are not embarrassed by severe changes in their lifestyles. It is also easier to discourage people who are unfit or unwell from seeking parenthood because no stigma attaches to being childless and, besides, the childless have others to love. Finally, children grow up more secure because they receive affection and help from hundreds of adults (Skinner, 1948, pp. 142–145).

On a more general level, Walden Two is governed by a Board of Six Planners, three of whom are usually women. The Planners are chosen by the board members themselves from names supplied by the Managers. Planners may serve for up to ten years but no more. They are responsible for policymaking and for the supervision of the Managers.

The Managers are responsible for providing adequate goods and services to community members. There are dozens of Managers—Managers of Food, Health, Dentistry, Play, Arts, Nursery School, Dairy, and so on. They are specialists who have been carefully trained and selected for their jobs through apprenticeship procedures (Skinner, 1948, p. 55).

The only other group besides the Workers, Managers, and Planners is the Scientists. The community supports research aimed at the improvement of the economy and the psychological well-being of its members. Experiments are often done in plant and animal breeding to improve the economy, and psychological experiments are performed to increase knowledge of the impact of the environment on behavior so that the environment can be effectively manipulated to increase community members' happiness.

In Walden Two there are no elections by the Workers to select the Planners, Managers, and Scientists. Skinner believes that the average citizen (worker) is unable to make such selections intelligently (Skinner, 1948, p. 267). These decisions are best left in the hands of the specialists who, he feels, will wield their power for the good of others. If they should take any steps that lessened the total happiness of the community, they would begin to experience a reduction in their power. Skinner is convinced that this potential reduction in power would serve as a check against misuse of the authority (Skinner, 1948, p. 264.

It could be argued that Skinner's view is naive and that concentration of power in the hands of a few people is likely to lead to a continuing misuse of the power, irrespective of the level of unhappiness of the community members. Yet such a view of the use of power sees it as a means to personal gain. Dictators exploit citizens to enhance their own feelings of esteem and to accrue wealth and possessions. In Skinner's utopia, however, a person's self-esteem is based on making contributions for the betterment of the community and not on personal gain. Recall also that possessions and wealth are shared by members so that the primary goal in life of community members is not the accumulation of goods. Moreover, a loss in power would signify to leaders that community members are less accepting of their efforts to help them, and the leaders would therefore be unhappy. Skinner also notes that the socialization process in Walden Two ensures that members do not see punishment as a primary means of controlling behavior. Rather, the emphasis is on using positive-reinforcement practices and on cooperative behavior (Skinner, 1948, p. 272). Furthermore, even if the Planners abused their authority, they could be replaced under the code adopted by community members to govern behavior. Despite these assurances, it is clear that Walden Two is a dictatorship (albeit a benevolent one) and, as such, is unsettling to most Americans, who prefer democratically oriented government.

Even more unsettling is Skinner's harsh indictment of democracy. He feels that democracy is really despotism because the minority is at the mercy of the majority (Freedman, 1972, p. 7 in Chap. 3). Moreover, Skinner sees little point in national elections, especially for president. He thinks that there is not much difference between the parties in their political platforms and that the election of either candidate does not make an appreciable difference in the lives of the electorate. To solve this problem, he would not strive to improve democracy but would instead abandon it (Freedman, 1972, p. 7 in Chap. 3).

Finally, in his version of the ideal society, people would be in a position to tell the experts (Planners, Managers, and Scientists) what they like or dislike about the life they are leading. Thus protests would be legitimate and would be taken "as seriously as the pilot of an airplane takes a sputtering engine" (Skinner, 1948, p. 269). If current practices were unsatisfactory, they would be changed, because Skinner's utopia is an experimenting society where the aim is maximization of the happiness of every community member.

Critical Comments

An examination and evaluation of the scientific worth of Skinner's theory on the basis of our six criteria are now in order.

Comprehensiveness. Skinner has constructed a theory of behavior that, until recently, focused almost exclusively on the functioning of lower animals. His primary concern seems to have been to generate a set of learning principles for certain types of simple, nonsocial performance. From this perspective, the range of topics actually covered by Skinner in his initial theorizing was highly limited. He has been severely criticized for this narrow focus by a variety of investigators. His primary rebuttal has been that, in all sciences, advances occur as investigators focus first on the simple and then progress to the more complex. The focus on simple behaviors allows scientists to control current situational conditions better and to record behavior over longer periods. In addition, genetic and environmental-history variables can be brought under control (Skinner, 1953, p. 38). Once the basic processes are revealed, this information can be utilized in the study of the more diverse and complicated behavior of human beings.

Such a research strategy is eminently reasonable, and, of course, it has had considerable payoff value in the important findings about behavior it has generated. Yet there is a kind of conservatism about it that may seem unnecessarily stultifying to investigators of human behavior. Science, as mentioned in the opening chapter, is a human enterprise and should, at least occasionally, be fun. Part of the enjoyment is based on taking risks—on testing hunches that are not firmly grounded in data. Of course, it would be unwise to pursue one's research goals by indiscriminately using such a risk-taking approach; and Skinner's allegiance to the strict simple-to-complex principle is generally cogent.

Recently, Skinner has argued that the imbalance in his work has been corrected because much of the current work in behavior modification focuses exclusively on human behavior. Still, it seems clear that he has not constructed a theory that rivals Freud's in comprehensiveness.

Precision and Testability. The terms of Skinner's theory are precisely defined, and the various relational statements are capable of experimental verification. The concern with rigor and precision in the study of behavioral phenomena is one of the impressive strengths of the work of Skinner and his operant colleagues.

Parsimony. Skinner's theory is relatively economical, especially when compared with some of the psychodynamic positions. It is not burdened by excess concepts and assumptions. In fact, it can be argued that the theory lacks a number of concepts that could help explain various social-learning phenomena. Skinner himself recognizes that there may be a need for additional concepts in a theory that attempts to account for complex and cognitively based human learning.

Empirical Validity. Skinner's position is firmly grounded in laboratory data, in sharp contrast to the psychodynamic positions we have considered thus far. Although there is strong empirical support for many aspects of his learning theory, critics have claimed that Skinner often gives the impression that a technology of behavior exists to solve the complex problems that confront us. In fact, they say, this is not the case, and he is making sweeping and unwarranted generalizations on the basis of limited empirical evidence (Black, 1973, p. 129). Skinner attempts to refute this criticism by acknowledging that he is indeed offering interpretations about the functioning of society from limited data but that this is perfectly legitimate and is done by scientists in other fields without attracting much attention. He maintains further that "when phenomena are out of reach in time or space, or too large or small to be directly manipulated, we must talk about them with less than a complete account of relevant conditions" (Skinner, 1973, p. 261). True, but we should also bear in mind that it is often easy to confuse speculation with fact and that Skinner's arguments about the efficacy of his approach in solving social problems are as yet unproven.

Heuristic Value. Skinner's theory has had tremendous impact on the thinking and research activities of investigators in many disciplines. He has become a controversial figure whose position has been severely criticized by a variety of critics, including psychologists, psychiatrists, politicians, philosophers, theologians, biologists, novelists, and journalists. Some people have taken these attacks as proof that Skinner is a revolutionary thinker whose position will eventually force a major shift in the way we view ourselves and others (Platt, 1973, p. 23). Although it is too early to comment on the validity of such an assertion, it is clear that Skinner's theory ranks high in heuristic value.

Applied Value. Skinner's position has far-reaching implications for the functioning of society. Beginning with experiments on the behavior of lower animals, he has, over approximately a half-century, derived a set of simple and precise reinforcement principles that have been applied to a number of significant problems faced by human beings. The theory's applied value can perhaps be seen most clearly in the areas of psychopathology and education.

Discussion Questions

1. Why does Skinner think there is a need for a scientific technology of behavior? Do you agree or disagree with him?
2. Do you ever use "mentalistic" explanations to account for behavior? If so, cite

some recent instances and try to reanalyze them in terms of possible environmental variables salient at the time.

3. How might the stereotypic belief that individuals are solely responsible for their behavior result in the continuation of discrimination against minority-group members?

4. Is all control of behavior bad? In what ways does control yield positive or negative outcomes for people? Why do many people dislike those who control the outcomes of others?

5. What is operant conditioning? How does it differ from classical conditioning?

6. Do you agree with Skinner that punishment is the most common technique of control in modern life? What are the limitations of punishment as a control technique? Is its use ever effective and desirable? Discuss the implications of the use of failing grades as a punishment technique. Can you propose alternate, more effective, and rewarding ways of evaluating students' performance, with accurate feedback to them of their progress or lack of it in a course?

7. What is extinction? Have you ever tried to extinguish someone's obnoxious behavior by ignoring it? What happened? What are some of the limitations of the technique?

8. Describe the various types of reinforcement schedules. Cite some examples in your everyday routine in which your behavior is controlled by the different schedule types.

9. What is behavior modification? What are its strengths and weaknesses? Do you think that token economies are useless, sterile, and unethical ways of changing undesirable behavior? Who decides which behaviors are undesirable? Who should decide?

10. Do you agree with Skinner's application of behavioral technology to education? What are the strengths and deficiencies of his arguments for reform of the educational system?

References

Ayllon, T., & Azrin, N. H. The measurement and reinforcement of behavior of psychotics. *Journal of the Experimental Analysis of Behavior,* 1965, 8, 357–383.

Black, M. Some aversive responses to a would-be reinforcer. In H. Wheeler (Ed.), *Beyond the punitive society.* San Francisco: Freeman, 1973.

Carpenter, F. *The Skinner primer.* New York: Free Press, 1974.

Ferster, C. B., & Perrott, M. C. *Behavior principles.* New York: Appleton-Century-Crofts, 1968.

Ferster, C. B., & Skinner, B. F. *Schedules of reinforcement.* New York: Appleton-Century-Crofts, 1957.

Flavell, J. H. *The developmental psychology of Jean Piaget.* New York: Van Nostrand, 1963.

Freedman, A. E. *The planned society: An analysis of Skinner's proposals.* Kalamazoo, Mich.: Behaviordelia, Inc., 1972.

Holland, J. G., & Skinner, B. F. *The analysis of behavior,* New York: McGraw-Hill, 1961.

Kazdin, A. E. *Behavior modification in applied settings.* Homewood, Ill.: Dorsey Press, 1975.

Kazdin, A. E. *The token economy: A review and evaluation.* New York: Plenum, 1977.

Krasner, L. Behavior modification, token economies, and training in clinical psychology. In C. Neuringer & J. L. Michael (Eds.), *Behavior modification in clinical psychology.* New York: Appleton-Century-Crofts, 1970.

Kushner, M. Faradic aversive controls in clinical practice. In C. Neuringer & J. L. Michael (Eds.), *Behavior modification in clinical psychology.* New York: Appleton-Century-Crofts, 1970.

Platt, J. R. The Skinnerian revolution. In H. Wheeler (Ed.), *Beyond the punitive society.* San Francisco: Freeman, 1973.

Skinner, B. F. *The behavior of organisms.* New York: Appleton-Century-Crofts, 1938.

Skinner, B. F. *Walden Two.* New York: Macmillan, 1948.

Skinner, B. F. *Science and human behavior.* New York: Macmillan, 1953.

Skinner, B. F. *Verbal behavior.* New York: Appleton-Century-Crofts, 1957.

Skinner, B. F. *Cumulative record.* New York: Appleton-Century-Crofts, 1961.

Skinner, B. F. *The technology of teaching.* New York: Appleton-Century-Crofts, 1968.

Skinner, B. F. *Contingencies of reinforcement.* New York: Appleton-Century-Crofts, 1969.

Skinner, B. F. An autobiography. In P. B. Dews (Ed.), *Festschrift for B. F. Skinner.* New York: Appleton-Century-Crofts, 1970.

Skinner, B. F. *Beyond freedom and dignity.* New York: Knopf, 1971.

Skinner, B. F. Answers for my critics. In H. Wheeler (Ed.), *Beyond the punitive society.* San Francisco: Freeman, 1973.

Skinner, B. F. *About behaviorism.* New York: Knopf, 1974.

Skinner, B. F. *Particulars of my life.* New York: Knopf, 1976.

Skinner, B. F. *Reflections on behaviorism and society.* Englewood Cliffs, N. J.: Prentice-Hall, 1978.

Skinner, B. F. *The shaping of a behaviorist.* New York: Knopf, 1979.

Skinner, B. F. *A matter of consequences.* New York: Knopf, 1983.

Skinner, B. F., & Vaughan, M. E. *Enjoy old age.* New York: Norton, 1983.

Walters, G. C., & Grusec, J. E. *Punishment.* San Francisco: Freeman, 1977.

Williams, R. L., & Long, J. D. *Toward a self-managed life style.* Boston: Houghton Mifflin, 1979.

Suggested Readings

Skinner, B. F. *Walden Two.* New York: Macmillan, 1948.

Skinner, B. F. *Science and human behavior.* New York: Macmillan, 1953.

Skinner, B. F. *Beyond freedom and dignity.* New York: Knopf, 1971.

Skinner, B. F. *About behaviorism.* New York: Knopf, 1974.

Skinner, B. F. *Reflections on behaviorism and society.* Englewood Cliffs, N. J.: Prentice-Hall, 1978.

Skinner, B. F., & Vaughan, M. E. *Enjoy old age.* New York: Norton, 1983.

Glossary

Behavior modification Series of procedures that seek to change behavior through reliance on reinforcement principles.

Conditioning Establishment of the linkage between the behavior and its consequences.

Continuous reinforcement   Schedule of reinforcement in which each response is followed by a reinforcer.

Discriminative stimulus   Stimulus whose presence leads an individual to respond because he or she has learned previously that its presence leads to particular reinforcing consequences.

Extinction   Reduction in behavior that eventually occurs as a result of the failure to reinforce the behavior.

Fixed-interval schedule   Schedule of reinforcement in which the first response that occurs after an absolute amount of time has elapsed is reinforced.

Fixed-ratio schedule   Schedule of reinforcement in which an absolute number of responses is required before a reinforcer is applied.

Functional analysis   Attempt to understand behavior by identifying the environmental conditions that determine its occurrence or nonoccurrence.

Intermittent reinforcement   Schedule of reinforcement in which reinforcers are applied to given responses occasionally or intermittently.

Law of effect   For Thorndike, the principle that behavior is determined by its consequences. In his view, behavior followed by reward was "stamped in," whereas behavior followed by punishment was "stamped out."

Mentalism   Pejorative term used by some learning theorists to indicate their dissatisfaction with the use of concepts that cannot be objectively validated as explanatory devices in attempts to account for behavior.

Negative reinforcer   Stimulus that maintains or strengthens the occurrence of a response through the removal of aversive stimuli.

Operant analysis   Study of the ways in which behavior is acquired, maintained, or modified by its reinforcing consequences.

Positive reinforcer   Stimulus associated with behavior that increases the probability of the occurrence of the behavior.

Punishment   Presentation of aversive stimuli following a behavior that results in a decrease in the performance of that behavior.

Reinforcement   In classical or respondent conditioning, the association formed through the repeated pairing of the conditioned stimulus and the unconditioned stimulus. In operant, or instrumental, learning, the association that is formed when an operant response is followed by a reinforcing stimulus.

Repertoire   Unique, acquired behavior patterns.

Self-control process   Actions instigated by a person to alter the conditions that influence his or her behavior.

Stimulus   Goad to behavior; a condition that affects behavior.

Stimulus control   Stimulus to which a person has learned to respond. If a person has been reinforced for a given behavior in the presence of certain stimuli and not in the presence of others, he or she learns to respond only in the presence of those stimuli that provide the opportunity for reinforcement.

Token economy   A behavior-modification procedure in which tokens are earned by patients for performing behaviors the hospital staff judges are necessary if the patients are to live effectively in the outside world. The tokens are conditioned reinforcers that can be exchanged for experiences and/or goods that are desirable to the patients.

C H A P T E R 12

Rotter's Expectancy-Reinforcement Model

Biographical Sketch

Julian Rotter was born in Brooklyn, New York, in 1916. He received his B.A. degree from Brooklyn College in 1937, his M.A. from the University of Iowa in 1938, and his Ph.D. in psychology from Indiana University in 1941. During his undergraduate and graduate days he was greatly influenced by the neoanalyst Alfred Adler and by Kurt Lewin, a prominent social psychologist. Rotter attended a series of Adler's clinics, demonstrations, and university seminars and also met informally with him at his home (Mosher, 1968). He credits Adler with focusing his attention on the goal-directedness of behavior and on the unity of personality. Many of the concepts in Rotter's position can be traced directly to Adler's influence. The similarities between various concepts in the two theories will become apparent later in the chapter.

Rotter was also affected by the field theory approach promulgated by Lewin. Two of the principal attributes of this approach are its emphasis on the interrelatedness of behavior and the premise that multiple factors are responsible for the occurrence of behavior at a given time. Rotter accepted

333

these assumptions as well as one that maintains that behavior must be described from the perspective of the person whose behavior is under scrutiny rather than from the viewpoint of the observer (Rotter &. Hochreich, 1975, p. 97). In addition to Adler and Lewin, Rotter reports that he was influenced by the writings of various learning theorists, including E. L. Thorndike, Edward C. Tolman, and Clark L. Hull. In general terms, his social learning position is an attempt to integrate two major trends embodied in the work of these theorists—reinforcement approaches and cognitive theories, or **field theories** (Rotter, Chance, &. Phares, 1972, p. 1).

After receiving his doctorate, Rotter served during World War II as a psychologist and personnel consultant to the U.S. Army. After the war, he accepted a position at Ohio State University, where he eventually became director of the Psychological Clinic. During his stay at Ohio State, he published *Social Learning and Clinical Psychology* (1954), a book in which for the first time he presented an extended treatment of his social-learning theory of personality. His stay at Ohio State was productive in research as well. Rotter attracted a number of capable students who worked with him to test various predictions derived from the theory. Some of these students have since become leading proponents of the social-learning view in contemporary psychology.

In 1963, Rotter left Ohio State and accepted a position as a full professor in the psychology department at the University of Connecticut. He is also director of the Clinical Psychology Training Program at the University of Connecticut and a diplomate in clinical psychology of the American Board of Examiners in Professional Psychology. He was elected president of the Eastern Psychological Association for 1976–1977. In 1972 he published *Applications of a Social Learning Theory of Personality* with his former students J. E. Chance and E. J. Phares. He also co-authored the text *Personality* (1975) with colleague Dorothy Hochreich. The most recent statement of his position can be found in "Social Learning Theory," a chapter he wrote for a book edited by N. T. Feather, *Expectations and Actions: Expectancy-Value Models in Psychology* (1981b). At present, Professor Rotter continues to be actively engaged in writing and research work in the social-learning area.

Basic Concepts and Principles

Rotter has constructed a theory of personality based on learning concepts and principles. It is an approach that focuses on learned behavior. The assumption is that most of our behavior is learned and that it is acquired through our experiences with other people (Rotter, Chance, &. Phares, 1972, p. 4). Such a social-learning view also makes use of a historical approach to the study of personality, for it is thought necessary to investigate the antecedent events in persons' lives to understand their behavior adequately. Unlike the Freudians, however, Rotter does not believe it is essential to sample the individual's past experiences in great detail to predict behavior adequately. Instead, he argues that we should focus on these past events only to the extent that they help us to meet our predictive goals (Rotter, Chance, & Phares, 1972, p. 5). For example, there may be no need to inquire into a student's traumatic experiences during the oral stage of infancy to predict his failure to attain a college degree. An examination of his relatively poor high school grades and low college-board scores may be sufficient.

To understand personality, Rotter also thinks that we must consider it to have unity, or interdependence (Rotter, Chance, & Phares, 1972, p. 7). One aspect of this belief is that a person's experiences or interactions influence one another. Past experiences influence current experiences, and current experiences change the things the person has learned in the past. For example, a student might reject potentially helpful advice from her college counselor because she has consistently been given poor advice by other counselors in the past. If she could be induced to accept the advice of this counselor, however, and it proved helpful, her general attitude toward counselors might become more positive. Thus personality is seen not only as involving change because the individual is continuously exposed to new experiences but also as having stability because previous experiences affect new learning (Rotter & Hochreich, 1975, p. 94).

The other aspect of the belief that personality has unity is that different behaviors are functionally related (Katkobsky, 1968, p. 215). A student may be successful in having his name added to the class list for a popular course in political science by engaging in such diverse behaviors as getting up earlier than the other students and securing a place in front of the line, asking a friend to register him, speaking directly to the instructor, getting approval from the college dean, and so on. Each of these behaviors then would be functionally related; that is, they would all operate to secure the same outcome. Reinforcements can also become functionally related (Rotter, Chance & Phares, 1972, p. 19). For instance, a star hockey player may learn that leading his team to the coveted Stanley Cup by scoring more goals than any other player in the league means not only a healthy increase in his annual salary but praise from teammates, the coach, and members of the media, as well as lucrative advertising contracts with major manufacturers whenever he has such a season.

In Rotter's position there is also the assumption that behavior is goal-directed. This directional aspect is inferred from the effect of reinforcing conditions (Rotter, Chance, & Phares, 1972, p. 8). In short, Rotter considers human behavior to be motivated. People strive to maximize rewards and to minimize or avoid punishment. In other words, Rotter, like Skinner, endorses the principle of the empirical law of effect. He maintains that "any stimulus complex has reinforcing properties to the extent that it influences movement toward or away from a goal" (Rotter, Chance, & Phares, 1972, p. 9). Some investigators have objected to this principle because it seems circular and because there is no attempt to define a reinforcer independently of behavior. Rotter maintains that such a view would be correct if we studied only the behavior of people from other cultures and were able to identify reinforcers only *after* they had occurred. In reality, the situation is quite different. We live in a culture in which it is possible to identify reinforcing events that have known effects both for groups and for individuals (Rotter, Chance, & Phares, 1972, p. 9). Thus it is possible to use this knowledge to make predictions about behavior.

A few other corollary points about human motivation should be made. First, when investigators using social-learning theory focus on the environmental conditions that determine the direction of behavior, they speak of goals or reinforcements. When they focus on the person determining the direction of behavior, they speak of needs. For Rotter, the distinction between goals and needs is a semantic one used merely for convenience (Rotter, Chance, & Phares, 1972, p. 10). Second, social-learning theory assumes that early goals are learned within a family setting. We are born with certain physiological needs that are satisfied by parents and parental surrogates. Their association with the satisfaction or frustration of our basic or unlearned needs provides the basis, in Rotter's judgment, for our later reliance on them and others for affection and love, praise, recognition, status, and dependency (Rotter, Chance, & Phares, 1972, p. 10).

This view, however, creates special theoretical difficulties. It assumes that all reinforcers are reinforcing because they have become associated with drive reduction. For example, a mother's praise of her son's performance in school is positively reinforcing to him because it is associated with earlier feeding experiences that reduced his hunger drive. Such a drive-reduction view of reinforcement may be fine when we are dealing with simple behaviors, but it becomes difficult to defend when we begin to consider complex social behavior (Rotter, Chance, & Phares, 1972, p. 9). For example, how can we show that an athlete with a high need for achievement has experienced reduction of an unlearned drive by winning the mile run in a track meet? There would seem to be no connection between her success and, say, the reduction of her hunger drive. To overcome this difficulty, social-learning theory relies instead on an empirical law of effect. It focuses on changes in behavior as a function of the introduction or removal of stimulating events as its criterion for reinforcement (see Chapter 11 on Skinner for a more detailed treatment of this view of reinforcement). In summary, social-learning theory assumes that the initial learning of goals occurs within a drive-reduction framework, but that the later acquisition of highly complex behaviors is better explained by using a reinforcement concept based on the empirical law of effect.

Social-Learning Concepts

There are four major concepts in the social-learning approach: behavior potential, expectancy, reinforcement value, and the psychological situation. In its simplest form, the formula for behavior is that "the potential for a behavior to occur in any specific situation is a function of the expectancy that the behavior will lead to a particular reinforcement in that situation and the value of that reinforcement" (Rotter, 1975, p. 57). Let us examine each of these concepts in order.

Behavior Potential. For Rotter, **behavior potential** refers to "the potentiality of any behavior's occurring in any situation or situations as calculated in relation to any single reinforcement or set of reinforcements" (Rotter, Chance, & Phares, 1972, p. 12). Like Skinner, Rotter is actually talking about the probability of the individual's responding when certain environmental conditions are present. Rotter's view, however, places more emphasis on the role of cognitive factors in the prediction of behavior than does Skinner's, because Rotter makes active use of our subjective interpretation of the events that confront us. For example, he assumes that our potential for behavior is affected by our perception of the other behaviors available to us in a given situation, along with the operation of other factors. Thus a complex set of internal or cognitive factors is typically involved in the prediction of behavior. Finally, it should be noted that Rotter's definition of behavior is quite broad:

> Behavior may be that which is directly observed but also that which is indirect or implicit. This notion includes a broad spectrum of possibilities—swearing, running, crying, fighting, smiling, choosing, and so on are all included. These are all observable behaviors, but implicit behavior that can only be measured indirectly, such as rationalizing, repressing, considering alternatives, planning, and reclassifying, would also be included. The objective study of cognitive activity is a difficult but important aspect of social learning theory. Principles governing the occurrence of such cognitive activities are not considered different from those that might apply to any observable behavior. [Rotter, Chance, & Phares, 1972, p. 12]

As we can see, the prediction of behavior is a monumental task.

Expectancy. Rotter defines **expectancy** as a cognition or belief about the property of some object(s) or event(s) (Rotter, 1981b, p. 13). Expectancies can vary in magnitude between zero and 100 (from 0% to 100%) and are subject to modification by experience. For example, some people may believe initially that a woman could never be elected president of the United States (0%), but as a result of the influence of the women's liberation movement, stories in the media about the number of women entering politics and being elected, and the nomination of a woman for vice-president, their expectations could change radically and even approach absolute certainty (100%).

There are three kinds of expectancy postulated in social-learning theory, according to Rotter (1981b, p. 4). They are (1) simple cognitions or labeling of stimuli ("I think that is a painting by Picasso"); (2) expectancies for behavior-reinforcement outcomes ("If I wear my three-piece Pierre Cardin suit, my employees will compliment me"); and (3) expectancies for reinforcement-reinforcement sequences ("When I graduate from college, I will become wealthy and respected").

Within social-learning theory, any behavior that has been associated with a reinforcement gives rise to an expectancy. Thus each expectancy is based on past experience (Rotter & Hochreich, 1975, p. 96). According to Rotter, simply knowing how important a goal or reinforcement is to a person is no guarantee that we can predict his behavior. A student may sorely want to obtain an "A" in a history course, but his previous experiences in other courses lead him to believe or expect that he will fail no matter how much effort he expends. It is virtually certain he will not study and will, as a consequence, fail.

Expectancies also vary in their generality; that is, we may acquire generalized expectancies or expectancies specific to a given situation (Rotter & Hochreich, 1975, p. 97). Generalized expectancies operate across a variety of situations. For example, a student may acquire a generalized expectancy for success in her courses. She may have obtained "A"s in a variety of different courses or situations so that she always expects to do well. Another student may have learned a specific expectancy in her academic career—that she is an excellent student in mathematics but horribly inept in literature and philosophy. She then expects to do well only in mathematics courses.

Later in the chapter, we will focus on another generalized expectancy called internal-external control of reinforcement, a construct that has generated a considerable amount of interesting research.

Reinforcement Value. Rotter defines **reinforcement value** as "the degree of preference for any one of a group of reinforcements to occur, if the probabilities of all occurring were equal" (Rotter, Chance, & Phares, 1972, p. 21). In simplest terms, reinforcement value refers to the importance we attach to different activities. For some of us, attending a symphony concert is important; others would find it dreadfully dull. Some of us like to play tennis; others do not. In addition to these differences between people, we can arrange our own activities in order of preference. Given the option, we may attach more importance to reading a novel by Dostoevsky than to playing a game of basketball or riding a bicycle. Like expectancies, the values associated with different reinforcers are based on our past experiences.

Psychological Situation. The fourth major concept utilized in the prediction of behavior is the **psychological situation**—that is, the situation as it is defined from the perspective of the person. In Rotter's view, this concept plays an extremely important part in the determination of behavior. As he points out, traditional theories tend to focus almost exclusively on an "inner core" of personality in which certain motives or traits are considered to control behavior, irrespective of the operation of situational demands (Rotter, Chance, & Phares, 1972, p. 37). For example, a man may be seized periodically by uncontrollable sexual impulses as manifested in his spouting of obscenities in a wide variety of situations. In trait theory, a person may be considered to have a strong "need for aggression" that erupts into fighting, irrespective of the situation. On the other end of the spectrum, approaches such as Skinner's emphasize the importance of situational influences and minimize, at least in research practice, individual differences based on idio-syncratic learning histories. Social-learning theory, in contrast, recognizes the importance of *both* dispositional and situational influences. In other words, it pays attention to the ways in which the unique past experiences of the person, as well as current situational cues, affect behavior. Thus a person may be described as having strong aggressive tendencies based on a learning experience, but she may not act aggressively in a given situation if such behavior is likely to lead to punishment by others.

In general terms, Rotter believes that the complex cues in a given situation arouse in the person expectancies for behavior-reinforcement outcomes and also for reinforcement-reinforcement sequences (Rotter, 1981a, p. 3). Thus, for example, a college student about to give a speech to her interpersonal-communications class might believe that she will do poorly and will therefore receive a low grade from her instructor and ridicule from several of her classmates. As a result, we might expect her to drop the course or to take other action designed to prevent the anticipated humiliating outcome.

Freedom of Movement and Minimal Goal. Two other concepts, freedom of movement and minimal goal, play a lesser but nevertheless important role in Rotter's position.

Freedom of movement is defined as the "mean expectancy of obtaining positive satisfactions as a result of a set of related behaviors directed toward obtaining a group of functionally related reinforcements" (Rotter, Chance, & Phares, 1972, p. 34). For example, students usually acquire general expectancies for how well they will do in various academic courses and situations. Some students have high general expectations for success, others very low ones. Thus we could say that the former students have high freedom of movement, whereas the latter are hindered by low freedom of movement. The second concept, **minimal goal**, is defined as the lowest goal in a con-tinuum of potential reinforcements for some life situation or situations which will be perceived as a satisfaction" (Rotter, 1954, p. 213). In other words, a minimal goal is conceptualized as the dividing point between those rein-forcements that are positively reinforcing and those that are punishing on some dimension. For instance, if we consider course grades on a continuum, one student may find a grade of "B" punishing, whereas another would be happy with it. The first student would be said to have a higher minimal goal than the second.

These concepts can be combined and used in the prediction of behavior, as shown in the following example. A student who is adjusted in academic achievement is probably one who has high freedom of movement in his academic expectations and who does not set exceedingly high minimal goals for himself in that area. He is a person who, on the basis of many successful experiences in a variety of courses, comes to expect to succeed. He is also a person who values such success. At the same time, he does not set his goals for positive reinforcement so high that he is bound to experience disappointment. For example, he does not set a minimal goal of "A" in all his courses. Such indiscriminate goal striving is unrealistic for most people. There is a striking parallel between Adler's conception of the neurotic person who sets fictional goals that cannot be attained and Rotter's conception of the maladjusted person who sets unattainable minimal goals. In a related way, a student would be considered maladjusted if he had low freedom of movement in academic achievement but continued to set high minimal goals for himself. In other words, if on the basis of past experiences he expected to fail in virtually all his courses and yet felt that he must attain all "A"s, he would be considered to be engaging in unproductive behavior. Once again, the similarity between Rotter's low freedom of movement concept and Adler's concept of feelings of inferiority should be apparent. More will be said about the ways in which the major theoretical concepts can be used to help understand abnormal and maladjusted behavior later in the chapter.

The Process of Personality Development

Rotter believes that a person's development hinges largely on the range, diversity, and quality of his or her experiences with other people. Early in life, these important figures are usually, and quite obviously, one's parents. The individual's early goals arise out of certain physiological needs that are then satisfied by the parents or parental substitutes. As a result of their association with need reduction, parents become reinforcing stimuli in their own right. The child comes to rely on them for affection, love, praise, recognition, and other reinforcers. Rotter assumes that **stimulus generalization** occurs and that other people who resemble the parents are perceived and evaluated in the same or similar ways. Once the parents and others (teachers, other adults, clergy) acquire value as conditioned reinforcers, Rotter assumes the child will work to secure their approval and avoid their disapproval, irrespective of whether their behavior toward him or her results in primary drive reduction.

In Rotter's view, language acquisition also plays a critical role in the child's development. Words serve as cues in directing the person's behavior. Parents issue instructions that often help children solve problems in a few trials rather than in the hundreds of trials it would take if they had to perform their actions in trial-and-error fashion. The parents thus direct their children to the relevant cues in given situations and show them how to avoid the irrelevant ones. Parents also use words as verbal reinforcers in statements of recognition, love, rejection, and shame to shape their children's behavior (Rotter, 1954, p. 218). Through these procedures, children learn different expectancies for success and failure in many different situations.

These expectancies are also subject to modification through the use of verbalizations. People can build up or tear down children's expectancies, and the value of their reinforcers for that matter, by directing their attention to new and previously neglected consequences of performing given behaviors. Or people can change their expectancies by analyzing children's previous experiences and showing them how they are responding to the wrong cues and how to rectify the situation (Rotter, 1954, pp. 219–220). Language can be used not only to help them make appropriate discriminations between events but also to increase generalization:

> Since the effect of language is to classify, to categorize, or to abstract similarity in events, it serves, therefore, to determine and enhance the nature of generalization. If an event is symbolized, it will increase generalization to other events that are similarly abstracted. Not only does language determine generalization . . . on the basis of the subject's implicit categorizing, . . . the language of others may be used by the observer as a stimulus to determine, control, or enhance generalization. (Rotter, 1954, p. 220).

Thus the developmental process involves the acquisition and modification of expectancies and reinforcement values through contact with various socialization agents. These socialization agents include not only adult authority figures but also the person's peers (Rotter, 1954, p. 414). In Rotter's opinion, development of individuals is, to a great extent, contingent on the standards, mores, goals, and techniques communicated to them by their classmates as well as by their parents. Next to the home, he believes that the school has the greatest influence on the child's development (Rotter, 1954, p. 416). Healthy or unhealthy behaviors are learned in the home, according to Rotter, and later transfer to the school situation. Characteristics of the home that promote health include parents who encourage the development and maintenance of behavior that leads to acceptance, love, and identification with others. Such behavior is most likely to occur in homes in which the parents themselves show affection and concern for the welfare and development of their offspring. In homes where parents do not provide such reinforcement, the child is unlikely to learn the kinds of behaviors that will permit him or her to adjust to the larger society (Rotter, 1954, pp. 406–407). Such an individual is likely to develop in an antisocial way and show selfish behaviors that produce hostility in others.

In addition to his speculation that neglect or rejection of the child may result in maladjustment, Rotter feels that overindulgence and overprotection can create problems. Under these circumstances, he thinks school life will be a traumatic experience. In contrast to the home, a child may perceive the school as a place where he is unwanted, unloved, and unprotected (Rotter, 1954, p. 418). Generally speaking, the rejected child is likely to enter school with low expectations for success, whereas the overindulged one will likely have expectations that are too high. Both attitudes are unrealistic. According to Rotter, the main importance of the school is to correct these views and help children attain a feeling of security and a realistic set of expectations for success that will serve them well when they assume adult responsibilities (Rotter, 1954, p. 419). To help a child grow into an effective citizen, then, Rotter believes that parents, teachers, and others should be warm, accepting, good-natured, democratic, and consistent in their disciplinary practice.

Techniques of Assessment

Rotter relies on various measurement procedures in his attempts to assess personality. In his early efforts at testing hypotheses derived from social-learning theory, he utilized the experimental method to good advantage. His concern centered on determining whether people learn tasks and perform differently in situations where they perceive reinforcing outcomes as related or unrelated to their behavior—that is, where skill or chance was seen as the controlling factor. After a series of experimental studies, he concluded that there were significant differences in behavior in the two situations. When people perceived the task as controlled by chance, they relied less on their past experiences in guiding their current behavior, learned less, and performed less well than people who perceived the task as skill-determined (Rotter, 1966).

These results were seen as having important implications for traditional learning theory and research. They suggested that reinforcement effects did not have a direct impact on behavior but were mediated by the person's perception of the relationship (or lack of it) between behavior and application of the reinforcer. Later, Rotter and his colleagues developed a personality measure to assess individual differences in perception. We will discuss research studies done with this internal-external control measure later. For now, though, we simply want to note that many of Rotter's studies have utilized the experimental method to secure data to test the validity of hypotheses based on his theoretical formulations.

In addition to this method, Rotter notes the potential usefulness of five major techniques for the clinical measurement of personality: (1) the interview, (2) projective tests, (3) controlled behavioral tests, (4) behavioral observation methods, and (5) the questionnaire (Rotter, 1954, p. 250). There are limitations as well as strengths associated with each of these techniques, and Rotter insists that investigators attempt to account for and try to minimize the weaknesses before utilizing the techniques. The interview is seen by him as a procedure to be used for the assessment of personality traits and for counseling and therapeutic purposes. In social-learning theory, it can be used to assess an individual's need potentials, freedom of movement, and need value (Rotter, 1954, p. 252).

In Rotter's view, projective tests like the Rorschach, Thematic Apperception Test (TAT), and his own Incomplete Sentences Blank can be used to advantage in clinical diagnostic work. He finds the Rorschach of relatively little use in measuring social-learning concepts (Rotter, 1954, p. 289). But since the social-learning position is concerned with the reactions of the person to stimuli such as mother and father, the TAT can be used to advantage. The incomplete-sentences method can also be used to measure freedom of movement. In this technique, people are asked to finish a sentence of which the first word or words are given by an investigator. Responses are assumed to give indications of underlying conflicts that determine expectancy levels for failure in given situations. Examples include sentences beginning with the words "I like," "I suffer," "I wish," "My father," "Sometimes I feel" (Rotter, 1954, pp. 302–304).

Controlled behavioral tests are assessment procedures in which people are placed in actual situations and their behavior is assessed as a reaction to stimulus changes engineered by the investigator (Rotter, 1954, p. 311). For example, if a clinician wanted to know how a client would react to stress, she would not simply ask him to report how he might behave but instead would place him under actual conditions of stress and watch his reactions. Such measures have been used to test hypotheses derived from social-learning theory, most notably in the area of expectancy changes after the experiencing of success or failure. The behavioral observation technique, in contrast to the controlled behavioral test, involves the relatively informal assessment of behavior by observers in natural settings (Rotter, 1954, p. 326). Rotter believes that such a technique should be employed to assess the generality of experimental findings to real-life situations. Rotter also thinks that questionnaires can be employed to test social-learning hypotheses. Rotter's I-E Scale is one such questionnaire, and we turn now to a consideration of this test and some of its personality and behavioral correlates.

Internal-External Control of Reinforcement

One of the key constructs in social-learning theory is called **internal-external control of reinforcement**. According to Rotter, people acquire generalized expectancies to perceive reinforcing events either as dependent on their own behavior or as being beyond their control (Rotter, 1966, p. 1). Internally oriented people tend to believe that reinforcers are subject to their own control and occur as a result of displaying their skills. Externals, in contrast, see little or no connection between their behavior and various reinforcers. Instead, they perceive the occurrence of the reinforcers as being determined by fate, luck, or powerful others. Constructs such as competence, powerlessness, helplessness, hopelessness, mastery, and alienation have all been used by other investigators in psychology and sociology to describe the degree to which people can control important events in their lives. All these constructs are related to a belief in internal-external control, but Rotter's construct has the advantage of being an integral part of a formal theory from which relatively precise predictions can be made.

Although there are a great variety of measures of control orientation for use with children and adults, the **I-E Scale** constructed by Rotter has been used most often by investigators in the area. It is a forced-choice scale consisting of 23 items (see Table 12.1). Scores are obtained by assigning one point for each external alternative endorsed by the subject and summing across all items. Thus scores can range from zero to 23, with higher scores indicating greater externality. Research using the measure is usually done by dividing the distribution of scores at the median or mean, classifying the subjects as either internals or externals, and then correlating these test responses with other personality variables and behavior. This split into two categories is not meant to imply a typology but is done for research convenience. Rotter conceptualized people as being more or less internal or external and not as being either internal or external (Rotter, 1975, p. 57). With this preliminary information in mind, let us turn to an examination of research that has utilized this individual difference construct.

Origins and Development of I-E Orientations

The bulk of the research literature indicates that beliefs in internal control are learned initially in families in which the parents are warm and supportive of children, praise them for their accomplishments, and do not try to exert authoritarian control over their behavior (Crandall, 1973, p. 2). In addition, these parents are consistent in their disciplining of the children. They do not change the rules continually or administer punishments that are much more severe than the offense. Under such warm and supportive conditions, the children learn to accept blame for failure as well as credit for success.

In late childhood, however, the family atmosphere tends to change from one of support and involvement to one of more parental detachment. At this stage, both parents, but especially the mothers, encourage their children to be independent. They do not reward dependency behaviors as often. They also show less involvement and less contact with their offspring (Crandall, 1973, p. 12). According to one prominent researcher, this parental "coolness" may force the child "into more active intercourse with his physical and social environment so that there is more opportunity for him to observe the effect of his own behavior [and] the contingency between his own actions and ensuing events" (Crandall, 1973, p. 13). Studies by Loeb (1975) and by Wichern and Nowicki (1976) provide support for Crandall's contention.

Table 12.1
Examples of Items from Rotter's Internal-External
Scale

1. a. I have often found that what is going to happen will happen (E).
   b. Trusting to fate has never turned out as well for me as making a decision to take a definite course of action (I).
2. a. Becoming a success is a matter of hard work; luck has little or nothing to do with it (I).
   b. Getting a good job depends mainly on being in the right place at the right time (E).
3. a. In the long run people get the respect they deserve in this world (I).
   b. Unfortunately, an individual's worth often passes unrecognized no matter how hard he tries (E).

Adapted from Rotter, 1966, p. 11.

Research has also indicated that children tend to acquire a progressive sense of personal efficacy as they grow older; that is, they become more internal with age (Milgram, 1971). Much research with college students shows that they are generally quite internal in their orientations (Rotter, 1966, p. 15). But what about the **locus-of-control** orientations of adults and the elderly? Are college students more internal than adults of varying ages? Are the elderly more external than college students? The answer to both questions is a tentative no. A study has shown that there is an increasing sense of personal efficacy from college age to adulthood, a stabilized sense of internal control through middle age, and no decrease in internality among the elderly (Ryckman & Malikiosi, 1975). This last finding runs contrary to popular stereotypes of the elderly as helpless and dependent. The study suggests that many of the elderly believe they are personally competent and not at the mercy of authority figures or a capricious environment.

Locus of Control and Performance Effectiveness. Various studies have shown that internals not only believe they have the power to affect their outcomes, but that they actually perform more effectively in both laboratory and academic situations. In academic settings, for example, Findley and Cooper (1983) have found very strong evidence that internality is associated positively with superior performance on a variety of standard achievement tests. Bar-Tal and Bar-Zohar (1977) found also that internality is associated positively with grade-point average.

There are several explanations for these general findings. Internals may outperform externals because they (internals) are more task-oriented, persistent, cognitively active and flexible, and efficient in learning the rules necessary for problem solving. They also have been found to gather more information than externals about their situations in an attempt to cope with and control outcomes. For example, internal inmates in a federal reformatory knew more about the way in which the institution was run and more about the conditions affecting their possible parole than did externals. Another study showed that internals even have more information about critical political events that have strong implications for their well-being than do externals. (See Ryckman, 1979, for a review of the extensive literature on locus of control and task-performance effectiveness.)

Locus of Control and Persuadibility. If internals have more information about their situations and greater problem-solving ability than externals, it should not be surprising that they are more resistant to influence from others. In fact, many of the early studies in the I-E literature reported findings consistent with that view. They found that internals tended to make judgments independently of the demands of others, whereas externals were much more compliant in the same situations (Lefcourt, 1971, pp. 3–4). You should not get the impression, however, that internals always act rationally; some data indicate that some internals are capable of acting quite irrationally under certain circumstances (Ryckman, Rodda, & Sherman, 1972). In circumstances in which they perceive that others are trying to manipulate their behavior, for example, internals tend to reject the requests of these people out of hand and to act in a strongly oppositional manner. Such behavior, of course, may eventually be detrimental to both them and others.

A concrete example may make these points clearer. A professor gives a lecture, and the students react in different ways to her message, depending, at least in part, on their own personality characteristics. An external student may react uncritically and accept whatever information is given, regardless of whether it is accurate. The external may pay more attention to the source and less to the message. The defensively internal student, on the other hand, may reject the information from the professor uncritically; that is, he or she may have learned to reject any statements from authority figures and therefore pays less attention to the message. Thus both internal and external students in this example pay less attention to the message but for different reasons. Both kinds of students also fail to acquire potentially useful information. Of course, other students who are nondefensive weigh information critically and act rationally without being unduly swayed by the source of the message. Future research on the relationship between I-E and conformity will probably provide us with more insight concerning the ways in which these individuals react to influence attempts in various situations.

Internals not only tend to resist influence attempts by others but, when given an opportunity, make more efforts to control the behavior of others (Phares, 1965). They also tend to like people they can easily manipulate and to dislike those they cannot influence (Silverman & Shrauger, 1970).

Some interesting research has shown that internal and external students differ in the number and kinds of romantic heterosexual experiences they have (Dion & Dion, 1973). Internals were found to have proportionally fewer romantic attachments than externals. They also reported experiencing romantic love as less mysterious and volatile than externals. In addition, internals were more strongly opposed to an idealistic view of romantic love than were externals. In comparison with externals, they disagreed more with these statements: (1) there is only one real love for a person; (2) true love lasts forever; and (3) true love leads to almost perfect happiness. But why do internals and externals differ in their orientations toward romantic love? The investigators who conducted the study suggest a number of reasons, all compatible with previous research findings. Romantic love implies that both parties "give themselves up" to their partners; that is, they become vulnerable and pliable to the wishes of the partner. But we have already learned that internals do not like to be influenced by others. In addition, internals are often concerned with manipulating others, so that strong feelings of attraction toward another may not serve their purposes; it is difficult to assume a calculating, manipulative attitude toward someone you love. For these reasons, then, perhaps it was not surprising that many of the internal students did not become as involved in romantic liaisons as externals.

I-E and Attribution of Responsibility

We have painted a general picture of internals as competent, responsible, and independent people who, in comparison to externals, perform more effectively on a variety of skill-determined tasks. Furthermore, it should be clear that a person's willingness to strive for excellence in performance depends on the way in which he or she accounts for success and failure experiences. With only one or two exceptions, a great variety of studies have shown that, unlike externals, internals tend to attribute success to internal factors (ability and effort) rather then to external factors (luck or task difficulty). In other words, internals attribute their success to ability and hard work, whereas externals attribute it to good luck or an easy task. Thus internals experience more pride in their achievements and a greater willingness to persist at tasks than do externals.

Research has also shown that internals attribute their failures to internal factors (a lack of ability and/or little effort), whereas externals blame them on external factors (bad luck or the difficulty of the task). Thus internals experience more shame and guilt than externals when they suffer defeat (Phares, 1976, pp. 113–115). Although extreme and indiscriminate reliance on either internal or external factors to account for one's experiences may be unhealthy, it seems reasonable that an internal-factor accounting system would be necessary if individuals are to attain competence with its attendant feelings of self-worth. It has therefore been proposed that an internal orientation is necessary for adequate social adjustment and functioning.

Externals also tend to devalue tests that they fail, using the old "sour grapes" gambit. Phares found that, after failing intelligence tests that they strongly wanted to pass, externals claimed success on these tests was not that important (Phares, 1971; 1979).

Phares and Lamiell (1974) also found that externals employ defensive strategies *before* task performance as well as after it. These investigators gave internals and externals choices of taking four kinds of intelligence tests. Two of the tests contained built-in rationalizations for subsequent failure (for example, on the task instructions for one test, the experimenter wrote, "Some of the symbols ... on this sheet did not print out very well.... I hope it won't affect your performance too much, but there is always that possibility"). The other two did not contain such rationalizations. Externals, more than internals, chose to take the tests that contained the excuses for failure already built in.

Research has also indicated that internals not only take responsibility for their own actions but also assume that others are responsible for theirs. Externals, in contrast, assume that their behavior and the behavior of others is controlled by outside forces (Phares, 1976, pp. 102–104). Internals are thus more likely, when given the opportunity, to mete out more severe punishment to rule violators in various situations than are externals. Thus they may be seen as being more punitive and less sympathetic than externals in their judgments and behavior toward wrongdoers (Kauffman & Ryckman, 1979).

This judgment about internals is corroborated indirectly by a study in which internal and external college women were asked to evaluate an autobiographical essay allegedly written by a woman applying for admission to a university and then to make a decision about whether to reject her application on the basis of the information in the essay. (Ryckman & Cannon, 1977). A photo of either an attractive or an unattractive woman was attached to the application form. It was predicted that when evaluating an essay of objectively good quality, as determined by ratings from a comparable and independent student sample, internal women would discriminate more against the unattractive person—and they did. They downgraded her essay and indicated a greater willingness to reject her application than one completed by an attractive person.

This prediction was based on a previous finding that people tend to see attractive people as having good personal qualities, whereas unattractive people are perceived as having negative qualities. Since internals tend to see internal factors such as ability and effort as causing a person's behavior, it was assumed they would see the attractive person as having good ability and strong motivation to do well, whereas the unattractive individual would be seen as lazy and having little ability. Thus it was assumed that an objectively good performance by an attractive person would be seen by internals as consistent with their expectations, and there would therefore be no need to downgrade her performance. In contrast, it was assumed that a good performance by an unattractive person would be seen as inconsistent with the internals' orientation. How could a lazy person with little ability perform well? The internals would say she could not, and thus it was assumed that they would downgrade her performance to make her performance fit their expectations. Externals were not expected to downgrade the work of either the attractive or the unattractive performer because they would assume that the outcomes were beyond the performer's control.

To reduce such discriminatory practices, the authors suggested that employers and admissions personnel in various academic, business, and government institutions make their judgments of the person's qualifications, where possible, without requiring a photo with the application. They also recommended that in conducting direct interviews with job applicants, prospective employers become aware of their own biases. This information might be especially enlightening to those internally oriented employers who see themselves as responsible and constructive members of society and who try to act accordingly but may be unaware of their prejudice against the unattractive.

I-E and Physical Health. There is considerable research evidence indicating internally oriented individuals are physically more healthy than externally oriented individuals (Ryckman et al., 1982; Strickland, 1979; Wallston & Wallston, 1981). One major explanation for this reliable finding is based on the early family experiences of internals and externals. Specifically, Lau (1982) has found that internals more than externals were encouraged by their parents when they were children to follow a good diet, to get enough exercise, to brush their teeth properly, and to have regular dental and medical checkups. As a consequence of these early experiences, internals have learned to see themselves as responsible for the maintenance or improvement of their physical health. Thus we would expect to find that internals know more about the conditions that cause poor health and to be more likely to take steps to improve or maintain their health.

Although the data are not completely consistent with these expectations (see Wallston & Wallston, 1982), a number of studies do support these ideas. For example, one early study concerned with the relationship between locus of control and information-seeking in tuberculosis patients showed the internal patients knew more about their particular medical problems and sought more information from their physicians than did external patients. Other research has shown that internals take more precautionary measures to protect their health than do externals. Internally oriented high school students report greater use of seat belts when driving than do externals. They also report going to the dentist for checkups and maintenance more often than externals, even when their teeth or gums do not hurt. Several studies have shown that internals are also more likely than externals to reduce or quit smoking (Strickland, 1978, pp. 1193–1194; Wallston & Wallston, 1982, p. 78). Studies also show that internals have more positive attitudes than externals about physical exercise and cardiovascular fitness (Strickland, 1979, pp. 223–224). Thus an internal locus of control is associated generally with good health, preventive health care, and more adequate coping with illness once it does occur.

As you can see from a consideration of the many research studies with the I-E variable, the composite picture of internals and externals formed by integrating study findings is a complicated and intriguing one. Although internals are more adjusted than externals in some respects, we see that they also have their limitations. Research with the I-E construct has proved highly informative, and there is little doubt that it will continue to be a popular area of investigation for personality psychologists.

Application of the Theory to the Treatment of Psychopathology

For Rotter, psychotherapy is a learning process, so that the same learning principles applied to change the behavior of people in everyday situations can also be utilized to advantage in a therapeutic setting (Rotter, 1954, p. 335). The problems of maladjusted people are seen as originating not in their heads but in their relationships with other people (Rotter & Hochreich, 1975, p. 109). In general, adjusted individuals experience satisfactions growing out of the performance of behaviors that society sees as constructive. Maladjusted people, in contrast, are perpetually dissatisfied with themselves and behave in ways that precipitate punishing responses from the members of society. Furthermore, Rotter believes that maladjusted people are often characterized by low freedom of movement and high need value (Rotter & Hochreich, 1975, p. 106). In his view, such individuals are convinced that they are unable to obtain the gratification they desire. As a result, instead of learning how to achieve their goals, they learn how to avoid or defend themselves against actual or anticipated failure.

The defense mechanisms postulated by Freud are accepted by Rotter and other social-learning theorists but are conceptualized as avoidance or escape behaviors. Projection, for example, involves blaming others for one's own mistakes to avoid anticipated punishment. Rationalization involves the construction of elaborate excuses for one's own inadequate behavior in an effort to stave off punishment. One of the unfortunate results of such maneuvering is that maladjusted people fail to learn new behaviors. They simply continue to gain temporary relief by avoiding the punishment, criticism, failure, or rejection they believe will follow if they attempt to perform behaviors that they doubt will succeed. In the long run, however, such defensive maneuvers have maladjustive consequences.

Maladjusted people not only have low expectations for success, but they also often inappropriately apply their low expectations in one area (say, their work situation) to other areas (say, their home lives), so that they come to perceive themselves as generally worthless. Clinicians have found that maladjusted people also tend to place too much importance on the gratification of one need (Katkovsky, 1968, p. 228). For example, a person may have a strong need to dominate others; that is, she finds it satisfying to be able to influence the behavior of others. Such a person may distort what others say in order to maintain and act in an aggressive manner when it is totally inappropriate (Katkovsky, 1968, p. 228). There is little doubt that such an individual will often be dissatisfied since her need to dominate will bring her into repeated conflicts with others.

Maladjusted individuals tend to engage in behaviors that lead to immediate rewards but are punishing in the long run (Katkovsky, 1968, pp. 229–230). The compulsive gambler finds gambling exciting but usually learns that his behavior has severe negative consequences for him and his family. To obtain money to pursue his passion, he may sell household property, reduce expenditures for food drastically, and even steal from other family members. Maladjusted people not only engage in behavior that others consider undesirable, but often fail to show behaviors that others consider desirable (Katkovsky, 1968, p. 230). Society encourages its members to communicate with one another, for example, and people who fail to do so in a wide variety of situations are considered maladjusted. It is often said that they lack the necessary verbal and social skills.

To change the behavior of such individuals, Rotter believes, it is necessary for therapists to be flexible. Because clients come into the therapeutic setting with different problems based on unique life experiences and motives, the environmental conditions that promote optimal change will vary from person to person. Treatment strategies can include recommendations for changes in the client's job, academic situation, home life, and so forth. For other clients, various behavior therapies, direct or indirect suggestions, or support and reassurance may be called for. All these procedures and others can be used singly or in combination to help clients (Rotter & Hochreich, 1975, p. 109).

In general, Rotter believes that therapy should be an evolving relationship between client and therapist in which clients are helped to discover how their present needs, attitudes, and behaviors developed, which are appropriate or inappropriate for effective living, and what alternatives are available to them. The therapist emphasizes that clients must take responsibility for change, be motivated to change, and be willing to try out new behaviors (Rotter, 1954, p. 353). Change advocated by the therapist may include teaching clients to discriminate between situations in which behaviors are likely to lead to failure and those likely to produce success, helping them lower unrealistically high expectations for punishment, and encouraging them to assess the importance of their goals more critically and appropriately.

To encourage adjustive discrimination between situations, for instance, the therapist may analyze and contrast a client's past life situation with his present situation and show him that his experiences of previous failure are unlikely to transfer into the present. The therapist might, for example, encourage a freshman to minimize past experiences of failure in elementary school and to believe instead that he can and will be successful in college on the basis of outstanding scores on aptitude and ability tests. In this case, the therapist's job is one of teaching the person to differentiate between two situations and to raise his expectations for success on the basis of solid evidence. Some clients may have inordinately high expectations for success that need lowering. We all know or have heard of people who brag about abilities they in fact do not possess. The mediocre student who claims to be brilliant is a pertinent example. The bragging done by such an individual may bring temporary gratification and a bolstering of self-esteem, but the long-range consequences of such behavior may be punishing. Therapy in such a case may center on lowering the person's expectations.

Therapy may also require changes in the importance a person attaches to certain goals. A person who has learned to value winning above everything else because it brought her acceptance and love from her parents may be encouraged to deemphasize the goal. The therapist might point out to her that her indiscriminate attempts to prove herself better than others, even when competing in a game of Ping-Pong with a neighbor, serve only to alienate others. She could be shown, for example, that her feeling of being disliked by everyone stems from indiscriminate pursuit of her goal and that a change in behavior is therefore necessary.

It should be emphasized that Rotter advocates a therapy that focuses not only on the elimination of undesirable and inadequate behaviors but also on the acquisition of desirable ones. The person is trained to learn methods of analyzing problems as a means of finding better solutions and to try out new behaviors. It is not enough, in Rotter's view, for therapists to help clients understand the sources of their problems. They must be shown how to perform new behaviors designed to overcome them (Rotter, 1954, p. 398).

Critical Comments

We now examine the scientific worth of Rotter's theory on the basis of our six criteria.

Comprehensiveness. Rotter's theory has its roots in both the clinical setting and the experimental laboratory. It covers a wide range of phenomena, including parental attitudes and behaviors, academic achievement, defensive behavior, interpersonal trust, social activism, alcoholism, maladjustment, mental retardation, and a host of psychopathological behaviors. As such, it is a theory that is quite comprehensive.

Precision and Testability. Compared to most of the other theories covered in the text, Rotter's is characterized by concepts that are well defined and hypotheses that are capable of being tested.

᙮ *Parsimony.* Rotter's position seems fairly parsimonious, at least in its attempts to account for individual performance phenomena. The picture is unsettled, however, when we consider the theory's treatment of abnormal and therapeutic phenomena. Rotter seems undecided, for example, about whether to retain, modify, or reject some of the psychoanalytic concepts. As a result, it is difficult to assess the parsimony of the position in accounting for abnormal phenomena.

Empirical Validity. Empirical support for the theory is strong. There have been many tests of hypotheses concerned with an understanding of the conditions that facilitate or hinder learning and performance but relatively few tests of hypotheses involving clinical phenomena. Many research tests of Rotter's position have centered on his I-E concept, but unfortunately, work with this concept has generally proceeded independently of the rest of the theory.

᙮ *Heuristic Value.* The theory has stimulated research in various areas, including learning theory, psychopathology, psychotherapy, personality development, and social psychology. Thus it has proved to have good heuristic value.

᙮ *Applied Value.* Rotter's theory has strong applied value. It has been used, for example, by clinical psychologists in their diagnoses of the origins of a variety of deviant behaviors, including alcoholism, depression, anxiety reaction, and shyness. The theory has also proved useful to clinical psychologists in their efforts to devise effective strategies for treating different types of patients. Abramowitz and colleagues (1974), for example, have shown that therapists who use treatment strategies that are congruent with their patients' control expectancies are likely to be more successful in helping their patients than are those therapists who use procedures that are incongruent with their patients' expectancies. Specifically, they found that nondirective therapies work better with internals, while more directive techniques work better with externals.

In the area of physical health, other investigators have found that treatments tailored to patients' control expectancies have proved useful in maximizing weight loss in the obese and in reducing cigarette smoking in smokers. Strickland (1978, 1979) has provided excellent reviews of this research.

Discussion Questions

1. Describe the four basic concepts of Rotter's social-learning theory of personality. Give some personal examples of how the concepts could be combined to predict the behavior of one of your friends.
2. What is a minimal goal? What is your minimal goal for academic grades? Do you

think it is realistic in terms of your abilities and motivation as a student? What is your minimal goal for establishing a friendship with someone?

3. Describe the behavior of a maladjusted person by using the terminology of Rotter's social-learning position.

4. What is meant by internal-external control of reinforcement? How much of your own behavior is controlled by forces beyond your own control? Are you an internal (or an external) in every situation? Is it healthy to be externally oriented in some situations? Which ones?

5. What are some of the determinants of a person's locus-of-control orientation? Are the elderly primarily external in their orientations?

6. Which concepts in Rotter's system bear striking resemblance to ones postulated by Adler?

7. Do you agree with Rotter that it is usually unnecessary to study in great detail the ways in which the person's early childhood experiences are related to his or her current behavior in order to predict such behavior accurately?

8. What is the empirical law of effect? Is a concept of reinforcement always necessary to account for behavior adequately?

9. What are some of the strengths and weaknesses of the social-learning approach to the study of maladjusted behavior?

10. How do you attribute responsibility for your successes and failures in school? Why?

References

Abramowitz, C. V., Abramowitz, S. I., Roback, H. B., & Jackson, C. Differential effectiveness of directive and nondirective group therapies as a function of client internal-external control. *Journal of Consulting and Clinical Psychology*, 1974, *42*, 849–853.

Bar-Tal, D., & Bar-Zohar, Y. The relationship between perception of locus of control and academic achievement. *Contemporary Educational Psychology*, 1977, *2*, 181–199.

Crandall, V. C. Differences in parental antecedents of internal-external control in children and in young adulthood. Unpublished manuscript, Fels Research Institute, 1973.

Dion, K. L., & Dion, K. K. Correlates of romantic love. *Journal of Consulting and Clinical Psychology*, 1973, *41*, 51–56.

Findley, M. J., & Cooper, H. M. Locus of control and academic achievement: A literature review. *Journal of Personality and Social Psychology*, 1983, *44*, 419–427.

Katkovsky, W. Social-learning theory and maladjustment. In L. Gorlow and W. Katkovsky (Eds.), *Readings in the psychology of adjustment* (2nd ed.). New York: McGraw-Hill, 1968.

Kauffman, R. A., & Ryckman, R. M. Effects of locus-of-control, outcome severity, and attitudinal similarity of defendant on attributions of criminal responsibility. *Personality and Social Psychology Bulletin*, 1979 *5*, 340–343.

Lau, R. R. Origins of health locus of control beliefs. *Journal of Personality and Social Psychology*, 1982, *42*, 322–334.

Lefcourt, H. M. *Internal versus external control of reinforcement revisited: Recent developments.* Research Report No. 27. Ontario, Canada: University of Waterloo, 1971.

Loeb, R. C. Concomitants of boys' locus of control examined in parent-child interactions. *Developmental Psychology,* 1975, *11,* 353–358.

Milgram, N. A. Locus of control in negro and white children at four age levels. *Psychological Reports,* 1971, *29,* 459–465.

Mosher, D. L. The influence of Adler on Rotter's social learning theory of personality. *Journal of Individual Psychology,* 1968, *24,* 33–45.

Phares, E. J. Internal-external control as a determinant of amount of social influence exerted. *Journal of Personality and Social Psychology,* 1965, *2,* 642–647.

Phares, E. J. Internal-external control and the reduction of reinforcement value after failure. *Journal of Consulting and Clinical Psychology,* 1971, *37,* 386–390.

Phares, E. J. *Locus of control in personality.* Morristown, N.J.: General Learning Press, 1976.

Phares, E. J. Defensiveness and perceived control. In L. C. Perlmutter and R. A. Monty (Eds.), *Choice and perceived control.* Hillsdale, N.J.: Lawrence Erlbaum Associates, 1979.

Phares, E. J., & Lamiell, J. T. Relationship of internal-external control to defensive preferences. *Journal of Consulting and Clinical Psychology,* 1974, *42,* 872–878.

Rotter, J. B. *Social learning and clinical psychology.* Englewood Cliffs, N.J: Prentice-Hall, 1954.

Rotter, J. B. Generalized expectancies for internal versus external control of reinforcement. *Psychological Monographs,* 1966, *80* (entire No. 609).

Rotter, J. B. Some problems and misconceptions related to the construct of internal versus external control of reinforcement. *Journal of Consulting and Clinical Psychology,* 1975, *43,* 56–67.

Rotter, J. B. The psychological situation in social learning theory. In D. Magnusson (Ed.), *The situation: An interactional perspective.* Hillsdale, N.J.: Lawrence Erlbaum Associates, 1981a.

Rotter, J. B. Social learning theory. In N. T. Feather (Ed.), *Expectations and actions: Expectancy-value models in psychology.* Hillsdale, N.J.: Lawrence Erlbaum Associates, 1981b.

Rotter, J. B., Chance, J. E., & Phares, E. J. *Applications of social learning theory of personality.* New York: Holt, Rinehart & Winston, 1972.

Rotter, J. B., & Hochreich, D. J. *Personality.* Glenview, Ill.: Scott, Foresman, 1975.

Ryckman, R. M. Perceived locus of control and task performance. In L. C. Perlmutter & R. A. Monty (Eds.), *Choice and perceived control.* Hillsdale, N.J.: Lawrence Erlbaum Associates, 1979.

Ryckman, R. M., & Cannon, D. W. Task evaluation as a function of the performer's physical attractiveness, quality of the performance, and the evaluator's locus of control orientation. Paper presented at the annual meeting of the Eastern Psychological Association, Boston, April 1977.

Ryckman, R. M., & Malikiosi, M. X. Relationship between locus of control and chronological age. *Psychological Reports,* 1975, *36,* 655–658.

Ryckman, R. M., Robbins, M. A., Thornton, B., & Cantrell, P. Development and validation of a physical self-efficacy scale. *Journal of Personality and Social Psychology,* 1982, *42,* 891–900.

Ryckman, R. M., Rodda, W. C., & Sherman, M. F. Locus of control and expertise relevance as determinants of changes in opinion about student activism. *Journal of Social Psychology,* 1972, *88,* 107–114.

Silverman, R. E., & Shrauger, J. S. Locus of control and correlates of attraction toward others. Paper presented at the annual meeting of the Eastern Psychological Association, Atlantic City, April 1970.

Strickland, B. R. Internal-external expectancies and health-related behaviors. *Journal of Consulting and Clinical Psychology*, 1978, 46, 1192–1211.

Strickland, B. R. Internal-external expectancies and cardiovascular functioning. In L. C. Perlmutter & R. A. Monty (Eds.), *Choice and perceived control*. Hillsdale, N.J.: Lawrence Erlbaum Associates, 1979.

Wallston, K. A., & Wallston, B. S., Health locus of control scales. In H. Lefcourt (Ed.), *Research with the locus of control construct*, Vol. 1. New York: Academic Press, 1981.

Wallston, K. A., & Wallston, B. S. Who is responsible for your health?: The construct of health locus of control. In G. Sanders and J. Suls (Eds.), *Social psychology of health and illness*. Hillsdale, N.J.: Lawrence Erlbaum Associates, 1982.

Wichern, F. & Nowicki, S. Jr. Independence training practices and locus of control orientation in children and adolescents. *Developmental Psychology*, 1976, 12, 77.

Suggested Readings

Lefcourt, H. M. *Locus of control: Current trends in theory and research*. Hillsdale, N.J.: Lawrence Erlbaum Associates, 1976.

Phares, E. J. *Locus of control in personality*. Morristown, N.J.: General Learning Press, 1976.

Rotter, J. B. *Social learning and clinical psychology*. Englewood Cliffs, N.J.: Prentice-Hall, 1954.

Rotter, J. B. Generalized expectancies for internal versus external control of reinforcement. *Psychological Monographs*. 1966, 80 (entire No. 609).

Rotter, J. B., Chance, J., & Phares, E. J. (Eds.). *Application of a Social learning theory of personality*. New York: Holt, Rinehart & Winston, 1972.

Glossary

Behavior potential Possibility that a particular behavior will occur as a function of the person's unique expectancies and the perceived value of the reinforcer to be gained for showing the behavior in a given situation.

Expectancy A cognition or belief held with a degree of certainty about the property of some object or event.

Field theory Theory that maintains that behavior is determined by the complex interplay between cognitive and environmental variables.

Freedom of movement In Rotter's theory, high freedom of movement refers to a person's expectancy that many of his or her behaviors will lead to success; low freedom of movement refers to his or her expectancy that behavior will be unsuccessful.

I-E Scale Test designed by Rotter to measure the person's belief that forces are or are not beyond his or her control. Internals (I's) are people who believe that events are under their own control; externals (E's) are people who believe that outcomes are controlled by outside forces such as luck, fate, God, or powerful others.

Internal-external control of reinforcement Term used by Rotter to refer to people's beliefs that their behavior is determined by themselves (internal control) or by outside factors (external control).

Locus of control Term used by Rotter to refer to people's beliefs about the location of controlling forces in their lives.

Minimal goal Dividing point between those reinforcers that produce feelings of satisfaction and those that produce dissatisfaction.

Psychological situation In Rotter's theory, the meaning of the situation as it is defined by the person.

Reinforcement value Importance of a given reinforcer to an individual in relation to other reinforcers if the possibilities for the attainment of all of them are equal.

Stimulus generalization Responses made by a person in the presence of an original stimulus come to be made in the presence of other stimuli that resemble the original one.

CHAPTER 13

Bandura's Social Learning Theory

Biographical Sketch

Albert Bandura was born on December 4, 1925, to a family of wheat farmers of Polish heritage. He grew up in the small town of Mundare in Alberta, Canada, and attended a high school that had only two teachers and 20 students. He received his B.A. degree from the University of British Columbia in 1949 and then earned an M.A. and Ph.D. in psychology from the University of Iowa in 1951 and 1952, respectively. After receiving his doctorate, he served a year's clinical internship at the Wichita Guidance Center and then accepted a position in the department of psychology at Stanford University, where he has remained ever since. He became a full professor in 1964. In 1974, he was awarded an endowed chair, the David Starr Jordan Professor of Social Science in Psychology.

During his tenure at Stanford, Bandura has been actively engaged in the development of a social-learning approach to the understanding of human behavior. He has also been a highly productive scholar, publishing several influential books and countless research articles in scientific journals. His early books, *Adolescent Aggression* (1959) and *Social Learning and Personality Development* (1963), were written in collaboration with Richard H. Walters. His *Principles of Behavior Modification* (1969) is an extensive review and summary of the the social-psychological principles that govern behavior. In 1971, he published a module entitled *Social Learning Theory*, an abbreviated treatment of these principles. In *Aggression* (1973), a review of current theory and research into the determinants of aggressive behavior, he shows how research on this important topic can help us understand the origins of such behavior, which is almost always harmful to us and others, and gives an exposition of the kinds of variables responsible for the reduction and elimination of the behavior. In his most recent book, *Social Learning Theory* (1977b), he has presented a concise overview of recent theoretical and research developments in his theory.

In recognition of his contributions to psychology, Bandura received the Distinguished Scientist Award in 1972 from the American Psychological Association and the Distinguished Scientific Achievement Award from the California Psychological Association in 1973. He was elected president of the American Psychological Association in 1974. He was also elected a fellow of the American Academy of Arts and Sciences.

Basic Concepts and Principles

Assumptions of the Social Learning Approach

According to Bandura, behavior is not caused solely by either inner forces or environmental influences. Bandura believes, like Rotter, that behavior occurs as a result of a complex interplay between inner processes and environmental influences (Bandura, 1971, p. 2). These internal processes are based largely on the previous experiences of the individual and are conceptualized as measurable and manipulable covert events. As he puts it, "These mediating events are extensively controlled by external stimulus events and in turn regulate overt responsiveness" (Bandura, 1969, p. 10). Unlike Skinner, who acknowledges that stimulus-response covariations are mediated by internal events but proceeds to neglect them in favor of causal explanations couched in terms of external manipulable events, Bandura places special emphasis on the role of the cognitive determinants of behavior (Bandura, 1969, p. 38). Thus he does not see cognitive events as mere epiphenomena, as does Skinner, but rather as actual causes of behavior. His theory analyzes behavior on the basis of **reciprocal determinism.** That is, Bandura believes that cognitive and environmental events affect each other. People do not simply react to environmental events. Instead they actively create their own environments and act to change them. Cognitive events determine which environmental events will be perceived and how they will be interpreted, organized, and acted on (Bandura, 1978, p. 345).

According to Bandura, we typically represent external events symbolically and later use both **verbal** and **imaginal representations** to guide our behavior. We also solve problems symbolically without having to resort to actual, overt trial-and-error behavior, and we foresee the probable consequences of our behavior and modify our actions accordingly. Thus our higher mental processes allow us to perform both insightful and foresightful behavior (Bandura, 1971, pp. 2–3).

The fact that Bandura places such emphasis on cognitive processes in his analysis of behavior should not mislead us—that is, cause us to think he ignores the effects of reinforcement. On the contrary, the reinforcement construct plays a major role in his theory, but a role that is compatible with a cognitive orientation, one that goes beyond the view offered by many traditional learning theorists. Skinner, for example, focuses on the changes in behavior that occur as a result of our direct experiences with the rewarding and punishing consequences of our actions. Responses that prove successful tend to be repeated; those that are punished tend to be inhibited. Bandura, in contrast, believes that reinforcers and punishers do not provide automatic strengthening or weakening of behavior. In addition, he thinks that reinforcement does not fully account for the ways in which our behavior is acquired, maintained, or altered (Bandura, 1971, p. 3). In his view, most of our behavior is not controlled by immediate external reinforcement. As a result of earlier experiences, we tend to expect that certain kinds of behavior will have effects we desire, that others will produce unwanted outcomes, and that still others will have little significant impact. Our behavior is therefore regulated to a large extent by **anticipated outcomes** (Bandura, 1971, p. 3). For example, we do not wait until we have a car accident to buy insurance. Instead, we rely on information from others about the potentially disastrous consequences of not owning insurance in making our decision to purchase it. We do not wait until we are caught in a blinding snowstorm to decide what to wear in extremely cold weather. We can imagine the consequences of being poorly prepared and take the proper precautionary steps. In countless ways, we make decisions based on the anticipation of consequences. This notion is similar to one espoused by Rotter; however, Rotter calls it expectancy rather than anticipation.

Bandura also maintains that behavior can be acquired without the administration of **external reinforcement**. We learn much of the behavior we eventually display through the influence of example: we simply watch what others do and then repeat their actions. Technically, we are also said to have acquired the behavior through **observational learning.** In Bandura's opinion, modeling figures prominently in our lives for several reasons. The environment is loaded with potentially lethal consequences, making trial-and-error behavior too costly. We do not rely on trial and error or direct experience to teach children to swim, people to drive automobiles, or pilots to fly planes. Some explanation and instruction must be provided before lessons can begin. Further, it would be too cumbersome to try to socialize people by selective reinforcement of their activities. Imagine trying to teach children language and the many rules and customs of the culture this way. The acquisition process can be shortened considerably by providing us with the appropriate models (Bandura, 1971, p. 5). Although early learning theorists tended to neglect the role of observational learning in their attempts to understand human behavior, Bandura and other proponents of the social learning approach have rectified this shortcoming and shed much more light on the ways in which we acquire, maintain, and modify our behavior through emulation of models.

Modeling Theory

At first glance, the modeling process seems simple and straightforward. We have an observer and a model, and the primary question is whether the observer will imitate the actions of the model. But the answer is far from simple because it depends on the operation of a host of factors, among them the personality characteristics of the observer. For example, the sex of the observer may play a part in determining whether the model's behavior will be followed. In addition, the sex of the model may influence the behavior of male and female observers. An early study by Bandura and his colleagues showed, for instance, that boys tended to show more aggressive behavior than girls after watching a male model who was aggressive than after watching a female model, whereas girls tended to imitate the aggressive actions of a female model more often than those of a male model (Bandura, Ross, & Ross, 1963b). It is debatable whether this study could be replicated today because of changes in the status of women during the past decade or so, but that issue should not obscure the general principle: people do learn sex-linked behaviors that influence the extent to which they will imitate the actions of others. Other research has shown that people who lack self-esteem or are incompetent, as well as those who have been rewarded in the past for imitative behavior, are likely to follow the behavior of a successful model (Bandura & Walters, 1963, p. 85).

Although it is true that certain characteristics and prior experiences affect observers' imitative behavior, there is also ample evidence that the characteristics of the model or models play a significant role. Observers imitate the behavior of a competent model more rapidly than that of an incompetent one (Rosenbaum & Tucker, 1952). People tend to be more strongly influenced by models who are similar to them in personal background and physical appearance (Rosenkrans, 1967). Observers also tend to learn more of the behaviors of models when the models are highly nurturant or rewarding and when they have control over the future resources of the observers (Grusec & Mischel, 1966).

Research indicates that rewards and punishments associated with the behavior of models as well as their personal characteristics can affect the imitative behavior of observers. We learn by observing the behavior of others and the occasions on which they are reinforced for their actions, and we alter our behavior accordingly. Such **vicarious reinforcement** has a special impact on our behavior, as the following study suggests. In this investigation, Bandura exposed nursery school children to a five-minute film on a television console showing an adult model behaving aggressively toward a large plastic doll:

> *The film began with a scene in which a model walked up to an adult-size plastic Bobo doll and ordered him to clear the way. After glaring for a moment at the noncompliant antagonist, the model exhibited four novel aggressive responses each accompanied by a distinctive verbalization.*
>
> *First, the model laid the Bobo doll on its side, sat on it, and punched it in the nose while remarking, "Pow, right on the nose, boom, boom." The model then raised the doll and pommelled it on the head with a mallet. Each response was followed by the verbalization, "Sockeroo ... stay down." Following the mallet aggression, the model kicked the doll about the room, and these responses were interspersed with the comment, "Fly away." Finally, the model threw rubber balls at the Bobo doll, each strike punctuated with "Bang." This sequence of physically and verbally aggressive behavior was repeated twice. [Bandura, 1965, pp. 590–591]*

The children in the control condition simply saw this film and observed no consequences to the model for his aggressive actions. Other children, however, saw a film sequence in which the model was rewarded or punished for his behavior. In the reward condition, a second adult praised the aggressive model for his behavior and rewarded him with soda pop and candy. In the punishment condition, the second adult spoke disparagingly to the aggressive model, accusing him of being a coward and a bully. The punishing adult also spanked the model with a rolled-up newspaper and threatened him with a beating if he was caught being aggressive again.

The independent variable in this study was the nature of the reinforcement administered to the model for aggressive actions. The dependent measure was the amount of aggression exhibited by the children in the three conditions when they were given an opportunity to display the behavior they had seen modeled. The children were escorted to a separate room that contained a Bobo doll, three balls, a mallet, and a pegboard, as well as an assortment of other toys. A wide variety of toys was presented so that the children had full opportunity to engage in either imitative or nonimitative behaviors. The experimenter then left the room, presumably to fetch other toys, and the children were left alone to play. Observers then recorded the children's responses after watching their behavior through a one-way mirror. As expected, the children exposed to the model who had been punished for his aggression showed significantly less aggression in the free-play sit-uation than the children who observed the rewarded model or the one who had incurred no consequences for his behavior. Thus the first phase of this study showed clearly that the differential reinforcements administered to a model can indeed have a profound impact on the performance of observers.

But a question with practical social implications still remained. Although we know that the children in the various reinforcement conditions *per-formed* differently, did they all actually *acquire* the model's behavior? In other words, is it possible that all the children learned the model's behavior but that only those who saw him rewarded or go unpunished decided to imitate him? In the second phase of the study, Bandura showed that this was the case. After their performances in the first phase were measured, all the children were offered attractive prizes contingent on their reproducing the model's aggressive responses. The introduction of these incentives com-pletely washed out the previously observed differences in performance, revealing that an equivalent amount of learning had taken place in the model-rewarded, model-punished, and no-consequences conditions. Thus the study suggests that people may learn a variety of behaviors but actively decide to perform or not to perform them depending on their estimates of rewards for performing them.

Why is this acquisition-performance distinction so important? Bandura suggests it is because it helps counter the arguments of critics who maintain that showing crime in the mass media is not harmful to young observers because the criminal is always punished for wrongdoing. These results show that punishment of the model (the criminal) may not prevent the acquisition of immoral and illegal behavior. It may eventually surface under the appro-priate circumstances—for example, under conditions in which peers reward a person for such behavior. The conclusion is that such activities should not be presented in the media because they may have potentially harmful effects.

Bandura has conducted many other studies showing further how mod-eling principles and research can be effectively applied to help us better understand the major social problem of violence in the media and its harm-ful effects on viewers. We now review his theorizing and some illustrative research in this important area.

Violence in the Mass Media and Imitative Behavior. As virtually all of us recognize, violence and aggressive acts permeate our society. We read in the newspapers every day about inhumane actions on the local, national, and international levels. We cannot help but notice the violence in the cartoons children watch on television. In the evenings, we watch the news and listen as commentators document for us the latest "kill counts" of faceless people who live in obscure foreign lands where political factions vie for power. A short time later, we are "treated" to law-and-order shows in which the good guys and bad guys resolve their problems by systematically blowing holes in one another with a wide assortment of weapons. Many of the films we watch provide the same gruesome cataloging of aggression. The old John Wayne shoot-'em-ups, though laden with aggression, are tame fare indeed in comparison to the films shown today.

It may be relatively easy to grant that we are exposed to a steady diet of violence in the media, but many people claim that such exposure does not lead inevitably to aggression. Further, they maintain that when such exposure does have an impact on viewers, the impact is minimal and relatively innocuous. In contrast, Bandura believes that media portrayal of violence can have harmful effects on our behavior and the behavior of others. He acknowledges that the portrayal of violence in the media is neither a sufficient nor a necessary cause of aggression but maintains vigorously that this does not preclude the possibility that such exposure can, under the right circumstances, facilitate aggression (Bandura, 1973, p. 267). In reply to the argument that the general impact of media violence on people is minor, Bandura maintains that such a contention flies in the face of the evidence: "The same stimulus can have weak or powerful effects for different individuals and even for the same individual on different occasions, depending on the presence of other aggression inducements" (Bandura, 1973, p. 267).

Another argument used by critics is that exposure to violence affects only disturbed individuals. Bandura counters by pointing out research that shows that models can get so-called normal people to aggress against others under the right circumstances. The Milgram study cited in Chapter 1 showed quite conclusively that many ordinary people are willing to act in violent ways under strong prompting from authority figures. By countering these and other arguments with an impressive mass of research evidence, Bandura has tried to make all of us aware of the potential danger involved in the unabated portrayal of violence in the media. Let us examine some of these findings to see how both personal and situational variables can act to facilitate or inhibit aggressive behavior.

Research on Modeling and Aggression

We have already learned that observers who watch models being punished for their actions tend not to repeat those actions, whereas observers who see models rewarded for certain behaviors tend to repeat them. We have also seen that even though observers tend not to perform the actions of punished models, they have still learned the disapproved behaviors. Research has also shown that observers will imitate the aggressive behavior of filmed as well as live models.

Another study has shown that even though young observers reported they disliked a model who had been rewarded for aggression, they still imitated him and reported wanting to be like him. It seems as though they knew aggression was wrong but also believed that it was fun. This finding suggested to the investigators an analogous situation in many television programs in which the bad guy is rewarded throughout an episode for his wrongdoing and punished only at the very end of the program (Bandura, Ross & Ross, 1963a). The viewers may know he is guilty of wrongdoing and has been punished for it, but they may, nevertheless, admire him for performing exciting and rewarding feats they themselves would love to perform. In other words, all the positive reinforcement he has received for his actions may easily override and outweigh the punishment he finally receives. Even if he suffers the ultimate punishment in the end, they may conclude that it was worth it since he had a "helluva good time along the way." In many programs and films, the "hero" may have only a fine imposed on him for his crimes. We can readily imagine the lessons being learned by young and naive viewers.

There is also a serious question about the advisability of using violence to punish wrongdoers. Although it is true that witnessing such punishment will indeed, at least temporarily, inhibit imitative behavior, we have already seen that viewers may learn the behavior anyway and show it under more favorable circumstances. More important, it gives viewers the impression that the use of violence is both justifiable and a ready solution for problems. It hinders their consideration of alternative nonviolent strategies. An experiment by Berkowitz has indicated that when people view acts of violence that seem justified, their inhibitions are lowered and aggressive responding is facilitated. If, on the other hand, they witness violence they consider inappropriate, their aggressive responding is inhibited (Berkowitz, 1962). A more recent study shows that similar results are obtained irrespective of whether the filmed violence represents real or fictional events (Meyer, 1972).

In that study, a group of students was divided into a subject group and a control group, and each subject was paired with a partner, a confederate of the experimenter. The subjects were individually introduced to an experimenter who informed each of them that the purpose of the study was to see how students react to grading another student's work. The subjects were also informed that grading would be by means of electric shocks to the student whose paper was being graded. That is, the grading scale ranged from one to ten shocks, and shocks were to be administered on the basis of how well the student performed on the task, according to the subject's evaluation: fewer shocks indicated a good performance; more shocks, a poor performance. Each subject was then asked to write an essay on the importance of obtaining a college education, and the composition was graded by the subject's partner. All subjects were then given eight shocks, regardless of what they wrote; naturally, this angered them. Under the pretext of giving their partners enough time to write their essays, all the subjects then were asked to participate in a second experiment in which they would see different film people react to news stories. Subjects were randomly assigned to eight different experimental conditions: (1) a real-violence segment, (2) an unjustified real-violence segment, (3) a justified real-violence segment, (4) a fictional-violence segment, (5) an unjustified fictional-violence segment, (6) a justified fictional-violence segment, (7) a nonviolent film, and (8) a control condition in which subjects were not exposed to a film.

The real-violence segment was two and a half minutes taken from the "CBS Evening News with Walter Cronkite." It depicted South Vietnamese soldiers on patrol who encounter the enemy and later execute a North Vietnamese prisoner by knifing him in the chest. Some subjects saw this film and heard a voice track that justified the execution by saying that the enemy soldier had previously killed innocent women and children. Other subjects saw the same film but heard a voice track that said the killing was unjustified because the enemy soldier was technically a prisoner of war and should have been turned over to South Vietnamese authorities. The fictional piece was a segment from the movie *From Here to Eternity* in which two soldiers engage in a knife fight and one of them stabs the other to death. In one condition, subjects heard a sound track that said the victim's punishment was justified; in another, the sound track informed subjects that the attack was unjustified. Still other subjects saw both films without a voice track. Other subjects were exposed either to a nonviolent film showing a cowboy breaking in a wild horse or to no film at all.

Following this part of the experiment, all subjects were given an opportunity to grade the essays of their partners. The results are depicted graphically in Figure 13.1. As you can see, subjects who viewed the films in which violence was justified showed more aggression toward their partners than those who saw violent actions that were unjustified. You might have also noted that levels of aggression in the control conditions of the real and fictional segments without the soundtracks differed, although such differences were not expected. The author of the study checked and found that these differences were obtained because the subjects seeing the fictional violence perceived the violence as justified despite the lack of a voice track saying that the attack was justified. Subjects who saw the real-violence segment without a voice track saying that the attack was unjustified perceived the violence as unjustified. In general, though, the results provided confirmation of the investigator's predictions. These findings suggest that typical film and television presentations in which the hero legitimately annihilates the villain by violent means may actually lead to an increase in aggressive behavior among viewers. The motto of such angry viewers may well be "Give it to him, he deserves it!" This primitive "eye for an eye and tooth for a tooth" philosophy, which still governs the behavior of many people, seems unfortunately to add to the problem of aggression in our culture.

Thus a number of factors, both personal and situational, can serve to instigate and facilitate aggressive effects. In addition to these variables, research has shown that viewers are more apt to behave aggressively if they identify with the victor, as in the case of moviegoers who imagine themselves to be the winners of fights in the films (Turner & Berkowitz, 1972). Observers are also more apt to aggress if they find themselves in the presence of stimuli

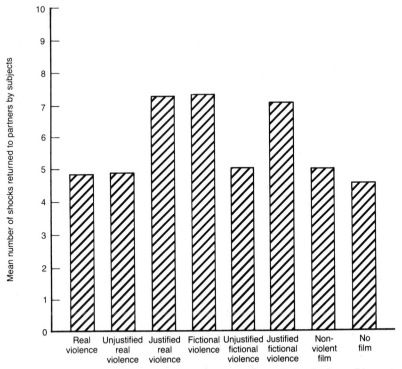

Figure 13.1 Comparisons of the average number of shocks by subjects to partners in the unjustified and justified real and fictional filmed violence conditions. Adapted from Meyer, 1972, p. 26.

previously associated with violence—for example, in the presence of guns and knives (Berkowitz & LePage, 1967).

Controlling Media Violence

If we grant the possibility that media violence can have harmful effects on viewers under the appropriate circumstances, what steps can people take to modify and control the showing of aggressive behavior? Bandura (1973, pp. 276–281) suggests a number of possible remedies. One popular but not very effective procedure, according to him, involves appeals by members of the public to government agencies to control the commercial marketing of violence. This procedure is ineffective because the Constitution guarantees free communication and restricts the government's tampering with program content. In addition, Bandura argues that we as a people have a strong tradition of opposing government control over what we watch. Some members of the broadcasting industry cater to our concerns and fear of government regulation and censorship by likening such controls to practices used in military dictatorships. Yet, as Bandura points out, most countries have adopted some regulations without jeopardizing their democratic institutions. He suggests that perhaps eventually the public will gain some control over program content through concerted legal action.

A second step that can and has been taken is to have members of the public protest loudly and strongly to government officials about the amount of violence shown in the media. Although officials cannot ignore such protests, Bandura feels they are relatively ineffective because the congressional committees formed to deal with the protests usually only issue threats to the broadcasting industry to stop their unsavory practices and do not follow through to see that the industry complies. A third procedure is to allow broadcasters to regulate themselves. According to Bandura, this method is unworkable because no matter how well-intentioned the media people are, content is dictated by profit. A fourth procedure is to create a public violence-monitoring system. It would be funded by private sources and would exercise control by publicized assessment of violence levels in the media. Publication of scientific surveys on this topic could be disseminated in a variety of sources, including TV guides, popular magazines, PTA publications, and newspapers. Bandura feels this approach might be effective because media advertisers are conscious of their public images and would act to change policies detrimental to their companies and stockholders.

A fifth procedure suggested by Bandura involves rewarding members of the media for desirable practices rather than focusing solely on the curtailment of undesirable practices. Creating shows that are interesting, informative, and nonviolent would probably lead to greater progress than simply condemning shows that reek with violence. One successful example is in the area of children's programming. "Sesame Street," which was designed with the help of psychologists, is informative as well as entertaining and has demonstrated that it can attract large audiences of children. It does not rely on violence, as do many of the morning cartoon shows, yet it has proved successful.

Bandura also suggests that parents, on a personal level, model nonaggressive behavior for their children and reward nonviolent behavior. In addition, they should try to limit their children's exposure to violence in the media by monitoring the content of programs in advance. Although these efforts may serve to curtail violence to some extent, Bandura does not delude himself that his recommendations would eliminate the problem. Yet, he believes that we must begin.

Like so many other problems confronting man, there is no single grand design for lowering the level of destructiveness within a society. It requires both individual corrective effort and group action aimed at changing the practices of social systems. Since aggression is not an inevitable or unchangeable aspect of man but a product of aggression-promoting conditions oper-

ating within a society, man has the power to reduce his level of aggressiveness. Whether this capability is used wisely or destructively is another matter. [Bandura, 1973, p. 323]

Let us now consider the ways in which modeling principles have been applied to behavioral problems other than aggression.

Modeling as a Therapeutic Technique. Modeling has been employed successfully in the treatment of language deficiencies in autistic children (Lovaas, 1967, pp. 108–159). Such children are typically not very responsive to environmental influences; the therapist must first gain their attention before employing modeling procedures. She accomplishes this goal by sitting directly in front of them so that they cannot ignore her. She also rewards them for maintaining eye contact and physically restrains any effort to move away from her. Once she has established attentional control, the therapist proceeds to model sounds, words, and phrases of speech and to administer rewards for appropriate responding. Under such training procedures, it has been possible to develop some language skills in autistic children. Modeling has also been used to increase communication skills in asocial psychiatric patients (Gutride, Goldstein, & Hunter, 1973).

Modeling has been used to reduce a variety of fears in children. In one particularly interesting study, two investigators showed that modeling procedures could be used to eliminate avoidance behaviors through observation of modeled approach responses (Bandura & Menlove, 1968). In more concrete language, the investigators were able to eliminate a fear of dogs in certain children by having them watch another person approach, pet, and handle the animals without being bitten. The study was conducted in the following way. A standardized test of avoidance behavior was administered to a group of nursery school children in order to identify those who were fearful of dogs. The test consisted of a graded series of 14 tasks in which the children were required to participate in increasingly intimate interactions with a dog. Some of these tasks included walking up to a playpen containing a dog and looking down at it, touching and petting it, opening the enclosure, walking the dog, and eventually getting into the playpen with it and petting it. Following the identification procedure, the dog-phobic children were assigned randomly to one of three experimental treatment conditions. In one condition, children observed a single model displaying progressively bolder approach responses to a cocker spaniel. In a second, multiple-model condition, other children observed the sequence of events just described and in addition watched other models of various ages playing with a wide variety of dogs, both small and large. In the control condition, still other children were shown movies of Disneyland and Marineland but no modeled interactions with dogs. After these procedures, all the children were again tested for their fear of dogs via a readministration of the standardized test used initially. They were given the test a third time approximately one month after the posttest in order to determine the stability of the modeling effects. The results showed clearly that the modeling procedures were instrumental in reducing and sustaining a reduction in the children's fears. These findings are shown graphically in Figure 13.2. Similar modeling procedures were used to reduce fear of snakes in adolescents and adults (Bandura, Blanchard, & Ritter, 1969).

Research has shown that high test-anxious college students tend to perform poorly because they spend much of their time paying attention to irrelevant cues. For example, such students tend to be self-centered and overly concerned with questions about their intellectual competence and the reaction of others to their performances. A recent investigation was conducted to determine whether disclosures by models about their own anxieties in evaluation situations and the strategies they had devised to cope with these interfering cues could improve the task performances of the highly anxious students (Sarason, 1975). All study participants filled out a personality questionnaire to determine their characteristic levels of test anxiety. Then groups of subjects who were classified as either high or low test-anxious were exposed to a variety of models. In one condition, they were

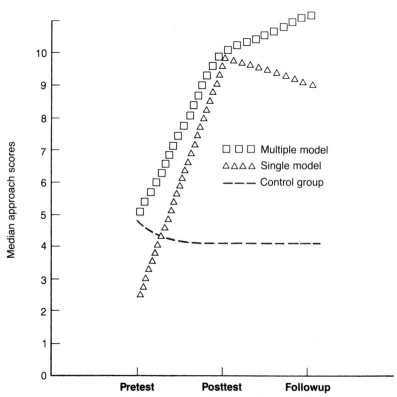

Figure 13.2 Median approach scores obtained by children under the various conditions of the experiment. Adapted from Bandura and Menlove, 1968, p. 102.

exposed to an anxious coping model who mentioned that she became anxious during testing situations. She also mentioned that she attempted to cope with her anxiety by (1) reminding herself periodically to stop thinking about herself and to concentrate on the task; (2) thinking about interesting aspects of the task; (3) not allowing herself to get flustered by errors; and (4) forcing herself not to think about the reactions of other people. In a noncoping anxious-model condition, the model simply mentioned that she became very anxious during testing, had difficulty in concentrating on the task, and was continually worried about what others would think of her if she failed. In a third condition, a neutral model did not mention testing or grading and talked instead about activities, programs, and issues on the campus.

All subjects then performed a task that involved learning a series of nonsense syllables. As expected, the model who not only mentioned that testing situations made her anxious but provided information on how to cope with her anxiety had the greatest positive impact on the high test-anxious students. Apparently the self-disclosures provided the subjects with modeled information about ways to improve their performances, and they utilized it. Figure 13.3 provides a graphic illustration of these results.

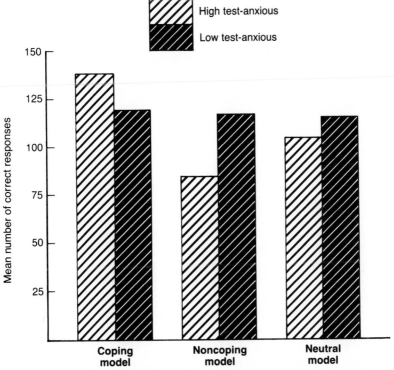

Figure 13.3 Mean number of correct responses on serial learning task for low and high test-anxious students under the different modeling conditions. Adapted from Sarason, 1975, p. 150.

The results of all these studies and countless others demonstrate quite conclusively the positive impact that modeling can have in changing undesirable behavior. Modeling is thus a viable alternative to traditional psychodynamic approaches that seek to give people insights into their behavior through protracted and costly analysis but provide little guidance as to how they might take specific courses of action to help themselves. Its continued usage as an aid in therapeutic settings seems assured.

The Process of Personality Development

For Bandura, social-learning experiences play a crucial role in the development and modification of each person's behavior. New behaviors are acquired as the individual watches the behavior of his or her caretakers. Imitation of the behaviors of parents often meets with reward but sometimes with punishment. Rewarded behavior tends to be repeated and, when performed in the presence of other people, is reinforced positively. As a result, children learn at an early age to match the behavior of successful models. They also learn to avoid imitating the behavior of unsuccessful ones. Unfortunately, the acquisition of complex forms of behavior is not always so simple and direct. Children are often exposed to multiple models who present behaviors that conflict with one another. One parent might reward them for speaking in the presence of guests, for example, whereas the other might punish them for doing so. Even when both parents are in agreement, other social agents such as teachers may disagree and communicate that information to the children. Peers might try to indoctrinate the children in still other ways. Thus the reinforcers for given behaviors are not always applied consistently.

Complicating the picture still more is the fact that behavior is not always imitated accurately or completely and must be shaped by the socializing agents through the application of the successive approximation principles pioneered by Skinner. The establishment of proper table manners in children provides a clear example of the necessity of applying reinforcers in a subtle manner to a variety of behaviors that initially bear little resemblance to the complicated set of behaviors that eventually "emerges."

In addition to imitation and successive approximation, Bandura thinks that the maintenance and extinction of behaviors in the person's repertoire depend on the application of various schedules of reinforcement. In particular, he contends that behavior is maintained through the application of combined schedules. To make his point, he uses the example of attention-seeking in children:

> In the training of children, the use of combined schedules certainly predominates. Let us take the example of attention-seeking behavior. Most young

children attempt many times in the day to elicit a nurturant response from their mothers. Sometimes the mother will respond immediately, but more often she is busy. At varying intervals she will reward the child with interest and attention. Many mothers are inclined to ignore mild forms of attention-seeking behavior and to respond only when this behavior is frequent or intense. It can be predicted ... that these mothers should have children who show persistent attention-seeking behavior occurring at the rates and intensities that have previously brought reward. One may suspect that most "trouble-some" behavior has been rewarded on a combined schedule by which unde-sirable responses of high magnitude and frequency are unwittingly rein-forced. The behavior is thus persistent, difficult to extinguish, and baffling for the parents. Perhaps the genesis of much aggressive behavior is to be found in the use of schedules which reward only responses of high magnitude; these could be attention-seeking, food-seeking, and other ... "dependency" responses, as well as responses of the kind more usually regarded as "aggres-sive." [Bandura & Walters, 1963, p. 7]

Thus, reinforcers appear to be dispensed in complicated ways by various socializing agents. In addition, and most important, children learn in the course of their development to apply reinforcers to their own behavior in various situations. Standards for self-reward and self-punishment can be acquired in a variety of ways. Children may be taught rules of behavior by their parents and others and be rewarded for following them and punished for violating them. Children may also learn these standards through expo-sure to books, newspapers, films, television, and radio. And, as you might expect, they may learn them through modeling procedures.

In one study, two groups of children participated in a miniature bowling game with adult models (Bandura & Kupers, 1964). In one condition, the children watched a model reward himself with candies only for excellent performances. In another condition, they watched a model reward himself for poor performances. After exposure to the models, the children were left alone to play the game with no models present. The results indicated that the children tended to match the behavior of the model to which they had been exposed. Although both groups of children had access to a generous supply of candy, those who were exposed to a high performance standard rewarded themselves sparingly and only when they had matched or exceeded the criterion, whereas those who were exposed to the low-standard model rewarded themselves quite often, even for poor performances.

In an extension of this work, two investigators sought to determine **multiple modeling effects** on imitative behavior (McMains & Liebert, 1968). Using the same bowling game as just described, adults in phase 1 imposed either a stringent criterion for self-reward (that is, they rewarded themselves only for attaining a particular score and told the children to do likewise) or a lenient standard for self-reward (that is, they rewarded themselves for attaining either one of two particular scores). In phase 2 of the investigation, a second model performed in the bowling game and either adhered to the stringent criterion set by the first model or violated it by rewarding himself for attaining the lenient standard. The results indicated that children trained on the stringent criterion by the first adult and who then saw the second model adhere to that standard deviated very little from the standard; that is, they rewarded themselves only when they met the stringent standard. Children who first trained on the stringent standard but who saw a second adult violate that standard were least willing to hold to the stringent standard in the absence of the models. They rewarded themselves for attaining various scores. These findings have some interesting implications. They suggest that parents and others who impose severe restrictions on children but do not follow through by example are likely to be quite ineffective in "training" their children to adopt certain social rules. It is not adequate, it seems, to use the old saw "Do as I say, not as I do" to instill appropriate values in children. Rather, our motto should probably be "Do as I say *and* do!"

Another implication of this study concerns the relationship between the learning of standards and the person's feelings of well-being. If the standards the individual learns to accept are too high or can be attained only rarely, he or she may experience stress. Under such conditions, the person is said to feel anxious, guilty, and depressed. Part of the tragedy here is that many people who adopt such standards are relatively competent but live in continual agony because they rarely consider their best efforts to be good enough. Approval—that is, the application of rewards and praise—by others may not be acceptable to such people. In such instances, external reinforcement may have little impact on their behavior.

You can see here the similarities between Rotter's concept of high minimal goals, Adler's concept of the unrealistic pursuit of fictional goals, and this notion of self-reward contingent on the attainment of extremely high standards. As Bandura well recognizes, an adequate social learning theory must account for the impact of self-determined reinforcement on behavior as well as for the effects of external reinforcement (Bandura, 1969, p. 39).

Finally, although Bandura places great emphasis on observational and instrumental learning and on self-reinforcement, he does not pay similar attention to the biological determinants of behavior. He does recognize, however, that constitutional factors inevitably influence the nature of the individual's social learning history:

> *Social manipulations can have relatively little influence on some biologically determined characteristics, such as the body type or facial features of an individual. Yet within a society that sets high value on the possession of certain physical attributes, the frequency with which social reinforcers are dispensed is partly dependent on the extent to which these cultural ideals are met. In North American society, where prestige and social rewards are bestowed for athletic ability and physique, boys who are small, lack muscular strength or dexterity, or who are obese and possess feminine-like physiques are relatively unsuccessful in obtaining positive reinforcement from peers. Similarly, a female who does not match the standards of beauty with her society evokes*

far fewer positive responses, especially from males than ones who possess these socially esteemed characteristics. The slender, petite female has been highly admired in North American culture; she may, however, be the recipient of relatively few positive reinforcers and considerable aversive treatment in cultures lacking in labor-saving devices. [Bandura & Walters, 1963, pp. 26–27]

Not only do constitutional factors exert an indirect influence on development, so do biochemical factors. Despite his recognition of the role of biology in personality development, Bandura deemphasizes it in his theory because he says there is currently little knowledge of the specific ways in which it operates to control behavior. As a consequence, he feels there is more to be gained by studying the role of social learning variables in personality development.

Techniques of Assessment

Bandura does not utilize dream analysis, free association, the method of amplification, or any of the other techniques utilized by practitioners in the psychodynamic tradition. Nor does he seem particularly interested in using personality questionnaires as assessment devices, although his position does not preclude the use of reliable and valid questionnaires, such as Rotter's I-E Scale, when they are helpful in understanding behavior.

For the most part, Bandura relies on experimental methods to assess personality functioning and change. He believes that the most stringent tests of a theory are provided by anchoring a hypothesized mediator (for instance, a cognitive event) in an independently measurable indicant and then confirming that external factors are linked to the indicant of the internal mediator and that it, in turn, is linked to overt behavior (Bandura, 1982a, p. 123). In other words, Bandura is interested in demonstrating that experimental manipulations of antecedent events influence cognitive functioning, which, in turn, influences the final, subsequent response(s) (Bandura, 1982a, p. 123). If the problem area is complex and uncharted, however, Bandura thinks it is advantageous to begin by conducting field studies that are essentially correlational in nature (Bandura & Walters, 1963, p. 391).

Application of the Theory to the Treatment of Psychopathology

Recently, Bandura has extended his social learning position by postulating a cognitive mechanism of self-efficacy to account for personality functioning and change (Bandura, 1977a; 1982a). In his view, healthy people have acquired high (but realistic) efficacy expectations that guide their actions, while abnormal people have acquired low and often unrealistic expectations that adversely influence their performances. **Efficacy expectations** are beliefs or convictions on the part of individuals that they can execute the behaviors required to produce certain outcomes or effects. According to Bandura, efficacy expectations influence people's choices of activities and environmental settings. Judgments of self-efficacy also determine how much effort people will expend on activities and how long they will persist on challenging tasks and in the face of aversive experiences. Because their efficacy expectations are poor, abnormal individuals are likely to avoid threatening situations they believe exceed their coping skills. If, for some reason(s), however, they have to perform in threatening situations, Bandura thinks their low efficacy expectations will lead them to expend little effort and give up after a short time. As a result, it is unlikely that they will gain corrective experiences that will enhance their sense of efficacy. They will, therefore, remain defensive and fearful.

For example, intensely shy people avoid social situations. If they must attend social functions, they will expend little effort in trying to meet and converse with people. They usually end up quickly becoming "wallflowers." Such people are wracked by self-doubts and persistently engage in debilitating self-criticism about their incompetence which, in turn, leads to poor performances in various social situations. These poor performances serve to reinforce low expectations of efficacy and to prevent the learning of new, assertive behaviors. Healthy people, in contrast, opt for challenging tasks that give them an opportunity to develop new skills. In such challenging situations, they are likely to expend maximum effort, to persist in the pursuit of their goals despite the presence of obstacles, and to engage in a minimum of debilitating self-criticism. As a result, they are able to increase the probabilities of eventual success.

According to Bandura (1977a; 1982a), the acquisition of high or low efficacy expectations has four major sources: performance accomplishments, vicarious experiences, verbal persuasion, and states of physiological (emotional) arousal. Let us examine each of these sources of efficacy expectations.

Performance Accomplishments. Bandura thinks that efficacy expectations are rooted primarily in personal mastery experiences. Success experiences tend to create high expectations, while failure experiences tend to generate low expectations. Moreover, once strong, high efficacy expectations are created, occasional failures are unlikely to have much impact on people's judgments of their capabilities. Conversely, once low expectations are generated by repeated failure, occasional successes are not very effective in changing people's judgments of their capabilities. However, low expectations can be changed by repeated and frequent successes fueled by determined effort. Through such efforts, people can eventually overcome and master the most difficult obstacles (Bandura, 1981, p. 203).

Vicarious Experiences. Although performance accomplishments provide the most influential source of efficacy expectations because they are based on actual mastery experiences, vicarious experiences also can influence the acquisition of efficacy expectations. That is, seeing or visualizing other people performing successfully can instill high self-perceptions of efficacy in observers so that they feel that they too possess the capabilities to master comparable activities (Bandura, 1982b, p. 27). Watching others of similar competence fail despite high efforts, however, lowers observers' judgments of their own capabilities and undermines their efforts.

Verbal Persuasion. Verbal persuasion is often used to convince people that they have the capabilities they need to accomplish their goals. Many parents, for example, encourage their children to believe that they have the abilities they need to succeed in different life spheres. To the extent that such encouragement persuades them to try hard enough to succeed, it may promote development of skills and a sense of personal efficacy. Of course, this encouragement must be kept within realistic bounds, because if, after persuasion, attempts to accomplish goals fail, they are likely to lessen the credibility of the source and to create low efficacy expectations (Bandura, 1977a, p. 198). Then, too, parents who continually discourage mastery attempts by their children through ridicule, criticism, and belittling are likely to leave them with low efficacy expectations.

Emotional Arousal. Stressful and difficult situations often generate high states of arousal in most individuals, and they use this arousal information to judge their capabilities. That is, because high arousal usually debilitates performance, individuals are more likely to expect failure when they are tense and physiologically aroused. Conversely, they are more likely to expect to succeed when they are not tense and highly aroused. In other words, low efficacy expectations can be generated when people rely on information from their bodily states that indicates they are highly aroused, while high efficacy expectations can be created when people perceive that they are relaxed when confronted by challenging tasks involving many obstacles.

Thus far in the exposition of Bandura's self-efficacy position we have focused primarily on the acquisition of efficacy expectations. However, Bandura's theory also explains how the four factors we have been discussing can be manipulated experimentally to reduce pathological behavior by raising clients' perceptions of their own efficacy. In particular, most of Bandura's recent research focuses on attempts to eliminate phobias in clients by raising efficacy expectations. We now turn to a discussion of some representative research in this area.

Phobia Reduction and Elimination. In several studies, Bandura has employed clinical treatments involving performance accomplishments to reduce or eliminate snake phobias in individuals. Specifically, snake phobics were guided by models to engage in progressively more threatening inter-actions with boa constrictors or corn snakes. The progression included (1) approaching a glass cage containing the snake; (2) looking down at the snake; (3) holding it with gloved and then bare hands; (4) letting it loose in the room and returning it to the cage; (5) holding it within 12 centimeters of their faces; and (6) tolerating the snake crawling in their laps while they held their hands passively at their sides. Bandura found that before the guided mod-eling occurred, the phobics' efficacy expectations for completing these tasks were very low but that, after the treatment, achievement of mastery was high and so were the phobics' efficacy expectations. Control subjects who did not receive the **guided-participation modeling** had lower levels of expec-tations throughout the experiment and did not achieve mastery.

In other experiments, Bandura has demonstrated further that vicarious-experience treatments, in which snake phobics simply watched models suc-cessfully engage in the increasingly threatening activities (without guided participation) and then independently tried to imitate the behavior of the models, resulted in higher efficacy expectations, lower physiological arousal (that is, reductions in heart rate and blood pressure), and more effective performances than was the case with phobic subjects who were not exposed to models at all (Bandura, 1977a, p. 206; Bandura, Reese, & Adams, 1982, pp. 14–21). It should be noted, however, that although exposure to models under vicarious conditions is effective in reducing snake phobia, it is not as effective as having the phobics engage directly in mastery experiences under guided-participation conditions.

Finally, Bandura and his colleagues have demonstrated that these ther-apeutic treatments work not only with subjects who are immobilized by fears of animals but also with people who are afraid of public places (ago-raphobics) (Bandura et al., 1980). These investigators utilized several thera-peutic treatments simultaneously in a highly successful way to change the behavior of agoraphobics. Many agoraphobics, for example, cannot shop in department stores and supermarkets because they find the crowds and checkout lines too threatening. Similarly, theaters, restaurants, buses, sub-ways, and even cars arouse highly negative emotions in many of them. Even-tually, if treatment is not forthcoming, most of these individuals cannot venture at all into public settings. They become virtual prisoners in their own homes.

To help these clients, Bandura and his associates began by forming group sessions in which the clients were taught how to identify the situa-tions that aroused varying levels of fear in them. They also learned how to identify self-debilitating thoughts and how to cope with them through the use of body-relaxation procedures and through the substitution of more positive, emboldening thoughts. But the primary treatment consisted of field mastery experiences. The emphasis in this treatment was on successful experiences with the feared objects and settings, because successes tend to raise mastery expectations. The exposure to these highly intimidating situations was done gradually by using graded subtasks and by carefully and slowly lengthening the time spent in the settings. For example, agoraphobics who feared automobile travel first rode cars in residential areas, then on busier streets, and eventually on freeways. Those clients who shunned supermarkets and department stores made shopping trips first to small, uncrowded stores and then to progressively larger stores. Those who feared restaurants gradually extended the amount of time they spent in them.

These performance accomplishments were generally aided by treatments that employed modeling by the therapists and by ex-agoraphobics using guided performance and encouragement. Whenever the clients became unduly distressed, they were encouraged to retreat momentarily and then to move forward again with proper guidance and support. As the clients developed their ability to cope, however, the field therapists gradually reduced their support and their guided participation. Clients were assigned progressively more challenging tasks to perform alone while the therapists remained in the vicinity. Using these multiple techniques, Bandura and his associates were able to substantially reduce the fears of these clients and to restore mastery behavior.

Critical Comments

We now turn to an evaluation of the scientific worth of Bandura's theory to see how well it meets our six criteria.

Comprehensiveness. In comparison with Freudian theory, for example, Bandura's position is quite limited in the range and diversity of phenomena it covers. It does, however, provide a relatively thorough analysis of the social learning variables responsible for the acquisition, maintenance, and modification of disordered behavior. These learning principles have been used to help increase our understanding of such disorders as alcoholism, academic anxieties, frigidity, impotence, exhibitionism, insomnia, nightmares, obsessive-compulsive problems, and phobias. In addition, much of Bandura's work and that of his associates has focused on illuminating the variables responsible for the acquisition of aggressive behavior and on modifying that behavior.

Social learning research has increased our knowledge of the ways in which childhood training practices influence personality development, how language is acquired and honed, and how self-reinforcement can be utilized in the acquisition, maintenance, and modification of behavior. This last area seems especially promising and exciting to investigators, as evidenced by the amount of research conducted on such phenomena in recent years.

Precision and Testability. Many of the cognitive variables in Bandura's theory are complex and difficult to define precisely. Yet Bandura has made strong efforts to define and measure his theoretical concepts objectively and reliably, and to a substantial degree these efforts have been successful. The ability to measure the cognitive variables objectively has allowed Bandura to incorporate them into experimental tests of his theory and to show how they can be utilized to enhance the predictive accuracy of the theory.

Parsimony. Social learning theory is based on relatively few assumptions, but those it does make are broadly stated and designed to encourage investigation of the ways in which social and cultural phenomena affect behavior and thought. The theory consists not only of the concepts traditionally associated with learning positions (reinforcement, discrimination, generalization, extinction) but also of new and different cognitive concepts. Although Skinner believes Bandura's position invents needless constructs to account for behavior, it is our judgment that these constructs are necessary for the development of an adequate theory of personality and that Bandura's theory is commensurate with the complexity of the phenomena it seeks to explain. Thus it is a parsimonious theory.

Empirical Validity. The evidence in support of Bandura's position is impressive. There have been countless empirical tests of the theory, and the results to date have been highly encouraging. For example, studies of observational learning have yielded evidence showing the importance of modeling in helping to mold, maintain, and vary behavior. Although much of this research has focused on the use of modeling to eliminate fears, anxieties, and disordered behaviors, modeling principles have also been applied to the study of nonneurotic behaviors. In addition to modeling, various other behavioral-therapy techniques derived from social learning theory have been successfully utilized in the treatment of an assortment of problems. In general, then, Bandura's position has a high degree of empirical validity.

Heuristic Value. Although Bandura's position has had considerable impact on the work of psychologists, especially in the clinical and social-psychology areas, it has not had much influence on the work of professionals in other disciplines. Certainly it has not had the interdisciplinary impact of Freud's theory. Still, its promise remains strong, and in the future we might see an increase in its heuristic value for professionals in other disciplines.

Applied Value. The applied value of social learning theory is high in the area of psychopathology. As mentioned earlier, social-learning principles have been successfully employed in the treatment of a variety of behavioral problems. Two basic problems, however, prevent the theory from having outstanding applied value in this area. One involves the stability of the behavioral changes following treatment. Most studies have been concerned only with the temporary effects of treatment of behavior. Bandura is acutely aware of this problem, and other investigators have begun to conduct research in an attempt to overcome it.

Another problem is the lack of solid evidence about the generalizability of treatment effects from the laboratory to natural settings. To what extent do the findings in the laboratory hold up in less artificial environments? This question is of the utmost importance in assessing the effectiveness of the various behavioral therapies that are part of the social learning position. If we reduce a person's aggressiveness through the use of modeling procedures in a clinical setting, will she also behave less aggressively in her relationships with the people she meets in her daily routine? Once again, there are smatterings of research addressed to this problem, and it seems clear that investigators will pay greater attention to it in the future.

Bandura's research in the area of aggression has increased our understanding of the origins of such behavior and has provided insights into the ways it can be modified and controlled. Unfortunately, the implications of these findings have not been utilized fully by government policymakers, despite long and persistent attempts by Bandura and his associates to transmit such information and to effect changes. In general, it seems reasonable to conclude that Bandura's theory has not reached its potential in helping generate new solutions to problems but that its applied value should become increasingly apparent.

Discussion Questions

1. Is it possible for a person to survive in his or her environment by relying solely on the trial-and-error method of learning? Cite reasons for your position.
2. Do you agree with the findings of the study cited that suggested that girls will more readily imitate female models, whereas boys will mimic male authority figures? Have there been any changes in the imitative behavior of boys and girls since the advent of the women's movement? Cite reasons for your answer.
3. Why is the distinction between acquisition and performance such an important one in the argument about the effects of television violence on children's behavior? Do you agree with Bandura on this point?
4. If positive reinforcers are such a potent determiner of behavior, why don't we praise and reinforce each other more often?
5. Do you believe that violence in the media has had an adverse effect on your behavior and that of your friends and relatives? Why or why not?
6. What are some of the primary personal and situational determinants of aggressive behavior?
7. What suggestions do you have for decreasing aggressive behavior in our culture, assuming you believe it should be brought under control?
8. Design an experiment that would utilize modeling procedures to rid a boy of his fear of bugs.
9. How anxious do you and your friends become before taking an examination? Does this anxiety interfere with your performance and theirs? If your answer is

yes in regard to their behavior or yours, how would you rearrange environmental conditions to minimize anxiety?

10. Bandura maintains that one of the sources of efficacy expectations is verbal persuasion. What are some of the limitations of using verbal persuasion to convince individuals that they have the abilities necessary to accomplish their goals?

References

Bandura, A. Influence of models' reinforcement contingencies on the acquisition of imitative responses. *Journal of Personality and Social Psychology,* 1965, *1,* 589–595.

Bandura, A. *Principles of behavior modification.* New York: Holt, Rinehart & Winston, 1969.

Bandura, A. *Social learning theory.* Morristown, N.J.: General Learning Press, 1971.

Bandura, A. *Aggression: A social learning analysis.* Englewood Cliffs, N.J.: Prentice-Hall, 1973.

Bandura, A. Self-efficacy: Toward a unifying theory of behavioral change. *Psychological Review,* 1977a, *84,* 191–215.

Bandura, A. *Social learning theory.* Englewood Cliffs, N.J.: Prentice-Hall, 1977b.

Bandura, A. The self system in reciprocal determinism. *American Psychologist,* 1978, *33,* 344–358.

Bandura, A. Self-referent thought: A developmental analysis of self-efficacy. In J. H. Flavell & L. Ross (Eds.), *Social cognitive development: Frontiers and possible futures.* Cambridge, England: Cambridge University Press, 1981.

Bandura, A. Self-efficacy mechanism in human agency. *American Psychologist,* 1982a, *37,* 122–147.

Bandura, A. The self and mechanisms of agency. In J. Suls (Ed.), *Psychological perspectives on the self,* Vol. 1. Hillsdale N.J.: Erlbaum, 1982b.

Bandura, A., Adams, N. E., Hardy, A. B., & Howells, G. N. Tests of the generality of self-efficacy theory. *Cognitive Therapy and Research,* 1980, *4,* 39–66.

Bandura, A., Blanchard, B., & Ritter, B. Relative efficiency of desensitization and modeling approaches for inducing behavioral, affective, and attitudinal changes. *Journal of Personality and Social Psychology,* 1969, *13,* 173–199.

Bandura, A., & Kupers, C. J. The transmission of patterns of self-reinforcement through modeling. *Journal of Abnormal and Social Psychology,* 1964, *69,* 1–9.

Bandura, A., & Menlove, F. L. Factors determining vicarious extinction of avoidance behavior through symbolic modeling. *Journal of Personality and Social Psychology,* 1968, *8,* 99–108.

Bandura, A., Reese, L., & Adams, N.E. Microanalysis of action and fear arousal as a function of differential levels of perceived self-efficacy. *Journal of Personality and Social Psychology,* 1982, *43,* 5–21.

Bandura, A., Ross, D., & Ross, S. A. Imitation of film-mediated aggressive models. *Journal of Abnormal and Social Psychology,* 1963a, *66,* 3–11.

Bandura, A., Ross, D., & Ross, S. A. Vicarious reinforcement and imitative learning. *Journal of Abnormal and Social Psychology,* 1963b, *67,* 601–607.

Bandura, A., & Walters, R. H. *Adolescent aggression.* New York: Ronald Press, 1959.

Bandura, A., & Walters, R. H. *Social learning and personality development.* New York: Holt, Rinehart & Winston, 1963.

Berkowitz, L. *Aggression: A social psychological analysis.* New York: McGraw-Hill, 1962.

Berkowitz, L., & LePage, A. Weapons as aggression-eliciting stimuli. *Journal of Personality and Social Psychology*, 1967, 7, 202–207.

Grusec, J., & Mischel, W. Model's characteristics as determinants of social learning. *Journal of Personality and Social Psychology*, 1966, 4, 211–215.

Gutride, M. E., Goldstein, A. P., & Hunter, G. F. The use of modeling to increase social interaction among asocial psychiatric patients. *Journal of Consulting and Clinical Psychology*, 1973, 40, 408–415.

Lovaas, O. I. A behavior therapy approach to the treatment of childhood schizophrenia. In J. P. Hill (Ed.), *Minnesota symposia on child psychology*, Vol. 1. Minneapolis: University of Minnesota Press, 1967.

McMains, M. J., & Liebert, R. M. The influence of discrepancies between successively modeled self-reward criteria on the adoption of a self-imposed standard. *Journal of Personality and Social Psychology*, 1968, 8, 166–171.

Meyer, T. P. Effects of viewing justified and unjustified real film violence on aggressive behavior. *Journal of Personality and Social Psychology*, 1972, 23, 21–29.

Rosenbaum, M. E., & Tucker, I. F. Competence of the model and the learning of imitation and nonimitation. *Journal of Experimental Psychology*, 1952, 63, 183–190.

Rosenkrans, M. A. Imitation in children as a function of perceived similarity to a social model and vicarious reinforcement. *Journal of Personality and Social Psychology*, 1967, 7, 307–315.

Sarason, I. G. Test anxiety and the self-disclosing coping model. *Journal of Consulting and Clinical Psychology*, 1975, 43, 148–153.

Turner, C., & Berkowitz, L. "Identification with film aggression (covert role taking) and reactions to film violence. *Journal of Personality and Social Psychology*, 1972, 21, 256–264.

Suggested Readings

Bandura, A. *Principles of behavior modification.* New York: Holt, Rinehart & Winston, 169.

Bandura, A. *Aggression: A social learning analysis.* Englewood Cliffs, N.J.: Prentice-Hall, 1973.

Bandura, A. Self-efficacy: Toward a unifying theory of behavioral change. *Psychological Review*, 1977, 84, 191–215.

Bandura, A. *Social learning theory.* Englewood Cliffs, N.J.: Prentice-Hall, 1977.

Bandura, A., & Walters, R. H. *Social learning and personality development.* New York: Holt, Rinehart & Winston, 1963.

Glossary

Anticipated outcome Person's expectancy that the performance of a given behavior will lead to the attainment of a given reinforcer.

Efficacy expectation Conviction of an individual that he or she can execute the behavior required to produce certain response consequences.

External reinforcement   Reinforcing environmental stimuli that control the occurrence of behavior. External reinforcement can vary in form; money is a reinforcer but so usually are praise, approval from others, a pat on the back, and a smile.

Guided-participation modeling   Mastery experiences for phobic subjects are arranged by models who first show the subjects how to cope successfully with increasingly threatening interactions with dreaded objects. Models then guide the subjects through these threatening activities (that is, there is a joint performance of the activities) until the the phobics are finally able to master their fears.

Imaginal representation   Image that a person has that is similar to the object in the environment. For example, the person can "picture," or imagine, his or her father, and the father is a real object.

Multiple modeling effects   Impact on a person's behavior as a result of being exposed to a variety of models.

Observational learning   Type of learning in which new responses can be made by the person as a result of watching the performance of others; also called imitative learning.

Reciprocal determinism   The belief that cognitive and environmental events mutually determine each other.

Verbal representation   Word that signifies an object in the environment. For example, the word *dog* is a verbal representation of a four-legged creature that barks and exists in the environment.

Vicarious reinforcement   Changes in a person's behavior due to witnessing a model being reinforced for the same behavior.

P A R T   6

Humanistic-Existential Perspectives

The materials in this section of the text are part of the Third Force movement in contemporary psychology (the other movements are psychoanalysis and behaviorism). The term was coined by Maslow to describe a position that focuses on the creative potentialities inherent in human beings and seeks ways to help them realize their highest and most important goals. The theories embodied by the movement tend to assume that human beings are basically good and worthy of respect. Virtually all these theories also postulate the existence of an innate "growth" mechanism within individuals that will move them toward the realization of their potentialities, if environmental conditions are "right." This growth process has been variously labeled by its numerous proponents as the drive toward self-actualization, self-realization, or selfhood.

The roots of the humanistic movement can be found in the writings of Jung, Adler, Horney, Fromm, Allport, Maslow, Rogers, May, and others. In each of these perspectives, we find an emphasis on the uniqueness of individuals and a belief that they should be free to make their own choices about the direction they want to take in their own lives. They should be allowed the opportunity to organize and control their own behavior; they should not be controlled by society. In most of these positions, society is generally seen as the "bad guy," as the enforcer of rules and regulations that stifle personal growth. According to the humanists, a benevolent, helpful attitude toward people allows them to grow and prosper. However, most societies attempt to coerce individuals into behaving "appropriately"—that is, "normally." The result is rather conventional, dull people who usually obey, without much question, the moral prescriptions of the majority. In other words, the result is the average, law-abiding man or woman.

The humanistic psychologists argue, instead, for allowing individuals to develop to their fullest potential. They see people as naturally striving to be creative and happy rather than mediocre and conventional. Of course, the assumption that what is conventional is very often mediocre is open to question, especially in a society that encourages people to try to attain excellence in their pursuits. Another assumption underlying many of the humanist positions is that it is possible to specify a universal set of values that will provide people with a moral anchor so that they will be able to decide what is right or wrong and good or bad. Such a set of values, rooted in the person's biology, would allow people to make moral decisions by looking inside themselves, instead of relying on the judgments of society. Yet, there has never been clear-cut agreement among philosophers or psychologists on a universal set of values, although numerous attempts to devise such a list have been made. Also the question of who will decide which values are universally valid has never been resolved. Is it the philosophers? the psychologists? the politicians? the artists? the theologians? As we learned in Chapter 11, Skinner thinks that behavioral psychologists can best make this decision, but surely not everyone will agree with him. Finally, despite the claims of the humanists, there is little scientific evidence for the existence of an innate mechanism that would allow us to make morally correct decisions.

Yet, instead of rejecting this aspect of the humanistic psychologists' position, we ought to give it a fair hearing. First, the fact that there is no agreement among scholars and others about the existence of a universal set of values does not mean that such a value system can never be devised. Second, although there is currently no evidence for the existence of an internal, biologically based mechanism that would guide moral behavior, it does not mean that such evidence will never be forthcoming. Even if these questions can never be answered, there may still be merit in the humanistic position. By raising significant questions and challenging the tenets of orthodox psychology, humanistic psychologists have forced more traditional psychologists to reconsider the directions and value of their work. The overall impact of the humanists has been most beneficial, although some of the more rigorous experimental psychologists would certainly disagree with this judgment. Let us review the two major challenges hurled by the humanists at orthodox psychology, and then you can make your own judgment.

The first challenge involves the claim that contemporary psychologies, like psychoanalysis and behaviorism, provide only a partial and limited view of human functioning, a view that needs drastic revision. Allport put the matter succinctly and picturesquely:

> It is especially in relation to the formation and development of human personality that we need to open doors. For it is precisely here that our ignorance and uncertainty are greatest. Our methods, however well suited to the study of sensory processes, animal research, and pathology, are not fully adequate; and interpretations arising from the exclusive use of these methods are stultifying. Some theories ... are based largely upon the behavior of sick and anxious people or upon the antics of captive and desperate rats. Fewer theories have derived from the study of healthy beings, those who strive not so much to preserve life as to make it worth living. Thus we find today many studies of criminals, few of law-abiders; many of fear, few of courage; more on hostility than on affiliation; much on the blindness in man, little on his vision; much on his past, little on his outreaching into the future. [Allport, 1955, p. 18]

In building his theory of self-actualization, Maslow also pointed out the limitations in the Freudian conception. Freud devoted most of his attention to understanding the unconscious forces that determine behavior and neglected the rational, conscious forces. The Freudian world is one in which neurotic people are continually struggling to adjust to the environment and to gain a feeling of security. Maslow, in contrast, posited a need hierarchy in human beings consisting of basic and growth urges. The need for security is one of the lower basic needs; if gratified, it frees the individual to pursue "higher" goals. Most of Maslow's attention was directed to the establishment of a psychology of personal growth and creative striving, as we will see in Chapter 14. Thus Maslow set out to study the behavior of psychologically healthy people in order to learn more about the growth process. Chapter 14 outlines his efforts and provides a review of the major characteristics of self-actualizing individuals.

In general terms, the first challenge Maslow and other humanistic psychologists advocate is a drastic revision of contemporary psychology in which primary attention would be paid to topics that have been relatively ignored by existing theories. These topics would include, among others, love, affiliation, creativity, spontaneity, joy, courage, humor, independence, and personal growth. Focusing on them should teach us about the "good" side of human nature and serve as a corrective to the more limited and pessimistic picture projected by the Freudians and the behaviorists.

The second challenge voiced by the humanists centers on the prevailing view in the discipline that psychology is a natural science and must therefore employ methods of study consistent with those used in physics, chemistry, physiology, and biology. The humanists claim this attitude has led to a psychology that does not do justice to the full range of human experience and behavior. To understand the arguments of the humanists more fully, let us look at the history of psychology and the reasons for its initial alliance with the natural sciences.

As you undoubtedly know, psychology as a science began in 1879 when Wilhelm Wundt established his experimental laboratory in Leipzig, Germany. Psychologists had originally been linked with speculative philosophers, but dissatisfaction with this relationship and the desire to establish an independent, more empirically oriented discipline led them toward the natural sciences and toward the use of the scientific method in the study of phenomena. The benefits of this move would be twofold: first, psychologists would have a ready-made approach to the study of behavior acceptable to members of the scientific community; second, psychology would gain status and respectability. So appealing was this prospect that psychologists adopted in rather uncritical fashion the scientific method used by the natural sciences.

The natural-science approach to the study of problems focuses on the accumulation of facts through the employment of objective and reliable measurement procedures. It avoids speculation and deduction in the attempt to understand phenomena and relies instead on induction. This tough-minded empiricism can be seen most clearly in the work of Watson and Skinner. Because of their concern with objective and precise measurement, advocates of this approach have focused on only those problems that can meet their criteria, so such phenomena as jealousy, hatred of a parent, and a man's love for a woman have been excluded from consideration.

The natural-science approach also insists that investigators be objective in their study of problems. There is a tendency to see the investigator as a potential source of bias whose influence on the inquiry process must be neutralized and controlled. There is also the implication that science is a value-free enterprise and that the investigator should study phenomena dispassionately as well as objectively. It is this depersonalized view of science that the humanistic psychologists have rejected. Rogers, for example, argues that

science exists only in people. Each scientific project has its creative inception, its process, and its tentative conclusion, in a person or persons. Knowledge— even scientific knowledge—is that which is subjectively acceptable. Scientific knowledge can be communicated only to those who are subjectively ready to receive its communication. The utilization of science also occurs only through people who are in pursuit of values which have meaning for them. [Rogers, 1965, p. 164]

Rogers would ask psychologists to develop a science and a psychology that has its primary focus within the person. Chapter 15 reviews Rogers' reasons for the establishment of such a science and his theory of personality. It presents the concepts and principles of a position based on personal growth and respect for the worth of the individual and his or her innate potential.

Rollo May (Chapter 16) has an orientation similar to that of Rogers. For example, he points out that we should consider science a human endeavor and begin our inquiry by asking "What is it in human nature that leads to the emergence of scientific attitude?" We should not, in other words, begin with an established methodology and try to fit human problems into that mold. Instead, we should start with our own experiences and formulations of problems and use procedures that will allow us to obtain answers. This orientation would mean emphasizing the problem rather than the use of elegant measurement techniques and equipment for the sake of being "scientific." It would make psychology, in other words, a "human" rather than a "natural" science.

The humanists do not think the natural-science approach is meaningless; their point is that psychology should adopt an expanded set of methods to help us understand reality better. We turn now to a treatment of theories in the humanistic-existential tradition that reflect these hopes for change.

References

Allport, G. W. *Becoming.* New Haven: Yale University Press, 1955.

Rogers, C. R. Persons or science? In F. T. Severin (Ed.), *Humanistic viewpoints in psychology.* New York: McGraw-Hill, 1965.

CHAPTER 14

Maslow's Self-Actualization Position

Biographical Sketch

Abraham Maslow was born in Brooklyn, New York, in 1908. His parents were Russian Jews who had immigrated to the United States, and Maslow was the eldest of seven children. At 18, he entered City College of New York to study law. Despite his high IQ, he began to do poorly in some of his courses. He had little interest in becoming a lawyer and had taken the courses only to satisfy his father's wishes. One day during the second semester of his first year, he quit school. Eventually, he matriculated at the University of Wisconsin, where he was first exposed to the scientific psychology of the Wundt-Titchener structuralism school. Advocates of the structuralist position were concerned with demonstrating that "mental life" could be studied in the same way as phenomena in chemistry—that is, by analyzing the various "elements" of sensation and perception and the ways in which they combined to affect behavior. Maslow found this approach boring, but his interest was piqued by the behavioristic approach being promulgated by John B. Watson. It is difficult to imagine Maslow being stimulated by the crude stimulus-response (S-R) treatment of human behavior that Watson was offering, and, in fact, later in his career he rejected the position. While Maslow was a student, however, Watson's approach did interest him because it seemed to imply that people could be understood and improved scientifically, a belief directly in line with Maslow's interest in helping people realize their potential.

During his Wisconsin days, Maslow worked with Harry Harlow, who later became famous for his work on curiosity and affectional motives in monkeys. Maslow was interested in the fact that monkeys would work to solve problems for long periods, even when they were not hungry. He observed similar behavior in pigs. The stronger and healthier pigs would explore their surroundings much more than the weaker ones. Maslow was also aware of an early experiment that showed that if chickens are allowed to choose their own diets, some of them would select a healthy diet and others would not. These results suggested to Maslow that there is a fundamental drive toward health in animals. Eventually, he came to believe that such a drive toward knowledge, power, and insight also existed in humans. Thus his initial work in animal biology provided the groundwork for the theory of self-actualization.

Maslow received his doctorate from Wisconsin in 1934, then worked for 18 months at Columbia University with the eminent learning theorist E. L. Thorndike. As Thorndike's assistant, Maslow was required to do research to discover the percentage of human behavior determined by genes and the percentage controlled by culture. Maslow found the project "rather silly" because he believed that "everything was determined by both." He made his views known to Thorndike, and much to his surprise, Thorndike gave him permission to pursue his own research on dominance and sexuality in monkeys and humans. Out of this work emerged Maslow's ideas about the existence of a hierarchy of needs in human beings. His classic paper was published in *Psychological Review* in 1943, after he had left Columbia and begun teaching at Brooklyn College. During Maslow's 14 years at Brooklyn College, he had an opportunity to meet and be exposed to the ideas of such prominent psychologists, psychoanalysts, and cultural anthropologists as Max Wertheimer, Karen Horney, Alfred Adler, Erich Fromm, and Ruth Benedict. The exposure had a considerable influence on his thinking, and it was at this point that he rejected the oversimplified S-R view of human behavior and embraced instead a more holistic and dynamic view of personality functioning.

In 1951, Maslow moved to Brandeis University, where he served as department chairman for many years. While at Brandeis, he produced two of his most creative works, *Motivation and Personality* (1970a), first published in 1954, and *Toward a Psychology of Being* (1962). In 1967, he was elected president of the American Psychological Association. The same year, he accepted a fellowship at the Laughlin Foundation in Menlo Park, California, to devote all his time to writing. Unfortunately, he died of a heart attack three years later at the age of 62 (Wilson, 1972, pp. 129–202).

Humanistic Biology and Self-Actualization

Maslow laid the groundwork for his theory of **self-actualization** by making the assumption that each of us has an intrinsic nature that is good or, at the very least, neutral (Maslow, 1962, p. 3). (The experimental evidence offered in support of this contention is not solid, however, as we shall learn in Chapter 15 when we discuss Rogers' "organismic wisdom" hypothesis.) Maslow proceeded to argue that since this inner nature is good or neutral, it is best to encourage its development. Further, he maintained that healthy development is likely only in a good society. In this theory of **humanistic biology,** such a society would be one that "offers all [the] necessary raw materials and then gets out of the way and stands aside to let the . . . organism itself utter its wishes and demands and make its choices" (Maslow, 1970a, p. 277). If the environment is restrictive and minimizes personal choice, the individual is likely to develop in neurotic ways because this inner nature is weak and subject to control by environmental forces. Maslow believed that the tendency, although weak, remains and continuously presses toward actualization (Maslow, 1962, pp. 3–4).

The objective of Maslow's theorizing about human nature was to establish a "scientific ethics, a natural value system, a court of ultimate appeal for the determination of good and bad, of right and wrong" (Maslow, 1962, p. 4). Such an ethic would allow investigators of human personality to overcome the relativism inherent in traditional appeals to moral authority. It would provide a set of ideals that would serve as guides for human conduct. If our inner natures, for example, told us that aggression against others is wrong, then no amount of preaching or exhortation by authorities that it is justified under certain circumstances would dissuade us from our inner conviction. Presumably, we would be able to cast out this evil in ourselves. Unfortunately, since the evidence for a natural ethic is unconvincing, we are left only with the word of a moral authority—Maslow—that such a set of values indeed exists.

Basic Concepts and Principles

Human Motivation and the Actualization Process

According to Maslow, human beings have two basic sets of needs that are rooted in their biology. These are the **deficiency,** or basic, **needs** and the **growth,** or meta, **needs.** The basic needs are more urgent than the growth needs and are arranged in a hierarchical order. Maslow acknowledged that there may be exceptions to this hierarchical arrangement. For example, he maintained that there are creative people whose drive to create is more important than any other need. There are also people whose values and ideals are so strong that they will die rather than renounce them. The meta needs, in contrast, are not arranged hierarchically. In general, they are equally powerful and can be easily substituted one for another. When any of these needs is not fulfilled, the person becomes sick. Just as we need adequate amounts of vitamin C to remain healthy, so we need love from others in sufficient quantities to function properly (Maslow, 1962, p. 21). To move toward self-actualization, we must have sufficiently gratified our basic needs so that we are free to pursue fulfillment of the higher, transcending, meta needs (Maslow, 1962, p. 23) (Figure 14.1).

The Basic Needs

From most to least powerful, the basic needs include the physiological drives, safety needs, belongingness and love needs, and esteem needs. The preconditions necessary for the satisfaction of these needs include the "freedom to speak, freedom to do what one wishes so long as no harm is done to others, freedom to express oneself, freedom to investigate and seek for information, freedom to defend oneself, justice, fairness, honesty, orderliness in the group" (Maslow, 1970a, p. 47). Without these freedoms, basic satisfaction of the needs is virtually impossible.

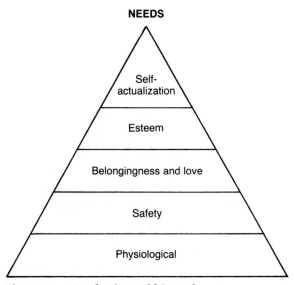

NEEDS

Self-actualization

Esteem

Belongingness and love

Safety

Physiological

Figure 14.1 Maslow's need hierarchy.

The physiological needs include, among others, hunger, thirst, and sex. A man deprived of food for long periods, for example, would begin to focus more and more of his attention on that deficiency. He would start to think and dream about food in an obsessive way. He would become less and less concerned with other activities such as a desire to buy a car, to fix the roof on his house, and to take his sons and daughters on camping and fishing trips. He would also become less interested in what other people might think of him and with trying to help others. In short, the person would be less concerned with safety needs, love and belongingness, esteem needs, and movement toward self-actualization. One of the implications of Maslow's scheme is therefore that not many poor people are involved in the quest for self-actualization. They use all their energies in finding enough work to feed themselves and their families.

Once the person's physiological needs are relatively well satisfied, however, a set of safety needs is presumed to emerge. This set includes needs for security, protection, structure, law, order, limits, and freedom from fear, anxiety, and chaos (Maslow, 1970a, p. 39). In Maslow's view, the need for security manifests itself in infants and children when there are disturbances in their environments. For example, they may be threatened by loud noises, flashing lights, rough handling, and inadequate support (Maslow, 1970a, p. 39). Their needs for safety may also be reflected in their preference for an environment in which reinforcers are dispensed in a systematic and consistent manner. Erratic behavior of parents can be especially debilitating. Children also need limits on their behavior, according to Maslow. Without them, they function poorly. Maslow maintained that the typical child will often react with panic in unfamiliar and unmanageable situations. For example, a mother may be surprised to find her young son crying and clinging to the handrail of a stairway that leads to his classroom a few minutes after she had received repeated assurances from the boy that he knows how to get there.

Like children, adults also have definite needs for safety, but they are more subtle and difficult to detect. The stable society is one that frees adults from worry about adequate food supplies and housing, about being assaulted on the streets or in their homes, about military coups or civilian takeovers of the government, and the like. In a more moderate way, people act to secure tenure in their jobs and to receive old-age pensions and medical coverage in case of illness or accidents.

The needs for belongingness and love tend to emerge once the physiological and safety needs have become routine. Like Fromm in his discussion of the need for rootedness, Maslow argued that all of us need to feel wanted and accepted by others. Some of us find gratification of these needs through our friends, others through family life, and still others through membership in groups and organizations. Without such ties, we would feel rootless and lonely. Of course, loneliness need not always have harmful implications for personal development; it can provide the basis for creativity and self-insight in some people. Often, however, loneliness is an unwanted and painful experience. Maslow believed that the current emphasis on sensitivity and encounter groups in our culture is evidence of our strong need for contact and affection. He felt that increased mobility, the breakdown of the traditional family, and depersonalization resulting from increased urbanization lend themselves to greater personal loneliness and alienation (Maslow, 1970a, p. 44).

The need for love that Maslow listed with the basic needs is different from Fromm's concept of mature love, discussed in Chapter 6. Mature love is concern for the welfare of others. Maslow's conceptualization of love as a deficiency need, on the other hand, is a selfish concern with seeking love from others. Maslow termed it **D-love**, or Deficiency-love. Once this need is relatively gratified, however, we become capable of loving others in the sense that Fromm proposed. Maslow called this type of love **B-love**, or Being-love, to distinguish it from the lower need to be loved. B-love, or mature love, becomes possible in Maslow's system only when the basic needs have been sufficiently gratified and the person is moving toward self-actualization.

Recent research by Dietch (1978) provides support for some of Maslow's ideas about mature love. He found that college men and women who scored higher on a test of self-actualization were more likely to have been truly in love with at least one person during the past three years than students who scored lower. These latter students reported not having been intimately involved with anyone. The implication was that students who were higher in self-actualization were more capable of giving affection and of intimately relating to others than those who were lower in the actualization hierarchy. Dietch also found a positive correlation between the capacity for mature love and self-actualization in this sample of students. Most interestingly, he also found that, among students who reported that their relationships had broken up, those who were higher in the self-actualizing tendency were less resentful toward their former lovers than those who were less actualizing. In accordance with Maslow's theory, this finding suggests that students higher in actualization were more mature and could accept the ending of an important relationship with more grace and understanding than those who were lower in the hierarchy.

Esteem needs are the last of the basic urges to emerge. Maslow divided them into two sets: esteem based on respect for our own competence, independence, and accomplishments, and esteem based on evaluation from others. Esteem in this latter sense is best seen in our striving for recognition from others and in attempts to secure status, fame, dominance, importance, and appreciation (Maslow, 1970a, p. 45). Maslow maintained that individuals become sick when these needs are thwarted. He also believed that we should base our self-esteem on actual competence and adequacy at the task rather than on praise or criticism from others. Surely there is little question that acceptance of undeserved praise from others may eventually have harmful consequences for our personal development. The young woman who has been continually praised by her high school teachers and her parents for academic prowess that she does not really possess and who is also encouraged to believe that she will excel at the college level may have a traumatic experience during her first year at the university. Conversely, undeserved criticism may hinder functioning. A young man may be creative and write marvelous poems but never share them with others because of excessive reliance on the opinion of various family members who continually derogate his efforts. Eventually he might even give up poetry completely.

In these extreme cases, it is not difficult to understand why these people should rely on themselves and not others in making their judgments. But other decisions we must make may not be as readily resolved. There may be numerous instances when we do not have the competence to make correct judgments and should rely on the advice of others. For example, a child on a picnic with her family might do well to heed the advice of her parents to avoid swimming in certain areas. In addition, self-diagnosis and treatment for illness have often had serious consequences for people. Listening to the advice of a competent doctor may be the wiser course of action, even though it is not infallible.

The general conclusion to be drawn from these examples is that Maslow's suggestion that we rely on ourselves and not on others in making decisions is questionable. We do not exist in a social vacuum, and we do not always know what actions are in our best interest. We simply cannot always rely on that "which comes naturally and easily out of one's own true inner nature, one's constitution, one's biological fate or destiny," as Maslow (1970a, p. 46) advocated. There is simply little evidence to support his contention, although it is difficult to disagree with a position that places such a high value on individualism, since individualism is viewed so positively in our culture. The most unfortunate outcome of such a biologically based individualism is that it sometimes deteriorates into a kind of idiosyncratic subjectivism that assumes that each person's comprehension of reality is just as accurate as that of others.

The Meta Needs

Once the basic needs in Maslow's hierarchy have been sufficiently gratified, the needs for self-actualization and cognitive understanding become salient. People's curiosity about themselves and the workings of the environment are aroused. There is a desire to know and understand phenomena that go beyond events associated with the gratification of basic needs. There is the possibility of moving toward the realization of one's own unique potentialities. But movement in this positive direction is not automatic. Maslow believed that we often fear "our best side, ... our talents, ... our finest impulses, ... our creativeness" (Maslow, 1962, p. 58). Discovery of our abilities brings happiness, but it also brings fear of our responsibilities and duties.

Sometimes it also brings a fear of the unknown. Maslow called this fear the **Jonah complex**.

Maslow pointed out that many women fear the best in themselves. They do not utilize their intellectual abilities to the fullest because they fear social rejection. Achievement is considered unfeminine and hence is avoided. In one study, researchers tested this contention by hypothesizing that sex-role training in our culture leads both men and women to value positively achievement by men but to value negatively similar accomplishments by women (Monahan, Kuhn, & Shaver, 1974). They asked both male and female students to make up stories in response to the statement "At the end of first term finals, Ann/John finds herself/himself at the top of her/his medical school class." They were also asked to describe Ann and John, to tell about the events leading up to their situation, and to guess what the future would be like for them. The results: 79% of the men and 70% of the women "projected" stories that showed little fear of success in regard to John's achievement, but 68% of the men and 51% of the women reported negative consequences for Ann because of her accomplishment. The following two excerpts illustrate the point:

> *Soon Ann became one of the leading doctors in the world. When she was in France, she met an American man. They both fell in love. Soon they were married. But after they had their first child, Ann turned all her attention to her work. So they got divorced. Ann always was involved in her work. The only people she talked to were fellow doctors and nurses. Soon she got very ill and died. No one even went to her funeral because she was very mean.*

> *Ann looks like a telephone pole and has purple eyes. Ann is a person who is a mental case which likes to cut up people. . . . We worry about the unfortunate people who have her as their doctor. [Monahan, Kuhn, & Shaver, 1974, pp. 62–63]*

These results support Maslow's arguments and suggest that many women will have difficulty moving toward actualization because environmental forces (socialization practices) restrict their options. It is also readily apparent that men may experience similar difficulties as a function of sex-role indoctrination, which prevents expression of emotion and feelings of tenderness toward others.

Poor socialization practices also contribute to the acquisition of a **desacralizing attitude** among young people that hinders movement toward self-actualization. Maslow believed this attitude emerges because many adolescents have "dopey" parents whom they do not respect, parents who are confused about their own values. They never punish their children or stop them from doing things that are wrong. They are terrified of them and let them do whatever they want. As a result, the children despise them, often with good reason. These adolescents then simplistically decide that all grown-ups are like their parents, so they will not listen to or respect any adults.

They become cynical and mistrustful of all grown-ups. They fail to see the goodness and value in many adults. Maslow believed that movement toward self-actualization is possible only when such young people learn to resacralize their lives. That is, progress toward self-actualization is possible only when they give up their cynicism and mistrust and begin to see not only the weaknesses in adults but also their virtues and strengths (Maslow, 1971, pp. 49–50).

In conclusion, "good" environmental conditions are needed if we are to begin moving toward actualization (Maslow, 1970a, p. 99). These conditions involve a socialization process that fosters equality and trust between people, along with respect and support of the individual's right to make his or her own decisions.

B-Cognition and Actualization

Assuming that good conditions are present and that people are willing and able to take risks, positive growth will occur. Individuals begin more and more to exist in a **B-cognition** state. In sharp contrast to **D-cognition** experiences that involve judging, condemning, and approving and disapproving of ourselves and others, B-cognition experiences are nonjudgmental, self-validating, nonstriving, and temporary (Maslow, 1962, p. 68). In such states of **peak experience**, we experience phenomena in their simplicity, "oughtness," beauty, goodness, and completeness. There is a lack of strain, an effortlessness, a spontaneity about the experience that is almost overwhelming (Maslow, 1962, p. 73). Typically there is a lack of consciousness of space and time. Intense emotions such as wonder, awe, and reverence are felt. During these intense experiences, individuals transcend their own selfishness. Events and objects are perceived as they truly are and are not distorted to meet the experiencers' needs or wishes (Maslow, 1970b, pp. 59–68). Examples include "perceiving the beautiful person or the beautiful painting, experiencing perfect sex and/or perfect love, insight, creativeness" (Maslow, 1962, p. 79). College students cite watching the beauties of nature, moments of quiet reflection, and listening to music, among other experiences, as "triggers" to peak experiences (Keutzer, 1978, p. 78). See Table 14.1 for a complete listing of these intense experiences.

But there are negative features to experiencing in the B-cognition realm, according to Maslow. It is not a perfect state in which people "live happily forever after." Thus self-actualizing people are more capable than ordinary people of B-cognizing, but they do not live in this state continuously (Maslow, 1962, pp. 109–110). Continual existence in such a passive and noninterfering state would prove fatal because action is often demanded for survival. The person who appreciates the beauty of the tiger without taking safety precautions may not survive the experience. As Maslow (1962, p. 111) put it, "The demands of self-actualization may necessitate killing the tiger, even though B-cognition of the tiger is against killing the tiger." As a con-

Table 14.1
Triggers to Peak Experiences among College
Students

Events	Percentage of Students Endorsing an Event*
1. Looking at the beauties of nature	45%
2. Moments of quiet reflection	42%
3. Listening to music	32%
4. Drugs	22%
5. Physical exercise	21%
6. Watching little children	19%
7. Reading a poem or novel	18%
8. Your own creative work	18%
9. Prayer	16%
10. Sexual lovemaking	14%
11. Looking at a painting	10%
12. Being alone in church	8%
13. Attending church service	7%
14. Reading the Bible	7%
15. Others (students cited meditation, theater, writing, my own poetry, dreaming, and so on)	33%

*Students could endorse as many or as few of the 14 events on the list as they wished. Adapted from Keutzer, 1978, p. 78.

sequence, self-actualization demands D-cognition, or the arousal of safety needs, as well as B-cognition. In a broader sense, this means that the actualization process will involve conflict, struggle, uncertainty, guilt, and regret as well as bliss and pleasure (Maslow, 1962, p. 111).

Another danger associated with B-cognizing is that it often leads to an indiscriminate acceptance of others. According to Maslow, this outcome occurs "because every person, seen from the viewpoint of his own Being exclusively, is seen as perfect in his own kind. Evaluation, condemnation, ... criticism, comparison [with others] are all then inapplicable and beside the point" (Maslow, 1962, p. 115). Yet there are times when people can be too tolerant of others. Maslow argued that they must also accept the responsibility for fostering growth in others by setting limits for them, by disciplining them, and by deliberately being the frustraters. Parents and teachers are confronted continuously by this dilemma (Maslow, 1962, p. 112).

There is also the danger that people who are B-cognizing will be misunderstood by others who will interpret the B-cognizer's inactivity as a lack of love, concern, and compassion. As a consequence, their own growth may be retarded because they may come to perceive others as "bad," as less deserving of their trust and respect (Maslow, 1962, p. 113).

Characteristics of Self-Actualizing People

To discover the distinguishing characteristics of **self-actualizers**, Maslow reported using the following procedure. He selected the best specimens of humanity he could find from among his friends and acquaintances and from among various public and historical figures. The latter included Abraham Lincoln in his later years, Thomas Jefferson, Albert Einstein, Eleanor Roosevelt, Jane Addams, William James, Albert Schweitzer, Aldous Huxley, and Baruch Spinoza, among others. These individuals were selected for intensive study because, according to Maslow, none showed neurosis, psychopathic personality, or psychosis and all had self-actualization tendencies. He admitted that his data were impressionistic and did not meet conventional scientific reliability, validity, and sampling standards. Yet he felt the problem of psychological health was so important that he was compelled to present this "evidence" for its heuristic value (Maslow, 1970a, pp. 149–152).

After extensive analysis of these individuals' lives, he found that actualizers have a more efficient perception of reality than nonactualizers. They are more capable than nonactualizers of perceiving the truth in many different situations. They are capable of detecting dishonesty and fakery in others. In addition, they are less guided in their judgments by stereotypes and prejudices (Maslow, 1970a, pp. 153–154). Actualizers show a greater acceptance of themselves, others, and nature than nonactualizers. They recognize their own shortcomings and those of others, but they do not feel excessively guilty or anxious about them. Instead, they tend to deal with them stoically in the same way that one accepts the workings of nature. Maslow also found that actualizers tend to be hearty in their appetites and enjoy themselves without regret or shame or apology (Maslow, 1970a, p. 156). They sleep well and enjoy sex without unnecessary inhibitions. They are not ashamed of their biological functioning—urination, defecation, menstruation, pregnancy, and growing older. These functions are part of reality and are accepted (Maslow, 1970a, p. 156).

Actualizing people are more problem-centered than nonactualizers. Nonactualizers tend to be very concerned with themselves and are characterized by feelings of inferiority. Actualizers, in contrast, are more concerned with undertaking tasks that will benefit others. They are less introspective and more task-oriented (Maslow, 1970a, pp. 159–160). Actualizers were also found to show greater resistance to enculturation than their more ordinary counterparts. They tend to be "ruled by the laws of their own character rather than by the rules of society" (Maslow, 1970a, p. 174). They show neither excessive rejection nor uncritical acceptance of the rules of society. Instead, they are more detached from the culture. They can yield to folkways perceived by them as harmless, yet react strongly against injustices. In general, though, they "show what might be called a calm, long-time concern with culture improvement that seems ... to imply an acceptance to slowness of change along with the unquestioned desirability and necessity of such change" (Maslow, 1970a, p. 172).

Finally, Maslow claimed that actualizers possess a democratic character structure. In contrast to nonactualizers, they are less likely to focus their attention on race, color, creed, sex, religious affiliation, educational level, or social class. Although they tend to be more creative than their more average counterparts, they do not consider themselves superior in all respects to others. They acknowledge their own limitations and can ask for help in areas in which they lack expertise. They honestly respect others and can be genuinely humble before people who can teach them something they do not know. Although they tend to select elite individuals for their friends, Maslow argued that this choice is made on the basis of talent and ability and not birth, race, sex, family, age, fame, or power (Maslow, 1970a, pp. 167–168).

After reviewing Maslow's list of characteristics for the actualizer, many students report having uncontrollable impulses to leap to their feet and recite the Boy Scout Oath. When they regain their senses, they say that Maslow's actualizers seem to be caricatures of the good human being. Maslow acknowledged this problem and said he found evidence in his studies that actualizers have a number of weaknesses. They "can be boring, stubborn, [and] irritating. They are by no means free from ... superficial vanity, pride, partiality to their own productions, family, friends, and children. Temper outbursts are not rare" (Maslow, 1970a, p. 175). They can also show extraordinary ruthlessness. For example, they can reject a friend totally and irrevocably if they find he or she has been dishonest with them. At times they can also show behavior and use language that is shocking and insulting. In brief, they are as capable as any other human being of displaying injurious and primitive behavior on occasion.

The Process of Personality Development

Maslow posited a universal stage-emergent theory of personal development, according to which the individual must, at least to a certain extent, satisfy the lower needs before higher ones can become operative. The emergence or nonemergence of the stages depends to a considerable degree on the kind of environment that confronts the individual. As noted earlier, environments that threaten the individual and do not allow for the satisfaction of basic needs are detrimental to growth, whereas environments that are supportive and provide for the gratification of these needs promote growth toward self-actualization. In Maslow's view, the role of the environment is crucial in the early stages of development when the person is struggling to gratify basic needs. For example, it is clear that needs for safety, love, and belongingness all depend on the cooperation of other people for gratification. Later on, as the higher needs emerge, the person becomes less dependent on the environment and relies on his or her inner experiences to guide behavior. That behavior is determined by his or her inner nature, capacities, potentialities, talents, and creative impulses (Maslow, 1962, p. 32). Such an individual is clearly less dependent on rewards or approval from others. Thus the shift is from instrumental learning (associative learning) to perceptual learning. Whereas instrumental learning generally involves voluntary responding to secure external rewards, perceptual learning involves an increase in insight and self-understanding. As Maslow put it:

> *The techniques of repeatedly acquiring from the outside world satisfactions of motivational deficiencies are much less needed. Associative learning . . . give[s] way more to perceptual learning, to the increase of insight and understanding, to knowledge of self and to the steady growth of personality. . . . Change becomes much less an acquisition of habits or associations one by one, and much more a total change of the total person. . . . This kind of character-change learning means changing a very complex, highly integrated, holistic organism, which in turn means that many impacts will make no change at all because more and more such impacts will be rejected as the person becomes more stable and more autonomous. [Maslow, 1962, p. 36]*

With the advent of persistent perceptual learning, the person is free to make his or her own spontaneous choices. These choices are made by listening to one's inner nature and not by relying on the values and expectations of others.

Techniques of Assessment

Maslow utilized a variety of research techniques in an attempt to identify self-actualizing individuals. He began by employing a selection technique called iteration (Maslow, 1970a, p. 151). It consisted of starting with his general belief concerning the meaning of self-actualization and then collating it and other existing definitions, as they were used by people in the culture, in an attempt to discover a common ground. A common definition was made possible by the systematic elimination of logical inconsistencies among the various definitions. Once the term had been refined and redefined, it was used to screen 3000 college students to determine whether they were high or low in self-actualization. Once the group had been divided into actualizers or nonactualizers, each person was examined in case-study fashion through use of the Rorschach test, Murray's Thematic Apperception Test, free association, and in-depth interviews to determine whether they possessed the characteristics of actualizers.

This effort can be thought of as an attempt to validate the concept of self-actualization empirically. The definition of the term was then changed and corrected further, where necessary, in light of the findings. Then the original subject pool was reselected on the basis of the new definition, and the retainees were restudied, using the same clinical procedures. On the basis of the new data, the self-actualization definition was again revised, and the new definition was used to reselect subjects from the remaining subject pool for further clinical study, and so on, until a precise identification of actualizers and nonactualizers was obtained. Thus the procedure involves beginning with a vague notion of the meaning of a term, then continuing with subsequent refinement on the basis of the collection of empirical evidence. As you might suspect, the use of such a procedure greatly reduced the number of individuals in 3000 who met this stringent criterion. Maslow then argued that perhaps young people had not had sufficient time and experience to develop the characteristics associated with actualization, so that it might be best to study middle-aged and older people. These people were chosen from among his personal acquaintances and friends and from public and historical figures.

The historical and public figures included approximately 60 definite, partial, and potential cases of self-actualization such as Lincoln, Jefferson, Eleanor Roosevelt, Einstein, Schweitzer, Spinoza, G. W. Carver, Eugene V. Debs, Pablo Casals, Adlai Stevenson, George Washington, Robert Benchley, and Camille Pissarro. Maslow employed the historical method because he found that it was possible to secure sufficient information about these individuals' lives from autobiographical sources to draw meaningful conclusions, whereas it was nearly impossible to do the same for living figures. He noted that many of the latter subjects, when informed of the purpose of his research, "became self-conscious, froze up, laughed off the whole effort, or broke off the relationship" (Maslow, 1970a, p. 151). The results of his investigations revealed that, although more older people than college students were self-actualized, the actual numbers of both were very small.

As noted earlier, Maslow's assessment procedures are fraught with ambiguities and imprecisions. We are not certain, for example, of how the various tests used in the interviews were administered or scored, what kinds of free associations led Maslow to conclude that his subjects were or were not actualized, or how he decided that some of his historical figures were definitely self-actualized and others were not. Most important, since Maslow chose for study people he greatly admired, it is distinctly possible that his definition of self-actualization was simply a reflection of his personal value system. Maslow, in short, may have superimposed his own values on the research process and selectively interpreted his data in line with his own orientation.

The Personal Orientation Inventory: A Measure of Self-Actualization. Although the aforementioned methodological problems plagued Maslow's position initially and prevented adequate research tests, investigations on certain aspects of the theory have been growing because of the construction of a more reliable and valid measure of self-actualization called the **Personal Orientation Inventory (POI)** (Shostrom, 1963). The POI is a self-report questionnaire consisting of 150 two-choice items that purportedly reflect the values and behavior of major importance in the development of a self-actualizing person. In responding to POI items, the person is asked to select the one statement in each of the 150 pairs that is most true of himself or herself. The subject's responses can then be scored by two major scales—one dealing with the effective use of time (time competence) and one assessing the extent to which the individual depends on himself or herself or on others in making judgments (inner direction)—and ten subscales. The subscales measure values important to the development of the self-actualizing person—self-actualizing values, existentiality, feeling reactivity, spontaneity, self-regard, self-acceptance, nature of man, synergy, acceptance of aggression, and capacity for intimate contact. Sample items and scoring for the two major scales and the subsidiary scales are presented in Table 14.2.

The scores have the following meanings and interpretations: High scores on the time-competence scale indicate that the respondents are living in the present. Self-actualizing individuals are considered to live most fully in

Table 14.2
Sample Items from Shostrom's Personal Orientation Inventory*

Time Competence

1. a. I strive always to predict what will happen in the future.
   b. I do not feel it necessary always to predict what will happen in the future.

2. a. I prefer to save good things for future use.
   b. I prefer to use good things now.

3. a. I worry about the future.
   b. I do not worry about the future.

4. **a. It is important to me how I live in the here and now.**
   b. It is of little importance to me how I live in the here and now.

Inner Direction

1. a. My moral values are dictated by society.
   b. My moral values are self-determined.

2. a. I feel guilty when I am selfish.
   b. I don't feel guilty when I am selfish.

3. a. I am bound by the principle of fairness.
   b. **I am not absolutely bound by the principle of fairness.**
4. a. I feel I must always tell the truth.
   b. **I do not always tell the truth.**

Self-Actualizing Values

1. a. **I often make my decisions spontaneously.**
   b. I seldom make my decisions spontaneously.
2. a. **It is possible to live life in terms of what I want to do.**
   b. It is not possible to live life in terms of what I want to do.

Existentiality

1. a. I feel I must always tell the truth.
   b. **I do not always tell the truth.**

Feeling Reactivity

1. a. I live by values which are in agreement with others.
   b. **I live by values which are primarily based on my own feelings.**

Spontaneity

1. a. I must justify my actions in the pursuit of my own interests.
   b. **I need not justify my actions in the pursuit of my own interests.**

Self-Regard

1. a. It is important that others accept my point of view.
   b. **It is not necessary for others to accept my point of view.**

Self-Acceptance

1. a. **I try to be sincere but I sometimes fail.**
   b. I try to be sincere and I am sincere.

Nature of Man Constructive

1. a. I have a problem in fusing sex and love.
   b. **I have no problem in fusing sex and love.**

Synergy

1. a. **People are both good and evil.**
   b. People are not both good and evil.

Acceptance of Aggression

1. a. **I find some people who are stupid and uninteresting.**
   b. I never find any people who are stupid and uninteresting.

Capacity for Intimate Contact

1. a. I am afraid to be tender.
   b. **I am not afraid to be tender.**

---

*A person who answers the items by choosing the alternatives noted in dark type is more self-actualizing than one who does not.
Adapted from Shostrom, 1963.

the here and now and to relate the past and future to current experiencing in a meaningful way. They do not dwell either on the past or on the future; instead, they use the past to illuminate current reflections about problems and aspirations for the future and to help make decisions. In regard to the inner-direction dimension, self-actualizing respondents show that the source of their behavior is essentially inner-directed but that, to a certain degree, they recognize they must be sensitive to other people's approval and affection. High scores on the self-actualizing-values dimension suggest that respondents hold and practice the values of self-actualizing people. High scores on the existentiality dimension measure respondents' ability to hold and practice self-actualizing values flexibly. Low scores indicate that respondents hold their values rigidly and compulsively. High scores on the remaining dimensions indicate that respondents have a sensitivity to their own needs, act spontaneously, consider themselves worthwhile, accept their weaknesses and like themselves in spite of these deficiencies, believe that human beings are essentially good, can see that the opposites of life are related, can accept their feelings of anger as natural, and have an ability to develop meaningful relationships with other human beings.

Much of the early work with the POI was concerned with establishing its reliability and validity as a research instrument. Test-retest reliabilities for various samples are satisfactory, although the coefficients for certain subscales are low to moderate in certain studies (Ilardi & May, 1968).

As for validity, a number of studies show that the measure can be used to distinguish between groups in society that we would ordinarily consider to differ in their actualization levels. For example, two studies have shown that groups of psychiatric patients scored lower (were less self-actualized) on virtually all the POI scales than groups of people judged by experienced clinical psychologists to be self-actualized (Fox, Knapp, & Michael, 1968). Another study has shown that all scales of the POI discriminated among groups of alcoholic wives, nonalcoholic wives, and clinically judged self-actualizers in the expected way. A group of normal subjects also scored higher on many of the POI scales than did the alcoholic wives (Zaccaria & Weir, 1967). In general, these studies and others indicate that POI is a valid discriminator between normal and abnormal groups.

A large number of studies have indicated that the POI can be utilized effectively to measure changes in self-actualization following sensitivity training and encounter-group experiences. Dosamantes-Alperson and Merrill (1980), for example, administered the POI to groups of people before and after they participated in a number of group-therapy sessions. Control groups (a ballet class and a waiting-list group drawn from the same population as the therapy groups) also filled out the POI at the same times but received no therapeutic experiences. The results indicated that in comparison to the controls, participants in the therapy sessions became more self-actualizing; that is, they became more inner-directed, spontaneous, and self-accepting. In another investigation there were also changes in POI scores on most of the subscales as well as on the two major scales in the direction of greater self-actualization following counseling that emphasized expression of feelings and the need to be sensitive to the desires of others, as compared to a variety of control groups who received no counseling (Pearson, 1966).

Despite these generally positive results, we cannot conclude that the scale has no methodological flaws. One primary, recurring problem is that subjects can deliberately fake their responses in ways designed to elicit positive impressions from others. It is possible for subjects who are familiar with the literature of **humanistic psychology** to deliberately present themselves as actualized when in fact they are not. Even though the POI has a built-in lie-detection scale to uncover such dissimulation, its usefulness as a research instrument would be weakened if it could be shown that sizable numbers of subjects do indeed fake their responses. The percentage of such subjects in a variety of populations has yet to be determined. At this point, a reasonable conclusion would be that the instrument is usable primarily with naive populations.

There are other problems with the measure. For example, subjects generally do not like to respond to forced-choice questionnaires because they feel that such instruments often do not provide them with an opportunity to present their feelings and opinions on a given topic fully and accurately. There is also the problem, common to most measures of personality, of neglecting to assess the person's traits in interaction with specific situations. How would you feel about being forced to select one of these alternatives for this POI item?

    a. I can cope with the ups and downs of life.
    b. I cannot cope with the ups and downs of life.

Perhaps you can cope with the "downs" or failures in life when they involve schoolwork but not when they involve the loss of a close friend. Maybe you can cope well with success in school but react poorly to praise from teachers or friends. Maybe you can cope well with the loss of your transistor radio but not with the theft of your new stereo set. The point is that a number of questions on the POI do not assess individual reactions in specific situations.

In conclusion, although the many investigations based on the POI have established that it has satisfactory reliability and validity (see Knapp, 1976), there has been a new attempt to improve the scale by extending and refining the concepts of actualizing measured by it. This new attempt involves the creation of a new testing instrument called the **Personal Orientation Dimensions (POD)** (Shostrom, 1975; 1977). Many of its scales are conceptually similar to ones in the POI, although a few are not. Preliminary work to establish the POD's reliability and validity is underway (Jansen, Knapp, & Michael, 1979; Knapp & Knapp, 1978; Rofsky et al., 1977), but for the most part, researchers will continue to use the POI until they are convinced that the POD has more adequate psychometric properties.

Application of the Theory to the Treatment of Psychopathology

For Maslow, neurotics are people who have been prevented and who have prevented themselves from attaining gratification of their basic needs. This hindrance stops them from moving toward the ultimate goal of self-actualization. They are individuals who feel threatened and insecure and who have little self-respect and esteem. Since the gratification of these basic needs can occur only through contact with other people, it follows that therapy must be interpersonal in nature (Maslow, 1970a, p. 242). Maslow likened the psychotherapeutic relationship between therapist and client to a relationship between friends. The therapy situation must involve mutual frankness, trust, honesty, and lack of defensiveness. It should also allow for the expression of a healthy amount of childishness and silliness (Maslow, 1970a, p. 249). The expression of these "weaknesses" is possible when the relationship is nonthreatening and supportive. In such a democratic context, the therapist should provide the client with the respect, love, and feelings of belongingness he or she must have in order to grow. In other words, the therapist must act to gratify the client's basic-need deficiencies. But effective therapy must go beyond this point. The therapeutic relationship should encourage not only the giving of love by the therapist to the client but also the expression of love and affection by the client toward the therapist and others (Maslow, 1970a, p. 250). The client should, in general, be encouraged to display those values associated with positive growth. He or she should be encouraged to "open up" to the world and learn to understand more about its complex nature.

Maslow realized that a warm, supportive therapeutic approach was unworkable with some clients, particularly those with chronic, stabilized neuroses involving deep mistrust and hostility toward others (Maslow, 1970a, p. 251). Under such conditions, Maslow believed that a depth analysis in the Freudian tradition might be more workable. Such an analysis would involve both a cognitive *and* an emotional "working through" by the person of his or her problems as a means of achieving change and self-improvement.

Critical Comments

We turn now to an evaluation of the scientific worth of Maslow's position on the basis of our six criteria.

Comprehensiveness. Maslow's theory is a pioneering and creative effort aimed at pushing personality psychology away from an exclusive concern

Limited

with psychopathology and toward a more positive and optimistic view of people concerned with their potential creativeness. His theory can be considered quite comprehensive in the sense that it incorporates much of the Freudian model of pathology and, in addition, addresses itself to the issue of positive growth; but technically speaking, its focus is primarily and explicitly on the latter rather than the former. In this sense, the theory is not quite as comprehensive as it appears at first. The theory itself does not spell out precisely the variables that control the occurrence, maintenance, and modification of self-actualization phenomena. Under these circumstances, Maslow's theory can be judged as somewhat limited both in the range and diversity of phenomena it explicitly encompasses and in the explanatory system it uses to account for these events.

Precision and Testability. Maslow's theory is not very precise and as a result is difficult to test properly. For example, his hierarchical scheme of human motivation, which is presumed to involve the emergence of our basic needs from most to least potent after their relative gratification, is marked by deficiencies. There are people who are willing to suffer hunger and thirst and eventually even to die for values Maslow assumed are less potent than the physiological needs. Although he recognized this problem, the theory does not account for the exceptions.

There is also a lack of precision concerning the exact amount of gratification the individual must experience before the next higher need will emerge. Maslow maintained that most people are partially satisfied and partially dissatisfied in their basic needs at the same time, so it is incorrect to assume that a given need must be completely gratified before the next will emerge. Instead, Maslow posited a gradual emergence of a higher need as the lower need becomes increasingly gratified. For example, if a lower need is 10% gratified, perhaps there will be no emergence of the next higher need. But if the lower need is 25% gratified, the higher need may emerge at 5% of potency; if the lower need is 50% gratified, there may be a 25% emergence, and so on (Maslow, 1970a, pp. 53–54).

Adequate definition of self-actualization and a number of other terms (purposefulness, inner requiredness, and "good" and "bad" situations) remains a major problem with the theory.

Parsimony. Maslow's theory fails to meet the parsimony criterion. The motivational deficiency scheme he uses to account for various behaviors, although more detailed than that employed by Rogers (see Chapter 15), is still too simplistic to account adequately for the phenomena within its domain.

Empirical Validity. Without adequate measures of the major constructs in Maslow's theory, tests of its empirical validity are impossible. Fortunately, however, researchers have constructed an adequate measure of actualization, as we have seen. Where the theory has been tested by utilizing the actualization measure, however, the research results have not been consistently supportive. For example, Mathes (1978) found no evidence for Maslow's hypothesis that self-actualizers are more creative than nonactualizers. Maslow also posits that actualizers tend to be physically strong, fit people, but Ryckman and co-workers (1983) could find no support for this hypothesis in two independent samples of undergraduate subjects. Despite these inconsistent findings, research interest in Maslow's theory continues to grow, as evidenced by the construction of new individual-difference measures of peak experiences (Mathes & Zevon, 1982) and of the basic needs (Haymes & Green, 1982).

Heuristic Value. Despite its many limitations, Maslow's theory has been provocative and has stimulated the thinking of many investigators in many disciplines. Not only has he encouraged theorists and researchers to consider the healthy side of human nature, but he has also forced some of them to reconsider their own myopic view of science and its limitations for understanding human functioning. Specifically, he has castigated them for their "inevitable stress of elegance, polish, technique, and apparatus [that] has, as a frequent consequence, a playing down of meaningfulness, vitality, and significance of a problem and of creativeness in general" (Maslow, 1970a, p. 11). As a result, he has gotten some of them to think of science as an enterprise in which people ask significant questions and then adopt techniques to help answer them rather than as a situation in which sophisticated techniques are used to study relatively unimportant problems.

Applied Value. Maslow's theory is also very strong in the applied area. His formulations have had a decided impact on pastoral and educational counseling programs and on various business-management programs.

Discussion Questions

1. What are the implications for the development of an individual's personality in light of Maslow's equivocal assumption that human nature is good or, at the very least, neutral?
2. Is it possible, in your opinion, to discover a universal set of ethical principles we can use to guide our behavior? What principles guide your life?
3. What are some of the limitations of Maslow's proposed self-actualization hierarchy of needs?
4. Do you agree with Maslow that children need limits on their behavior? Why or why not?
5. Have you experienced B-love? How could you be certain?
6. What is the need for cognitive understanding? In what ways can this need be satisfied?
7. Maslow maintains that we not only fear failure but often are afraid to be successful. Why does he hold such a belief? What great work are you planning in your own life? Are you satisfied with your progress toward your goals?

8. What are some of the dangers associated with B-cognition states?
9. In the self-actualization hierarchy, how would you characterize yourself?
10. List and discuss the strengths and weaknesses of self-actualizing people.

References

Dietch, J. Love, sex roles, and psychological health. *Journal of Personality Assessment,* 1978, *42,* 626–634.

Dosamantes-Alperson, E., & Merrill, N. Growth effects of experiential movement psychotherapy. *Psychotherapy: Theory, research, and practice,* 1980, *17,* 63–68.

Fox, J., Knapp, R. R., & Michael, W. B. Assessment of self-actualization of psychiatric patients: Validity of the Personal Orientation Inventory. *Educational and Psychological Measurement,* 1968, *28,* 565–569.

Haymes, M., & Green, L. The assessment of motivation within Maslow's framework. *Journal of Research in Personality,* 1982, *16,* 179–192.

Ilardi, R. L., & May, W. T. A reliability study of Shostrom's Personal Orientation Inventory. *Journal of Humanistic Psychology,* 1968, *8,* 68–72.

Jansen, D. G., Knapp, R. R., & Michael, W. B. Construct validation of concepts of actualizing measured by the Personal Orientation Dimensions, *Educational and Psychological Measurement,* 1979, *39,* 505–509.

Keutzer, C. S. Whatever turns you on: Triggers to transcendent experiences. *Journal of Humanistic Psychology,* 1978, *18,* 77–80.

Knapp, R. R. *Handbook for the Personal Orientation Inventory.* San Diego, Calif: EdITS/Educational and Industrial Testing Service, 1976.

Knapp, R. R., & Knapp, L. Conceptual and statistical refinement and extension of the measurement of actualizing concurrent validity of the Personal Orientation Dimensions (POD). *Educational and Psychological Measurement,* 1978, *38,* 523–526.

Maslow, A. H. A theory of motivation. *Psychological Review,* 1943, *50,* 370–396.

Maslow, A. H. *Toward a psychology of being.* New York: Van Nostrand, 1962.

Maslow, A. H. *Motivation and personality* (2nd ed.). New York: Harper & Row, 1970a.

Maslow, A. H. *Religions, values, and peak-experiences.* New York: The Viking Press, 1970b.

Maslow, A. H. *The farther reaches of human nature.* New York: Viking Press, 1971.

Mathes, E. W. Self-actualization, metavalues, and creativity. *Psychological Reports,* 1978, *43,* 215–222.

Mathes, E. W., & Zevon, M. A. Peak experience tendencies: Scale development and theory testing. *Journal of Humanistic Psychology,* 1982, *22,* 92–108.

Monahan, L., Kuhn, D., & Shaver, P. Intrapsychic versus cultural explanations of the fear of success. *Journal of Personality and Social Psychology,* 1974, *29,* 60–64.

Pearson, O. Effects of group guidance upon college adjustment. Unpublished doctoral dissertation, University of Kentucky, 1966.

Rofsky, M., Fox, J., Knapp, R. R., & Michael, W. B. Assessing the level of actualizing of psychiatric in-patients: Validity of the Personal Orientation Dimensions. *Educational and Psychological Measurement,* 1977, *37,* 1075–1079.

Ryckman, R. M., Robbins, M. A., Thornton, B., Gold, J. A., & Kuehnel, R. H. Physical self-efficacy and actualization. Colloquium presented at the Department of Psychology, Tilburg University, The Netherlands, 1983.

Shostrom, E. L. *Personal Orientation Inventory*. San Diego, Calif.: EdITS/Educational and Industrial Testing Service, 1963.

Shostrom, E. L. *Personal Orientation Dimensions*. San Diego, Calif.: EdITS/Educational and Industrial Testing Service, 1975.

Shostrom, E. L. *Manual for the Personal Orientation Dimensions*. San Diego, Calif.: EdITS/Educational and Industrial Testing Service, 1977.

Wilson, C. *New Pathways in Psychology*. London: Gollancz, 1972.

Zaccaria, J. S. & Weir, W. R. A comparison of alcoholics and selected samples of nonalcoholics in terms of a positive concept of mental health. *Journal of Social Psychology*, 1967, *71*, 151–157.

Suggested Readings

Goble, F. *The third force: The psychology of Abraham Maslow*. New York: Pocket Books, 1970.

Maslow, A., A theory of human motivation. *Psychological Review*, 1943, *50*, 370–396.

Maslow, A. *Toward a psychology of being*. New York: Van Nostrand, 1962.

Maslow, A. *Motivation and personality* (2nd ed.). New York: Harper & Row, 1970.

Maslow, A. *The farther reaches of human nature*. New York: Viking Press, 1971.

Glossary

B-cognition state State of experiencing that is nonjudgmental and self-validating.

B-love Being-love, a mature form of love in which the person is more concerned with giving love to benefit others than in receiving love from others for gratification of his or her needs.

D-cognition state State of experiencing that involves judgments of approval and disapproval.

Deficiency need Basic need that must be gratified to a large extent before an individual can progress toward self-actualization.

Desacralizing attitude The tendency to be disrespectful, cynical, and mistrustful of others. Such an attitude causes the perceiver to overlook the virtues and strengths of the perceived.

D-love Deficiency-love, a selfish love in which the individual is concerned more with receiving love and gratifying his or her needs than with giving love to another.

Growth need Higher need that may emerge once the basic needs have been satisfied (meta need).

Humanistic biology The view that the basic nature of human beings is potentially good and capable of pushing people in the direction of self-realization if the "right" social conditions prevail.

Humanistic psychology Type of psychology concerned primarily with helping individuals to reach their maximum. It is also a psychology that emphasizes and tries to foster the dignity and worth of each human being.

Jonah complex The fear that the exercise of our abilities to the maximum will bring with it responsibilities and duties that we will be unable to handle. Thus there is an unwillingness to sacrifice current safety and security for the unknown.

Peak experience Intense, mystical experience in which an individual exists in a temporary state of joy and wonderment.

Personal Orientation Dimensions (POD) New test to measure self-actualization in adolescents and adults in a more reliable and valid way than the Personal Orientation Inventory.

Personal Orientation Inventory (POI) Test designed to measure the self-actualizing tendencies of the individual.

Self-actualization Process postulated by Maslow as involving the healthy development of the abilities of people so that they can fulfill their own true natures.

Self-actualizers Individuals who have gratified their basic needs and developed their potentialities to the point that they can be considered healthy, fully functioning human beings.

C H A P T E R 15

Rogers' Person-Centered Theory

Biographical Sketch

Carl Ransom Rogers was born in 1902 in Oak Park, Illinois, a suburb of Chicago. He was the fourth in a family of six children. His father was a successful civil engineer and contractor. Rogers reports that he was raised in a home marked by close and warm family relationships but also by strict and uncompromising religious principles. His parents controlled his behavior and would allow no alcoholic beverages, no dancing, no card playing or theatergoing, and very little contact with other people. Instead, they extolled the virtues of the Protestant Ethic—hard work, responsibility for one's actions, and the importance of personal success. Rogers reports that "even carbonated beverages had a faintly sinful aroma, and I remember my slight feeling of wickedness when I had my first bottle of 'pop'" (Rogers, 1961, p. 5). His wife, who was his childhood sweetheart, also remembers him as a "shy, sensitive, and unsocial boy who preferred to live in his books and his dream world rather than encounter the rough [and] tumble of the play yard or

414

enter into competitive sports" (H. E. Rogers, 1965, p. 94). Thus Rogers seems to have been a rather solitary figure who had strong scholarly interests from an early age.

When he was 12, his parents bought a farm a short distance from Chicago, and Rogers spent his adolescence there. His father encouraged his sons to raise animals for profit, so Rogers reared chickens, lambs, pigs, and calves. The venture caused him to become interested in scientific agriculture and how scientific methods could be applied to farming. In retrospect, Rogers believes the experience taught him a healthy respect for science and the ways in which it could be used to solve problems (Rogers, 1961, p. 6). He entered the University of Wisconsin and chose scientific agriculture as his field of study. Shortly afterward, his professional goals shifted dramatically as a result of some emotion-laden experiences at student religious conferences. After graduation, he entered Union Theological Seminary in New York City. There, he and a group of other students decided they were being unilaterally presented with ideas by their instructors but were not being given an opportunity to fully explore their own personal doubts and questions. Accordingly, they petitioned the administration for a seminar without a formal instructor. To their surprise, the request was granted. Rogers found the seminar most gratifying and reports that, as a result of the experience, he thought himself right out of religious work (Rogers, 1961, p. 8).

As he had taken some courses in psychology and enjoyed them, he decided to enter that field and began his studies at Columbia University, which was located across the street from the seminary. At the end of his clinical internship, even though he had not completed his doctorate, Rogers felt he had to have a job to support his growing family. He took a position as a psychologist in the Child Study Department of the Society for the Prevention of Cruelty to Children, in Rochester, New York, and completed his doctorate in 1928. Rogers reports that the 12 years spent at Rochester were valuable ones. During most of these years, he was immersed in practical work, the diagnosis and treatment of delinquent and disadvantaged children. Rogers' unique nondirective or client-centered therapy approach evolved during this period and culminated in the book *Clinical Treatment of the Child* (1939). In 1940, he accepted an academic position at Ohio State University as a full professor. He began to attract capable students and to conduct research tests of his theory; it was also at this point that he achieved international recognition. *Counseling and Psychotherapy* (1942), a book designed to provide therapists with procedures he felt would engender constructive changes in their clients, was written during this time.

In 1944, Rogers was given an opportunity to establish a counseling center at the University of Chicago. He then wrote *Client-Centered Therapy* (1951), in which he provided readers with the theory that underlies his approach to an understanding of human relationships. Still later he published *On Becoming a Person* (1961), a collection of papers on a variety of issues relating to Rogers' basic approach to understanding personal growth.

In 1957, Rogers returned to the University of Wisconsin. He recalls that his experiences there were generally unpleasant as he became aware of the restrictions under which graduate students were forced to work. He called for massive reform in the graduate program, arguing that students have the potential for learning and development within themselves but that this potential can be realized only when they are provided with freedom and a supportive environment (Rogers, 1968, pp. 687–703). Shortly after he released the reasons for his disagreement with current educational policies, he resigned from the department.

In 1963, he became a member of the Western Behavioral Sciences Institute in La Jolla, California. Five years later Rogers left the institute to help form the Center for the Studies of the Person in La Jolla, where he has remained to the present time.

In 1967, he wrote *Person to Person: The Problem of Being Human* in collaboration with Barry Stevens. This book was followed by *Freedom to Learn* (1969), *Carl Rogers on Encounter Groups* (1970), *Becoming Partners: Marriage and Its Alternatives* (1972a), *Carl Rogers on Personal Power* (1977), and, finally, *A Way of Being* (1980). In the book on personal power, Rogers attempts to illustrate the revolutionary impact of his person-centered approach on psychotherapy, family life, education, administration, and politics. He also discusses the implications of his approach for the emergence in the culture of a new type of self-empowered person who will spearhead the revolution in human relationships that Rogers believes is occurring.

Died Feb, 1987 (Same yrs studied)

Basic Concepts and Principles

The Fundamental Perspective: The Person's Experiences as the Ultimate Authority

Rogers' psychology starts and ends with the subjective experiences of the individual. The subjective experiencing of reality is critically important, in Rogers' view, because it serves as the basis for all the individual's judgments and behavior. It is this phenomenological, inner reality rather than external, objective reality that plays the key role in determining the person's behavior.

Inner experience includes everything that is occurring within the organism at a particular moment. All this experience, conscious and unconscious, is said to comprise the person's phenomenal field. Conscious experience or awareness is the aspect of the phenomenal field that involves the symbolization of experience. Symbolized experience, in turn, involves the ability to verbalize or imagine experience. Unconscious experience, in contrast, is experience that cannot be verbalized or imagined by the person. The healthy person, in Rogers' view, can symbolize his or her experiences accurately and completely, whereas the unhealthy person distorts or represses his or her experiences and is unable to symbolize them accurately and sense them fully.

Self-Actualizing Tendency: The Master Motive. There is also within each of us, according to Rogers, an innate motivation called the actualizing tendency. He conceptualizes it as an active, controlling drive toward fulfillment of our potentials, a drive that enables us to maintain and enhance ourselves.

Rogers' conclusion that this positive tendency exists was based primarily on his varied and prolonged experience with many troubled individuals in therapy. He noticed in them

> a growth tendency, a drive toward self-actualization.... It is the urge which is evident in all organic and human life—to expand, extend, become autonomous, develop, mature.... This tendency may become deeply buried under layer after layer of encrusted psychological defenses ... but it is my belief that it exists in every individual, and awaits only the proper conditions to be released and expressed. [Rogers, 1961, p. 35]

Rogers also infers the existence of this tendency by citing experiments that show that even the "lowly" rat prefers an environment involving more complex stimuli over one involving less complex stimuli. Human beings also seek new experiences and avoid environments that are lacking in stimulation. As Rogers points out, experiments have shown that when human beings are suspended weightless in a soundproof tank of water for long periods of time, they experience aversive hallucinations. For Rogers, then, these studies and his many experiences in therapy suggest that there is a directional tendency in each of us to grow, to seek new and varied experiences.

The actualizing tendency has both a biological and a psychological aspect to it. The biological aspect includes drives aimed at the satisfaction of needs essential for our survival—the needs for water, food, and air. The psychological aspect involves the development of potentials that make us more worthwhile human beings. In Rogers' judgment, we are all basically good. The actualizing tendency is, thus, selective and directional, a constructive tendency. Organisms do not, according to Rogers, develop their capacity for nausea or self-destruction except under the most perverse circumstances (Rogers, 1977, p. 242). Instead, they develop their innate goodness but only if society acts toward them in a helpful, encouraging way. Although Rogers is clearly optimistic about human nature, he is nevertheless keenly aware that human beings are sometimes immature and antisocial and that they sometimes act out of fear, ignorance, and defensiveness. Such behavior, however, is not in accordance with their basic natures, according to Rogers, but is instead the result of faulty socialization practices. In general, then, society can facilitate or hinder movement toward self-actualization. We now turn to a discussion of exactly how society does so.

The Process of Personality Development

The Valuing Process in Infants

Rogers maintains that infants perceive their experiences as reality. They operate from an internal frame of reference and are unencumbered by the evaluations of others. He also believes that infants interact with their reality in terms of their basic actualizing tendency (Rogers, 1959, p. 222). That is, their behavior is directed toward the goal of satisfying their need for self-actualization as they perceive it. As a result, infants engage in an **organismic valuing process** in which they use their actualization tendency as a criterion in making judgments about the worth of a given experience. Experiences that help promote actualization are "good," or positively valued; experiences that hinder actualization are "bad," or negatively valued. In support of his argument, Rogers cites the example of an infant who values food when he is hungry but rejects it when satiated. He contends further that infants have a built-in mechanism that allows them to select the diet that, in the long run, enhances their development (Rogers, 1959, p. 210; Rogers & Stevens, 1967, p. 6). Thus Rogers maintains that infants "know" instinctively which foods and experiences are good for them and which are bad. Yet the scientific evidence in support of Rogers' "organismic wisdom" hypothesis is weak.

The Davis Infant Study. Let us examine the investigation most cited by Rogers, Maslow, and others who have attempted to build a psychology on the notion that people not only know what foods are best for them but also know the answers to their problems instinctively. Davis (1928) reports that three infants ranging in age from 8 to 10 months were given thorough physical examinations by a medical doctor, including a blood count, urinalysis, and X rays of the bones. After the examination, the infants were given an opportunity to select their own diets from saucers holding different foods and from glasses filled with different liquids. A list of a typical meal is shown in Table 15.1. Nurses were present at each feeding but did not offer any food to the infants. If the infants reached or pointed to a food or liquid, however, the nurses were allowed by the experimenter to offer them a spoonful. Two infants were on such a diet for six months and one for a year. At the end of each period, the infants were again given complete physical examinations. The results showed that, in general, the diets selected were optimal and the infants were healthy.

What is wrong with this study? With acumen born of hindsight, we could point to several major deficiencies. The role of the nurses introduces a possible source of error because they could have misjudged random arm waving and reaching as signs of the infants' wanting a particular food. Moreover,

Table 15.1
Typical Meal Served to Test for Adequacy of Self-Selection Diet

Milk, grade A	Beets, cooked
Milk, lactic	Carrots, raw
Seasalt (Seisal)	Carrots, cooked
Rye-Krisp	Turnips, cooked
Bone marrow, raw	Cauliflower, cooked
Bone marrow, cooked	Cabbage, raw
Beef, raw	Cabbage, cooked
Lamb, cooked	Spinach, cooked
Beef, cooked	Peas, cooked
Chicken, cooked	Peas, raw
Lettuce, raw	Cornmeal, cooked
Potatoes, cooked	

Adapted from Davis, 1928, p. 659.

because the experiment lasted a relatively short time, it is impossible to assess its impact on development. Harmful effects could have surfaced after much longer periods had elapsed. Further, all the foods offered were nutritious, so the choices available to the infants could only promote health. Of course, it would have been unethical to provide infants with nonnutritive food choices, but this does not negate the fact that most of the available choices contained nutrients necessary for maintaining health. Finally, only three infants participated in the study, so it is clearly unwarranted to generalize these results to all infants in the culture.

Of course, numerous studies with lower animals do support the notion of specific hungers—that is, animals tend to select those foods that enable them to compensate for specific nutritional deficiencies (Krieckhaus, 1970), but still other investigations in the same research literature show that these innate propensities in lower animals can be rather easily overriden by learning experiences (Garcia, Kimeldurf, & Hunt, 1961). Thus, even if we could generalize the results of studies conducted on rats to the behavior of human beings, we might still conclude that humans would have an extremely difficult time getting in touch with their organismic-wisdom mechanism in order to make good decisions, because their learning experiences would interfere. Rogers hints at this problem when he states that the drive toward self-actualization may be "deeply buried under layer after layer of encrusted psychological defenses" (Rogers, 1961, p. 35). At the very least, then, the process of getting in touch with our innermost feelings would be difficult.

The Valuing Process in Adults

In adults, the valuing process is much more complex than it is in infants. At this point in the developmental process, the adult is making more complicated judgments about experiences relating to issues in art, politics, career, ethics, personal relationships, and so forth. Moreover, the value judgments being made in these areas are often changing. A painting that was satisfying to the person last year may be abhorrent to him or her now. Judgments about friends, acquaintances, politicians, doctors, teachers, clergy, parents, and others do not remain constant. The judgments are more difficult to make. In addition, adults, unlike infants, are exposed to a variety of opinions about the correct stand on issues and come to incorporate them into their value systems. Yet, in Rogers' view, adults, though listening to what others think, must ultimately trust the wisdom of their bodies if they are to grow constructively. They realize that if they can trust themselves fully, their feelings and intuitions may be wiser than their thinking or than what they have learned from others about these matters (Rogers & Stevens, 1967, pp. 15–16).

Although it is critical that people rely on their own intuitions about what is correct or incorrect, they often grow up thinking and evaluating their experiences in terms of the values of others. In fact, their self-concept is very often based primarily on the acceptance of the evaluations of others concerning what is appropriate or inappropriate behavior. We turn now to a more detailed examination of the emergence of the self.

The Self-Concept. The self-concept is a central concept in Rogers' theory. It is the organized set of characteristics that the individual perceives as being peculiar to himself or herself. It is primarily a social product and is acquired through social contact. Rogers believes that as we interact with significant people in our environment, like parents, brothers, sisters, friends, and teachers, we begin to develop a concept of self that is largely based on the evaluations of others. In short, we come to evaluate ourselves according to what others think rather than what we feel. We rely so heavily on the evaluation of others, according to Rogers, because we have a **need for positive regard**. Rogers is uncertain concerning whether this need is innate or learned, but he maintains that its origins do not really matter that much. What does matter is its impact on the individual. It is a strong need and is responsible for our tendency to rely more on others than on ourselves for judgments about personal self-worth. We are aware that when we satisfy another's needs, we necessarily experience satisfaction of our own need for positive regard (Rogers, 1959, p. 223). As a consequence, the desire for positive regard from others may become more compelling than our organismic valuing process (Rogers, 1959, p. 224). If, for example, we feel that aggression against others is wrong but significant others place a positive value on it, we may ignore the validity of our feelings and act in line with their expectations to gain their approval.

This need to seek approval from people and avoid disapproval is respon-sible for the emergence of a self-concept that is conditional on the perfor-mance of only given kinds of behavior (Rogers, 1959, p. 209). With this emer-gence the person is said to have acquired a **condition of worth**. Experiences and behaviors are perceived as acceptable by the person only if they meet with the approval of others. Experiences and behaviors that meet with dis-approval from others are perceived as unacceptable.

If, on the other hand, the person experienced only **unconditional pos-itive regard** from others, no conditions of worth would be present. In such a case, there would be **congruence** between self and experience, and the person would be psychologically healthy. This state of affairs, however, is an ideal. We all have conditions of worth placed on our behavior. We all learn in the course of socialization that some of our feelings and behaviors are "appropriate" and others are "inappropriate." When these normative rules are congruent or in line with our organismic evaluations, we continue our movement toward self-actualization. When the expectations run counter to our innate evaluations, however, problems occur and movement toward actualization is hindered. Congruence between self and organismic expe-riencing leads to accurate symbolization of experiences and positive growth. Incongruence leads to inaccurate or distorted symbolization, psychological maladjustment, and vulnerability. Under such incongruent conditions, the person may experience a vague sense that something is wrong. The threat, in Rogers' view, may be "subceived" before it is clearly perceived. That is, the person may experience an increased heartbeat and breathing rate and a sense of anxiety without being able to accurately identify the source of the difficulty. This anxiety then leads to the use of defense mechanisms for coping with the threat. If the incongruence between self and organismic experiencing is too great or significant, defense may be unsuccessful and a profound state of disorganization occurs. Such a person may be labeled psychotic.

Empirical Support for the Self Theory

If Rogers' theorizing about the relationship between the self and organ-ismic experiencing is correct, we would expect persons who deny threats to their self-picture—that is, persons who are defensive—to be more malad-justed than those who are less defensive. A study by Chodorkoff (1954) has provided supportive data for this reasoning. This investigator hypothesized that the greater the agreement between a person's self-description and a description of the person provided by others, the less perceptual defense he will show. This hypothesis was based on the assumption that the non-defensive person is open to all his experiences, threatening or otherwise. He should be able to assimilate them into his self-concept, providing they are organismically valid. Of course, it is assumed that the descriptions of the person provided by the judges mirror the individual's own assessment on an organismic level. (This is a questionable assumption in view of Rogers' repeated warnings that judgments based on diagnostic tests violate the individual's integrity and are, at best, only crude approximations of the person's experiencing.)

In the study, clinical judges provided descriptions based on biographical information and the results of two projective tests—the Rorschach and the Thematic Apperception Test (TAT). Scores based on the degree of agreement between the two sets of ratings were then correlated with the person's perceptual defense score, as measured by the time it took the subject to react to tachistoscopic presentations of threatening words (for example, "bitch" and "whore") compared with time latencies for nonthreatening words (for example, "chair" and "table"). As mentioned initially, the prediction was confirmed.

Another hypothesis tested was that the greater the agreement between the personal and objective descriptions of the person, the greater would be his personal adjustment. Adjustment was measured by having the judges check on a list any number of adjectives they thought described the subject, such as kind, confident, and well-liked. The more checks the person received, the greater his personal adjustment. This hypothesis was also confirmed.

Rogers' self theory also predicts that persons who are nondefensive (self-accepting) should also be more accepting of the behavior of others. In Rogers' words, "When the individual perceives and accepts into one consistent and integrated system all his sensory and visceral experiences, then he is necessarily more understanding of others and is more accepting of others as separate individuals" (Rogers, 1951, p. 520).

The data for this aspect of the theory are largely supportive, although Wylie (1979) does outline some unresolved problems with the kinds of self-report measures used to assess self-and-other acceptance. In any event, a supportive study by Phillips (1951), reported by Wylie, showed positive correlations ranging from +.51 to +.74 with groups of high school and college students, indicating that students who had greater self-acceptance also were more accepting of others. The correlations were +.35 and approximately +.57 for introductory psychology students (Suinn & Geiger, 1965; Suinn & Hill, 1964). In general, then, there seems to be solid support for the major aspects of Rogers' self theory.

Techniques of Assessment

Rogers believes that assessment of the individual's personality must be based on an exploration of the person's feelings and attitudes toward himself or herself and others. It is the client who subjectively interprets experiences and who provides the therapist with valid information about his or her functioning. Rogers recognizes that this phenomenological extremism has its limitations. For example, the therapist can gain only that experiential information about the client that he or she is able or willing to articulate. In addition, the client may purposely distort reports to the therapist and reveal information he or she believes will win approval. Despite these limitations, Rogers stands by his person-centered approach. The therapist provides a supportive and nonthreatening milieu for the client so that distortions and evasions are minimized. The therapist also tries actively not to prejudge the client by fitting him or her into a preconceived theoretical structure. Under these conditions, the therapist may gain an increased and accurate understanding of the unique strengths and weaknesses of the client, who will then probably move toward self-realization.

Although Rogers argues against the use of formal assessment techniques in the study of the client's personality, he is forced to rely on measurement procedures to test his theory. In the Chodorkoff study, for example, judges' ratings were used to assess the person's organismic experiencing. Rogers has also been a pioneer in developing a technique for assessing the nature of the interactions between client and therapist and in showing how these data are related to the therapeutic outcome. The technique involves the use of video and audio tape recordings of the therapeutic process. These tapes provide a more comprehensive and available set of data for analysis and interpretation than has ever before been possible, for earlier assessment procedures relied on written records of therapy sessions as recalled by the therapist.

Rogers has also conducted research on the impact of person-centered therapy on personality functioning by using an assessment procedure pioneered by Stephenson (1953) and labeled the Q-sort. The **Q-sort** technique is designed to measure a person's self-concept. Rogers maintains that a person's self-concept should change over the course of therapy. He believes that the initial discrepancies between the way in which clients actually view themselves and the way in which they like to view themselves are reduced by effective counseling. The Q-sort technique enables investigators to measure these discrepancies between actual and ideal selves.

On entering therapy, clients are asked to sort (arrange) a large number of self-referent statements on a 7-point continuum ranging from "not like me" (1) to "like me" (7). The list might include statements such as "I am tolerant," "I am confident," "I am intelligent," and "I am emotionally mature." After sorting these statements (usually 100 or so), clients are asked to re-sort them, in line with their views of their ideal selves, on a 7-point continuum ranging from "unlike my ideal" (1) to "like my ideal" (7). The two sets of scores are then correlated. Correlations between arrangements for clients entering therapy are generally low, suggesting that clients see their actual selves as very different from their ideal (or wanted) selves, whereas correlations following therapy tend to be high and positive, suggesting that clients see fewer discrepancies between their actual and their ideal selves—that is, their views of their actual and ideal selves are more closely matched. (We will present more details about the effectiveness of person-centered therapy, based in part on research using the Q-sort, after discussing Rogers' theory of therapy.)

In conclusion, Rogers utilizes various assessment procedures to ascertain the validity of this theory and the efficacy of his approach to therapy. His reliance on these measures may seem to be in direct contradiction to his statements about the need to avoid the use of techniques in therapy. But a more reasonable interpretation might be that assessment procedures, although an inevitable part of the therapeutic process, should be deemphasized. They should not be allowed to become so important that they prevent the therapist from understanding the experiencing of clients.

Application of the Theory to the Treatment of Psychopathology

Rogers has not only created a theory of how the self evolves and is related to actualization, he has also posited a theory of psychotherapy that focuses on the kind of relationship between the therapist and client that must be attained before positive growth is possible.

These theories had their roots in the soil of his personal experience. When he first started practicing psychotherapy with children and adults at the guidance center in Rochester, he reported having very definite preconceptions about the nature of personality functioning. His ideas were based on an acceptance of Freudian thinking because such thinking was an important part of the guidance center orientation. In practice, however, Rogers found that the Freudian formulations were unworkable. All too often, constructive changes in his clients were not forthcoming. As a consequence, he abandoned the Freudian view and adopted instead a more pragmatic orientation toward therapy. This is, the only criterion he used to judge the validity of his work with his patients was "Does it work? Is it effective?" (Rogers, 1961, p. 10). Out of this inductive approach, then, Rogers established the therapeutic conditions necessary for positive growth.

Therapeutic Conditions That Facilitate Growth

To identify the conditions that promote growth, Rogers focused not only on his direct experiences with clients, but also on the history of attempts by counselors and others to change behavior. He notes that four major techniques have been used: (1) ordering and forbidding, (2) exhortation, (3) suggestion (which includes reassurance and encouragement), and (4) advice (Rogers, 1942, pp. 20–27). As none of these techniques have been successful, Rogers thinks it is time they were abandoned. But what is wrong, for example, with reassuring someone who is experiencing doubts about his personal worth? Rogers maintains that there is a tendency for counselors to use the technique indiscriminately. Telling the client repeatedly that he is improving leads to a denial of the problem and no exploration of the client's feelings about it. Under these conditions, Rogers maintains, it is impossible for the client to improve.

In a broader sense, Rogers holds that all these techniques have directive aspects. That is, one person (the therapist) thinks of herself as an authority figure who understands the nature of the other person's problems and the best way or ways to solve them. In the therapeutic process, the counselor perceives herself as an expert who discovers, diagnoses, and treats the person's problems. In Rogers' nondirective, person-centered approach, the focus is primarily on the client himself. Instead of asking "How can I treat, or cure, or change this person?" Rogers asks, "How can I provide a relationship which this person may use for his own personal growth?" (Rogers, 1961, p. 32).

Rogers believes the person has the capacity for change within himself and will change in constructive ways if the therapist creates the appropriate conditions for growth. These conditions are as follows:

1. *The client and the therapist must be in psychological contact; that is, both must make an impact on the phenomenological field of the other.*
2. *The client is in a state of incongruence and feels anxious about it.*
3. *The therapist is congruent in the relationship.*
4. *The therapist experiences unconditional positive regard for the client.*
5. *The therapist experiences an empathic understanding of the client's internal frame of reference.*
6. *The client perceives the therapist's unconditional positive regard for him and the therapist's empathic understanding of his difficulties. [Rogers, 1959, p. 213]*

For growth to occur, then, the therapist must be congruent—that is, genuine and without a "front." The congruent therapist is, in other words, not playing a role but is, instead, openly displaying the feelings that are flowing within him at that moment. He is aware of these feelings, is able to live with them and communicate them to the client if it is appropriate to do so (Rogers & Stevens, 1967, p. 87). For example, if the therapist feels bored with the client at a particular moment, he may not be willing to tell her immediately that he has this feeling; but if she continues to be boring through many sessions, he may then mention this fact to her in the hope of dealing with it openly and constructively. Thus the therapist's job, in Rogers' view, is not to impulsively blurt out every passing feeling and accusation under the guise of being real and genuine. If and when he does express negative feelings, however, he voices them as his own reaction and not as an indication that the client has some characterological flaw (Rogers & Stevens, 1967, p. 88). Thus he might say "I am feeling bored," not "You are a boring person and must change immediately." The therapist is, in other words, not passing judgment on the client's character.

The second essential ingredient in a facilitative therapeutic relationship is the therapist's empathic understanding of the client. The therapist should be able to accurately sense the client's inner world of private meanings (Rogers & Stevens, 1967, p. 89). The congruent therapist is able to sense the client's confusion, joy, anger, hostility, and tenderness and is able to communicate this information accurately. Under these conditions, then, the client will be more trusting and accepting of the therapist's communications even concerning experiences of which the therapist is scarcely aware (Rogers & Stevens, 1967, p. 89).

Finally, the facilitative therapist is one who feels unconditional positive regard for the client. This regard is "an outgoing, positive feeling without reservations and without evaluations. It means *not* making judgments" (Rogers & Stevens, 1967, p. 91). In other words, the therapist should prize the client in a total rather than in a conditional way; he or she should not accept certain feelings in the client and reject others.

Although Rogers still endorses the concept of unconditional positive regard as being highly important for the implementation of positive growth, he has expressed some uncertainty about whether this concept applies to all clients. In work with schizophrenics, for example, he notes that some therapists are more effective when they appear to be highly conditional— that is, when they do *not* accept some of the bizarre behavior of these psychotics (Rogers & Stevens, 1967, p. 94). At the very least, however, Rogers believes that clients must be treated with respect and dignity and be given positive support by their therapists.

In Rogers' view, if the previously stated six conditions are operative, the following changes will be observed in clients:

1. *Clients will increasingly express their feelings about their lives and problems.*
2. *They will become increasingly accurate in their assessment of the meaning of their feelings.*
3. *They will begin to discern the incongruity between their self-concepts and their experiences.*
4. *They will feel threatened by the incongruity. The experience of threat is possible only because of the continued unconditional positive regard of the therapist.*
5. *They will then begin to experience fully, in awareness, feelings that have in the past been denied to awareness or distorted in awareness.*
6. *They will then become capable of reorganizing their self-concepts by assimilating these previously threatening experiences.*
7. *As therapy continues, their self-concepts will become increasingly congruent with their experiences. Their self-concepts will now include experiences that previously would have been too threatening to be in awareness. Defensiveness will be decreased.*

8. *They will become increasingly capable of experiencing the therapist's unconditional positive regard for them.*
9. *They will become increasingly positive in their regard for themselves.*
10. *They will come to evaluate their own experiences more in terms of their organismic valuing process and less in terms of the values endorsed by other people. [Rogers, 1959, p. 216]*

Rogers feels that, as an outgrowth of this process, people will become what they organismically *are* and not what other people want them to be (where these desires run contrary to their organismic valuing process).

Empirical Support for the Theory of Therapy

To determine whether or not this theory of therapy had any validity, Rogers and his colleagues embarked on an ambitious research program. The data were generally supportive. For example, Butler and Haigh (1954) found that the average correlation between actual and ideal self for 25 clients before therapy was − .01, indicating no link between perceived actual and ideal selves. Following counseling, however, it was + .34, indicating that clients changed their view of themselves by moving toward their ideal self-picture. A control group of 16 normal individuals who did not undergo therapy, but who did the Q-sorts during the same periods (pre- and postcounseling periods) as the treatment groups, had correlations of + .58 during the precounseling and + .59 during the postcounseling sessions. These correlations indicate that normals tend to see less discrepancy between their actual and ideal selves and that this relationship remains stable over time. Unfortunately, this study has several methodological flaws, as noted by Eysenck (1960). One flaw, for instance, is that the investigators failed to equate their control and treatment groups in initial psychological adjustment, so that it is impossible to assess the effectiveness of the person-centered therapy in producing changes in self-concept among the clients. (If you are interested in further elaboration of these criticisms, see Eysenck, 1960.)

In a study of a single case not subject to such methodological criticisms, Rogers (1954) analyzed the case of "Mrs. Oak," a dependent, inarticulate, passive person who had experienced rejection by others both at home and in social groups, as revealed by her responses before therapy. Mrs. Oak reported her feelings and thinking about herself by using a self-sort before therapy and several times during the course of therapy. The correlations of the self-sort *before* therapy with ones done during therapy were as follows: after the seventh therapeutic session, + .50; after the 25th session, + .42; after therapy, + .39; and 12 months after therapy, + .30. As you can see from the decreasing correlations, during the course of therapy Mrs. Oak became increasingly unlike the person she described herself as being before therapy. She perceived herself, after therapy, to be much more secure, confident, emotionally mature, and expressive, to be warmer in relationships, and to be less afraid than she was before therapy began (Rogers, 1954, pp. 274–276). Although not every person who undergoes Rogerian therapy shows such improvement, Rogers notes that the Mrs. Oak case does indicate that positive changes *may* occur in other individuals utilizing this type of psychotherapy (Rogers, 1954, p. 343).

If we accept the view that person-centered therapy can be effective in some cases, the next question that arises is "Why does it work in such cases?" As we know, Rogers maintains that it is likely to work when the therapist is facilitative—that is, when he or she is accurately empathic, genuine, respectful, and unconditionally supportive. Does any research evidence validate or invalidate Rogers' position? A host of research studies summarized by Truax and Carkhuff (1967) indicate generally that empathy, genuineness, respectfulness, and unconditional support are all essential ingredients in promoting positive personality changes in clients and successful therapeutic outcomes. Thus the success of therapy rests on the therapist's level of psychological health as he or she relates to clients.

Despite the generally positive nature of these findings, there are several problems associated with many of the investigations. For example, in most of the studies the measurement of successful therapeutic change is based only on clients' or therapists' verbalizations or clients' self-reports, *not* on clients' behavior. There is also a lack of long-term follow-up studies. That is, most studies of treatment effectiveness assess only immediate changes in clients' functioning and do not make any attempt to assess the permanence of the changes.

All in all, however, the research support for Rogers' model at present is clearly positive enough to warrant further exploration and testing. Given the complexity of the therapeutic process and the difficulty in measuring its various concepts, enormous strides have been made and are being made toward understanding the variables that facilitate or hinder personality change. (Carkhuff & Berenson, 1977).

A Possible Outcome of Facilitative Therapy: The Fully Functioning Person

If therapy is successful, clients will be able to understand the sources and consequences of their difficulties and be in a position to modify them. They will then be on their way to becoming all that they are capable of becoming. In Rogers' terminology, they are moving toward becoming **fully functioning persons**. Such individuals have the following characteristics (Rogers, 1961, pp. 187–196):

1. *They are open to experience*. That is, fully functioning people are nondefensive individuals who are open to all their feelings—for

example, feelings of fear, discouragement, pain, tenderness, courage, and awe. They are fully aware of their experiences and accept them rather than shutting them out.

2. *They are characterized by existential living*. They are open to their experiences and live them as they occur in the present. They do not try to superimpose preconceived meaning on the experiences. Instead, they are open and flexible and deal with the experience as it is. As they live the experience, they discover its meaning for themselves.

3. *They trust their organisms*. Fully functioning people do what feels right. This does not mean they are inevitably right in their choices but rather that they make their own choices, experience the consequences, and correct them if they are less than satisfying.

4. *They are creative*. Creative products and living emerge when individuals are open to new experiences, able to trust their own judgments, and willing to take risks if they feel good about a new venture.

5. *They live richer lives than other people*. They live "the good life," but its aim is not happiness, contentment, security, and bliss, although fully functioning people would experience each of these feelings at appropriate times. Instead, their lives could be characterized as exciting, challenging, meaningful, and rewarding. It is not a life for the fainthearted. It involves taking risks, experiencing pain occasionally, and facing challenges courageously.

The Wave of the Future: The Emerging Person

Recently, Rogers has extended and amplified his view of the fully functioning person by discussing the emergence of a "new political figure" in our culture (Rogers, 1977). These **emerging persons**, as he calls them, are found everywhere in our culture. They are corporate executives who have given up the rat race to live a simpler life. They are young people who have defied many of the current cultural values and formed a counterculture. They are priests and nuns who have rejected the dogma of their churches to live more meaningful lives. They are Blacks, Chicanos, women, and other minority group members who have shed their passivity and begun to live more assertive and positive lives (Rogers, 1977, p. 264).

These new emerging people have the following characteristics (Rogers, 1977, pp. 255–274):

1. *They are honest and open*. They reject the sham and hypocrisy of the government, Madison Avenue, and parents, teachers, and clergy. They are open about their sexual relationships and open in their dealing with others. These humanistically oriented people are opposed to highly structured, inflexible bureaucracies. They believe that institutions exist for human beings and not vice versa.

2. *They are indifferent to material comforts and rewards*. Blue jeans replace expensive clothes, sleeping bags replace Holiday Inn beds,

and simple (natural) foods replace fine cuisine. Emerging people are not power-hungry or achievement-hungry. They are not concerned with status but prefer to relate to people in informal, egalitarian ways.

3. *They are caring persons*. They have a deep desire to help others, to contribute to society. They are suspicious of people in the "helping professions"—counselors, social workers, and drug counselors, for example—who earn their livelihood by offering help for pay and very frequently hide behind a professional facade. Instead, emerging people voluntarily help others in crisis. They share food and lodging without question. Their caring is gentle, subtle, and nonmoralistic. When they help people down from a bad drug trip, for example, they do not hassle or preach to them.

4. *They have a deep distrust of cognitively based science and a technology that uses that science to exploit and harm nature and people*. Emerging people have an intuitive belief that significant discoveries involve feelings. They also respect the environment and do not want to see technology used to destroy it. For example, they are opposed to the nuclear arms race between the superpowers and see our political leaders as having a profound disregard for human life as they continue to advocate the construction of increasingly destructive weapons (Rogers, 1982). These comments do not mean that emerging persons are against technology per se. They can support the use of technology but only when it is used wisely to promote human welfare.

5. *They have a trust in their own experience and a profound distrust of all external authority*. Neither the pope nor the president nor intellectuals can convince emerging persons of anything that is not borne out by personal experience. They do not obey laws just for the sake of obeying them. They obey when it feels right for them to do so. They also will disobey the law and accept the consequences when the law seems unjust or immoral.

6. *They are people who are always in process*. These new people expect to change unjust political and social situations. They are not afraid of change but are fully aware that change is the one constant in life.

Rogers recognizes that emerging persons are a small minority of the total population. Yet he believes that they are having, and will continue to have, a significant impact on society out of proportion to their numbers.

Applied Value of Rogers' Theory

Rogers believes his theory has applicability in areas besides therapy, including family life, marriage, group leadership, politics, and education. Let us now review how it might be applied to two of these areas, education and marriage.

Education

In Rogers' view, current educational practices at all levels are basically authoritarian and coercive. In such settings, the teacher is perceived as the sole possessor of knowledge and the student the recipient of it. Teachers use lectures as the primary means to transmit information to the student. Rogers believes that too much emphasis is placed on the acquisition of cognitive skills (the learning of facts and problem-solving skills) and not enough is placed on the development of affective skills (learning how to be a sensitive and loving person). Moreover, not enough of an effort is made to deal with issues of importance to students—for example, sexual relationships and friendship. Educational settings are thus typically impersonal, in Rogers' opinion, with too much emphasis being placed on performance and the evaluation of performance by testing and grading. According to Rogers, the educational establishment unfortunately bases its program on the following kinds of faulty assumptions (Rogers, 1968; 1977):

First Faulty Assumption—Students Cannot Be Trusted to Pursue Their Own Educational Goals. Rogers maintains that teachers exhibit their mistrust of students by constantly supervising and checking on them and their work. He believes that if students were allowed to choose their educational goals, there would be no need to continually monitor their behavior because they would be positively motivated to study and learn. Surveillance is necessary to ensure compliance only when teachers set goals that are irrelevant or radically at variance with student concerns and interests. Rogers' view in this regard certainly seems reasonable, assuming that it is indeed the case that most (all?) teachers who are part of the traditional education establishment do mistrust their students as Rogers contends.

Rogers also maintains that students should be allowed to make their own educational choices and set their own goals because they are the ones who know best what is right for them. This assumption is dubious in view of the continual shifting of goals by many students throughout their school years. In addition, even if they could choose the goals that are right for them, they nevertheless do exist in a society that may not agree with them regarding the worth and usefulness of their aims. Obviously, people should have the right to pursue whatever goals they wish, but this does not mean that others need find them meaningful. Society also has the right to express its views and reward those it considers worthy.

Second Faulty Assumption—Creative People Develop from Passive Learners. Rogers objects strongly to what he considers the primary emphasis in education—that students be passive learners. University students, for example, are typically given information by professors and are expected to regurgitate that information on examinations. Rogers believes that such an emphasis stifles the production of original and creative ideas. Students are taught to conform, to defer coming to grips with their own ideas, and to accept unquestioningly the ideas of their professors. He argues further that in an atmosphere of trust and mutual respect and freedom from constraints, students would be free to test their own ideas and to become creative individuals. Graduate students, for example, should be selected on three criteria: originality, intelligence, and independence of thought. In Rogers' view, if students who meet these standards are educated in the atmosphere just described, both students and society will benefit.

Not everyone agrees with Rogers on this point, however. Brown and Tedeschi, for instance, maintain that many creative individuals throughout history have been impatient with the constraints of institutions but that their complaints "are interesting not because they tell us anything about the development of genius but because they tell us of [the geniuses'] reactions to the formalities of the learning environment" (Brown & Tedeschi, 1972, p. 5). They maintain further that child prodigies such as John Stuart Mill, Charles Sanders Pierce, and Ludwig von Beethoven all learned under demanding circumstances and their creative impulses were not stifled. In addition, Brown and Tedeschi state:

> It is clear both from the evidence and from history that the mere absence of constraint or evaluation is not a necessary condition for the development of creative persons. Great ideas are not gathered while sitting under the banyan tree waiting for them to drop. Edison once said that creativity was 99% perspiration and 1% inspiration. What was meant is that the individual must gather a great deal of information that may be relevant for solving a problem. This assimilation process can be quite tedious and tests the motivational intensity of the individual's interest in the problem. Hence, there are times when the work takes on the form of sheer drudgery and there are times when the work is intensely exciting and exhilarating. [Brown & Tedeschi, 1972, p. 6]

Rogers' rebuttal is that Brown and Tedeschi ignore the fact that self-discipline is one of the most demanding and fruitful of all constraints, one that is present in almost every creative experience. But conformity does not breed this self-discipline. To the contrary, it breeds undisciplined people dependent on the evaluations of others (Rogers, 1972b, pp. 17–18).

Third Faulty Assumption—Evaluation Is Education: Education Is Evaluation. Rogers argues that "examinations have become the beginning and the end of education" (Rogers, 1968, p. 691). They are, in his view, stultifying the student. He points out further that the graduate student at one university faces the following major evaluation obstacles (Rogers, 1968, p. 692):

1. *examination in first foreign language*
2. *examination in second foreign language*
3. *first six-hour qualifying examination*

4. *second six-hour qualifying examination (both of these in the first grad-uate year)*
5. *three-hour examination in methodology and statistics*
6. *four-hour examination in a chosen major field of psychology*
7. *two-hour examination in a minor field*
8. *oral examination on master's thesis*
9. *committee evaluation of Ph.D. proposal*
10. *committee evaluation of Ph.D. thesis*
11. *oral examination on Ph.D. thesis*

In addition to these hurdles, the student faces endless quizzes and final examinations in his or her courses. Such obstacles prevent the student from doing the real independent learning necessary to a creative life. Rogers' point here seems valid. Research does indicate that many graduate departments in psychology still require examinations of the graduate student similar to those just listed (Merenda, 1974). It is doubtful that students have sufficient time to pursue their own interests under such a grueling schedule. It would seem more reasonable to first ensure that students grasp the basic concepts that are a prerequisite of creative activity by testing them early in their graduate career and then to provide them with the latitude Rogers advocates.

In conclusion, Rogers believes that the education system is in desperate need of reform. In his view, there is a need for more participation by students in the decisions that affect their academic and social development and a need for better communication and cooperation between faculty and students and administrators. Students should be able to choose their own goals and to pursue them with the help and encouragement of faculty (Rogers, 1970, p. 154).

Marriage

In Rogers' opinion, marriage is a failing institution. He attributes its decline to the fact that couples can now prevent conception through the use of various contraceptive devices. This situation means that women need no longer be fully occupied with pregnancy, nursing, and child rearing. They are now as free as men to explore relationships outside of marriage and to have a choice between family and career. For the first time in history, women are physically free agents and are liberated from their subjugated role. The women's liberation movement has also played a part, according to Rogers, because it encourages women to make their own choices and not stay in unsatisfactory marriages that stifle their growth. Finally, Rogers attributes the decline in marriage as an institution to the increasing life expectancies of women and men. Women and men can expect, on the average, to live into their seventies. As a result, Rogers believes that flaws in a relationship that would be endured in previous times (when life expectancies were con-siderably lower) will no longer be tolerated in a relationship that is expected to endure for approximately 50 years.

As a result of this decline, Rogers believes that people, especially the young, are searching for fulfilling alternatives—hence the upsurge in cohabitation without benefit of legal ties, swinging communal lifestyles, and so forth. One other alternative, in Rogers' view, is the possibility of a new kind of marriage that is radically different from the traditional kind in which the husband is the sole provider and the ultimate authority and the wife occupies a subservient role. Thus it is clear that Rogers is not opposed to marriage per se but only to the kind of marriage that is not egalitarian, enriching, satisfying, and a growing experience for both partners. He also opposes the kinds of marriages that are consummated only to please parents or to resolve a crisis in the relationship—for example, one person threatening to break up the relationship if the other does not agree to marry (Rogers, 1972a, p. 39). Rogers also insists that marriages in which couples make the following kinds of remarks to each other may experience difficulties (Rogers, 1972a, p. 200):

1. "I am more concerned for you than I am for myself." Although a loving relationship certainly does involve a deep concern for the welfare of the other person, the statement could also mean that the speaker may be uncritically willing to submerge his or her identity to please the partner, and that could eventually prove lethal to the relationship.
2. "We will work hard on our marriage." This statement is not completely wrong, in Rogers' view, but if it implies that the couple will work hard to salvage the marriage at any cost, even when it is proving persistently unsatisfying to the participants, then it may be destructive.
3. "We pledge ourselves to each other until death do us part." Again, in Rogers' opinion, the sentiment expressed here is fine, but it should not be adhered to if the cost is too great. Otherwise the parties are likely either to demean or to destroy themselves or each other or to break the bonds.

As Rogers sees it, marriage is a free-flowing, changing process, not a contract with a list of unalterable stipulations. It does not involve a rigid commitment at any cost but rather a dedication on the part of both people to try to enhance and enrich the relationship: "We each commit ourselves to working together on the changing process of our present relationship, because that relationship is currently enriching our love and our life and we wish it to grow" (Rogers, 1972a, p. 201). In such a relationship the following kinds of events are likely to occur (Rogers, 1977, pp. 45–53):

1. *Difficulties always present in the partnership will be brought into the open.* The parties will be willing to take risks, to explore the differences between them, and to therefore (usually) deepen the bonds of partnership.
2. *Communication will be more open, more real, with mutual listening.* Trust will be in evidence, and the parties will be more willing to listen to each other rather than just to attack and make accusations.

3. *The partners will come to recognize the value of separateness*. The partners will begin to recognize that each one has separate needs and desires and that they do not have to pursue the same activities and goals together to be happy.

4. *Women's growing independence is recognized as valuable in the relationship*. Wives are able to discuss their needs with their husbands instead of submerging their resentments. As a result, the husbands have more respect for the wives and the relationship is more mutually satisfying.

5. *Roles and role expectations tend to drop away and are replaced by the person choosing his or her own way of behaving*. The expectations inherent in the traditional marriage relationship are given up. Men no longer see themselves as superior to their wives, as the controllers of all activities, including sexual ones. Women no longer see themselves as having to be submissive to their husbands. These changes lead to role flexibility and to behavior that is sometimes in line with role expectations, sometimes not. At no time, however, is the behavior governed totally by the role the person is expected to play.

6. *Satellite relationships may be formed by either partner, often causing great pain as well as enriching growth*. Close secondary relationships outside the marriage may or may not involve sexual intercourse; they are valued for themselves. When two people, according to Rogers, learn to see each other as separate persons, with separate as well as mutual needs and interests, they are likely to discover that **satellite relationships** are one of those needs. Thus married people may feel the need to date others or to have sexual intimacy with others.

This last aspect of better "partner-process" relationships should be elaborated on. Rogers sees the formation of satellite relationships as part of healthy marriages. Others would speak very negatively of such arrangements and would label them "extramarital affairs" and "adultery." They would maintain that such relationships are immoral and illegal and that they serve, and rightly so, as the grounds for divorce in many states. Rogers says that these concepts are old-fashioned and ridiculous (Rogers, 1972a, p. 214). He thinks that we should give up considering such relationships as immoral and should declare, instead, that any partnership entered into by mutually consenting adults is legal, providing it does no injury to others. Although many of us might endorse such a statement, it is clear that not everyone would. Many people with conventional moral orientations, for example, would frown on adultery, even under the conditions that Rogers is stating, because it runs counter to their own religious upbringing. These people have been taught that adultery is wrong under any conditions and cannot be condoned.

Let us assume for the moment, however, that Rogers' position is a reasonable one (for many people) and that partnerships entered into by mutually consenting adults are legal, providing they do not injure others. Under such conditions, if two people agreed that it was acceptable for each of them to pursue relationships, sexual or otherwise, with others, then no harm to either party (by definition) could be done. Yet, very often, partners who agree to such arrangements wind up in divorce court. Theoretically, then, Rogers' position makes some sense, but practically, it seems a disaster. Rogers maintains, however, that these disasters occur because, though both parties agree to the arrangement, their agreement is more intellectual than emotional. In other words, intellectually both parties give consent (it sounds like a logical and reasonable idea) but emotionally they are not ready for it. As a result, they are often jealous and hurt if their partner has a sexual relationship with someone else (Rogers, 1977, p. 53). In Rogers' opinion, the agreement must be fully acceptable to both partners on an intellectual *and* an emotional level if it is going to prove workable. He hopes that couples in the future will be more sophisticated and be able to accept these experiences on both levels. They will then be motivated to enhance each other and to promote mutually positive growth by allowing the other to satisfy his or her needs outside the relationship.

Critical Comments

Let us examine how well Rogers' theory meets the criteria outlined in Chapter 1 for acceptance of scientific theories.

Comprehensiveness. Until recently, Rogers' theory was restricted in scope, being concerned primarily with explaining the origins of pathological behavior and the means of treating it in therapy. Now Rogers has extended his theory to explain a number of other phenomena, including the ways in which problems in human relationships arise in marriages, family life, education, race relations, and politics. He has also begun to discuss the means by which these difficulties can be overcome. As a result, his theory is now much more comprehensive than it was originally.

Precision and Testability. To Rogers' credit, he has made a tremendous effort to construct a precise and testable theory. There are still problems with measuring the key concepts like empathy, genuineness, and unconditional positive regard that Rogers utilizes in his theory of therapy. Nevertheless, Rogers has made significant strides toward the creation of a theory with explicitly stated concepts and hypotheses that are capable of being tested. His efforts have been commendable when one realizes that such creative efforts have been traditionally lacking.

Parsimony. Rogers' theory fails to meet the parsimony criterion. Although the phenomena he chooses to examine are complex, he relies on only a few concepts and assumptions to account for them. Thus the explanatory base of his theory is restricted in scope and clearly reductionistic in nature. For example, Rogers' proposed solutions to help minimize racial and international conflict, hostility, and aggression rely primarily on a *psychological* analysis of problems in these areas and the application of the same principles to promote positive change that he utilizes in his work with troubled individuals in therapy. That is, Rogers discusses the clear possibility of significantly reducing these tensions by having the concerned parties communicate with each other under facilitative group conditions (Rogers, 1977). Although Rogers' proposal is provocative and undoubtedly would be helpful in promoting better relationships between antagonists, it unfortunately ignores, for the most part, the complex set of historical, political, economic, and cultural factors that serve to preserve the status quo. In the area of race prejudice, for example, discriminations in the job market, in pay, and in education, among other factors, all conspire to keep minority groups in bondage. Although sensitive communication under facilitative conditions is an important beginning in trying to resolve conflicts in this area, it is clearly not enough. Radical changes in the political and economic arenas are needed if solutions are ever to be forthcoming. A psychological analysis of the problem is useful but limited if not coupled with social, economic, and political analyses as well.

 † *Empirical Validity.* There have been numerous tests of Rogers' theory to date, and the results are generally positive. They thus provide encouragement for investigators to continue their explorations and testing.

 † *Heuristic Value.* Rogers' views have been highly controversial in some quarters of psychology and have provoked continued, vigorous debate. His strong stand on the sanctity of the person is an asset. His humanistic concern for the integrity and uniqueness of the individual has led many investigators to question views of men and women that picture them as automatons who simply react uncritically to environmental forces. His theorizing has forced many people to reconsider the importance of the self-concept in their theorizing and research.

 † *Applied Value.* Rogers' theory is also strong in the applied area. Aspects of it have been fruitfully applied to such diverse areas as education, race relations, politics, family relationships, administration, leadership, and counseling.

Discussion Questions

1. Why did Rogers abandon the Freudian view of personality functioning?
2. In what ways is Rogers' position different from Freud's?
3. Discuss Rogers' concept of the organismic valuing process and how it is related

to the development of the person. What scientific evidence is there to support the organismic-wisdom hypothesis?

4. What are the consequences of an individual's need for positive regard?

5. What are some of the "conditions of worth" that you have placed on your parents? What conditions of worth have they attached to your behavior?

6. Why does Rogers feel that many educators are doing an ineffectual job? Do you agree with him? Can you cite additional problems with the current educational system? What are some of its strengths?

7. Do you believe it is possible to be creative without learning the basic concepts in a discipline first? Why or why not?

8. What are some of the major problems of the Chodorkoff study cited in this chapter?

9. Do you think that cohabitation is a meaningful alternative to marriage?

10. What is your opinion of Rogers' view that sexual relationships outside marriage can be healthy, providing both partners agree that such relationships are an acceptable means of satisfying their needs?

References

Brown, R. C., & Tedeschi, J. T. Graduate education and psychology: A comment on Rogers' passionate statement. *Journal of Humanistic Psychology*, 1972, *12*, 1–15.

Butler, J. M., & Haigh, G. V. Changes in the relation between self-concepts and ideal concepts consequent upon client-centered counseling. In C. R. Rogers & R. F. Dymond (Eds.), *Psychotherapy and personality change.* Chicago: University of Chicago Press, 1954.

Carkhuff, R. R., & Berenson, B. G. *Beyond counseling and therapy* (2nd ed.). New York: Holt, Rinehart & Winston, 1977.

Chodorkoff, B. Self-perception, perceptual defense, and adjustment. *Journal of Abnormal and Social Psychology*, 1954, *49*, 508–512.

Davis, C. M. Self-selection of diet by newly weaned infants. *American Journal of Diseases of Children*, 1928, *36*, 651–679.

Eysenck, H. J. The effects of psychotherapy. In H. J. Eysenck (Ed.), *Handbook of abnormal psychology: An experimental approach.* London: Pitman Medical Publishing, 1960.

Garcia, J., Kimeldurf, D. J., & Hunt, E. L. The use of ionizing radiation as a motivating stimulus. *Psychological Review*, 1961, *68*, 383–395.

Krieckhaus, E. E. Innate recognition aids rate in sodium regulation. *I.C.C.P.*, 1970, *73*, 117–122.

Merenda, P. F. Current status of graduate education in psychology. *American Psychologist*, 1974, *29*, 627–631.

Phillips, E. L. Attitudes toward self and others: A brief questionnaire report. *Journal of Consulting Psychology*, 1951, *15*, 79–81.

Rogers, C. R. *The clinical treatment of the problem child.* Boston: Houghton Mifflin, 1939.

Rogers, C. R. *Counseling and psychotherapy: Newer concepts in practice.* Boston: Houghton Mifflin, 1942.

Rogers, C. R. *Client-centered therapy: Its current practice, implications, and theory.* Boston: Houghton Mifflin, 1951.

Rogers, C. R. The case of Mrs. Oak: A research analysis. In C. R. Rogers and R. F. Dymond (Eds.), *Psychotherapy and personality change*. Chicago: University of Chicago Press, 1954.

Rogers, C. R. A theory of therapy, personality, and interpersonal relationships, as developed in the client-centered framework. In S. Koch (Ed.), *Psychology: A study of a science*, Vol. 3. New York: McGraw-Hill, 1959.

Rogers, C. R. *On becoming a person*. Boston: Houghton Mifflin, 1961.

Rogers, C. R. Graduate education in psychology: A passionate statement. In W. G. Bennis, E. H. Schein, F. I. Steele, & D. E. Berlew (Eds.), *Interpersonal Dynamics* (2nd ed.). Homewood, Ill.: Dorsey Press, 1968.

Rogers, C. R. *Freedom to learn*. Columbus, Ohio: Merrill, 1969.

Rogers, C. R. *Carl Rogers on encounter groups*. New York: Harper & Row, 1970.

Rogers, C. R. *Becoming partners: Marriage and its alternatives*. New York: Delacorte Press, 1972a.

Rogers, C. R. Comments on Brown and Tedeschi's article. *Journal of Humanistic Psychology*, 1972b, *12*, 16–21.

Rogers, C. R. *Carl Rogers on personal power*. New York: Delacorte Press, 1977.

Rogers, C. R. *A way of being*. Boston: Houghton Mifflin, 1980.

Rogers, C. R. A psychologist looks at nuclear war: Its threat, its possible prevention. *Journal of Humanistic Psychology*, 1982, 22, 9–20.

Rogers, C. R., & Stevens, B. *Person to person: The problem of being human*. New York: Simon & Schuster, 1967.

Rogers, H. E. A wife's view of Carl Rogers. *Voices*, 1965, *1*, 93–98.

Stephenson, W. *The study of behavior*. Chicago: University of Chicago Press, 1953.

Suinn, R. M., & Geiger, J. Stress and the stability of self- and other attitudes. *Journal of General Psychology*, 1965, 73, 177–180.

Suinn, R. M., & Hill, H. Influence of anxiety on the relationship between self-acceptance and acceptance of others. *Journal of Consulting Psychology*, 1964, 28, 116–119.

Truax, C. B., & Carkhuff, R. R. *Toward effective counseling and psychotherapy*. Chicago: Aldine, 1967.

Wylie, R. C. *The self concept*, Vol. 2. Lincoln: University of Nebraska, 1979.

Suggested Readings

Eysenck, H. J. The effects of psychotherapy. In H. J. Eysenck (Ed.), *Handbook of abnormal psychology: An experimental approach*. London: Pitman Medical Publishing, 1960.

Rogers, C. R. A theory of therapy, personality, and interpersonal relationships, as developed in the client-centered framework. In S. Koch (Ed.), *Psychology: A study of a science*, Vol. 3. New York: McGraw-Hill, 1959.

Rogers, C. R. *On becoming a person*. Boston: Houghton Mifflin, 1961.

Rogers, C. R. *Becoming partners: Marriage and its alternatives*. New York: Delacorte Press, 1972.

Rogers, C. R. *Carl Rogers on personal power*. New York: Delacorte Press, 1977.

Rogers, C. R., & Stevens, B. *Person to person: The problem of being human*. New York: Simon & Schuster, 1967.

Glossary

Conditions of worth People's beliefs that they are worthwhile only if they perform behaviors that others think are good and refrain from performing those actions others think are bad.

Congruence State of harmony that occurs when there is no discrepancy between the person's experiencing and his or her self-concept.

Emerging persons People of the future whose interpersonal relationships are characterized by honesty, cooperation, and concern for others and an avoidance of sham, facades, and hypocrisy. Such individuals welcome change and opt for growth even when it is painful to do so.

Fully functioning person Individual who is utilizing his or her potentials to the maximum degree.

Need for positive regard An individual's learned or innate tendency to seek the approval of others.

Organismic valuing process An innate bodily process for evaluating which experiences are "right" or "wrong" for the person. The person experiences satisfaction in those behaviors that maintain and enhance him or her and aversion to those behaviors that do not.

Q-sort Self-report assessment procedure designed to measure the discrepancy between the person's actual and ideal selves.

Satellite relationships Relationships with others that are formed outside the marriage and that may or may not involve sexual intimacy.

Unconditional positive regard An attitude that the therapist has toward the person. It involves the therapist's complete acceptance of the person's expression of negative as well as positive feelings. It is a total caring or prizing of the person for what he or she is without any reservations or any conditions of worth.

C H A P T E R 16

May's Existential-Analytic Position

Biographical Sketch

Rollo May was born in Ada, Ohio, in 1909. He earned a bachelor of arts degree from Oberlin College in Ohio in 1930. After his graduation, May pursued an early interest in art by touring Poland with a group of artists and painting pictures of its citizens (Reeves, 1977, p. 252). He then traveled extensively through Europe, taught at a college in Greece, and attended summer classes led by Alfred Adler.

When he returned to the United States in 1934, he served as an adviser to students at Michigan State University. Later he enrolled at Union Theological Seminary in New York not to become a preacher but rather to ask fundamental questions about human existence (Reeves, 1977, p. 252). At the seminary he was exposed to the existential thinking of Sören Kierkegaard and Martin Heidegger in classes led by the theologian Paul Tillich. May reports being greatly influenced by Tillich and using Tillich's work to illuminate and support some of his own insights into human existence that grew out of his psychotherapeutic experiences as a counselor to students at City College of New York. He received a bachelor of divinity degree cum laude from the seminary in 1938.

In the mid-1940s, May not only served as a counselor to college students but also studied psychoanalysis at the William Alanson White Institute of Psychiatry, Psychoanalysis, and Psychology in New York. He opened a private psychotherapeutic practice in 1946 and also became a member of the faculty at the White Institute in 1948 (Reeves, 1977, p. 256). In 1949 he submitted his dissertation on anxiety to the Columbia faculty and was awarded the university's first Ph.D. in clinical psychology. The dissertation was published in modified form in 1950 as *The Meaning of Anxiety*.

During this period of his life, May contracted tuberculosis and lived for a few years at a sanitarium in upstate New York. This was a particularly terrifying and depressing time for May. Several times he was close to death. During his illness, he studied Kierkegaard's and Freud's views on anxiety and concluded that, although Freud had brilliantly analyzed the reactions of the individual made anxious by threat, it was Kierkegaard who had seen most clearly that anxiety is ultimately the threat of becoming nothing (Reeves, 1977, p. 257).

Following his recovery, May continued to write, teach, and practice therapy. He has served as a faculty member at the New School for Social Research, New York University, Harvard, Yale, and Princeton. He has also published several texts, including *Man's Search for Himself* (1953), *Psychology and the Human Dilemma* (1967), *Love and Will* (1969), *Power and Innocence* (1972), *Paulus: Reminiscences of a Friendship* (1973b), *The Courage to Create* (1975), *The Discovery of Being: Writings in Existential Psychology* (1983), and an edited volume, with E. Angel and H. F. Ellenberger, of articles by leading advocates of the existential view, entitled *Existence: A New Dimension in Psychiatry and Psychology* (1958).

Professor May has been honored by his colleagues with numerous awards for his outstanding achievements. He is a fellow in the American Psychological Association, emeritus fellow and faculty member at the White Institute, and a fellow in Brantford College, Yale University, and in the National Council of Religion in Higher Education (Reeves, 1977, p. 263). He currently resides in Tiburon, California.

Basic Concepts and Principles

What Is Existentialism?

The term **existentialism** has become popular in academic and literary circles and is used in so many different ways by philosophers, psychologists, theologians, novelists, actors, and others that it has almost lost its meaning. In the popular mind, it is a term equated with things like gloom and despair, not to mention suicide and death. For some, it suggests that the world is an absurd place with no meaning and is invoked self-righteously when any misfortune befalls them. Because the concept is so central to an understanding of May's position, it might be wise to trace its use historically by leading philosophers and exponents.

Existentialism has its roots in the 19th-century writings of the Danish philosopher Sören Kierkegaard. Kierkegaard's attempts to understand human functioning were based to a large degree on his rejection of G. W. F. Hegel's monumental effort to understand reality by identifying it with abstract thought and logic (May, 1973a, p. 200). Kierkegaard, and later Friedrich Nietzsche, sought to correct the one-sidedness of Hegel's arguments by starting the analysis with a focus on the basic realities of people's existence, or **Dasein.** Thus existentialism is concerned with **ontology,** or the study of the core of one's being. It focuses directly on personal experiences and tries to avoid analyzing the lives of people by means of logical systems that treat human beings as abstracted, impersonal objects.

Proponents of this philosophy, and especially Kierkegaard, argued that we must not treat truth as something detached from human experience. Truth can be known, according to Kierkegaard, only by starting with the person's perception of it as it relates to natural phenomena. According to Rollo May, Kierkegaard's insight changed our way of thinking about truth, and his radical stance has had tremendous implications for all scientific endeavors, including psychology. Kierkegaard has given us the concept of relational truth, an idea that was the forerunner of the notion of relativity. In other words, May (1958b, p. 26) believes Kierkegaard has shown us that "the *subject*, man, can never be separated from the *object* which he observes." Thus existentialism can be defined as "the endeavor to understand man by cutting below the cleavage between subject and object which has bedeviled Western thought and science since shortly after the Renaissance" (May, 1958b, p. 11).

What exactly do existentialists see as some of the major problems with Western science? One is that the traditional approach to the study of human beings uses scientific methods that treat people as *objects*. Orthodox scientists have tended to view us in an impersonal way and to restrict themselves to detached and objective measurements of our behavior. According to the existentialists, this value-free approach is incorrect. In their view, we are human beings first, and the scientific approach should emerge from that fundamental fact. As one prominent existentialist puts it:

> Man may seek the meaning of science by approaching it as a typically human endeavor and asking: What is it in human nature that leads to the emergence of the scientific attitude? . . . Once I have the answer to this question . . . I may begin to grasp what science really means. From that moment on, I may be able to trace back to man's existence all forms, aims, and methods of science and to demonstrate that they are manifestations of his nature. [Van Kaam, 1969, p. 15]

What the existentialists are maintaining, in effect, is that we bring the *subject*—that is, our own "inner world" of experiences—into our view of science. This does not imply that they think the object side of the reality equation should be dismissed. Rather, they believe we should focus first on our own subjective experiences in the formulation of problems to be studied and then proceed to study them in as objective a way as possible. By proceeding in this manner, the horse is put before the cart and not the cart before the horse. Scientists should also try to adapt their methods of study to meaningful human problems and not tailor their problems to a restricted methodology borrowed from physics or physiology (Van Kaam, 1969, p. 26). May tells us an amusing story of what might eventually happen to psychologists who avoid studying the complexities of human experience and focus solely on behavior that can be precisely and objectively quantified:

> *A psychologist—any psychologist, or all of us—arrives at the heavenly gates at the end of his long and productive life. He is brought up before St. Peter for the customary accounting. . . . An angel assistant in a white jacket drops a manila folder on the table which St. Peter opens and looks at, frowning. St. Peter's frown deepens. He drums with his fingers on the table and grunts a few nondirective "uhm-uhms" as he fixes the candidate with his Mosaic eyes.*
>
> *The silence is discomfiting. Finally, the psychologist opens his briefcase and cries, "Here! The reprints of my hundred and thirty-two papers."*
>
> *St. Peter slowly shakes his head. . . . At last [he] speaks, "I'm aware, my good man, [of] how industrious you were. It's not sloth you're accused of." . . . [Then he] slaps his hand resoundingly down on the table, and his tone is like Moses breaking the news of the ten commandments. "You are charged with Nimis simplicandum [oversimplifying]! You have spent your life making molehills out of mountains—that's what you're guilty of. When man was tragic, you made him trivial. . . . When he suffered passively, you described him as simpering; and when he drummed up enough courage to act, you called it stimulus and response. . . . You made man over into the image of your childhood Erector Set or Sunday School Maxims—both equally horrendous." [May, 1967, pp. 3–4]*

In May's story, there is no ending. There is only the implication that eternal damnation is waiting for psychologists and other investigators in the sciences who study human beings by dissecting the human experience, and who, by so doing, tend to trivialize it. May also takes issue with proponents who utilize only the subjective or objective views of reality in their formulations (May, 1967, pp. 15–20). As examples, he mentions the positions of Rogers and Skinner. He maintains that Rogers overemphasizes the subjective side of our natures. Rogers is also guilty, in May's view, of assuming that we are "exquisitely rational" and will always make the "right" choices if we are given the opportunity. In May's opinion, Rogers is wrong because he ignores the irrational side of our nature. Skinner, in contrast, places too much emphasis on the objective side of human behavior. He is concerned almost exclusively with the ways in which the manipulation of precisely defined environmental variables determine behavior and ignores the subjective side of human functioning.

May believes both views of human nature are necessary for a science of psychology and for meaningful living. He maintains that we are all faced with the dilemma of living in both modes, or "worlds," at once. In his words, "The human dilemma is that which arises out of a man's capacity to experience himself as both subject and object at the same time" (May, 1967, p. 8). A major aspect of the dilemma is that we know we are subject to illness, death, the limitations of intelligence and experience, and other deterministic forces. At the same time we realize we have the subjective freedom to choose to relate to these objective and deterministic forces. We alone can assign meaning to them. We are responsible for our own destinies. Of course, strict determinists like Skinner would say that all our behavior is determined, including our belief that we are free to make our own decisions. They would maintain further that we consider only those options determined by our past experiences and by current stimulation from the external environment.

Besides the compelling points made by early existentialists concerning the subject-object dichotomy, a number of other interesting ideas put forth by prominent figures in the movement have contributed to existentialism's growth in popularity since World War II. These contributors include the philosophers Martin Heidegger, Karl Jaspers, Maurice Merleau-Ponty, Paul Tillich, Albert Camus, and Jean-Paul Sartre, among others, and the psychotherapists Ludwig Binswanger, Medard Boss, Viktor Frankl, and May. Although existentialism cannot be called a systematic and unified philosophy, these positions do have certain features in common.

One such commonality concerns the fact that all take the *person* as the starting point in their analyses of human existence. They all ask fundamental questions about existence. Who am I? What is the meaning of life? Is there a meaning to life? Is life worth living? How do I realize my potentialities? How do I become an individual?

Another similiarity is that in order to move toward answers, the existentialists focus on the immediate experience of the person as he or she exists in the world. We each view the world of natural phenomena from a subjective perspective. We face a world filled with uncertainties, a world that, in many respects, is absurd. The greatest absurdity from the existentialists' viewpoint is that we each realize we are finite and must die. Death is the great equalizer. All accomplishments, all hopes and dreams will inevitably be blasted into oblivion at some point. The key question for the person under these circumstances is: What should I do? Should I retreat into nothingness or should I, in Tillich's words, "have the courage to be"? It is up to the person to make a choice and take action. As Kierkegaard said, "Truth exists only as the individual himself produces it in action" (May, 1958b, p. 12).

The individual must also be committed to the goals he or she chooses to pursue.

Thus it is clear that the person assumes almost godlike status in the existential design. We must each assign meaning to our existence and act accordingly. We must exercise our freedom and act authentically. To be authentic, we must be who we are. We act inauthentically when we let other people define our goals and tell us how we should behave.

The fundamental choice certainly seems obvious if we assume that nothingness and suicide are synonymous. But how many people choose suicide, the ultimate form of nothingness? Nothingness can be seen in less extreme terms as well. We may choose not to exercise our freedom to be. We may avoid commitment to goals and responsibilities. We may decide to follow the moral dictates of the crowd. These are all forms of nonbeing or nothingness. We may make these decisions because it is easier than facing our responsibilities. The exercise of freedom is costly. In many instances it creates severe anxiety, and an immediate and easier way of coping with it is to lose oneself by accepting the moral values dictated by society. Such acceptance of values at variance with one's being leads to self-alienation, apathy, and despair. We can see clearly, here, the similarity between the existentialists and Rogers and Maslow. Human existence is seen as a continuous struggle for each of us as we try to deal with the problems of life and to move toward the realization of our potentialities.

Existentialism and Psychoanalysis

The major applications of existentialism to personality and psychotherapy have come from the work of people trained in classical psychoanalysis. To better understand May's **existential-analytic perspective**, which is an integration of the Freudian and existentialist positions, let us look at some of the similarities and differences between the two approaches to the study of human behavior.

Both psychoanalysis and existentialism ask fundamental questions about human existence. Although Freud was distrustful of philosophy and mere speculation, he nevertheless frankly acknowledged at an early point in his career that he was vitally concerned with the great problems of human existence and with understanding human nature (see Chapter 2). Both positions also focus on the irrational as well as the rational side of our natures. The existentialists talk about the inevitability of death and nothingness and the varied ways in which we try to cope with it. Freud too recognized the overwhelming importance of death in the psyche of the individual and incorporated it into his theory as a self-destructive urge he called the Death Instinct. Freud was also quite pessimistic about our long-range chances for survival as a species because he believed that we have within us the seeds for our own destruction.

Although the existentialists have generally been reproved for being unduly concerned with death and being highly pessimistic, a careful reading of their work suggests that the criticism is not entirely warranted. It is true death is given a high priority in their formulations, but they argue that their stance is quite reasonable because death "touches" us all. They maintain further that their focus may be seen as morbid because many of us have an unrealistic view of death and have been taught from a very early age to avoid thinking about it. Accordingly, they argue that we are the ones with the unhealthy attitude, not they.

> Throughout the ages men have shunned the sight of death and the mention of death, and they have devised innumerable ways of assuring themselves, when the reality of death inevitably confronts them, that death does not really change anything and that after death it will be business as usual. In contemporary America the attempts to deprive death of its reality are just as frantic at they ever were in any culture—the embalming of bodies, the expensive caskets designed to delay as long as possible decay and decomposition, soft music piped into tombs. Then there is the deep-freezing of bodies, in the hope that one day medicine will have discovered a cure for the victim's disease, and there can take place a joyous(?) resurrection.
>
> It is, of course, natural to fear death or to be anxious in the face of death. But this is very different from constructing a vast cultural illusion (to say nothing of a highly profitable industry) to help us forget about death or to persuade ourselves that it is unreal. [Macquarrie, 1972, pp. 154–155]

In addition, not all existentialists treat death in the same way. Some are more optimistic than others. For example, Sartre sees death as the final absurdity, but Heidegger maintains that an honest acceptance of death can help us to live more authentically and happily (Macquarrie, 1972, p. 155). Thus the existentialists disagree among themselves as to the meaning of death for human existence.

The next point of agreement between advocates of the two positions lies in their concern with the alleviation of human suffering. Both Freudians and existentialists discuss the ways in which conflict and anxiety disrupt functioning. Some existentialists focus on the positive features of anxiety, on anxiety as a prerequisite of self-affirmation. Both groups also assume that people often deal with severe anxiety by avoiding responsibilities. For the existentialists, people deny what they really *are* (Boss, 1963, p. 68). Freudians talk about the avoidance of responsibility through the repression of impulses that are an integral part of human nature.

Both positions blame society, to a large extent, for not allowing people to be true to their natures. In the Freudian scheme, society works through superego mechanisms to restrain the expression of "uncivilized" impulses. In the existential design, society often waylays individuals by inducing them to behave in inauthentic and self-alienating ways. Advocates of both positions are deeply concerned with understanding human nature. Freud, like the existentialists, sought to free people from illusions about themselves and to get them to recognize who they really are (Boss, 1963, p. 62).

Despite these commonalities, there are a number of interesting and provocative differences between the two positions. As you probably guessed from our discussion of the subject-object dichotomy, the existentialists disapprove strongly of Freud's attempts to fashion a science of human nature by relying on an abstract and logical system of thought. The existentialists want to avoid creating "lofty" theories removed from human experience. As Kierkegaard proclaimed, we must get "away from Speculation, away from the System, and back to reality" (May, 1958b, p. 25). By reality he meant experience as it is immediately given to us. This phenomenological stance, which is so characteristic of existential thought, is quite different from Freud's attempts to objectify experience, to measure and calculate it precisely.

In the existential view, Freudian theorizing also led to a reductionism that violates the unity of experience. Reductionism means lessening an entity by changing it from one state to another. For example, the existentialists accuse Freud of changing complex human experience into a few hypothetical components that he called id, ego, and superego. They accuse him of intellectualizing and analyzing the interplay of these three components in a structure he called the psyche. Such a reductionism destroyed his primary understanding of our "being-in-the-world," according to them.

According to the existentialists, one further result of Freud's emphasis on the use of objective techniques to study behavior was that it limited his sphere of investigation. Existentialists contend that the stress on technique dictated the kinds of problems Freud considered worthy of investigation. They maintain that these techniques led Freud to investigate problems in the *Umwelt*, or the world of man in his biological environment, but prevented him from dealing with or comprehending the problems faced by people in their *Mitwelt*, their sphere of personal relations with others, or their *Eigenwelt*, the world of their relationships with themselves (May, 1958b, p. 34). Existentialists take a much more interactionist stance in their inquiries and stress problems and issues that involve not only the biology of humans but their attempts to relate to others and to themselves. Existentialists want to develop a science that aims to understand the unique problems of men and women but not by fragmentizing their humanity (May, 1958b, p. 36).

With these distinctions firmly in mind, we turn now to an examination of May's position.

The Disintegration of Values in Modern Society

May begins his theory by pointing out that we live in an age of transition in which our values and goals are continually being called into question. According to him, in the 19th century one central value that did have a positive impact on our society in some respects was individual competitiveness. It was necessary for people to utilize a philosophy of "each man for himself" to ensure the clearing of the frontier and economic growth and to secure benefits for the community. Fromm and others might argue that the barons of industry who operated in the last century continually exploited the members of society as they sought to maximize their own gains (see Chapter 6). May, however, is talking not about the unbridled capitalism of the 19th century but about the competitiveness that emphasized social welfare during frontier times (May, 1953, p. 48). He argues that today we have lost the notion of individual competition designed to maximize the prosperity of all. Instead, we have adopted an unhealthy, exploitative competitiveness that "makes every [person] the potential enemy of his neighbor, . . . generates much interpersonal hostility and resentment and increases our anxiety and isolation from each other" (May, 1953, p. 48). To hide our feelings of hostility, May contends, we have become a nation of joiners. As adolescents, we give allegiance to peer groups. As adults, we belong to civic organizations and social clubs. We develop strong needs to be accepted and well-liked, and this orientation has led to a deepening self-alienation and dissatisfaction.

Another central value we have lost is a belief in the efficacy of reason in solving problems (May, 1953, pp. 49–50). May maintains that during the Enlightenment in the 18th century, this belief led to magnificent advances in science and education. In the 19th century, the belief became corrupted. People began to split reason from emotion. To reason was rational and good; to feel was irrational and bad. In the present century, reason was supposed to provide the answers to our problems, but it has not. This fragmentation of reason and emotion is also seen in the Freudian scheme of human nature in which unacceptable instincts and emotions are repressed by ego and superego functions based, in part, on rational input from others in the environment. Such compartmentalization has led, in May's view, to a splitting of the personality and of the person so that we act inappropriately—that is, by applying either reason or emotion—in situations that call for unity in our experiencing.

A third value we have lost is our sense of worth and dignity (May, 1953, p. 55). In May's view, this loss of sense of self grows partially out of the fact that people feel they are powerless to change the operations of government and business. Government and business are seen as huge, impersonal enterprises unresponsive to the needs of society. In the recent past, for example, government leaders arbitrarily committed us and our resources to an undeclared war that did untold damage to the national psyche. Feelings of powerlessness also accrue in a worsening economy in which inflation and recession operate simultaneously to raise the cost of living almost beyond the capacity of its citizens to pay and to terminate the jobs of millions of workers with little or no warning. In such a threatening and uncertain world, people feel that the situation is beyond their control, that they are pawns in a terrifying game in which a few mediocre men make moves that affect their destinies. Of course, the situation is not quite as simple and one-sided as May would have us believe, but he has pointed out an orientation that characterizes some people in our culture. (See the material on internal and external individuals in Chapter 12 for a review of the characteristics and behavior of people who feel powerless and of how they differ from those who feel they are in control of their destinies.)

Next, May maintains that many of us have lost not only our sense of identity but also our sense of relatedness to nature (May, 1953, p. 68). In his opinion, we have been too concerned in Western society with the development of techniques to master nature and not concerned enough with understanding our relationship to it. Perhaps the romantic, back-to-earth movement in this country can be seen as a reaction to an indiscriminate emphasis on technology. Because of our anxiety and emptiness, we have lost our feelings for and sense of awe about nature (May, 1953, p. 69). Our task, as May sees it, is to fill the impersonality of nature with our own aliveness and awareness. We must confront the power and vastness of nature and relate to nature creatively (May, 1953, p. 75). (Note the similarity between May's ideas and those of Fromm presented in Chapter 6.)

Finally, May (1969) maintains that many of us have lost our ability to relate to others in a mature, loving way. We have confused sex with love. The media have contributed to this confusion by glorifying sex and by suggesting that people who do not engage in continual sexual affairs are unhealthy. Thus people are pressured to have innumerable temporary liaisons. In May's opinion, sex is used like a narcotic to dull the senses and to keep individuals from becoming fully aware of their essential separateness from others. The ability to perform the sexual act with many different partners is taken as an indication of the person's worth and adequacy as a human being. The more partners, the more worthwhile the human being. Unfortunately, this production-line mentality is not ultimately satisfying, and people who are tied to it feel vaguely dissatisfied and lonely. In May's view, mature relationships are difficult to achieve and take time to develop. They involve a commitment to and concern for the welfare of the other person. Sex is the natural expression of affection and caring between people in this kind of evolving, deepening relationship. It is not an experience that should be forced on individuals before they are ready for it. In a world fraught with troubles and anxiety, however, this lesson is difficult to learn, according to May. Although sex decreases anxiety, its effects are temporary. The eventual result is an increase in feelings of alienation and worthlessness.

In conclusion, May maintains that our sense of worthlessness leads to a loss of the sense of the tragic significance of human life (May, 1953, p. 75). For May, tragedy is an integral part of the human experience. It implies the fall of someone who believes strongly in his or her dignity and worth. It also implies a final optimism because it suggests that we take our freedom seriously and continue to struggle to achieve our potentialities.

Emptiness and Loneliness

The primary result of the confusion that comes from the disintegration of values is that we feel "empty" inside and isolated from other men and women. The vastness and complexity of the problems that confront us contribute to these feelings. For May, however, a sense of emptiness should not be taken to mean that we are literally empty or without potential for feeling (May, 1953, p. 24). Instead, the experience of emptiness comes from feelings of powerlessness in which events seem beyond our control. We do not seem to be able to direct our own lives, to influence others, or to change the world around us. As a result, we tend to have a deep sense of despair and futility. Eventually, if we see that our actions make no difference, we give up wanting and feeling. We become apathetic. In May's opinion, the greatest danger at this point is that the attempt to defend ourselves against despair will lead to painful anxiety. If this occurs and if the situation goes uncorrected, the result is the restriction of our potential to grow as human beings or our surrender to some destructive form of authoritarianism (May, 1953, pp. 25–26).

May also believes there is a close association between emptiness and loneliness. He contends that when we do not know what we want or feel and when we stand in the midst of a general upheaval and confusion about values in our society, we sense danger and turn to the people around us for answers (May, 1953, p. 27). We may turn to them because we have been taught by society to rely on others in times of crisis. Yet, paradoxically, the more we attempt to reach out to others to ease our feelings of loneliness, the more lonely and desperate we become. Many of us need to be "going with someone" all the time to feel safe and secure. We tend to cling to partners we really do not like or respect. We are afraid that others will think less of us if we do not have a "steady." As a result, we suffer in silence and try to make the best of a bad situation. We learn to "adjust" to the person and to stifle our own individuality in order to protect the status quo. We yearn for security and yet are constrained by it.

Part of the syndrome also involves seeking invitations to parties or dinners or other outings with people. Often we do not especially want to go but feel compelled to as a means of proving to ourselves that we are not alone and that we are acceptable to others. We know we have "made it" if we are continually sought after and if we are never alone. We do not even see the positive value of solitude (May, 1953, p. 26). We must be accepted in order to consider ourselves alive. This compulsive need for acceptance may not manifest itself among college students in some of the ways described, but consider the frantic search for acceptance among some students in the form of the same clothes and the same opinions. The search for acceptance is also seen in attempts to be as average academically as possible. There is an effort not to be different. There is ridicule of academic excellence and an extolling of mediocrity. There is safety in being average and anti-intellectual.

There is also security. But May maintains that such pursuits are illusory and, in the final analysis, harmful to human growth. They are temporarily comforting, but the eventual price is that we give up our existences as identities in our own right. We avoid relying on ourselves and renounce the one thing that would help us overcome our loneliness in the long run—the development of our inner resources and values (May, 1953, p. 33).

The Emergence of Anxiety

According to May, feelings of anxiety stem from loneliness and emptiness. Like Freud, he believes that anxiety signals a conflict within us. But May's theorizing about the nature and source of the conflict differs from Freud's. For Freud, the conflict was nearly always sexual in nature. It generated anxiety, and the person reduced these unpleasant feelings by banning the conflict from consciousness. For May, anxiety is not simply an unpleasant feeling; it is "the human being's basic reaction to a danger to his existence, or to some value he identifies with his anxiety" (May, 1953, p. 40). It is "the experience of the threat of imminent nonbeing" (May, 1958b, p. 50). An example is the rejection of friendship overtures. In such a case, the threat or anxiety may strike at the core of the individual's being. Another example is the student who flunks out of the university. Such an outcome may strike at the very center of the person's sense of self, for "anxiety can be understood only as a threat to *Dasein*" (May, 1958a, p. 51). Thus anxiety, in May's theory, is to be understood in ontological terms.

In May's position, the conflict that generates ontological anxiety is between being and nonbeing. Anxiety occurs as the individual attempts to realize his or her potentialities. If, for example, a man's overtures at friendship have been rejected, he faces a fundamental conflict between being and nonbeing: he can try to understand the reasons for the rejection by questioning the other person, or he can avoid asking questions that may prove embarrassing. He is thus faced with a fundamental choice, but a choice that generates anxiety. He has the freedom to move forward or backward, and it makes him anxious. Kierkegaard describes this feeling of anxiety as the "dizziness of freedom" (May, 1958a, p. 52). If the person decides to assume responsibility and questions the person, he is using the experience of anxiety constructively. If he fails to ask the pertinent questions, he is denying his responsibility and blocking the realization of his potentialities. In this case, May would say he is guilty. Like anxiety, then, guilt is also an ontological characteristic of human existence (May, 1967, p. 52). But ontological guilt does not occur because the person fails to act in accordance with cultural prohibitions, as Freud thought. It occurs because an individual who can choose fails to do so (May, 1958a, p. 55). Such a person fails to act in accordance with his central need in life—the fulfillment of his potentialities (May, 1953, p. 93).

Coping with Anxiety and the Expansion of Consciousness

In May's theory, individuals can not fulfill their potentialities if they are largely unconscious. The unconscious involves "those potentialities for knowing and experiencing which . . . individual[s] cannot or will not actualize" (May, 1983, p. 18). May therefore believes that the more conscious of our being we are, the more spontaneous and creative we will be and the more capable we will be of choosing our plans and reaching our goals (May, 1953, pp. 94–104). Our objective, then, would clearly be an increase in consciousness. Severe anxiety tends to restrict our consciousness, according to May, and we try to defend ourselves from pain through various defense mechanisms, including those first postulated by Freud. These defenses help us avoid coping with our own being and are thus detrimental to growth.

In May's view, the sense of being that needs to be uncovered refers to our capability of seeing ourselves as beings-in-the-world who can deal with the problems of our existence. This sense of being is fundamental and not identical with the ego. The Freudian ego, according to May, was conceived of as weak and passive and as being buffeted by id impulses and admonishments from the superego. It has little of the vitality and aliveness associated with a sense of being. Movement toward realization begins with awareness of our potentialities as we journey toward becoming fully human (May, 1958a, pp. 46–47). In such a state, there is a gradual unfolding of our potentialities.

The Process of Personality Development

May's discussion of the development process centers on the physical and psychological ties between us and our parents or their substitutes—teachers, friends, clergy. He begins by noting our physical dependence on our mothers because we are all fed as fetuses through the umbilical cord. This tie is severed at birth, but physical dependency remains. As we grow older, physical dependence tends to subside, but psychological dependence often does not. This to May is a major problem, and the way in which we handle it will determine in large degree whether we will move toward maturity and personal growth. We must decide to assume responsibility for our actions or to let others make our decisions for us. So "the conflict is between every human being's need to struggle toward enlarged self-awareness, maturity, freedom and responsibility, and his tendency to remain a child and cling to the protection of parents or parental substitutes" (May, 1953, p. 193).

This dependency struggle is May's reinterpretation of the classic Oedipal conflict postulated by Freud. Whereas Freud believed the conflict was sexual in nature, May sees it as a power confrontation. The struggle focuses on our attempts to establish autonomy and identity in our relationships with people who are very powerful. This battle for freedom also involves our going through several stages of consciousness (May, 1953, pp. 138–139). The first stage is simply our innocence as infants before a consciousness of self is created. The second stage is one of rebellion in which we seek to establish our inner strength. This struggle typically takes place, in May's view, at age 2 or 3 and during adolescence. Although rebellion is seen as a necessary step in the evolution of consciousness, it should not be confused with freedom. Rebellion involves defiance and an active rejection of parental and societal rules. Such behavior is automatic, rigid, and reflexive. True freedom, in contrast, involves "*openness*, a readiness to grow; it means being flexible, ready to change for the sake of greater human values" (May, 1953, p. 159).

The third stage involves the ordinary consciousness of self. At this point we are capable of understanding some of our errors and of recognizing some of our prejudices. We are also capable of learning from our mistakes and assuming responsibility for our actions. May maintains that many people identify such a state of consciousness with being, maturity, and health. But, he argues, there is still another stage, a fourth stage of consciousness, that, if attained, actually signifies maturity. He calls this stage the creative consciousness of self. It is a stage that transcends the usual limits of consciousness. We are able to see the truth without distortion. These moments of insight are joyous ones and occur only occasionally. Note the similarity between May's ideas of the various levels of consciousness and Maslow's argument about the self-actualization process. *Peak experiences* and *creative consciousness* appear to be interchangeable terms.

We attain maturity and move close to self-realization when we experience these joyous moments. We are able to make choices, confront our problems, and take responsibility for our actions. We are not pushed along by deterministic forces. We are not bound by the past, by our role training, by the standards we have been taught by others. We are conscious of these forces but are capable of coping with them and freely choosing to act in line with them or not. As May puts it, "Consciousness of self gives us the power to stand outside the rigid chain of stimulus and response, to pause, and by this pause to throw some weight on either side, to cast some decision about what the response will be" (May, 1953, p. 161). Opponents might argue that this view is nonsensical and that our behavior is not really determined by some incredibly vague term called "consciousness of self." "How can a phantom make a decision for us?" they might ask.

May might counter this criticism with the argument that, although behavior is often determined by other events, we still have the freedom to make choices. May maintains that we move away from self-realization and maturity when our consciousness is restricted or stifled. Such a lessening of consciousness results from threats to our sense of being or existence.

Neurosis and psychosis are seen by him as attempts to adjust to these threats. They are ways of accepting nonbeing so that some aspect of being can be preserved (May, 1967, p. 117). To cope with the threats to our being, we repress or distort our experiences through defensive maneuvers. The overwhelming threats then recede into unconsciousness. But through these maneuvers we deny our own freedom to make choices. We shrink from our responsibilities and reject our own potentialities (May, 1958a).

Techniques of Assessment

Like Rogers, May is not primarily concerned with the use of various techniques in his attempts to understand human functioning. Instead, his main focus in the therapeutic relationship is on the dynamic encounter between the two participants. In fact, May believes that a premature emphasis on technique may actually hinder understanding:

> *Existential analysis is a way of understanding human existence, and its representatives believe that one of the chief (if not the chief) blocks to the understanding of human beings in Western culture is precisely the overemphasis on technique, an overemphasis which goes along with the tendency to see the human being as an object to be calculated, managed, "analyzed." Our Western tendency has been to believe that* understanding follows technique; *if we get the right technique, then we can penetrate the riddle of the patient.... The existential approach holds the exact opposite; namely, that* technique follows understanding. [May, 1958a, pp. 76–77]

May maintains that existential analysis is an *attitude* rather than a set of psychotherapeutic techniques. It involves a stress on understanding the special meanings of the person's existence. In the pursuit of this understanding, the therapist may derive new techniques or utilize existing ones. Thus the therapist may employ dream analysis, free association, and transference, as do the Freudians, or personality measures, as do the Rogerians. But the therapist would also seek to interpret dreams and symbols to ferret out their meaning for the patient's existence now and their implications for his or her future (May, 1958a, p. 77).

May's approach to the understanding of his patients is also characterized by flexibility and versatility, so that the techniques will vary from patient to patient and from time to time during the therapeutic process (May, 1958a, p. 78). This process implies an eclectic orientation, but one that systematically uses each selected procedure to shed light on the person's unique potentialities and existence.

Application of the Theory to the Treatment of Psychopathology

The primary task of the therapist, according to May, is to make empty and lonely people more aware of themselves and their potential for growth through the expansion of their consciousness and experience (May, 1967, p. 126). To accomplish these goals, the therapist must seek to understand patients as human beings and as beings-in-the-world (May, 1958a, p. 77). The focus is not on a detailed analysis of the patients' problems but on how past experiences and aspirations shed light on where they are at the moment and where they are headed. In May's words, "The context is the patient not as a set of psychic dynamisms or mechanisms but as a human being who is choosing, committing, and pointing himself toward something right now; the context is dynamic, immediately real, and present" (May, 1958a, p. 77). In short, the focus is on the ontological basis of the person's problem. These problems can be understood only in a therapeutic situation where the relationship between patient and therapist is a real one. The therapist, if he or she is to be successful, must relate to the person as "one existence communicating with another" (May, 1958a, p. 81).

Under such conditions, May believes the patients can experience their existence as real. Under these conditions, they also become aware of their potentialities and develop the courage to act on the basis of them (May, 1958a, p. 45). The patients are "cured," according to May, not when they come to accept the standards of the culture but when they become oriented toward the fulfillment of their unique existence (May, 1958a, p. 87).

In his most recent work, May provides an actual case study to illustrate some of the assumptions and principles that guide him in therapy.

The Case of Mrs. Hutchens. According to May, Mrs. Hutchens is a suburban woman in her mid-30s who suffers from a hysterical tenseness of the larynx. The result is that she can speak only with a perpetual hoarseness. May's analysis revealed that the woman felt that if she said what she really believed to people, and in particular to her parents, she would be rejected. Thus she concluded that it was safer to be quiet. Although May believed that he understood the childhood origins of her problem (that is, her need to protect herself against the authoritarian criticisms of and belittling by her mother and grandmother), he felt that the most important part of the therapy was not this interpretation but rather the person now "existing, becoming, emerging . . . in the room with [him]" (May, 1983, p. 25). Focusing on his patient, May realized that she, like every human being, was *centered* in herself. That is, she was making an attempt at preserving her existence by speaking in a hoarse voice. In addition, she also was protecting herself by being too controlled and proper in her behavior.

In the course of analysis, she revealed that she had a dream in which she was searching room by room for a baby in an unfinished house at an airport. When she found the baby, she placed it in a pocket of her robe and then was seized by anxiety that it would be smothered. Much to her joy, she found that the baby was still alive. She then had a terrifying thought: "Shall I kill it?"

Analysis revealed that the house was located near an airport where she had at age 20 learned to fly solo, an act that asserted her independence from her parents. The baby was revealed to be her youngest son, whom she regularly identified with herself. The baby was therefore herself. The baby also was a symbol of her growing consciousness, a consciousness that she considered killing in her dream.

Moreover, approximately six years before Mrs. Hutchens entered therapy, she left the religious faith of her parents. She then joined another church whose denomination she dared not tell her authoritarian parents. Although during therapy she considered telling them, whenever May brought the topic up, she became faint. She would report feeling empty inside and would have to lie down on the couch for a few minutes. Finally, she wrote her parents about her change in religious faith and told them it would accomplish nothing if they tried to change her mind. In the next therapeutic session she told May that she felt tremendous anxiety and wondered if she might become psychotic. May informed her that he thought this outcome was highly unlikely.

May interpreted her fainting and her anxiety attacks as attempts to kill her emerging consciousness. She was struggling to accept her hatred of her mother and her mother's hatred of her, to free herself from her mother's painful dominance, and to accept responsibility for her own actions and choices, even though they might not always have the best consequences. In brief, Mrs. Hutchens was actively confronting herself in these areas. The result was an opportunity for fuller independence, positive growth, and the development of a healthier lifestyle.

Critical Comments

We turn now to an evaluation of May's theory in terms of our six criteria.

Comprehensiveness. Like the other humanistic psychologists, May seems most concerned with the development of a model of positive growth as a means of alleviating human suffering. Thus his focus seems to be on understanding abnormal behavior and changing it. Yet his position seems more comprehensive than those of Rogers and Maslow because he does a more thorough job of integrating psychoanalytic and existential principles into his theory. Maslow focuses more on the growth aspects of his model, and

Rogers presents a more global and undifferentiated view of the defense process. May's treatment of the development process is also more detailed than the views presented by these other two theorists.

May also attempts a compromise with American behaviorism and its assumptions. In some of his earlier work, for example, he attempted to utilize learning principles and experiments to increase our understanding of the meaning of anxiety, although he did see this approach as limited. In general, then, May's system seems comprehensive, especially when compared with the other major humanistic positions.

Precision and Testability. May's theory is quite imprecise and difficult to test. Numerous terms like *daemonic, being, potentiality,* and *ontological guilt* are vague and nearly impossible to define accurately. In addition, the theory consists of a series of disjointed and unconnected propositions that do not lend themselves readily to scientific inquiry. Instead, his position appears to retain close ties to philosophy. This link, of course, is not a weakness in itself, as some psychologists seem to think, but it does become a liability if May hopes to convince investigators of his theory's scientific status. In such a case, his theory would have to meet the precision and testability standards ordinarily applied to such efforts by members of the scientific community. But at this point, its deficiencies in this sense are so painfully apparent that May will probably not even get a fair hearing from members of the scientific establishment. This situation is unfortunate because there are many interesting and provocative ideas in his position, especially in his arguments about the need for the change in our ideas about science, that will not have the impact on investigators that they merit. At best, he will be seen as a gadfly to be endured. Some constructive changes may eventually be forthcoming, but the full impact of his message about the need for a humanistic science of psychology will go unheeded. It is a message that deserves a better fate.

Parsimony. In its present state of development, it is difficult to make a judgment about how well May's position meets the parsimony criterion. A tentative judgment is that it has an excess of concepts. And as we have seen, the scientific utility of many of the terms in the system is doubtful.

Empirical Validity. Empirical support for the theory is limited. Much of the evidence for the position is based on clinical observation in therapy sessions and is largely unsystematic and retrospective. So research on May's position is still in an exploratory stage.

Heuristic Value. May's position has proved highly stimulating to investigators in the humanistic psychology movement and to members of the public, but for the most part his efforts have been ignored by traditional investigators within psychology.

Applied Value. May's theory has been fruitfully applied to problems in areas such as education, pastoral counseling, family life, and religion.

Discussion Questions

1. How would you define existentialism?
2. Do you agree with May that many psychologists tend to study human behavior and experience in abstract and oversimplified terms? Give reasons for your judgment.
3. What does it mean to "act authentically"? Would you ever be willing to let others define your goals for you?
4. Compare and contrast psychoanalysis and existentialism.
5. Do you agree with May that we have lost our sense of values? Do you feel powerless to control your own destiny?
6. Has there been too much emphasis in our society on the development of new technology to help us master the environment? Do we have a good understanding of our relationship to the environment? Have you seen any progress in our attempts to preserve the environment in recent years?
7. How often do you feel "empty," in the sense of being powerless to control your own outcomes? What are the causes of such feelings in you and others?
8. Do you agree with May that many people continue to endure basically unsatisfying relationships because they want to alleviate feelings of loneliness?
9. Do you think that many students yearn for uncritical acceptance from others? Do you believe that some students are anti-intellectual because it makes them more acceptable to others?
10. Do you think that many students are struggling to become independent of parental control? Do you agree with May that one of the basic struggles in life involves our attempts to accept ultimate responsibility for our actions? Is dependency always harmful to the person?

References

Boss, M. *Psychoanalysis and Daseinsanalysis.* New York: Basic Books, 1963.

Macquarrie, J. *Existentialism.* Baltimore: Penguin Books, 1972.

May, R. *The meaning of anxiety.* New York: Ronald Press, 1950.

May, R. *Man's search for himself.* New York: Norton, 1953.

May, R. Contributions of existential psychotherapy. In R. May, E. Angel, & H. F. Ellenberger (Eds.), *Existence: A new dimension in psychiatry and psychology.* New York: Basic Books, 1958a.

May, R. The origins and significance of the existential movement in psychology. In R. May, E. Angel, & H. F. Ellenberger (Eds.), *Existence: A new dimension in psychiatry and psychology.* New York: Basic Books, 1958b.

May, R. *Psychology and the human dilemma.* New York: Van Nostrand, 1967.

May, R. *Love and will.* New York: Norton, 1969.

May, R. *Power and innocence.* New York: Norton, 1972.

May, R. Existential psychology. In T. Millon (Ed.), *Theories of psychopathology and personality.* Philadelphia: Saunders, 1973a.

May, R. *Paulus: Reminiscences of a friendship.* New York: Harper & Row, 1973b.

May, R. *The courage to create.* New York: Bantam Books, 1975.

May, R. *The discovery of being: Writings in existential psychology.* New York: Norton, 1983.

Reeves, C. *The psychology of Rollo May.* San Francisco: Jossey-Bass, 1977.

Van Kaam, A. *Existential foundations of psychology.* Garden City, N.Y.: Image Books, 1969.

Suggested Readings

Macquarrie, J. *Existentialism.* Baltimore: Penguin Books, 1972.

May, R. *Man's search for himself.* New York: Norton, 1953.

May, R. *Love and will.* New York: Norton, 1969.

May, R. *Psychology and the human dilemma.* New York: Van Nostrand, 1967.

May, R. *The meaning of anxiety.* New York: Ronald Press, 1950.

May, R., Angel, E., & Ellenberger, H. F. (Eds.). *Existence: A new dimension in psychiatry and psychology.* New York: Basic Books, 1958.

Glossary

Dasein Term existentialists use to describe the unique character of human existence. Each of us can become aware of the fact that we exist in a particular place at a particular time. We can then make our own behavioral decisions in a responsible way.

Existential-analytic perspectives Theoretical positions that combine elements of existential philosophy with Freudian concepts as a means of furthering understanding of human personality. Both positions, for example, focus on the ways in which people try to cope with the anxieties that result from the inability to love others and from the inevitability of death.

Existentialism Philosophy that focuses on people's attempts to make sense of their existence by assigning meaning to it and then taking responsibility for their own actions as they try to live in accordance with their values and principles.

Ontology Branch of philosophy that examines the nature of being or reality.

PART 7

Constitutional Perspectives

The view that differences in behavior are produced by differences in our biological functioning is an ancient one. Historically, efforts to understand the nature of this relationship have included emphases on the ways in which behavior is determined by the operation of certain fluids in the body and on the role played by body shape and size. There have also been numerous attempts to understand how differences in skull shape and facial features produce variations in behavior. More recently, scientific investigations have focused on temperament differences in children, on individual differences in physiological reactivity patterns as a result of stress, and on showing how chromosomal abnormalities lead to Down's syndrome and other forms of mental retardation.

It is popularly believed that the Greek physician Hippocrates first undertook to study the nature of the relationship between body type and individual differences in behavior. He was an advocate of the position that changes in the amount of internal fluids, or "humors," in the body produced distinctive temperaments and behaviors. He maintained that there were four distinctive kinds of personalities: a predominance of black bile caused a person to be melancholic and depressed, whereas an excess of yellow bile made one irritable and short-tempered; too much phlegm, on the other hand, caused a person to be slow and lethargic, whereas disproportionate amounts of blood caused an individual to be hopeful and sanguine. Hippocrates also believed that body type was related to physical disease. On the basis of his many observations of patients, he concluded that people with short and thick bodies were prone to stroke (*habitus apoplecticus*) and that people who were tall and thin were susceptible to tuberculosis (*habitus phthisicus*).

The inadequacies of such typologies are painfully clear. They involve unsophisticated and oversimplified theoretical and empirical treatments of differences in behavior along with medical "explanations" that are obsolete in light of current knowledge. But useful vestiges of Hippocrates' legacy to the medical profession and to behavioral science can still be seen in research on hormonal therapy and the effects of various hormones on performance in people and lower animals.

The assessment of personality from the study of facial features also had its origins in antiquity and has throughout history commanded the attention of theologians, poets, philosophers, artists, writers, and scientists. Interest in the subject seems to have reached a peak in the late 19th century, but even today there are occasional books and studies on the topic. Before the beginning of the 19th century, devotees of physiognomy tended to make their judgments about personality on artistic grounds. They offered lyrical descriptions of the beauties of the various aspects of the face and sometimes presented their version of truth in aphorisms like the following:

> *A beard on a woman is a sign of little honesty.*
> *Bright eyes are the sign of wantonness.*
> *The smallness of the forehead indicates a choleric man.*
> *Men with curved noses are magnanimous. [Mantegazza, 1899, p. 13]*

The primary orientation in the 19th century was scientific, with attempts to measure the features of the face and relate these measurements to psychological characteristics. Unfortunately, virtually all these findings are meaningless in a scientific sense because they are based on the biased and subjective impressions of the investigators and the use of woefully inadequate methodologies.

Scientific research that examines the effects of physical attractiveness on behavior is extremely popular today. Most contemporary researchers in this area assume, however, that standards of beauty are learned and not biologically based. Their judgment is based on cross-cultural evidence that standards of beauty vary from country to country. Their work shows that physically attractive people are better liked by their peers and by adults than are unattractive people. For example, teachers tend to assume that socially undesirable acts committed by attractive children are less reprehensible than those committed by unattractive children (Dion, 1972). For college students, physically attractive people are seen as possessing more socially desirable traits than unattractive people. Beautiful people, for instance, are seen as more altruistic, genuine, sensitive, sincere, modest, poised, and sophisticated than those with less physical appeal. Attractive men and women are also expected to attain more prestigious occupations and to have better prospects for happy social and professional lives. It does seem, then, that people who are seen as beautiful are also seen as good, a finding that was, incidentally, accurately predicted by a number of early physiognomists (Dion, Berscheid, & Walster, 1972).

Phrenology was still another attempt to relate constitutional factors and individual differences in behavior. This system purports to assess personality from a knowledge of skull shape and contours. Popularly known as the study of bumps on the head, phrenology originated in the 19th century as a serious attempt to relate knowledge about brain structure and function to behavior (Davies, 1955, p. 3). Its foremost proponent was Franz Gall (1758–1828), a German anatomist and physician who believed that the mind was composed of approximately 40 independent faculties. These faculties were variously cataloged by him and later by other disciples under such headings as combativeness, benevolence, amativeness, language, secretiveness, self-esteem, destructiveness, and hope (Davies, 1955, p. 6). Gall claimed that these faculties were located in various "organs" or regions of the brain and that the development or lack of development of these organs affected the size and shape of the skull. To judge a person's character or personality, therefore, he believed it was necessary only to study these contours. A person with a well-developed benevolence region, for example, would be judged as having a kindly character; one with an underdeveloped region would be characterized as cruel.

Gall had a single-minded passion for scientific inquiry about brain structure and function. His pupil and colleague Johann Spurzheim did not. Spurzheim's view of phrenology was based on religious and philosophical speculations as well as on scientific research. He sought to popularize phrenology and to discuss, in public lectures, its applications to education, medicine, mental health, and penology (Davies, 1955, p. 8). These efforts and those by other disciples proved very successful, and phrenology flourished. During the last half of the 19th century, however, phrenology was attacked by numerous critics on religious and philosophical as well as scientific grounds (Davies, 1955, pp. 65–75).

Opponents argued that phrenology was atheistic and immoral because it held that behavior had natural and not divine causes and that acceptance of it necessarily meant an endorsement of fatalism. This latter argument was not consistent with the aims of the movement, however, because phrenology was directly linked with social reform by its proponents. For example, people who were judged insane were considered by phrenologists to have diseased brains that resulted from violations of "natural laws." To overcome these deficiencies, it was recommended that these people should once again follow these natural laws. This meant that they they should get plenty of fresh air and physical exercise, eat bland foods, and avoid liquor and tobacco. In the crudest sense, the phrenologists were arguing that the establishment of a warm, supportive environment for the insane was therapeutic—an idea still acceptable to those in the contemporary mental-health movement.

Despite the irrational nature of the attacks on phrenology, its critics were effective in damaging the movement. Scientific evidence also took its toll. Pierre Flourens demonstrated in his experiments with pigeon brains in 1845 that large portions of the brain could be destroyed without impairment of any of the functions. In 1861, Paul Broca showed conclusively that the faculty of speech was located not near the eyeballs, as Gall maintained, but in the temporal region (Davies, 1955, p. 142). Despite these overwhelming criticisms, phrenology is credited with having an important impact on the field of neurology in the sense that it directed the attention of researchers to the problem of cerebral structure and function. There is still sporadic interest in the topic, not within the scientific community but among people who also embrace pseudosciences like astrology and palmistry.

Although there have been numerous other investigators of the relationships between body build and behavior since Hippocrates, the leading researcher in this area in modern times is William Sheldon. Chapter 17 focuses primarily on his theory, because it is the most comprehensive and systematic statement of the constitutional position and the most thoroughly researched.

We note first that Sheldon adopted as a guide for his theorizing and research the radical premise that biological structure determines behavior. He did so because he felt that American psychologists had largely ignored the contributions made by biology to behavior and had instead focused too strongly on the contributions made by environmental forces.

Our review of the basic concepts and principles of the theory includes a discussion of the elaborate measurement procedures Sheldon used to establish the primary and secondary components of physique. We then turn to the manner in which Sheldon proceeded to identify the basic components of temperament. To assess temperament, he rated approximately 30 graduate students and instructors on 50 personality traits over a one-year period during weekly clinical interviews. In intercorrelating the ratings, he found three basic, underlying temperament dimensions. He then proceeded to correlate the data on the body type and temperament of his subjects. The major results of his correlations are presented, along with corroborative data. But, in opposition to the constitutional view, a social-learning hypothesis is suggested as a possible alternative explanation of these data.

Sheldon's theory of personality development is outlined next, along with the implications of his position for child rearing and parental use of discipline. Inferences are also drawn concerning the relationships between morphology and abnormality. There is a brief treatment of Sheldon's techniques of assessment and of the kinds of therapy that should be employed in the treatment of pathology.

References

Davies, J. D. *Psychology: Fad and science.* New Haven, Conn.: Yale University Press, 1955.

Dion, K. Physical attractiveness and evaluations of children's transgressions. *Journal of Personality and Social Psychology*, 1972, 24, 207–213.

Dion, K., Berscheid, E., & Walster, E. What is beautiful is good. *Journal of Personality and Social Psychology.* 1972, 24, 285–290.

Mantegazza, P. *Physiognomy and expression.* New York: Scribner, 1899.

C H A P T E R 17

Sheldon's Somatotyping Position

Biographical Sketch

William Sheldon was born in 1899 in Warwick, Rhode Island. The son of a naturalist and animal breeder, Sheldon reported that, as a boy, he was trained to judge the quality of poultry and dogs. He had attended many livestock exhibits by the time he reached 15 and said he was a competent judge of livestock. Quantitative scales were used by the judges at such exhibits, and agreement on ratings was uniformly high. Sheldon clearly remembered the keen disappointment on his father's face when the boy gave a rooster a score of 83 on a 100-point scale after the other officials had rated the bird at 80 (Sheldon, Hartl, & McDermott, 1949, pp. 20–21). It seems likely that these early experiences had a lasting effect on his view of human behavior and his advocacy of a biologically based psychology.

Sheldon attended Brown University and received a B.A. in 1919. Later he earned a master's degree from the University of Colorado and, in 1926, a

Ph.D. in psychology from the University of Chicago. In 1933, he added an M.D. from Chicago to his credentials.

After brief academic stints at Chicago and at the University of Wisconsin, he moved to Harvard. At this time he also began a collaboration with the eminent experimental psychologist S. S. Stevens. Stevens seems to have heightened Sheldon's interest in and concern with the need for precise measuring instruments to assess physique and temperament. The result was the construction of a measurement system of the human body decidedly superior in most respects to any of the systems devised by his predecessors.

Sheldon was an active researcher and a productive writer. Some of his more notable books include *The Varieties of Human Physique* (1940) (written with S. S. Stevens and W. B. Tucker), *The Varieties of Temperament* (1942) (written with S. S. Stevens), *Varieties of Delinquent Youth* (1949) (written with E. M. Hartl and E. McDermott), and the *Atlas of Men* (1954) (written with C. W. Dupertuis and E. McDermott). In 1947, Sheldon accepted an appointment as director of the Constitution Laboratory at Columbia University. Later he was affiliated with the Biological Humanics Foundation in Cambridge, Massachusetts, a position he held until his death in 1977.

The Radical Premise of Sheldon's Psychology

It should be clear at the outset that although Sheldon's position is firmly rooted in human biology, he is not simplemindedly arguing that environmental forces such as our past experiences with other people have no impact on our behavior. He recognized the importance of our social experiences but decided quite consciously and deliberately to adopt the radical premise that biological structure determines our behavior because of his belief that such an orientation has been largely ignored by American psychologists and that this unbalance must be rectified (Sheldon, Hartl, & McDermott, 1949, pp. 3–6). The value orientation of many American psychologists stresses the importance of equality among people and the goodness of self-improvement and social progress. A frequently accompanying belief is that endorsement of a strong hereditarian position precludes the attainment of these social goals. Although the **constitutional position** does stress innate differences between people, it does not necessarily follow that proponents of the position are incapable of endorsing and supporting a social philosophy that emphasizes equality of opportunity under the law. Biological superiority does not necessarily imply social superiority, but the strong liberal bias of psychologists leads them to fear, perhaps rightly, that such a distinction is often difficult to maintain. The specter of Hitler and his Aryan race is not easily forgotten, nor should it be.

Basic Concepts and Principles

The Primary Components of Body Build

Sheldon and his associates set out to examine the physiques of thousands of college students in an attempt to determine whether there were any basic regularities among them. He first photographed them in the nude from the front, side, and rear. After careful examination, he concluded that there were three extreme variations. Repeated efforts to find a fourth major type failed. These three basic types correspond approximately to the pyknic (plump), athletic (muscular), and leptosomatic or asthenic (thin and frail) types identified by Sheldon's historical predecessor and acquaintance, Ernst Kretschmer (1856–1926). Sheldon insisted, however, that he did not simply borrow Kretschmer's classification scheme and add new labels to the various types. He maintained that the three types were determined solely by empirical investigation; that is, they were found by examining the photographs. Whether this was actually the case is debatable.

The first component identified by Sheldon is labeled **endomorphy,** the second **mesomorphy,** and the third **ectomorphy.** According to Sheldon,

> Endomorphy *means relative predominance of soft roundness throughout the various regions of the body. When endomorphy is dominant, the digestive viscera are massive and tend relatively to dominate the bodily economy. The digestive viscera are derived principally from the* endodermal *embryonic layer.*
>
> Mesomorphy *means relative predominance of muscle, bone, and connective tissue. The mesomorphic physique is normally heavy, hard, and rectangular in outline. Bone and muscle are prominent, and the skin is made thick by a heavy, underlying connective tissue. The entire bodily economy is dominated, relatively, by tissues derived from the* mesodermal *embryonic layer.*
>
> Ectomorphy *means relative predominance of linearity and fragility. In proportion to his mass, the ectomorph has the greatest surface area and, hence, relatively the greatest sensory exposure to the outside world. Relative to his mass, he also has the largest brain and central nervous system. In a sense, therefore, his bodily economy is relatively dominated by tissues derived from the* ectodermal *layer. [Sheldon, Stevens, & Tucker, 1940, pp. 5–6]*

Each of these dimensions was considered to be a continuous variable that varied along a 7-point scale. Each person was assigned a set of three numerals from 1 to 7. The patterning of these nonpsychological components yielded a **somatotype.** For example, a 711 is an extreme endomorph, a 171 an extreme mesomorph, and 117 an extreme ectomorph. Note that the order of the primary components is always endomorphy, mesomorphy, and ectomorphy (Sheldon, Hartl, & McDermott, 1949, p. 14). The advantage of such a measuring system is that it is possible to obtain a much more reliable, complex, and differentiated picture of an individual's **morphology** than with any of the systems constructed previously. Theoretically, the system yields 343 different somatotypes, although Sheldon focused his attention on only 76 (Sheldon, Hartl, & McDermott, 1949, pp. 62–63). The system also avoids extreme types like the 777 or the 111 by stipulating that the sum of the ratings cannot be less than 9 or more than 12.

Sheldon treated extreme types as ideals. He labeled God as a 777, for example. God is a projection of our wish for perfection, in Sheldon's view. In other words, God is a reflection of our deepest needs to attain maximum ratings on the three components—that is, to be all-loving, all-powerful, and all-knowing. The Devil, in contrast, was labeled a 177. Such a projection would be devoid of compassion and feelings of affection for others, as reflected in the low rating on the first component, but would be rated extremely high on the second and third components, reflecting extreme aggressiveness and hyperawareness (Sheldon, Stevens, & Tucker, 1940, p. 61). Why the highest ratings on the second and third components can indicate positive characteristics in the case of God and negative characteristics in the case of the Devil is unclear and was not explained by Sheldon.

Sheldon maintained that the somatotype is genetically determined and does not change despite advances in age and changes in diet or the environment (Sheldon, Stevens, & Tucker, 1940, pp. 221–226). He distinguished between the phenotype, or physical appearance, and the genotype, or what the person actually is morphologically. Changes in diet, for example, may change a person's phenotype but not the genotype. Although it is rather easy to mistake the two, Sheldon maintained that the error can be avoided by keeping careful case-history records and taking a series of photographs over the years. In this way, the somatotype can be accurately identified. If the investigator is not careful in his or her determination of the somatotype, errors can occur. One striking instance of such an error, according to Sheldon, is the **pyknic practical joke** (PPJ). Somatotyped typically as a 443, 442, or 452, this person appears

> stocky but not fat, sturdy but not blocky, and all his features tend to be blunt or rubbery. There are no sharp corners and there is nothing about [him] . . . that appears easy to break. He can be picked up and dropped. . . . In youth he generally has and expresses tremendous energy, but if too well fed or too successful in the middle decades he is prone to grow fat and sodden. The female . . . PPJ . . . is highly active, and is generally a "pep" girl [cheerleader]. Before marriage she remains extraordinarily slender, like the bud of a late-blossoming tree. The unpracticed eye does not perceive the latent first component. After marriage the joke is sprung. [Sheldon, Stevens, & Tucker, 1940, pp. 198–199]

The Secondary Components of Physique

As a result of further examination of the photographs, Sheldon was able to isolate a number of secondary dimensions. These he labeled dysplasia, gynandromorphy, texture, and hirsutism. Sheldon defined **dysplasia** as an aspect of disharmony or disproportion between different regions of the same body. An example of a type of dysplasia is a person with unusually long legs and a short trunk; another is a person who has a very large body but a very small head. **Gynandromorphy** refers to the bisexuality of the body. For example, a man may have large, soft breasts and wide hips like a woman; a woman may have a hard body with little or no breast development and narrow hips. **Texture** refers to the person's aesthetic attractiveness. Some people are strikingly handsome or beautiful and have fine features; others are physically unattractive and have coarse features. Sheldon likened those who are aesthetically pleasing to the thoroughbreds of the animal world. **Hirsutism** refers to the general hairiness of the body (Sheldon, Stevens, & Tucker, 1940, pp. 68–79).

The Primary Components and Temperament

After establishing the primary and secondary aspects of physique at the morphological level, Sheldon proceeded to search for the basic components of temperament. Drawing on the personality-trait literature, he eventually decided to use a list of 50 traits in his investigation. He then rated approximately 30 graduate students and instructors on these characteristics on the basis of observations made over a one-year period during weekly clinical interviews. He then intercorrelated the ratings, looking for basic clusters or dimensions. The basic clusters included ratings on traits that correlated positively with one another and negatively with the traits of other clusters. He eventually decided there were three basic dimensions, which he labeled **viscerotonia, somatotonia**, and **cerebrotonia**. The traits associated with each temperament type are listed in Table 17.1. In general, viscerotones have a love of comfort and need approval and affection from people; somatotones like action and are assertive and vigorous; and cerebrotones tend to be tense and withdrawn. If Sheldon's radical premise has any validity, there should be a reliable relationship between morphology and temperament. In fact, Sheldon reported very high positive correlations between the three morphological and three temperament dimensions. Specifically, he found correlations of .79 between endomorphy and viscerotonia, .82 between mesomorphy and somatotonia, and .83 between ectomorphy and cerebrotonia (Sheldon & Stevens, 1942, p. 400). Unfortunately, Sheldon himself made both sets of ratings, so that investigator bias may have affected the judgments and produced the very high correlational outcomes. In short, Sheldon may have found what he was looking for.

In two more methodologically sound studies by Child (1950) and by Cortes and Gatti (1965), however, in which investigator bias was minimized

Table 17.1
The Scale for Temperament

Viscerotonia	Somatotonia	Cerebrotonia
1. Relaxation in posture and movement	1. Assertiveness of posture and movement	1. Restraint in posture and movement, tightness
2. Love of physical comfort	2. Love of physical adventure	2. Physiological overresponse
3. Slow reaction	3. Energetic characteristic	3. Overly fast reactions
4. Love of eating	4. Need and enjoyment of exercise	4. Love of privacy
5. Socialization of eating	5. Love of dominating and lust for power	5. Mental overintensity, hyperattentionality, apprehensiveness
6. Pleasure in digestion	6. Love of risk and chance	6. Secretiveness of feeling, emotional restraint
7. Love of polite ceremony	7. Bold directness of manner	7. Self-conscious motility of the eyes and face
8. Sociophilia	8. Physical courage for combat	8. Sociophobia
9. Indiscriminate amiability	9. Competitive aggressiveness	9. Inhibited social address
10. Greed for affection and approval	10. Psychological callousness	10. Resistance to habit and poor routinizing
11. Orientation people	11. Claustrophobia	11. Agoraphobia
12. Evenness of emotional flow	12. Ruthlessness, freedom from squeamishness	12. Unpredictability of attitude
13. Tolerance	13. The unrestrained voice	13. Vocal restraint and general restraint of noise
14. Complacency	14. Spartan indifference to pain	14. Hypersensitivity to pain
15. Deep sleep	15. General noisiness	15. Poor sleep habits, chronic fatigue
16. The untempered characteristic	16. Overmaturity of appearance	16. Youthful intentness of manner and appearance

(Table continues)

Table 17.1
The Scale for Temperament (continued)

Viscerotonia	Somatotonia	Cerebrotonia
17. Smooth, easy communication of feeling, extraversion of viscerotonia	17. Horizontal mental cleavage, extraversion of somatotonia	17. Vertical mental cleavage, introversion
18. Relaxation and sociophilia under alcohol	18. Assertiveness and aggression under alcohol	18. Resistance to alcohol and to other depressant drugs
19. Need of people when troubled	19. Need of action when troubled	19. Need of solitude when troubled
20. Orientation toward childhood and family relationships	20. Orientation toward goals and activities of youth	20. Orientation toward the later periods of life

Adapted from Sheldon, Hartl, and McDermott, 1949, pp. 26–27.

by having one investigator rate the somatotypes and having the subjects independently rate their own personality characteristics (temperament), the results yielded lower correlations but ones that are still consistent with Sheldon's theorizing. The data for the more recent study are presented in Table 17.2. In regard to specific trait assignments, Cortes and Gatti found that endomorphs saw themselves as relaxed, warm, and generous; mesomorphs as adventurous, confident, and energetic; and ectomorphs as withdrawn, shy, tense, and reserved. Yates and Taylor (1978) reported essentially similar results.

In addition to these studies, further support for Sheldon's position can be found in a recent study by Gacsaly and Borges (1979). These investigators asked 100 subjects to attribute various viscerotonic, somatotonic, and cerebrotonic traits to the three major body types, as they deemed appropriate. Their results are shown in Table 17.3. Thus mesomorphs were judged by college students as the most aggressive, the most athletic, and the most likely to be chosen as leaders of groups; ectomorphs as the most likely to be college professors and as shy and nervous; and endomorphs as lonely and in need of friends and as likely to be alcoholics. An earlier study by Lerner (1969) reported similar findings with samples of children. As would be predicted by Sheldon's theory, Lerner found that mesomorphs were seen as being the most aggressive, making the best soldiers, and being able to endure pain better than their endomorphic and ectomorphic counterparts. Ectomorphic adults were also seen as eating the least and as being the most susceptible to nervous breakdowns.

In a massive study of over 1000 Scottish teenagers' involvements in sports, leisure activities, and peer relations, Hendry and Gillies (1978) also provided

Table 17.2
Correlations Between the Primary Components of
Physique and Sets of Adolescent Self-Ratings

	Boys		
	Viscerotonia ($N=47$)	Somatotonia ($N=38$)	Cerebrotonia ($N=51$)
Endomorphy	+ .51	− .14	− .27
Mesomorphy	− .39	+ .69	− .37
Ectomorphy	− .15	− .26	+ .43
	Girls		
	Viscerotonia ($N=100$)	Somatotonia ($N=100$)	Cerebrotonia ($N=100$)
Endomorphy	+ .36	− .03	− .33
Mesomorphy	− .21	+ .47	− .23
Ectomorphy	− .20	− .30	+ .49

Adapted from Cortes and Gatti, 1965, pp. 435 and 437.

cross-cultural support for aspects of Sheldon's theorizing. For instance, they found that mesomorphic teenagers of both sexes perceived themselves as more physically skilled than teenagers with endomorphic and ectomorphic body builds. Their teachers also saw the mesomorphs as having greater physical skills. Mesomorphs were also quite popular with their peers, although endomorphs (particularly the girls) were even more popular with peers of both sexes. Ectomorphs were least popular with their peers. They were perceived by their teachers as lacking social poise and physical skills. They had very few friendships with members of the opposite sex, and it should not be surprising to learn that they spent large amounts of their leisure time in solitary activities, particularly in television watching. Recent research by Kellett, Marzillier, and Lambert (1981) provides further corroboration for the view that ectomorphs lack social skills. These investigators tested the social skills of endomorphs, mesomorphs, and ectomorphs by videotaping their performances during an interview session. They found that ectomorphs smiled less, had fewer head nods, fewer gestures, looked less at the interviewer, and had a slower rate of speech than endomorphs and mesomorphs. These results suggest that ectomorphy is associated with deficits in verbal and nonverbal skills.

Finally, the results of the studies in this section suggest that mesomorphs (who are assigned many favorable traits by observers) should be more confident and have a greater sense of self-worth than endomorphs

Table 17.3
Frequency of Assignment of Traits to Three Major
Body Types by 100 College Students

Which Man Is Most Likely to	Endomorph	Mesomorph	Ectomorph
1. Need friends	65	2	33
2. Be the worst athlete	91	2	7
3. Be aggressive	8	83	9
4. Be a college professor	14	28	58
5. Be lonely	62	7	31
6. Be a good doctor	11	49	40
7. Assume leadership	5	79	16
8. Be an alcoholic	52	13	35
9. Get lung cancer	43	17	40
10. Have many friends	5	72	23
11. Be a good father	13	58	29
12. Be generous	48	20	32
13. Be a political leader	4	66	30
14. Have a nervous breakdown	34	9	57
15. Be quiet	23	6	71
16. Worry	40	9	51
17. Help others	35	27	38
18. Be convicted of a felony	15	52	33
19. Be intelligent	9	36	55
20. Be chosen a leader	3	85	12
21. Be preferred as a personal friend	9	59	32
22. Lie	37	42	21
23. Be cynical	35	29	36
24. Put his own interests before others	32	41	27

Adapted from Gacsaly and Borges, 1979, p. 100.

and ectomorphs. Two studies by Tucker support these speculations (Tucker, 1982; 1983). He found that mesomorphs reported having greater self-confidence than endomorphs and ectomorphs and that they demonstrated a stronger and more positive self-concept. Endomorphy, in particular, was associated with a poor self-concept.

Body Stereotyping: A Social-Learning Explanation as an Alternative to Sheldon's Genetic View

Although there is clearly an impressive amount of data that support the major hypotheses concerning the relationships between different physiques and temperaments derived from Sheldon's theory, there is no direct proof that the correlations were caused by biological factors, as Sheldon maintained. Social-learning theorists claim, as an alternative to his constitutional position, that the relationships between body build and behavior are determined by learning factors. Particularly, the social-learning position stipulates that people have specific stereotypes about the kinds of traits that are associated with specific body builds (probably learned through books, films, magazines, and television as well as from contact with other people). They then transmit these stereotypes to children, who eventually come to conform to them in the course of their development. Thus children learn to incorporate these traits into their own body concepts, and these traits eventually become a central part of their own self-concept (Hendry and Gillies, 1978). This theory would also lead to the research outcomes we have cited. Therefore a reasonable conclusion would be that at present it has not been determined conclusively whether the behaviors associated with the major body types are determined by biological or by learning factors. What we can conclude is that people seem to agree in their behavioral descriptions of various body builds. *Why* they do so is still unknown.

The Process of Personality Development

The Somatotypes and Movement toward Self-Actualization

From Sheldon's theorizing, it seems reasonable to assume that he believed the socialization process should be geared to the child's unique constitutional background if his or her potentialities are to be developed to the maximum. On this point, Sheldon is curiously aligned with Maslow, Rogers, and other proponents of the human potential movement. He also thought discipline should be tailored to the child's biology:

It is possible that some children need rigid discipline for their best development. This may be true in general of somatotonic children—those given to vigorous assertive characteristics. It may well be that a premature attempt at "reasoning" with somatotonic children is even more baffling and frustrating, and it may in the end be more devastating to character than is the ruthless whipping of a sensitive cerebrotonic child—one marked by sharp inhibition and hyperattentionality. Perhaps viscerotonic children—those characterized by emotional and social warmth, relaxation, gluttony—need to be handled in groups and "socialized" early in their development, whereas the cerebrotonics may need above everything else to be protected from this influence.

> *Watch young children in a nursery school. There are often a few vigorous-bodied somatotonics who take the lead in all enterprises, a few round, healthy-looking viscerotonics who join in with excellent fellowship, and a few little pinch-faced cerebrotonics who constitute a watchful and unsocialized periphery. These little cerebrotonics seem to want to stay on the sidelines and watch. Their eyes are sharp as needlepoints and nothing seems to escape their quick attention, but they do not want to be pushed into the swim. They are under stern internal check, and they seem to want to see without being seen. Should these children be sent to nursery schools and forced into the social press with a score of other children? Should they be sent to boys' camps and girls' camps? We do not know about these things. Modern educators might want to ponder this problem. It may be that late maturing personalities need a high degree of privacy and seclusion and protection during the formative years. It is possible that loneliness is an essential to the full development of a creature "mentally inclined" as sociability is essential to a viscerotonic or aggressive self-expression to a somatotonic youth. [Sheldon, Stevens, & Tucker, 1940, pp. 260–261]*

Modern child psychologists decry the use of "rigid" discipline, which presumably involves the use of physical punishment. Sheldon, however, seems to imply that such punishment may be entirely appropriate for children with mesomorphic builds and somatotonic temperaments. Sheldon went even further by arguing that perhaps enforced loneliness and isolation are virtues under some circumstances. In fairness to Sheldon, however, he did state that he was offering only hypotheses. It may turn out that environmental influences are even more important in determining the course of development. The crux of his argument seems to be that adequate development will take place if parents use disciplinary practices consistent with the child's basic nature and that abnormal behavior may be the result of applying discipline incongruent with this nature. If discipline is consistent with constitution type, the person will develop along viscerotone, somatotone, or cerebrotone lines, with the temperament and personality characteristics peculiar to these types.

Somatotyping and the Normal-Abnormal Continuum

Sheldon rejected the traditional view in psychiatry that mental disorders are diseases to be cured. In such a view, a person is thought either to have a disease or not to have it. She either has the measles or she does not. Similarly, he either suffers or does not suffer from manic-depressive psychosis, paranoid schizophrenia, or hebephrenic schizophrenia. Such a scheme posits qualitative differences in the behavior of people: normals, neurotics, and psychotics are different kinds of people (Sheldon, Hartl, & McDermott, 1949, p. 43).

Sheldon's view, in contrast, treats normal and abnormal behavior as different points on the same continuum. Normals, neurotics, and psychotics are not characterized by different kinds of behavior but by differences in the extremity of particular behaviors. These differences in the degree of behavior are then linked with the primary and secondary components of the body, which also vary along continua. Sheldon's scheme is thus much more complicated and allows for the assessment of subtle differences in both temperament and body build.

The Association between Normality and Balance in the Primary Components

The relationship Sheldon postulated between the primary components and normal behavior is difficult to express accurately. In general terms, he seems to be arguing that the normal person is one who has a somatotype that is moderate on all three components. For example, the healthy man or woman would be classified as a 444. Because endomorphy is strongly associated with viscerotonia, mesomorphy with somatotonia, and ectomorphy with cerebrotonia, it follows that the 444 somatotype implies well-balanced and moderate temperaments on the three primary components. Such a person, according to Sheldon, would be characterized as humorous. Sheldon defined "humorous" in an unusual way, however:

> Whatever else humor may be it certainly is characterized by two qualities: (1) An inclination toward detachment—the quality of regarding life and self lightly; (2) An inclination to tolerate and to enjoy incompatibilities at a high level of awareness. This second quality may contain the essence of humor, and if it does it may contain the essence of human salvation. [Sheldon, Hartl, & McDermott, 1949, p. 93]

Thus the humorous person is one who has probably achieved high status in life and who can easily tolerate conflict and uncertainty. He or she possesses all three temperaments to a moderate degree, and they serve to regulate one another. For example, the person's cerebral cortex serves to inhibit his or her visceral and muscular energies (Sheldon, Hartl, & McDermott, 1949, p. 94). Otherwise, the individual would be given to outbursts of emotion and aggressiveness.

The Association between Abnormality and the Primary Components

Somatotypes that suggest abnormality seem to be characterized by excesses or deficiencies in the primary body components (Sheldon, Hartl,

& McDermott, 1949, p. 90). For example, a delinquent characterized by loudness, restlessness, directness, and bluntness, as well as by amiability and a love of food, might have the somatotype 731 (Sheldon, Hartl, & McDermott, 1949, p. 414). In such a person, the cerebrotonic component is lacking, so that there are few restraints on his or her behavior.

In regard to the severe behavior disorders, Sheldon presented scientific evidence that particular body types are associated with different psychotic reactions. Manic-depressives are characterized by continual shifts in moods, ranging from extreme elation and euphoria to utter sorrow, dejection, and self-deprecation. Sheldon found that their somatotypes are high on the first two primary components (endomorphy and mesomorphy) but low on the third (ectomorphy). The primary problem with such people is that there is a pathological absence of inhibition (Sheldon, Hartl, & McDermott, 1949, p. 46). In other words, manic-depressives are characterized by extreme deficiencies in cerebrotonia. There are, as a consequence, few restraints on their tendencies to be expansive and energetic. According to Sheldon, it is pyknic individuals with 551 body types who most often and most easily become manic-depressives (Sheldon, Hartl, & McDermott, 1949, p. 62).

People labeled as paranoid schizophrenics tend to be hostile and suspicious of the intentions of others. They are also egocentric, conceited, condescending, and sarcastic (Sheldon, Hartl, & McDermott, 1949, p. 83). Sheldon discovered that their somatotypes are high on the last two components but very low on the first. They tend to be aggressive and have a hyperawareness of their surroundings, but they lack compassion and feeling toward others. They tend to overreact and to be indiscriminate in their judgments. Paranoid schizophrenics are especially high on mesomorphy and have somatotypes that approximate 253½ (Sheldon, Hartl, & McDermott, 1949, p. 82).

Individuals labeled as hebephrenic schizophrenics tend to be withdrawn, inadequate, and helpless (Sheldon, Hartl, & McDermott, 1949, p. 90). They are also characterized by bizarre and irrelevant feelings toward others (Sheldon, Hartl, & McDermott, 1949, p. 67). Hebephrenic schizophrenics have somatotypes that are high on the first and third components but low on the second. Although they are high on endomorphy, they are even higher on ectomorphy. Their somatotypes approximate 316 (Sheldon, Hartl, & McDermott, 1949, pp. 70–71).

Techniques of Assessment

Sheldon's theory is an attempt to provide a basic taxonomy of human beings through the use of somatotyping procedures. The taxonomy focuses on the identification of morphological characteristics in the hope of providing a conceptual scheme that can be used as a framework for the analysis of other related variables, such as physiological function, susceptibility to disease, temperament, and social adjustment.

The identification and measurement of the three primary and several secondary components of the person's physique were accomplished through the use of a photographic technique and several other anthropometric procedures. Photos were taken of the individual from the side, front, and back using a special long-focus lens to ensure that the length and breadth dimensions of the individual's body were not distorted in any way and, in fact, matched the measurements taken of the living body (Sheldon, Stevens, & Tucker, 1940, p. 30). Observers of the photos then proceeded to identify three extreme types—the endomorph, mesomorph, and ectomorph—as well as several minor components.

The next step in the somatotyping procedure involved an empirical determination of the physical characteristics associated with each major type. In general, endomorphs were found to have round and soft bodies, whereas mesomorphs had a relative predominance of muscle, bone, and connective tissue. Ectomorphs were characterized by large brains and nervous systems. Part of the identification process involved the examination and measurement of the principal internal organs of cadavers during autopsy work. This latter procedure showed that, of the three major types, endomorphs were endowed with relatively large intestines, livers, and other digestive viscera; and mesomorphs had the largest hearts and arteries (Sheldon, Stevens, & Tucker, 1940, pp. 32–35). Sheldon and his associates then developed 7-point rating scales for the three types that allowed for the assessment of variations in the characteristics associated with each component. This measurement procedure made it possible to precisely delineate and identify many body types.

Once proper somatotyping procedures were established, Sheldon developed scales for assessing the different kinds of temperaments. He collected a list of 650 traits of temperament by combing the research literature. Observers then combined terms that had similar meanings and eliminated those that seemed insignificant. The list was thereby reduced to 50 traits, which were then incorporated into 5-point and later 7-point rating scales. Subjects could then be rated according to the degree to which they possessed the characteristic (Sheldon and Stevens, 1942, p. 13). These assessments were made by repeatedly interviewing subjects and judging their temperament dispositions. Sheldon also had investigators watch the subjects during their daily routines throughout the year and make assessments on the basis of their observations.

Later, Sheldon computed the degree of association between the individual's physical type and temperament type (these results were reported earlier in the chapter). Sheldon relied on correlational procedures to assess the relationship between these two sets of variables. Although such measurements yield noncausal data that are open to various interpretations, Sheldon's reliance on them was appropriate because he was conducting work in an unexplored area where even the basic relationships between events were unclear. It would have been premature and inappropriate to attempt experimental analyses under such conditions.

Application of the Theory to the Treatment of Psychopathology

Sheldon was not able to develop a systematic position concerning the kinds of treatment that should be used to help alleviate the suffering of troubled individuals. He readily admitted that the constitutional approach has little or nothing to offer in these areas. Instead, he suggested that investigators focus most of their attention on diagnosis and "postpone the thought of treatment just as long as postponement can reasonably be tolerated" (Sheldon, Stevens, & Tucker, 1940, p. 257). Constitutional psychology is in a primitive state, and there is little basic information about the ways in which heredity influences our somatotypes and temperament (Sheldon, Stevens & Tucker, 1940, p. 227). How can the therapist recommend specific kinds of treatment if he or she is ignorant of the constitutional processes that underlie behavior? Sheldon maintained that, before they attempt to prescribe treatment, investigators must be able to describe and measure accurately the ways in which our genes exert influence indirectly through the physiology and chemistry of our bodies or directly on our behavior.

Despite this advocacy of a focus on diagnosis at this stage of our knowledge, Sheldon did make some suggestions concerning treatment. In our previous discussion on the socialization process, we noted that Sheldon strongly believed disciplinary practices should be consistent with the person's basic nature if the person is to develop his or her potentialities. Discipline that is inconsistent with one's basic nature, on the other hand, leads to the development of abnormal behavior. Accordingly, the person who is characterized by conflicts exists in an environment that restricts his or her growth. An example is the boy who represses his aggressive tendencies (his somatotonia) because they are forcefully prohibited by his parents. Such a person can be helped via psychoanalysis because his ability to think and analyze—that is, his cerebrotonic tendencies—are intact. He can also be helped by sympathetic discussion and explanation and thus be freed to express his aggressive tendencies under appropriate circumstances.

If this boy, however, had become abnormally dominant and aggressive and had repressed his cerebrotonia, he would not be able to resolve his conflicts through psychoanalysis. According to Sheldon, Freudian analysis can reach the person only through the cerebrotonic aspects of his or her personality, and in this case that component is unavailable. One solution is to confront the boy with strict disciplinary measures, including physical punishment, in order to bring his aggressiveness under control so that he can be trained to live effectively in society. Accordingly, the therapist might suggest to the parents that they establish a "benevolent dictatorship" over the child and teach him habits that allow him to function effectively (Sheldon, Stevens, & Tucker, 1940, pp. 262–263).

On a more general level, Sheldon advocated a eugenics program in which officials would discover the people who would produce the "best stock" of children. Such parents would then be encouraged by state authorities to breed, and people with "inferior" constitutions would be discouraged from breeding. Sheldon believed that in this way the number of people who are potentially dangerous to society could be drastically reduced. He offered this plan as an alternative to suppressing the unfit and eliminating or sterilizing people with the "wrong" body types. He did not want the state to subject people to such extreme and harsh treatment (Sheldon, Stevens, & Tucker, 1940, pp. 229–230). Yet, for all his humanitarian concern, in a later publication Sheldon did advocate a position that is clearly antihumanistic in nature. He proposed that war may be the "solution" to the problem of a society populated with a certain percentage of misfits:

> We are . . . scheduled for such inconveniences as social chaos, wars of increasing and crescendic violence, general frustration, and the confusion necessarily attendant upon the pathology of increasing urbanization and loss of zest in human life. All of this we have already earned by irresponsible reproduction in the recent past. No amount of regret or prayer or pacifism can cancel that debt, and nature generally collects her debts. Pacifism might be defined as the expression of a hebephrenic wish to escape the consequences of delinquent reproduction already committed. This delinquency is everybody's for since we all participate in the future unless we die out, the one thing that is everybody's responsibility is guardianship of the quality of the reproduction of his own time. If that responsibility is shirked, war is perhaps the least ungentle of natural punishments.
>
> We cannot be now declaring how much we would like to have peace [in order to] escape the devastating wars of the next few generations, nor do I think that a morally responsible person should want to escape them. That punishment is needed for without it the delinquency would continue. [Sheldon, Hartl, & McDermott, 1949, pp. 837–838]

We can now perhaps understand the liberal's concern with the potential for a totalitarian state based on a position like Sheldon's. Although the constitutional position, which maintains that biological superiority and inferiority are realities, does not necessarily imply that its proponents are incapable of supporting a democratic philosophy, it does lend itself quite readily to the establishment of an antidemocratic philosophy. Fortunately for us, Sheldon's social philosophizing and moralizing about the "treatment" have been largely ignored.

Critical Comments

We turn now to an assessment of the scientific worth of Sheldon's position in terms of our six criteria.

Comprehensiveness. The theory Sheldon offered is grossly inadequate in its comprehensiveness and ability to generate testable hypotheses outside its narrow province. Sheldon seemed more interested in the classification of physique and related behaviors than in constructing an internally consistent conceptual system capable of generating testable hypotheses. The attractiveness of his position for many people, however, lies in this very simplicity. They find it easy to understand and easy to apply to people in their everyday encounters. If they meet a fat man who turns out to be jolly and sociable, they find their view of the "basic nature" of human beings confirmed. If they meet a thin man who is also jolly and sociable, they tend to ignore this apparent incongruence or to judge him as an exceptional case, thus leaving their views intact. Even if knowledge of body type allowed us to predict the sociability of people perfectly, there are still countless other behaviors left untouched and unassessed by the system Sheldon presented. In particular, he ignored the impact of social-learning phenomena on behavior.

Precision and Testability. In his favor, Sheldon constructed a somatotyping scheme that is more sophisticated and precise than any devised by his predecessors. By using a 7-point rating scale instead of simple dichotomies, Sheldon made it possible for other investigators to gauge more precisely the somatotypes and temperaments of people and to assess more accurately the relationship between the two factors. Despite his painstaking attention to measurement procedures, we should not conclude that the concepts and relational statements in Sheldon's theorizing are clear and lead to precise hypothesizing and rigorous research. Many of the terms are global and ambiguous in nature (for example, viscerotonia and somatotonia) and do not have clear and unequivocal operational referents. The relational statements of the theory are also in a rudimentary stage of development. In spite of these limitations, however, Sheldon deserves credit for attempting needed research in a largely unexplored and undefined area. Under these conditions, he did a tremendous job in trying to assess precisely the relationships between physique and temperament.

Parsimony. Sheldon's theory fails to meet the parsimony criterion. It has too few concepts and too few assumptions to account adequately for the range and diversity of phenomena involved in a theory of personality. Sheldon recognized that the environment has a tremendous impact on the acquisition, maintenance, and modification of behavior, but his theory virtually ignores social-learning phenomena and concepts. The theory, in brief, is too simple and does not do justice to the full range of variables that determine behavioral outcomes.

   ✢ *Empirical Validity.* There have been many tests of Sheldon's theory, and the bulk of the results is highly supportive. Although the major hypotheses about the relationships between body build and behavior have been confirmed, there is as yet no direct proof that these relationships are the product of genetic inheritance. In fairness to Sheldon, however, there is no direct proof that the associations are determined by social experience either. Thus the issue of whether the correlations between body build and behavior are determined by genetic or learning factors remains open and subject to debate and further empirical study.

   N̷ *Heuristic Value.* Sheldon's theory has had little impact on the thinking and research efforts of other investigators. Most are trained in an environmentalist orientation and are convinced that learning phenomena play the major role in determining behavior. As a consequence, they usually pay lip service to the importance of the biological determinants of behavior but proceed to study problems from an environmentalist perspective. Where investigators have displayed an interest in assessing the role of biology in determining behavior, most efforts have been directed at examining the behavior of lower animals in an attempt to generate principles also applicable to human behavior.

   N̷ *Applied Value.* Sheldon's theory has had little, if any, practical value. As mentioned previously, most investigators have ignored Sheldon. It is not uncommon to hear students exclaim that they "thought Sheldon was a dead issue!" This chapter should have convinced you that the issues raised by Sheldon have not yet been resolved and that they are worth further investigation. His position has considerable strengths. He succeeded, for example, in calling our attention to the importance of the bodily determinants of behavior. He also studied these problems empirically and helped generate some interest in the area among investigators. His measuring system is superior to any constructed by his predecessors and provides a much more objective way of assessing physique.

   Despite the empirical orientation of his efforts, however, it should be recognized that research in this area is still exploratory. Sheldon himself pointed out that body build and structure are direct results of heredity and of the way in which the development of the genes influences the physiology and chemistry of the body. Our knowledge of these influences is scant at the present. There can be little question that heredity sets limits on our activities and influences our behavior in conjunction with our environmental experiences. If he did nothing else, Sheldon succeeded in alerting us to the need for redress of the imbalance in our theoretical and research work on human behavior.

Discussion Questions

1. Describe Hippocrates' typology linking the activity of humors to behavior. What are some of the inadequacies of such a typology?
2. What is phrenology? In what ways was it a serious scientific endeavor? What were some of the criticisms leveled at it by those in a variety of disciplines?
3. Are physiognomy and phrenology completely outdated? If so, how can you explain their continued popularity in certain quarters?
4. List the three basic body types postulated by Sheldon and describe the ways in which he related each to human behavior.
5. Discuss Sheldon's theory in relation to the socialization of children. Do you believe in the use of physical punishment to discipline certain types of children? Why or why not?
6. Discuss the implications of Sheldon's position for the treatment of individuals with behavioral problems.
7. Do constitutional positions necessarily imply the endorsement of an anti-egalitarian philosophy? What are some of the possible dangers of such positions for democratically oriented societies?
8. Why is Sheldon's position so attractive to many people?
9. Can an adequate theory of personality exist without accounting for the operation of genetic variables? Give your reasons.
10. Why do many academics continue to ignore biologically based theories of personality?

References

Child, I. L. The relation of somatotype to self-ratings on Sheldon's temperamental traits. *Journal of Personality*, 1950, *18*, 440–453.

Cortes, J. B., & Gatti, F. M. Physique and self-descriptions of temperament. *Journal of Consulting Psychology*, 1965, *29*, 432–439.

Gacsaly, S. A., & Borges, C. A. The male physique and behavioral expectancies. *Journal of Psychology*, 1979, *101*, 97–102.

Hendry, L. B., & Gillies, P. Body type, body esteem, school, and leisure: A study of overweight, average, and underweight adolescents. *Journal of Youth and Adolescence*, 1978, *7*, 181–194.

Kellett, J., Marzillier, J. S., & Lambert, C. Social skills and somatotype. *British Journal of Medical Psychology*, 1981, *54*, 149–155.

Lerner, R. M. The development of stereotyped expectancies of body build–behavior relations. *Child Development*, 1969, *40*, 137–141.

Sheldon, W. H., Dupertuis, C. W., & McDermott, E. *Atlas of men: A guide for somatotyping the adult male at all ages.* New York: Harper, 1954.

Sheldon, W. H., Hartl, E. M., & McDermott, E. *Varieties of delinquent youth: An introduction to constitutional psychiatry.* New York: Harper, 1949.

Sheldon, W. H., & Stevens, S. S. *The varieties of temperament: A psychology of constitutional differences.* New York: Harper, 1942.

Sheldon, W. H., Stevens, S. S., & Tucker, W. B. *The varieties of human physique: An introduction to constitutional psychology.* New York: Harper, 1940.

Tucker, L. A. Relationship between perceived somatotype and body cathexis of college males. *Psychological Reports*, 1982, *50*, 983–989.

Tucker, L. A. Self-concept: A function of self-perceived somatotype. *Journal of Psychology*, 1983, *113*, 123–133.

Yates, J., & Taylor, J. Stereotypes for somatotypes: Shared beliefs about Sheldon's physiques. *Psychological Reports*, 1978, *43*, 777–778.

Suggested Readings

Hartl, E. M., Monnelly, E. P., & Elderkin, R. D. *Physique and delinquent behavior: A thirty-year follow-up of William H. Sheldon's varieties of delinquent youth.* New York: Academic Press, 1982.

Sheldon, W. H., Hartl, E. M., & McDermott, E. *Varieties of delinquent youth: An introduction to constitutional psychiatry.* New York: Harper, 1949.

Sheldon, W. H., & Stevens, S. S. *The varieties of temperament: A psychology of constitutional differences.* New York: Harper, 1942.

Sheldon, W. H., Stevens, S. S. & Tucker, W. B. *The varieties of human physique: An introduction to constitutional psychology.* New York: Harper, 1940.

Glossary

Cerebrotonia Temperament type attributed by Sheldon to the ectomorphic individual. The cerebrotone is characterized by emotional restraint, tenseness, and withdrawal from others.

Constitutional position Theoretical perspective that emphasizes the biological and genetic determinants of behavior.

Dysplasia Secondary body component identified by Sheldon. It refers to disharmony between different regions of the same body.

Ectomorphy One of three basic body dimensions studied by Sheldon. The ectomorph is characterized by thinness and a large surface area and nervous system in proportion to body mass.

Endomorphy One of three basic body dimensions studied by Sheldon. The endomorph is characterized by softness, roundness, and a large digestive system.

Gynandromorphy Secondary body component identified by Sheldon. It refers to the bisexual nature of the body.

Hirsutism Secondary body component identified by Sheldon. It refers to the general hairiness of the body.

Mesomorphy One of three basic body dimensions studied by Sheldon. The mesomorph is characterized by strong bones and muscles.

Morphology Body structure of the individual.

Pyknic practical joke Person who appears to have a relatively normal physique but who later in life changes dramatically in appearance and becomes obese.

Somatotonia Temperament type attributed by Sheldon to the mesomorphic individual. The somatotone is characterized by boldness, aggressiveness, and love of physical danger and risk.

Somatotype Establishment of a person's general body type or pattern through the assignment of a set of ratings on the three primary components. For example, an extreme mesomorph would have a somatotype of 171.

Texture Secondary body component identified by Sheldon. It refers to the attractiveness of the person's physique.

Viscerotonia Temperament type attributed by Sheldon to the endomorphic individual. The viscerotone is characterized by relaxed posture, love of comfort, and a need for approval and affection from others.

PART 8

The Future of Personality Psychology

Approximately 20 years ago, psychologist Walter Mischel presented a critique of the inadequacies of many of the personality theories currently in existence. His provocative criticisms unleashed a barrage of counterarguments by other leading personality psychologists. Several major conceptual and methodological gains and a new direction for the discipline have emerged from this stimulating and intricate debate. There is now a consensus that the creation of an interactional theory of personality is needed to increase our understanding of human functioning. The last chapter reviews the gist of this debate, the gains from it, and the prospects for the future of the discipline.

New Directions in the Discipline

We have now completed a long and complicated, yet perhaps interesting and enlightening, journey through several major perspectives on human personality. It should be apparent to you at this point that none of the theoretical systems we have reviewed ranks high on all the criteria used by investigators in judging the scientific worth of a theory. For example, some theories excel in organizing a mass of unrelated facts into a coherent frame-work. A few are clearly superior in parsimony, internal consistency, and precision, so that they are likely to generate testable predictions. Some are comprehensive in the number and variety of phenomena they treat; others are much more limited in scope. Some are stimulating and provocative; others are less influential. Some of the theories have greater applied value, allowing investigators to help solve social problems.

All our theories, however, have made major contributions to our under-standing of personality functioning. Yet there is clearly a need to develop new approaches that build upon the strengths and overcome the limitations in the current positions. Fortunately, substantial progress toward this goal has been made recently. There has been lively debate among prominent personality psychologists about the inadequacies of the current positions and about the means of overcoming their deficiencies.

This debate has long historical roots (Ekehammar, 1974; Epstein, 1985). It centers on attempts to answer two fundamental questions: To what extent does our behavior change as a result of situational changes, and to what extent does our behavior remain the same despite situational changes? In recent times, Walter Mischel reopened this **person-situation debate** by noting that virtually all current personality theories rely almost exclusively on person variables (for instance, traits, motives, needs) or situation variables to explain and predict personality functioning and behavior, whereas a more adequate model would incorporate *both* person and situation variables. In brief, like other prominent personality psychologists before him, Mischel argued for the development of an interactional model of personality as the best framework for generating a theory that would most adequately account for personality functioning and change. As we will see, the debate that Mischel sparked involves a new look at historical issues and the consideration of new issues and possibilities.

Needed: An Interactional Model of Personality

Mischel proposes that personality psychology adopt an **interactional model of personality** that would explain personality functioning in terms of the joint contributions of person variables and situation variables (Mischel, 1973). **Person variables** are conceptualized as cognitive and motivational structures within persons that are utilized by them to adapt to the demands of situations. **Situation variables** are the environmental conditions or eliciting stimuli that confront the individual and affect him or her in some way. The response may be a thought or an emotional reaction or an overt behavior—or sometimes all three. For example, you may respond to a difficult academic test by thinking negatively ("I am going to fail"), experiencing anxiety, and chewing your pencil to a stump. In the interactional view, not all students would react to the test in the same way. Their responses would be modified by their personality characteristics, such as their traits and motives. For instance, a classmate with a low need for achievement might be less prone to think negatively about the test outcome (he may not care), to experience anxiety, or to show fidgety behavior than would a student with a high need for achievement. Thus, within the interactional framework, we are not "empty organisms" buffeted by external stimuli, but rather active, thinking human beings who select or modify situations to suit our own purposes (Raush, 1977, p. 294). We reinterpret incoming stimuli in light of our past experiences, e.g., in terms of our needs, values, and goals. We engage in active and continuous transactions with the environment. That is, we are influenced by the environment, but we also influence it (Magnusson & Endler, 1977, p. 4).

General Limitations of the Person-Oriented Theories. Although the interactionist position just cited may seem reasonable and perhaps even obvious to you, Mischel notes that personality psychologists have traditionally deemphasized or even ignored the situation side of the equation. That is, they acknowledge theoretically the interaction between person and situation, but in practice, most of their attention has been focused on person variables (Mischel, 1968, p. 281). This one-sided emphasis can be seen clearly in the psychodynamic Freudian and Jungian positions and in the works of prominent trait theorists like Allport and humanistic psychologists like Maslow. Sheldon's position, too, favors person variables (that is, genetic and temperament factors) because he was primarily concerned with understanding how biology determines behavior, and, as a result, he paid little attention to the role of the environment. Finally, Kelly's position is strongly cognitive and emphasizes the ways in which the person's unique construct system influences behavior.

According to Mischel, the classic-person approaches (for example, the psychodynamic and trait theories) postulate the existence of broad and stable characteristics that cause the person to behave consistently across many situations (Mischel, 1968, p. 6). Thus the assumption in these positions is that situational influences play only a minor role in the modification of behavior. Yet we know that people alter their behavior in response to environmental influences at many points of their lives. The person who marries changes in many ways as a result of that new status. Entering into careers and the playing of new roles—for example, athlete, lover, or student—also change behavior. We are changed as a result of births in our families, by the deaths of loved ones, by educational experiences, and by increases in taxes and unemployment. The point should be clear, yet many of the **person-oriented theories** deemphasize the situational determinants of behavior. Thus Mischel believes these psychologies present an oversimplified and inaccurate view of the means by which behavior is acquired, maintained, and modified.

General Limitations of the Situation-Oriented Theories. In contrast to the one-sided person-oriented theories that typically have their roots in the clinical tradition, there are **situation-oriented theories** that rely almost exclusively on the role played by environmental or situational factors in the prediction of behavior. These theories typically have their historical roots in the experimental laboratory. In these positions, person variables tend to be ignored or deemphasized. Instead, situations or environmental conditions are seen as the primary causes of behavior. Skinner's position can reasonably be characterized as situationist despite his recent acknowledgment of the importance of cognitive mediating processes.

Specific Limitations of the Person-Oriented Theories

Imprecise Concepts

Mischel argues that the person-oriented perspectives—the psychodynamic, trait, and humanistic views, among others—have limited scientific utility because the constructs they use to describe underlying dispositions that direct behavior are too global in nature and ill-defined. Examples include Freud's id, ego, and superego; Jung's anima and animus; Adler's striving for superiority; Fromm's need for transcendence; Allport's central traits; Cattell's ego strength, dominance, and venturesome (parmia) and imaginative (autia) traits; Erikson's identity-crisis concept; Maslow's peak experience; Rogers' drive for self-actualization; and May's concept of anxiety, which he defines as a threat to *Dasein*. To illustrate Mischel's point further, let us examine the measurement and definitional problems associated with two other constructs—Freud's death instinct and Jung's shadow.

Freud's Death Instinct. Freud first postulated the existence of a death instinct to explain the eruption of aggressive impulses that resulted in destructive behavior toward others or oneself. He based his concept on the idea in biology that all human beings are composed of organic materials that eventually decompose and return to an inanimate state. He then gave this simple description explanatory power. Thus he saw the death instinct as an agency causing the person to be aggressive and destructive.

What were the parameters of the death instinct? Freud himself acknowledged that they were not easy to specify. He thought that it was a "special physiological process" that eventually directed behavior (Freud, 1960, p. 30). He then talked about this process in terms of a blending of life forces (Eros) and death forces (Thanatos) because, for him, every action was the result of the combined forces of life and death. In his view, the death instinct operated in the following way:

> It appears *that, as a result of the combination of unicellular organisms into multicellular forms of life, the death instinct of the single cell can successfully be neutralized and the destructive impulses be diverted on to the external world through the instrumentality of a special organ. This special organ would seem to be the muscular apparatus; and the death instinct would thus seem to express itself—though* **probably** *only in part—as an instinct of destruction directed against the external world and other organisms. [Freud, 1960, p. 31. Boldface added.]*

As you can see, this description is speculative. The referents in the example are vague, and Freud begs the question by assuming there is a "death instinct" in every single cell. It is clear that cells die but not that a death instinct causes them to die. Furthermore, even if we grant the validity of his argument, why should a death-instinct cell that is successfully neutralized by a life-instinct cell have any energy or impulses left to divert into muscular channels? How are they diverted into muscular channels?

In fairness to Freud, he did recognize that the physiological process underlying the death instinct was vague. But he then proceeded to talk about the instinct as though it existed and controlled much of human behavior. He used it as a post hoc device to explain a variety of behaviors he observed among his patients and believed it was a scientifically useful tool. The problems with both its measurement and its explanatory status should be evident.

Jung's Shadow. In regard to Jung's shadow construct, we can also ask: What exactly are its referents? That is, what are the publicly observable and agreed-on indicators of the shadow? If we knew what they were, and if we could establish a reliable means of measuring them, then perhaps the construct would have potential scientific utility. Under these conditions, investigators could incorporate it into their hypothesizing and use it to make differential predictions about behavior. If we examine Jung's definition of the term, however, we begin to see the extreme difficulty in establishing such a measure. For him, the shadow

> *is a* **moral problem** *that challenges the* **whole ego personality**, *for no one can become conscious of the shadow without considerable effort. To become conscious of it involves recognizing the* **dark aspects** *of the personality as present and real. . . . Closer examination of the dark characteristics—that is, the* **inferiorities** *constituting the shadow—reveals that they have an emotional nature, a kind of* **autonomy**, *and accordingly an* **obsessive** *or, better,* **possessive** *quality. Emotion, incidentally, is not an activity of the individual but something that happens to him. Affects occur usually where adaptation is weakest, and at the same time they reveal the reason for its weakness, namely a certain degree of inferiority and the existence of a lower level of personality.* [Jung, 1958, p. 7. Boldface added in the first sentence only.]

What does Jung mean by *moral problems?* What are the *dark aspects* of personality? Although we may have some intuitive understanding of these terms and others in his definition, it would be difficult, if not impossible, to define these referents of the shadow. In addition, Jung's attempts to have us understand the meaning of the shadow construct hinge on an exploration of the psyche. In short, we would have to plunge even further into the "depths" of the psyche if we were ever to attain even an approximation of its meaning. Such a procedure takes us further from the observables of external reality and leaves us tangled in a web of mystery that may be interesting and entertaining but is scientifically not very useful. Considering that Jung believed the shadow was easier to define than his anima and animus archetypes, you can imagine the efforts required to begin to make scientific sense of these constructs, if indeed it is possible at all.

Although we have emphasized here the use of global and imprecisely defined constructs by theorists who focus on person variables, similar arguments could be mustered in regard to the ambiguity of many other constructs. Recall the ambiguities in Fromm's definition of conscience as the "reaction of ourselves to ourselves," Freud's concept of the "life instincts," and the construct of "potentiality" that is utilized by the humanistic psychologists.

Interpretational Difficulties

Mischel maintains that in the person-oriented theories there is an added problem of confusion and lack of precision because of the assumption that the various dispositions (traits, id impulses, strivings for superiority, needs for self-actualization) are not observed directly but are inferred from various behavioral signs. In short, overt behavior is merely an indicator of the operation of underlying causal factors. The investigator's job, then, is to try to understand the underlying meaning of the overt behavior. To accomplish this goal, he or she must plunge into the "depths" of the person's psyche and untangle the complex interweavings of underlying motives that produce the surface behavior. The investigator's primary focus, in other words, is on understanding the "dynamics" of the behavior in question.

In the Freudian scheme, for example, there is the continual attempt by the ego and superego to distort or deny the expression of id impulses in surface behavior. If the behavior ever does reach the surface, it is usually disguised. Dancing, for instance, may be seen as a kind of sublimated activity in which undesirable impulses are converted into a socially acceptable form of behavior. The same is true for creative painting. Harmless slips of the tongue are seen as indicators of underlying conflicts, as you know. Even healthy statements like "I love my mother" may be taken by Freudian therapists under certain circumstances to be a distortion of one's "true" feelings. As you can imagine, it is extremely difficult to determine the precise meaning of overt behavior in such a theoretical framework.

Although the concepts and propositions in Kelly's theory are clearly defined, it, too, assumes that overt behavior is merely a sign of underlying causal factors—in this case, personal constructs. Thus his Role Construct Repertory Test is conceptualized as a rough indicator of the kinds of personal constructs that guide the person's behavior in certain channels (Kelly, 1955, pp. 204–205). Like Cattell, he believed that the raw data provided by the test can be factor-analyzed to reveal the underlying sources of the person's behavior. Once again, precision in interpreting the meaning (or meanings) of overt behavior becomes difficult.

Finally, Mischel maintains that clinicians guided by psychodynamic concepts about underlying causal factors have not been able to predict behavior better than investigators using more direct methods. As he puts it, "Predictions [of behavior] should be most accurate when the past situations in which the predictor behavior was sampled are most similar to the situations at which predictions about future behavior are aimed" (Mischel, 1968, p. 140). Thus, if you want to predict a student's grade in a calculus course, you should be able to predict it best from a knowledge of his previous grades in mathematics courses. If, for example, he never obtained a grade higher than "D" in his prior mathematics courses, you would predict that he is not likely to be a whiz at calculus. Prior academic accomplishments in mathematics would, in Mischel's view, be a better predictor of the student's performance than an indirect predictor based on a dynamic interpretation of early id, ego, and superego conflicts between the student and his parents. For Mischel, then, it is best to discard the indirect approach to the assessment of personality. At the very least, Mischel thinks investigators using the indirect approach will have to demonstrate its usefulness empirically.

Lack of Ability to Predict Accurately

As we have seen, an adequate theory should lead eventually to the testing of hypotheses and the collection of supporting data. Mischel thinks that person-oriented theories generally lack the ability to predict accurately the behavior of individuals in specific situations. He maintains, for example, that knowledge of people's global, underlying traits does not allow investigators to predict their current behavior in particular situations very well. These traits are assumed to cause people to behave in similar ways despite differences in the situations confronting them. In Sheldon's theory, for example, part of the definition of viscerotonia is *indiscriminate* amiability. It implies that endomorphs will be friendly and happy in all situations, a rarity for virtually all of us regardless of body type. Consider our behavior at family funerals, at boxing matches, at bankruptcy proceedings, during lovers' quarrels, at divorce proceedings, after academic suspensions, and so forth.

Low correlations would also be expected, according to Mischel, because most of the traditional, person-oriented theories utilize constructs, such as viscerotonia, somatotonia, and cerebrotonia, that are global and that contain many ambiguous and diverse dimensions (Mischel, 1968, p. 60). For example, somatotonia is measured by rating people on dimensions like lust for power, claustrophobia, love of risk and chance, overmaturity of appearance, orientation toward goals and activities of youth, competitive aggressiveness, and so forth.

Not only do the trait positions lack predictive utility, but so, in Mischel's opinion, do the psychodynamic theories. In his view, psychodynamic theorists, such as Freud, Jung, and Adler, typically use a highly restricted sample of patients' self-reported behavior to infer the existence and operation of underlying dynamic forces. These underlying forces—for example, the id, ego, superego, shadow, anima, animus, and the need for superiority—are then speculated to control much of the individual's behavior in many different situations. But because their existence is inferred on the basis of only a few behavioral signs, Mischel believes they exist more in the imagination of the therapist than in the actual life experiences of the person being observed and analyzed (Mischel, 1976, pp. 632–633). As a result, a prediction of actual behavior is poor if it utilizes these speculative concepts.

In summary, Mischel levels the following major criticisms at person-oriented theories:

1. The theories are populated with constructs that are poorly defined; definitional ambiguity hinders the accurate prediction of behavior.
2. Person-oriented constructs (for instance, traits, motives, needs) are not observed directly but are inferred from examination of overt behavior. This inference process is plagued by difficulties when one tries both to interpret the meaning of that behavior and to predict other behavior precisely.
3. In the prediction of behavior, there is too much emphasis in these theories on the role played by person variables and not enough emphasis on the role played by situational demands.
4. Person variables are supposed to predict behavior across many situations. Yet they do not seem to have much predictive power because behavior is very responsive to and regulated by situational demands. Thus behavior is not determined typically by broad dispositions (for instance, traits, motives) that manifest themselves stably more or less independently of situational change.

Defense of the Person-Oriented Theories

We turn now to the vigorous defense of the person-oriented theories by several prominent investigators and to attempts by Mischel and his supporters to rebut the arguments. The primary focus of Mischel's critics is on his view that the traditional global-trait concept is untenable and does not allow for the accurate prediction of behavior. As you will see, they are able to show rather convincingly that such broad dispositions (that is, traits) do exist and can be utilized to predict behavior accurately if precautions are taken to measure the constructs precisely and to ensure that they are highly reliable.

Individual Differences and the Prediction of Behavior

In their opening salvo, Mischel's critics maintained that it is blatantly obvious to everyone that any theory that purports to adequately account for personality functioning must incorporate measures of individual differences. They argued further that Mischel's attacks on the scientific utility of the trait and psychodynamic models indicate that he views individual differences (person variables) as unimportant, holding instead that situations are the primary determinants of behavior (see, for example, Bowers, 1973).

Mischel (1977) vigorously denied the accusation. His denial has some validity, as can be seen by the following quotation taken from one of his early major writings on the subject. At the end of a chapter in which he attacked the scientific utility of the person-oriented models, he explicitly stated:

> It would be a complete misinterpretation . . . to conclude that individual differences are unimportant. To remind oneself of their pervasive role one need merely observe the differences among people's responses to almost any complex social stimulus under most supposedly uniform laboratory conditions. The real questions are not the existence of differences among individuals but rather their nature, their causes and consequences, and the utility of inferring them for particular purposes. [Mischel, 1968, p. 38]

Thus Mischel did not reject totally the role played by person variables in the prediction of behavior, but only those (for example, global traits) that are assumed to have pervasive cross-situational generality and that thereby lead one to underestimate the impact of situational circumstances. However, it is easy to understand why Mischel's critics could make the accusation, for he continuously pointed out in the course of this writing the importance of the situation in determining behavior. In fairness to Mischel, though, his exaggeration of the importance of the situation was probably his way of underscoring the fact that the traditional trait and psychodynamic positions had largely ignored the situation's role in the determination of behavior and that a correction for this deficiency was sorely needed.

In any event, it is now abundantly clear from his more recent writings that Mischel thinks that person variables are very important and must be incorporated into any theory that presumes to account adequately for personality functioning (Mischel, 1973; 1984). Specifically, he has included several individual differences constructs in his proposal of a **cognitive social-learning** model as an integral part of the new interactional theory of personality. These cognitive (and motivational) variables include the person's ability to generate diverse behaviors under appropriate situational circumstances and his or her unique ways of encoding and organizing events. They also include attention to the person's expectancies about outcomes, the subjective value of such outcomes, and self-regulatory systems and plans.

Psychodynamic Theories and Situational Influences

Next, advocates of the psychodynamic approaches argued that Mischel falsely accused them of ignoring situational influences on behavior. They maintained that their theories explicitly recognize that a person's behavior can and often does vary from situation to situation, so that Mischel's view of their theories is wrong (see, for instance, Wachtel, 1973). Mischel responded that his critics were knocking a straw man about because he had in fact *always* maintained in his writings that the psychodynamic theories do attempt to account for such situational influences. The psychodynamists' criticism of him on this matter was, he asserted, actually an attempt to divert attention away from the real issue—that is, the limited clinical and scientific usefulness of their theories. Although psychodynamists assume that a person's behavior varies from situation to situation, Mischel contends that these inconsistencies are treated as *merely superficial symptoms* that mask underlying motives that actually press for expression across diverse situations. In other words, the task of the clinician is to organize inconsistent behaviors into a fundamental, unified, underlying trait or motive, which they should then use to accurately diagnose the person's personality and/or predict his or her behavior. Mischel notes that, unfortunately, such attempts have usually failed (Mischel, 1968, pp. 103–148). Using such global and dynamic procedures, clinicians have often arrived at conflicting personality diagnoses even when their interpretations are based on the same information. These global assessments also have a poor record in predicting the adjustment behavior of patients.

The Predictive Utility of Person-Oriented Theories

Finally, Mischel's most controversial contention is that the person-oriented approach has little empirical utility. That is, he maintains that person variables like traits, needs, and motives do not exercise major control over behavior in the face of fluctuations in situations. He cites evidence showing that the correlations between the person's traits and behaviors across situations are typically between .20 and .30. Mischel coined the term **personality coefficient** to describe these low correlations. In his view, the personality coefficient is likely to be "found persistently when virtually any personality dimension inferred from a questionnaire was related to almost any conceivable criterion [behavior]" (Mischel, 1968, p. 78). The low correlations suggest that behavior is controlled primarily by situational influences and that knowledge of a person's traits does not allow investigators to predict his or her behavior accurately. If knowledge of the traits did allow investigators to predict the behavior perfectly, the correlations would be 1.00.

Mischel's critics took immediate issue with his statements, for his argument implied to them that there was little or no consistency or stability in people's behavior over time and across situations. They contended that the personalities of individuals in fact reveal impressive organization and stability, and they set out to show that "traits were alive and well" (Epstein, 1977). They used the following four arguments to attack Mischel's position.

Argument 1: Mischel's Review of the Research Literature Is Biased. One prominent researcher, Robert Hogan, maintained that Mischel's review of the empirical literature was selective and that there is ample evidence that the cross-situational correlations obtained in many studies are much higher than .30. He cited numerous studies in which the correlations range from .40 to .73, suggesting that Mischel's contention was erroneous (Hogan, DeSoto, & Solano, 1977).

Argument 2: Reliance on Multiple Traits in Behavioral Prediction Increases Predictive Power. Another researcher contended that trait-behavior correlations would be higher than .30 if investigators relied on several personality variables (traits) in making their predictions about particular behaviors (Alker, 1972). That is, according to Alker, it is possible to increase the magnitude of the correlations (and thereby the accuracy of predicting certain behaviors from a knowledge of people's traits) by *combining* several trait measures in the statistical analysis of the data. The statistical technique to be used is called a multiple-correlation analysis (see Chapter 1). If we wanted, for example, to predict the performance of students on a particular test, we might compare not only the scores of the low-anxiety students to those of high-anxiety students, but also the test scores of students with high test anxiety, low intelligence, low self-esteem, and an external orientation to those of students with low test anxiety, high intelligence, high self-esteem, and an internal control orientation.

Bem (1972) defended Mischel by pointing out that Mischel had already noted in his earlier writings that such multiple-correlations analyses could indeed be used to increase the magnitude of trait-behavior correlations. Alker (1977, p. 244), however, maintained that although Mischel mentioned the utility of such analyses, he never seriously considered them as providing a major counterargument to his view that traits are poor predictors of behavior.

Argument 3: The Design and Implementation of Well-Conceived Studies and the Use of Reliable Measures Increase Predictive Accuracy. Even where the correlations in many studies are actually low, defenders of the trait position maintain there are valid reasons for these outcomes. One major reason is that many personality studies have been weak both conceptually and methodologically. Thus the use of unreliable, poorly conceived trait measures has prevented investigators from obtaining results that show that people behave consistently over time and across diverse situations (Block, 1977; Epstein, 1977, 1979, 1980, 1983a, 1983b; Pervin, 1981).

Since traits are conceptualized as generalized tendencies for people to behave in a certain manner over time and across situations, questionnaires that measure these dispositions must consist of items that assess subjects' reports of past behaviors in a variety of situations. Thus the Internal-External Control Scale (see Chapter 12) consists of items assessing internal versus external beliefs in political, academic, occupational, and social situations, among others. Because total scores for subjects are obtained by summing their responses to these items (thereby summing across situations), the result is a score that indicates the measurement of a generalized trait. Unfortunately, not all the tests designed to measure traits in personality psychology are constructed with the care that was used in the development of the Internal-External Control Scale. Thus, as Pervin pointed out, many of the tests utilize items that do not mention situations at all (Pervin, 1981, p. 344). These unreliable measures prevent the demonstration of trait stability. In addition, even where this problem has been resolved in particular studies, all too often the **temporal stability** of the measures has not been established in a satisfactory way. Temporal stability entails assessment of consistency in behavior (trait stability) over time (that is, on many occasions in the same situation) (Epstein, 1979, p. 1105).

To illustrate the concept of temporal stability concretely, assume for a moment that you applied for employment as an office manager during your summer vacation, did poorly on the typing test, and, consequently, were not hired. It may well be that your test score (as measured by the total number of words you typed per minute less the number of words on which you made errors) did not reflect your actual typing ability. It may instead have reflected the fact that you were particularly anxious on that day because of a serious illness in your family or that you were fatigued because of insufficient sleep the night before or that you were simply nervous about taking the test. Or perhaps the employer inadvertently misscored your test.

The prospective employer might better have assessed your typing ability by giving you the test several times on different occasions in the same setting so as to obtain your *average* score on the tests. Such an **aggregation procedure,** while costly and time-consuming, would have reduced errors in measurement, yielded a more accurate assessment of your typing ability (trait), and given the employer a better gauge of your ability to perform the duties of office manager successfully.

Epstein has argued cogently and demonstrated empirically that correlations between traits and behaviors routinely exceed .30 when the traits and the behaviors are sampled (and then *aggregated* by averaging) over a sufficient number of occurrences (Epstein, 1979).

Block (1971) also has presented impressive evidence for consistencies in behavior. In a complicated longitudinal study, he assessed the personality traits of 150 subjects at three different times in their lives—during junior high school, during senior high school, and during adulthood (subjects were in their mid-30s). Different sets of judges assessed the personality characteristics of the subjects during the junior and senior high school years, and these ratings were then correlated with the subjects' own assessments of their present personality characteristics. Block found considerable consistency in the subjects' behavior over time. For example, individuals who were seen by judges as talkative in junior high and senior high reported being talkative as adults, and those who were seen as productive in adolescence were also productive as adults. This consistency was found to exist for a wide variety of traits. In a more recent study, Costa and his colleagues also have found very strong evidence for behavioral consistency over time (Costa, McCrae, & Arenberg, 1980).

Mischel's rejoinder to the trait theorists (and to Epstein in particular) centered on the distinction between temporal stability and cross-situational consistency. **Cross-situational consistency** involves stability in people's behavior across many situations. Mischel maintained that temporal stability was never a central issue in the debate. He noted that in his early work he said that "considerable stability over time has been demonstrated" (Mischel, 1968, p. 36). Thus, though Mischel agreed with Epstein and the other trait theorists that temporal stability is an important phenomenon, he identified the crux of the debate as "the cross-situational consistency or discriminativeness of social behavior and the utility of inferring traits for the prediction of an individual's actions in particular contexts" (Mischel & Peake, 1982, p. 732).

After assuming cross-situational consistency to be the basic issue, Mischel and Peake proceeded to present their own data showing that cross-situational consistencies for the traits of friendliness and conscientiousness were quite low (averaging .13). In addition, they argued that the earlier data Epstein (1979) had presented in favor of the idea that behavior is stable across situations did not actually support his conclusion. Epstein (1983b) countered that Mischel and Peake had focused on the wrong correlations in his data and that if they had attended properly to only the correlations that described relationships between the *same* behavior in *different* situations (that is, cross-situational correlations), they would have seen that the reliability coefficients ranged from .70 to .94.

Argument 4: The Use of New Strategies Reveals That Predictive Accuracy Can Be Increased. Finally, Bem and Allen (1974), in still another effort to demonstrate the incorrectness of Mischel's view, utilized a **personality-moderator analysis** to show that knowledge of individual differences among people can be used to predict certain cross-situational behaviors very accurately. Such an analysis involves an assessment of the ways in which cross-situational behaviors depend on certain differences in the personality characteristics of subjects. In particular, Bem and Allen argued that cross-situational consistency could be demonstrated for only certain kinds of subjects. They compared subjects who reported that they were consistent in their traits with those subjects who reported they were not consistent. The subjects were preselected for trait consistency or trait inconsistency on certain dimensions *before* the cross-situational behaviors relevant to their dimensions were examined. Bem and Allen hypothesized, "Individuals who identify themselves as consistent on a particular trait dimension will in fact be more consistent cross-situationally than those who identify themselves as highly variable" (Bem & Allen, 1974, p. 512). Their results strongly supported their hypothesis. That is, subjects who identified themselves as consistently friendly behaved in a friendly way in a group discussion *and* in a waiting room before the experiment, while subjects who identified themselves as inconsistent behaved inconsistently in both situations. Bem and Allen also attempted to show that similar results would be obtained for the subjects when they were classified as consistently conscientious or inconsistently conscientious on the basis of self-reports and then had their actual levels of conscientiousness checked across three situations. Conscientiousness was measured in terms of: (1) whether the subjects had turned in to their instructor several evaluation forms of their introductory psychology course; (2) whether they had completed the supplementary readings for the course; and (3) whether they were personally neat. The neatness measure consisted of the cleanliness and neatness of each individual's hair and clothing as rated by independent judges and the neatness (orderliness, cleanliness, and so on) of his or her living quarters during a surprise visit by judges during the last week of school. The results did not entirely support Bem and Allen's position. Consistently conscientious subjects had completed the course readings *and* the evaluation forms for the course, whereas inconsistently conscientious subjects showed more variability in their behavior across the same two situations, as predicted. However, the results for the neatness variable were negative; that is, consistently conscientious subjects were not more neat in their personal appearance and in their living quarters than were inconsistently conscientious subjects. Consistently conscientious subjects did not see personal neatness as being related to returning course evaluations ($-.01$) or completing course readings ($-.11$).

Mischel and Peake's review of Bem and Allen's data (particularly for the conscientiousness dimension) led them to conclude that these researchers had not demonstrated the existence of cross-situational consistency in some of their subjects' behavior. Furthermore, Mischel and Peake conducted a replication of Bem and Allen's study and failed to replicate the findings. They then concluded that subjects identified as consistent on certain dimensions did not show high levels of cross-situational consistency (Mischel & Peake, 1982, pp. 745–747).

In Bem's (1983) rejoinder to Mischel and Peake, he did not comment directly on their assertion that he and Allen had failed to demonstrate convincingly that there is cross-situational consistency in certain subjects' behavior. Instead, Bem chose to focus on the negative findings in the Bem and Allen study and to argue that these findings (that is, that personal neatness did *not* correlate with either course evaluations or completed course readings) were, in fact, supportive of the key argument in the Bem and Allen article. And, according to Bem, it was this argument that Mischel and Peake unfortunately failed to recognize or understand. This key argument centered on (1) whether *investigators* should provide the subjects with those behaviors that they thought composed a trait in various situations or (2) whether *subjects themselves* should decide on the behaviors that make up a particular trait. Bem himself clearly favors the second approach, yet ironically, as he himself acknowledged, he and Allen relied on the first approach in their study. That is, they assumed that personal neatness, course evaluations, and completed course readings were all intercorrelated positively and thus were measuring conscientiousness. However, it turned out that the subjects themselves did not perceive these same three variables as intercorrelated positively and as falling into the same class (that is, conscientiousness). Thus, according to Bem, the lesson to be learned is that investigators should rely on subjects' perceptions, not on investigators' perceptions, of what behaviors are equivalent and can therefore be included in a trait class. Bem believes that if this approach were followed, personality psychology would be moving in the right direction of developing a more idiographic view of personality. In a rebuttal, Mischel (1983) maintained that he understands Bem's position. He praised Bem for his candor in acknowledging that he should have relied on the subjects' perceptions in the Bem and Allen study, but he still concluded that Bem and Allen failed to demonstrate strong cross-situational consistency in behavior.

In a later study, Bem and another associate offered a **template-matching procedure** that was designed, at least in part, to demonstrate cross-situational consistencies (Bem & Funder, 1978). The procedure generally involves the definition of a given situation in terms of the different behaviors shown by idealized types of persons in that setting. These definitions can be obtained by using observers' ratings of the characteristics of the situation or through derivations from theory (Bem & Funder, 1978, p. 486). The personality descriptions of the specific ways in which idealized types of persons are expected to behave in that setting are called templates. Once the situation has been characterized according to these templates, the subjects' own ratings of their unique sets of behaviors are obtained. Then the behavior of a particular individual is predicted by correlating his or her unique behavior ratings with the behaviors of the various idealized types of persons. The highest correlation (that is, the closest person-template match) identifies the behavior the person will probably show. As Bem and Funder put it, "The probability that a particular person will behave in a particular way in a particular situation is . . . postulated to be a monotonically increasing function of the match or similarity between his or her characteristics and the template associated with the corresponding behavior" (Bem & Funder, 1978, p. 486).

Consider this concrete example (adapted from Bem and Funder). Assume that you are the parent of a high school senior and that she is thinking of applying to Stanford University for her undergraduate education. As a parent, you basically need to know whether Stanford is the best place for your daughter. One way to help her make a good decision is to secure information about how several idealized types of people function at Stanford (that is, the situation). For example, you might have the following three bits of information: (1) Students who are hardworking but shy tend to earn excellent grades but do not interact much with the faculty; (2) students who are very bright and assertive tend to get involved in too many extracurricular leadership activities and obtain good (but not excellent) grades as a result; and (3) students who are highly friendly, sociable, and noncompetitive make many friends but tend to ignore their coursework and obtain poor grades as a consequence. Now all you as a parent have to do is match your daughter's personality characteristics with the three templates. You can then predict her grades. Specifically, if she described herself primarily as hardworking but shy, her self-description matched template 1 best, and you would predict she would earn excellent grades. If she described herself as very bright and assertive, thereby matching template 2 best, you would predict good, but not outstanding grades. And if she described herself as highly friendly, sociable, and noncompetitive, thereby matching template 3 best, you would predict poor grades. In this last case, you would obviously not advise her to apply to Stanford, because her personality characteristics indicate that she would be highly similar to students at Stanford who get poor grades and flunk out.

In the description of the template-matching procedure outlined thus far, we have described the personality characteristics associated with ideal types in *one* situation. To assess whether or not cross-sectional consistency in behavior exists, Bem and Funder had to utilize at least one more situation. (Obviously you can try to demonstrate cross-situational consistency only if you observe behavior in two or more situations.) In a case where you have information on two situations, Bem and Funder propose that often you will see inconsistencies in behavior (thereby supporting Mischel's position) because the two situations are superficially similar but functionally different. For example, people might erroneously conclude that Stanford (situation 1) and Harvard (situation 2) are highly similar. After all, they are both prestigious institutions with high-quality faculty and students, and so on. Yet the personal qualities students need to earn excellent grades at Stanford may differ from the qualities needed to do so at Harvard. That is, the templates at the two institutions may differ, and therefore the qualities needed to match the templates at the two institutions may differ. Hardworking but shy students may earn excellent grades at Stanford, but perhaps at Harvard the crucial characteristics needed for excellent grades are a high degree of competitiveness and assertiveness. Thus only if the two institutions had identical templates would students who matched the templates in both situations be expected to show consistency in behavior—that is, earn excellent grades in both institutions.

Bem and Funder then proceeded to demonstrate empirically that two situations that appeared to be similar but that produced inconsistencies in behavior were actually functionally different. Yet Mischel and Peake argued that Bem and Funder's evidence did not resolve the cross-situational consistency debate for the following reasons:

> *The design of their study [that is, the Bem and Funder study] does not allow them even to make any estimates about potential consistency because evidence for cross-situational consistency can only be obtained if the same subjects are observed in at least two or more situations. Rather, their conclusions are based on a comparison of . . . two different sets of [subjects], where samples were not even matched in age. Their paper thus raises the prospect of improving evidence for cross-situational consistency in behavior, but it does not take the essential step of doing so. [Mischel & Peake, 1982, pp. 740–741]*

Mischel and Peake then conducted a study utilizing a design that adequately tested Bem and Funder's arguments in favor of cross-situational consistency through the use of the template-matching procedure, but they found no evidence to support those arguments.

Bem and Funder responded to their critics by noting that Mischel and Peake had focused on only *one* of three studies in their article and that the study they critiqued was not intended to be a demonstration of the unique advantages of the template-matching procedure for showing cross-situational consistencies in behavior. They noted further that their template-matching procedure has a variety of other important uses, including the testing of competing theories, which Mischel and Peake never discussed. Thus Bem and Funder maintained that Mischel and Peake's judgment that the template-matching procedure is a failure is completely unwarranted (Bem, 1983; Funder, 1983).

Mischel and Peake replied that they were interested just in the cross-situational issue and that since only one of the three studies in the Bem and Funder article specifically addressed that issue, they focused on it alone. They also maintained that their criticisms were not addressed to the other uses of the template-matching procedure (Mischel & Peake, 1983, p. 400).

Mischel concluded, after reviewing all of the studies conducted by his critics, that there is little support for the idea of cross-situational consistency in behavior (that is, trait consistency). He then wondered why people intuitively believe in trait consistency even though the evidence is essentially negative and shows instead that behavior is typically highly situation-specific. He calls this contradiction between intuition and research evidence the **consistency paradox** (Mischel & Peake, 1982, p. 730). After noting that his critics had failed to resolve the paradox, Mischel offered his own solution. His proposal is termed the **cognitive-prototype approach**. It holds that impressions of trait consistency result not from actual cross-situational consistency but rather from the observation of the temporal stability of those behaviors that are highly relevant (central) to the trait. Conversely, the perception of variability in behavior arises from the observation of temporal instability in highly relevant features of the trait. Specifically, the cognitive prototype view sees the broad cognitive categories (for example, traits) we use to represent our experiences as consisting of features or dimensions (for instance, behaviors) that vary in their prototypicality. That is, traits can be conceptualized as categories that encompass a variety of behaviors that vary in relevance (centrality) in denoting the categories. For example, we might define student conscientiousness (trait category) in terms of the following dimensions or behaviors: (1) attending classes regularly, (2) completing course assignments, (3) returning books to the library when they are due, and (4) writing letters home on a regular basis. Let us assume that each of these behaviors varies in defining the trait. Perhaps attending classes is most relevant (highest prototypicality) in defining student conscientiousness, while writing letters home is least relevant (lowest prototypicality). Thus when subjects judge their own conscientiousness they will be more likely to do so by taking into account their frequency of class attendance rather than their regularity in writing letters home. Observers will follow the same reasoning, according to Mischel. Therefore both subjects and observers are more likely to conclude that a student is highly conscientious across situations if he or she attends classes regularly (the behavior has temporal stability) even if he or she does not complete course assignments, return books to the library, or write letters home regularly. In other words, even though the student's behavior is not consistent across situation 2 (completing course assignments), situation 3 (returning library books), and situation 4 (writing letters home), the student and others will still be led to conclude erroneously that the behavior is cross-situationally consistent, because it is temporally stable in situation 1 (attending classes) and is highest in prototypicality. Thus Mischel attributed trait consistency *primarily* to perceptual error— that is, overestimation of the importance of specific stable features of the trait under consideration. He then proceeded to conduct a study that generally provided empirical support for his cognitive-prototype solution.

Despite Mischel's pessimistic conclusions concerning the existence of cross-situational consistency in behavior, a recent study by Small, Zeldin, and Savin-Williams (1983) reported evidence of highly impressive cross-situational correlations for the traits of dominance and prosocial behavior in four groups of adolescents participating in a camping program. Specifically, trained observers rated the adolescents in terms of their dominance (for example, argumentativeness, monopolizing of conversations, verbal challenges threatening bodily harm, and fighting) and their prosocial behavior (for example, sharing food or possessions with others without being asked, explaining how to put up a tent or make a bed, and praising and encouraging others) in three different situations. These situations were (1) camping, (2) mealtime, and (3) free time. Then the data were analyzed. The results are presented in Table 18.1. As you can see, all of the correlations exceed .30 and *75% of them are larger than .70.*

Table 18.1
Cross-Situational Correlations for Dominance and
Pro-social Behavior in Four Groups of Adolescent Campers

Situations	Group 1		Group 2		Group 3		Group 4	
	Prosocial Behavior	Dominance Behavior	Prosocial Behavior	Dominance Behavior	Prosocial Behavior	Dominance Behavior	Prosocial Behavior	Dominance Behavior
S1–S2*	.99	.93	.91	.95	.48	.63	.79	.89
S2–S3	.73	.72	.85	.33	.60	.87	.92	.70
S1–S3	.78	.76	.85	.49	.80	.79	.72	.72

Adapted from Small, Zeldin, and Savin-Williams, 1983, p. 10.
*Situation types: S1 = camping; S2 = meals; S3 = free time.

In addition, Epstein (1984) has presented strong evidence for the cross-situational generality of behavior in a laboratory setting in which the identical behavior was examined across experimentally manipulated changes in situations. His data suggest, at least for certain traits, that behavior is more cross-situationally consistent than Mischel thinks.

So there you have the essence of this interesting debate. It has had tremendous heuristic value, and there have been several important positive outcomes as a result.

Gains from the Person-Situation Debate

The debate has made clear that broad, cross-situational response dispositions do indeed exist (Epstein, 1983a; Mischel, 1983). Nevertheless, leading personality psychologists recognize that the strategy, employed by many person-oriented theorists, of using such broad, stable dispositions or traits to predict behavior in specific situations is not very useful because it typically yields poor predictive outcomes (Epstein, 1983a, 1983b; Mischel & Peake, 1983). Most important, a consensus now exists that there is substantial coherence and continuity in the lives of individuals, but *also* substantial discriminativeness in the patterning of their behavior from situation to situation and over time within situations (Mischel, 1983, p. 600). There is a recognition that individual behavior is sometimes cross-situationally consistent, while at other times it is highly situation-specific and that an adequate theory of personality must be able to account for *both* stability and change in behavior.

The debate has also encouraged investigators to reexamine the person-oriented theorists' view of traits as underlying causes (and explanations) of behavior and to replace it with a view of traits as categorical-summary statements of behavior in a manner consistent with Mischel's cognitive-prototype approach (Buss & Craik, 1983). In this new view, traits are not assigned explanatory power in a causal sense but instead are seen as useful in identifying regularities in behavior and in making predictions (in correlational terms) about future trends in behavior. This development is promising because it points to a more precise way of measuring the behaviors within trait categories, and it also raises a host of new researchable questions (for example: What are the prototypical behaviors of important trait categories? Are there age-specific variations in prototypical acts for some trait constructs?).

Relatedly, many of the instruments traditionally utilized to assess these broad dispositions were psychometrically unsound, and the debate has made researchers acutely aware of the necessity of using reliable instruments in order to predict behavior accurately (see, for instance, Epstein, 1983a). There also is a consensus that poor predictive accuracy can be avoided in many cases by developing more specific behavioral measures—that is, measures that assess past behaviors in the domain of the behavior to be predicted. Furthermore, predictive accuracy can be improved considerably if measures of the relevant psychological environment or situation are used. For example, if we know the quality of a boy's intellectual environment and his opportunities for learning as well as his IQ, we can more accurately predict his achievement-test scores. Accuracy of prediction can also be increased if measures of relevant future conditions are utilized. For instance, knowing the kind of job and housing opportunities that await a discharged mental patient, as well as his scores on a personal-adjustment scale following therapy, would allow investigators to better predict his success in the environment outside the institution (Mischel, 1983, pp. 581–582).

It is apparent from the preceding examples and from the arguments in the debate that knowledge of the situation and its impact on the individual are highly important for the accurate prediction of behavior. Although, historically, most person-oriented theorists have been aware of that fact (for instance, Allport, 1937), they typically have not attempted to account for its influence in a systematic way, as mentioned earlier. So another exciting development in the discipline is the almost universal recognition among personality psychologists of the critical need for systematic knowledge about situations, along with the initial movement by researchers to fulfill that need by developing a **psychology of situations**. According to Magnusson, this need is obvious because behavior takes place in situations and cannot be understood or explained in isolation from them. Moreover, it is in actual situations that we confront the world, learn from it, form our conceptions of it, and develop our unique behaviors and strategies for coping with it. Thus the physical, social, and cultural aspects of the environments that people experience in the course of their development are of fundamental importance in shaping their personalities (Magnusson, 1981, pp. 9–10).

Efforts to fulfill that need have included the development of situational taxonomies and the construction of measures to assess various physical and social environments (see, for instance, Craik, 1981). In regard to the development of situational taxonomies, investigators face the unfortunate fact that there are almost an infinite number of ways that situations can be classified, so that the search for a single basic taxonomy is probably futile (Mischel, 1977, p. 337). For example, situations can be classified not only by their multifaceted physical, social, and cultural properties, but also according to their clarity, cohesiveness, competitiveness, complexity, efficiency, familiarity, formality, goals, intimacy, organization, riskiness, roles, rules, strength, and stressfulness. Yet investigators tend to be a pragmatic lot. They are aware that, though a single basic taxonomy is beyond reach, the construction of situational taxonomies is necessary if the solutions to pressing research questions are to be found (Hettema, 1979; Van Heck, 1984). So they have proceeded to develop such taxonomies to meet specific research needs, while recognizing that their taxonomies are not suitable for all purposes.

Along with an awareness of the need to revamp the traditional trait conception (which has been accomplished) and to generate a systematic analysis of situations (which is moving forward in rapid fashion), the final major gain from the debate involves the acceptance by leading personality psychologists of the critical need for developing a coherent integrated interactional theory of personality that would account for both stability and change in behavior. While not all investigators agree that this approach is the best solution to the problem (see Epstein, 1983a), the general acceptance of the idea means that, in the past, some theorists have overemphasized the role of person variables and neglected situation variables, while others have done just the opposite, the result being the lack of a theory that examines person-situation interactions. Of course, investigators are not saying that *only* the study of person-situation interactions is important. There are times when these are most important, but there are other times when person variables are most critical, and still other times when situation factors account for most of the variation in particular behaviors. Therefore investigators realize that the question "Which is most important in the prediction of behavior—person, situation, or person-situation interactions?" addresses a pseudo-issue because research conditions can be (and have been) constructed that demonstrate the superiority of each of the three factors (see, for example, Alker, 1977; Epstein, 1977; Olweus, 1977).

Let us consider a nonresearch example, centering on people who run races (Epstein, 1977). By selecting races (situations) that vary little in distance and runners who vary greatly in speed (large person-variable differences), we can show that individuals (person variables) account for almost all the variation in running speed. If the distances were 50, 100, and 200 meters, for instance, and some individuals were very fast and others very slow, we would expect the very fast runners to have faster running times in all three events than the slower runners. Individual differences (person variables) matter here; the situations do not. Assume, however, that we allow only runners of highly similar ability to run and that we vary the race distances (situations) considerably. Under these conditions, we would expect situations (races) to account for running speed. If the distances were 50 meters, 1500 meters, and 3000 meters, the differences in running speeds would be due primarily to differences in distance (situations) and not to differences among individuals. Finally, if we select races of different types—say, dashes and hurdle races—and runners who excel in one type and not in the other, it can be shown that person-situation interactions account for most of the variation in running times. Hurdle specialists would do well in hurdle races but not in dashes, while dash specialists would perform well in dashes but not in hurdle races.

With this basic understanding (after much debate and research) of the futility of trying to ascertain which one of the three factors is most important, investigators have shifted their attention to more substantive issues in their efforts to create a viable interactional psychology. Recall that the essence of the interactional model is that behavior is a function of a continual set of transactions between individuals and their environments. Within this framework, individuals are affected by their environments and also influence them. They do not simply react to situational demands; they often act to create, select, or modify situations to suit their own purposes (Snyder, 1983). This description implies that a viable interactional theory of personality will have to focus on the process of change in individuals during the course of their lives as well as on the consistencies in their behaviors. Accordingly, the model must incorporate conceptions of personality development and individual learning experiences within the limits imposed by biology (Hettema, 1979, p. 4). It also will have to emphasize the roles played by cognitive, emotional, and motivational factors in personal development and functioning. Although the incorporation of adequate formulations of social learning into the interactional model are considered necessary, they are seen as not being sufficient for a complete interactional theory of personality, at least by some investigators (for instance, Hettema, 1979; Kenrick & Dantchik, 1983). In their judgment a complete theory must incorporate the biological underpinnings of behavior within the context of evolutionary behavior.

In particular, Hettema (1979) offers the construct of adaptation as the unifying principle of the new theory. He sees it as the root of all individual functioning. It involves efforts by organisms to enlarge the range of environments in which they can survive, to extend the ecological niche defined by their species-specific behavior. According to Hettema, adaptation is acquired gradually during the course of development. Individuals are continuously utilizing information from their environments to acquire, maintain, and promote control over them. This construct of adaptation is compatible with the cognitive social-learning position that is postulated by many investigators to be an integral part of the new emerging interactional theory (Mischel, 1973). Also generally consistent with this social-learning/interactional view is Hettema's judgment that in effective transactions with the environment, individuals are flexible enough to show behaviors that satisfy the requirements posed by situations (Hettema, 1979, p. 46). Such transactions allow individuals to obtain subjectively valuable outcomes while avoiding or escaping those that are aversive or punishing. The key here for both Hettema and the cognitive social-learning theorists is that individuals need to acquire discriminative facility in their behavior and in their assessment of situations in order to function adaptively. That is, they need to learn to modify their behavior as the contingencies between behavior and outcomes in various situations change so as to maximize the attainment of subjectively valued outcomes.

A lack of sensitivity to changing circumstances is often characteristic of an organism adapting poorly (Mischel, 1977, p. 335). Let us say a boxer acts very aggressively in his bouts, wins, and is rewarded. Now if, once outside the ring, he shows the same aggressive behavior toward nonboxers (for example, traffic cops, his father, store clerks), he is apt to be punished by fines and/or a jail sentence. Likewise, the student who studies only 12 hours a week and earns excellent grades in high school may very well be punished by low grades if she does not change her study behavior at a university. So it is important that individuals learn when it is appropriate and healthy to change their behavior.

It is also important to know, however, when it is appropriate to maintain the same behavior in different situations. These are likely to be situations that are functionally similar in that they are all perceived to be similar in their reinforcement contingencies. Under such circumstances, individuals should (and do) behave in the same way to obtain subjectively valued outcomes (Pervin, 1981, pp. 352–353). For instance, if being friendly toward one's fellow students (situation 1), teachers (situation 2), and parents (situation 3) is followed typically by rewards of different kinds, it would be foolish to change one's behavior and to act in an unfriendly way upon meeting some new students or teachers.

From the preceding discussion, it should be apparent that there are several important convergences between the adaptation and cognitive social-learning models and that it may well be possible to utilize aspects of both models in the creation of a new and more comprehensive interactional theory of personality.

Prospects for the Future of the Discipline

The consensus concerning the need to develop an interactional theory of personality provides the motivation and direction for the discipline and makes the realization of the goal more probable. We can speculate that, when it is fully developed, this theory will increase our understanding of the individual immeasurably. Since cognitive social-learning principles will play a large part in this theory, personality psychologists will obviously have to pay serious attention to the role played by cognitive processes in the determination of behavior. People are often flooded with environmental information that somehow must be reduced and simplified to allow efficient processing and to avoid an overwhelming overload. To predict people's behavior, we must know how they organize and use this information to secure their goals (Mischel, 1979). The strategies they devise may either prove useful and satisfying or have highly negative consequences. The theory therefore must be able to account for how people categorize information and then how they act in terms of their categorizations.

The foregoing discussion implies that people are always aware of their experiences, can adequately categorize them, and, as a consequence, are in a position to act effectively. Yet we know that such a viewpoint is overly simplistic. People are not always aware of their experiences; so they cannot categorize them adequately and may, as a result, act ineffectively. At times individuals are unaware of the actual determinants of their actions, and they therefore attempt to account for them by invoking plausible (but false) explanations (Nisbett & Wilson, 1977). At other times people may make good judgments and show effective behaviors, but the judgments are based on *implicit* information. On such occasions we talk about the role of intuition in the determination of behavior (Bowers, 1981). The new interactional theory will have to account for the roles played by both conscious and unconscious factors in the production of behavior.

The new theory undoubtedly will also have to incorporate conceptions of motivation. Motives are the underlying springs of behavior. People pursue goals, for example, because their attainment brings valued consequences; they also avoid taking certain actions because they fear the consequences of doing so. The new theory will have to explicate the dynamic and complex interrelationships between cognition and motivation in the production of behavior. People have knowledge of their preferences and values, their goals and motives, and their rules and strategies for regulating their own behavior (Markus, 1983). This self-knowledge is based in part on an organized understanding of their behaviors and their consequences in various situations in the past. But self-knowledge is organized also in terms of the possible or potential. Individuals make plans for the future. They have hopes and dreams and act on the basis of their ideals. They also have fears at times about what the future may bring. Thus the new theory will have to incorporate conceptions of the self that are based on aspirations for the future as well as on experiences rooted in the past (Mischel, 1973; Markus, 1983). The result should be the development of a more adequate theory of personality, an outcome that could prove beneficial to all of us. This is the challenge now facing personality psychologists. If the past two decades of exciting debate and growth are any indication, the future of the discipline looks promising indeed.

Discussion Questions

1. What are some of the limitations of the person-oriented view? What are some of the major problems with the situation-oriented view? In what ways will the new interactional theory overcome the deficiencies of these viewpoints?
2. Do you think it is necessary to retain concepts like the shadow and the death instinct to explain human behavior adequately?
3. Why does the use of broad trait categories lead to poor predictive outcomes in specific situations?
4. What is a "personality coefficient"? Why is it considered by many investigators to be a disparaging and unfair term?
5. What is the evidence in favor of the view that there is cross-situational consistency in behavior?

6. Describe how Epstein uses an aggregation procedure to demonstrate trait consistency.
7. Describe the differences between temporal stability and cross-situational consistency. Explain the perception of trait consistency in the cognitive-prototype approach.
8. Why is there a need to develop a "psychology of situations"?
9. What are some of the major gains from the person-situation debate?
10. Why would an adequate theory of personality have to incorporate motivational as well as cognitive factors?

References

Alker, H. A. Is personality situationally specific or intrapsychically consistent? *Journal of Personality*, 1972, *40*, 1–16.

Alker, H. A. Beyond ANOVA psychology in the study of person-situation interactions. In D. Magnusson & N. S. Endler (Eds.), *Personality at the crossroads: Current issues in interactional psychology*. Hillsdale, N. J.: Lawrence Erlbaum Associates, 1977.

Allport, G. W. *Personality: A psychological interpretation*. New York: Holt, Rinehart & Winston, 1937.

Bem, D. J. Constructing cross-situational consistencies in behavior: Some thoughts on Alker's critique of Mischel. *Journal of Personality*, 1972, *40*, 17–26.

Bem, D. J. Further déjà vu in the search for cross-situational consistency. *Psychological Review*, 1983, *90*, 390–393.

Bem, D. J., & Allen, A. On predicting some of the people some of the time: The search for cross-situational consistencies in behavior. *Psychological Review*, 1974, *81*, 506–520.

Bem, D. J., & Funder, D. C. Predicting more of the people more of the time: Assessing the personality of situations. *Psychological Review*, 1978, *85*, 485–501.

Block, J. *Lives through time*. Berkeley, Calif.: Bancroft Books, 1971.

Block, J. Advancing the psychology of personality: Paradigmatic shift or improving the quality of research? In D. Magnusson & N. S. Endler (Eds.), *Personality at the crossroads: Current issues in interactional psychology*. Hillsdale, N. J.: Lawrence Erlbaum Associates, 1977.

Bowers, K. S. Situationism in psychology: An analysis and critique. *Psychological Review*, 1973, *80*, 307–336.

Bowers, K. S. Knowing more than we can say leads to saying more than we can know: On being implicitly informed. In D. Magnusson (Ed.), *Toward a psychology of situations: An interactional perspective*. Hillsdale, N. J.: Lawrence Erlbaum Associates, 1981.

Buss, D. M., & Craik, K. H. The act-frequency approach to personality. *Psychological Review*, 1983, *90*, 105–126.

Costa, P. T., Jr., McCrae, R. R., & Arenberg, D. Enduring dispositions in adult males. *Journal of Personality and Social Psychology*, 1980, *38*, 793–800.

Craik, K. H. Environmental assessment and situational analysis. In D. Magnusson (Ed.), *Toward a psychology of situations: An interactional perspective*. Hillsdale, N. J.: Lawrence Erlbaum Associates, 1981.

Ekehammar, B. Interactionism in personality from a historical perspective. *Psychological Bulletin*, 1974, *81*, 1026–1048.

Epstein, S. Traits are alive and well. In D. Magnusson & N. E. Endler (Eds.), *Personality at the crossroads: Current issues in interactional psychology*. Hillsdale, N. J.: Lawrence Erlbaum Associates, 1977.

Epstein, S. The stability of behavior: I. On predicting most of the people much of the time. *Journal of Personality and Social Psychology*, 1979, 37, 1097–1126.

Epstein, S. The stability of behavior: II. Implications for psychological research. *American Psychologist*, 1980, *35*, 790–806.

Epstein, S. Aggregation and beyond: Some basic issues on the prediction of behavior. *Journal of Personality*, 1983a, *51*, 360–392.

Epstein, S. The stability of confusion: A reply to Mischel and Peake. *Psychological Review*, 1983b, *90*, 179–184.

Epstein, S. The stability of behavior across time and situations. In R. Zucker, J. Aronoff, & A. I. Rabin (Eds.), *Personality and the prediction of behavior*. San Diego, Calif.: Academic Press, 1984.

Epstein, S. The person-situation debate in historical and current perspective. Unpublished manuscript, University of Massachusetts at Amherst, 1985.

Freud, S. *The ego and the id*. Translated by J. Riviere; revised and edited by J. Strachey. New York: Norton, 1960.

Funder, D. C. Three issues in predicting more of the people: A reply to Mischel and Peake. *Psychological Review*, 1983, *90*, 283–289.

Hettema, P. J. *Personality and adaptation*. Amsterdam: North-Holland Publishing Co., 1979.

Hogan, R., DeSoto, C. B., & Solano, C. Traits, tests, and personality research. *American Psychologist*, 1977, *32*, 255–264.

Jung, C. G. Aion. In V. S. de Laszlo (Ed.), *Psyche and symbol*. Garden City, N.Y.: Doubleday Anchor, 1958.

Kelly, G. A. *The psychology of personal constructs*, Vol. 1. New York: Norton, 1955.

Kenrick, D. T., & Dantchik, A. Interactionism, idiographics and the social psychological invasion of personality. *Journal of Personality*. 1983, *51*, 286–307.

Magnusson, D. Wanted: A psychology of situations. In D. Magnusson (Ed.), *Toward a psychology of situations: An interactional perspective*. Hillsdale, N. J.: Lawrence Erlbaum Associates, 1981.

Magnusson, D., & Endler, N. S. Interactional psychology: Present status and future prospects. In D. Magnusson & N. S. Endler (Eds.), *Personality at the crossroads: Current issues in interactional psychology*. Hillsdale, N. J.: Lawrence Erlbaum Associates, 1977.

Markus, H. Self-knowledge: An expanded view. *Journal of Personality*, 1983, *51*, 543–565.

Mischel, W. *Personality and assessment*. New York: Wiley, 1968.

Mischel, W. Toward a cognitive social learning reconceptualization of personality. *Psychological Review*, 1973, *80*, 252–283.

Mischel, W. On the empirical dilemmas of psychodynamic approaches: Issues and alternatives. In N. S. Endler & D. Magnusson (Eds.), *Interactional psychology and personality*. Washington, D.C.: Hemisphere Publishing, 1976.

Mischel, W. The interaction of person and situation. In D. Magnusson & N. S. Endler (Eds.), *Personality at the crossroads: Current issues in interactional psychology*. Hillsdale, N. J.: Lawrence Erlbaum Associates, 1977.

Mischel, W. On the interface of cognition and personality: Beyond the person-situation debate. *American Psychologist,* 1979, *34,* 740–754.

Mischel, W. Alternatives in the pursuit of the predictability and consistency of persons: Stable data that yield unstable interpretations. *Journal of Personality,* 1983, *51,* 578–604.

Mischel, W. Convergences and challenges in the search for consistency. *American Psychologist,* 1984, *39,* 351–364.

Mischel, W., & Peake, P. K. Beyond déjà vu in the search for cross-situational consistency. *Psychological Review,* 1982, *89,* 730–755.

Mischel, W., & Peake, P. K. Some facets of consistency: Replies to Epstein, Funder, and Bem. *Psychological Review,* 1983, *90,* 394–402.

Nisbett, R. E., & Wilson, T. D. Telling more than we can know: Verbal reports on mental processes. *Psychological Review,* 1977, *84,* 231–259.

Olweus, D. A critical analysis of the "modern" interactionist position. In D. Magnusson & N. S. Endler (Eds.), *Personality at the crossroads: Current issues in interactional psychology.* Hillsdale, N. J.: Lawrence Erlbaum Associates, 1977.

Pervin, L. A. The relation of situations to behavior. In D. Magnusson (Ed.), *Toward a psychology of situations: An interactional perspective.* Hillsdale, N.J.: Lawrence Erlbaum Associates, 1981.

Raush, H. L. Paradox levels, and junctures in person-situation systems. In D. Magnusson & N. S. Endler (Eds.), *Personality at the crossroads: Current issues in interactional psychology.* Hillsdale, N. J.: Lawrence Erlbaum Associates, 1977.

Small, S. A., Zeldin, R. S., & Savin-Williams, R. C. In search of personality traits: A multimethod analysis of naturally occurring prosocial and dominance behavior. *Journal of Personality,* 1983, *51,* 1–16.

Snyder, M. The influence of individuals on situations: Implications for understanding the links between personality and social behavior. *Journal of Personality,* 1983, *51,* 497–516.

Van Heck, G. L. M. The construction of a general taxonomy of situations. In H. Bonarius, G. Van Heck, & N. Smid (Eds.), *Personality psychology in Europe.* Lisse: Swets & Zeitlinger, 1984.

Wachtel, P. L. Psychodynamics, behavior therapy, and the implacable experimenter: An inquiry into the consistency of personality. *Journal of Abnormal Psychology,* 1973, *82,* 324–334.

Suggested Readings

Endler, N. S., and Magnusson, D. (Eds.). *Interactional psychology and personality.* Washington, D.C.: Hemisphere Publishing, 1976.

Magnusson, D. (Ed.). *Toward a psychology of situations: An interactional perspective.* Hillsdale, N. J.: Lawrence Erlbaum Associates, 1981.

Magnusson, D., & Endler, N. S. (Eds.). *Personality at the crossroads: Current issues in interactional psychology.* Hillsdale, N. J.: Lawrence Erlbaum Associates, 1977.

Mischel, W. *Personality and assessment.* New York: Wiley, 1968.

West, S. G. (Ed.). Personality and prediction: Nomothetic and idiographic approaches. *Journal of Personality* (Special Issue), 1983, *51,* No. 3.

Glossary

Aggregation procedure A basic procedure for reducing errors of measurement and for establishing trait consistency by averaging behavioral measurements of traits over situations and/or over occasions (repeated measurements of the behaviors in the same situation).

Cognitive-prototype approach An approach to understanding the perception of trait consistency. It maintains that impressions of consistency arise not from actual cross-situational consistency in behavior but from temporal stability in those behaviors that are especially relevant to the trait.

Cognitive social-learning model Theoretical position that attempts to account for individual differences in thought and behavior by examining the unique ways in which people actively utilize cognitive strategies based on prior learning experiences in reacting to and coping with demands posed by the environment.

Consistency paradox The contradiction between people's strong, intuitive beliefs that there is cross-situational consistency in behavior even though (in Mischel's view) the empirical evidence in support of the belief is essentially negative.

Cross-situational consistency Term that refers to the stability in people's behavior across many situations.

Interactional model of personality Position that attempts to account for personality functioning by examining the joint effects of person and situation variables on behavior.

Personality coefficient Disparaging term used to indicate that knowledge of people's traits does not allow investigators to predict their behaviors accurately. The suggestion is that the low correlations between traits and behaviors mean that behavior is determined primarily by situational forces.

Personality-moderator analysis The view that behavior in given situations will vary for people who differ in their personality characteristics.

Person-oriented theories Positions that focus almost exclusively on the ways in which underlying, internal characteristics (person variables) control behavior.

Person-situation debate A long-standing controversy in personality psychology, the issue being whether behavior is stable despite situational variation or variable in the face of situational change.

Person variables Internal characteristics of the person such as cognitions, emotions, motives, traits, needs, and urges that are involved in the production of behavior.

Psychology of situations The development of theory and procedures to describe and explain the role of situations in the determination of behavior.

Situation-oriented theories Positions that focus almost exclusively on the ways in which situational parameters control behavior.

Situation Variables The physical (e.g., temperature, furniture, size of room) and social (e.g., the number and different kinds of people) aspects of the environment that affect behavior.

Template-matching procedure A procedure designed to predict an individual's behavior by matching his or her self-reported behavior with the behavior of various idealized types of persons for particular situations.

Temporal stability Term that refers to consistency in behavior over time in the same situation.

Author Index

Subject Index